PLEASE RETURN THIS BOOK TO

MR. DIETTE

WORLD WAR II

A Day-by-Day History

WORLD WAR II

A Day-by-Day History

Edited by
Peter Darman

This edition published in 2005 by Crestline, an
imprint of MBI Publishing Company,
Galtier Plaza, Suite 200, 380 Jackson Street,
St. Paul, MN 55101-3885 USA

The information in this book is true and
complete to the best of our knowledge.
All recommendations are made without any
guarantee on the part of the author or Publisher,
who also disclaim any liability incurred
in connection with the use of this data or
specific details.

We recognize that some words, model names and
designations, for example, mentioned herein are
the property of the trademark holder.
We use them for identification purposes only. This
is not an official publication.

Crestline titles are also available at discounts in
bulk quantity for industrial or sales-promotional
use. For details write to Special Sales Manager at
Motorbooks International Wholesalers &
Distributors, Galtier Plaza, Suite 200, 380 Jackson
Street, St. Paul, MN 55101-3885 USA.

ISBN 0-7603-2400-X

Printed in China

Editorial and design:
The Brown Reference Group plc
8 Chapel Place
Rivington Street
London
EC2A 3DQ
UK
www.brownreference.com

PICTURE CREDITS
Front Cover: Robert Hunt Library
Back Cover: Robert Hunt Library

All Images The Robert Hunt Library except the following:
Chris Ailsby: 6, 8t, 8b, 9t, 10, 11b, 11t, 14/15, 15b, 19t, 19b, 21b,
21t, 22l, 23t, 24, 25tr, 26, 27, 27/28, 28/29, 28, 29b, 29t, 30b, 30t,
33b, 33t, 36, 37, 37/38, 38b, 38t, 44b, 44t, 45b, 45t, 46, 47, 48, 58b,
63b, 65tr, 66b, 77tr, 78b, 78tr, 79br, 90b, 90t, 91b, 91t, 92/93, 93,
95tr, 97t, 100b, 101c, 101t, 104b, 104t, 105t, 108t, 110/111, 110b, 110t,
111b, 111t, 112, 117b, 120t, 121t, 123t, 126/127, 126b, 126t, 133b, 133t,
134t, 136b, 137b, 138/139, 138b, 140, 141t, 145t, 146t, 147b, 147t, 148b,
148tl, 148tr, 149b, 150/151, 151, 154, 155, 156/157, 160t, 161b, 161tl,
162tl, 164b, 164t, 165c, 166bl, 166tl, 167tr, 168/169, 169b, 169c, 169tr,
170r, 172/173, 172bl, 172br, 172cl, 173tr, 174tc, 175b, 176cl, 176tl,
177b, 178, 180b, 181bl, 181t, 183b, 184b, 184tl, 184tr, 185/186, 185br,
185tr, 186, 187b, 187tl, 187tr, 189bl, 189br;
AP Pictures: 572b;
Corbis: 423, Bettmann 542t, 562/563, 564/565; Hulton Archive 499b, 562t;
John Swope Collection 565b;
David King Collection: 192/193, 194tl, 194/195t, 194/195b;
Getty Images: 191t, 192t, 196b, 197t, 198b, 198/199, 200b, 498t, 499t;
US National Archives: JFK Library 465.

CONTENTS

INTRODUCTION
Deutschland Erwache

The Third Reich, which was spawned on January 30, 1933, was born out of the National Socialist Workers' Party, which was the very embodiment of Adolf Hitler himself. On April 20, 1889, its Führer (Leader) was cast upon the unsuspecting world at Braunau, Upper Austria. At the age of nine he became a choirboy in the Catholic Church at Lambach, and claimed in later years that his great vocal power had developed while singing hymns. He was an average, lazy and rebellious student, with a talent for drawing. This talent decided him on a career in art. His oratorical rehearsals were not overlooked. August Kubizek, his close boyhood friend, recalled young Adolf practising elocution in an open field. From his schooldays Hitler was a fanatical German Nationalist with a rancorous hatred of others, mostly Slavic races which made up the Austro-Hungarian Empire.

With the aim of entering the Academy of Art or the School of Architecture, Hitler moved to cosmopolitan Vienna in 1907, which at the time housed a large Jewish community. His failure in the entrance examinations was to have dire consequences for the future of Europe. Angry at his rejection, Hitler also caught the infection of anti-Semitism and became a prey to a morbid loathing of the Jews, which affected his whole outlook on life. A fierce nationalism and a corresponding intolerance of other races soon furnished Hitler with a distorted view on life from then on. His German nationalism was derived from Fichte, Hegel, Treitshed, Nietzsche and Richard Wagner. Wagner's operas, with their emphasis on Teutonic and German mythology, had an enormous influence on him, while the writings of the philosopher Nietzsche also attracted him.

▶ Adolf Hitler, the extremist who founded the Third Reich, which he regarded as the greatest of all German Empires.

6

Nietzsche expounded the notion of the "superman" (*Ubermensch*), a being perfect in mind and body who disdained man-made laws and goals, and who discarded morality for the virtue of "hardness". In this way Nietzsche extolled the ideas of force and strength. Hitler and the Nazis would later appropriate and pervert these ideas to create a ruthless totalitarian state. In Hitler's eyes the Nordic German hero was the archetypal superman, but he had to be freed from the shackles of Christian morality, which Hitler condemned for its Judaistic origins.

In May 1913 Hitler was 25 and had moved from Vienna to Munich. By this time, he was to claim later, his character was fully formed and his fundamental philosophy was already worked out, though materially he was little better than a vagrant, making a living from selling his paintings. In January 1914, and overdue for Austrian military service, he was summoned to military service in Austria and the Munich police obliged him to return. At Salzburg he was found to be medically unfit, though, and was allowed back to Munich. In August he joined the crowds demanding action

▼ **At the end of World War I, a Hessian regiment marches back across the Rhine at Koblenz to a Germany in chaos.**

against Russia and calling for a pan-German movement against both Russia and Serbia. The Austrian Empire had already declared war against Serbia since the heir to its throne had been assassinated in the town of Sarajevo. August 1914, with the outbreak of World War I, gave the wandering Hitler an opportunity. He threw himself into it with an ardour extraordinary even in those euphoric first days. He promptly addressed

▲ **Revolution in Germany, October 1918. Troops loyal to the Kaiser battle with communists on the streets of Hamburg.**

a petition to the Kaiser seeking permission, although he was an Austrian, to join a Bavarian regiment.

The disability which had kept him out of the Imperial Austrian Army having been apparently overlooked, Hitler's wish was

INTRODUCTION

granted. He served during World War I as an infantry volunteer in the 1st Company of the 16th Bavarian Regiment known, after its founding colonel, as the *List* Regiment. By October Hitler's regiment was at the front before the town of Ypres. By his own choice he served in the dangerous role of regimental message runner for the duration of the war, refusing promotion beyond the rank of corporal. In 1914 he won the Iron Cross second class. In the regiment were Lieutenant Wiedemann and Sergeant Max Amann, both of whom later became prominent Nazi Party members. In October 1916 Hitler was injured in the thigh and sent to a military hospital in Berlin. On recovery he was sent to the reserve

▲ The very first SS members, whose task was to be Hitler's bodyguard.

◄ Two SA members. The Sturmabteilung (Brownshirts) was the Nazi Party's private army of ex-servicemen.

battalion in Munich, returning to his regiment in March 1917. The *List* Regiment participated in Ludendorff's April 1918 offensive, when Hitler was awarded the Iron Cross first class for his bravery. The act of heroism for which he received his award is not known, but apparently he captured an enemy officer and about a dozen soldiers. The award to a soldier of his rank was unusual, and marked him out as a distinguished frontline soldier. In the fighting near Ypres he was blinded by gas in October 1918 and sent to hospital in Pasewalk in eastern Germany, until discharged fit and posted back to the Munich barracks in November 1918

World War I ended on November 11, 1918, leaving Hitler not yet having reached Munich and Germany in chaos and revolt under the frail Weimar Republic. The chancellor of Germany was the social democrat Friedrich Ebert, who in 1919 would become president of the country. Under the terms of the armistice, the army was reduced to a 100,000-man force called the *Reichswehr*.

Germany was far from a united country. On the one hand, the disbanded troops and their officers viewed the new republic with distaste, while the socialists and communists were fomenting revolution, culminating in January 1919 when the Spartacist revolt broke out at the beginning of that month.

The new republic's army decided to defend itself against subversion. Munich, for example, was first under the rule of a Bavarian socialist government, which was subsequently crushed by central government troops with the aid of its *Freikorps* allies. The *Freikorps* were groups of right-wing ex-soldiers which sprang up all over Germany following the end of the war. Essentially gangs of brutalized men

▲ *An early SA and Nazi Party member and later editor of the* Völkischer Beobachter, *Max Amann.*

normality and felt himself drawn to exploit the chaos which engulfed Germany after her defeat. This unusual combination produced a detestable personality that was to be his ultimate undoing. He had remained in the army after the war and fought in Ritter von Epp's Freikorps to crush the revolutionary Bavarian socialist government. He was also at this time secretly employed by the army to establish ammunition and weapons dumps in the Munich region for monarchist and nationalist groups, and to organize a special political intelligence unit for the army. Hitler, still a corporal awaiting his discharge from service, was selected for training in this new unit as an education officer in February 1919. Hitler's deeply held nationalistic views and anti-Semitic prejudices were bolstered by the political instruction that he received during his training. In September 1919, his army intelligence masters sent him to investigate this small group. Drexler's ideas appealed to Hitler, for he was bitterly opposed to the "capitalist Jews" and the "Marxist conspiracy" (these ideas were to form the very core of Nazi ideology). Hitler joined Anton Drexler's German Workers' Party in

1919. Drexler wrote confidentially to a colleague about Hitler, describing him as, "An absurd little man", and commenting on how in such a short time Hitler had become steering committee member No 7 of the party. Drexler's position in the party was under threat by Hitler's forceful personality and his persuasive oratory. Hitler later wrote of Drexler in *Mein Kampf*: "His whole being was weak and uncertain, nor did he have the ability to use brutal means to overcome the opposition to a new idea inside the party. What was needed was one fleet as a greyhound, smooth as leather, and hard as steel." In less than a year the "absurd little man" had become the dominant force in the party. Soon afterwards, Hitler had created the *National Sozialistische Deutsche Arbeiter Partei* (National Socialist German Workers' Party – NSDAP) to succeed the DAP.

To inflate its importance and size, Hitler massaged the membership numbers, but the party desperately needed a kick-start. Ernst Röhm, who was chief of staff to the

▼ *German Army troops in Berlin in 1919 during the Spartacist revolt. The* Freikorps *assisted in the suppression of this uprising.*

whose allegiance was to their commanders only, the *Freikorps* fought for the elimination of all "traitors to the Fatherland". They brutally suppressed the Spartacist revolt in Berlin, and then helped to put out the embers of left-wing revolt that had spread to other parts of Germany (ironically, the *Freikorps* fought with British and French approval when they fought against the Bolsheviks in Lithuania and Latvia in 1919).

Onto the political stage during this turbulent time appeared two luminaries, both of which Hitler would eclipse. The first was an insignificant railway locksmith, Anton Drexler. He was a harmless-looking, bespectacled man who worked with the Fatherland Party during and after World War I, whose aim was to get a fair peace for Germany. Drexler merged two tiny groups of malcontents into the *Deutsche Arbeiterpartei*, the German Workers' Party, or DAP, in January 1919. It was an organization with no assets except a cigar box in which to put contributions. The second was a far more sinister character named Ernst Röhm, who could be best described as short, overweight and bullet-scarred, with flushed cheeks and a savage smile. He was a non-conformist, a roistering lecher, homosexual and adventurer who by his own admission detested bourgeois

commandant of the Munich military region, now chose to support Hitler, thus helping the fledgling Nazi Party to grow. Röhm fancifully considered himself a revolutionary and had heady ambitions of forming a revolutionary army with himself at its head. His chosen vehicle was the Bavarian Home Guard, which possessed clandestinely secreted weapons, which Röhm hoped he could use in his revolution. The Berlin government, having collected intelligence about revolutionary activity, disbanded this and other military groups who were covertly gathering in various districts of Germany in early 1921. This thwarted Röhm's ambitions. Hitler's embryonic Nazi Party acted as a magnet and seemed the obvious receptacle for his inflated ego (Röhm was confident he could mould Hitler to his will and usurp his powers). He courted Hitler with introductions to influential persons like General Erich Ludendorff, World War I hero and right-wing nationalist, and General Franz Ritter von Epp, the commandant of the Munich military region. These introductions subsequently bore fruit. Hitler and his party gained credibility and

financial help began to materialize. Money equates to power, a fact not wasted on Hitler. He now needed to improve the party's programme, and its visual aspect would be its best advert. Men were now used to military life and uniforms and the pageantry that went with it. What was more natural than to harness these patriotic feelings, which had been instilled and burned into them during the four years of carnage? Hitler chose the female form of the ancient swastika emblem as his symbol, and planned the design of the Nazi flag, which he described as "something akin to a blazing torch".

With a visual political message and growing financial support, Hitler's party was making progress, but he needed a major confrontation with his political enemies to attract more attention. This occurred on November 4, 1921.

Hitler was informed that at the Hoffbrauhaus, the venue for a speech he was going to make that evening, the left-wing social democrats and the communists were going to try to crush his party. The meeting went ahead, but during his speech fighting broke out in the hall. Hitler later

▲ **The Reichswehr, the 100-000 man post-Versailles Treaty German Army, was forced to train with dummy tanks.**

described the event poetically: "The dance had not yet begun when my stormtroopers, for so they were called from this day on, attacked like wolves. They flung themselves in packs of eight or 10 again and again on their enemies, and little by little actually began to thrash them out of the hall. After five minutes, I hardly saw one of them who was not covered with blood. Then two pistol shots rang out and now a wild din of shouting broke out from all sides. One's heart almost rejoiced at this spectacle which recalled memories of the war."

THE BIRTH OF THE SA
In the early days of Nazism, Hitler was surrounded by the unwieldy *Sturmabteilung* (Storm Detachment), or SA, who were in the main tough, unemployed ex-soldiers who frequented Munich beer halls such as the Torbräukeller near the Isar Gate. They were recruited by Röhm to protect Nazi speakers at public meetings. The Brownshirts, as they became

▲ *Ernst Röhm (second from left), homosexual, bully and freebooter, turned the SA into a powerful arm of the Nazis.*

▼ *The Stosstrupp (Shock Troop) Adolf Hitler provided the Nazi leader with protection in Munich in the early 1920s.*

known, were party uniformed supporters who acted as bodyguards. They were to grow in number, acting under Röhm's orders rather than Hitler's.

The Nazi Party, being small and relatively insignificant, needed the oxygen of publicity to keep its cause alive. In 1922 there occurred an incident that kept the Nazis in the public mind and was later to become part of party folklore. Coburg's city fathers had decided to hold a "German Day"

that was to be a folk festival to encourage German rural life. Coburg's geographical position is some 192km (120 miles) east of Frankfurt on Main and about 64km (40 miles) from Schweinfurt. The city had a population of approximately 30,000, was Marxist controlled and was largely insignificant – until October 1922.

COBURG, OCTOBER 14–15, 1922

Hitler with his party were invited to the gathering (one wonders by whom considering the political persuasion of those who controlled the city), which afforded him the public platform that he so desperately needed to publicize his fledgling party. The chances of political violence were high, but the greater the disturbance, the more media attention it would attract. First, though, Hitler had to overcome an initial problem: transportation to the venue. Although without visible funds, he managed to hire a train, and the tickets bought by almost every party member who boarded the train defrayed the cost. With what was virtually the entire membership of the party – some 700 accompanied by a 42-piece band – set off from Munich in the "special train". Such was the devotion of some of the Nazi membership that many had bought tickets with their last Reichmarks.

The Marxist city officials were far from elated when they perceived the full

INTRODUCTION

ramifications of what was descending on the carefully controlled Coburg festival. A police captain was dispatched to greet the train, who pronounced that the Nazis could not enter the city with flags flying and band playing, as this was contrary to the law. The police officer was brushed aside by Hitler, and the Nazi Party marched off in formation. Eight massive Bavarians carrying Alpenstocks and clad in lederhosen led the cortege, and formed an escort for Hitler and his confidants: Max Amann, Hermann Esser, Dietrich Eckhart, Christian Weber, Ulrich Graf, Alfred Rosenberg and Kurt Ludecke.

Word had spread concerning the approach of the Nazis and a crowd, some thousands strong, threatened to bar their way. One of its Marxist members began to throw projectiles, sparking off a furious fight which lasted approximately 15 minutes. A curious thing now happened, for the crowd began to go over to the Nazis, who proceeded to march into the town. Hitler addressed a meeting in the town hall that evening attended by the Duke and

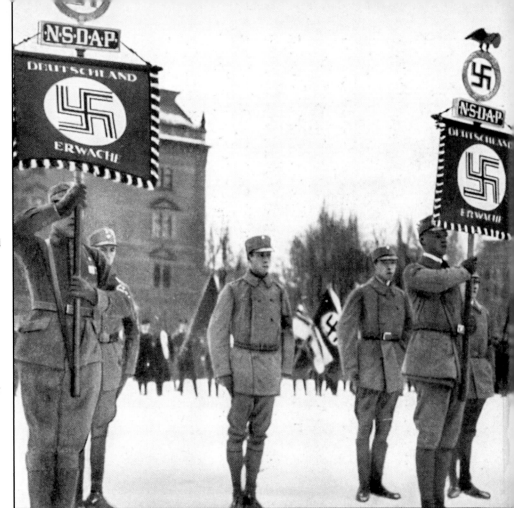

▼ *The swastika flies at the 1st Nazi Party Day on January 28, 1923, held in the snowy streets of Munich.*

▲ **SA men carry Deutschland Erwache (Germany Awake) standards at the 1st Nazi Party Day, January 1928.**

Duchess of Coburg, who were later to become active Nazis. This speech was to be hailed as one of his triumphs, and after it fights raged between Marxists and the Nazis long into the night. In the morning the city was festooned with notices calling for a "People's Demonstration" that would eject the Nazis. The Marxists had made their move. Hitler grouped his men and marched them into the city's main square. Here, it was thought, would be gathered as many as 10,000 townsfolk waiting to annihilate them. Instead, there were only a few hundred die-hard Marxists, whose stranglehold over the city was broken before the day was out. Imperial flags were festooned from windows and the rock-throwing crowds were replaced by cheering throngs. The Marxists, reeling from the defeat, announced that they would not let the "special train" leave. Hitler, buoyed up by his victory, told the officials that he would take hostages of every communist he could find and transport them to Munich on his train. The outcome was not lost on the Marxists, who capitulated to Hitler's demands. Hitler had won his first decisive

victory. In Nazi circles the event entered folklore and led to the expression in later years: "But were you at Coburg?"

The mass meetings continued. A party rally to be held on the outskirts of Munich on the Marsfeld was planned by Hitler during 1922 and proposed for January 27–29 the following year. It was to be the NSDAP's largest rally to date, with 5000 SA men from all over Bavaria converging on Munich. To increase popular appeal, bands and traditional dance groups had been hired, in addition to 12 meeting halls. Also planned were marches of SA and party supporters through the streets of the city on the way to the massed meetings. This *Parteitage* (Party Day) was to be all-important, as Hitler's first four *Deutschland Erwache* ("Germany Awake") standards were to be consecrated on the Marsfeld along with other NSDAP flags. The government, however, became increasingly uneasy upon hearing rumours of a *Putsch* (*coup d'état*), and so a ban was issued against the outdoor ceremony of consecrating the flags and standards, plus half of Hitler's publicly announced meetings throughout Munich. Upon hearing of these bans, Hitler flew into a rage and went to the Munich police commissioner, Eduard Nortz. Hitler demanded that the ban to be lifted, but Nortz would not be moved and reiterated that the ban would remain. Hitler shouted at the commissioner that the rally would still take place in its original

▼ **A lone voice in the political wilderness: Hitler speaks to Nazi Party members outside Munich on April 15, 1923.**

form and, in the defiance of the ban, he would march at the front of the SA through the streets of Munich. Nortz convened a session of the Council of Ministers. They proclaimed a "state of emergency" which automatically banned all the activities planned for the party rally. Hitler now had only one possible solution – the *Reichswehr* – which was sympathetic to the National Socialists. Hitler arranged for Röhm and Ritter von Epp to persuade Lossow, its commander in Bavaria, to meet with him to discuss the situation. After the meeting Lossow informed the government that he considered "the suppression of the Nationalist Socialist organisation unfortunate for security reasons". The ban was subsequently lifted. However, Commissioner Nortz demanded a second meeting with Hitler, where he requested that the number of meetings remained at six instead of 12 and, more importantly, Hitler was to stage the consecration of the standards and flags inside the "Krone Circus" and not outside on the Marsfeld. Vaguely, Hitler indicated compliance with the request.

1ST NAZI PARTY DAY

The *Parteitage* was held between January 27 and 29, 1923, under the slogan *Deutschland Erwache*. Two brigades of men marched through the city of Munich and Hitler held all 12 mass meetings. He declared the swastika would be the national symbol of the future Germany. Furthermore, he stated: "The German spirit cannot be broken in these men, Germany is awakening, the German freedom movement

is on the march.' All the party members swore to be true to the party and the man who led and guided them, i.e. Hitler. It was proclaimed that the name of this movement was the NSDAP. The consecration of the first four *Deutschland Erwache* standards and NSDAP flags as originally planned on the Marsfeld amidst the typical January snowy weather took place on the third day of the *Parteitage* of the NSDAP.

BIRTH OF THE SS, MARCH 1923

Hitler realized the necessity of organizing a more dedicated élite personal guard. This guard should not be large, but it had to consist of men of proven calibre, of Nordic blood and of good character. They had to act as bodyguard and spearhead with an unequivocal allegiance to Hitler. They had to protect both Hitler and important members of his party while they travelled the breadth of Germany furthering the Nazi cause. The Brownshirts could be relied on to meet violence with violence, but they acted under Röhm's orders when they acted on orders at all. Many SA were ex-*Freikorps* members, and they were

▼ *A Nazi supporter in Bavaria in the early 1920s. Many Germans believed the Nazis could solve their nation's economic ills.*

accustomed to swearing loyalty to their immediate commander. They were too unreliable as far as Hitler was concerned; they fulfilled a short-term necessity, but for the future he needed a totally loyal Praetorian Guard. That guard would be later be the *Schutzstaffel* (Defence Squad), the SS.

In March 1923 the embryo SS consisted of just two men – Josef Berchtold and Julius Schreck – who called themselves the *Stabswache* (Staff Guard). Two months later a new unit, the *Stosstruppe Adolf Hitler* commanded by Josef Berchtold, was formed. In August 1923 Heinrich Himmler, its future leader, joined the NSDAP.

By the autumn of 1923 Hitler had made the Nazi Party a rallying point of opposition to the government in Berlin, but he now committed a major error in trying to seize power by force rather than constitutional means. He had seen Mussolini take power in Italy in October 1922 by marching on Rome, thus why could he not do the same?

Perhaps not as sole leader of right-wing forces, but certainly part of a small group that would include Ludendorff, a notable anti-republican and hero of the right.

Circumstances seemed to favour a coup against the Weimar government: Germany was almost bankrupt, a fact not helped by the world slump of 1921. She defaulted on reparations payments (one of the hated clauses of the Treaty of Versailles), which prompted the French to occupy the Ruhr, the centre of German industry, in January 1923, which acted as the catalyst for destroying the value of German currency. The fault was laid at the feet of the "November Criminals", those individuals who had signed the Treaty of Versailles, plus the communists, Jews, profiteers and social democrats who had betrayed the army during World War I – the "stab-in-the-back" theory – and who still worked for the downfall of Germany. All fanciful stuff, but very popular with ex-soldiers, serving

▲ Hitler and senior Nazis stand before a huge swastika banner. The swastika (Hakenkreuz) became the most powerful political symbol of the twentieth century.

▶ Ulrich Graf, ex-soldier and butcher, was Hitler's personal bodyguard.

▲ Brownshirts in a Munich beer hall in the early 1920s. Battles with communists in beer halls became part of Nazi folklore.

soldiers and the vast reservoir of anti-Semitism and anti-democratic resentment that existed in Germany at the time. To Hitler and the right, the time appeared right to take power by force of arms, and restore Germany's pride and place in the world. Unfortunately for the Nazis, events conspired against them. A communist uprising in Hamburg was defeated on October 23, and by the end of that month the *Reichswehr* had defeated communists in the governments of the states of Saxony and Thuringia. This denied the Munich plotters the excuse of the threat of communism. However, as far as Hitler was concerned the die was cast: the coup would go ahead. On the eve of the November 9 Munich *Putsch*, Gustav von Kahr, head of the Bavarian government, was to speak in the Bürgerbräukeller (Kahr was

sympathetic to the right and Hitler had tried to recruit him to his cause, but Kahr had prevaricated and withdrawn his support). Unnoticed, Hitler, Max Amann, Alfred Rosenberg and Ulrich Graf took up position in the hall. After Kahr had been speaking for about 20 minutes, 25 armed Brownshirts, accompanied by Hermann Göring – World War I air ace and now commander of the SA – burst into the hall. At this moment Hitler leapt upon a chair, fired a shot into the ceiling and shouted: "The National Revolution has begun. This hall is occupied by 600 armed men. No one may leave the hall. The Bavarian and Reich Governments have been removed and a provisional National Government formed. The army and police barracks have been occupied, troops and police are marching on the city under the swastika banner."

THE MUNICH *PUTSCH*

Most of what Hitler said was bluff, though the audience did not know it. Hitler ushered Kahr, General Otto von Lossow and Colonel Hans von Seisser into a side room and announced that they must join him in the new government with General Ludendorff. Hitler then rushed from the room and declared to the stunned audience that the three had agreed to join him in a new government. In a wild sense of

euphoria he returned to the three men as General Ludendorff arrived. The latter was in total ignorance of any of the proceedings and was furious that all of this was taking place using his name without his permission. But he supported the general principles of what was taking place and went along with Hitler. In apparent unity they all filed back into the hall. It was now that Hitler made the first of many mistakes, leaving the hall to attempt to settle a disagreement between army engineers and SA stormtroopers that had broken out. Everyone left the hall, including the generals. At the same time the *Reichskriegsflagge*, the Reich Flag of War, another right-wing organization, was holding a "social" in the Augustiner Beer Cellar, when Ernst Röhm, its commander, was ordered to seize the former *Reichswehr* ministry in the Leopoldstrasse.

KAHR WITHDRAWS
Lossow returned to his own headquarters and began to call up the troops from outlying garrisons. Kahr publicly denounced the whole episode, which should have signalled the collapse of the *Putsch*. Ludendorff, however, was now

heavily committed, and he persuaded Hitler to go ahead with the coup.

On what happened incidentally to be the 124th anniversary of Napoleon's *coup d'état* of Brumaire, Hitler had assembled over 2000 men to help him overthrow the Bavarian State government. At midmorning on November 9 they gathered into file and began to march towards the Ludwig Bridge leading to the centre of the city. At the head of the column marched Hitler between Ludendorff, Max Erwin von Scheubner-Richter and Ulrich Graf on one side, and Dr Christian Weber, Gottfried Feder and Colonel Kriebel on the other. Julius Streicher, Nazi rabble rouser, who had been ranting at the crowd in the Marienplatz, joined the second rank. Rosenberg and Albrecht von Graefe, representative of the North German Nationalists and who had come only at Ludendorff's summons, trudged resentfully along with the rest. Behind the leaders were three units marching abreast in columns of four. On the left was Hitler's 100-man bodyguard, steel helmeted and armed with carbines and "potato masher" grenades. On the right was the *Bund Oberland*, a paramilitary organization that had once been a

▲ The SA marches to the War Memorial in Munich in 1923. A hatless Hitler reviews the parade from the pavement.

Freikorps, and in the middle was the battle-seasoned Munich SA Regiment. Himmler, carrying the imperial war flag, led the *Reichskriegsflagge* column. Behind followed a motley collection of men, some in uniform or parts of tattered World War I uniforms, and some wearing work clothes or business suits. The cadets from Infantry School, smart and ultra military, were sandwiched between students, shop-keepers, middle-aged businessmen and hard-faced "Freebooters". The only common mark among them was a swastika brassard on the left arm.

FARCE
From the Marienplatz they turned down the Residenzstrasse towards the Odeonsplatz. Beyond was the old War Ministry where Ernst Röhm with other stormtroopers stood surrounded and impotent. At the end of the street the police were drawn up with carbines. There was only room enough in the street for eight abreast. Hitler locked arms with Scheubner-

Richter in preparation for trouble. Ludendorff touched no one, still supremely confident that no one would fire on him. Those who participated claimed the police shot first. Some said Streicher screamed: "Ludendorff! Don't shoot your General! Hitler and Ludendorff!" Others said it was Graf. At any rate the police fired. Ludendorff was unhurt and marched ahead. Scheubner-Richter dropped to the ground, fatally wounded, pulling Hitler to the ground with him, wrenching the latter's shoulder as he did so. Ulrich Graf, Hitler's bodyguard, covered Hitler with his body and received 11 bullets. Kurt Neubauer, Ludendorff's valet, who had sprung in front of the general to protect him, lay dead, shot in the head. As Hitler sprawled on the ground, thinking he had been shot in the left side, comrades tried to shield him. In all 18 men lay dead in the street, 14 followers of Hitler and four state police (all incidentally more or less sympathetic to National Socialism).

▼ **Hitler's attempt to seize political power by force: arms being distributed to his followers prior to the Munich Putsch.**

The crowd jammed up behind only heard firecracker explosions ahead, but then a rumour spread that both Hitler and Ludendorff had been killed. The *Putschists* scrambled to the rear; the crowd panicked and fled. Hitler, accompanied by a towering young local physician and chief of the Munich SA medical corps, Dr Walther Schultze (who would later become Reich Leader of Teachers), made good his escape. At Max Joseph Platz they finally reached Hitler's old grey Selve, and Dr Schultze bundled Hitler into it. After taking various routes of escape and increasing the pain in Hitler's dislocated shoulder, they took refuge 59km (37 miles) away at Uffing in the Hanfstaengl's villa (Ernst Hanfstaengl was the only literary member of Hitler's early inner circle; tall and a practical joker, he became a sort of court jester to the Führer before and after he came to power. He eventually fell out with Hitler and had to flee to the United States to save his life). Göring, also wounded, was carried into another car and driven by his wife Karin across the Austro-German frontier. Röhm surrendered at the War Ministry two hours

later. The *Putsch* ended in a fiasco: the rank and file surrendered their weapons, identified themselves to the police and returned home, while the leaders were arrested. Himmler returned to Landshut where he sold advertising space in the *Völkischer Beobachter* (*The Racial Observer*, the official newspaper of the Nazi Party).

THE *VÖLKISCHER BEOBACHTER*
The paper had originally been a weekly sheet devoted to spreading gossip, though immediately after World War I it became more anti-Semitic. In February 1923 Hitler, having raised money with the help of Hansfstaengl, made it a daily newspaper. The chief editor was Nazi racial "expert" Alfred Rosenberg, who filled its columns with anti-Jewish literature. He praised the Nordic race and launched scathing attacks on "coloured subhumanity". The treasurer of the *Völkischer Beobachter*, Max Amann, was Rosenberg's great rival, and they often fought with each other over editorial content. Rosenberg wanted to politicize readers by stressing the Nazi way of life, whereas Amann was only interested in making money for the party. Following the Munich Putsch, the paper ran a front-page headline proclaiming "Hitler's Triumph". The

issue was priced at eight billion Marks, a reflection of the state of Germany's currency at the time.

THE BANNING OF THE NSDAP

The Munich Beer Hall *Putsch* died with the men who fell in the streets. Though it was a failure, Hitler didn't consider it as such, but rather a success for what it ultimately achieved. It had created martyrs, and Hitler needed martyrs. The red flag blazoned with a black swastika on a white circular field that had been carried as the emblem and clarion call at the head of the march became another of those Nazi propaganda concepts which walked the fine line between the ridiculous and genuinely effective. The banner, made sacrosanct by the blood of the martyrs of the *Putsch*, was to become the icon of the party as well as the primary flag of the Nazi movement.

On the same date as the failed Putsch, the General State Commissar issued an order dissolving the NSDAP and stipulated heavy

▼ *The Munich* Putsch. *In this photograph are Rudolf Hess (second from left) and Heinrich Himmler (holding flag).*

penalties for anyone attempting to carry on the work of the party. The SA and the *Stosstruppe Adolf Hitler* were banned. Röhm was one of those put on trial; although found guilty of treasonable acts, he was released and dismissed from the army. Shortly afterwards he went to Bolivia to work as a military instructor. Berchtold, the *Stosstruppe Adolf Hitler* commander, managed to escape to Austria and remain in exile there. On the following day the police searched the headquarters of the NSDAP in the Corneliusstrasse and confiscated everything they could lay their hands on. It was during this difficult period for the Nazi movement that Julius Streicher tried his best to keep the banned NSDAP together as a unit. To evade the ban he set up a new party, the *Völkischer-Freiheits-Bewegung*. Streicher founded his own paper in 1923. Entitled *Der Stürmer* (*The Stormer*), he later claimed that it was the only paper that Hitler read from cover to cover. Among its more notable "achievements" was the discovery that Jesus was not a Jew. Following the *Putsch* Streicher worked as a teacher, though he clashed with his superiors on numerous occasions, not least

because he insisted that his pupils greet him each day with "*Heil Hitler!*". In many ways he was the archetypal Nazi: brutal, violent and sadistic, he advocated the use of force as the solution to any problem. Probably insane, after the war he was tried at Nuremberg, an event he denounced as "a triumph for world Jewry". Found guilty and condemned to death, his last words on the scaffold were "*Heil Hitler!*".

DEFEAT

The Nazi Party had been defeated and was in disarray, its leaders either arrested or having fled into exile. The Weimar government had seemingly triumphed. The party had 70,000 members in Bavaria before the *Putsch*, but by the middle of July 1925 this had fallen to 700. The original members had been mostly believers in *Völkish* ideas, which sought to promote Germanic culture and eliminate the influence of other peoples. The *Völkish* movement provided the ideological starting point of National Socialism. Hitler wrote in *Mein Kampf*: "The basic ideas of the National Socialist movement are *Völkish* and the *Völkish* ideas are National

▲ *The failed* **Putsch** *became a central part of Nazi myth. This Blood Order was later presented to those who took part.*

deeds. And out of this time, which also included the period before 1923, came the *Alte Kämpfer* (the "old fighters"), the early members of the Nazi Party who were later revered for their role in the rise of National Socialism. When Hitler gained power the old fighters were given preference for jobs in the Nazi bureaucracy, and those who had been injured in street battles with communists were given the same benefits as the ones allowed to disabled World War I veterans.

Thus was the myth of the Munich *Putsch* created, which propelled Adolf Hitler onto the national stage. As Hitler was to state: "As though by an explosion, our ideas were hurled over the whole of Germany." It had been a semi-farcical affair, and had stood little chance of success, even with the revered Ludendorff on board (he had walked right through the police lines on November 9, the policemen having turned their weapons away as a sign of respect). Hitler also learned a valuable lesson: that he would not achieve political power through direct action, especially without the support of the armed forces. He would have to achieve political victory by winning over the masses to his side, plus enlisting the support of wealthy industrialists. In this way he could gain power through legitimate channels.

Socialist." However, he was keen to stress that the Nazis were different from the numerous discussion groups that existed to debate the finer points of what *Völkish* actually meant.

The Nazi Party's Programme, which contained 25 points, provides an example of these Völkish ideas. Point 1 advocated the union of all Germans within a Greater Germany; Point 8 called for the halting of all non-German immigration; Point 19 proposed the replacing of Roman Law, which was materialistic, with "German law"; and Point 23 stated that newspapers must be German-owned.

Though the party had been seemingly destroyed, many thousands still believed in its principles, hence it would be relatively easy to rebuild its power base. This is not to underestimate the task facing senior Nazis in the aftermath of the Putsch. Indeed, the period became known as the *Kampfzeit* (the "time of struggle"), which later was portrayed as a time of heroes and great

▶ *The shrine to the fallen of the Munich* **Putsch,** *the Feldherrnhalle in Munich, where the 16 martyrs were buried.*

1923-32

The failure of the Munich Putsch was the low point in the Nazi Party's fortunes. However, Hitler's lenient sentence meant he could rebuild the party relatively quickly. Though the party performed poorly at the elections in the 1920s, the world economic depression in 1929 gave Hitler and his followers a much-needed boost, as the German people saw their economy and standard of living nose-dive, and they began to listen to Hitler's rantings about Jews, communists and international conspiracies against Germany.

POLITICS, *BAVARIA*
A diffident young state police lieutenant, accompanied by two other officers, discovers Hitler at the Hanfstaengl Villa. Hitler shakes hands with the young man and says he is prepared to leave. Hitler arrives at the district office at about 21:45 hours and is formally arraigned, before being hustled to the prison at Landsberg. Throughout the tiring trip over winding, deserted roads, Hitler is depressed and sullen. At Landsberg Prison the chief warder is preparing for a possible attempt by *Putschists* to free him. An army detachment is on its way to stand guard but has not arrived by the time the great nail-studded iron entrance gate creaks open to admit him. He is brought to the fortress section of the prison and put into cell 7, the only one

▼ *General Erich Ludendorff, who took part in the Munich Putsch but was acquitted at the subsequent trial.*

▲ *The aftermath of the Putsch. Empty Munich streets as the Bavarian government rounds up Nazi participants.*

with an anteroom large enough for a military guard.

FEBRUARY 24, 1924

LEGAL, *MUNICH*

All Germany watches Munich this morning for the political significance of the treason charges against Hitler, Ludendorff and eight co-defendants, the ramifications of which go far beyond their personal fate. The new republic and democracy is as much on trial as one of Germany's most respected war heroes and a fanatic from Austria. Though they are on trial for treason, the odds are stacked in the defendants' favour. First, public opinion favours them; second, the minister of justice, Franz Gürtner, is openly sympathetic to the Nazi cause; and finally, the presiding judge, Georg Neithardt, is a fervent nationalist who regards Ludendorff as a national treasure. Hitler defends himself

brilliantly, though considering those who are judging him, he would have difficulty doing otherwise. In his closing remarks he portrays himself as a man of destiny: "Gentlemen, judgment will not be passed on us by you; judgment will be passed on us by the eternal court of history. This court will judge the accusations that have been made against us. The other court, however, will not ask: 'Did you or did you not commit high treason?' That court will pass judgment on us, on the General in command of the Quartermaster Corps of the old army, on his officers and soldiers, who as Germans wanted the best for their people and their country, who were willing to fight and die for it. Even if you find us guilty a thousand times over, the goddess of the eternal tribunal of history will smilingly tear apart the proposal of the Prosecutor and the sentence of the Court, because she will acquit us." The trial that only the *Putschists* wanted comes to an end on April 1, and although Hitler has won the battle of propaganda, he is back in prison and for all he knew would remain there four and a half years. However, he becomes a national hero in Germany, while Ludendorff is acquitted altogether. To a large segment of the German public and to the Western world in general, though, the sentence is ridiculously mild for treason and armed uprising. The whole affair has been a stunning defeat for the Weimar Republic, but a triumph for right-wing nationalism.

▶ *Kurt Daluege, who formed the Frontbann-Nord unit in Berlin following banning of the SA.*

APRIL 1924

NAZI PARTY, *REFORM OF THE SA*

Ernst Röhm is charged with the reconstruction of the officially still-illegal SA. In an attempt to get around the government law, Röhm founds an organization known as the *Frontbann*, basically the SA under another name. The *Frontbann*, meaning "Front Band", is formed as a substitute for the SA. Units are formed in various parts of Germany. *Frontbann-Nord* is founded in Berlin by Kurt Daluege, an ex-*Freikorps* member, and is destined later to be the basis of SA *Gruppe Berlin-Brandenburg*. In all the *Frontbann* numbers some 30,000 men.

MAY 1924

POLITICS, *ELECTIONS*

With the Nazi Party outlawed and Hitler in prison, some members stand as the National Socialist Freedom Movement. In the first election of 1924 this grouping win nearly two million votes and 32 of its 34 candidates – among them Strasser, Rohm and Ludendorff – enter the *Reichstag*, the German parliament. The

second election in December 1924, however, sees the National Socialist vote more than halve as the National Socialist Freedom Party loses 18 seats (the *Reichstag* has a total of 472 seats).

DECEMBER 20, 1924

LEGAL, *LANDSBERG*

It is during his time in prison that Hitler dictates to Rudolf Hess, who has taken the position of his secretary, his book. Hitler initially titles it: *Four and a Half years of Struggle against Lies, Stupidity and Cowardice.* In it he attempts to set out his political dreams. However Amann, a rough, uncouth but shrewd and intuitive man, changes the title to *Mein Kampf - My Struggle.* He also arranges the publication of the book and organizes the royalties, which are to become Hitler's main source of income. He later supervises the dozens

▶ *Adolf Hitler photographed in 1926. He wears the Iron Cross and Wound Badge, both of which he won in World War I.*

▲ *Julius Schreck, who in 1925 formed the Stosstruppe Adolf Hitler to guard the leader of the Nazi Party.*

of editions published during Hitler's life, and with *Gleichschaltung* (the complete fusing of every element of German life into the Nazi social machine) of the press would become president of the Reich association of newspaper publishers and president of the Reich press chamber.

FEBUARY 1925

POLITICS, *NAZI PARTY*

It was not until January 1925 that the official ban was lifted on the NSDAP, and on February 27, 1925, in the Bürgerbräukeller in Munich, Hitler assembles the party faithful to re-establish the NSDAP. After re-establishment of the NSDAP the "interim" *Völkischer-Freiheits-Bewegung* is dissolved. Service time with the party is counted from February, with the time from that date to January 30, 1933 counting double in recognition of the *Kampfzeit* ("time of struggle") by members of the Old Guard. Himmler acts as General Secretary to Gregor Strasser who, in February 1925, agrees to disband his party and assimilate it into the reformed NSDAP.

APRIL 1925

NAZI PARTY, *REBIRTH OF THE SS*

Hitler orders the former member of the *Stosstruppe Adolf Hitler* and his chauffeur, Julius Schreck, to form a new guard unit. Two weeks later, Schreck forms a new headquarters guard and re-christens it the *Schutzstaffel* or SS Protection Squad,

though still called the *Stosstruppe Adolf Hitler*. Initially the new SS consists of only eight men, most of whom have previously been members of the *Stosstruppe Adolf Hitler*. Schreck, however, devises a plan to set up SS units throughout Germany.

A circular was sent out in September 1925 which called on party groups to set up Schutzstaffeln. These were to be small, élite squads of 10 men and one commander,

▲ *After his release from Landsberg, Hitler worked hard to rebuild the Nazi Party. Here, he speaks in a Munich beer hall.*

made up of respected young men in their communities and totally loyal to Hitler. By January 1926 Schreck's plan had worked and the SS had established itself on a national level. Josef Berchtold, the original commander of the Stosstruppe Adolf Hitler, returned to Germany from exile in Austria and in April 1926 took over command of the SS from Schreck.

JULY 1926

NAZI PARTY, *SECOND PARTY DAY*

It is at this rally, held in Weimar, that Adolf Hitler turns over the coveted "Blood Flag" to the SS and proclaims the SS to be his élite organization. As such, these small SS units have become the élite units of the SA. It is because of this that the SS is given the honour of bearing the *Deutschland Erwache* standards of the SA at party meetings and rallies.

SEPTEMBER 1926

NAZI PARTY, *INTERNAL POLITICS*

Gregor Strasser is appointed Reich propaganda leader of the NSDAP, and Himmler accompanies him to party headquarters as his secretary. Himmler now

◀ *Hitler at a meeting of the party hierarchy in the mid–1920s. To his left are Strasser, Himmler and Rosenberg.*

KEY MOMENTS

The Nazis in Decline?

A forecaster in 1928 would have predicted nothing but doom and gloom for the NSDAP. In fact the Nazi Party was in steep decline; it was going to "hell on a handcart". It suffered a significant humiliation in the polls that year. The political situation was dire, there was little to celebrate, and hence there was no Party Day in 1928 (at times the Nazis gave the appearance of being sulky children). The Weimar Republic, which Hitler had so bitterly criticized, was defeating the Nazis resoundingly in one political skirmish after another. Hitler had raved about the occupation of the Ruhr, which had been occupied by the French and Belgians in January 1923 following German failure to make timely reparations payments, when the French withdrew; the Weimar government reaped the reward. Hitler ranted about inflation; again the Weimar government stabilized the situation. Hitler's protestations on Law and Order were overlooked; when it was temporarily restored again the Weimar government received the applause. Politically, the Nazis were fading fast. The world economic depression of 1929, however, would see them become a force again in German politics, as Hitler blamed Jews and communists for Germany's economic troubles.

finds himself a local party official with command over the tiny SS in his district.

Strasser was de facto leader of the Nazi Party during Hitler's time in Landsberg. He established the National Socialist Freedom Movement with Ludendorff and Röhm, and also set up a newspaper, the Berlin Workers' Paper. He appointed Josef Goebbels to be editor.

Goebbels was born the son of a director of a small textile factory in Rheydt, a small industrial town in the Rhineland. His mother was a devout Catholic and he had two brothers and a sister. At four years old he contracted polio and the physician advised immediate surgery, but this could not prevent him having a crippled left leg and foot. This disability remained with him for the rest of his life, and gave rise to him having to wear special shoes, braces and bandages. Because of its visible effects he became a quiet boy who withdrew into himself, not being able to join in games with his brothers, sister or other children. Being physically inferior, the young Goebbels developed his intellectual powers. He would criticize at every

▼ *A Nazi Party rally in the 1920s. Military style parades were an important part of Nazi ritual for giving an image of strength.*

opportunity; his continual hateful remarks earned him the reputation of being arrogant and difficult to get along with. When World War I broke out he volunteered for the army, but inevitably was pronounced unfit for military service. He, as many German students of the time, attended no less than eight universities. He became superbly educated in philosophy, Greek and Latin. Slowly, feelings of nationalism began to grow in him, and as a result of this he was alienated from almost everything that surrounded him in these days: his family, hometown, leftist intellectuals, the leftist press and his communist friend of several years standing, Flisges. When he became a nationalist he betrayed everything he had formerly adhered to. His chauvinism was peppered with mysticism. He began to believe that Germany had a special mission to fulfil, and after some time came to the conclusion that non-Germans were by nature inferior and therefore of no importance. In consequence, he broke off all contact with Jews as, according to him they were not German. He once said later: "I treasure an ordinary prostitute above a married Jewess." In 1922, Goebbels returned to Munich where he studied, and soon became

▲ *The Nazi Party Day in Weimar in 1926, at which Hitler proclaimed the SS to be his élite organization.*

▲ *Hitler consecrates Nazi standards while holding the "Blood Flag", the banner that was carried during the Munich Putsch.*

a member of the NSDAP. He became Gregor Strasser's secretary, the man responsible for NSDAP activities in northern Germany. In 1925 important differences of opinion arose between the National Socialists in the north and those in the south. A meeting was held for all northern party officials. The discussion became so heated that at one point Goebbels cried out: "I propose that the insignificant bourgeois Adolf Hitler be thrown out of the party." The corruption and the confusing reports about the party in the south had undermined his faith in

Hitler and had reached the point of no longer accepting Hitler's leadership. He led the *Gau* Ruhr from March 7 to June 20, 1926 with Kaufmann and Pfeffer. On November 9, 1926, he was appointed by Hitler *Gauleiter* (a *Gau* was a Nazi Party adminstrative region, each headed by a *Gauleiter*) for Berlin. Hitler knew only too well that the young intellectual would

come into his own in the turbulent streets of the capital. On arriving there Goebbels found a corrupt and divided local NSDAP department. There were hardly any members and the communists and socialists were by far the larger movements. In early 1927, speaking to only 600 party members, he said: "We must break through the wall of anonymity. The Berliner can insult us, slander us, beat us, as long as they talk about us. Today we are 600 strong, but in six years time there will be 600,000 of us."

As for Gregor Strasser, he regarded himself as an intellectual, and he emphasized the socialist side of Nazism, and called for land nationalization and profit-sharing in industry. He began to wage a war of words with Hitler over this issue. However, at Bamberg in February 1926 Hitler spoke so strongly against the Strasserites that he won over Goebbels to his cause and ended Strasser's claim to ideological leadership of the party. His Berlin stronghold was put under Göbbels as *Gauleiter*, who at the same time was given full authority to write party propaganda. To an extent Strasser was

◀ *Hitler at the party Day held at Nuremberg in 1927. On the right is Franze Pfeffer von Salomon, SA commander.*

mollified by his new position, and giving him charge of party organization used his skills. Nevertheless, Hitler had defeated a major threat.

NOVEMBER 1, 1926

NAZI PARTY, *THE SA*

Hitler places *Hauptmann* Franz Pfeffer von Salomon as commander of the SA throughout Germany. A condition of Pfeffer von Salomon taking the position is that the SS also comes under the overall authority of the appointed SA leader. Hitler agrees to this because he needs Pfeffer's influence over the North German SA. Pfeffer von Solomon is unsentimental and a Prussian rather than Bavarian in outlook, and is not taken in by Hitler's image. "That flabby Austrian", the taut and austere Pfeffer von Solomon has reportedly called him.

▼ **Deutschland Erwache (Germany Awake) standards on parade. Hitler borrowed the phrase from one of Wagner's works.**

Under Pfeffer, recruitment to the SA continues, largely from the unemployed, bringing the strength from 2000 to over 60,000 by 1930. Many have joined it in the hope that in time it will be absorbed into the army. Röhm has encouraged this idea. As it grows, political elements in the SA begin to challenge the Nazi Party and demand a greater say in its running. In particular, they insist on nomination of SA men as party candidates in the Reichstag elections. Hitler views with alarm the increasing dissension of the Brownshirts, which appears to be encouraged by their leadership. The SS, meanwhile, remains totally obedient.

AUGUST 1927

NAZI PARTY, *THIRD PARTY DAY*

Hitler's speeches of the last few months have indicated that he is obsessed with his personal ideology, his *Weltanschauung* (World View). This states that the Aryan-Nordic race was the founder and is the maintainer of civilization, whereas the Jews are destroyers. Again and again he hammers at race and the fact that Germany's future lies in conquest of Eastern territories. Over and over he preaches his pseudo-Darwinist

Lebensraum was an integral part of Nazi ideology, which linked the twin concepts of space and race. Hitler believed that Germany needed more farmland to support itself – the need to be self-sufficient. Given the Nazi theory of race, it was only natural that she should take lands from the "inferior" Slav peoples of Poland and the Soviet Union.

JANUARY 9, 1928

NAZI PARTY, *INTERNAL POLITICS*
Hitler appoints Goebbels head of propaganda for the entire nation.

Goebbels later became Minister of Propaganda in Hitler's first cabinet. His ministry was situated in the heart of Berlin across from the Reich Chancellery. After an extensive renovation, he boasted that he was in charge of the smallest but most efficient ministry in the Reich. It consisted of 300 civil servants and 500 other employees. His heads of department were given a free hand and he expected a considerable amount of initiative from them. His top assistants were Otto Dietrich as press officer and Max Amann, head of *Eher Verlag*, the NSDAP Publishing

◀ **Hermann Göring (left), one of the first Nazis to be elected to the Reichstag, with Rudolf Hess, deputy party leader.**

Company. All aspects of German artistic life came under the Reich Culture Chamber after September 22, 1933. The purpose of this institution was the furtherance of "German culture" and to bring together artists from all fields in a single organization under the control of the Reich. Any artist who had a reputation for being outspoken against the regime or critical of it was prohibited from carrying out their professional career. It was Goebbels who introduced national holidays, such as May Day and the *Erntedant*, the harvest celebration. These holidays, which became more and more inflated and extensive, offered excellent opportunities for speeches and for showing the people how fortunate they were to be living under National Socialism. With these holidays, Goebbels also created a Nazi tradition, and after a few years it seemed to most Germans that they had been celebrating them all their lives.

The outbreak of war in 1939 started a new chapter in Goebbel's propaganda programme. The people had to be prepared for war, and that war had to be justified. Therefore, in addition to domestic enemies

▼ **Hitler in his supercharged Mercedes electioneering in the late 1920s. On the right is Kurt Daluege.**

sermon of nature's way: conquest of the weak by the strong. This programme is carried a step forward at the third Party Day. Almost 20,000 members, 8500 of them in uniform, flood into the ancient city of Nuremburg accompanied by the usual pageantry: marching with flags and standards to the strains of rousing military airs. It is on the last day of the celebrations, Sunday August 21, that Hitler connects the the central concept of *Lebensraum* (Living Space) with anti-Semitism, but few realize the significance of this misbegotten marriage, for the terms are too vague. He reiterates his demands for more living space for the German people, then points out that power and power alone is the basis for acquisition of new territory. But, he says, Germany has been robbed of her God-given power by three abominations: internationalism, democracy and pacifism. Hitler then links this evil trinity with racism. Are not internationalism, democracy and pacifism all creations of the Jew? Surely, if obscurely, Hitler has mated *Lebensraum* with anti-Semitism. His unsystematic search for *Weltanschuung* is close to realization.

▲ *Hitler gives a speech to the party faithful in the late 1920s. By this time he had powerful industrial supporters.*

and the Jews, the injustice of the Treaty of Versailles was expounded, attention was directed towards the "cruel fate" of the pan-Germans in Czechoslovakia and Poland, and the "historical unity" of Austria and Germany was stressed. The propaganda had begun with "Germany Awake" and "The Jews are our Misfortune", but now the emphasis was placed on "Blood and Soil" and "People without Living Space" and "Guns for Butter".

Away from his work, Goebbels had a fancy for beautiful women, and he struck up a relationship with a young Czech actress, Linda Baarova. This blossomed into a serious love affair and when his wife Magda heard about it she considered divorce. She approached Hitler to seek his permission, whereupon he intervened. He summoned Goebbels and asked him for an update on the position. Goebbels informed him that he was in love and wanted to marry Baarova. Hitler became extremely agitated and demanded to know how could the German Minister of Propaganda get a divorce? Goebbels asked permission to resign, enabling him to seek a divorce and marry Baarova. He also sought to be made ambassador to Japan. Hitler flew into one of his manic rages: "Those who make history may not have a private life!" Goebbels was unmoved, so Hitler finally agreed on a compromise. He might divorce Magda and remarry should he feel the same way a year later. But he was not allowed to see Baarova during the year. Goebbels gave his word of honour that he would obey. Goebbel's throne was shaky and many party leaders, among them Himmler, were convinced Goebbels would break his word. Göring and Ribbentrop also wished to usurp his position. As a result of these threats, Goebbels never saw Baarova again.

MAY 1928

POLITICS, *REICHSTAG ELECTIONS*

The Social Democrats increase their vote from 7.8 million to 9 million, whereas the extreme right-wing German National Party drop from 6.2 million to 4.3 million. The Nazis manage to win only 810,000 votes, giving them only 12 of the 491 seats in the *Reichstag*. Although a group of National Socialist deputies, among them Strasser and Goebbels, take their place in the House for the first time, closer analysis reveals that the right is suffering in German politics. Ironically, the elections were the best thing that could have happened to Hitler considering the circumstances. As right-wingers lose more and more positions and power through elections, they begin to search for another cause around which to rally. That cause is the Nazi Party.

1929 saw things moving in Hitler's favour. Germany's big industry began to support him. Alfred Hugenberg, a millionaire and right-wing politician, was to be a prime mover. Hugenberg owned a huge propaganda empire, which included a chain of newspapers, news agencies and the leading film company in Germany, UFA. It was through this propaganda machine that Hitler managed to gain power (Hugenberg put the resources of his papers at Hitler's disposal). Following Hugenberg's lead were other important groups that added their weight to the Nazi cause. The *Stahlhelm* (Steel Helmet), for example, a militant right-wing nationalist ex-servicemen's association, had nearly one million members. The Pan-German League, Alberg Voegler, president of the United Steel Corporation and Hjalmar Schacht, president of the German Reichsbank (who was opposed to reparations payments), all lent their support to the Nazi cause. With this favourable climate, the Nazis deduced they

▼ *Hitler Youth girls take part in gymnastics. The Nazis made great effort to recruit youngsters.*

could and should hold their rally, which was planned to be held at Nuremburg in August 1929. It was to upstage all spectacles held thus far. In 1927 Nuremburg had completed a war memorial in the form of a statue to commemorate the dead of World War I. Little did the city fathers know it would be used by the Nazis as the centrepiece of their rallies from this time on.

AUGUST 2-4, 1929

NAZI PARTY, *FOURTH PARTY DAY*

On August 2, the Nazi Party convenes its rally; there are 60,000 men and 2000 Hitler Youth present. At 11:00 hours in the Kulturvereinshaus, Gregor Strasser convenes the congress. Hitler sits passively

▶ Hitler Youth members welcome their Führer to a Nuremberg rally. Boys found the militarized Hitler Youth very attractive.

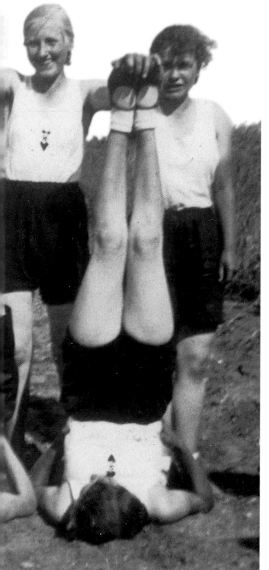

by as Julius Streicher welcomes the delegates and Adolf Wagner reads Hitler's opening statement. This rehashes all of the old dogmas: the injustice shown to German soldiers by the home front during World War I; those of the Treaty of Versailles; and finally a vitriolic attack on the communists and of course the Jews. Gottfried Feder speaks during the afternoon, discussing the Young Plan which required Germany to pay reparation for 59 years. Even though the reparations are less than those imposed

under the previous Dawes Plan (which proposed a rate of payment by Germany of 2000 million gold Marks a year), they are ammunition for the Nazis and employed with great advantage.

Nuremberg watches with amazement the pageantry that it would witness over the next years. The highlight of August 3 is a vast

▼ Hitler said of his aims regarding German youth: "A violently active, dominating, brutal youth – that is what I am after."

torchlight parade followed by a fireworks extravaganza. The most spectacular display takes place when five bands accompany the crowd in the singing of the national anthem. The centrepiece of the display is a swastika surrounded by a circle of green leaves and topped with a huge eagle.

A memorial celebration to commemorate the dead of World War I takes place in front of the new war memorial the following day. A stone coffin is topped by a helmet and covered with hundreds of wreaths. Hitler, escorted by dozens of flags, makes his entrance and General von Epp makes a short address. Then the highest leaders of the Nazi Party, accompanied by standard bearers, make their way onto the field while the band plays a march. There are 34 new standards, and as each new standard passes Hitler he touches it with one hand while holding the "Blood Flag" in the other. This part of the ceremony concludes with the massive crowd chanting *Deutchland Erwache* in unison; the party's rallying cry for the years to come.

Delegates have marched from the northern, middle and southern provinces of Germany to take part in this event, and it takes those from the south more than an hour just to march by. Many Hitler Youth also march. Delegates have even come from other countries: Austria, Sudentenland, Sweden, South Africa, and the Americas.

That evening in the Kulturvereinshaus, Alfred Rosenberg, Nazi ideological "expert"

◀ The party created awards to inculcate a sense of belonging. This is the Germanic Proficiency Runes introduced by Himmler.

and rabble-rouser, lashes out against his favourite foe – communism – in a vitriolic speech to the roar of the crowd.

One of the most prophetic speeches, though, comes from another delegate, Konstantin Hierl, who virtually proclaims that the Nazis, once they have achieved power, will prepare the state to be ready and willing to resort to war if necessary. These are strong words when the world is attempting to recover from the "War to End all Wars". Hierl leaves no one in doubt when he states: "As long as free nations exist that are willing to work towards their political goals, only war will be able to achieve the ultimate political aim."

Hitler closes the congress on the evening of August 5 with a final address on the

deterioration of German national power and says Germany's leaders to date have turned a great nation into nothing more than a state tourist country. As he calls his country to his version of greatness, which will banish the weak, the political opposition and the Jews from any role in society, and includes the resort to war if necessary to obtain what is "rightfully" Germany's, Hitler watches with pride as the audience roars its approval. In his own mind he has no doubts that he has taken the first step towards immortality, rather than his first leap towards infamy. However, he and his party are elated by their success. This was to be the last party day until the Nazis came to power in 1933.

JANUARY 6, 1929

PERSONALITIES, *HIMMLER*

Berchtold takes the new title of Reichsführer-SS as commander, although his power has been undermined by having his SS subordinate to the SA. Berchtold tries to keep the SS as independent as possible from the manoeuvring of the SA and also from party officials, but this becomes more difficult when the SA increases its numbers still further. Berchtold then resigns.

Erhard Heiden, Berchtold's deputy, was appointed Reichsführer-SS. Himmler's organizing ability had not gone unnoticed and he was appointed Deputy SS Leader.

▼ The "Adolf Hitler" cuff band worn by members of Hitler's bodyguard, which later became the Leibstandarte Division.

▲ Hitler at Nuremberg in 1929. This would be a pivotal year for the Nazis, with the World Slump dealing Weimar a fatal blow.

Himmler

Appointed Deputy SS Leader and then National Leader in January 1929 when he commanded approximately 1000 men, when the SS was still part of the SA. He gradually asserted the separation of the SS from the SA. Himmler became *Polizeipräsident* of Munich after Hitler became Chancellor in January 1933. This modest post enabled him to gradually gain control of the German police network except in Prussia, where Göring was Minister of the Interior. But he finally achieved complete control in 1936. Himmler devoted his life to the expansion of the SS, giving it many facets. These included the SS-financed research organization, the *Ahnenerbe*.

From the security point of view he took over the Gestapo and made it a Europe-wide organization. He controlled the concentration camp system, and in 1943 became Minister of the Interior as well. Himmler was appointed Chief of the Home Army in 1944, and a week before Hitler's suicide he made an effort to negotiate the surrender of Germany. Hitler, having heard of Himmler's treachery, dismissed him from all posts. Captured by the British in May 1945, he bit on a cyanide phial and was dead within seconds.

Heiden held the post until Hitler gave Himmler the appointment. Himmler retained his personal rank of *SS-Oberführer*, as *Reichsführer-SS* was not a personal rank at this time but rather a title as leader of the SS organization. He was born in Landshut on October 7, 1900, Bavaria, into a solid, respectable middle-class family. His father was a headmaster who was conservative in outlook and staunchly monarchist. Heinrich was named after his godfather, Prince Heinrich of Bavaria, to whom his father was tutor. As well as being a sickly child, he had to endure the discomfiture of attending his father's school. He welcomed the outbreak of war in 1914 enthusiastically, but it was not until January 1918 that he was able to report for duty as an officer cadet in the 11th Bavarian Infantry Regiment. But on December 17, 1918, after the war had ended, he was discharged and returned to school in Landshut. He attended the München Technical High School where he studied for a degree in agriculture. He became embroiled in right-wing politics, first joining the *Freikorps Oberland* and then the *Reichskriegsflagge*. He joined the NSDAP in August 1923 and during the Munich *Putsch* carried the imperial war flag and led the column as it marched through the streets of the city. The *Putsch* ended in a fiasco, the rank and file surrendered their weapons, identified

themselves to the police and returned home, while the leaders were arrested. He returned to Landshut where he sold advertising space in the *Völkischer Beobachter*. He acted as general secretary to Gregor Strasser who, in February 1925, agreed to disband his National Socialist Freedom Movement and assimilate it into the reformed NSDAP. Himmler now found himself a local party official with command over the tiny SS in his district. Strasser was appointed Reich propaganda leader of the NSDAP in September 1926, and Himmler accompanied him to party headquarters as his secretary. However his party career still allowed him time to run a chicken smallholding, where he carried out breeding experiments. He married Margarete Bodern, the daughter of a German landowner from Conerzewo, west Prussia, on the July 3, 1928. She was known as Marge and was eight years older than Himmler. She specialized in homeopathy and herbs, and when he met her in 1927 he became fascinated by her work and fell for her charms. It was in fact her money that enabled the setting up of the smallholding.

When the Nazis came to power Himmler had the power to indulge his fantasies. The

▲ *The streets of Meiningen are flooded with SA men in this 1931 photograph. By this time Röhm was in charge of the SA.*

castle of Wewelsburg was rebuilt at immense expense as a shrine to a Germanic civilization. Here, the Hold Order of the SS was founded and from 1934 held ceremonies several times a year. Karl Wolff, Himmler's adjutant, ushered each SS leader into a monastic cell, where he steeped himself in Germanic mysticism surrounded by treasures from ancient Germany. Beneath their mock medieval coats of arms the leading 12 high SS officers were assigned places around an Arthurian table. Himmler started a ceramics works in Dachau concentration camp, which produced fine porcelain as well as earthenware. A Damascus smithy was also established. Himmler concerned himself with the perfecting of a future German élite through the SS. Not only would they be of guaranteed Aryan stock, but they would be encouraged to form the new race through the *Lebensborn* network of maternity homes (which ensured that the children of SS men and Aryan women were cared for).

The SS at the beginning of 1929 numbered 280 men, but it was still a part of the SA. Himmler began gradually to assert the separation of the SS from the SA, bringing in biological criteria and the concept of racial purity into new recruitment plans to trawl through the large number of applications from ex-*Freikorps* and unemployed bourgeois volunteers. The army, which perceived Röhm and his SA as a rival, took a favourable view to the SS as a force. This, combined with Himmler's considerable organizational skills, provided him with a personal power base.

SEPTEMBER 1929

PERSONALITIES, *HITLER*

Early in September Hitler moves from his monastic room to one of the most fashionable quarters of Munich. Here, he rents a luxurious nine-roomed apartment covering the entire second floor of 16 Prinzregentplatz. He brings along Frau Reichert, his landlady from the Thierschstrasse, and her mother Frau Dachs, together with his niece, Geli Raubal. He installs Geli in her own room while she

pursues her medical studies in Munich. They are occasionally seen together in public at the theatre or at his favourite table in the garden of the Café Heck, where he often holds court late in the afternoon. There is vicious gossip in Munich that Hitler should stop cavorting with Geli or marry her. It is likely that Hitler's relationship with her at this time is platonic, for he obviously adores her and, according to many of his intimates, intends to marry her. Heinrick Hoffmann, however, holds a different view, especially after Hitler told him: "I love Geli and could marry her. But you know my views. I am determined to remain a bachelor."

JANUARY 14, 1930

NAZI PARTY, *HORST WESSEL*

Horst Wessel, the son of a Protestant clergyman from Bielefeld, was a songwriter who abandoned his law studies to live with a former prostitute in the slums of Berlin. He joined the party at 19 and became the leader of a troop of Brownshirts. He wrote the lyrics for the celebrated "Horst Wessel" song, originally titled by him "Raise High the Flag". A gang of communists that burst into his room murdered him. The supposed killer is Ali Höhler. The "official" Nazi Party version has it that Wessel was surprised by communists at his home at Grosse Fraankfurter Strasse 62 on January 14, 1930, and was shot in the mouth and died nine days later. Other more critical, but possibly more objective, reports go so far as to claim he was a procurer of prostitutes and was killed in a brawl over a girl. His untimely death has transformed him into a Nazi symbol, an idealist who has given his life for the Nazi cause.

Gobblels, never one to let an opportunity slip and in typically verbose language, calls him, "a Socialist Christ". The "Horst Wessel" song becomes the official anthem of the Nazis and takes second place only to the national anthem, "Deutschland, Deutschland". The tune is said to have been originally a Salvation Army hymn.

▼ The massed ranks of the SA at a Nuremberg rally. Hitler described them affectionately as his "rough fighters".

▲ Rudolf Hess (centre), Hitler's deputy, became increasingly overshadowed during the early 1930s by men such as Himmler.

▲ *Alfred Rosenberg, Nazi racial philosopher, giving an anti-Semitic speech. Many Nazis regarded him as a crank.*

Die Fahnen hoch, die Reihe dicht geschlossen!
SA marschiert mit ruhig festem Schritt.
Kam'raden, die Rotfront und Reaktion erschossen,
Marschiern im Geist in unsern Reihen mit.

The flags held high! The ranks stand tight together!
SA march on, with quiet, firm forward pace.
Comrades who, though shot by Red Front or Reaction,
Still march with us, their spirit in our ranks.

MARCH 27, 1930
POLITICS, *GERMANY*
The outside world is changing rapidly. The Muller coalition government resigns and Henrich Brüning, head of the Catholic Centre party, succeeds him and promises to cure Germany's economic problems of deflation and unemployment, but the Nazis and communists have voted against him in the *Reichstag*. Finally, on July 16, Brüning persuades President Hindenburg to use his emergency powers to put his decrees into effect. When his coalition partners refuse to vote for him, however, he dissolves the *Reichstag* and calls for new elections for September 14.

MAY 1930
NAZI PARTY, *ORGANIZATION*
With the money from the Ruhr magnates continuing to pour into the Nazi coffers, Hitler re-equipps and enlarge his SA. He purchases the Brown House in Munich on the Briennerstrasse, which he has re-designed as party headquarters. Originally built in 1828, it had by the 1920s fallen into some disrepair, which left it open for the internal changes that will be necessary for its use by the NSDAP. Contributions have been pouring in from many party members to help defray the costs. Professor Troost, Hitler's favourite architect, has been brought in to deal with the architectural and design features and is working closely with Hitler.

Inside the Brown House was stunningly impressive, at least by Nazi values. The conference room was garish red leather, and the black and red entrance hall was highlighted with swastikas, and there was a restaurant in the basement. The SA man from the country who visited his party headquarters left in awe, but possibly depressed, for many of the SA were in dire financial straits during this period.

SEPTEMBER 1930
SA, *STENNES MUTINY*
Many SA men, being unpaid and hungry, and exhausted from non-stop campaigning, are becoming disillusioned. So the districts under *Oberster SA-Führer Ost*, Walther Stennes, have gone on strike. Stennes a former *Freikorps* leader and follower of Strasser's radical Nazism, has become Pfeffer von Salomon's deputy and leader of the SA in eastern Germany. His men are for

the most part unemployed and in poverty, and have heckled a speech by Goebbels, the *Gauleiter* of Berlin, and beat up his SS guard. Hitler's oratorial skills have not worked and he fears an SA revolt.

Hitler was in Munich at the time of the revolt. He raced to Berlin, because if the revolt continued or spread all would be lost in the coming elections. Hitler went from group to group, begging, pleading even sobbing. They were angry and frustrated. One SA-Führer actually grabbed Hitler by the tie and shook him.

Ernst Röhm, Hitler's long-time ally, is in Bolivia assisting that country in training its army. Hitler believes that Röhm is the one man who can control the uneasy SA. So he decides it is time to call Röhm back. In the meantime he quietly takes steps which assures his ultimate control of the SA. He names himself Oberster SA-Führer on September 2 with the second-in-command to be Stabschef answerable only to him.

Pfeffer von Solomon, following the SA mutiny and a dispute with Hitler over the nomination of SS rather than SA men to the *Reichstag*, was relieved of command of the SA. Hitler took it over personally and recalled Röhm from Bolivia to command it, demanding a personal loyalty oath from the men of the SA. For a time in 1930 it looked highly unlikely that there would be an SA rally in Braunschweig to pay homage to Hitler. During this period the Nazis took advantage of every opportunity provided to them.

During 1930 Strasser organized the party for the *Reichstag* elections, concentrating on key seats, making the party the second largest in the *Reichstag*. But again he quarrelled with Hitler over Nazi Party policy. His younger brother, Otto, was thrown out of a party meeting in Berlin and called for other radicals to form a new party with him. Gregor disowned him and remained at the centre of Nazi power, but his position was seriously weakened. It was further weakened when Otto Strasser and Stennes later fled to Prague and established the *Schwarze Front* (Black Front), an organization of dissident Nazis who represented "true National Socialist views".

SEPTEMBER 14, 1930

POLITICS, *REICHSTAG ELECTIONS*

In the elections, 30 million Germans have gone to the polls. The Nazis become the second-largest party in the *Reichstag* with 107 seats, second only to the Social Democrats with 143 seats. The communists are a poor third with 77 seats. A total of 6,409,000 votes have been cast for the

Nazis, and most of the men whose names would later become synonymous with National Socialism are now party deputies in the *Reichstag*.

While the Nazis are celebrating their gains, Heinrich Brüning, the Social Democrat Chancellor is faced with an appalling predicament. Not only does he not command an absolute majority but also there is obviously no way in view of the political mix that he can hope to get one.

All in all 1931 augured well for Hitler, save for the discontent in the SA. He had suddenly become a best-selling author. *Mein Kampf* had sold an average of a little more than 6000 annually until 1930, when the amount rose to 54,086. This got him a respectable personal income. Furthermore the Brown House, the new party headquarters, was opened on the first of the year. At the same time he was profoundly disturbed by a personal crisis. He learned that his chauffeur and companion Emile Maurice had become secretly enged to his niece Geli Raubal, who had been living a restricted life in the

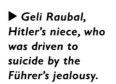
▶ *Geli Raubal, Hitler's niece, who was driven to suicide by the Führer's jealousy.*

Prinzregentplatz apartment. Ironically it was the Führer himself, the perpetual matchmaker, who had given the idea to Maurice. "I'll come and have supper with you every evening when you are married," he urged the young man. "Following his advice," Maurice confided in a colleague, "I decided to become engaged to Geli, with whom I was madly in love, like everybody else. She gladly accepted my proposal." Finally he steeled himself to confess. Hitler flew into a rage, accused Maurice of disloyalty and dismissed him as chauffeur.

JANUARY 15, 1931

SA, *RÖHM RETURNS*

Röhm returns as chief of staff of the SA, answerable only to the Führer. Hitler is pursuing his personal goal with a vengeance, but the SA is venting its fury. It wants a bloody revolution to sweep away

the old order, not legal manoeuvrings, and it
wants that revolution now.

APRIL 1931

LAW AND ORDER, *GERMANY*

Hitler submits to a government ban on
public demonstrations. Stennes, meanwhile,
is not placated and continues to fight for
economic aid for the SA men in SA group
Ost, but it is a losing battle. It is rumoured
that Hitler is about to dismiss him. Stennes
therefore holds a secret meeting of SA
leaders which declares for him and against
Hitler. But his men have no funds and
cannot sustain a revolt. The party therefore
expels them and Göring takes over the
Berlin organization with SS men. Goebbels'
role in the affair is not clear; it is possible
that as a former radical himself he may have
had some sympathy with the SA.

SEPTEMBER 18, 1931

PERSONALITIES, *GELI RAUBAL*

Hitler became increasingly possessive and
jealous of his niece. So zealously did he
guard her that in the end she was little
more than a slave to his whims. That
summer she announced to Hitler that she
planned to continue her voice studies in
Vienna. Hitler objected violently and the
storm between the two intensified. On
September 17, as Hitler boarded his car to
drive to Hamburg, Geli called from the
window: "Then you won't let me go to
Vienna." Hitler retorted sharply: "No." Geli
was found dead in her room the next
morning, a bullet in her heart, having shot
herself with Hitler's pistol. So great a loss
has this been for him, that for two days and
nights his friend Gregor Strasser has had to
stay with him to prevent the Nazi Party
leader from taking his own life.

SEPTEMBER 1931

NAZI PARTY, *ORGANIZATION*

Hitler spends the autumn consolidating the
party and revamping the SA in light of the
weakness made evident by the Stennes
revolt. Hitler knows he needs Röhm, and
Röhm knows he needs Hitler. Goebbels and
Goring, meanwhile, feeling threatened by
Röhm's position next to Hitler, cleverly
acquire some "love letters" which the
homosexual Röhm has written. These are
then published in the newspapers. Röhm
could have been destroyed by events, but
he is not. Hitler comes to his rescue with a
statement that includes these words; "the
SA is not a moral institution for the
education of well-to-do-daughters, but an
association of rough fighters".

▲ *Josef Goebbels, propaganda supremo of
the Nazi Party, was a philanderer who was
nicknamed "the cripple" by his enemies.*

OCTOBER 17–18, 1931

SA, *RALLY AT BRUNSWICK*

On Saturday and Sunday October 17–18, *SA-
Gruppe Nord*, under the leadership of *SA-
Gruppenführer* Victor Lutze, hosts a rally at
Brunswick, a town of 100,00 about 64km
(40 miles) east of Hanover and about
240km (150 miles) west of Berlin. Some
104,000 members of the SA, SS, NSKK
(*National Sozialistisches Kraftfahrer Korps*
– National Socialist Motor Corps) and the
Hitler Youth take part in a "token
mobilization" of Nazi strength. Brunswick is
the only state where the Nazis hold office
and are allowed to wear uniform in public.
There, just 10 months after Röhm's return,
Hitler receives the salute. The parade takes
six hours to pass the podium. He seems to
sense that this is the "true beginning" of his
awesome power.

It was at this assembly, which followed
closely on the heels of the Stennes *Putsch*,
that Hitler gained in public the assurance of
the SA rank and file of its unqualified
support for his leadership. Despite earlier
revolts by certain elements in previous
months, it never again wavered from that
loyalty, the Röhm bloody weekend not
withstanding. Hitler awarded the name
Horst Wessel to *SA-Standarten* 5 Berlin,
consecrated the SA *Deutschland Erwache*
standard *Danzig*, and authorized the

creation of 23 other new standards, thus expanding the SA, and recognized the Motor-SA and NSKK. Lutze gained a reputation as a totally loyal party member and Hitler did not forget this act of loyalty in 1934, when he named Lutze to replace the executed Röhm.

In the disturbances that followed the rally two people were killed and some 50 or 60 more wounded.

NOVEMBER 1931

ESPIONAGE, *BOXHEIM PAPERS*

A Nazi group in Hesse under Werner Best, a Rhineland law student who was imprisoned by the French during their occupation of the Ruhr and who subsequently became a legal advisor to the Nazi Party, has drawn up plans to deal with the contingency of a communist revolution in Germany. The so-

▼ *By the early 1930s Hitler had created a cult of admiration around himself, which was particularly strong among the youth.*

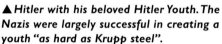

▲ *Hitler with his beloved Hitler Youth. The Nazis were largely successful in creating a youth "as hard as Krupp steel".*

called Boxheim Papers have been seized by the state and subsequently become known by the name of the house where the meetings were held: Boxheimer Hof. The plans contain a proclamation to be issued by the SA and emergency decrees which a provisional Nazi government would make, including the immediate execution of anyone resisting or failing to cooperate or found with weapons. Private property rights would be suspended, interest debts annulled, work made compulsory without reward, while people would be fed through public kitchens and issued with food ration cards. There would be courts martial under Nazi presidents. The discovery of the documents has resulted in a public scandal and Hitler has been forced to disavow the Boxheim Papers, assuring Rhineland industrialists that he would take power only by legal means.

This scandal did not do any lasting harm to the Nazis's election hopes. In 1932 there were four separate elections. The first two polls were for the presidency in which Hitler, though losing to Hindenburg, received 30.1 percent of the total vote in the first election and 36.8 percent in the second. The affair also did little to harm Best's rise: he was made Polie Commissioner of Hesse in 1933 and State Governor in July.

JUNE 1932

LAW AND ORDER, *SA BANNED*

Chancellor Brüning, feeling confident enough to take measures against the Nazis, orders the disbandment of the SA and SS under a decree which prohibits uniformed political organizations (when Brüning's decree came into effect, the SS had grown to 30,000 members or approximately 10 percent of the SA's strength). This is followed by police swoops to ensure the ban is respected. In some SA quarters there is an inclination to stand and fight, but Hitler immediately overrules this sentiment. People other than the Nazis are involved, however, and many Rightist and Nationalist groups had their own uniforms seized, including some like the *Stahlhelm* which were ostensibly veterans' organizations. Brüning may therefore have made a grave mistake, for the decree may be interpreted as an insult to those who have fought for Germany.

JULY 31, 1932

POLITICS, *REICHSTAG ELECTIONS*

The Nazi Party is very successful in the *Reichstag* elections of July 1932. Travelling by aeroplane, Hitler has appeared in the last two weeks of the campaign in almost 50 cities – "Hitler over Germany" – a ploy that has reaped dividends. In Berlin 120,000 people heard him in the Grünewald Stadium, while 100,000 more listened via loudspeakers outside. When the polls close, 13,732,779 Germans have voted for him, giving the NSDAP 230 *Reichstag* members. Hitler immediately demands the chancellorship and passage of an Enabling Act to run Germany by decree, in effect a dictatorship, but he is turned down on both counts by President Hindenburg.

▶ *Honour Badge of the Technical Emergency Service, which under Hitler became a large emergency force.*

▲ *The SS Long Service Cross, awarded to SS members for 4, 8, 12 and 25 years of service (military service counted as double).*

The last of the year's elections was held on November 6 and resulted in a setback. In it the party lost two million votes and was reduced to 196 seats, while the communists gained 750,000 votes and now had 100 seats. Even in alliance with the Nationalists, the Nazis could not command an overall majority.

NOVEMBER 17, 1932

POLITICS, *SCHLEICHER INTRIGUE*

General von Schleicher, chief military intriguer of the Weimar period and Minister of Defence, succeeds in organizing the downfall of Chancellor Papen's cabinet and thus his government. Informing Papen that the army and police would not defend his government, he stresses to Hindenburg that he should be chancellor. Hindenburg refuses, especially as he states he could obtain the support of Gregor Strasser and at least 60 Nazi *Reichstag* members to support his aims, and recalls Papen as chancellor. However, Hindenburg finally accepts that Schleicher has the support of the army and police forces, again dismisses Papen and now appoints Schleicher as chancellor.

He was to last as Chancellor for 57 days, and later stated that he was betrayed on each separate day.

DECEMBER 1932

POLITICS, *GERMANY*

The end of the year sees the political situation in Germany degenerate and take on the guise of near civil war. The socialists and the Communist Party field armed militia to battle the right-wing street fighters. The SA and SS reply with force and 10 SS men are killed with several hundred wounded during the violent street battles with the *Rötfrontkämpferbund*, or Red Front Fighters' Association. It suits the NSDAP's agenda to create the illusion that the country is on the slippery slope to all-out anarchy, especially with the crucial 1933 elections approaching, and that the party and its "valiant" street fighters hold the key to the political problems that grip Weimar Germany.

▶ *SS headquarters in Munich. Though the SS was smaller than the SA, it had a ruthless and determined head in Himmler.*

▼ *A Nazi Nuremberg rally in the early 1930s. The power of the party at this time can be judged by comparing this picture with the one on page 12.*

1933

The Nazis gained power via the ballot box, and some political dealings. But once in power Hitler quickly consolidated his control over the German state. New laws were introduced giving him dictatorial power, their passage made easier by the *Reichstag* fire in February. From then on, Nazi Germany became a centrally controlled totalitarian regime.

POLITICS, *GERMANY*

"The hour of the birth of the Third Reich"; Papen and Hitler agree on a coalition with Hitler as its head. Papen has pledged the support of the Rhineland industrialists in exchange for the vice-chancellorship, which Hitler has readily agreed to. Chancellor Schleicher fails to win over breakaway groups from the Nazis, such as that headed by Strasser, and is unable to keep control over the *Reichstag* parties. He resigns and President Hindenburg is persuaded to give Hitler the chancellorship, which is celebrated by Nazi parades in Berlin.

▼ *Chancellor Hitler and President Hindenburg. The latter had once vowed he would never make Hitler chancellor.*

Lubbe, but it is so convenient for the Nazis that they are suspected of complicity. On the eve of the arson attack on the Reichstag, for example, Rudolf Diels, Prussian State Police, reported to Hitler that the culprit, van der Lubbe was in custody and it was the work of a single demented pyromaniac. Hitler blamed the communists and burst out in fury: "This is a cunning plot! Every communist official must be shot. All communist deputies must be hanged this very night."

The police have quickly made some arrests: Göring, head of the Prussian State Police, has arrested 100 communist *Reichstag* deputies (the leader of the communists in the *Reichstag*, Ernst Torgler, has voluntarily surrendered himself to the police). Cynics are saying that it is a Nazi ploy to increase their popularity as defenders of the nation.

◀ **The** Reichstag *burns in February 1933. This convenient event gave Hitler the excuse to strangle democracy in Germany.*

JANUARY 30

NAZI PARTY, *BERLIN*

Hans E. Maikowski proudly heads his *Sturm* (Storm – an SA unit) during a parade at the Brandenburg Gate on this historic day. It isn't until the evening that *Sturm* 33 finally makes its way back to Charlottenburg. En route it is attacked by a mob of communists. During the bloody street-fighting Maikowski is severely wounded and taken to hospital. At midnight he dies, becoming the first martyr to the cause after the assumption of power by the NSDAP. Maikowski is given a lavish funeral, which takes place at the Charlottenburg Cathedral, and is buried in the Invaliden Friedhof.

FEBRUARY

GERMANY, *LEGAL*

Thirty-three decrees are published, including the banning of rival political meetings or publications and the dissolution of the Prussian parliament. Raids on Communist Party offices begin.

FEBRUARY 27

GERMANY, *ESPIONAGE*

The *Reichstag* Fire: the parliament building burns to the ground.

There are some mysteries concerning the Reichstag blaze. It was thought to be started by the Dutch ex-communist Marinus van der

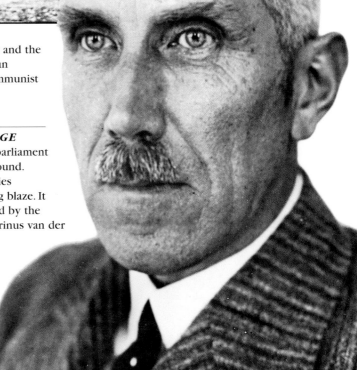

▶ *Ex-chancellor Franz von Papen, who persuaded Hindenburg to make Hitler chancellor in January 1933.*

MARCH 1

GERMANY, *LEGAL*

Hitler is given emergency powers by presidential decree. Whereupon he issues a "Decree for the protection of people and State" which gives police powers to the SA and SS. Some 25,000 SA and 15,000 SS men have been issued with firearms and deployed as *Hilfspolizei* or auxiliary policemen. This also empowers the police presidents to take anyone into protective custody considered to be a political opponent in the broadest sense of the term. The *Reichstag* fire, the "affront to democracy perpetrated by communists", permits Hitler to flex his political muscle and the party's left-wing protagonists begin to be unceremoniously ushered into prisons and makeshift unofficial camps or "wild man camps", so-called due to the lack of supervision and the frightful stories of brutality which comes from them. By the end of July 1933, it is estimated that there are nearly 27,000 people being held in protective custody.

MARCH 3

NAZI PARTY, *INDIVIDUALS*

Göring assures a Frankfurt audience: "I don't have to worry about justice, my mission is only to destroy and exterminate, nothing else." On the same day Hitler is busy bending the law so that he can deal "legally" with any opponents. He is slowly

but surely increasing his iron grip over Germany and her people.

MARCH 5

GERMANY, *ELECTIONS*

Reichstag elections; the Nazis win a working majority. The Nazis poll 17,277,180 votes out of a total of 39,343,300. This is an increase of 5.5 million votes since the last election but still less than a majority. However, with the help of the Nationalists the Nazis can add an additional 52 seats to their own 288, giving them a majority of 17. The Nazis set about filling local and state government posts with their supporters, while Göring declares that there is no longer any need for individual state governments. Using the state of emergency decree, the Nazis slowly take control of Germany with "planned terror".

◀ **Baldur von Schirach, Reich Youth Leader. Once the Nazis came to power he sought to re-educate youth in the spirit of Nazism.**

The procedure was simple but effective: local SA and SS groups would start violent protests and unrest, which would be followed by the appointment of Nazi Reich commissioners who would take over local governments in order to restore order. During this period suspects were rounded up and herded into abandoned army and police barracks, where they were beaten and tortured. They were then sent to camps, which later would become infamous as concentration camps. Those rounded up were mostly social democrats and communists, and of course Jews. Most of the first concentration camps sprung up near Berlin, though the one at Dachau was near Munich in the south.

When Hitler came to power in 1933, the most pressing economic problem was high unemployment (it totalled over five million in 1933). Those on the socialist side of the Nazi Party pushed for nationalization and state control. Hitler, however, had no intention of dismantling large industrial machine. This will have two consequences: first, the consolidation of his dictatorship; second, the eradication of organizations with differing political views.

MARCH 17

NAZI PARTY, *ORGANIZATION*

With Hitler's coming to power in January 1933, he decided that he was in need of a Praetorian Guard. The state protection rendered by the *Reichswehr* or police elements cannot, in his eyes, be entirely replied upon. Europe is a hotbed of plot and coup which he himself had been party to, so the Fatherland itself must be seen as suspect. Without delay Hitler decrees that there be formed a new full-time armed SS unit whose primary role would be exclusively to escort him wherever he was in Germany. "Sepp" Dietrich, one of Hitler's closest associates, is entrusted with the formation of the unit. Dietrich undertakes the task with zeal. By March 17, 1933, the embryo of a new Headquarters Guard named the SS *Stabswache Berlin* was founded. It comprised 120 hand-picked volunteers, of whom some were former

▲ Hitler, Germany's new chancellor, photographed in Berlin in March 1933. To his right stands Papen, to his left, Goebbels.

enterprises that would be useful for his war economy. To reassure big business, Hitler brought into his government a former president of the Reichsbank and a brilliant economist, Hjalmar Schacht, to run the economy. Nazi economic theory was slender and therefore Hitler turned to Schacht, who had resigned in 1930 in protest at reparation repayments and turned to the Nazis. "I desire a great and strong Germany and to achieve it I would enter an alliance with the Devil," Schacht exclaimed.

MARCH 12

NAZI PARTY, *IDEOLOGY*

Hitler speaks on *Gleichschaltung*, "the Co-ordination of the Political Will". Hitler is determined to fuse every element of German national life into the Nazi social

members of the *Stosstrupp Adolf Hitler* and whose loyalty to the Führer was unswerving. They were garrisoned in the Alexander Barracks on Friedrichstrasse and lightly armed with rifles, bayonets and pistols.

Two months later the unit was reformed as the *SS Sonderkommando Zossen* and enlarged with three training companies. The terms of engagement for the unit were expanded and the unit could now be employed for armed police and anti-terrorist activities, as well as the guard duties it already undertook. There was another metamorphosis during the proceeding months when a further three companies were formed as the *SS Sonderkommando Jüterbog*. This was the beginning of a unit that would become one of the greatest fighting formations in the German armed forces: the *Leibstandarte*.

MARCH 21

POLITICS, *GERMANY*

The new National Socialist *Reichstag* opens in the Kroll Opera House after the *Reichstag* building itself had been burnt down. To their eternal credit, the German people still did not give Hitler a majority in the elections, which took place in the first week of March. By then the Nazis were beyond any constitutional refinement and any communist

▼ *"Sepp" Dietrich (centre), the commander of the SS Stabswache Berlin, Hitler's bodyguard.*

▲ An early photograph of the inmates of Dachau concentration camp. The camp was filled with communists and Jews.

and social democrat deputies who turned up for duty at the Kroll Opera House were simply arrested. Once they were out of the way, the Nazis and their allies had the necessary two-thirds majority to effect major constitutional change. Only one thing still commanded Hitler's respect: the German Army and its loyalty to Hindenburg.

Before opening the new *Reichstag* session Hitler lays on a service in the garrison church at Potsdam, shrine of the old Prussian Army, which is attended by the Brownshirts, Nazi deputies and high-ranking officers of the Kaiser's regime in a show of continuity between the old and new nationalist ideas. As a climax to this display Hitler makes an obsequious tribute to Hindenburg to keep the old

soldier content. He then speeds back to Berlin to start the business of dealing with his remaining lesser opponents.

MARCH 21
POLITICS, *REICHSTAG*

The Nazi-controlled *Reichstag* opens. Decrees are passed on a general amnesty for all Nazis who committed offences during the so-called "struggle". On the other hand, punitive measures are introduced

▼ Camp guards at Dachau. In 1933 there was little discipline among the guards, who committed many atrocities.

against malicious gossip. Finally, the setting up of a special court, the "People's Court", is approved. This is set up in Berlin to deliver quick verdicts for accused traitors of the Third Reich, though impartiality appears well down the list.

MARCH 22
GERMANY, *LEGAL*

Enabling Law is passed, giving special powers to Chancellor Hitler for four years. In essence the law provides the constitutional foundation for dictatorship. It gives the Nazis the right to pass laws without the consent of the *Reichstag*, to deviate from the constitution, to conclude treaties with foreign powers, and to place the right of issuing a law into the hands of the chancellor. Hitler said in 1932: "Once we have power, we will never surrender it unless we are carried out of our offices as corpses." It appears he means to honour his chilling pledge. The fact that the communists have already been eliminated from the *Reichstag* means the passing of the law is a mere formality.

MARCH 23
POLITICS, *REICHSTAG*

The surviving deputies to the *Reichstag* attend the Kroll Opera House to sanction an Enabling Bill to give Hitler supreme, untrammelled power. To make sure that all deputies have a rough grasp of the way they are expected to vote, the building has been surrounded and packed inside and out with ranks of SA and SS, who keep up a menacing chant demanding blood if the bill does not go through. With amazing courage, Otto Wels, leader of the Social Democratic Party, rises to oppose the bill, although he is alone and defenceless and the baying of the

stormtroopers could be clearly heard in the chamber. The last pretences are abandoned, as Hitler leaps to his feet and screams at Wels that his death-knell had sounded. The bill is then hurriedly passed by an enormous majority. From this moment on Germany is a dictatorship.

MARCH 29
GERMANY, *LEGAL*
Lex van der Lubbe gives retrospective sanction to execution by hanging for arson.

MARCH 31
GERMANY, *LEGAL*
First Coordination Law of States and Reich establishes new state and local assemblies, with membership in the same proportions as the *Reichstag* parties, i.e. a Nazi majority.

Thousands are rounded up and put into camps by police and the "auxiliary police", the SA. Dachau concentration camp is opened. SA troops in all states force state government resignations; the Bavarian state government is suppressed. Epp is appointed new Nazi Governor in Bavaria with Himmler as State Police President.

APRIL 1
GERMANY, *LEGAL*
Official boycott of Jewish shops and professional men begins. The attitude of the German population towards the Jews is curious. Though Nazi propaganda would have the world believe that every German hates the Jews, this is not the case. It is true that in places where National Socialism was able to attach itself to deeply rooted anti-Semitic traditions, the racially based anti-Semitism of the Nazis has found receptive ears. However, the mass of the population has not been induced into

▲ Cuff band of the concentration camp guards. Hitler said of the camps: "Terror is the most effective instrument."

actively supporting the persecution of the Jews. That said, the persecution of the Jews has not prompted any wide-scale popular criticism.

The Nazi Party has pledged to create a Germany in which Jews will be set apart from their fellow Germans and denied their place in German life and culture. Jews have been expelled from a number of smaller towns and forced to move to larger towns or cities, or emigrate. All but Nazi-controlled publications have been effectively suppressed.

The Law on the Reconstruction of the Professional Civil Services is introduced,

▼ The Death's Head symbol, seen here on a concentration camp guard's sleeve insignia, became synonymous with Nazi terror.

which makes no distinction between Reich, state or civil service cadres and giving transferability between each. All unqualified, disloyal or Jewish staff are to be dismissed (in the event, however, 90 percent of the civil service remained). Himmler is made Commander of the Bavarian Political Police.

APRIL 1
MILITARY, *NAVY*
The pocket battleships *Deutschland* was commissioned and the *Admiral Scheer* launched. *Deutschland* was one of three armoured ships – the so-called "pocket battleships" – laid down between 1928 and 1931. *Deutschland* was the first of the class, being launched in May 1931 and completed in April 1933. She was originally used as a seagoing training ship, to familiarize crews with her new technology.

Designed as long-range commerce raiders, powerful enough to sink anything they could not outrun and fast enough to outrun anything they could not sink – except for the Royal Navy ships HMS *Hood*, *Renown* and *Repulse*. – and they often classed as "pocket battleships". Officially listed as *Panzerschiffe* ("armoured ships"), in reality they were raiding cruisers built to light cruiser standards and equipped with an exceptionally heavy main battery. They were built under a clause in the Treaty of Versailles that allowed Germany to build ships up to 10,605 tonnes (10,000 tons) with guns of up to 11in; this was intended to allow coast-defence battleships. Two further ships of this class were redesigned to become the "Scharnhorst" class in response to the French "Dunkerque" class. *Deutschland* varied in the style and arrangement of the superstructure. The Washington Treaty of 1921 left Germany quite limited in the amounts of ships that she could construct. Admiral Raeder had a vision of a fleet of ships that would tie up the Royal Navy and disrupt the sea line of communication for France and England, but this was not possible with the tonnage permitted by this treaty. There was only one solution to the problem – Germany would have to under-report the weights of her ships. Lying or not, in 1933 the *Deutschland*. was commissioned. She was underreported in her weight by at least 20 percent (reported at 12,294 tonnes [12,100 tons] but actually displacing 15,748 tonnes [15,500 tons]), but even this was a violation of the weights granted in the treaty. The French and British, the enforcers of this treaty, were not worried because they knew that the new French "Dunkerque" class and British ships like the HMS *Hood* could outgun and outrun this new class of German ship.

APRIL 7

GERMANY, *LEGAL*
Second Coordination Law appoints state governors.

APRIL 8

GERMANY, *LEGAL*
Law on the Reconstruction of the Professional Civil Service is introduced, making no distinction between Reich, state or local cadres, giving transferability between each.

APRIL 26

GERMANY, *POLICE*
A decree on the establishment of the *Geheime Staats Polizeiamt* (Gestapa), which was later renamed *Geheime Staats Polizei* (Gestapo), as a new department of the Prussian state police affiliated with the Minister of the Interior, to be headed by Diels. Göring is persuaded by his friend Diels that a secret police force was necessary to monitor the activities of the communists. The Gestapo becomes the political police of Nazi Germany.

The Gestapo ruthlessly eliminated opposition to the Nazis within Germany and its occupied territories and was responsible for the roundup of Jews throughout Europe for deportation to extermination camps. Hermann Göring, Prussian minister of the interior, detached the political and espionage units from the regular Prussian police, filled their ranks with thousands of Nazis, and, on April 26, 1933, reorganized them under his personal command as the Gestapo. Simultaneously, Heinrich Himmler, head of the SS, together with his aide Reinhard Heydrich, similarly

reorganized the police of Bavaria and the remaining German states.

The Gestapo operated without restraints. It had the authority of "preventative arrest", and its actions were not subject to judicial appeal. Thousands of leftists, intellectuals, Jews, trade unionists, political clergy, and homosexuals simply disappeared into concentration camps after being arrested by the Gestapo. The political section could order prisoners to be murdered, tortured, or released. Together with the SS, the Gestapo managed the treatment of "inferior races," such as Jews and Gypsies. During World War II the Gestapo suppressed partisan activities in the occupied territories and carried out reprisals against civilians. Gestapo members were included in the *Einsatzgruppen* (Special Action Squads), which were mobile death squads that followed the German army into Poland and Russia to kill Jews and other "undesirables." Bureau IV B4 of the Gestapo, under Adolf Eichmann, organized the deportation of millions of Jews from other occupied countries to death camps.

◄ *The badge of the German High Seas Fleet, which Hitler was determined to restore to its former greatness.*

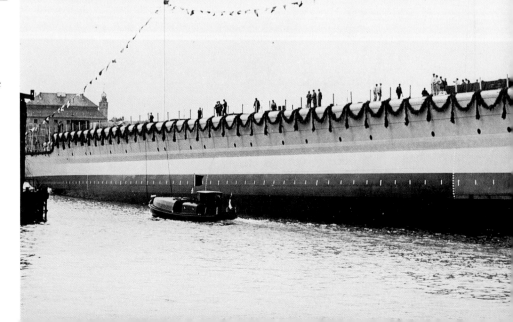

MAY 2

GERMANY, *INDUSTRIAL RELATIONS*

All German Free Trade unions are dissolved, and their 5.5 million members incorporated into the newly formed German Labour Front, an affiliated organization of the NSDAP with virtually a parallel organizational structure. It is headed by Dr Robert Ley.

To weld German labour into a solid organization backing Hitler, Ley abolished the democratic trade unions and built up a powerful labour organization designed to facilitate German militarization and war preparations. He was also head of the *Bund der Auslanddeutsche* (Union of Germans Living Abroad).

MAY 6

NAZI PARTY, *IDEOLOGY*

Goebbels organizes a national "Burning of the Books". The Nazis begin an action against unwanted books. Many important literary works are also proscribed because their authors or subjects are considered subversive or "un-German".

Göebbels rationalizes the burnings by proclaiming: "Fellow students, German men and women! The age of extreme Jewish intellectualism has now ended, and the success of the German revolution has again given the German spirit the right of way.... You are doing the proper thing in

committing the evil spirit of the past to the flames.... This is a strong, great, symbolic act, an act that is to bear witness before all the world to the fact that the November Republic has disappeared. From these ashes there will arise a phoenix of a new spirit.... The past is lying in flames. The future will

▲ *The trappings of absolute power: the headquarters of Hermann Göring's air force, which was a secret in 1933.*

rise from the flames within our hearts ... Brightened by these flames our vow shall be: The Reich and the Nation and our Führer Adolf Hitler."

Hermann Göring summed up the Nazis' attitude to culture and art in his famous quip: "Whenever I hear the word 'culture', I reach for my revolver." Göring's attitude was echoed by most senior Nazis. Hitler hated the intelligentsia and all things intellectual, and seriously toyed with the idea of doing away with them once he was in power. After 1933, many German intellectuals saw the writing on the wall, especially those of Jewish descent, and emigrated. The list of those who fled says much for the strength of opposition to Nazism among German intellectuals, and this wave of emigration was a great loss for German culture: writers such as Thomas and Heinrich Mann, Arnold and Stefan Zweig, Franz Werfel and Jakob Wassermann; masters of the Bauhaus school such as Walter Gropius, Mies van der Rohe and Marcel Breuer; painters such as Max Beckmann, Oskar Kokoschka and Kurt Schwittens; film directors Fritz Sternberg and Fritz Lang; and actress Marlene

◀ *The pocket battleship* Deutschland. *The British and French were initially unconcerned about this class of ships.*

Dietrich. The loss of talented musicians and composers was particularly pronounced: Paul Hindemith, Otto Klemperer, Kurt Weill, Hanns Jelinek, Ernst Toch, Arnold Schönberg and Richard Tauber. Academics also left in their droves: Max Wertheimer, William Stern, Sigmund Freud, Paul Tillich, Ernst Bloch, Theodor Adorno, Ernst Cassirer, Kurt Goldstein, Erich Fromm, Fritz Reiche, Hans Bethe, Richard Courant, James Frank and Albert Einstein. Einstein's loss would be sorely felt when Germany embarked on its atomic weapons programme: it was Einstein's Theory of Relativity that was the basis of America's atom bomb dropped on Japan in August 1945. In total, some 2500 writers left Germany once the Nazis took power.

MAY 19

GERMANY, *INDUSTRIAL RELATIONS*
Establishment of Trustees of Labour. There are 13 departmental offices, each one headed by a Trustee of Labour. Their task is the "negotiation of work contracts between employer and labour".

MAY 20

GERMANY, *POLITICS*
Seizure of the assets of the Communist Party (KPD).

JUNE 1

GERMANY, *LEGAL*
First Law for the Reduction of Unemployment.

JUNE 9

GERMANY, *LEGAL*
Law on Payments Abroad.

JUNE 12

GERMANY, *LEGAL*
Law on Betraying the German Economy; notification of assets abroad.

JUNE 14

GERMANY, *LEGAL*
Law on the New Formation of the German Peasantry.

JUNE 22

GERMANY, *LEGAL*
Decree dissolving political parties: the Social Democrats.

JUNE 27

GERMANY, *LEGAL*
Decrees dissolving political parties: DNVP.

JUNE 28

GERMANY, *LEGAL*
Decrees dissolving political parties: State Party. Theodor Eicke becomes Commandant of Dachau. He is brutal and dedicated to ensuring that the "enemies of Germany" are securely held in the camp.

JULY 4

GERMANY, *LEGAL*
Decrees dissolving political parties: DVP and Bavarian Party.

▶ **The leader of German women in Nazi Germany: Gertrud Scholtz-Klink. Women had little influence in the Third Reich.**

◀ *Part of the Nazis's drive to increase the birthrate – a badge awarded to mothers who produced babies.*

JULY 5

GERMANY, *LEGAL*
Decrees dissolving political parties: the Centre Party.

JULY 8

GERMANY, *TREATIES*
Concordat between Germany and the Vatican. Negotiated by the Catholic Franz von Papen, it conferred a

▲ Dr Robert Ley (seated in the front of the car next to the driver), the head of the German Labour Front.

◀ The reality of Nazi power: an SA man stands outside a Jewish shop in Berlin as the boycott of Jewish businesses begins.

certain legitimacy on the Nazi regime. Hitler sought to end Vatican support for the Catholic Centre Party while he proceeded to subordinate the churches and to corrupt Christianity into a state-centred form of neo-paganism. Pope Pius XI, like every other European statesmen after him, thought that he could appease and moderate the Nazis.

The Concordat gives Germans the right to practise religion and allows the church to administer itself. In return, Catholic priests are not to take part in politics. Some have charged that the Vatican, lured by guarantees for its schools and other institutions, has secured the Concordat by sacrificing the Centre Party, which had fought the *Kulturkampf* (Culture Battle). In fact, Pius XI does not believe that Catholic political action anywhere should serve as the primary means of defending church interests. Furthermore, it is clear from the

beginning of July that Hitler does not need the Concordat to remove the clergy from German politics.

JULY 14

GERMANY, *LEGAL*
Law against the Establishment of Parties is introduced.

JULY 15

GERMANY, *LEGAL*
Reich Regulations for the Corporate Reorganization of Agriculture. German agriculture is in dire straits, and under Minister of Agriculture Walter Darré the Nazis are making genuine efforts to improve the lot of German farmers.

AUGUST

NAZI PARTY, *INTERNAL POLITICS*
Röhm had always regarded the SA as his personal revolutionary army, but the power of the SA, conjoined with the ambitions of its leaders, were to consume it. Röhm's quest for personal power was not to Hitler's liking, and his concern over Röhm

was fuelled by the whisperings of Göring and Himmler. Himmler's objective was to eliminate the power of the SA, which had grown to be the largest of the Nazi formations, gathering considerable strength in the process. Hitler was looking to the future and decided to cast his lot with the generals of the army. Röhm had been aware of what was happening when he declared: "Anyone who thinks that the days of the SA are over must make up his mind that we are here and that we will remain."

AUGUST 31–SEPTEMBER 3

NAZI PARTY, *RALLIES*
A rally is held at Nuremberg which is called the *Parteitag des Siegers* or Victor's Party Rally. It marks the Nazi accession to power on January 31, 1933. At this rally Hitler formally recognizes the *Adolf Hitler SS Standart* and the dedication of the SS *Standarten* or regiments takes place. The *Adolf Hitler SS Standart* has been formed from *SS-Sonderkommando Zossen* and *SS-Sonderkommando Jüterbog*. A total of 785 men from these two units are present and

▲ *Young Germans take part in Goebbels' burning of literature considered by the Nazis to be "un-German".*

on the last day a salutary round is fired by a *Reichswehr* battery. *Grüppenführer* "Sepp" Dietrich receives the banner with the name *Adolf Hitler* on the box that surmounts it. The two *Sonderkommandos* have been granted the honour and right to wear the name *Adolf Hitler* on a cuff band on the left arm. The merged formation will later be renamed the *Leibstandarte-SS Adolf Hitler* or LSSAH.

SEPTEMBER

GERMANY, *RELIEF AGENCIES*
First *Winterhilfe* Campaign; the Help for the Winter campaign. It is an enormous charity for the better-off to help their poorer national and racial comrades. Collections are made by SA men on the streets, and though most people give voluntarily and a great deal of work is carried out, the threat of violence is used to back up donations.

SEPTEMBER 13

GERMANY, *LEGAL*

Law on Reich Food Costs. The Reich Food Estate will guarantee profitable prices for German farmers in an effort to make Germany self-sufficient in agricultural production.

SEPTEMBER 22

GERMANY, *CULTURE*

The tightening of control on the arts begins with a law that establishes a National Chamber of Culture, or *Reichskulturkammer*, which is a nationwide organization embracing all those whose professional remuneration comes from art, music, the theatre, press, radio, literature or the cinema. Its purpose is to act as a coordinating point for the various cultural and culturally related arts, with the ultimate control of the chamber vesting in the minister of propaganda, Dr Joseph Goebbels. The chamber consists of seven sub-elements: architecture and sculpting arts, music, theatre, literature, press, film and radio, with a president at the head of each element. Each chamber president has the power to regulate his respective field. Membership is compulsory for any person engaged in these fields.

OCTOBER

GERMANY, *TREATIES*

Hitler takes Germany out of the League of Nations. Germany has been a member of the league since 1925, but it has always been regarded by many nationalists as an agency of the Allied powers and an enforcer of the hated Treaty of Versailles.

OCTOBER 1

GERMANY, *LEGAL*

Reich Entailed Law stabilizes small firms.

OCTOBER 14

GERMANY, *PARLIAMENT*

The *Reichstag* is dissolved.

OCTOBER 27

GERMANY, *LEISURE*

On a visit to Italy in 1929 Dr Robert Ley had been impressed by the fascist *Dopolavoro* (After Work) Organization, and on his return plans for a German equivalent were formulated. It was launched at a joint Italian German ceremony at Koblenz, although a formal press announcement was not made until November 17, when it was referred to as *Nach der Arbeit*. Shortly thereafter the name was changed to "Strength through Joy". It was the opportunity to travel which caught the public imagination. To visit theatres, to own a car, or to holiday abroad were, before Hitler, a daydream for the average German worker. Ley was determined to make them a reality, and to a large extent he succeeded. Although principally associated with leisure and travel, the organization also included a "Beauty at Work" office under a then little-known architect called Albert Speer. The function of this office was to enhance the interiors and exteriors of workplaces, improve their amenities, ensure good ventilation and adequate light, and generally make the factory or workplace a more pleasant and agreeable place in which to work.

NOVEMBER 9

NAZI PARTY, *RALLIES*

The ceremonial consecration of the *Leibstandarte SS Adolf Hitler* is formalized in front of the Feldherrnhalle on the occasion of the Commemoration of the Munich *Putsch*. Here, the members of the *Leibstandarte* take a personal oath of allegiance to Hitler. This dispels any thoughts that these men are anything but his personal cohort. Himmler theoretically has control over the unit, however in reality the ultimate director of its function is Hitler, conjoined with the fact of his personal friendship with the Guard Commander, "Sepp" Dietrich, assumes an independence within the SS organization for the *Leibstandarte* that no other unit enjoys. This led Himmler to complain that it was "a complete law unto itself." Dietrich has scant regard for Himmler, addresses him on equal terms and is often engaged in arguments with him. The rivalry between the two men and the regard the officers of the *Leibstandarte* have for their commander can best be summed up by the gift he received on the occasion of his 50th birthday. A collection had been made among the officers so that an honour sword could be presented in the name of the entire officer corps. The gift was made by *Untersturmfübers* Brohl and Peiper, and on the blade were the 105 names of the men. After wearing it during the Olympic Games in Berlin, Himmler forbade Dietrich from wearing the unofficial sword. The unruly Dietrich obviously upstaged the "Boss" and the officer corps had acted without obtaining Himmler's permission. This

KEY PERSONALITY

Goebbels

It is a little-known fact that the Minister of Propaganda was opposed to a European war. He realized that Germany would be taking unnecessary risks and that her position of power would be weakened. Despite the victories of 1940 Goebbels said: "We must not fool ourselves. It will be a long and difficult war. Its outcome will not depend on boisterous victory parties but on a determination to do one's daily duty." He was probably the only Nazi leader to correctly judge the length and gravity of the war. As the war turned against Germany, Goebbels now saw himself as a general, his ministry as a general staff and the propaganda war as important as that at the front. In Berlin in May 1945, in the bunker with Hitler, Goebbels and his wife Magda commited suicide. He shot himself while she took poison, then an SS orderly gave them the *coup de grâce* to ensure that the couple were indeed dead.

amounted to insubordination that was too much to bear.

NOVEMBER 10

ARMED FORCES, *AIR FORCE*

When Hitler came to power in 1933 he introduced the *Deutscher Luftsport-Verband*. This organization is to stimulate air-minded young men. The club offers its members, most of whom have been in the armed forces, the active disciplined life for which they yearned, to such an extent that on November 10, 1933 Hitler introduces for the DLV a special uniform with rank and trade insignia. Under the direction of this organization the members will learn the three main aeronautical skills: ballooning, glider and powered flight.

Previously the *Reichswehr*, fearing that it was being left behind in its capacity to defend itself, secretly negotiated with the Red Army early in 1923 and finally signed

▼ *The* **Leibstandarte, Hitler's bodyguard, on parade in Berlin in 1933. They were the Führer's Praetorian Guard.**

▲ *Disgruntled SA men in 1933. Röhm's SA wanted more from the Nazi takeover of power than Hitler was prepared to give.*

an agreement in April 1925, which made the Lipezk Airfield in Russia available for German military training. In 1926, besides the fighter pilot training that was already underway, observer training began. Added to this, a special unit for testing new aircraft and weapons was also included. Between 1925 and 1933 approximately 120 officers returned from this flying school in Russia, being fully trained as fighter pilots.

Now Hitler has abandoned the school at Lipezk and relies on the DLV to train the new personnel of his clandestine *Luftwaffe* (Air Force).

NOVEMBER 12

GERMANY, *ELECTIONS*

A national referendum is held, in which 95 percent of the electorate approve Nazi policy. This vote is the culmination of the Nazis' work throughout the 1920s and early 1930s. Though the Nazis have undoubtedly

played on anti-Semitic feelings, scare-mongering and "stab-in-the-back" theories, they have also made expert use of newspapers, the radio and mass demonstrations of power. The *Kraft durch Freude* (Strength through Joy) movement is founded. Cardinal Faulhaber speaks out against Nazi anti-Christianity. Old *Freikorps* units are given a ceremonial dismissal parade by a grateful regime.

DECEMBER

GERMANY, *LEGAL*

Law to Secure Unity of Party and Reich. End of the *Reichstag* Fire trial. Only van der Lubbe is found guilty. This semi-blind, simple Dutch youth is sentenced to death by beheading to show the world that old German traditions were being brought back to the Third Reich.

In retrospect 1933 was one of the most successful years in the history of the Third Reich. The *Reichstag* fire of February 27 had provided Hitler with the pretext to begin consolidating the foundations of an authoritarian one-party state, and the

"enabling laws" forced through the *Reichstag* legalized intimidatory tactics and suspended civil rights in Germany.

The extraordinary "achievement" of the Nazis compared with other fascist and authoritarian regimes of the period was the speed with which they eliminated opposition. Within 18 months of coming to power, for example, they had erased all forms of political opposition by successfully preventing their opponents from organizing collectively. Within six months political opponents had been rounded-up, incarcerated and outlawed.

However, the reality of Nazi rhetoric soon became apparent as political opponents disappeared into concentration camps, and the quality of life of Jews deteriorated rapidly. These things obviously did not concern Hitler and the Nazi leadership. What did concern them, however, was the attitude of Ernst Röhm and his SA. The two million Brownshirts represented a possible alternative power base, and this issue would have to be addressed. It would be, in 1934.

▼ *German agricultural workers. The Nazis made great effort to alleviate the poor state of German agriculture.*

1934

The tensions between the SA leadership and Hitler exploded in 1934. Ernst Röhm, believing that the Nazi revolution should be taken a step further, began to talk of the SA replacing the army. Hitler, however, now firmly in power, did not want to alienate the army or the conservative élites that were backing him. Egged on by other senior Nazis, the Führer decided to eradicate the SA threat. The result was the Night of the Long Knives, during which the senior leadership of the SA, including Röhm, was killed.

FEBRUARY 3

NAZI PARTY, *SA*

In a clear attempt to strengthen his hold on the veteran membership, Röhm issues an order authorizing all SA as well as SS leaders and subordinates who were members prior to December 31, 1931, and still members, to receive and wear a specially inscribed Honour Dagger. Röhm's dedication is inscribed on the reverse of the blade. The inscription *In herzlicher freundschaft Ernst Röhm*, "in cordial comradeship Ernst Röhm", was acid etched onto the blade from a template bearing Röhm's own handwriting. A total of 135,860 daggers are awarded, of which the SS receives 9900.

Röhm states "The SA and SS will not tolerate the German revolution going to sleep or betrayed at the halfway stage by

▼ *An image of more harmonious times –
Ernst Röhm, SA leader (left) with "Sepp"
Dietrich, SS Leibstandarte commander.*

▲SS supremo Heinrich Himmler, who was outraged by the SA's sedition and disgusted by Röhm's homosexuality.

GERMANY, *INDIVIDUALS*

Ex-Chancellor Brüning leaves Germany, for safety, settling in the USA. As a politician who opposed the Enabling Act, he has been at risk from arrest or violence from the Nazis for some time.

APRIL

NAZI PARTY, *SS*

Himmler becomes Inspector of the Prussian Gestapo and Heydrich heads the Gestapo.

JUNE 1

ARMED FORCES, *NAVY*

The pocket battleship *Admiral Graf Spee* is launched.

JUNE 5

NAZI PARTY, *SA*

Röhm is summoned to a private conference with Hitler which results in a month-long leave for the whole of the SA in July.

▼ Hitler with the bullet-scarred Röhm. The Führer was quite fond of the SA leader, and went ahead with the purge reluctantly.

non-combatants." He further assures his SA: "You won't make a revolutionary army out of the old Prussian NCOs ...You only get the opportunity once to make something new and big and that'll help us lift the world off its hinges."

Röhm once again begins to make plans to merge the SA with the *Reichswehr* to form a "people's army" and also continues talking about a second National Socialist revolution. The party leadership clearly does not approve of these ideas, not least due to the fact that Hitler needs the support of the *Reichswehr*.

FEBRUARY 20

NAZI PARTY, *SA*

Röhm gives a speech in which he claims that the SA is the true army of National Socialism, that the regular army should be relegated to a training organization and that the Ministry of Defence should be reorganized. The inferences are unequivocal; this is a treasonable statement aimed at the Nazi Party and the German Army. Röhm holds the allegiance of over three million SA members. Things are moving to a head between Röhm and the Nazi hierarchy.

KEY MOMENTS

Night of the Long Knives

The killing of Röhm and the emasculation of the SA was prompted by such senior Nazis as Himmler, Göring and Goebbels, who were united in their dislike of Röhm. Hitler to the end tried to reach an accommodation with the SA leader, but to no avail. The army was also delighted that the SA would no longer be a threat to its position as sole bearer of the nation's arms, and was grateful to Hitler for dealing with the SA. However, just over a month later the army had a new master, when Hitler, following Hindenburg's death, became supreme commander of the armed forces. All German soldiers henceforth had to swear an oath of allegiance to him: "I swear before God this sacred oath: I will render unconditional obedience to Adolf Hitler, the Führer of the German nation and people, Supreme Commander of the armed forces, and will be ready as a brave soldier to risk my life at any time for this oath." In this way the army had been outman-oeuvred by Hitler, who had deftly taken advantage of the vacuum left by the death of Hindenburg and the army's gratitude over the Röhm Purge.

JUNE 14

GERMANY, *INTERNATIONAL RELATIONS*

German diplomats arrange a meeting between Hitler and Italian dictator Mussolini in Venice. Hitler stated in his writings from *Mein Kampf* "that it would be an advantage for Germany to improve relations with Italy in the future". The pursuit of this policy has not been possible after his coming to power due to one major stumbling block: Hitler's own birthplace, Austria.

The peacemakers of 1919 had granted this small country which was the last fragment of the Hapsburg Empire to Italy to be her guarantee of security – it served as a buffer zone. For this reason Italy could not allow Austria to be absorbed into Germany or fall under German control. In 1934, civil war broke out between the Austrian Clericals and the Austrian Socialists. These hostilities in turn stirred up the Austrian Nazis. German diplomats hope that Hitler will not actively push the Austrian question at this meeting between him and Mussolini. They believe that by meeting Mussolini face to face Hitler can be pushed into concessions. At this meeting

▼ *Röhm at an SA rally. The man mounted next to him is his lover, who was also shot during the Night of the Long Knives.*

military intelligence organization, claims to have secret SA orders to stage a *coup d'état*. The army has cancelled all leave.

JUNE 26

NAZI PARTY, *SA*

Himmler warns senior SS and SD (*Sicherheitsdienst* – the party's intelligence and security body) officers of an impending SA revolt.

JUNE 27

NAZI PARTY, *SA*

"Sepp" Dietrich, commanding the SS Guard in Berlin, goes to army headquarters and is

given extra weapons and transport for his men. A rumour spreads that the SA plans to kill the army old guard.

JUNE 28

NAZI PARTY, *SA*

Hitler travels from Berlin to Essen to attend the wedding of the local *Gauleiter* Terboven.

JUNE 29

NAZI PARTY, *SA*

The *Völkischer Beobachter* prints an article by Minister of Defence Blomberg pledging loyalty to Hitler and asking for curbs on the

▲ *Minister of Defence General Werner von Blomberg, who ordered that the army take an oath of allegiance to Hitler.*

Hitler and Mussolini pronounce their mutual dislike of France and the Soviet Union and Hitler renounces any desire to annex Austria. The *Duce* requests that the Austrian Nazis drop their campaign, and in return Dollfuss, the Clerical Chancellor, will treat them more sympathetically.

JUNE 20

NAZI PARTY, *SA*

The meeting between Hitler and Röhm seems to have done little to ease tensions. A shot fired at Hitler wounds Himmler; it is thought to have been fired by an SA escort.

JUNE 25

NAZI PARTY, *SA*

The "League of German Officers" disowns Röhm and expels him. The *Abwehr*, the

▶ *Hermann Göring directed operations from Berlin during the Röhm Purge. Like other Nazis, he disliked Röhm intensely.*

JUNE 30

SA. Hitler visits Labour Camps and goes on to Bad Godesberg near Bonn, on the Rhine, where he is joined by Goebbels. Göring, meanwhile, mobilizes his Berlin police and SS units. The SA in Munich have been ordered out aimlessly on the streets by anonymous notes – the local *Gauleiter* tells Hitler this is proof of the SA's disloyalty.

JUNE 30

NAZI PARTY, *RÖHM PURGE*

Hitler accepts an invitation to attend a conference of SA high leaders at the Vierjahreszeiten Hotel in Bad Weissee, hosted by Röhm. Hitler drives to Bad Weissee where Röhm and other SA men are staying at the hotel. But then Hitler flies at dawn to Munich with Goebbels, Dietrich and Lutze of the SA. The Führer is in a highly volatile state, ranting and making threats. He orders Schmidt and Schneidhubber, leading SA officers, to be sent to Stadelheim jail. The Munich *Gauleiter* is given lists of SA men and others in Bavaria to arrest. He orders them all to Stadelheim, some 200 of them, except for Heines, the SA commander of Silesia, who is found in bed with a man and is shot immediately. Goebbels now sends a codeword *Colibri* to Berlin for action. SA leaders in Berlin are taken to the army cadet school at Licherfelde and shot immediately. Murders of hundreds thought to be dangerous to the Nazis take place, including ex-Chancellor von Schleicher. Hitler prepares announcements from the Brown House in Munich and flies back to Berlin. Röhm is still alive, but the Night of the Long Knives is over.

JULY 2

NAZI PARTY, *RÖHM PURGE*

Röhm is shot after refusing to take his own life. In recognition of the part Eicke played

▲ *Italian Fascist dictator Mussolini moved troops towards the Austrian border to halt German designs on Austria.*

▼ *The cuff band of one of Theodor Eicke's newly created* **SS-Totenkopfverbände** *battalions –* **Thüringen.**

in the Night of the Long Knives, Himmler appoints him Inspector of Concentration Camps and head of the *SS-Totenkopf-verbände*. As a direct result of the Röhm *Putsch* most of the unofficial camps or "wild man camps" are closed. The remaining SA camps are removed from the jurisdiction of the civil authorities and taken over by the SS. The first full-time SS *Konzentrationslager*, concentration camp, unit was recruited from members of the *Allgemeine-SS* (General SS – the overall SS body) and is placed entirely under the overall command of the SS district south, who makes it a depository for its unwanted personnel in its ranks. The conditions that the guards live under are little better than the inmates.

Eicke improved conditions, lifted the morale and discipline of his men and formulated service regulations for both guards and prisoners which remained virtually unchanged until the end of the war. With his new inspectorate firmly established at Oranienburg, near Berlin, Eicke reorganized and enlarged the *SS-Totenkopfverbände* into five numbered *Sturmbanne* or battalions: I *Oberbayern*, II *Elbe*, III *Sachsen*, IV *Ostfriesland* and V *Thüringen*.

JULY 4

NAZI PARTY, *SS*

Three days after the SS has successfully carried out the purge of Röhm and his supporters, Himmler personally presents specially dedicated SS Honour daggers to 200 of the major participants in the action. The dagger follows the same pattern as the dagger given out by Röhm, but with Himmler's name replacing Röhm's and the inscription being in Himmler's hand writing. This was his final stamp of authority on the proceedings.

JULY 14

GERMANY, *LEGAL*

A law is issued legitimizing all the killings that took place during the Night of the Long Knives. Hitler makes a speech in the *Reichstag* explaining and justifying the affair, claiming that only 19 senior and 42 other SA men had been shot, while 13 had been shot resisting arrest and three had committed suicide (other estimates put the number of dead at 1000). The SS is now formally separated from the SA.

▶ *General Werner Freiherr von Fritsch was appointed the commander of the Germany Army in 1934.*

JULY 25

AUSTRIA, *POLITICS*

Hitler has done nothing to fulfil Mussolini's demands. The Nazis of Vienna occupy the Chancellery, murder Dollfuss and attempt to seize power, all with Hitler's support. At this critical moment Mussolini makes his first major bid as an international leader. He mobilizes Italy's crack mountain regiments in the mountain gorges leading to the Brenner Pass, threatening to beat any German force into Austria if necessary. This gesture is sufficient to halt the German plans for the absorption of Austria into the Reich. It should be noted that Mussolini is very disappointed that the Western Powers have stood aside and failed to support Italy. He later remarked to his wife: "I expected more from our Western friends, Rachele. They've let me down. Their apathy could have been disastrous." Hitler can do nothing to help his Austrian adherents and stands helplessly by while Schuschnigg, successor to Dollfuss, restores order under Mussolini's protection.

AUGUST 2

GERMANY, *PERSONALITIES*

Field Marshal Paul von Hindenburg dies at Neudeck; the only barrier between Hitler

KEY PERSONALITY

Heydrich

He was born in Halle, Saxony, on March 7, 1904, the son of the founder of the Halle Conservatory. He was a rounded individual, possessing exceptional intellectual ability, as well as being an accomplished sportsman. In 1922 he joined the navy as a cadet and was under the orders and tutelage of Canaris, but in April 1931, due to allegations of dishonourable conduct towards a young lady who declared that he had impregnated her, he was brought before an honour court, presided over by Canaris, which found him guilty and dismissed him from the service. He became engaged to Lina von Osten and it was she who was to convert him to Nazism, and he joined the NSDAP in 1931. Lina enlisted the help of Frederich Karl von Eberstein to bring him to Himmler's notice, which he did on the June 14, 1931. Himmler found him appealing; the interview was short and he came straight to the point: "I want to set up a security and information service within the SS and I need a specialist. If you think you can do this management job, will you please write down on paper how you think you would tackle it, I'll give you 20 minutes."

His considerable organizational abilities, his total ruthlessness, the intensity of anti-Semitism and his Nordic appearance were self-evident. Himmler perhaps perceived the perverse view that Heydrich's fear of being considered Jewish, or partly Jewish, would be a means of controlling his talented associate. Whatever the truth in this, Heydrich rose quickly within the SS and became Protector of Bohemia and Moravia in September 1941. Tipped to be a future leader of the Third Reich, he was assassinated in 1942.

▲ *Hitler at Hindenburg's Memorial Chamber at Tannenberg in late 1934. Hitler now had absolute power.*

and unrestrained power disappears with Hindenburg's demise. Within three hours Goebbels announces that the office of president is abolished, and the fusing of the two roles of chancellor and president. The Führer of the NSDAP is now the Führer of Germany. Hitler also becomes commander of the armed forces.

SEPTEMBER

ARMED FORCES, *HIGH COMMAND*
General Werner Freiherr von Fritsch becomes chief of the High Command of the German Army.

SEPTEMBER 5–10

NAZI PARTY, *PARTY DAY*
Party Rally of Unity is held in Nuremberg. It is the first rally to last for over a week. The event is recorded by the film-maker Leni Riefenstahl, who makes a three-hour film entitled *Triumph of the Will*.

SEPTEMBER 24

NAZI PARTY, *WAFFEN-SS*
The chief of the three branches of the *Wehrmacht* (armed forces) are officially advised of the creation of the *SS-Verfügungstruppe* (SS Militarized Troops) by means of a circular letter. It states that the *SS-Verfügungstruppe* is to be formed on a basis of three regiments modelled on infantry regiments of the army, each to contain three battalions, a mortar company and a motorcycle company, as well as being supported by a signals battalion. It also provides for three officer cadet schools. The formation will be under the personal command of the *Reichsführer-SS* except in time of war, when it will come under the control of the army.

OCTOBER 24

GERMANY, *LEGAL*
Hitler issues a decree establishing the scope and aims of the DAF, "The German Labour Front is the organization of all German professional and manual workers. It includes, in particular, the members of the former labour unions, of the unions of employees, and of the former associations of employers, which are united in the

NOVEMBER 12

ARMED FORCES, *NAVY*

The pocket battleship *Admiral Scheer* is commissioned.

DECEMBER 14

SS, *WAFFEN-SS*

The *Leibstandarte*'s "first blooding" was over when the Röhm *Putsch* shooting finally ended on July 2. As a reward for their loyalty and involvement, Dietrich was promised by Hitler that he would see that the *Leibstandarte* became a fully equipped regiment. A rare honour was conferred on the *Leibstandarte* in early October 1934 when it was decided that it should be fully motorized. At this time the *Reichswehr* in the main is still horse-drawn and this decision leads to whispers of discontent in military circles. The Political Readiness Detachments were to be reorganized into battalions and then amalgamated within the *Leibstandarte* under Himmler's orders. The *Leibstandarte* now consists of: one Staff, three motorized infantry battalions, one motorcycle company, one motor company, one signals platoon, one armoured car platoon, one regimental band.

▶ *Party Day at Nuremberg, 1934. Beside Hitler stand Himmler (left) and Victor Lutze (right), the new SA commander.*

Labour Front on a footing of complete equality. The aim of the Labour Front is the formation of a real national community of all Germans. The Labour Front has the duty of adjusting the legitimate interest of all parties in a manner conforming with National Socialist principles. Attached to the Labour Front is the organization 'Strength through Joy'. The Labour Front has the further duty of looking after the professional education of its adherents." Thus Dr Ley is given responsibility for the social, educational and political well-being of the entire German working population. Membership in the DAF is of two kinds, individual and corporate. Hitler charges *Reichsleiter* Dr Robert Ley, leader of the DAF and all affiliated labour organizations, with leading the German labour effort. The term *Reichsleiter* is the official designation for Hitler's position as leaders of the Third Reich. However, it is also applied to departmental heads, and is highly regarded by senior Nazis.

1935

This year was a pivotal period for the Third Reich's relations with the rest of the world. Adolf Hitler announced he was reintroducing universal conscription, which was a repudiation of the hated Treaty of Versailles, and was warmly welcomed at home. In addition, as German troops marched into the Saar, he was determined to reintegrate those ethnic Germans who were living outside Germany back into the Reich. On the domestic front, more laws were introduced against Jews, who were becoming second-class citizens in their own country.

◀ **German troops march into the Saar in March following the plebiscite. It had been under League of Nations control.**

▲ **Heinkel He 42 floatplanes fly over the Fatherland, part of Hitler's new Luftwaffe and a breach of the Treaty of Versailles.**

JANUARY 13

GERMANY, *ELECTIONS*

The inhabitants of the Saar overwhelmingly vote to return to the Reich, which in 1919 was placed under League of Nations control for 15 years under the terms of the Treaty of Versailles. The Saar plebiscite is the instrument upon which Hitler founds his "return of the Saar to Germany" campaign.

JANUARY 20

NAZI PARTY, *SS*

The great SS Leaders' conference is held in Breslau. An interesting illustration of the British policy of appeasement has been given in a British newspaper report: "Germany's secret police are not always the sinister beings they are supposed to be", and goes on to note "the happy faces of the SS chief and his men as they arrive at the meeting".

FEBRUARY 26

ARMED FORCES, *AIR FORCE*

As the NSDAP begins to feel its political might, Hitler becomes more confident and announces the official formation of the new *Luftwaffe* (German Air Force). All the secrecy that has surrounded it is blown away, as if as a prelude to events that were to come, by the winds of war. The DLV is

◀ **Counting the votes in the Saar plebiscite, which overwhelmingly favoured returning to the Reich.**

disbanded and all its former members are encouraged to join the new *Nationalsozialistisches Fliegerkorps* (NSFK) that has been introduced in its place. In this manner the party brings together under its control all of the country's flying clubs into one organization, which in fact is paramilitary. The NSFK can thus operate with the fledgling *Luftwaffe* and both can grow and gather strength together.

MARCH 1

GERMANY, *THE SAAR*

The German Army, accompanied by armed SS units, marches into Saarbrücken.

MARCH 16

GERMANY, *TREATIES*

Adolf Hitler renounces the Treaty of Versailles' disarmament clauses. He makes his famous proclamation in which he repudiates the Treaty of Versailles and reintroduces military conscription, announcing this to the German parliament as a political statement, in direct contravention to the Treaty of Versailles, which expressly forbids a standing army of over 100,000 men. Parts of the speech are word-for-word those written seven years earlier by Defence Minister Groner. Hitler appears to have been the first frontline politician prepared to stand up and present it. He certainly expects some repercussions

▶ **Aircraft of the new Luftwaffe entertain the crowd at a mass Nazi rally, while antiaircraft guns let loose salvos of blanks.**

from the Allies, but they are too engrossed with their own internal affairs and actually take very little no notice.

MARCH 16

SS, *WAFFEN-SS*

Hitler officially establishes the *SS-Verfügungstruppe*, although at this time it

APRIL

already consists of 11 battalions. The intention was always that the *SS-Verfügungstruppe* would benefit from the highest possible standards of training available. To facilitate this, two highly regarded former army officers, Paul Hausser and Felix Steiner, have been recruited to supervise training. Both were ultimately to become among the finest field commanders of the Waffen-SS.

APRIL

ARMED FORCES, *AIR FORCE*

The *Luftwaffe*'s existence is formally declared. The first German fighter squadron emerges under the command of Major Ritter von Greim, which bears the title *Jagdgeschwader Richthofen* 2.

The first Luftwaffe fighter school was established at the *Deutsche Verkehrsfliegeschule* (German Commercial Pilots School) at Schlelssheim, thus completing the formation of the new Luftwaffe and the *Nationasozialistische Flieger Korps*. Hitler's conjuring trick had worked; through skilful propaganda and deception an astonished world was convinced that he had been able to produce a force as technically involved as the *Luftwaffe* virtually out of a hat. This feat added to Hitler's international diplomatic aura and as the *Luftwaffe* gained experience in Spain later in the Civil War, the fear of this "terror machine", which was interlaced with the chivalry of those knights of the air from the former days, often settled a diplomatic disagreement.

APRIL 10

NAZI PARTY, *PERSONALITIES*

Göring finally asks the actress Emmy Sonnemann to marry him. Emmy, in her youth, was a provincial actress who developed into a beautiful and gracious lady who captivated Göring. Congratulatory telegrams and presents pour in from all over the world, which includes jewels, oriental rugs and two paintings by Cranach. This is a union that meets with Hitler's approval. Their wedding is one of the "grandest social occasions" of the Third Reich that rivals any Hollywood spectacular. The ceremony is held in Berlin, where more than 30,000 members of the paramilitary organizations line the streets. Bells sound, and a formation of the latest German aircraft fly overhead as Hermann and Emmy drive in an open-topped

▼SS soldiers are inspected by Hitler. Paul Hausser and Felix Steiner were appointed as SS military instructors in March.

▲ Joachim von Ribbentrop, the head of the Ribbentrop Bureau, which was set up as a rival to the German Foreign Office.

▲ Erich Raeder inspects men of his newly titled Kriegsmarine. The building of surface ships and submarines was increased in 1935.

Mercedes to the cathedral. Here, Hitler greets the bridal couple on the steps in front of the cathedral. The Reich Bishop, and armed forces chaplain, Ludwig Müller conducts the service, while Hitler undertakes the duties of best man. In all its riotous details, the proceedings are reported live on radio. The couple left the cathedral accompanied by an enormous band, which played the celebrated march from Lohengrin. The Görings saluted the large crowd that had gathered to view their marriage pageant.

MAY 21

ARMED FORCES, *NAVY*
The German Navy, formerly the *Reichsmarine*, is renamed *Kriegsmarine*.

▶ A prime example of garish vulgarity at its worst – the marriage of Hermann Göring to Emmy Sonnemann.

JUNE 18

NAZI PARTY, *RIBBENTROP BUREAU*

Under Hess' secretariat the Ribbentrop Bureau is established in the Wilhelm Strasse, provocatively across the street from the foreign office. This is in direct opposition to the ministry, with the avowed objective of proving Nazi methods are more effective than the foreign ministry's traditional policies. Careerists and journalists of dubious qualifications staff it.

Joachim von Ribbentrop, having served in 1934 as special commissioner for disarmament, seized his big chance when he was able to conclude the Anglo-German naval treaty in May 1935, unaided by foreign ministry officials, let alone having informed the ministry. The German object was to trap the British Government into an agreement to flout the naval restrictions of the Versailles Treaty. The British Government, with Anthony Eden the main negotiator, with what now seems a mixture of credulity and arrogance, fell into Ribbentrop's trap.

▲ *Hitler attacks the Treaty of Versailles, which he described as a "shame and an outrage" designed to destroy Germany.*

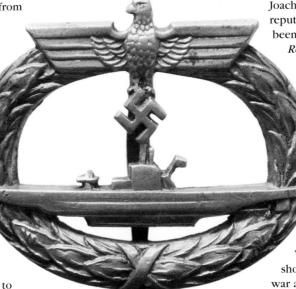

▲ *The Submariner's Badge, one of the awards given to the members of Hitler's new U-boat service.*

Neither the League of Nations nor Italy and France were consulted. The Anglo-German Naval Agreement was signed by Sir Samuel Hoare for Britain and by Special Envoy Joachim von Ribbentrop for Germany. His reputation, especially with Hitler, had now been definitely established. From *Reichsführer-SS* Himmler he received the honourary rank of *SS-Gruppenführer*. Hitler told Admiral Erich Raeder, Commander-in-Chief of the German Navy, that the day the agreement was signed was the happiest of his life. Raeder himself told his officers they could not have hoped for better conditions during the coming decade. He went on to say that the Agreement ruled out the possibility of Germany having to fight another war against Britain.

With this agreement, Hitler hoped to show that he had no desire to conduct war against Britain. Germany volunteered to restrict her maritime strength to 35 percent of that of the Royal Navy. However, submarines were considered as a separate case, and a 45 percent ratio was agreed. Parity in submarines was also agreed in principle, but in that event Germany would have to sacrifice tonnage in other categories, and Britain would have to approve the move.

JUNE 29

ARMED FORCES, *NAVY*
The first of the new submarines, *U-1*, is commissioned.

JULY 30

NAZI PARTY, *SS*
The *SS-Hauptamt*, or Main Office, is established to organize all branches of Himmler's SS.

SEPTEMBER 10–16

GERMANY, *LEGAL*
Party Rally of Freedom takes place. It is at the seventh Party Congress that the new Reich Citizen's Law, and Law for the Protection of German Blood and German Honour, which were known thereafter as the Nuremberg laws, are proclaimed. The laws define two degrees of humanity: the *Reichbürger*, the Citizen of Pure German Blood, and the *Staatsangebörige*, the subject of the state, i.e. Jews. Intermarriage between the two groups is strictly forbidden. The lot of Jews living in Germany is getting progressively worse, and many are leaving the country.

The Nazi swastika banner is made the official national flag.

SEPTEMBER 27

ARMED FORCES, *NAVY*
Karl Dönitz, who had previously been the commander of the light cruiser *Emden*, commissions the 1st U-boat Flotilla, called Flotilla *Weddigen*.

NOVEMBER

GERMANY, *LEGAL*
National Law of Citizenship comes into effect, which provides the definition of who is a Jew and *Mischling*, or mixed race. To be Aryan is a precondition for public appointments. First Decree of the Law for the Protection of German Blood and Honour (see above); marriages between Aryan and Jew or *Mischling* are forbidden.

NOVEMBER 2

ARMED FORCES, NAVY
The light cruiser *Nürnberg* is commissioned.

▶ *Berlin Jews who, by the National Law of Citizenship, became second-class citizens in their own country.*

NOVEMBER 15

GERMANY, *CULTURE*
Dr Goebbels has long controlled communications and the media, but the establishment of the National Senate of Culture offers him the opportunity to extend his control still further, and utilize various art forms to convey his National Socialist propaganda themes to a wider audience. The chamber is composed of individuals connected with the various arts or those who have assisted in the advancement of German culture and it is from these members that the Senate appointments are chosen.

It is doubtful that the membership of the Senate underwent very many changes during the proceeding years, which would have limited the membership to probably less than 300.

1936

The Olympic Games gave Nazi Germany a chance to show the world that the Third Reich was a well-ordered, powerful society. For propaganda purposes measures against Jews were relaxed, and Berlin became the home of fraternal international friendship, albeit temporarily. However, away from the Olympics the Germans re-occupied the demilitarized Rhineland and began to channel military aid to the Franco's Nationalists fighting a civil war in Spain. As they did so, Great Britain and France, the major powers of Europe, did nothing but watch idly.

JANUARY 6

ARMED FORCES, *NAVY*
The pocket battleship *Admiral Graf Spee* is commissioned.

FEBRUARY

SS, *GESTAPO*
The Gestapo is given national status with Heydrich as its head.

   On October 5, 1931, Heydrich became a member of the SS and after a short spell at the Brown House, decided to set up the SD out of the view of enquiring eyes. Certainly from this time on Heydrich experienced a meteoric rise, becoming the second most powerful man in the RSHA. Heydrich's ancestry was in SS terms questionable, however; his father had been listed in the *Lexicon of Music and Musicians* under Heydrich's real name Süss, a clear

▼ *German troops move into the Rhineland in March 1936. They had orders to withdraw if opposed by the French.*

MARCH

GERMANY, *TREATIES*

The Locarno Treaty is renounced. This was a non-aggression treaty signed in 1925 between Germany, France and Belgium. It recognized the demilitarization of the Rhineland as being permanent, with the post-Versailles Treaty borders of the three signatories being mutually accepted.

MARCH 7

GERMANY, *THE RHINELAND*

It had been another specification of the hated Treaty of Versailles that the Rhineland should be demilitarized. This turned the Rhineland into an unoccupied buffer zone between Germany and France. It comprised all German territory west of the Rhine and a 48km (30-mile) strip east of the river which included Köln, Düsseldorf and Bonn.

Hitler has been burning to send troops marching back into the Rhineland, both in order to assert that it is an indivisible part of his new Germany and to show his contempt for the Treaty of Versailles. His chance came in February 1936 when the nervous French ratified a treaty with the Soviet Union, a power which Hitler

indication that he was Jewish. However, investigations carried out into this later tended to indicate that Süss was in fact not Jewish. It is said that Heydrich had erased the name Sarah from his mother's gravestone because of its Jewish connotations.

FEBRUARY 4

SWITZERLAND, *NAZI PARTY*

Wilhelm Gustloff was born in Schwerin and went to live in Davos, Switzerland. He joined the *Ausland* Organization of the NSDAP in 1929 and went on to found his

▲ *Potsdam Naval Academy, which in 1936 was producing personnel to crew such ships as the new* **Admiral Graf Spee.**

own group in Davos in 1931. On this day David Frankfurter, a Jewish student, murders him in a Davos Hotel.

The body of Wilhelm Gustloff was brought back to his home town of Schwerin for burial. Gustloff is declared a martyr of the Nazi movement.

Frankfurter was found guilty and imprisoned, since there was no capital punishment in Switzerland.

▼ *Images to fool the world: well-fed concentration camp inmates receive their cigarette rations from the SS.*

GERMANY, *RAD*

The Labour Service, *Reichsarbeitsdienst* (RAD) is created. Its began in 1931 when Chancellor Heinrich Brüning authorized the formation of state-sponsored labour camps to help ease unemployment, the *Freiwillige Arbeitsdienst* (FAD). These camps were controlled by individual states and their use varied greatly across the country. When Hitler became chancellor he soon appointed Konstantin Hierl as Secretary of State for the Labour Service, the control of which was transferred from the states to the central government. The RAD was used for various tasks, mainly for reclaiming land for farming, helping with the harvests and construction roads, but also for various emergence relief projects.

claimed, at the time, was particularly detestable to his Nazi State because it is Asiatic and Bolshevik. In response to this threat, and against the advice of his more cautious associates, he orders his army to march into the Rhineland in an operation codenamed Winter Exercise on the morning of March 7. The new *Luftwaffe* fighters make their first public display, while the *Leibstandarte* provides the advance guard in the retaking of the Rhineland demilitary zone. Orders to the *Wehrmacht* are to retreat immediately should French forces move to oppose the occupation. That evening the Führer makes a gloating speech in the packed *Reichstag*.

The occupation of the Rhineland has been an enormous risk, which only a man as determined as Hitler would have taken. The German Army had only mustered one division to make the march into the Rhineland, and of that only three battalions had crossed the Rhine. If the worst had come to the worst, these puny forces could only have been strengthened by a few brigades, while the French, with their Polish and Czech allies, could immediately mobilized 90 divisions and brought up reserves of 100 more.

To make the situation even more dangerous, the re-occupation of the Rhineland is not a mundane breach of the Treaty, but a *casus foederis*; that is to say that it virtually obliges France to declare war. However, despite the terrifying prospect of a humiliating climb-

▲ *General Francisco Franco (centre, waving), leader of Spain's Nationalists whom Hitler supported from 1936.*

down, Hitler was confident that the French would make no move against him and he has been proved right.

After this success Hitler's diplomacy began to take on a new edge. This operation was achieved without the predicted political and military consequences. In the ensuing crisis Hitler's resolute position split Great Britain and France diplomatically, ensuring the international acceptance of his fait accompli and giving him confidence to undertake his other expansionist desires.

MAY 8

SS, *CONCENTRATION CAMPS*

Reichsführer-SS Himmler conducts a group of Nazi Party officials around Dachau concentration camp. He is extremely proud of this new institution. The SS camp guards have formed as *Totenkopfverbände*, and currently number 3000 men.

JUNE 20

GERMANY, *SS*

By decree of the Führer the party post of *Reichsführer-SS*, held by Himmler, is formally combined with the newly established government post of Chief of the German Police. Himmler is steadily increasing his powers.

SS, *IDEOLOGY*

Himmler lays a wreath on the empty tomb of the Saxon King Heinrich I, who was nicknamed Henry the Fowler, on the occasion of the thousandth anniversary of his death. Himmler also participated in a solemn ceremony in the crypt of Quedlinburg Cathedral. He regards himself as the embodiment of this warrior king, who had defeated the Slavs and was founder of the German Reich.

JULY 17

SPAIN, *CIVIL WAR*

The Spanish Civil War begins. A revolt against the Spanish Republic breaks out in

▲ *Nationalist troops in Spain during the Civil War. Assistance given by Nazi aircraft was crucial to the Nationalist cause.*

▼ *One of the Junkers Ju 52 transport aircraft used to ferry Franco's men to the Spanish mainland in 1936.*

many of the military garrisons in Spanish Morocco. The revolt is led by General Mola and General Francisco Franco Bahamonde, who has been the governor of the Canary Islands until his dismissal from his post by the Popular Front Government. The revolt spreads rapidly throughout Spain, resulting in serious fighting between government troops and anti-government forces. For several years Spanish generals and other Nationalists agents had been in contact with, and successfully seeking support from, both Hitler and Mussolini. Hitler, who is wholly committed to oppose what he sees as the communist threat in Western Europe, makes the decision within a few days of the Nationalist rebellion to stand by General Franco and actively to support him in his "fight against Bolshevism". It will also be an excellent testing ground for Germany's new tanks and aircraft.

▼ *A model of the grand Berlin Olympic Stadium, plus the swimming pool, is shown to foreign and German guests.*

JULY 11

GERMAN, *TREATIES*

The "Gentleman's Agreement" between Hitler and Schuschnigg of Austria, in which Hitler recognizes the full sovereignty of Austria and in return Schuschnigg acknowledges that Austria is an "German State", agrees to admit members of the so-called "National Opposition" into his government and give amnesty to Nazi political prisoners in Austria. The final stumbling block regarding close German-Italian relations has eliminated by this agreement.

JULY 31

SPAIN, *GERMAN AID*

The first detachment of 85 German air and ground crew volunteers drawn from Sonderstab W, and travelling as a party of tourists, leaves Hamburg for Cadiz in the Woermann liner *Usamoro*. They take with them six Heinkel He 51 fighters. Simultaneously, 20 Junkers Ju 52 transport planes piloted by German airmen are

▲ *A clearly bored Führer watches an ice hockey game between Great Britain and Hungary at the Olympic Games.*

▲ *The games were an ideal opportunity to show off Nazi militarism. Here, 2000 military musicians entertain the crowd.*

flown from Berlin to Morocco. It has been recognized that the most valuable service Germany can render General Franco at this stage is to help him ferry his Moorish troops into Spain. Under the command of Hauptmann Henke, 42 Luftwaffe pilots began to ferry Franco's Moroccan troops of the Spanish Foreign Legion from Tetuan to the aerodrome of Tablada at Seville. The first flight is made with 22 soldiers and their equipment on board each plane. On subsequent flights the number of passengers carried on each plane was increased to 30. Untiring, Henke and his pilots flew to and fro sometimes four or five times a day. By the beginning of September this small unit had transported from Africa to the mainland the astonishing number, for its time, of 8899 soldiers, 44 field guns, 90 machine guns and 137 tons of ammunition and equipment.

August

BERLIN, *OLYMPIC GAMES*
The Olympic Games open in Berlin. The occasion is used by the Nazis to present the success of National Socialism to the world.

▶ *Black athletes winning gold medals was not part of the Nazi plan. This is Mitte Woodruff, winner of the 800 metres.*

As such, it has resulted in a quietening of the anti-Semitic campaign. The opening ceremony is conducted by 40,000 SA men and a choir of 3000 sings *Deutschland* and the *Horst Wessel* song. On the first day of the games Hitler presents medals to the winners. German athletes do well in the games, winning the most gold, silver and bronze medals. However, Hitler declines to award any more medals when black American athletes start winning

competitions, especially Jesse Owens, who wins four gold medals.

August 11

GREAT BRITAIN, *DIPLOMACY*
Joachim von Ribbentrop is appointed German Ambassador to the court of St

73

▲ **Great Britain's King George V, whom Ribbentrop greeted with a "Heil Hitler!" salute whilst Ambassador to Great Britain.**

James in London. He accepts his appointment as ambassador grudgingly, and shows his reluctance by taking up his post three months after his appointment. Once there he travels back and forth between London and Berlin so often that the British satirical magazine *Punch* calls him "the roving Aryan", while a highly placed official in the German Foreign Office suggests the possibility that von Ribbentrop regards his appointment to the Court of St James's as a part-time job. He is convinced, not without justification, that Foreign Minister Neurath is trying to get him out of the way with this position. It now becomes Ribbentrop's ambition to replace Neurath as Minister of Foreign Affairs.

Ribbentrop made the unforgivable mistake of greeting George V, King of England with "Heil Hitler" at a court reception in 1937. He was rejected by British society as a result, which deeply offended him. After this episode he had a deeply ingrained hatred for everything British, a hatred that certainly played a role in the turbulent developments leading up to the outbreak of World War II.

SEPTEMBER

SPAIN, *GERMAN AID*

In September a further flight of fighters, a flight of reconnaissance aircraft, a heavy battery of antiaircraft guns and two tank companies are sent to Franco from Germany through Portugal. The pocket battleship *Deutschland* appears off Ceuta. The German submarines *U-33* and *U-34* have been in Spanish waters since the outbreak of the civil war, having been sent there to represent German interests. Also in September, *Oberstleutnant* Walter Warlimont, a general staff officer from the army general staff, is appointed Plenipotentiary delegate of the *Wehrmacht* in Spain. The German Minister of Justice, Hans Frank, conveys to the *Duce*: "The Führer desires to receive you in Germany at the earliest possible moment, not only in your capacity as head of the government but also as founder and *Duce* of a party with affinities to National Socialism." Mussolini expresses his wishes to undertake the trip: "It must, however, be well prepared so as to produce concrete results. It will cause a great stir and must therefore be historically important in its results." The *Duce* was anxious to prove that he could excite a Berlin crowd to the same heights of enthusiasm as he had done in Rome. Count Ciano personally makes the plans for the state visit, scheduled for September 25–29, 1937. He also emphasizes the importance of uniforms during the visit: "We must appear more Prussian than the Prussians."

SEPTEMBER 8–14

NAZI PARTY, *RALLIES*
Party Rally of Honour, Nuremberg.

OCTOBER

GERMANY, *ECONOMICS*
Göring initiates the Four-Year Plan, which is designed to make Germany industrially independent.

Despite the grand promises, there was no coherent national programme to ensure Germany's military spending was pegged to economic capacity. Göring was a hopeless administrator, with the result that each of the services pursued its own rapid expansion, setting ludicrous targets and then competing for the necessary allocations of capital investment and raw materials. The truth was that Germany did not have the money or raw materials to meet the demands of the armed services. The *Luftwaffe*, for example, had plans to build 19,000 frontline and reserve aircraft by 1942. Even if this target had been met, fuel needs to keep such an air fleet flying would have required 85 percent of the world's oil production. To make matters worse, Germany required vast amounts of iron ore, copper, bauxite, nickel, petrol and rubber, and these had to be imported as Germany was rich only in coal. Though the Four-Year Plan encouraged the development and production of synthetic substitutes, none of these products could balance the demands made by the arms buildup. In fact, the armaments industry was constantly in crisis, with stocks of raw materials being exhausted and no money for fresh supplies.

▶ Hans Frank, Reich Leader of the NSDAP.

▼ *The pocket battleship* Deutschland *was active in supporting the Nationalists in Spain in 1936.*

▲ *Ribbentrop, Ciano, Italian foreign minister, and Hitler develop the Rome-Berlin axis in November 1936.*

OCTOBER 1

SS, *WAFFEN-SS*

A special Inspectorate of the *SS-Verfügungstruppe* has been created to supervise administration and military training. The new inspectorate has the objective of moulding the mainly ill-trained and far flung units of the *SS-Verfügungstruppe* into an efficient fighting force. *SS-Oberstgruppenführer und Generaloberst der Waffen-SS* Paul Hausser, who was to become known affectionately as "Papa" Hausser to his men, is chosen as inspector of the *SS-Verfügungstruppe*, although he has only just been appointed inspector of the *SS-Junkerschule* (Officer Schools) at Bad Tölz and Brunswick.

OCTOBER 3

ARMED FORCES, *NAVY*

The battlecruiser *Scharnhorst* is launched. Based on a World War I design, she is a fast battlecruiser that is designed to be faster than any enemy she will encounter on the seas. She will need this speed because she is terribly undergunned for her size, being armed with 11in guns. Part of Raeder's Plan-Z, she is designed to be a stopgap. She will eventually compliment the larger *Bismarck* and *Tirpitz* in the new German fleet.

NOVEMBER

SPAIN, *GERMAN AID*

With the realization that the Civil War is likely to last a long time, the German Government decides to increase its economic and military commitment to the Nationalists. Hermann Göring, as the Commander in Chief of the German Air Force, is eager to advertise the power of his *Luftwaffe* and to test its new aircraft under combat conditions. Because the German Army is reluctant to commit any substantial numbers of regular troops, German participation in the Spanish Civil War becomes primarily a *Luftwaffe* affair. This force, the Condor Legion, is sent to Spain to fight the communists.

NOVEMBER 1

ITALY, *TREATIES*

Mussolini publicly announces a German-Italian agreement, which constitutes an "Axis" around which the other European powers might work together. In the shaping of the Axis, Galeazzo Ciano goes to Germany where he meets Hitler and Joachim von Ribbentrop, the Führer's special advisor on foreign policy. The birth of the Rome-Berlin Axis is now imminent. Italy's relations with England and France have been severely strained by the opposing interests brought about by the Abyssinian conflict. The advisability of standing with Germany and confronting the Western powers is clear. At this and subsequent meetings at Berchtesgaden, Hitler's retreat in the Bavarian Alps, five points are worked out in collaboration between the two countries, and the viewpoints of both dictators are carefully examined. Ciano's report of the meetings was found satisfactory and Mussolini publicly announces the agreement.

Despite the Axis and the repeated mutual professions of friendship, the relations between the two leaders remain strained with certain suspicions. They watch each other's diplomatic activities with Great Britain closely, and also the pressures each exert over Austria, the piece of territory sandwiched between the two.

NOVEMBER 2

NAZI PARTY, *AWARDS*

Hitler introduces an order that formalizes the awards of the party and forbids the wearing on party uniforms badges that have, by tradition, become considered genuine party commemorative or honourary awards. Badges and awards are an important part of Nazism. The order

reads as follows:

"They may be worn on the civilian overcoat or jacket by all party members on the left lapel. All party members who were permitted to wear their party badge or the national emblem badges which were issued at the party gatherings may now not be worn at all, except that issued in the year 1929, but the ones which will be issued in future at such gatherings may only be worn for the duration of the

gathering. The wearing of club medals on duty or party uniform is herewith forbidden or any of the party's associated branches."

NOVEMBER 3

SPAIN, *GERMAN AID*

Warlimont returns to Germany and

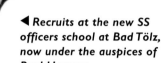

◀ **Recruits at the new SS officers school at Bad Tölz, now under the auspices of Paul Hausser.**

▲ **Eagle's Nest at Bertchesgaden, Hitler's retreat in the Bavarian Alps, where he often entertained cronies and guests.**

Generalmajor Hugo Sperrle is appointed by Göring to command the Condor Legion, which at the outset comprises, in addition to those German forces already in Spain, the following assets:

1 bomber group with 3 squadrons of Junkers Ju 52s
1 fighter group with three squadrons of Heinkel He 51s
1 reconnaissance squadron with 12 Heinkel He 70 aircraft
4 batteries of 88mm antiaircraft guns
2 batteries of light antiaircraft guns
1 air signals unit with a wireless, telephone, a communication and an air security company
1 Air Park with machine shops
1 leadership staff

NOVEMBER 6

GERMANY, *TREATIES*

Germany joins the London Submarine Protocol. This international treaty was originally signed by the major naval powers in 1930, and seeks to impose rules on submarine warfare. Surprise submerged attacks on merchant vessels are not permitted. Instead, the submarine should surface, stop the vessel and inspect its papers. It can only be sunk if its cargo comes under a specified list of contraband and the safety of the crew can be ensured. As lifeboats are not

▶ **The head of the Inspectorate of the SS-Verfügungstruppe, Paul "Papa" Hausser.**

considered suitable accommodation on the high seas, the ship's crew are supposed to be taken aboard the submarine.

NOVEMBER 9

SS, *WAFFEN-SS*

Felix Steiner is the luminary when it comes to the actual training programme of the *SS-Verfügungstruppe*. In 1935, he joined the *SS-Verfügungstruppe* and helped to

▲ *A Heinkel He 111 of the Condor Legion. Early operations were not a success: in one raid the Legion bombed Nationalists.*

develop the 3rd battalion of the *SS-Standarte Deutschland*, stationed in Munich and the SS training camp at Dachau concentration camp. He applied his military training to the men, instituting rigorous training schedules in application of his motto "sweat saves blood".

One recruit in three fails basic training the first time round. However, for the successful candidates there is a passing-out parade where they take the SS oath, which is taken separately from members of the other SS branches. At 22:00 hours on the occasion of the November 9 anniversary celebrations of the Munich *Putsch*, the ceremony takes

▲ *Hermann Göring, the head of the Luftwaffe, whose Condor Legion aided the Nationalists in Spain.*

▶ *Hugo Sperrle (right), appointed by Göring to be commander of the Condor Legion in 1936.*

place. They have been described as a "uniquely holy event on which the venerated cadre of the survivors of the Munich *Putsch* silently re-enacted their march through the crowd-lined streets of the Bavarian capital in a bombastic travesty of the Passion Play". The finale is the torch-lit oath-taking ceremony for candidates of the *SS-Verfügungstruppe*, which takes place in Hitler's presence before the Feldherrnhalle and the 16 smoking obelisks, each of which bear the name of the first

► *The battlecruiser* Gneisenau *was launched in December 1936. She was sister to the Scharnhorst.*

fallen party faithful. The oath is a major ingredient in the SS mystique, binding each successful candidate in unswerving loyalty to Adolf Hitler. During the ceremony a voice intones the 16 names, and after each one a thousand voices chant "Hier".

NOVEMBER 25

GERMANY, *TREATIES*

The Anti-Comintern Pact is signed with Japan. The agreement was concluded first between Germany and Japan and then between Italy, Germany, and Japan (November 6, 1937). Ostensibly it was directed against the Communist International (Comintern), but

► *The annual ceremony held at the Feldherrnhalle in Munich to commemorate the fallen of the 1923* Putsch.

by implication, specifically against the Bolshevik Soviet Union.

The treaties were sought by Adolf Hitler, who at the time was publicly inveighing against Bolshevism and who was interested in Japan's successes in the opening war against China. The Japanese were angered by a Soviet-Chinese non-aggression treaty of August 1936 and by the subsequent sale of Soviet military aircraft and munitions to China. For propaganda purposes, Hitler and Benito Mussolini were able to present

themselves as defenders of Western values against the threat of Soviet communism.

DECEMBER 8

ARMED FORCES, *NAVY*

The battlecruiser *Gneisenau* is launched. She is a small battleship, with smaller guns and armour on the battleship scale. Designed to allow replacement of triple 11in guns with dual 15in, she and her sister *Scharnhorst* is a reply to the French "Dunkerque" class.

1937

Germany and Italy had not always been close allies; indeed, during the early 1930s Mussolini had moved troops up to the Austrian border to deter Hitler from influencing events in Austria. However, Hitler had supported Mussolini's war in Ethiopia and both dictators found themselves supporting the anti-communist cause in Spain. It was, therefore, perhaps logistical that they should ultimately become allies. That process was cemented by the *Duce*'s historic trip to Germany in 1937, when the Nazis pulled out all the stops to win over Italy's leader.

FEBRUARY 6

ARMED FORCES, *NAVY*

The heavy cruiser *Admiral Hipper* is launched. This ship is part of Germany's Plan-Z, a plan to build a navy that will be able to meet the British Royal Navy on their own terms.

Admiral Raeder was told by Hitler to develop a plan for a major fleet rebuilding that would be able to defeat the British merchant navy shipping in the Atlantic and be able to suppress the naval forces that would be there to protect them. Raeder planned on doing this by having a well-balanced fleet and dividing his ships in battle groups to strike when and where he needed to. This reflected Raeder's experience with the Kaiser's Navy, where German raiders were able to disrupt the seas in favour of Germany. It was a long-

▼ *Hjalmar Schacht (left), the Minister of Economics and Plenipotentiary General for the War Economy, resigned in 1937.*

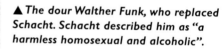

▲ The dour Walther Funk, who replaced Schacht. Schacht described him as "a harmless homosexual and alcoholic".

decree further empowers the Minister of the Interior, Dr Frick, to take the necessary measures to prevent the departure or transit through Germany of volunteers, German or foreign. It should be noted that this decree has been promulgated over three months after the formation of the Legion Condor. Few are deceived by this decree.

▲ The heavy cruiser Admiral Hipper, part of Germany's Plan-Z to build a fleet to match those of Great Britain and France.

▶ Minister of the Interior Wilhelm Frick, who carried out a cosmetic exercise to prevent aid to Franco.

term plan that was to be complete by 1948. The following ships were planned:

6 battleships of 50,800 tonnes (50,000 tons), plus the *Bismarck* and the *Tirpitz*.
8 Heavy Cruisers of 20,329 tonnes (20,000 tons), later increased to 12.
4 aircraft carriers of 20,329 tonnes (20,000 tons).
A large number of light cruisers.
233 U-boats.

FEBRUARY 20

SPAIN, *GERMAN AID*

Despite the setting up of a European non-intervention committee, of which Germany is a member, intended to prevent the possibility of international participation in the Spanish Civil War, Germany very swiftly, and secretly, sets about organizing a powerful, semi-autonomous air component for collaboration with General Franco. An example of the lengths to which the German Government is prepared to go in order to deny to the world the existence of the Condor Legion and its commitment of arms and men to Franco can be seen from the decree published in Germany on February 20, 1937. This forbids German nationals to enter Spain or Spanish possessions, including Spanish Morocco, in order to take part in the Civil War. The

KEY MOMENTS

Deutschland Incident

The importance of the attack on the *Deutschland*, both militarily and politicaly, to the Nazi government cannot be under-estimated. It was therefore of the highest importance to Hitler to see that this outrage was fully recognized. The *Deutschland* was in the Ibiza harbour and this was a declared war zone. On the evening of May 29, she was lying in a roadstead of Ibiza along with the tanker *Neptune* and the torpedo boat *Leopard*. Although assigned to international sea control and off duty, the *Deutschland* was attacked by two unidentified aircraft, which dropped two bombs. The attack was carried out by two Soviet pilots flying SB-2 Katiuskas who thought they were bombing Franco's flagship, the *Canarias*.

For political reasons, the Republican government in Spain attributed the attack to two Spanish pilots, José Arcega and Leocadio Mendiola. The first bomb fell on the crewmen's mess, resulting in 22 killed and 83 wounded. The second fell on the side deck which caused little damage. The *Deutschland* then sailed to Gibraltar where it disembarked the dead and wounded. The wounded were attended to by the British at the British Military Hospital. Nine more soldiers died, bringing the death toll to 31 with 74 wounded. This led to a number of awards to British medical personnel of the German Red Cross Decoration 1937–1939 in varying grades. A temporary funeral was conducted in Gibraltar, where the cortege with the coffins draped in the German battle flag was escorted by Royal Marines. The coffins were disinterred and returned on board the *Deutschland*, which then sailed to the port of Kiel.

MARCH

GERMANY, *RELIGION*

Pope Pius XI issues *Mit brennende Sorge* (*With Burning Anxiety*), a paper listing violations of the Concordat and Nazi persecution of the Catholic church.

APRIL

GERMANY, *LOCAL GOVERNMENT*

Carl Gördeler resigns as Mayor of Leipzig. Formally a Nazi supporter, he has become disillusioned by rearmament and growing anti-Semitism.

APRIL 20

NAZI PARTY, *PERSONALITIES*

On the occasion of his 48th birthday, Hitler receives the good wishes and an expensive hand-crafted SS sword bearing the inscription:"In good times and bad, we will always be the same", from the leadership corps of the SS.

APRIL 26

SPAIN, *GERMAN AID*

The bombers of the German *Luftwaffe* are sent to help Franco destroy Guernica, the cultural and spiritual home of the Basques. It is market day and the square is crowded

when the bombers, Heinkel He 111s and Junker Ju 52s, escorted by fighters, appear and pound Guernica with high explosives. They then set the town alight with incendiary bombs and strafe it with machine-gun fire. Eyewitnesses later tell of the death that rained down on them. The bombing has shocked the world.

There were military targets in Guernica: it was a communications centre and it had a

▼ The Deutschland, *seen here behind the* Admiral Scheer, *was badly damaged in a Republic air attack in Ibiza in May.*

▲ *Nazi Party Day in 1937. The figure on the extreme right is Martin Bormann, who at the time was a* **Gauleiter.**

▶ *Another shot of the 1937 Party Day. Here, Hitler talks with Rudolf Hess, whose influence was beginning to wane.*

munitions factory. But there is no evidence that the German bombers aimed for them. They simply unloaded their bombs indiscriminately on this undefended town.

MAY 5

ARMED FORCES, *NAVY*
In the presence of Hitler, a new "Strength through Joy" ship was named *Wilhelm Gustloff* is launched by Gustloff's widow.

JUNE

NAZI PARTY, *GESTAPO*
Secret orders are issued from Heydrich ordering "protective custody", meaning concentration camp, for those jailed for "racial offences" after release from jail, i.e. Jewish liaisons with Aryans. Heydrich now heads both the SD and Gestapo under the structure of the Reich Security Administration.

By this time the Gestapo was joined with the *Kriminalpolizei* (Kripo - Criminal Police) under the umbrella of a new organization, the *Sicherheitspolizei* (Sipo - Security Police)

JUNE 8

ARMED FORCES, *NAVY*
The heavy cruiser *Blücher* is launched.

JUNE 17

ARMED FORCES, *NAVY*
A state funeral, attended by Hitler, is held at Kiel for the 31 dead of the *Deutschland*.

Their names are:
Lobitz, Martens, Schmitz, Martin, Zimmermann, Busche, Sehm, Denno, Gerhardt, Männing, Oelrich, Schübert, Inglen, Bochem, Faltin, Wille, Gallus, Brüchner, Mies, Manja, Röbers, Schöslkopf, Bismark, Eckart, Schubert, Holzwarth, Meyer, Woftweber, Fischer, Steiger and Dürr.

AUGUST

GERMANY, *ECONOMICS*

Hjalmar Schacht resigns as Minister of Economics. Though he had stated that he would support Hitler and the Third Reich as long as he had breath in his body, he has become disillusioned by the regime's anti-Semitism and also the Night of the Long Knives. He has played an important part if Germany's rearmament programme, but has found it difficult to battle inflation. After reading *Mein Kampf* he decided that Hitler was a genius who could restore Germany's greatness. Walther Funk replaces him.

SEPTEMBER 6–13

NAZI PARTY, *RALLIES*

Party Rally of Labour.

SEPTEMBER 24

GERMANY, *DIPLOMACY*

As Mussolini boards the train in Rome for his visit to Germany, he wears a splendid uniform specially designed for the occasion: a grey-blue Corporal of Honour uniform with a cornflower blue sash across his chest and a black militia cap adorned with a red cord. His staff, which consists of Ciano, Alfieri, the minister of press and propaganda, Storace, the party secretary, and about 100 officials, journalists and subordinates, are also bedecked in finery. From Rome Mussolini's train stops at Forli where he pauses for family kisses and well-wishes. His special nine-coach armoured train then progresses on its historic journey, which will be one of the pivotal moments in the history of the Third Reich and Fascist Italy.

When the train pulled into the Alps, it stopped for five hours during the night to give the *Duce* an opportunity for a rest.

SEPTEMBER 25

GERMANY, *DIPLOMACY*

The following morning the train enters Austria. There, Chancellor Dr Kurt von Schuschnigg's cabinet is deeply concerned at the possibility of the *Duce*'s assassination. This trip not only exposes him to the usual danger of anti-Fascist attacks, but also the bitter hatred of the Tyrolese as a result of Italy's annexation of South Tyrol. Some 4300 Austrian soldiers have been stationed along the 160km (100 miles) of railway line, their backs to the "Mussolini Special" with orders to shoot to kill without question anyone suspected of bombing, shooting at or stoning the train.

▼ *A beaming Mussolini arrives in Germany on September 25 to begin his historic trip to the Third Reich.*

of Staff; Dr Robert Ley, Leader of the German Labour Front; Victor Lutze, commander of the SA; General Franz Ritter von Epp, Governor of Bavaria; Adolf Wagner, Gauleiter of Munich; Ernst Wilhelm Bohle, leader of Germans living abroad; Konstantin Hierl, Labour Corps leader; and a number of less known dignitaries. They exchange the Fascist salute with their Italian guest, then Hitler and Mussolini shake hands, who subsequently introduces the members of his immediate party. The Duce and the Führer march side by side through the station on a crimson carpet and emerge to the roar of heavy German guns crashing 21 times in salute. As they come in sight of the decorated Bahnhofplatz, a wide square in front of the station, they are met by the glitter of steel and standards from the army and Nazi honour detachments. Massed bands

◀ *Hitler shows off his bodyguard to the Duce. Mussolini was visibly impressed by Germany's military strength.*

When Mussolini arrives in Innsbruck, the *Duce* openly admires the scenic beauty of the country.

At 08:52 hours Mussolini's train stops at the German boarder town of Kiefersfelden. There, Reichsminister Rudolf Hess and the Italian Ambassador Attolico meet the Duce and board his special carriage. The trip from the German border to Munich is lined with *Bund Deutscher Mädel* (BDM – League of German Girls) and *Jungvolk* (Young People – junior division of the Hitler Youth) members, who muster on the platforms of every station to wave their welcome. As the train slowly enters the outskirts of Munich, the city seems aflame with masses of red, white and black swastika flags fluttering beside the warmer Italian combination of red, white and green. At 10:00 hours the train arrives at the station, and a smile lights Mussolini's face. Everywhere he sees tall pillars surmounted

▶ *Constantin Freiherr von Neurath, senior diplomat, was one of those wheeled out to meet Mussolini.*

by Roman Eagles and a spectacular scarlet and gold Caesarean festoons set off by Nordic fir and laurel. When the train halts he is the first to step off. Adolf Hitler and his group of diplomats, which comprise Dr Josef Goebbels, Minister of Propaganda; Heinrich Himmler, head of the German Police and commander of the SS; Dr Alfred Rosenberg, in charge of party ideological schooling; Baldur von Schirach, Reich Youth leader; Colonel-General Werner von Fritsch, Chief

▲ The Brown House welcomes Mussolini. There was a restaurant in the basement of the party's Munich headquarters.

spontaneously break into "Giovinezza", the Fascist hymn, and cheering squads set up rounds of "Heil Hitler" and "Duce, Duce!"

After an inspection of the guard of honour, which was comprised of one company each from the army, navy, air force, SS, Labour Corps and the SA, the dictators entered an open Mercedes. They were slowly driven through the Munich streets where double-lined SS troops stood shoulder to shoulder. Mussolini and his retinue were taken to Prince Karl Place where they would stay while in Munich. A short time later, Hess called on the *Duce* and escorted him to the Fuhrerhaus at 6 Prinzregentstrasse. At 11:32 hours the two leaders met for an extended conversation. Count Galeazzo Ciano and Baron Constantin von Neurath, the German Foreign Minister, also participated in these talks. The discussions were general rather than particular and all that emerged was a firm agreement on a friendly attitude towards Japan and the greatest possible support to Franco in Spain. At this time the *Duce* presented Hitler with a commission as a Corporal of Honour in the Fascist

Militia, which had been created for himself alone. In turn the Führer bestowed upon the *Duce* one of Germany's highest awards, the Eagle Order, Grand Cross in Gold with Diamonds, which was not to be repeated for any future holder.

The early part of the afternoon was spent touring the carnival-decked streets and palaces and laying wreaths on various Nazi monuments in the Bavarian capital. Among these was the Feldherrnhalle in Königsplatz, which held the bodies of 16 Nazi heroes killed in the 1923 Munich *Putsch*. The two leaders later attended a lunch at the Führerhaus with members of the *Alt Kämpfer* of the Party. The Königsplatz resounded to the stomp of boots as Mussolini looked on in admiration from his saluting base. He later commented to Hitler: "It was wonderful!", as they stood side by side on the small reviewing stand in front of the Temples of Honour: "It couldn't have been better in Italy." This massive

demonstration left an indelible impression on the *Duce*.

An afternoon reception was held in their honour at the Museum of German Art. Fräulein Leni Riefenstahl, feminine arbiter of the Nazi film world, gathered more than 100 of Germany's most beautiful stage and cinema actresses for the occasion. Hitler proudly toured Mussolini through the new museum, pointing out favourite specimens and explaining at length his elaborate plans for beautifying Berlin, Munich and other cities. After the tour, the two dictators attended a tea in the museum's restaurant. It is interesting to note, however, that at the tea the female glances were towards boxer Max Schmeling who was also a guest. At this time, Mussolini spoke of an impending visit to Rome by Hitler. "It will be an occasion for wearing my new uniform," replied Hitler, commenting on his newly acquired rank of Corporal of Honour.

That evening Hitler and Mussolini boarded separate trains, lest perchance one wreck killed them both, which sped across Germany to the Baltic province of Mecklenburg-Schwerin.

SEPTEMBER 26

GERMANY, *DIPLOMACY*

Hitler and Mussolini arrive in the morning at the little village of Lalendorf, near the centre of the manoeuvre area, to witness the final stages of post-World War I Germany's greatest military manoeuvres. Hitler and Mussolini's entourage are met at the station by high officials of the German defence forces, which are led by War Minister Werner von Blomberg, Air Minister Hermann Göring, the Army Chief of Staff, Colonel General Werner von Fritsch, and Naval Chief of Staff Admiral Erich Raeder. In an open touring car, Hitler and Mussolini dash from area to area observing the latest in artillery, infantry and armoured

▶ *As the two dictators were driven through the streets of Munich, 36,000 guards lined their route.*

▼ *Then came a display of Nazi standard bearers, rank upon rank of Brownshirts marching in perfect unison.*

techniques. Throughout the lightning tour, they are cheered by German soldiers who are of the class of 1935. These troops are the first to have been called up when Hitler restored universal conscription to the German way of life.

At the conclusion of the manoeuvres, Hitler and Mussolini boarded a special train to Kröpelin, in the northwestern corner of Mecklenburg-Schwerin. There they inspected the new flying field at Wustrow, examined several new types of military aircraft and later observed air exercises. The famous slow-flying "Storch" was demonstrated by Major-General Udet, with Air General Milch as passenger. Flying the versatile aircraft at minimal speeds of 19–24km/h (12–15 mph), once again the *Duce* was visibly impressed. Up until now Mussolini had seen German art, laid wreaths on monuments, inspected honour guards and observed war games. He now wanted to inspect one of Germany's most closely guarded secrets, the mighty Krupp munitions works at Essen. The German schedule had called for a short trip to Berlin from the Baltic for a triumphant welcome, but Mussolini's insistence now called for the dictators to travel across

▲ *Then came a parade of NSKK vehicles. This was a paramilitary unit that oversaw the training of the army's motorized units.*

▶ *Among the dignitaries present was air ace Ernst Udet, who at this time was Technical Officer of the Air Ministry.*

Germany to Essen and then cross it once more, back to Berlin. Immediately German Minister of Propaganda and Public Enlightenment Dr Josef Goebbels broadcast to the astonished citizens of Essen that they were to deck their city with green branches and flags in honour of the Italian leader, who would arrive the next day. To ensure that all arrangements would be in readiness, he and several assistants rushed by special train to Essen.

SEPTEMBER 27

GERMANY, *DIPLOMACY*
After travelling across Germany in separate trains, the Hitler and Mussolini specials rumble into Essen at 08:07 hours. Essen and Krupp have done themselves proud; all is in readiness. Due to security precautions, correspondents are not allowed to join in the tour while the *Duce* and Hitler inspect

the hush-hush realm of munitioneer Dr Gustav Krupp von Bohlen und Halbach. At the company's offices, the dictators are received by the director of Krupp, who presents the members of his family. He then explains the growth and organization of his gigantic concern. The party was then escorted to the main plant by car. There they see the production of artillery, tanks and every conceivable weapon of war. Mussolini is highly impressed by the discipline of the workers, scale of operation and tremendous output of weaponry. The Krupp inspection ends at 10:45 hours. Once again the leaders travel in separate trains from Essen.

Elaborate measures were taken with true German thoroughness to ensure that for the last 24km (15 miles) of the journey to Berlin, the two trains would run side by side, signifying the equality of the two revolutions. Before arriving at the station, Hitler sped ahead, enabling him to be on the platform to properly greet his guest. The arrival in the German capital was, as Count Ciano stated in his diary, "Triumphal".

The first three days of the state visit had been for indoctrination, but the culmination was the welcoming in Berlin. Never before in German history had Berlin witnessed such a display. This spectacle dwarfed the Munich pageantry to the dimensions of a country fair. With the aid of professional stage designer Benno von Arendt, Berlin's central sections were transformed into a prop fairyland. The city was decorated with thousands of German and Italian flags from the station at the Heerstrasse to the Presidential Palace in the centre of the city. A 38.4m (126ft) flag tower erected in Adolf Hitler Platz, midway between the railway station and the Brandenburg Gate, was bedecked with German and Italian flags 36.5m (120ft) long. The Pariserplatz before the Brandenburg Gate had two coloured water fountains and four massive towers covered alternately with Italian and German flags. Dusk fell as the leaders drove through the floodlit Brandenburg Gate onto the famous Unter den Linden. There, four rows of white, illuminated pylons, 10m (33ft) high bearing golden eagles and Nazi and Fascist emblems, glowed in the night. Banners in the German and Italian colours hung from rooftops to the pavements and in the Wilhelmstrasse. It is estimated that approximately 50,00 square metres (55,000 square yards) of bunting had been woven for the decoration of these two streets. As the crowds roared a welcome to the Italian dictator, Mussolini stood up to let himself

be seen, obviously delighted with his reception. The Führer remained seated at his left, allowing his guest to enjoy the full glory of the moment. Work had ceased in Berlin at 16:00 hours on the day of the arrival, enabling the total population to be present. Hitler took personal precautions in the security measures to protect the *Duce*. Approximately 60,000 troops lined the route of travel. In some places they stood

▲ *Colonel-General Erhard Milch (right), Luftwaffe commander, laid on a flying display for the Italian dictator.*

three and four deep. The city's police was reinforced by detachments from Saxony. Plainclothes men mixed in the crowd while armed launches patrolled the River Spree. That evening a state banquet was held in Mussolini's honour. Members of the government and all leading members of the party were present at the Berlin reception. Hitler, a strict vegetarian and teetotaller, nibbled throughout the banquet and toasted his guests with sweet German champagne.

SEPTEMBER 28

GERMANY, *DIPLOMACY*

This day has been given as a national holiday. Mussolini visits the Arsenal Museum on Unter den Linden where he views mementos from previous wars.

He stood reverently for a few minutes before President von Hindenburg's death mask. He and his party then motored to Potsdam near Berlin and inspected Sanssouci, Frederick the Great's palace. After walking to the famous Garrison Church, Mussolini placed a wreath on the tomb of Frederick the Great. The *Duce* then returned to Berlin and called on the Italian Embassy and the headquarters of *Fascio*. There he was saluted by 25,000 Italian Fascists now resident in Germany and 3500 members of the Fascist youth organization. At noon he drove with Ciano and Bernardo Attolico, his new ambassador to Berlin, to Schorfheide 64km (40 miles) from Berlin. He then attended a luncheon given by Göring and his wife at their beautiful hunting lodge Waldhof Karinhall. It was at this time that he was presented with the Luftwaffe's highest award, the Pilot-Observer Badge in gold with diamonds. Later he took afternoon tea with Dr Goebbels and then retired to the Presidential Palace where he dined privately that evening.

Simultaneously that day a mammoth demonstration was being organized on the Maifeld, the polo ground adjoining the Olympic Stadium. Since early that morning a crowd of approximately 650,000 had gone to the city's outskirts and gathered before the official tribune. At 18:00 hours the Olympic Bell began to ring, signifying that Hitler and Mussolini were en route. Their arrival was announced by trumpets, while the large personal standards of the *Duce* and the Führer were hoisted on either side of the tribune. Despite threatening rain clouds, the crowd was good natured. Dr Goebbels mounted the speakers tribune and stated: "Three million people have taken part in this historic demonstration of the National Socialist movement, either along the route, on the Maifeld or in the stadium." All of Germany's radio stations were connected to the

▲ *Once proceedings had finished in Munich the tour moved on to Berlin. Here, a torchlit display entertains Mussolini.*

▼ *Mussolini was treated to seeing Hitler's Berlin at its zenith. This is the Bismarckdenkmal und Siegessaule.*

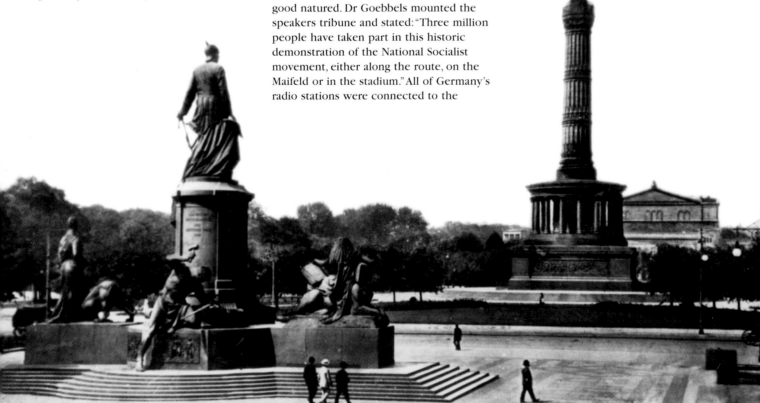

Maifeld speaker system. Twenty countries in Europe and North and South America were also united in the gigantic hook-up, which the Propaganda Ministry had arranged for this occasion. Great Britain did not accept the broadcast, however, and Russia was not invited to do so. As Dr Goebbels, the man who had supervised this engineering wonder, told the two dictators in presenting them to the audience: "The whole world is listening to you."

Hitler was the first to speak to the German nation by wireless. He introduced the *Duce*: "What moves us most at the moment is the deep-rooted joy to see in our midst a guest who is one of the lonely men in history. These two men are not put

stress on the 115 million Germans and Italians and the need for them to unite "in one single, unshakable determination".

After the speeches, Hitler and Mussolini walked across the field to the Olympic Stadium. There, in the huge green and brown Olympic arena, marched the massed bands of three army corps. There were 4000 musicians in all, 33 brass bands, 25 fife and drum corps and 10 trumpet bands. They goose-stepped in perfect precision to the tune of "Preussens Gloria", a favourite military march, and wheeled into three

◄ *Panzer II tanks in a side street in Berlin wait to move out to parade past Hitler and Mussolini.*

▲ *The memorial to the unknown soldier in Berlin, where Mussolini laid a wreath to commemorate the dead of World War I.*

to trial by historic events but determine the history of their country themselves." Mussolini then stood up and climbed the podium to speak. Before him thousands of Germans arms rose in the Roman salute. Mussolini delivered his carefully prepared speech in fluent German, but with an Italian accent. In the midst of the *Duce*'s speech a darkening sky suddenly opened and a torrential rain fell on the Maifeld. Unfortunately, he became overcome by the excitement generated by the dynamic spectacle before him and spoke faster and faster. This, plus the sounds of the downpour, caused his words to be almost inaudible. His script was soon a sodden

mass but he continued as the patient crowd became soaked to the skin. In the course of his speech the *Duce* pronounced: "Fascism has its ethical principles, to which it intends to be faithful, and they are also my morals; to speak clearly and openly, and, if we are friends, to march together to the end." He also spoke of the awakening of Germany through the Nazi revolution, Bolshevism, the common enemy, and Germany's friendly stand during the Ethiopian War. The speech ended with a

columns in the centre of the arena. The trumpet bands came from the cavalry and artillery and the rest of the units from the army, navy and air force. As the floodlights shone on them, the massed musicians sent forth strains of the great marches from Verdi's "Aida", for the Italians' benefit, Wagner's "Rienzi" for the Germans. Then the "Bavarian March Past" was struck up and from under an arch at the side of the Stadium, a battalion of torchbearing *Schultzstaffeln* appeared. They flowed into the arena like a living flame, wheeling halfway around, dividing and moving to each side in columns of four. These again divided and became streamlets of twos, which in turn divided, countermarched and passed each other in single file just as a second torchbearing battalion came from under the arch. The first battalion marched in single file around the arena and took rigid stations at its edges, approximately 3m (9ft) apart. The second battalion divided, subdivided and moved through the massed musicians forming with them a huge "M" with its base towards the dais on which Hitler and Mussolini stood. After this complicated manoeuvre, the musicians began a march to Beethoven. Simultaneously, three "honour companies" from the army, navy and air force entered. They goosestepped halfway around the arena, then wheeled to the front and came to attention. Their mounted commander came forward, faced the dais, and reported to Hitler: "1600 of your defence forces, Mein Führer."

Outside the stadium, 50 concealed searchlights threw up long beams of light, forming "the tent of light" which was now a feature at German pageants. The troops came to present arms and the massed bands very softly played the German Army

hymn, followed by the Italian national anthem, "Giovinezza," "Deutschland uber Alles" and the "Horst Wessel Lied".

As the spectacle came to an end, the rain began to fall once more. Standing equally unprotected, side-by-side, Mussolini made a remark to Hitler. Hitler made a gesture to a nearby SS officer, who threw rain capes around the shoulders of both leaders. The end of this massive pageant came when the huge swastika and Fascist standards, above the host and guest, were lowered as they departed from the stadium.

SEPTEMBER 29

GERMANY, *DIPLOMACY*

The mornings activities are confined to placing a magnificent wreath at the German War Memorial on Unter den Linden by Mussolini, Count Ciano and Marshal Badoglio. After reviewing the guard of honour at the War Memorial, Mussolini marches past about 100 war invalids in self-propelled wheelchairs and salutes them. He then joins Hitler in a salute to 14,000 men of the army, navy and air force on Charlottenburger Chaussee. The parade, which is led by General Witzleben, commander of the Third Army Group, takes one hour and 20 minutes. Some 591 officers, 13,000 rank and file, 2000 horses, 600 motorized vehicles and 144 motorcycle

▼ *Nazi supporters the Duke and Duchess of Windsor arrive in Berlin to ingratiate themselves with Germany's leaders.*

▲ *One of Berlin's most famous landmarks, the Brandenburg Gate, which was riddled with shells by the Red Army in 1945.*

units, all drawn from Berlin and neighbouring garrisons, pass by.

The army contingent was comprised of five infantry regiments, four artillery, one cavalry, besides pioneer, armoured, signal and machine-gun battalions. The air force contributed three motorized antiaircraft regiments, while the navy contributed two

companies of cadets. During the parade an incident occurred that Mussolini later recalled: "During the military review the mace bearer was too quick and struck a soldier behind him on the head, and an artillery horse kicked over the traces and bolted right in front of the box. Hitler laughed and so did I. Then he turned to me and remarked confidentially, 'I don't like to think what'll happen to the wretched private. Our perfect German organization will set in motion. The general will go for the colonel; the colonel will go for the major; the major will go for the captain; the captain will go for the lieutenant; the lieutenant will go for the sergeant-major; the sergeant-major for the sergeant; the sergeant for the corporal; and finally poor private!'" After the impressive review, Mussolini was taken to the Reich Chancellery for a farewell luncheon. He was then escorted to the Lehrter Station in Berlin. There, he and Hitler shook hands heartily and continued an animated conversation from his window after the *Duce* had boarded the train. Personal gifts accompanied him: three crates of geese presented by the curator of the Berlin Zoological Gardens. Hess, Hitler's deputy, travelled with the Italian party as far as the German frontier. The Rome-Berlin axis had been pronounced for all the world to see.

OCTOBER 22

GERMANY, *DIPLOMACY*
Nazi leaders, including Hitler's adjutant, *SA-Obergruppenführer* Wilhelm Brückner, are among the party who wait on the platform

▼ *Leading from the Brandenburg Gate, stone pillars surmounted by swastikas reminded visitors who ruled Germany.*

to meet the Duke and Duchess of Windsor as they arrive in Berlin. Flowers and cries of "Heil Edward" greet the couple from the large crowds that throng the station to watch. Dr Robert Ley, leader of Hitler's Labour Front, hands the Duchess a bouquet of pink and yellow roses. The Duke and Duchess of Windsor later meet the Führer. They are ostensibly in Berlin to "study social conditions and housing problems". They visit the first "National Socialist model factory", where they lunch with the workers before attending a concert given by the Nazi district orchestra.

NOVEMBER 1

GERMANY, *LEGAL*
The Enabling Law is renewed, ensuring Germany remains a National Socialist dictatorship. Confiscation of Jewish businesses without legal justification continues.

NOVEMBER 1

ARMED FORCES, *AIR FORCE*
Generalleutnant Hellmuth Volkmann is appointed commander of the Condor Legion. He will hold the command from November 1, 1937 until November 1, 1938. Volkmann won promotion to *General der Fliege* and on his return to Germany was appointed Commandant of the *Luftkriegsakademie* in Berlin.

1938

Though the early years of World War II saw a string of German military triumphs, 1938 was probably the most successful year for Adolf Hitler. The removal of Blomberg and Fritsch ensured the total loyalty of the army, which *de facto* became an unthinking tool of Hitler's will. On the international front the union of Austria and the Sudetenland with the Third Reich was a stunning coup, and one achieved without firing a shot. At home Hitler was viewed as a genius, a leader who could do no wrong and who had kept his promise to bring ethnic Germans back into the Reich.

JANUARY

ARMED FORCES, *POLITICS*

Minister of War Blomberg is dismissed after a scandal, and Fritsch, commander-in-chief of the army, is forced to resign on false charges of homosexuality.

The slight irritation which Hitler felt towards Blomberg and Fritsch (the former had opposed the march into the Rhineland and the latter was hostile to the Nazis, especially the SS), was increased by the events which followed his decision to reoccupy the Rhineland. The generals were only too aware that the operation carried a grave military risk as insignificant forces could only carry it out – Germany's rearmament had not by then advanced far. Hitler was contemptuous of their fears and later compared them with his own aplomb in bluffing his way through the crisis. This was the beginning of the constantly reiterated claim that the Führer was always right and his timid generals often wrong. In November 1937, Hitler warned the army to prepare for action against Austria and Czechoslovakia and stated that he was prepared to risk war with the Western powers. Blomberg and Fritsch were anxious about this

▶ Field Marshal Werner von Blomberg. He opposed Hitler's plans to march into the Rhineland and the Sudetenland, and was therefore removed.

▲ General Freiherr Werner von Fritsch, army commander-in-chief, disliked Nazism. He was removed following a sex scandal.

▲ Nazi troops march in Vienna following the Anschluss with Germany. Chancellor Schuschnigg was sent to Dachau.

▲ Wilhelm Keitel, Hitler's new chief of staff. His total subservience to Hitler earned him the nickname "lackey".

▶ Ribbentrop, the new ambassador to Great Britain, had a wretched time in his new post. He was disliked by the British.

and Fritsch even had the temerity to warn the Führer against such a suicidal course. While these two senior soldiers were low in Hitler's esteem as a result of such faint-heartedness, they were framed and disgraced in a conspiracy which was probably organized by Göring and Himmler. Blomberg was a widower who was considering marriage to his secretary. This would have been a slight misalliance by the strict standards of the officer corps, but Göring encouraged the wretched "rubber lion" and even shipped off a rival for the young lady's affections to South America. The 60-year-old field marshal married his secretary Fraulein Gruhn on January 12,

1938. On January 25, 1938, Göring brought the Führer startling evidence that Blomberg's new wife was a prostitute with an extensive history with the German police. There were even salacious photographs of the new Frau Blomberg in pornographic poses. Blomberg was forced to resign, but before he left for an extended honeymoon on Capri to console himself with the arts which his new wife had learned in a Berlin massage parlour, he was given a word of encouragement by Hitler. As far as is known, Hitler told Blomberg that he would be recalled to the supreme command in the event of war. This promise was never fulfilled.

At that moment Himmler's Gestapo was also moving against Fritsch. It produced a dossier which allegedly proved that Fritsch was a homosexual susceptible to blackmail. When Fritsch protested his innocence, the Gestapo produced a degenerate called Hans Schmidt who claimed to have seen the army chief committing an unnatural act with a certain "Bavarian Joe" in a dark corner near Potsdam railway station.

▼ *General Walter von Brauchitsch (right) became the new army commander-in-chief following the removal of Fritsch.*

Although Fritsch was later found innocent of this ludicrously clumsy frame-up, he was relieved of his command "for health reasons" on February 4, 1938.

FEBRUARY

ARMED FORCES, *HIGH COMMAND*

Hitler becomes Minister of War and Commander-in-Chief of the armed forces with Keitel his chief of staff and Brauchitsch succeeding Fritsch. Ribbentrop is appointed Foreign Minister. Austrian Chancellor Schuschnigg is called to Berchtesgaden and given an ultimatum to allow the Nazis in Austria a free hand.

MARCH 12

AUSTRIA, *POLITICS*

The *Anschluss* (Union) with Austria. Seyss-Inquart becomes

Reich Governor of *Ostmark*. All laws of Germany, including racial laws, are now in operation in Austria.

In July 1934, Austrian and German Nazis together attempted a coup but were unsuccessful. An authoritarian right-wing government then took power in Austria and kept perhaps half the population from voicing legitimate dissent; that cleavage prevented concerted resistance to the developments of 1938. In February 1938 Hitler invited the Austrian Chancellor Kurt von Schuschnigg to Germany and forced him to agree to give the Austrian Nazis virtually a free hand. Schuschnigg later repudiated the agreement and announced a plebiscite on the *Anschluss* question. He was bullied into cancelling the plebiscite, and he obediently resigned, ordering the Austrian Army not to resist the Germans. President Wilhelm Miklas of Austria refused to appoint the Austrian Nazi leader Arthur

▲ *The cuff band of the SS-Polizei Division, one of the Waffen-SS units created from the SS-Verfügungstruppe.*

▶ *The Dresden Hotel at Bad Godesberg, where Hitler and Chamberlain met to discuss the Czech problem in September.*

Seyss-Inquart as chancellor. The German Nazi minister Hermann Göring ordered Seyss-Inquart to send a telegram requesting German military aid, but he refused, and the telegram was sent by a German agent in Vienna. On March 12 Germany invaded, and the enthusiasm that followed persuaded Hitler to annex Austria outright on March 13. A controlled plebiscite of April 10 gave a 99.7 percent approval.

APRIL

GERMANY, *LEGAL*
All Jewish wealth is to be registered.

MAY 21

ARMED FORCES, *NAVY*
The battlecruiser *Gneisenau* is commissioned.

JUNE

GERMANY, *ANTI-SEMITISM*
Destruction of Munich synagogue by Nazi thugs. A new decree demands registration of all Jewish businesses.

JULY

GERMANY, *RESISTANCE*
Carl Gördeler, ex-Mayor of Leipzig, goes to London but fails to convince the British of the strength of anti-Hitler resistance. Chamberlain visits Hitler at Berchtesgaden to consult with him on Czechoslovakia.

JULY 11

SPORTS, *GREAT BRITAIN*
The International Motorcycle Six Day Trials is held at Donnington Park in England. It is

▲ *A destroyed synagogue following Crystal Night, the anti-Jewish pogrom organized by Reinhard Heydrich.*

forces already in existence. Therefore, it is able to be legitimately trained by the *Reichsführer-SS* in Nazi theories of race and also to be manned by volunteers who have completed their commitment in the *Reichsarbeitsdienst*, the Reich Labour Service. The Führer decree also states that in time of war, elements of the *Totenkopfverbände* will reinforce the *SS-Verfügungstruppe*. If mobilized, it will be used firstly by the commander-in-chief of the army under the jurisdiction of the army, making it subject only to military law and order, but still remaining a branch of the NSDAP and owing its allegiance ultimately to that organization. Secondly, in the event of an emergency within Germany, the *SS-Verfügungstruppe* will be under Hitler's control through Himmler.

The army had always been suspicious of the SS. As the supposed sole arms bearers of the state, it regarded the creation of armed units within the SS as a betrayal by Hitler. It

▼ *German troops receive a rapturous welcome as they march into the Sudetenland in September.*

won by the SS motorcycle team made up of Mundhenke, Patina, Knees and Zimmermann.

When the SS-emblazoned green leather-clad team marched up to receive the Adolf Hühnlein Trophy and gave the Hitler salute, a loud raspberry was blown by the director of the British team.

AUGUST

GERMANY, *RESISTANCE*
General Ludwig Beck, Chief of the General Staff, having sent Ewald von Kleist-Schmenzin to London to try and warn the British of Hitler's plans, submits a paper on the danger of going to war to Brauchitsch, who informs Hitler. Beck is forced to resign.

GERMANY, *ANTI-SEMITISM*
The destruction of the Nuremberg synagogue. A decree is issued requiring all Jews to carry the first name of either "Israel" or "Sarah" from 1939.

AUGUST 17

NAZI PARTY, *WAFFEN-SS*
Hitler defines the *raison d'être* of the *SS-Verfügungstruppe* as being an armed force at his personal disposal, stating that it is not a part of the armed forces nor of the police

had been hypothesized that Hitler was playing a double game and allowing the expansion of the *SS-Verfügungstruppe* as a counter to any possible coup by the army.

In the early stages of his regime this was extremely unlikely, and Hitler bent over backwards in his efforts to appease the army. From these provisions emerged the first four of what were to become known in 1940 as the *Waffen-SS* divisions: the *Leibstandarte Adolf Hitler*, *Das Reich*, *Totenkopf* and *Polizei*, plus the nucleus of a fifth, *Wiking*.

AUGUST 22

ARMED FORCES, *NAVY*

The heavy cruiser *Prinz Eugen* is launched.

SEPTEMBER

GERMANY, *DIPLOMACY*

British prime minister Chamberlain meets first with Hitler at Godesberg, then with Daladier and Mussolini at Munich, where they agree that the Sudetenland should go to Germany (see box right). This signals the collapse of the army generals' plot against Hitler's regime.

KEY MOMENTS

The Munich Agreement

After his success in absorbing Austria into Germany proper in March 1938, Adolf Hitler looked covetously at Czechoslovakia, where about three million people in the Sudeten area were of German origin. It became known in May 1938 that Hitler and his generals were drawing up a plan for the occupation of Czechoslovakia.

The Czechs were relying on military assistance from France, with which they had an alliance. As Hitler continued to make inflammatory speeches demanding that Germans in Czechoslovakia be reunited with their homeland, war seemed imminent. Neither France nor Britain felt prepared to defend Czechoslovakia, however. In mid-September, Hitler agreed to take no military action without further discussion, and Chamberlain agreed to try to persuade his Cabinet and the French to accept the results of a plebiscite in the Sudetenland. The French premier, Édouard Daladier, and his foreign minister, Georges Bonnet, then went to London, where a joint proposal was prepared stipulating that all areas with a population that was more than 50 percent Sudeten German be returned to Germany. The Czechs were not consulted. The Czech government initially rejected the proposal but reluctantly accepted it on September 21.

On September 22 Chamberlain again flew to Germany and met Hitler, where he learned he now wanted the Sudetenland occupied by the German Army and the Czechoslovaks evacuated from the area by September 28. The Czechs rejected this, as did the British Cabinet and the French. On the 24th the French ordered a partial mobilization: the Czechoslovaks had ordered a general mobilization one day earlier.

In a last-minute effort to avoid war, Chamberlain then proposed that a four-power conference be convened immediately to settle the dispute. Hitler agreed, and on September 29, Hitler, Chamberlain, Daladier, and Mussolini met in Munich, where Mussolini introduced a written plan that was accepted by all as the Munich Agreement: the German Army was to complete the occupation of the Sudetenland by October 10, and an international commission would decide the future of other disputed areas. Czechoslovakia was informed by Britain and France that it could either resist Germany alone or submit to the prescribed annexations. The Czechs capitulated.

Before leaving Munich, Chamberlain and Hitler signed a paper declaring their mutual desire to resolve differences through consultation to assure peace. Chamberlain returned home a hero.

SEPTEMBER 5-12

NAZI PARTY, *RALLIES*

Party Rally of Greater Germany.

SEPTEMBER 27

SS, *WAFFEN-SS*

SS *Totenkopf* units are moved into the Sudetenland to reinforce the frontier guards and provide the cadre for the Sudeten Free Corps, whose overt mission was the protection of the German minority and covert mission the maintenance of disturbances and clashes with the Czechs.

OCTOBER

GERMANY, *ANTI-SEMITISM*

Passports for Jews are to be stamped "J" henceforth. The expulsion of 17,000 former Polish Jews from Germany takes place.

OCTOBER 1

CZECHOSLOVAKIA, *SUDETENLAND*

Germany occupies the Sudetenland in accordance with the terms of the Munich Agreement reached in September (see box on page 99).

▲ The heavy cruiser Prinz Eugen, which was launched in August as part of the Kriegsmarine's rearmament policy.

▼ The army parades its standards in salute of Hitler in 1938. The army was delighted that he had restored its pride.

NOVEMBER 9

GERMANY, *ANTI-SEMITISM*

Ernst von Rath was a young diplomat holding a secretarial position in the German Embassy in Paris. A Jew named Herschel Grynszpan had the idea of assassinating the German Ambassador, Count Johannes von Welczek. Grynszpan went to the embassy and asked the receptionist for an interview with the ambassador. The receptionist inquired as to the nature of his business, to which he gave no reply and began to act suspiciously. The

NOVEMBER 1

SPAIN, *GERMAN AID*

The last commander of the Legion, *Generalmajor* Wolfram Freiherr von Richthofen, has served as Chief of Staff to both Sperrle and Volkmann. He now takes over the command of the unit and retains it throughout the remaining months of the Spanish Civil War. Though many of the aircraft are in a poor state of repair, many pilots have gained valuable combat experience. Richthofen would lead the Condor Legion back on its triumphant return to Germany in 1939.

▲ *The cutting edge of Hitler's army: panzers. German propaganda always exaggerated their number.*

▼ *The map of Europe in 1938. Within months, Austria and the whole of Czechoslovakia would be German.*

▲ *Tanks and armoured cars (shown here) spearheaded the takeover of Austria and the Sudetenland to show German strength.*

receptionist rang for assistance from the inner office. Ernst von Rath answered the call and proceeded to the entrance hall to assist the receptionist. Grynszpan, thinking Ernst von Rath was the ambassador, pulled out a revolver and shot at him six times. Only three of the rounds found their mark, one hitting him in the foot, another in the shoulder and the third in the stomach. He was rushed to hospital, but died later.

In response, Heydrich organizes "Crystal Night", a pogrom against the Jews. More than 20,000 Jews are imprisoned, 74 killed, decrees eliminate Jews from the economy and demand a collective fine of 12,500 million Marks to pay for the destruction caused by the Nazi mob. The expulsion of all Jews from schools follows. Roosevelt, US president, recalls his ambassador.

DECEMBER

GERMANY, *LEGAL*

Compulsory Aryanization of all Jewish shops and firms.

FINLAND

NORWAY

SWEDEN · ESTONIA

USSR

LATVIA

DENMARK · LITHUANIA

EAST PRUSSIA

UK · NETHERLANDS

GERMANY · POLAND

BELGIUM

CZECHOSLOVAKIA

FRANCE

AUSTRIA

SWITZERLAND · HUNGARY

ROMANIA

ITALY

YUGOSLAVIA

BULGARIA

PORTUGAL

ALBANIA

SPAIN

TURKEY

GREECE

1939

Despite the appeasement of Great Britain and France, Hitler's territorial ambitions could only be satisfied by the conquest of Poland. Great Britain and France finally realized that Hitler was determined to absorb Poland just as he had the Austrians and Czechs. They therefore signed treaties with the Poles guaranteeing to declare war on Germany should Hitler invade. But the world was stunned by the Russo-German Non-Aggression Treaty, which sealed the fate of Poland. On September 1 German forces attacked Poland. World War II had begun.

JANUARY 12

NAZI PARTY, *PERSONALITIES*
The SS leadership pay their respects to Göring on his 46h birthday. Present are Heissmeyer, Daluege, Himmler, Heydrich, Nebe, Wolff, Besr, Darré, Backe and Greifelt.

GERMANY, *MEDIA*
Members of the SS show-jumping team are interviewed on German television. The team comprises Hermann Fegelein (who would later marry Eva Braun's sister) and his brothers Waldemar and Temme.

FEBRUARY 14

ARMED FORCES, *NAVY*
The battleship *Bismarck* is launched. The ship was ordered to be built by the shipbuilding firm Blohm & Voss. The keel was laid down on July 1, 1936 at the Blohm & Voss shipyard facilities in Hamburg. By September 1938, the hull was already complete to the level of the upper deck. The launching ceremony is attended by thousands of people, military personalities, government officials, and yard workers. Adolf Hitler delivers the pre-launch speech and the hull is then christened by Frau Dorothea von Loewenfeld, granddaughter of the German chancellor Otto von Bismarck, after whom the ship was named. Moments afterwards, at 13:30 hours, *Bismarck*'s hull slipped into the water.

▶ *The pride of the German fleet, the battleship* **Bismarck**, *glides into the water on the day of her launch.*

After launching, the ship was moored to the equipping pier where the boilers, turrets and all other parts of the superstructure began to be installed. In addition, the original straight stem was replaced with a new "Atlantic" bow that offered better sea-keeping capabilities and a different arrangement for the anchors. The war started in September 1939, but despite this and the hard winter that came after, the construction work continued as scheduled to produce a potent warship.

MARCH

GERMANY, *AGGRESSION*
Germany occupies Bohemia and Moravia as "Protectorates" – Czechoslovakia has disappeared from the map of Europe. Memel is also annexed from Lithuania. The

▲ The Germany Army rolls into Bohemia in March as Hitler declares it and Moravia German "Protectorates".

Free City of Danzig and the "Polish Corridor" is also demanded. German nationalists were outraged when Poland was given the narrow strip of land that divided Prussia from the rest of Germany. At this time, Nazis within Danzig are agitating for union with Germany.

▲ The waterfront in Danzig, The Free City that Hitler wanted back. Note the Nazi flags; there were many Nazis in the city.

◄ Another German conquest on the Baltic. These smiling troops are the new rulers of Memel.

▼ Grand-Admiral Erich Raeder, commander of the Kriegsmarine, which grew dramatically under the Nazis.

APRIL

GERMANY, *LEGAL*
Confiscation of all Jewish valuables. A law on Tenancies is passed, foreseeing all Jews living together in "Jewish houses".

APRIL 1

ARMED FORCES, *NAVY*
The battleship *Tirpitz* is launched. Erich Raeder is promoted from General-Admiral to Grand-Admiral, a rank unused since World War I.

SS, *TOTENKOPFVERBÄNDE*
The organization of the *SS-Totenkopfverbände* was fixed at: four *Standarten* of three *Sturmbanne* with three infantry companies, comprising 148 men each, one machine-gun company comprising 150 men, and medical, transport

and communications units. By the end of 1938 Eicke's men had all received some basic military training. The *SS-Totenkopfverbände* made no tactical contribution to the German campaign in Poland, but was extensively employed in the Führer's social plan for that country where the *SS-Totenkopfverbände* received its initiation in blood, being employed in terrorizing the civilian population.

APRIL 2

SPAIN, *GERMAN AID*
The end of the Spanish Civil War is officially announced in the last Nationalist military communiqué, issued in Madrid at

▲ *The Roman Triumph laid on in Berlin for the returning Condor Legion.*

▶ *Wolfram Richthofen (far right), the last commander of the Condor Legion.*

▼ *Veterans of the Condor Legion march past Hitler during the parade in Berlin.*

midnight on this day. It states:
Today the Red Army is captive and disarmed and the Nationalist troops have achieved their final military objective. The war is over.

APRIL 14

NAZI PARTY, *AWARDS*
Hitler, in response to the last Nationalist military communiqué from Spain, announces the institution of an award for the bravery of the members of the Condor Legion, which is also to serve as a campaign medal. It is worthy of note that the title bestowed on the entire series of this new award at the time of request for design approval was that of the Spanish Cross of the Legion Condor.

APRIL 27

GERMANY, *DIPLOMACY*
Hitler repudiates the Anglo-German Naval Treaty, which had been signed four years earlier.

APRIL 29

ARMED FORCES, *NAVY*
The heavy cruiser *Admiral Hipper* is commissioned.

MAY 12

SPAIN, *GERMAN AID*
Barajas Field, some 13km (eight miles) from Madrid, serves on as the venue for Generalissimo Franco to bestow 15 German and eight Italian flyers with Spain's second-highest military decoration, the Military Medal. As each man is decorated, a Spanish aviation staff officer pronounces: "In the name of Spain this is given in recognition of your technical service and bravery in the anti-Bolshevist crusade."

MAY 19

SPAIN, *GERMAN AID*

The victory parade celebrating the Nationalists triumph in the Civil War is held in Madrid. Over 42,000 troops representing all units of the Nationalist forces march past General Franco, who takes the salute. The parade is headed by 10,000 Italians under the command of General Gambara, leader of the Italian Legionnaires; the rear of the parade is brought up by 3500 men of the German Legion Condor under Richthofen. Apart from Spanish, Moorish, Italian and German infantry units, there is a prominent display of artillery, tanks and antiaircraft guns, while 880 aircraft fly past overhead.

▲ *A final roll call for German troops serving with the Nationalists in Spain, who will return to Germany in triumph.*

The parade, which lasts several hours, concludes with a short speech by a jubilant General Franco.

MAY 23

SPAIN, *GERMAN AID*

A final farewell parade is held for the Condor Legion at Leon in northwest Spain. On the aerodrome of "Our Lady of Travellers" *Generalmajor* von Richthofen presents his troops with Spanish decorations of varying grades in the name of Generalissimo Franco. Franco then addresses the men of the Condor Legion drawn up for their final inspection. In his speech to the Legion he states that it was with the feeling of great pride that he has under his orders German leaders, officers and men. He asks them to take back with them to Germany "the imperishable gratitude of Spain".

MAY 24

NAZI PARTY, *PERSONALITIES*

Hitler attends the funeral of Friedrich Graf von der Schulenburg, the former Prussian general, and one of the most eminent names to hold honourary SS rank. Honourary members of the SS were allowed to wear uniform but had no duties or powers.

MAY 25

SPAIN, *GERMAN AID*

The German troops begin to embark on six "Strength through Joy" ships that have arrived at Vigo, and shortly afterwards they set sail for Germany. Before leaving Spain, the German and the Italian Legionnaires hand over their arms and war materials to the Spanish Government.

▼ *Franco shows his gratitude: honours are showered on the Condor Legion by Spain's new ruler.*

▲ The Soviet dictator Stalin (left) and his foreign secretary Molotov, who negotiated the Non-Aggression Treaty with Germany.

MAY 30

ARMED FORCES, *RALLIES*

The Condor Legion lands at Hamburg where it receives an official welcome from *Generalfeldmarschall* Göring. Göring announces that Hitler has instituted a new decoration, The Spanish Cross, in four classes of Bronze, Silver, Gold and Gold with Brilliants. All volunteers from the Civil War are to receive one of the four classes. It is further announced that the Condor Legion is to be officially disolved within a few days, and that in proud memory of the Legion's battle against international communism, the name "Condor" has been bestowed by Hitler himself on a *Luftwaffe* aircraft wing, an antiaircraft regiment and a signals battalion.

A few days after their arrival in Hamburg, the troops of the Legion proceeded to Döberitz, the military centre near Berlin.

JUNE 4

ARMED FORCES, *RALLIES*

At Döberitz, the Legion is visited by Grand-Admiral Raeder, the commander-in-chief of the German Navy. The Grand-Admiral distributes decorations to the naval contingent and *Generalfeldmarschall* Göring presents decorations to the *Luftwaffe* members of the Legion.

JUNE 6

ARMED FORCES, *RALLIES*

The Condor Legion undertakes its last public appearance. At a special military parade held in the Reich capital, over 14,000 troops from the Legion, which includes 3000 sailors and 1000 men from the army, march past Hitler in review order. The Legion is led by *Generalmajor* von Richthofen and the three previous commanders: Volkmann, Sperrle and Warlimont. The population of Berlin give them a reception worthy of a victorious army. The Marble Gallery of the new Reich Chancellery is the venue for a special ceremony where Hitler, accompanied by Göring, presents the Spanish Cross in Gold to air force officers of the Condor Legion and naval officers from the pocket battleship *Deutschland*.

It would appear that there was no prerequisite for having a higher award, and the grade of the cross tended to be related to the rank of the person to whom it was

▲ *The British ambassador to Berlin, Sir Neville Henderson (left), who at first believed that Hitler would not go to war.*

▼ *Preparations for world war – the pocket battleship Admiral Graf Spee slips out of Wilhelmshaven.*

awarded. Who received which grade was dependant upon the highest Spanish decoration a German volunteer received.

JULY

GERMANY, *DIPLOMACY*

Hitler's foreign minister, Ribbentrop, starts trade talks between the Soviet Union and Germany, which include secret talks on improving political relations and mutual spheres of influence.

AUGUST 18

ARMED FORCES, *NAVY*

The German Naval High Command orders the previously planned "Three Front War Programme" to come into effect as an emergency measure.

AUGUST 19

ARMED FORCES, *NAVY*

14 submarines leave Germany and sail to their war stations in the North Atlantic.

AUGUST 21

ARMED FORCES, *NAVY*

The pocket battleship *Admiral Graf Spee* sails from Wilhelmshaven.

AUGUST 23

GERMANY, *TREATIES*

Ribbentrop and his Soviet counterpart, Molotov sign the Russo-German Non-aggression Treaty, by which neither party would attack the other and spheres of influence were agreed regarding the Baltic states and Poland.

▲ *Cuff band of the SS-Heimwehr Danzig, an SS unit set up in the city to assist the German invaders.*

In order to avoid a two-front war Hitler decided that the Soviet Union would have to be neutralized; to which end Hitler directed Ribbentrop to open negotiations with the Soviets. His first diplomatic overtures in Moscow were not successful. The Soviets were stalling for time as they were already negotiating with Great Britain and France. Hitler, desperate to conclude an agreement, decided to intervene personally and on August 20 sent a telegram to Stalin asking him to receive his foreign minister immediately and adding: "The conclusion of a non-aggression pact for me means the fulfilment of a long-standing German policy.

▲ *Members of the SS-Heimwehr Danzig in action against Polish troops in Danzig at the beginning of September.*

◄ *German motorized infantry tackle one of Poland's dirt roads during the Blitzkrieg (Lightning War) campaign.*

Germany now resumes a political course that was beneficial to both states in past centuries. In view of the intention of both states to enter into a new relationship to each other it seems to me best not to lose any time. I therefore propose that you receive my Foreign Minister on Tuesday, August 22, or at the latest Wednesday August 23. The Reich Minister has the fullest power to draw up and sign the non-aggression pact as well as the protocol. In view of the international situation a longer stay by the minister in Moscow is impossible. A crisis may arise any day. Germany is determined to use all measures at her disposal to protect the interests of the Reich. I should be glad to receive your early answer."

On the evening of August 21, Hitler was handed a telegram from Stalin. The Führer was overcome with uncontrollable excitement. "To the Chancellor of the German Reich, A. Hitler. I thank you for your letter. I hope that the German-Soviet non-aggression pact will bring about an important improvement in the political relations between our countries. The people of our countries need to live in peace with each other. The Soviet government have instructed me to inform you that they agree to receiving your Herr von Ribbentrop on the August 23 in Moscow."

Hitler was apprehensive about the meeting and its outcome, feeling that his good fortune may not hold. During the negotiations Stalin made claims on the Baltic states of Estonia, Latvia and Lithuania. Ribbentrop telephoned Hitler who authorized him to accept the Soviet proposals. The protocol reached now achieved the aims of both dictators, as all of Eastern Europe had been divided up into spheres of influence between the two countries. Hitler's attitude – that he could confidently localize any Polish conflict – was reinforced with the conclusion of the pact with the Soviet Union.

Despite British guarantees, the situation for Poland had become intolerable. Not withstanding the many assurances she received, speedy assistance from the West was most improbable. Powerful enemies,

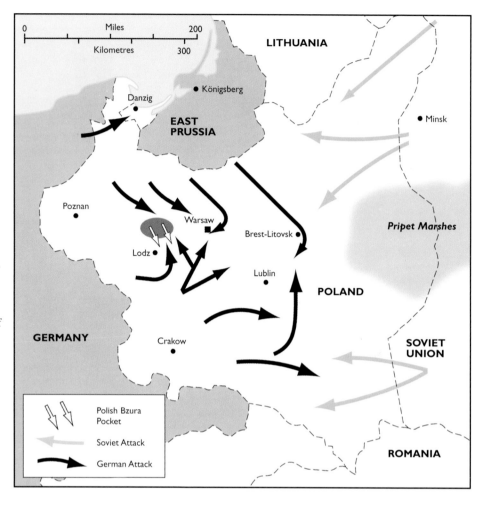

▲ Poland's strategic situation was hopeless. She had German armies on three sides and the Soviets in the rear.

who had just become reconciled to each other and were hungry to devour her, now hounded her on both sides. Hitler for his part counted on a Western renunciation of military intervention similar to those which had taken place in 1936, 1938 and again in the spring of 1939.

AUGUST 24

ARMED FORCES, *NAVY*
Two more U-boats depart to their war stations. The pocket battleship *Deutschland* (Hitler does want to risk a ship named after the Fatherland being sunk in any hostilities), now renamed *Lützow*, leaves Wilhelmshaven.

AUGUST 25

GERMANY, *AGGRESSION*
Hitler orders the attack against Poland in the afternoon, and about two hours later the German Army in the East leaves its position of readiness for the fateful march over the Polish frontier between the Carpathian Mountains and Lithuania. Later that afternoon Hitler has a change of heart when he receives a letter from the British

▼ Danzig, assaulted by the German Army externally and riddled with Nazi sympathizers, fell almost at once.

GERMANY, *MERCHANT MARINE*
German merchant ships are instructed to return home to Germany or to make for the nearest neutral port. The threat of war hangs over Europe like a black cloud.

GERMANY, *ARMED FORCES*
In German military circles there is little

◄ *Warsaw burns following a Luftwaffe raid on September 25, carried out on Hitler's personel orders.*

government that reaffirms the British intention to help Poland if Germany invades that country, and that a mutual assistance programme between England and Poland has been worked out in detail. Hitler orders Keitel: "Stop everything at once, I need time for negotiations."

The Anglo-Polish treaty was signed on the same day at 17:40 hours and, following the advice of his commander-in-chief who was seeking to preserve the peace, Hitler decided to call off the attack. Despite the imposed radio silence, the order to halt was passed right up to the frontline, a masterly achievement in communication techniques. The army generally regarded the halt as a psychological and diplomatic weapon in the political war of nerves; similar to that used in the previous autumn before entering Czechoslovakia. But since the Poles had observed the advance and had secretly begun to mobilize, the Germans lost their planned operational surprise and with it all the advantages which might have ensued. On the other hand, they too were able to use the time for further mobilization.

◄ *Germans in Poland. Having achieved complete air superiority on the first day of the campaign, victory was certain.*

enthusiasm for war, leading to rumblings of disquiet. Most of the officers are well aware of the possible military and political difficulties which its armed forces might encounter. These objections, which Hitler regards as defeatist, he overrides, believing in his own intuition.

The Polish mobilization on the March 25, 1939, caused Hitler to decide that the German-Polish question could now only be resolved by force, even at the risk of a probable outbreak of war. Hitler was confident he could localize any such conflict, grossly underestimating both his opponents and his influence on world opinion. War on two fronts was Hitler's great fear, stemming from the bitter experience gained by Germany in World War I, one which, as yet, he was not ready to risk.

AUGUST 28

GREAT BRITAIN, *DIPLOMACY*

At 22:00 hours at the Chancellery in Berlin, Sir Neville Henderson, the British ambassador, meets Hitler to deliver another letter from the British Government stating it intends to stand by Poland. Henderson's observation was that "Hitler was once again friendly and reasonable and appeared to be not dissatisfied with the answer which I

▲ The bombing of Warsaw broke the back of Polish resistance in the capital. The Luftwaffe *had established its reputation.*

arrival, then effusive greetings at the door by Chief of the Chancellery, Otto Meissner. However, it was another matter once inside the Chancellery. Henderson's recollections were vivid: "I immediately sensed a more uncompromising attitude than the previous evening on Hitler's part." The British Government's letter received a reply from

Hitler that was starkly uncompromising, stating that the Danzig problem must be settled peacefully on German terms by the following day or he would use force. Henderson left the Chancellery noticing that the anteroom was filled with German Army officers. The die was cast.

AUGUST 30

POLAND, *ARMED FORCES*

The Polish mobilization is officially announced. Hitler can wait no longer and

▲ Little thought was given to the vanquished. These Polish refugees have had their homes destroyed by bombing.

▶ Though the campaign in Poland was quick and decisive, over 10,000 German soldiers were killed fighting for the Führer.

had brought him. Our conversation lasted for well over an hour."

AUGUST 29

GREAT BRITAIN, *DIPLOMACY*

At 21:15 hours, Henderson again goes to the Chancellery, this time to receive Hitler's reply to the British Government's letter. His reception outside the building was the same as usual: SS guard of honour at the main door, roll of drums announcing his

on the next day he gives the order to invade Poland at 04:45 hours.

The time has come to undertake the deception Hitler perceived was necessary to legitimize the invasion. *SS-Sturmbannführer* Alfred Naujocks was chosen by *SS-Obergruppenführer* Heydrich to lead a simulated attack on the Gleiwitz radio stations. Formerly an engineering student at Kiel University; *SS-Sturmbannführer* Naujocks became an official of the *Amt* (Office) VI of the SS security service and was one of the most audacious commanders in the SD. He wasn't an intelligent leader and lacked the mental capacity for creating plans such as those which *SS-Obergruppenführer* Heydrich conceived. However, he was an expert at carrying out an operation once it was explained. He helped Heydrich with some bombings in Slovakia, which were blamed on Slovak nationalists. At 16:00 hours on August 31, *SS-Obergruppenführer* Heydrich alerted *SS-Sturmbannführer* Naujocks in Gleiwitz and ordered him to be at the radio station at 21:45 hours that evening.

The Dachau concentration camp corpses loaded on Müller's lorries were expected to arrive at approximately 21:25 hours. The dead "Polish soldiers" could then be scattered "convincingly" around the station. The deception party arrived on time at the station, finding a 1.8m- (6ft-) high wire

fence surrounding it, but the two attached buildings which were used for living quarters were unguarded. The German operational staff of the station were not privy to Heydrich's plan, so when Foitzik, an engineer, encountered *SS-Sturmbannführer* Naujocks and his companions entering the station, he mentally questioned what they were doing. As they ascended the steps leading to the broadcasting studios, he called out to them – where did they think they were going? He was silenced by the muzzle of a pistol being pointed at a spot between his eyes.

On reaching the broadcasting studios, *SS-Sturmbannführer* Naujocks and his men began making as much noise as possible, hoping to give the impression that the station was under attack by a large Polish insurgent force. The ceiling of the studio received several shots, adding to the bedlam and petrifying the radio personnel. The staff of the station, who had by this time decided that resistance to the strangers was futile, surrendered, were handcuffed and taken to the basement of the building. Meanwhile, a flaw was discovered in the plan: Naujocks and his SS men did not know how to operate the

▼ *A beaming Hitler inspects men of the Leibstandarte as he tours newly conquered Poland.*

radio equipment. The SS men were frantically turning dials and flipping switches until they finally found the storm switch. This permitted them to interrupt the programme in progress, allowing Naujocks' Polish-speaking announcers to broadcast anti-German statements, to the background accompaniment of shots fired by other SS men for the next five minutes. Having decided they had convinced the listeners that the radio station was under attack by armed Poles, *SS-Sturmbannführer* Naujocks and his men withdrew.

A successful mock attack on the German customs station at Hochlinden was also made by Heydrich's SS detachment. Additional concentration camp corpses were dressed in Polish uniforms. The fact that the dead inmates' bodies were rigid due to the time of their death many hours earlier was of little importance to the SS leaders. The Polish military forces and police would not be able to investigate the bodies at Gleiwitz or Hochlinden. Hitler now had his justification for invading Poland. In fact, his soldiers and tanks were on the move before the SS men had returned to their bases.

SEPTEMBER 1

POLAND, *GERMAN AGGRESSION*
The incident at Gleiwitz is reported by the *Völkischer Beobachter* as being "clearly the signal for a general attack on German

▲ *Swastikas fly in Danzig following the end of the Polish campaign. The city was once more part of the Reich.*

territory by Polish guerrillas". Feigning outraged indignation regarding the attack on the radio station, Hitler sends a message to the German armed forces the same day: "The Polish Government, unwilling to establish good neighbourly relations as aimed at by me, wants to force the issue by way of arms. The Germans in Poland are being persecuted with bloody terror and driven from their homes. Several acts of frontier violations which cannot be tolerated by a great power shows that Poland is no longer prepared to respect the Reich's frontiers. To put an end to these mad acts, I can see no other way but from now onwards to meet force with force."

Hitler solemnly mounts the rostrum in the Kroll Opera House that morning and announces to a hushed *Reichstag* that Germany is at war with Poland, declaring towards the end of his speech: "From now on I am just the first soldier of the German Reich. I have once more put on the coat that was the most sacred and dear to me. I will not take it off again until victory is secured, or I will not survive the outcome." Those in the audience noticed that Hitler

▶ *Some of the 750,000 Poles captured by the Germans in a campaign that was characterized by speed and ruthlessness.*

had discarded his customary brown party jacket for a field-grey uniform blouse resembling that of a junior officer in the Waffen-SS.

SEPTEMBER 2–11

NAZI PARTY, *RALLIES*
Party Rally of Peace is held at Nuremberg without any sense of irony.

SEPTEMBER 3

SEA WAR, *NORTH SEA*
German ships start laying mines in the North Sea, concentrating on the defence of the German bight. Such mining operations continue through out the year, and become one of the navy's most important contributions to the war during its first winter.

EUROPE, *INTERNATIONAL RELATIONS*
Great Britain and France declare war on Germany. The Soviet Union invades Poland.

GERMANY, *LEGAL*
Jews are forbidden to be out of doors after 2000 hours in winter or 21:00 hours in summer. Confiscation of all radios from Jews is carried out.

SEPTEMBER 7

SEA WAR, *BALTIC*
Operational submarines are withdrawn from the Baltic Sea.

SEPTEMBER 16

SEA WAR, *ATLANTIC*
U-31, commanded *Kapitänleutnant* Hans Habekost, is the first U-boat to attack a British convoy.

SEPTEMBER 17

SEA WAR, *ATLANTIC*
The British aircraft carrier HMS *Courageous* is sunk by *U-29*, commanded by *Kapitänleutnant* Otto Schuhart.

SEA WAR, *GERMANY*

The heavy cruiser *Blücher* is commissioned.

OCTOBER

EASTERN FRONT, *POLAND*

German armies advance rapidly through Poland. *Fall Gelb*, Operation Yellow, the invasion of France through the Low Countries, is planned.

The intention had been expressed in *Mein Kampf* in 1925 that Britain and France would stand in the way of German expansion to obtain *Lebensraum*, and thus the only solution was by force.

In 1939 began the subjugation of non-German-speaking nationalities to the totalitarian Nazi police state. When Germany started World War II, it came as the logical outcome of Hitler's plans. Thus, his first years were spent in preparing the Germans for the approaching struggle for world control and in forging that instrument which would enable Germany to establish its military and industrial superiority and thereby fulfil its ambitions. With mounting diplomatic and military successes, the aims grew in quick progression. The first aim was to unite all people of German descent within their historic homeland on the basis of "self-determination."

▲ *The British battleship* Royal Oak *was sunk in Scapa Flow in a daring attack by Günther Prien's U-47.*

The next step foresaw the creation of a *Grosswirtschaftsraum* (Large Economic Unified Space) or a *Lebensraum* (Living Space) through the military conquest of Poland and other Slavic nations to the East. Thereby the Germans would acquire sufficient soil to become economically self-sufficient and militarily impregnable. There, the German master race (*Herrenvolk*) would rule over a hierarchy of subordinate peoples and organize and exploit them with ruthlessness and efficiency.

At the beginning of October the Polish campaign was at an end. For the loss of 10,572 dead, Germany had conquered the Polish nation. The Poles lost 50,000 dead and 750,000 captured. The country was divided into two zones of occupation divided by the River Bug. The Blitzkrieg proved to be devastatingly effective.

OCTOBER 4

SEA WAR, *ATLANTIC*

The war against Allied merchant shipping is intensified by the German Naval Command, which lifts various restrictions on the types of vessels that can be attacked.

OCTOBER 13

SEA WAR, *SCAPA FLOW*

U-47, commanded by Günther Prien, penetrates the Royal Navy defences of Scapa Flow during the night of 13/14 October on a mission that is near-suicidal considering the strong currents, shallow draft, mine nets and other defensive measures. The 31-year-old Prien, commanding his first submarine, surfaces on a moonless night. Beginning his attack on the morning of the 14th, he selects as his first target the battleship HMS *Royal Oak*. He fires three of his four bow torpedoes, of which one hits and the other two miss or are duds. He then fires his stern tube, knowing that he may have already been sighted, but this also misses. By this time two of his bow tubes had been reloaded. These two, plus his remaining one, are then fired, all of which hit the aged Royal Navy battleship.

The *Royal Oak* quickly sank, taking 883 men and officers with her. Prien also hit and damaged the aircraft carrier HMS *Pegasus* and mistakenly reported it as the *Repulse*. Hitler awarded Prien the Knights Cross of the Iron Cross, which earned him the distinction of becoming the second naval officer to be so decorated. This victory was a great boost to German morale.

NOVEMBER 9

GERMANY, *RESISTANCE*

A bomb explodes in the Bürgerbräukeller in Munich shortly after Hitler leaves the hall on the 16th anniversary of the Munich *Putsch*.

▼ *French sailors parade in Paris, 1939. Great Britain and France failed to launch attacks to relieve pressure on the Poles.*

WESTERN FRONT, *FRANCE*

There is little military activity on the Western Front. This is the period of the "Sitzkrieg" or phoney war.

NOVEMBER 20

SEA WAR, *GREAT BRITAIN*

First mines are dropped in British waters by German aircraft.

▲ *Hitler in the Bürgerbräukeller on November 9, 1939. Moments after he left the hall, a bomb exploded.*

NOVEMBER 30

EASTERN FRONT, *FINLAND*

Russia attacks Finland, but the invasion only penetrates the border areas and is carried out so inefficiently that Germany and the world thinks the Red Army is of poor quality. But the Soviet Union had purged its officer corps three years before, on suspicion of political disloyalty, and had not

▲ *French troops near the German border in September 1939. The French Army adopted a defensive posture in the West.*

yet completed the training of enough new officers.

DECEMBER

SEA WAR, *NORWAY*

Admiral Raeder, commander of the German Navy, urges Hitler to seize Norway to make sure that Britain does not block the sea route from northern Norway, used to carry Swedish iron-ore to Germany. Rosenberg introduces Vidkun Quisling, leader of a Norwegian nationalist party with pro-Nazi views, to Hitler as a possible puppet leader for Norway.

When World War II broke out Norway, together with Sweden, Denmark and Finland, announced its neutrality. In September 1939 Germany assured Norway that it would respect its territorial integrity, but warned her that the Third Reich would not tolerate an infringement of that neutrality by a third power. Germany at this time was sincere about respecting Norwegian neutrality, but Raeder kept reminding Hitler that naval bases in Norway would be very useful in carrying the war to Great Britain. In addition, Raeder reminded the Führer, a British occupation of Norway would be disastrous for Germany because Sweden would then come entirely under British influence. This would interfere with iron-ore supplies and operations in the

Baltic. In addition, Allied aid that was being sent to the Finns might lead to an occupation of Norwegian ports. Hitler thus began to consider an invasion of Norway more carefully.

DECEMBER 1

SS, *WAFFEN-SS*

Gottlob Berger created the *Ergänzungsamt der Waffen-SS* (Waffen-SS Recruiting Office) within the *SS-Hauptamt* (SS Central Office). The remarkable growth of the Waffen-SS must be attributed to Berger rather than Himmler. He had generally been able to outmanoeuvre and outwit his military counterparts with a cunning cocktail of diplomacy, threat and duplicity. His successes also encouraged him to undertake increasingly ambitious schemes to expand the wartime role of the SS, thus fulfilling the desires of his *Reichsführer-SS*. Berger, who had proved his organizational ability by directing the activities of the Henlien *Freikorps* during the 1938 Sudetenland crisis, was appointed by Himmler to command the new *SS-Hauptampt*, with responsibility, amongst other duties, for recruitment. One of the functions of the district leaders of the *Allgemeine-SS* had always been recruiting for the SS, but with the threat of impending war it became necessary to centralize and consolidate this increasingly important role.

The establishment of a nation-wide SS recruiting network was Berger's first task, and on December 1 he created the *Ergänzungsamt der Waffen-SS* within the SS-Hauptamt with himself as its chief, with an order he prepared and signed by Himmler. In each of the 17 *SS-Oberabschnitte* (Higher Sections), an *SS-Ergänzungsstelle* (Recruiting Centre) was established. Since the *Wehrkreise* (Army Defence Districts) were coterminous with these SS districts, Berger possessed a

▼ *French troops in the Ardennes in the winter of 1939–40. French and British inactivity would cost them dear in 1940.*

◄ *Gottlob Berger worked tirelessly to establish recruiting centres for Reichsführer-SS Himmler's Waffen-SS.*

▲ *The Admiral Graf Spee burns in Montevideo harbour after being scuttled by her crew in December.*

recruiting organization which geographically paralleled that of the army. The *Oberkommando der Wehrmacht* (OKW), High Command of the Armed Forces, at the same time issued an order to military district commanders explaining the function of the new bureaus and ordering them to deal directly with the *SS-Ergänzungsstelle* in all SS personnel matters.

DECEMBER 13

SEA WAR, *ATLANTIC*
The British submarine HMS *Salmon* scores torpedo hits on the cruisers *Leipzig* and *Nürnberg*.

DECEMBER 15

SEA WAR, *ATLANTIC*
The damaged *Leipzig* is torpedoed again, this time by HMS *Ursula*.

DECEMBER 17

SEA WAR, *ATLANTIC*
The Battle of the River Plate. After sinking several merchant ships in the

Atlantic, the *Admiral Graf Spee* was sighted on December 13, 1939, off the Río de la Plata estuary by a British search group consisting of the cruisers *Exeter*, *Ajax* and *Achilles*, commanded by Commodore H. Harwood. At 06:14 hours Harwood's three ships attacked, but in a little more than an hour the *Admiral Graf Spee* had damaged the *Exeter* and driven off the other two cruisers. The *Admiral Graf Spee* then made for Montevideo, Uruguay, where its commander, Captain Hans Langsdorff, obtained permission to stay for four days to repair damage. The British devoted the period to intense diplomatic and intelligence activity in order to keep the *Admiral Graf Spee* in harbour while they brought up heavy reinforcements. On December 17, however, when the *Admiral Graf Spee* put to sea again, only the *Cumberland* had arrived to reinforce the *Ajax* and the *Achilles*. The fight that the British had anticipated never took place: Captain Langsdorff, believing that a superior force awaited him, had his crew scuttle their ship; three days later Langsdorff shot himself.

1940

This year Germany maintained her series of military victories by defeating the combined armies of Great Britain and France in a quick campaign. The victory against Poland had been won against a foe that was inferior to the German Army, but in the West in 1940 the *Wehrmacht* defeated opponents who were technologically equal, and who actually had more tanks and aircraft. But the German Army used its weapons and men more imaginatively. At sea, meanwhile, the U-boat campaign in the Atlantic gathered momentum.

▲ The **Altmark** *photographed after the incident with HMS* **Cossack** *in mid-February 1940.*

JANUARY 10

WESTERN FRONT, *BELGIUM*

News received from the German embassy in Brussels puts *Luftwaffe* headquarters into turmoil when it learns of the crash-landing of a German military plane near the Belgian town of Mechelen-sur-Meuse. The aircraft, on a flight from Münster to Cologne, became lost in thick cloud. After it came down, one of the passengers jumped out and raced for a clump of bushes, where

he set fire to papers he had taken from his briefcase. Belgian soldiers closed in and retrieved the partly burnt papers. The man has been identified as Major Helmut Reinberger, a *Luftwaffe* staff officer, and the papers are operational plans, complete with maps, for a German airborne attack on the West, to begin on January 14 with saturation bombing attacks on French airfields. When distraught aides gave news

▼ *Great Britain's lifeline:* an Atlantic *convoy bringing supplies from the United States, now under U-boat threat.*

118

the gloves off in the battle to stop essential supplies of food and war materials reaching Great Britain from the United States. Any ship which is likely to come under British control can now be torpedoed without warning.

The policy was already in effect, as was made evident by the sinking of Danish, Dutch, Norwegian and Swedish ships in the days that preceded the order. Danish newspapers protested loudly at the sinking of one of their ships, the *5177*, to Chastine Maersk by a U-boat.

FEBRUARY 16

SEA WAR, *BALTIC*
The destroyer HMS *Cossack* rescues some 299 British seamen held prisoner on the

▼ *The* **Altmark** *after having been driven farther into the Norwegian fjord following the engagement with HMS* **Cossack***.*

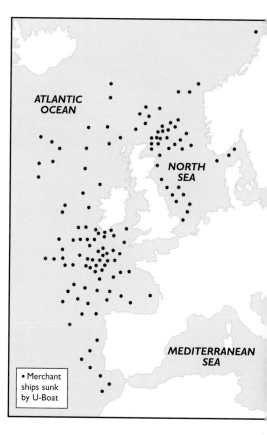

▲ *This map shows the success the U-boats enjoyed against merchant shipping between September 1939 and May 1940.*

of the lost plans to Hitler, the Führer exploded in anger and retorted: "It's things like this that can lose us the war."

FEBRUARY

GERMANY, *ANTI-SEMITISM*
First deportations of Jews from Germany begin, mainly from Pomerania.

FEBRUARY 15

SEA WAR, *ATLANTIC*
Hitler gives the order for unlimited U-boat war. U-boat commanders are ordered to take

▶ *A German U-boat in the Atlantic in February 1940. Hitler gave his submarines licence to attack any potential enemy.*

Altmark. The *Altmark* was the supply ship for the German pocket battleship *Admiral Graf Spee*, and the prisoners had been taken from merchant ships captured by her. After the sinking of the *Admiral Graf Spee*, the *Altmark* sailed for Europe, taking a route near the Arctic to avoid detection. Incredibly, the Norwegians, who stopped and searched her, found neither her

▲ *Airborne troops were used extensively by the Germans in Norway and Denmark to seize airfields and strongpoints.*

concealed guns nor the prisoners. Two British destroyers then chased her into Jossing Fjord. The *Cossack* lowered two boats, but they could not move through the ice. The *Altmark* then made two attempts to ram the *Cossack*. As the two ships scraped together, several members of a

boarding party leapt aboard the German ship. The *Altmark* then ran aground and the rest of the Royal Navy party scrambled over the side, opening fire with their rifles and charging with fixed bayonets. Four German crewmen were killed. One prisoner said: "It was a hit-and-run affair along the decks and round corners, more of a rathunt than anything. You can imagine our joy when we heard an English voice shouting down 'The Navy's here!'"

The captain of the *Altmark* had denied the existence of prisoners right up to the end. One prisoner told how they had shouted, hammered and blown SOS whistles to attract the attention of the Norwegian search party at Bergen. The Germans turned a fire hose on them to stop them, and to drown the noise they turned on a winch. Even so, the prisoners found it difficult to understand why the Norwegians had not noticed something of their presence. Afterwards the Germans told them that their behaviour was mutiny and put out a notice saying: "On account of today's behaviour of the prisoners, they will get bread and water tomorrow instead of their regular meals."

FEBRUARY 22

SEA WAR, *NORTH SEA*
The Dutch destroyers *Leberecht Maass*, commanded by *Korvettenkapitän* Fritz Bassenge, and *Max Schultz*, commanded by *Korvettenkapitän* Claus Trampedach, while trying to avoid an attack by German aircraft, run onto mines laid by a British submarine.

MARCH 11

EASTERN FRONT, *FINLAND*
Finland signs a peace treaty with the Soviet Union, ceding territory around the Baltic to

▼ *The* Admiral Hipper *sinks the Royal Navy destroyer HMS* Glowworm *after the latter had rammed her.*

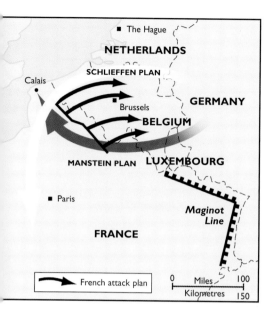

▲ The German plan for the attack on the West in May 1940 compared to the Schlieffen Plan of World War I.

improve Soviet defences. The war has not been a great success for the Red Army. It has lost 200,000 men, while the Finns lost only 25,000.

NORTHERN FRONT, *SCANDINAVIA*
Hitler, convinced of his military planning ability after the victory against Poland in 1939, orders an attack on Norway. Denmark is also included in the plan. He takes personal charge, issuing orders through Keitel and his OKW rather than planning through *Oberkommando des Heeres* (OKH), the Army High Command.

MARCH 31

SEA WAR, *ATLANTIC*
The auxiliary cruiser *Atlantis*, commanded by *Kapitän zur See* Bernhard Rogge, leaves German coastal waters, the first auxiliary cruiser to do so. The many days at sea stretched into months, and the total shipping tons of enemy vessels sunk reaches 93,803. Rogge went on to become

▼ The Blitzkrieg in operation in Norway. German troops go into the attack following an artillery barrage.

▲ Major-General Eduard Dietl (centre) commanded the German 3rd Mountain Division at Narvik in northern Norway.

the most successful and famous of the auxiliary cruiser commanders. His success is directly attributed to the courage displayed by the men of his command, the manoeuvring tactics, and his ability to disguise his ship. In recognition of the outstanding success achieved by the ship, Rogge was awarded the Knights Cross of the Iron Cross on December 7, 1940.

APRIL 6

SEA WAR, *ATLANTIC*
The *Orion* under the command of *Kapitän zur See* Weyher, becomes the second auxiliary cruiser to leave Germany.

APRIL 8

SEA WAR, *NORWAY*
The British lay mines off Norway. The *Admiral Hipper* sinks the British destroyer HMS *Glowworm*.

APRIL 9

NORTHERN FRONT, NORWAY
The invasion of Denmark and Norway, codename *Fall Weserübung* or Operation Weser Exercise, begins in the early dawn. The operation is characterized by lightning speed, meticulous planning and total secrecy. In Denmark it is met with virtually no resistance. Two German aircraft are shot down and a few armoured cars damaged.

Thirteen Danish soldiers are killed and another 23 wounded. It is nothing more than a skirmish.

Before the Danes had had breakfast, it was all over. There was no "fifth column". The *Volksdeutsche* (ethnic Germans) and the pro-German Danes were as surprised as any by the fate which literally fell from the sky upon them. It was the first example in any war of a successful airborne operation. Once they had recovered from their shock, the North Schleswig Germans welcomed the arrival of "their" army. They offered hospitality, directed traffic and in some cases even took it upon themselves to round up and guard Danish prisoners of war. But nowhere did any Danish citizen indulge in any act of premeditated sabotage. Before the invasion the Germans had dispatched a small commando unit to Pagborg to ensure that the Danes did not try to impede their advance by blowing up the important bridge there – an unnecessary precaution, as the Danes had not even mined it.

The German Navy sailed into Norwegian ports from Oslo to Narvik in the north and landed troops. German naval losses were heavy, with three cruisers, *Karlsruhe*, *Königsberg* and *Blücher*, being sunk and a battleship badly damaged. In southern Norway German troops were also landed by air. *Luftwaffe* units took over airfields and gained air superiority over Norway. The

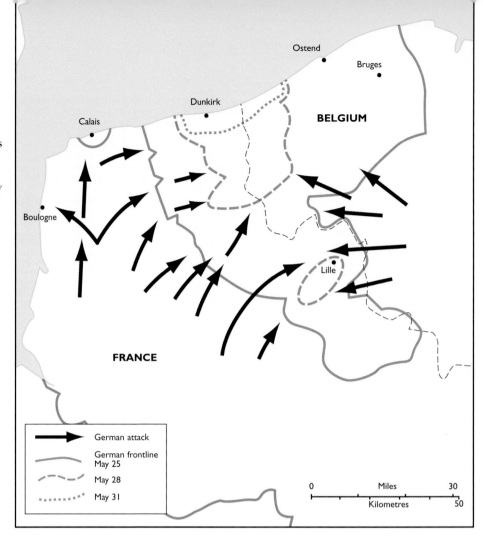

German attack

German frontline
May 25

May 28

May 31

▼ **The Belgian fortress of Eben Emael, reckoned to be impregnable, was captured by German paratroopers in gliders.**

▲ **The fight to hold the Dunkirk perimeter was fierce, though Hitler did not permit his panzers to attack the port.**

next morning the lookouts spotted the outline of the *Blücher* approaching in the darkness. Two 280mm shells hit her director control tower, and lighter guns demolished the bridge. Wrecked and ablaze, the *Blücher* tried to creep out of range, but as she passed the fortress, two torpedoes were fired by the fixed tubes ashore. Both hit the mark and she rolled over and sank. The guns then turned on the *Brummer*, and within a few minutes the whole of the force was in retreat down the fjord. In Norway the Germans were not a moment too soon; the British Navy was almost simultaneously mounting Operation Wilfred, the laying of mines off the

▲ *Hitler poses with some of those paratroopers who captured the fortress of Eben Emael in May 1940.*

▶ *Rotterdam burns following the devastating Luftwaffe attack on the city, which demoralized the citizens.*

heavy cruiser *Blücher* was part of a task force which tried to seize Oslo by surprise on April 8. With the pocket battleship *Lützow*, the light cruiser *Emden* and the gunnery training ship *Brummer*, she went up Oslo Fjord that night. The arrival of the force had been reported to the coastal fortress of Oskarsborg on the Island of Kalholmen and although the guns were old and the gunners were elderly reservists, both were adequate to the task for which they had been designed. At 03:30 hours

◀ *General Erwin Rommel (centre), commander of the 7th Panzer Division, led the panzers to the Channel in May 1940.*

Norwegian coast. But in the terminology of the "Gun fighter" the Germans had the drop on the British. It was the *Kriegsmarine*, not the Royal Navy, that sailed first into Norwegian waters. In spite of all the ominous portents, the Norwegian authorities were taken completely by surprise. The campaign lasted 62 days and cost the lives of 5000 casualties on both sides. Eduard Dietl, the "Hero of Narvik", stated later: "Had the British held on for another two hours I would have withdrawn." But they did not and the conquest of Norway was assured. For his decisive leadership during the battle of Narvik, he was awarded the Knights Cross of the Iron Cross on May 9, 1940. No SS troops were used in either of these countries, which is a little surprising considering Himmler's eagerness to test his racial warriors. With the occupation of these strategic countries complete, Hitler was free to make his next move.

APRIL 10

SEA WAR, *NORWAY*

The light cruisers *Karlsruhe* and *Königsberg* are sunk in Norwegian waters. *Königsberg*'s presence at Bergen was noted by British reconnaissance aircraft and word was passed to a group of 15 Skua dive-bombers based at Hatston in the Orkneys by the carrier HMS *Ark Royal*. At their maximum range the Skuas took the cruiser by surprise and sank her at her moorings with three 500lb bombs. The *Karlsruhe* was torpedoed off Kristiansund by the British submarine HMS *Truant* shortly after landing troops during the invasion of Norway, and had to be sunk by her escort after the crew had been rescued.

APRIL 14

NORTHERN FRONT, *NORWAY*

Anglo-French troops are landed at Narvik and near Trondheim, but are unable to do more than hold some of their landing areas.

SEA WAR, *ATLANTIC*

U-49, commanded by *Kapitänleutnant* Johann Egbert von Gossler, is sunk by HMS *Brazen* and HMS *Fearless*. Secret documents, probably connected with the German "Enigma" cyphering machine, float to the surface and are then captured by the British.

▲ *Field Marshal Walther von Brauchitsch, commander of Germany's forces in the attack on the West in May 1940.*

▶ *The spearhead of the Blitzkrieg: a Panzer III tank races through the French countryside in May 1940.*

▲ *The leader of a gallant but hopelessly outnumbered and outclassed nation: King Leopold of Belgium.*

MAY 10

NORTHERN FRONT, *NORWAY*

The re-embarkation of Allied troops leaves the Germans in control of southern and central Norway. At Narvik in the north, 2000 German Alpine troops are slowly pushed back by 20,000 Allied troops.

WESTERN FRONT, *BELGIUM*

Hitler moves to his forward

artillery pieces in four casements and three revolving turrets. The field of fire from these guns allowed them to cover Maastricht to the north and Vise to the south, as well as the three bridges across the Albert Canal that were also to be taken. The two 120mm guns were encased in a huge rotating steel dome. All the artillery positions were connected by 4.5km (2.8 miles) of corridors, stairs and lifts, and officers even used bicycles to move around the complex. Some 500 Belgian artillery troops manned the large guns, with an additional 500 men manning the immediate defences on the flat roof of the fortress, consisting of 60mm antiaircraft guns, searchlights and heavy machine guns. Two heavy machine-gun bunkers sat atop the surface. Eben Emael also had dummy installations to fool any attacker. The only downside to Eben Emael was the lack of surface trenches and defences against infantry attack.

Before the Netherlands are attacked, a key frontier bridge is taken by "Brandenburgers'", small groups of Dutch-speaking and sometimes Dutch-uniformed troops. Parachute troops are landed near The Hague and communications are soon in German hands. "Brandenburgers" dressed as tourists pass into Luxembourg,

▲ *The lucky ones: some of the 300,000 Allied troops taken off the beaches of Dunkirk by British ships.*

▶ *Behind them they left all their heavy equipment and vehicles. These are spiked British antiaircraft guns on the Dunkirk beaches.*

headquarters, Felsennest (Cliff Nest) at Bad Munstereiffel, about 48km (30 miles) from the Belgian frontier, and issues the codeword Danzig which sets *Fall Gelb*, Operation Yellow – modified by General Erich von Manstein in operation – a strike through the Ardennes towards the English Channel to defeat the British and French.

On May 10 aircraft hit pre-arranged targets, while paratroopers prepared to seize vital objectives, one of these being the Belgian fort of Eben Emael. It was a well-situated, well-armed and well-defended strongpoint built into the side of the Albert Canal, with the natural defences on one side and an antitank ditch and barbed-wire defences on the other. Eben Emael was considered to be virtually impregnable due to its location. It measured approximately 700m (2296ft) east to west and 900m (2952ft) north to south. It had a formidable arsenal of 16 75mm and two 120mm clearing minefields and roadblocks and keeping bridges intact.

MAY 11

WESTERN FRONT, *BELGIUM*

Fort Eben Emael, guarding a bridge on the Belgian border, is taken by German troops landing gliders on top of the caissons. Two panzer divisions move into Belgium.

MAY 14

WESTERN FRONT, *ARDENNES*

Rotterdam is heavily bombed on the fourth day to hasten the Dutch surrender. Rundstedt's Army Group A moves through southern Belgium, with a panzer corps under Guderian moving through the Ardennes' hills and forests. The French, taken by surprise at armour coming through the "unpassable" Ardennes, wait for them to halt at the River Meuse. But Rommel's 7th Panzer Division crosses the river. The same day, all of Guderian's panzers are across and racing through the open country beyond, with Junkers Ju 87 Stuka dive-bombers clearing opposition before them. This is classic Blitzkrieg strategy: to sustain the momentum of the advance by avoiding centres of resistance to strike the enemy's rear areas and his lines of communication and supply. Bold commanders take advantage of new opportunities as they arise.

▼ *The Waffen-SS in the West. These are troops of the Totenkopf Division moving through northern France.*

▲ *Panzers parade in Paris. The Blitzkrieg in the West took just six weeks, and established German military prowess.*

MAY 15

WESTERN FRONT, *HOLLAND*

The Dutch Army surrenders. One of Guderian's divisions is 64km (40 miles) beyond the Meuse and still advancing west.

MAY 17

WESTERN FRONT, *BELGIUM*

The Belgian capital, Brussels, is taken.

▲ *The leader of Vichy France, Marshal Pétain. He felt it was his duty to establish a new regime after the French defeat.*

◀ *In 1940 French military defeat was accompanied by humiliation as German troops took possession of Paris itself.*

MAY 19

FRANCE, *POLITICS*
French Premier Reynaud appoints Marshal Pétain as Vice Premier.

MAY 20

WESTERN FRONT, *FRANCE*
The German Army reaches the English Channel, cutting the Allied forces in two. The commander-in-chief, von Brauchitsch, wants to round up the trapped Anglo-French and Belgian troops, but Rundstedt decides to halt and regroup his forces; Hitler confirms these orders to give Göring's *Luftwaffe* the chance to distinguish itself by destroying the Allied armies in the Dunkirk Pocket. However, the sands reduce the effect of aircrafts' bombs.

MAY 27

WESTERN FRONT, *DUNKIRK*
British start evacuations of troops, including French and Belgian, from beaches of Dunkirk to England. The Belgian King Leopold of Belgium surrenders.

▶ *Under the terms of the Armistice the Germans left Vichy areas, but they retained control of he vital Atlantic ports.*

SEA WAR, *PACIFIC*
The German auxiliary cruiser *Orion* passes Cape Horn on her outward voyage.

JUNE 3

WESTERN FRONT, *DUNKIRK*
The Dunkirk evacuation ends; over 300,000 soldiers are taken to England, but without their equipment and weapons. Another 200,000 are evacuated from other ports.

JUNE 5

WESTERN FRONT, *FRANCE*
The German Army resumes its offensive, moving south and west into France. Guderian takes the French defensive Maginot Line in the rear and encircles a

large part of the remaining French Army, which is now totally demoralized.

JUNE 7

NORTHERN FRONT, *NORWAY*
The Norwegian King and Government are taken to Great Britain on board a British destroyer, and a government-in-exile is formed. In Norway, Quisling is proclaimed sole political head with a state council of 13 Nazi-appointed commissioners. Josef Terboven, *Gauleiter* of Essen, is made Reich Commissioner as the effective ruler.

JUNE 8

NORTHERN FRONT, *NORWAY*
The last British troops are evacuated from Narvik in northern Norway as the Anglo-French military position disintegrates in France.

SEA WAR, *ATLANTIC*
The British aircraft carrier HMS *Glorious* is sunk by the *Scharnhorst* and the *Gneisenau*.

JUNE 10

WESTERN FRONT, *FRANCE*
Italy declares war on Great Britain and France, and moves troops into southern France. The French Government leaves

▶ *Stockpiling supplies and ammunition at the Channel ports for the proposed amphibious invasion of Great Britain.*

▼ *German troops practice with landing craft for Operation Sea Lion, the German invasion of southern England.*

▲ With the fall of France the danger to Atlantic convoys increased as the U-boats started using French ports.

Paris, first to Tours, then to Bordeaux, but defeat is only a matter of time.

JUNE 14

WESTERN FRONT, *FRANCE*
German troops enter Paris.

JUNE 17

SEA WAR, *FRANCE*
The first U-boats arrive in France to use the French Atlantic ports for refuelling.

JUNE 21

WESTERN FRONT, *FRANCE*
The French surrender is signed at Compiègne, the same railway carriage where the Germans surrendered in November 1918. France is divided into occupied and unoccupied "Vichy" zones. After the fall of France, Hitler is secure in Western Europe. He imminently expects the surrender of Great Britain, which will enable him to turn his attention to the East. Meanwhile, the Soviets move into Estonia, Latvia and Lithuania and make them Soviet Republics.
SEA WAR, *BALTIC*
The German auxiliary cruiser *Pinguin*

▶ The aftermath of a German air raid on London in September 1940 during the Battle of Britain.

passes through the Denmark Strait on her outward voyage.

JUNE 25

WESTERN FRONT, *FRANCE*
The ceasefire in France comes into effect at 01:35 hours. French casualties are 85,000, British 3475 and the Germans 27,074.

JUNE 27

SEA WAR, *ATLANTIC*
Great Britain announces a total blockade of the Continent.

JULY

GERMANY, *ALLIES*
Romania, attacked by the Soviet Union, becomes an ally of Germany.

JULY 3

SEA WAR, *PACIFIC*
The German auxiliary cruiser *Komet* leaves Gotenhafen in the Baltic for the Pacific Ocean, sailing under the command of *Konteradmiral* Robert Eyssen, around the North Cape of Norway and heading east via the Siberian Sea passage.

JULY 19

BERLIN, *PARADES*
A victory parade is held in Berlin to celebrate the stunning victory in the West. The *Leibstandarte-SS Adolf Hitler* takes part, and for the first time the achievement of the Waffen-SS is brought to the attention of the German public at large.

However, what was not disclosed was that the SS dash and élan had resulted in disproportionately high casualty rates among its members. In addition, the fact that the SS had committed atrocities during the campaign was also kept secret. The army is angry at these outrages.

AUGUST

EASTERN FRONT, *SOVIET UNION*
Hitler secretly orders his staff to prepare a plan for the invasion of the Soviet Union, to be codenamed "Otto", while making provisional plans for an invasion of Britain. The attack on Russia will be two-pronged: against Moscow and Kiev. Nazi Germany always intended to attack the Soviet Union, regarded as the centre of Jewry and Bolshevism and thus the ideological enemy.

AUGUST 1

SEA WAR, *GERMAN NAVY*
The heavy cruiser *Prinz Eugen* is commissioned.

AUGUST 8

AIR WAR, *GREAT BRITAIN*
Adlertag or Eagle Day, the codename for the first day of the air offensive against Great Britain, is launched. The Germans need to establish air superiority over Great Britain before they can launch an invasion. *Luftwaffe* attacks occur on British targets, first Royal Air Force (RAF) bases, developing later in the year into night attacks on London and other cities – the "Blitz" – in an effort to destroy civilian morale.

▼ *Surprisingly cheerful Greek civilians watch Italian bombers fly overhead towards their targets.*

AUGUST 17

SEA WAR, *ATLANTIC*
Germany announces a total blockade of Great Britain and an area in which all ships are to be sunk without prior warning.

AUGUST 20

MEDITERRANEAN, *GIBRALTAR*
The German High Command plans to capture Gibraltar with a plan codenamed Operation "Felix".

AUGUST 24

SEA WAR, *GERMAN NAVY*
The battleship *Bismarck* is commissioned.

AUGUST 27

WESTERN FRONT, *GREAT BRITAIN*
The plan to mount an initially large-scale invasion of Great Britain is abandoned in favour of landings on a small front from Eastbourne to Folkestone.

AUGUST 30

WESTERN FRONT, *GREAT BRITAIN*
With the failure of the *Luftwaffe* to clear the skies of the RAF, the invasion of Great Britain is postponed indefinitely.

SEPTEMBER 27

POLITICS, *AXIS*
The Axis Treaty is joined by Japan. Germany, Italy and Japan pledge to fight any state that declares war on an Axis nation. This is the central element of the Tripartite Pact.

OCTOBER 7

FRANCE, *NAZI IDEOLOGY*
Deportations of "non-Germans" from Alsace-Lorraine, Saar and Baden take place.
EASTERN FRONT, *ROMANIA*
Germany invades Romania, seizing the vital oilfields at Ploesti. The pretext is the training of the Fascist Iron Guard.

OCTOBER 9

SEA WAR, *ATLANTIC*
The start of one of the most important and critical convoy battles: 21 ships are sunk from convoy SC7 and another 12 from convoy HX79, making this also one of the most successful U-boat "wolf pack" attacks.

OCTOBER 23

SEA WAR, *ATLANTIC*
The pocket battleship *Admiral Scheer* leaves Gotenhafen for the Atlantic under the command of *Kapitän zur See* Theodor Krancke. Some of the German heavy cruisers were classed as pocket battleships before the war.

OCTOBER 23

SPAIN, *DIPLOMACY*

Reichsführer-SS Himmler visits Spain to discuss various questions to include those arising out of the shared frontier between France and Spain, now that France has been occupied.

OCTOBER 28

BALKANS, *GREECE*

Hitler did not want a conflict on his southern flank in the Balkans, and had restrained his Axis partner Mussolini on several occasions during the spring and summer of 1940 from initiating plans for an Italian invasion of Yugoslavia and Greece. Mussolini reluctantly accepted Hitler's wishes as he was dependent on Germany for raw materials needed for armaments. On this morning, though, Italian forces based in Albania crossed the frontier into Greece to initiate one of the most surprising campaigns of World War II.

To understand why the Italian dictator finally ignored Hitler's directives and drew Germany into the conflict it is necessary to view the situation through Mussolini's eyes. Benito Mussolini proclaimed the birth of a "New Roman Empire" that was to take shape under his direction and would recreate the ancient glories of Roman history, celebrated in the rhetoric of the Fascist poet D'Annunzio. He was a man obsessed with thoughts of personal greatness and this proclamation was to satisfy his belief that he was indeed a genius. He had no master plan, unlike Hitler, to make his dream a reality. His decisions were frequently coloured by the prevailing condition of his health, which

▲ *November 1940. Italian artillery pounds Greek positions from Albania during Mussolini's ill-fated campaign.*

was affected by the aftermath of syphilis contracted in his youth, as well as a duodenal ulcer. His arbitrary behaviour added to his intensely vain and theatrical nature. On occasions he exercised great shrewdness, on others he acted on impulse. Under Mussolini's rule Italy had already overrun two weak states: Abyssinia in 1936 and Albania in March 1939. Mussolini was a realist and recognized that he did not possess the raw materials to wage war on a grand scale. This realization did not,

however, prevent him before the outbreak of World War II from uttering bellicose sentiments illuminating the fact that Italy was ready to fight by Germany's side. Privately he considered it folly to wage war at this time, and he attempted unsuccessfully to persuade Hitler not to attack Poland. In March 1940, an official German communiqué roundly presenting Germany's military achievements, after only six months of war, brought Mussolini's

▼ *Italian heavy bombers on their way to Greece. Italy was confident of victory, but Greek resistance stunned the world.*

▲ *Romanian leader Ion Antonescu listens glumly as Hitler dictates the terms of Romania's alliance with Germany.*

grudging admiration and deep envy. He had nothing to show in comparison to Hitler's territorial gains. He felt his prestige as Europe's first Fascist dictator demanded that he should occupy the stage and bask in the limelight the Führer now enjoyed. In May 1940, Mussolini's frustration was further heightened when the German armies drove the British forces off the

▼ *RAF Sunderland flying boats were operating against U-boats in November.*

continent and brought France to her knees. It now seemed certain to him that Germany would win the war. He had an understanding with Hitler that in the "New Europe" Italy would be rewarded with pickings from the French Empire. To reinforce this right and give Italy these spoils by force of arms, Mussolini announced on June 10, 1940, her declaration of war on Great Britain and France. Unfortunately, *Il Duce* was caught in

what his Foreign Minister Ciano ironically called "an outbreak of peace".

OCTOBER 31

SEA WAR, *ATLANTIC*
The German auxiliary cruiser *Widder* arrives in Brest after a cruise in American waters.

NOVEMBER

GERMANY, *TREATIES*
Hungary, Romania and Slovakia, a puppet state taken from the dismemberment of Czechoslovakia, sign treaties with Germany. The resettlement treaty between Germany

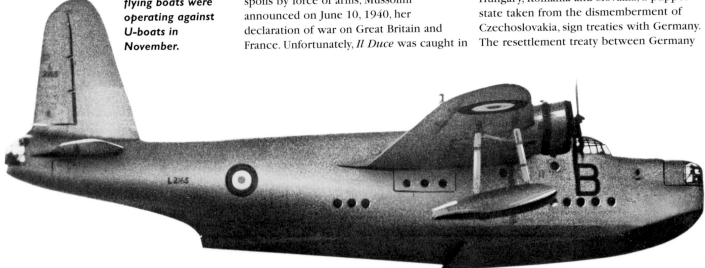

SEA WAR, *ATLANTIC*
The first U-boat located, but not sunk, by radar fitted in a Sunderland flying boat.

SEA WAR, *ATLANTIC*
The German auxiliary cruiser *Komet* returns to Hamburg after 516 days at sea.

EASTERN FRONT, *SOVIET UNION*
Directive No 21 calling for an invasion on or about May 15, 1941, is issued. Operation Barbarossa (named after a medieval German emperor nicknamed "Redbeard") mapped out a lightning attack by three million troops organized in 186 divisions equipped with 2500 tanks, 28,800 aircraft and 6000 artillery pieces. The assault would be three-pronged. Army Group North under Field Marshal von Leeb would strike through the Baltic states to Leningrad where it would link up with Finnish forces allied with Hitler. Army Group Centre under Field Marshal von Bock, including panzer groups under Generals Guderian and Hoth, would strike through central Poland and Belorussia all the way to Moscow itself. Army Group South under Field Marshal von Rundstedt, including two Romanian armies and one Hungarian corps, would smash into the Ukraine and beyond into the Crimea and Caucasus to conquer the USSR's vast agricultural lands and its richest oilfields.

and the Soviet Union in regard to ethnic Germans living in Soviet-annexed Bessarabia and northern Bukovina has to be completed by November 1940. Throughout October, some 45,000 settlers make the long and so-called "final trek" to reception camps in Pomerania, Eastern Prussia and Warthegau before leaving for permanent settlement in the newly incorporated Polish territory. Each family was limited to 50kg (110lb) of personal possessions or two wagonloads. On arrival at the reception

▲ *Field Marshal Wilhelm Keitel (wearing gloves), chief of OKW, was deeply involved in the planning of Barbarossa.*

camp at Galatz, settlers are screened and processed before proceeding by train. Types of ethnic Germans from Bessarabia were given identity tags, but many families become separated.

This policy was part of the grand Nazi scheme to colonize the conquered Eastern territories with "Nordic" blood.

▼ *Troops of the Totenkopf Division on their way east to take part in the forthcoming attack on the Soviet Union.*

1941

Hitler launched his invasion of the Soviet Union, and thus fulfilled his ideological dream of locking horns with the home of Bolshevism and Jewry. At first the German armies carried all before them, but as the campaign continued, his armies seemed to be swallowed up by the endless Russian terrain. The panzers began to falter, and the attack on Moscow in December failed. Then came the Red Army counterattack; for the first time in the war, the *Wehrmacht* was on the defensive.

GERMANY, *TREATIES*
Germany signs trade and frontier pacts with the Soviet Union, to import from the Soviets essential commodities, such as rubber and petroleum.

NORTH AFRICA, *GERMANY*
The *Afrika Korps* is formed for the Libyan campaign. Italy's forces under the command of Marshal Rodolfo Grazziano have suffered a series of heavy defeats at the hands of the British in Cyrenaica. Indeed, the remaining Italian troops are in no condition to defend Mussolini's remaining North African possessions, and Hitler is therefore forced to come to the aid of his ally.

EASTERN FRONT, *BULGARIA*
Hitler, pre-empting a suspected Soviet move, occupies Bulgaria from his Romanian bases.

NORTH AFRICA, *TRIPOLI*
Hitler issues Führer Directive No 22 to create a special force: the 5th Light Division, later renamed 21st Panzer Division, as the nucleus of an *Afrika Korps* under the command of General Erwin Rommel, which lands at Tripoli in Libya.

◀ The cuff band of Rommel's **Afrika Korps**, which arrived in North Africa in February 1941.

▼ The Focke Wulf Fw 200 Condor long-range bomber, which operated against Allied ships in the Atlantic.

MARCH 6

GERMANY, *IDEOLOGY*

Reichsführer-SS Himmler visits the Austrian concentration camp at Mauthausen in which the "scum of mankind were exploited for the good of the great folk community by breaking stones and baking bricks so that the Führer can erect his grand buildings". Himmler views the prisoners, already weakened by undernourishment and exploitation, who negotiate the *Totensteige*, where in cold or heat in a continuous column five prisoners wide, they carry stones up 148 steps hour after hour, day after day, year after year. They carry the stones until they die, or are killed by their guards.

MARCH 17

SEA WAR, *ATLANTIC*

HMS *Vanoc* locates *U-100* on the surface with radar, the first success with the Type 286 radar, which leads to the sinking of

▲ The Afrika Korps *arrives at the port of Tripoli in February, just in time to reverse Axis fortunes in North Africa.*

FEBRUARY 4

AIR WAR, *ATLANTIC*

Some 40 Focke Wulf Fw 200 Condor long-range bombers come under the direct control of the U-boat arm, to be used for reconnaissance purposes in the Atlantic.

FEBRUARY 25

SEA WAR, *GERMAN NAVY*

The battleship *Tirpitz* is commissioned.

MARCH 2

EASTERN FRONT, *BULGARIA*

German troops march into Bulgaria. To control the Balkans, Hitler persuades

Yugoslavia to join the Axis treaty. Hitler makes his intentions clear to the German Army by briefing 250 senior officers on his plans for war against the Soviet Union.

GERMANY, *IDEOLOGY*

Some 5000 ethnic Germans from Bukovina were presented with Reich citizenship in Breslau by *Reichsführer-SS* Himmler. Such gestures are the physical manifestation of the Nazis' racial purity theories.

MARCH 3

GREAT BRITAIN, *ESPIONAGE*

The British capture an "Enigma"-type cipher machine from an E-boat.

▼ *Otto Kretschmer, the commander of U-100, which was sunk in March.*

▲ *German panzers enter the Greek port of Thessalonika in April. Greece's mountains did not hinder the panzers.*

▲ *Yugoslav troops surrender to German forces during the invasion. Belgrade was bombed heavily.*

▼ *The Waffen-SS in Greece. The standing figure is "Sepp" Dietrich, commander of the Leibstandarte Division.*

U-100, commanded by Joachim Schepke, and *U-99*, commanded by Otto Kretschmer.

APRIL 6
BALKANS, *YUGOSLAVIA AND GREECE*

Invasion and occupation of Yugoslavia and Greece by Germany. Hungarian troops also attack Yugoslavia, and its government surrenders. German troops occupy Greece, brushing aside the small British Army. Germany has been forced into the Balkans by events inside Yugoslavia. Following the *Anschluss* of 1938, the Yugoslav Government attempted to sustain a position of

independence while being pressured to ally itself ever more closely with Germany. When, on March 25, 1941, the government succumbed to Axis pressure and signed the Tripartite Pact, the news was greeted by demonstrations of protest, especially in Belgrade. On March 27 the regency was replaced in a coup headed by senior officers, who declared the majority of Prince Peter and repudiated the pact. Belgrade was immediately bombarded and

the country invaded by Germany and its allies. Resistance collapsed with surprising speed in view of the size, reputation, and equipment of the Yugoslav Army. On April 14 the king and government fled to Athens.

NORTH AFRICA, *LIBYA*

With three reinforced Italian Army corps and the German 15th Panzer Division, Rommel moves on through Libya towards Egypt, bypassing Tobruk, where the 1st Australian Division holds him off and is left in a state of siege.

APRIL 23

SEA WAR, *ATLANTIC*

The German auxiliary cruiser Thor, commanded by *Kapitän zur See* Otto Kähler, arrives in the Bay of Biscay after a successful cruise in the South Atlantic.

APRIL 27

BALKANS, *GREECE*

The advance guard of the *Leibstandarte-SS Adolf Hitler* crosses the gulf of Corinth in requisitioned Greek fishing boats. German troops occupy Athens as Commonwealth troops are evacuated to the island of Crete. The Greeks have lost over 15,000 men in the campaign; German losses are 1518.

▲ *One of Rommel's Panzer III tanks advancing east towards Egypt during the Afrika Korps' first offensive.*

▼ *An early German casualty in North Africa: the grave of an Afrika Korps soldier killed on April 26, 1941.*

APRIL 30

SEA WAR, *ATLANTIC*

The German auxiliary cruiser *Thor* arrives in Hamburg from France after 329 days at sea.

MAY

GERMANY, *IDEOLOGY*

Heydrich prepares the SS for its part in the forthcoming war in the Soviet Union, instructing the leaders of the *Einsatz-gruppen* (Special Task Force) on their work of murdering all Jews, "Asiatics", communist officials, intellectuals, professionals and gypsies.

MAY 7

SEA WAR, *ATLANTIC*

The German floating weather station *Munchen* is sunk by a British cruiser force. Men from the destroyer HMS *Somali* manage to get aboard her before she goes down. In the event, they capture valuable radio equipment and a naval cipher machine of the "Enigma" type, plus various important related documents.

MAY 8

SEA WAR, *ATLANTIC*

The auxiliary cruiser *Pinguin* is sunk.

KEY PERSONALITY

Hess

He served in World War I in the same regiment as Hitler. After the war he served in the *Freikorps*. He was seduced by the oratory of Hitler and joined the NSDAP in 1920. He marched in the 1923 *Putsch* and was imprisoned at Landsberg with Hitler. By 1932 he had been appointed chairman of the central political commission of the party. With Hitler coming to power, Hess became Deputy Leader, and in June 1933 Reich Minister without portfolio. In 1935 Hess was a selector of all senior Nazi officials. By 1939 his great days had been eclipsed by the generals and admirals on one hand and Göring and Himmler on the other. He felt himself estranged from Hitler and excluded from the centre of the web. It was his loyalty to Hitler which led to his flight to Britain in May 1941 with the intention of recovering his position with Hitler. He was incarcerated for the rest of his life, and committed suicide in 1987.

MAY 10

SEA WAR, *ATLANTIC*
U-110, commanded by Fritz Julius Lemp, is captured by British forces. Valuable secret material falls into British hands, including a working model of the secret cipher machine set up with the code of the day.

NAZI PARTY, *POLITICS*
Rudolf Hess flies to Great Britain. Hess believes a diplomatic coup is possible if he can have an audience with George VI, whom he might persuade to dismiss Churchill. Peace could then be implemented between the two countries and they could act in concert against a common enemy: the Soviet Union. The piloting of the aircraft and the final roll to allow his parachute descent was masterful. On landing he gave his name as Captain Horn and asked to be escorted to the Duke of Hamilton, whom he had met at the 1936 Berlin Olympic Games. The British, however, immediately imprison Hess.

MAY 19

SEA WAR, *ATLANTIC*
The *Prinz Eugen* and *Bismarck* leave Gotenhafen for the *Bismarck*'s first and only operational cruise.

MAY 20

BALKANS, *CRETE*
German paratroopers land on Crete and, despite heavy casualties, conquer the island in a daring air assault.

MAY 21

SS, *WAFFEN-SS*
Reichsführer-SS Himmler attends the oath-taking ceremony of the Norwegian SS in Norway, where he addresses the assembled volunteers: "The formation of the *Norges* SS is a new and important step forward for the Germanic community. The honour of its foundation will fall upon Norway."

▼ *The cuff band worn by those who took part in the airborne assault on Crete, where one in four paratroopers died.*

MAY 24

SEA WAR, *ATLANTIC*
The British battlecruiser HMS *Hood* is sunk by the *Bismarck*.

MAY 27

SEA WAR, *ATLANTIC*
The *Bismarck* is sunk during a battle with Royal Navy ships, with the Fleet Commander and the entire Fleet Command on board.

BALKANS, *GREECE*
"Sepp" Dietrich accepts the surrender of Greek General Tsolakaglu's Centre and Epirus Armies.

JUNE 4

SEA WAR, *ATLANTIC*
The German tanker *Gedania* is abandoned and scuttled when the British auxiliary cruiser *Marsdale* appears. Royal Navy personnel manage to get on board before the tanker sinks and capture secret material relating to the "Enigma" cipher machine.

JUNE 22

EASTERN FRONT, *SOVIET UNION*
Operation Barbarossa, the German invasion of the Soviet Union, begins. The "Commissar Order" is issued to the army, under the signature of Hitler's chief of staff, Keitel. It states that Red Army political commissars are to be killed on capture. General orders are addressed to all troops to be ruthless against the "Bolshevik" Russians. Despite reports from his own intelligence agents and from the British that an attack is imminent, Stalin refuses to believe them. The Russian news agency TASS issues a statement seven days before the invasion: "To counter absurd rumours, responsible bodies in Moscow judge it necessary to declare that these rumours are sheer propaganda put out by the forces opposed to the USSR and Germany, attempting to spread and intensify the war."
Accompanying German forces are Romanian, Finnish, Hungarian and Slovak troops. Italian and volunteer Spanish and French troops were to follow. The Russian command is taken by surprise, in spite of warnings from British intelligence and their own agents in Germany, the *Rote Kapella*.

JUNE 15

SEA WAR, *ATLANTIC*
The German supply ship *Lothringen* is captured by the British cruiser *Dunedin*. Once again, secret documents fall into British hands. By this time, Great Britain has captured vital documents and machinery for deciphering German secret codes, which is unknown to the Germans.

▲ *U-boats in the Atlantic. Dönitz forbade attacks on US warships in order not to provoke Washington.*

▼ *German troops in June 1941 during the opening phase of Operation Barbarossa.*

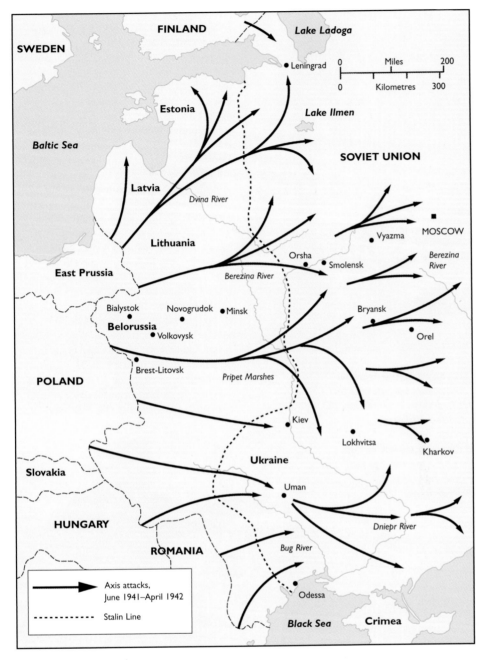

Axis attacks,
June 1941–April 1942

---------- Stalin Line

was the most successful commander, but he commanded two different boats and *U-48* was responsible for sinking more tonnage than either of the two. During this month, U-boat command began to suspect that some Allied convoys were being deliberately routed around the German submarine "wolf packs".

JUNE 23

GERMANY, *MEDIA*
Dr Goebbels announces on the radio at 05:30 hours the invasion of the Soviet Union.

JUNE 30

SEA WAR, *ESPIONAGE*
The German floating weather station *Launenburg* sinks in the North Atlantic. Men from the British destroyer HMS *Tartar* manage to get on board before she goes down and capture yet more top-secret German documents.

JULY

EASTERN FRONT, *SOVIET UNION*
Göring orders Heydrich to clear the occupied lands in the Soviet Union of Jews. The SS *Einsatzgruppen* follow the German armies according to plan, and begin executing Jews and "sub-humans". German troops enter the Ukraine. By the end of the month the German Army has occupied Latvia, the River Dnieper is reached and Smolensk captured. Nearly 750,000 prisoners are taken. Most will die as slave labourers or starve to death.

◄ *During the first weeks of Barbarossa the Germans experienced phenomenal success in the Soviet Union.*

▼ *Waffen-SS soldiers in the Soviet Union during Barbarossa. Himmler's racial warriors fought a savage war in Russia.*

The British immediately declare themselves as allies of the Russians.
SEA WAR, *ATLANTIC*
An incident occurs between the USS *Texas* and *U-203*, commanded by Rolf Mötzelburg. As a result, Dönitz forbids German submarines attacking American warships, even if they appear inside the blockade area around the British Isles.

U-48, the most successful U-boat of the war, returns to port from her last operational war cruise. She is subsequently used for training.

It has been stated that *U-99* was the most successful U-boat of the war; however, this is not so. Her commander, Otto Kretschmer,

▲ *German troops on the outskirts of Uman in August 1941. Entire Soviet armies were being destroyed by the Wehrmacht.*

JULY 5

SEA WAR, *ARCTIC*
U-boats start to operate in the Arctic seas.

AUGUST

EASTERN FRONT, *SOVIET UNION*
The German advance in the East continues. Estonia is occupied and incorporated into a new territory, subject to the Third Reich, called *Ostland*. The British and Soviets move into Iran to secure Russia's southern flank and prevent any German linkup in the Middle East.

AUGUST 23

SEA WAR, *ATLANTIC*
The German auxiliary cruiser *Orion* returns to France after a successful voyage that lasted 511 days.

AUGUST 28

SEA WAR, *ATLANTIC*
British forces capture the *U-571* which later becomes HMS *Graph*.

▶ *A Red Army soldier captured during Barbarossa. He and his comrades were regarded by his captors as "sub-human".*

SEPTEMBER 1

GERMANY, *LEGAL*
Yellow star becomes compulsory attire for Jews living in Germany. The general deportation of German Jews to concentration camps starts.

SEPTEMBER 3

NAZI PARTY, *PERSONALITIES*
Heydrich, perhaps in reward for his efforts, certainly in recognition of his considerable talents, is appointed to succeed Neurath as Protector of Bohemia and Moravia. His administration of the territory is masterful. It begins in brutality, but within months adroitly combines stick and carrot.

Czech industrial production began to rise. Fuelled with this, Heydrich issued additional ration cards on a productivity basis. The message was unequivocal: collaborate and prosper, or resist and perish. Heydrich was shown the crown jewels of Czechoslovakia

by President Hacha, who told him of an intriguing legend that surrounded them. It is said that any person not the true heir who put the crown on his head is sure to die. It is said that he laughed and tried it on.

SEPTEMBER 19

EASTERN FRONT, *UKRAINE*
German troops take Kiev, having already occupied most of the Ukraine and begin siege of Leningrad. The Shah of Iran is

▲ *An ammunition ship explodes en route to the Soviet Union as part of American and British aid to Stalin.*

▶ *Reinhard Heydrich, the new Protector of Bohemia and Moravia. His reign would be characterized by brutality and cleverness.*

▼ *The hazardous Arctic convoy routes, which were prey to German air and naval attack from bases in Norway.*

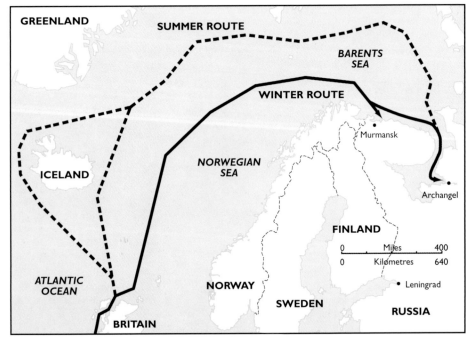

forced to abdicate and two zones of control, Soviet and British, are established in Iran. The specially equipped and trained 90th Light Division reinforces the *Afrika Korps*. U-boats experience difficulties in finding and attacking enemy convoys.

OCTOBER 1

EASTERN FRONT, *SOVIET UNION*

The German Army begins Operation Typhoon, the offensive against Moscow. Meanwhile, Hitler in Berlin speaks to the German public and describes the extent of his victory: 2.5 million prisoners, 22,000 guns captured, 18,000 tanks destroyed and 145,000 Russian aircraft eliminated. After such losses he may wonder why the Red Army is still in existence.

OCTOBER 11

SS, *WAFFEN-SS*

Dutch volunteers join in the SS parade in The Hague before leaving for training in eastern Prussia. German stupidity, broken promises and contempt for the nationals of countries they had defeated has adversely affected recruitment, though, and many volunteers return home disillusioned. This is an inauspicious beginning for Himmler's brotherhood of "Nordic" nations.

NOVEMBER 14

SEA WAR, *MEDITERRANEAN*

The British aircraft carrier HMS *Ark Royal* is sunk by *U-81* commanded by *Kapitänleutnant* Friedrich Guggenberger.

NOVEMBER 15

SEA WAR, *GERMAN NAVY*

U-459, the first purpose-built supply submarine, is commissioned by *Korvettenkapitän* Georg von Wilamowitz-Möllendorf.

NOVEMBER 19

SEA WAR, *PACIFIC*

The German auxiliary cruiser *Kormoran*, after a successful career in the South Atlantic and the Indian Ocean that lasted 350 days at sea, falls in with the Australian cruiser HMAS *Sydney*. Apparently the cruiser was taken in by the disguised raider's pretence of being an innocent Dutch freighter and came too close. The concealed guns quickly inflicted serious damage and a torpedo hit damaged the *Sydney* seriously. The cruiser replied effectively with her guns, but both ships caught fire and were heavily damaged. The *Sydney* drifted away and was never seen again, and the *Kormoran* sank. Nothing was

▲ *A German Jew complete with yellow Star of David, the wearing of which was made compulsory in September.*

known about the action until months later, when a few of the *Kormoran*'s survivors were found on a South Pacific island. It was the only case of a mercantile auxiliary cruiser sinking a regular warship of any size during the war.

NOVEMBER 22

SEA WAR, *ATLANTIC*

The German auxiliary cruiser *Atlantis*, after being at sea for 622 days and sailing over 160,000 km (100,000 miles), is intercepted and sunk by HMS *Devonshire*.

NOVEMBER 27

EASTERN FRONT, *MOSCOW*

The German drive towards Moscow begins to falter. In November, a new Hitler directive ordered the resumption of the Moscow drive. And so the Germans pushed on. The plan this time was for Guderian's Second Panzer Army to take Tula, then move north and loop around behind Moscow. In the north the Ninth Army and the Third Panzer Army would cross the Moscow-Volga canal and swing south for Moscow. In the centre, the Fourth Army and the Fourth

centre north of Moscow, littering the road to the west for 40km (25 miles) with the charred and frozen remnants of tanks and men from two panzer divisions. On that day the Siberians killed 3000 German soldiers. South of Moscow, the Red Army's cavalry corps crossed frozen rivers. Tanks pulled armoured sleds packed with more infantry. Soldiers fought on the run, carrying sacks of dry bread crusts and raw vegetables, and feeding their horses with straw stripped from thatched roofs. The Red Army forced

▲ *The Kriegsmarine suffered mounting U-boat losses in 1941, and the Bismarck (above), pride of the fleet, was sunk.*

▶ *A case study in folly: the Reichstag salutes Hitler following his unnecessary declaration of war on the United States.*

Panzer Group would make a frontal attack on the city. It was an ambitious plan for German troops who were hungry and sick with fatigue. The offensive is slowed by heavy rains then halted by severe frost, although German tanks eventually reach to within 32km (20 miles) of Moscow. The intense cold halts the Germans, who are not equipped for a winter campaign.

DECEMBER 5

EASTERN FRONT, *SOVIET UNION*

To the surprise of the German General staff and the bewilderment of the frontline

troops, Russian counterattacks come through the snow using reserves fresh from training in Siberia and signalling the commencement of the Soviet Union's effort to drive the German Army from the outskirts of Moscow. In the days that were to follow, the Siberians distinguished themselves. Kept warm by sheepskin coats, as well as quilted pants, fur hats and felt boots, they could travel almost silently over the snow and wait patiently for hours in snow before launching an attack at night.

The Siberians broke through on December 14 near Klin, a transportation

▼ *The British aircraft carrier* Ark Royal *photographed just before she sank after being torpedoed.*

the Germans back 160–240km (100–150 miles) before stabilizing the line.

Stalin, gambling that Japan would not attack Russia in the East, moved the Siberians across Asia to the European theatre. In the south Rundstedt was forced to evacuate Rostov, which he had just taken. Shocked by the news of his first major military setback ever, Hitler dismissed Brauchitsch and assumes his role. Other army commanders are dismissed, including Rundstedt and Guderian.

DECEMBER 7

PACIFIC, *PEARL HARBOR*
The Japanese attack Pearl Harbor and part of the US Pacific Fleet is destroyed.

DECEMBER 11

GERMANY AND ITALY, *TREATIES*
Germany and Italy declare war on the United States, an absurd gesture of solidarity with Japan which is to have significant consequences for Germany.

DECEMBER 14

SEA WAR, *ATLANTIC*
A dramatic and very significant convoy

▼ *German troops trudge through the snow as they retreat from Moscow. Suddenly the Supermen appeared fallible.*

▲ *Red Army soldiers escort Germans into captivity during the Red Army's counteroffensive of December 1941.*

battle takes place in the Atlantic Ocean. Swordfish aircraft from the British escort carrier *Audacity* succeed in keeping U-boats away from convoy HX76. *U-751*, commanded by *Korvettenkapitän* Gerhard Bigalk, manages to sink the *Audacity* after a ferocious battle. However, Dönitz records in his war diary: "The risk of being sunk is greater than the possible success. The presence of aircraft make 'wolf pack' tactics impossible." U-boat High Command now issues standing directives to U-boat commanders telling them to make the location and destruction of aircraft carriers their prime objective.

1942

This year marked the high point of the Third Reich. Hitler's armies were at the gates of Cairo and were on the Volga in the Caucasus. However, two military defeats turned the tide of war against Germany. In North Africa Rommel was decisively defeated at El Alamein, while at Stalingrad Hitler refused to allow the Sixth Army to withdraw from the city when faced by encirclement. The Third Reich was suddenly on the defensive.

▲ *Adolf Eichmann, head of the Gestapo's "Jewish Evacuation Department" and organizer of the "Final Solution".*

JANUARY 1

POLITICS, *ALLIES*
"United Nations" conference in Washington, Britain, USA and Soviet Russia agree on no separate peace with Germany.

JANUARY 20

GERMANY, *ANTI-SEMITISM*
Reinhard Heydrich hosts a conference of Nazi Party and government officials in the SS RHSA headquarters at Wannsee, a Berlin suburb. The meeting is chaired by Heydrich and attended by 15 SS and government officials, including Stukart, Heinrich Müller, Adolf Eichmann, head of the "Jewish Evacuation Department" of the Gestapo, and Freisler.

In July 1941, Heydrich had been appointed the officer in charge of planning the "Final Solution" of the Jewish "problem". In the early years of the Nazi regime, they promoted the idea of achieving Aryan racial purity. They decided that undesirables – Slavs, Gypsies, homosexuals, and the handicapped and mentally ill – were to be disposed of. But the chief target of the regime's campaign was the Jewish population of Germany; later, of all Europe. A policy of consistent persecution was

▼ *Afrika Korps officers watch an artillery bombardment of the garrison of Tobruk, which fell to Rommel in June.*

▲ **Afrika Korps** *infantry and armour on the advance in Libya during Rommel's drive towards the Egyptian frontier.*

followed during the 1930s, but a more ambitious programme was crafted under the cover of the war. Hitler announced that about 11 million European Jews yet remained to be dealt with. He had decided that a "Final Solution" to the Jewish problem must be implemented while the war was going on.

The Wannsee Conference, as it was known, lasted only a few hours, and proposed the "Final Solution". The idea of mass deportation was ruled out as impractical, considering the ongoing war. Forced sterilization was discussed, but no decision was made at the conference. But as a result of it, directives were sent to move Jews to the East as part of the "territorial solution". No doubt was left that this meant the physical destruction of all Jews, accelerating the process that had already started. The *Einsatzgruppen* had already been in action for six months and the first extermination camp, at Chelmno, was by then in operation. The conference decided that the best policy was to round up the Jews from all parts of Europe and send them eastward to work in labour gangs. Hard enough work, it was believed, would result in significant loss of life. Within a few weeks the first poison gas chambers in concentration camps were built in Poland.

▲ *A German E-boat badge. These vessels accompanied German warships during the so-called "Channel Dash" in February.*

Responsibility for carrying out the policy of extermination was given to *Reichsführer-SS* Heinrich Himmler. The conference gave Eichmann the necessary authority for his actions in the various ministries, and 30 copies of the conference records were distributed to them. At no point was killing mentioned. Recipients were expected to understand the meaning of "final solution" and "deportation to the East". The policy of extermination went forward until the end of the war. Accurate numbers are impossible to obtain, but the estimates run as high as 15 million people, including six million Jews. They were liquidated in the camps or by mass executions in isolated places.

JANUARY 21

NORTH AFRICA, *LIBYA*

Rommel, having retreated, allowed the British Eighth Army into Libya again. Two Australian divisions are moved from Egypt to the Pacific theatre of war to hold Japanese advances, while Rommel receives reinforcements from Germany. Rommel then attacks and smashes the British armour. Benghazi falls by the 29th.

FEBRUARY 4

NORTH AFRICA, *LIBYA*

Rommel again nears Tobruk, though his lines of communications are stretched.

▲ The German Wound Badge, which was awarded to soldiers, and, on the insistence of Goebbels, later civilians hurt in air raids.

FEBRUARY 11

SEA WAR, *ENGLISH CHANNEL*
The start of the "Channel Dash". The *Gneisenau*, *Scharnhorst* and *Prinz Eugen* sail through the English Channel from Brest in France to Germany and Norway. This is a major embarrassment for the Royal Navy and Royal Air Force (RAF), and a great propaganda victory for the *Kriegsmarine*.

FEBRUARY 26

SEA WAR, *ENGLISH CHANNEL*
The *Gneisenau* is put out of action by bomb damage, but manages to make her way to Kiel.

◀ The Funeral Pillow of Reinhard Heydrich showing his various awards, during his funeral in Berlin.

▼ In commemoration of Heydrich, the 11th SS Gebirgsjäger Regiment was formed. This is the unit's cuff band.

Reinhard Heydrich

▶ *The German Order, the Party's highest decoration. Hitler pinned the medal on Heydrich's Funeral Pillow.*

▲ *The coffin of Reinhard Heydrich, draped in the swastika flag, at his funeral in Berlin, June 8, 1942.*

MARCH 13

SEA WAR, *ATLANTIC*
The German auxiliary cruiser *Michel* passes through the Strait of Dover on the outward voyage of her first operational cruise.

APRIL 4

SEA WAR, *BALTIC*
The *Gneisenau* is moved to Gotenhafen.

APRIL 24

SEA WAR, *KRIEGSMARINE*
The motor torpedo-boats, which previously had been under the jurisdiction of the Flag Officer for Destroyers, are given their own autonomous command under *Kapitän zur See* Rudolf Petersen.

MAY 8

EASTERN FRONT, *CRIMEA*
Manstein's army enters the Crimea and besieges Sevastopol, which falls in July.

Satisfied with this, Hitler moves Manstein north to tackle the siege of Leningrad, which has been going on since September 1941. Bock's Army Group South defeats Russian tank forces in the Ukraine and takes Kursk, but when Bock pauses in his attack on Voronezh, Hitler dismisses him.

MAY 12

SEA WAR, *BALTIC*
The *Stier* leaves Kiel on her first war cruise as an auxiliary cruiser.

MAY 26

NORTH AFRICA, *LIBYA*
Rommel's *Afrika Korps* outflanks the British and attacks towards Tobruk, and although delayed by Free French outpost at Bir Hacheim, takes the offensive, driving British out of Libya.

AIR WAR, *GERMANY*
British air raids on German cities intensify.

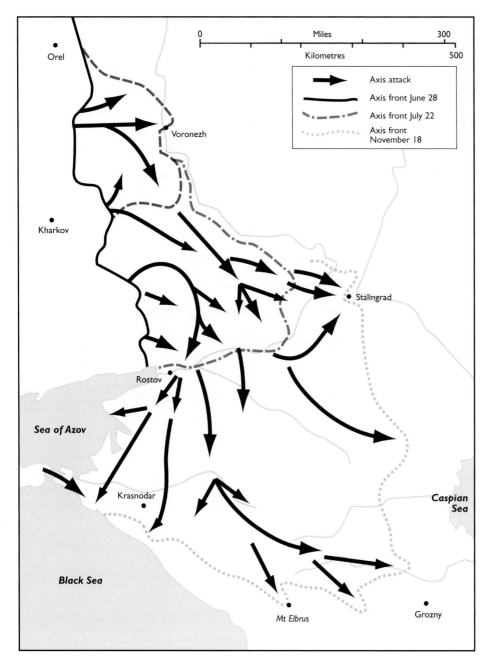

▲ *German Army soldiers hear the Führer's words on the eve of their summer offensive on the Eastern Front.*

MAY 27

CZECHOSLOVAKIA, *RESISTANCE*

A plan, implemented in London for the assassination of Heydrich, is carried out by British-trained Czech assassins.

This decision has always caused speculation, as he was the only Nazi leader thus targeted. In late spring of 1942, a section of Czech soldiers flew from England and were dropped outside Prague. Heydrich, possibly through bravado, rode in an open-topped, unprotected car on his way from his residence to the palace. The assassination team struck during the journey. His car was machine-gunned on the Kirchmayer Boulevard. Heydrich was

▲ *The German 1942 summer offensive in the East was initially very successful, but the Soviets were trading space for time.*

injured and drew his pistol. Then the Czech Sten gun jammed. Heydrich was about to pursue the assassin when a grenade, thrown by another member, Kubis, exploded, impregnating him with horsehair stuffing and pieces of metal springs from the car seat. At 21:10 hours that evening, Karl Hermann Frank, former deputy leader of the Sudeten German Party, Secretary of State and Chief of Police in Bohemia and Moravia under Heydrich, was ordered by Himmler via telegram to arrest 10,000

hostages from amongst the Czech intelligentsia and to shoot 100 of the most important that same night.

JUNE 4

CZECHOSLOVAKIA, *RESISTANCE*

Heydrich dies from septicemia – caused by foreign bodies – in Prague at the Bulov hospital. Himmler's first act after he has recovered from the shock of Heydrich's death is to locate the key to the safe in which Heydrich kept his "personal" files.

Heydrich's coffin lay in state in the main courtyard of Hradcany Castle and the people of Prague filed by in resemblance of homage, some giving the Nazi salute.

JUNE 8

NAZI PARTY, *PERSONALITIES*

At 15:00 hours, Heydrich's coffin is carried into the courtyard of the Reich Chancellery for the state funeral. Hitler and 600 of Germany's leading officials and industrialists attend to pay homage to him. In addition, there is evidence that the Czech puppet government, headed by President Emil Hácha and his staff, was supporting the Nazi attitude that a great

crime had been committed when Heydrich was killed. Hitler bestows upon him the German Order, the highest party and state award. It is well known that Heydrich kept files on all the leading Nazis, even on Hitler himself, and many are relieved to see him dead. However 50,000 Czech workers march in protest in Prague on the day of the funeral, angry about the assassination. Heydrich is buried with full military honours at the Invalidenfriedhof cemetery.

JUNE 10

CZECHOSLOVAKIA, *ATROCITIES*

Karl Frank, Heydrich's deputy, immediately threatens reprisals unless the assassins are found. Although there is very little evidence to support his assumption, Frank decides that Lidice should be punished for having harboured the assassins. Hitler orders that this mining village be "wiped from the face of the earth" in retaliation.

During the night of 9/10 June, SS troops surrounded Lidice and at 02:00 hours the

▼ As they head east once more, the morale of these Germans is high. The easy advance was like a repeat of Barbarossa.

151

villagers were woken and driven to the main square. The men were separated from the women and children. They were told to take food to last for three days and any valuables if they so wished. This was for an "inspection" they were told, and then they would be returned. The women and children were taken to the schoolhouse and the men to the farm of the Horak family. At the school there were two SS men with two suitcases where they were told to deposit their valuables. Then they assembled in the classroom and were checked against their police identity cards to ensure all were present. Trucks to the city of Kladno then transported the women

▲ British infantry capture one of Rommel's Panzer IIIs near El Alamein in July 1942.

▶ Rommel near El Alamein. Though he was near Alexandria, his supply lines were long and his troops were exhausted.

▶ Field Marshal Wilhelm List commanded an army group during the German offensive into the Caucasus.

and children. Some 197 men were killed and the women and children were sent to concentration camps. On June 12 it was announced that the village of Lidice had been destroyed. The village was then bulldozed and it took volunteers almost a year to raze it completely.

JUNE 18

CZECHOSLOVAKIA, *RESISTANCE*

The Czech Orthodox Church of Saints Cyril and Methodius in Prague is where the Czech assassins of Heydrich and their helpers have taken sanctuary. The chaplain Vladimir Petrek hid them in the crypt under the floor. Here, members of the Czech Fire Brigade have had to pump water into the crypt in an attempt to flush out their countrymen after they had been engaged in a heroic battle against SS units. The remaining parachutists take their own lives with their last rounds of ammunition.

JUNE 21

NORTH AFRICA, *LIBYA*
The British retreat into Egypt, losing Tobruk to the *Afrika Korps* following an intense battle to the south of the port. Rommel is promoted to field marshal.

▶ *The aftermath of the Dieppe raid: British prisoners are led away into captivity. It was a total disaster.*

JULY 1

SEA WAR, *BALTIC*
The battlecruiser *Gneisenau* is decommissioned.

JULY 4

EASTERN FRONT, *CRIMEA*
The Germans take Sevastopol.

JULY 13

EASTERN FRONT, *UKRAINE*
Hitler moves to his Ukraine headquarters at Vinnitsa, called "Werewolf", to supervise the the summer offensive and the Sixth Army's advance on Stalingrad and the Caucasus. The Germans make great initial advances

AUGUST 11

SEA WAR, *ATLANTIC*
The British aircraft carrier HMS *Eagle* is sunk by *U-73*, commanded by *Kapitänleutnant* Helmuth Rosenbaum.

AUGUST 17

AIR WAR, *FRANCE*
18 American Boeing B-17E "Flying Fortresses", personally led by General Ira Eaker, bomb Rouen-Sotteville, France, and return to England without loss. It is the modest beginning of the United States Army Air Force's (USAAF's) daylight bombing operations in Europe. The USAAF under its Commanding General H.H.

The *Africa Korps* reaches El Alamein in Egypt, within 96km (60 miles) of the Nile Delta. The *Afrika Korps* now has three divisions with supporting units, and under Rommel are three Italian corps, including élite Italian armoured forces. The British have divisions from South Africa, India, New Zealand and Australia. Rommel is at the end of a very long and vulnerable supply line. The British, on the other hand, are receiving fresh supplies on a daily basis.

POLAND, *FINAL SOLUTION*
Mass gassings begin at Auschwitz concentration camp in Poland.

▶ *Men of the Sixth Army near Stalingrad in August 1942. During this offensive the Red Army yielded space for time.*

Arnold had until now favoured daylight attacks by well-armed bombers. The rationale of the policy was that they could deliver higher degrees of industrial damage and lower civilian casualties than the RAF's night attacks. They were convinced that unescorted daylight bombing could be successful if the bombers were sufficiently well armed.

The American four-engine bombers "bristled" with .50-calibre heavy machine guns and flew in a formation designed for mutual defence and maximum combined firepower. Although the Rouen raid was insignificant in itself, it argued ill for the future of the *Luftwaffe* in the West.

AUGUST 19

WESTERN FRONT, *FRANCE*

5000 Canadian and 1000 British troops raid Dieppe in France as part of a "reconnaissance in force". It is a total disaster, with almost 4000 men being captured or killed.

GERMANY, *ESPIONAGE*

The *Rote Kapelle* communist spy network in Germany is uncovered by the *Abwehr*.

SEPTEMBER 1

EASTERN FRONT, *CAUCASUS*

German troops enter Stalingrad and reach the Elbruz Mountains in the Caucasus. Hitler had, however, hoped to reach the oilfields at Baku. He dismisses Field Marshal List for not advancing fast enough. At "Werewolf" there are arguments between Hitler and his military advisors, who claim

▲*American B-17 bombers in the skies over Germany. US daylight raids resulted in heavy losses in bombers.*

that his strategy has stretched out his forces too widely. When General Halder, the chief of the army general staff, warns that the Soviets with growing strength could soon counterattack, he too is dismissed and eventually sent to the concentration camp at Dachau. Paulus' Sixth Army takes most of Stalingrad and with control of the air seems to be on the way to break through the town to the river. But the Red Army holds on, its backs to the river, artillery supporting it from the other bank.

NORTH AFRICA, *EGYPT*

A strengthened British Eighth Army, now commanded by Bernard Montgomery, halts Rommel's offensive at Alam Halfa.

SEPTEMBER 12

SEA WAR, *ATLANTIC*

The liner *Laconia* is torpedoed and sunk by *U156* commanded by *Korvettenkapitän* Werner Hartenstein. More than 1400 of the 2491 men and sailors on boards are drowned, despite Hartenstein's efforts to help the survivors.

SEPTEMBER 27

SEA WAR, *ATLANTIC*

The German auxiliary cruiser *Stier* is scuttled after damage inflicted by action with the American armed freighter *Stephen Hopkins*.

▼ *Cologne Cathedral and its surrounding buildings after a bombing raid. Air raids failed to break German civilian morale, but did hit industry hard.*

SEPTEMBER 28

SEA WAR, *BERLIN*
The German Naval High Command, including leaders of the U-boat arm, meet with Hitler in Berlin to discuss new trends in the Battle of the Atlantic and the deterioration of the U-boat impact on Allied convoys.

OCTOBER 8

SEA WAR, *NORTH SEA*
The German auxiliary cruiser *Komet* leaves Hamburg for her second war cruise, under the command of *Kapitän zur See* Ulrich Brocksien.

OCTOBER 9

SEA WAR, *PACIFIC*
The German auxiliary cruiser *Thor* arrives at Yokohama in Japan at the end of her second cruise.

OCTOBER 14

SEA WAR, *ATLANTIC*
The German auxiliary cruiser *Komet* is torpedoed by a British torpedo boat.
AIR WAR, *GERMANY*
The catastrophic raid by 291 American Boeing B-17E "Flying Fortresses" on Schweinfurt to destroy its ball-bearing factories demonstrated that daylight bombing is bedevilled with practical

▼ **Luftwaffe *personnel direct fighters against Allied bombers. Ground defence of cities was in the hands of the* Gauleiters.**

difficulties. The "Flying Fortresses" are attacked by continuous waves of German fighters, and by the time the American force returned to England, 60 bombers have been shot down and 138 suffer heavy damage. Such a loss rate cannot be sustained.

OCTOBER 23

NORTH AFRICA, *EGYPT*
The British defeat Rommel at El Alamein.

By mid-October the British Eighth Army had 230,000 men and 1230 tanks ready for action, while the German–Italian forces numbered only 80,000 men, with only 210 tanks of comparable quality ready; and in air support the British enjoyed a superiority of 1500 to 350. Allied air and submarine attacks on the Axis supply lines across the Mediterranean, moreover, had prevented Rommel's army from receiving adequate fuel, ammunition, and food; and Rommel was convalescing in Austria.

The British launched their infantry attack at El Alamein, but found the German minefields harder to clear than they had foreseen. Two days later, however, some of those tanks were deploying 9.6km (six miles) beyond the original front. When Rommel, ordered back to Africa by Hitler, reached the front in the evening of October 25, half of the Germans' available armour was already destroyed. Nevertheless, the impetus of the British onslaught was stopped the next day when German antitank guns took a heavy toll of British armour. During the night of October 28,

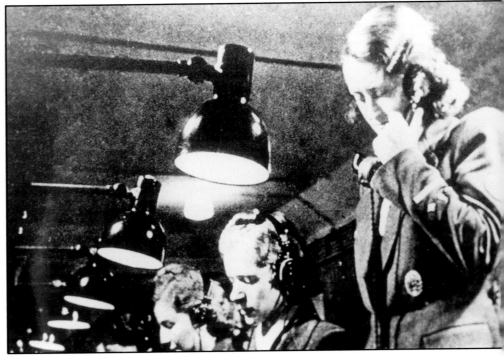

DECISIVE MOMENTS

Stalingrad

During the summer of 1942 the Germans advanced to the suburbs of Stalingrad but failed to take the city itself against a determined defence by the Red Army, despite repeated attacks by the Sixth Army under Friedrich Paulus and part of the Fourth Panzer Army under Ewald von Kleist. By September they reached the city's centre, where they encountered stiff resistance from the Soviet Sixty-Second Army under General Vasily I. Chuikov. The city's Soviet defenders had been driven almost to the Volga by mid-October, but the Germans' supplies were beginning to run low and their tanks were of little value in the constant street fighting.

On November 19 the Soviets launched a counterattack in the form of pincer movements north and south of the city, and by the 23rd they had encircled the Sixth Army and part of the Fourth within Stalingrad. A German attempt to relieve Paulus failed in mid-December. Under orders from Hitler, Paulus continued to fight on, but in early January 1943 he surrendered, and on February 2 the last of his remaining 91,000 troops turned themselves over to the Soviets. The Soviets recovered 250,000 German and Romanian corpses in and around Stalingrad, and total Axis losses are estimated to have been 800,000 dead. Official Russian military historians estimate that 1.1 million Soviet soldiers lost their lives in the campaign.

▶ *Stores are loaded onto one of Göring's Junkers Ju 52 transport aircraft for the relief of the Sixth Army at Stalingrad.*

Montgomery turned the offensive northwards, but this too failed. In the first week of their offensive the British lost four times as many tanks as the Germans but still had 800 available against the latter's remaining 90. Rommel had no choice but to order a withdrawal, or see his *Afrika Korps* destroyed where it stood.

OCTOBER 24

GERMANY, *POLITICS*

Hitler holds a meeting with Marshal Pétain, which gives rise to secret accords known as *Montoir*. Pétain agrees to support Germany in every way short of military involvement: "The Axis Powers and France have an identical interest in seeing the defeat of England as soon as possible." In return for Vichy support, France is to be accorded "the place to which she is entitled" in the new Europe. Pétain possibly has no choice but to pay lip service to Hitler's ambitions. However, the aged Pétain has succeeded at Montoire in keeping France out of the war.

▼ *German heavy artillery in Tunisia in December. The Germans now faced a war on two fronts in North Africa.*

NOVEMBER 8

NORTH AFRICA, *MOROCCO*

Anglo-American troops land in Morocco.

NOVEMBER 9

EASTERN FRONT, *STALINGRAD*

The Russian counterattack at Stalingrad begins. Hitler is in Munich at the annual celebration of the 1923 Beer Hall *Putsch*

when news comes of the counteroffensive that threatens to encircle the Sixth Army. The new chief of the Army general staff, Zeitzler, suggests a withdrawal to the River Don, but Hitler insists that he will not leave the Volga.

NOVEMBER 23

EASTERN FRONT, *STALINGRAD*

The whole of the German Sixth Army, a quarter of a million men, is encircled. If they do not withdraw now, while they still can, they face annihilation. The Germans are forced to eat horses' bones, and as temperatures drop to minus 30 degrees Centigrade the German bread ration, already as low as 100 grammes (4oz) a day, is reduced to just 50 (2oz). The starving German soldiers are forced to slaughter their horses and later still to dig up their frozen carcasses to eat the bones. Despite the desperate situation and the urgent advice of his military commanders,

Hitler refuses to contemplate a withdrawal. However, after General Manstein's attempts to relieve them in December failed, Paulus's men have neither the supplies nor the strength to break through the Soviet lines.

DECEMBER 31

SEA WAR, *ARCTIC*

Battle of the North Cape. Hitler threatens to "throw the surface fleet into the dustbin" as a result of the failure of the German North Norway Naval Squadron to drive home its attack on convoy JW51B.l

EASTERN FRONT, *STALINGRAD*

Göring's *Luftwaffe* fails to drop adequate supplies to the trapped Sixth Army.

▶ *The poor weather, combined with Red Army antiaircraft gun, made the airborne relief operation at Stalingrad a failure.*

1943

The disasters on the Volga and in North Africa threw the Third Reich onto the defensive, while in the Atlantic the U-boats began to lose the war against the convoys. Worse still for the German population, the Allies continued their strategic bombing campaign, bringing death and destruction on a daily basis. And with the German defeat at Kursk in July, Hitler lost all hope of winning the war on the Eastern Front.

JANUARY 1

EASTERN FRONT, *CAUCASUS*
A Red Army offensive retakes Voronezh on the River Don. A Soviet drive might have cut off the *Wehrmacht* in the Caucasus, but the retreat of the Germans from the southeast is well managed and they elude the Soviet net.

JANUARY 30

SEA WAR, *BERLIN*
Grand-Admiral Erich Raeder resigns as Supreme Commander-in-Chief of the *Kriegsmarine* and is replaced by Karl Dönitz.

FEBRUARY 2

EASTERN FRONT, *STALINGRAD*
Paulus surrenders with his army at

Stalingrad and with the 90,000 survivors becomes a prisoner of the Soviets. Hitler is furious: "The man should have shot himself just as the old commanders threw themselves on their swords. That's the last field marshal I shall appoint in this war." From now on, Hitler gives preference to the Waffen-SS over the regular army.

Relying on the original six SS divisions as his élite troops, he allows the Waffen-SS to take in conscripts and double in size. The Red Army now retakes Kursk although the Germans, hoping to begin a spring offensive this year, hold Kharkov and Orel.

GERMANY, *ECONOMY*
Hitler orders Albert Speer, minister of armaments, and Heinz Guderian, inspector

▲ *A haggard Field Marshal Paulus surrenders his remaining troops at Stalingrad to the Red Army.*

general of tank forces, to improve the production and design of tanks. The successful Soviet Yak-9 fighter plane becomes operational.

FEBRUARY 12

HOLLAND, *TECHNOLOGY*
The "Rotterdam Radar", as it was known, falls into German hands after being taken

▼ *Red Army troops in the ruins of Stalingrad in February 1943. This battle cost the Germans their finest field army.*

▲ *Karl Dönitz, the new Grand-Admiral of the Kriegsmarine. After Hitler's death in 1945 he would be Führer for a few days.*

from a crashed British aeroplane near Rotterdam in Holland.

FEBRUARY 14

NORTH AFRICA, *TUNISIA*

Rommel retreats into Tunisia, but then makes a stand at Mareth and launches an attack. He defeats green American units at Kasserine Pass, but lacks the reserves to effect a decisive breakthrough. His attacks eventually run out of momentum and he is forced to retreat. Meanwhile, Montgomery closes in from the southeast.

FEBRUARY 22

GERMANY, *RESISTANCE*

The execution of Hans and Sophie Scholl of the White Rose resistance takes place in Munich. They were found guilty of distributing traitorous literature and beheaded.

MARCH 2

SEA WAR, *PACIFIC*

The German auxiliary cruiser *Michel* arrives at the port of Kobe in Japan to end her first war cruise.

MARCH 13

GERMANY, *RESISTANCE*

The Smolensk Plot, an attempt to assasinate Hitler, was organized by General von Tresckow, a Prussian officer who fought with

▲ *Red Army antiaircarft guns deployed at Stalingrad. Batteries such as this one shot down many Luftwaffe transports.*

▲ *Axis troops retreat following the disaster at Stalingrad, a defeat that put the southern Eastern Front in jeopardy.*

distinction in Poland and France, but who became convinced that Germany would face ruin in the war with Soviet Russia. The plan, involving Gördeler, Tresckow, General Friedrich Olbricht and Fabian von Schlabrendorff, was for Hitler to be enticed to army headquarters in the Smolensk area, where Tresckow was serving, and there murdered. In the event it was decided to place two bombs, disguised in a parcel to look like bottles of brandy, on the Führer's plane. But technical problems with the bombs meant that the conspirators waited in vain for news of the explosion. When Hitler landed safely at Rastenburg the bombs were removed by Schlabrendorff and a new date was fixed, a week later, for another attempt, this time at the memorial day for World War I heroes at the Zeughaus in Berlin.

▼ *German panzers advance to meet American forces at Kasserine Pass, Rommel's last victory in North Africa.*

MARCH 14

EASTERN FRONT, *KHARKOV*

German tanks and infantry enter Kharkov. After two months of bitter fighting, the SS Panzer Corps manages to hold the German line, recapture Kharkov and encircle and destroy part of the Soviet First Guards Army and an army group. But in doing so it has lost 11,500 dead, wounded and missing.

Two of the young Waffen-SS officers that were instrumental in the fighting were Joachim Peiper and Fritz Witt; the latter was to become the youngest general in the German Army. Prisoners of war and the inhabitants of the city were immediately put to work cleaning up the mess and restoring vital services. To commemorate the recapture of the city of Kharkov the Red Square was renamed "Platz der Leibstandarte" in honour of the SS Panzer Corps' exploits.

MARCH 16

SEA WAR, *ATLANTIC*

The start of the largest convoy battle of World War II, with U-boats attacking convoys HX229 and SC122.

MARCH 25

SEA WAR, *ATLANTIC*

The battle for convoy HX231, which lasted until April 8, was the first time since the fighting began that a convoy had managed to cross the Atlantic Ocean and beat off all the attacking U-boats, despite the "air-gap" still being 724km (450 miles) wide.

APRIL 1

SS, *WAFFEN-SS*

The Waffen-SS victors of the battle of Kharkov – Buchner, Jüttner, Kraas, Macher and "Panzer" Meyer – are received by Dr Goebbels in Berlin. At the same time, *Generaloberst* Heinz Guderian visits the SS Panzer Corps' repair shops in the former tractor factory in Kharkov. The Eastern Front has been stabilized.

▲ *The Close Combat Bar, nicknamed the "Eyeball-to-Eyeball" medal, was regarded as the highest German infantry award.*

▼ *A Tiger tank of the Das Reich Division, SS Panzer Corps, west of Kharkov prior to Manstein's attack in March.*

▲ *Fritz Witt, one of the young Waffen-SS officers who distinguished himself in the battle to retake Kharkov.*

▲ *Kharkov's battled-scarred Red Square following the German recapture of the city after Manstein's counterattack.*

▼ *Joachim Peiper was an officer in the élite Leibstandarte Division during the fighting in Kharkov in early 1943.*

APRIL 19

RESISTANCE, *WARSAW*

The Jews of the Warsaw ghetto rise. The defence has been organized by the Jewish Combat Organization.

The Germans expected to liquidate the ghetto in three days. However, the fighters held off attacks for four weeks, some survivors fighting on in the ruins for months. By mid-May the ghetto no longer existed, and around 60,000 Jews had been killed. However, they had inflicted 1300 casualties on their German tormentors

RESISTANCE, *YUGOSLAVIA*

In the Balkans, the Yugoslav partisans grow in strength and increase from 20,000 men at the beginning of the year to nearly 250,000 by the end. They are led by Tito.

MAY 13

NORTH AFRICA, *TUNISIA*

Some 150,000 *Afrika Korps* and Italian troops surrender to Allied forces at Tunis. Only Rommel and a small number escape.

MAY 21

SEA WAR, *PACIFIC*

The German auxiliary cruiser *Michel* leaves Yokohama in Japan after fitting out.

MAY 23

SEA WAR, *ATLANTIC*

U-boat losses rise dramatically, and Grand-Admiral Karl Dönitz admits defeat in the Battle of the Atlantic by withdrawing U-boats from the troubled waters. Up to May there were 40 U-boats in place each day in the Atlantic, but between February and May 91 U-boats have been lost and such losses cannot be sustained. A combination of long-range bombers, radar and submarine hunter groups have made the Atlantic a hazardous place for U-boats.

MAY 29

AIR WAR, *GERMANY*

On a single night, 90 percent of Barmen-Wuppertal is destroyed by the RAF in a bombing raid. The reaction of the Nazi leaders differs greatly. Hitler, despite requests from the *Gauleiters* of bomb-damaged cities, refuses to visit them to see for himself the extent of the damage (in Berlin he even arranges for his chauffeur to avoid bombed areas of the city while driving him around). Göring, who said that if the RAF ever raided Berlin "you can call me Meier", makes fewer and fewer public appearances as civilian casualties mount.

KEY PERSONALITY

Göring

Born in Rosenheim, Bavaria, to minor gentry, he joined an infantry regiment in World War I, but arthritis made him unfit for his duties. By pulling strings he became a fighter pilot and established himself as one of Germany's aces with 22 victories. During 1939 he was made Chairman of the Reich Council for National Defence and named as Hitler's successor. He planned the *Luftwaffe*'s role in the invasions of Poland, Norway and France. In 1940, when Hitler made nine of his generals field marshals, Göring was given the unique rank of *Reichsmarshall*. He had reached the height of his career. Self-indulgence softened him and more ambitious Nazis, Himmler, Bormann, Goebbels and Speer, began to bypass him and reduce his importance. At the Nuremberg trial he was found guilty on all counts and condemned to death. He cheated the hangman by taking cyanide on October 15, 1946.

The RAF is under the command of Arthur Harris. Made an air commodore in 1937, he was named air vice marshal in 1939 and rose to air marshal in 1941 and commander-in-chief of the RAF bomber command in February 1942. As a firm believer in mass raids, Air Marshal Harris has developed the "saturation" technique of mass bombing: concentrating clouds of bombers in a giant raid on a single city, with the object of completely demolishing it, a tactic he used to the end of the war.

▲ *In the Jewish ghettos the inhabitants organized their own services: this is a postage stamp from Litzmannstadt.*

MAY 31

GERMANY, *ECONOMY*
U-boat construction is handed over completely to Albert Speer's Department of Military Armaments.

JUNE 4

SEA WAR, *PACIFIC*
The last German auxiliary cruiser still operational, *Michel*, leaves Yokohama, Japan, for her second cruise under the command of *Kapitän zur See* Günther Gumprich.

JULY 5

EASTERN FRONT, *KURSK*
Unsuccessful German assault on the Soviet salient around the city of Kursk. The salient is a bulge in the Soviet lines that stretches 240km (150 miles) from north to south and protrudes 160 km (100 miles) westwards

▼ *A British warship escorting an Atlantic convoys opens fire against attacking German aircraft, probably Condors.*

successes encouraged them to develop a broad offensive that recovered the nearby city of Orel on August 5 and Kharkov on August 23. The Battle of Kursk was the largest tank battle in history, involving some 6000 tanks, two million troops and 4000 aircraft. It marked the decisive end of the German offensive capability on the Eastern Front and cleared the way for the great Soviet offensives of 1944–45.

JULY 10

MEDITERRANEAN, *SICILY*

Anglo-American forces comprising General Montgomery's British Eighth Army and General George Patton's US Seventh Army

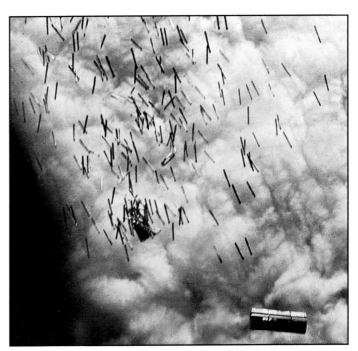

▲ *Jews of the Warsaw ghetto are lined up against a wall prior to being executed.*

◄ *Artillery and mortar rounds pound the Warsaw ghetto as the Jews fight back.*

► *The RAF's "saturation" bombing in action: incendiaries being dropped on Kiel.*

▼ *Some of the tens of thousands of Axis prisoners captured by the Allies in North Africa.*

into the German lines. In an attempt to recover the offensive on the Eastern Front, the Germans launch a surprise attack on the salient from both north and south, hoping to surround and destroy the Soviet forces within the bulge. Hitler orders Kluge in the north and Manstein in the south to attack. The object is to encircle and destroy the Russian armies and then move on to Moscow. The German assault forces consist of almost 50 divisions containing 900,000 troops, including 17 motorized or armoured divisions having 2700 tanks and assault guns.

However, the Soviets had realized the German attack beforehand and had withdrawn their main forces from the obviously threatened positions within the salient. The Germans soon encountered deep antitank defences and minefields, which the Soviets had emplaced in anticipation of the attack. The Germans advanced only 16km (10 miles) into the salient in the north and 48km (30 miles) in the south, losing many of their tanks in the process. At the height of the battle on July 12, the Soviets began to counterattack, having built up by then a preponderance of both troops and tanks. Their subsequent

land on the shores of southern Sicily. The landings are codenamed Operation Husky, and are opposed by General Guzzoni's Sixth Army: 230,000 Italian and 40,000 German soldiers.

JULY 11

ITALY, *POLITICS*

Mussolini is dismissed as Prime Minister of Italy, overthrown and imprisoned. The King regains temporary power and Marshal Badoglio forms a government. Italy is in turmoil, and it looks as if the whole

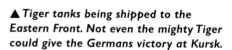

▲ *Tiger tanks being shipped to the Eastern Front. Not even the mighty Tiger could give the Germans victory at Kursk.*

country will fall into Allied hands. Against the advice of his generals, Hitler withdraws the *Leibstandarte* from the fighting at Kursk and rushes it to Italy that day. He justifies the weakening of the line in a vital sector by saying that, "down there I can only accomplish something with élite formations that are politically close to Fascism. If it weren't for that I could take a couple of army panzer divisions, but as it is

▲ *An officer of the élite Grossdeutschland Panzer Division in the turret of his tank at the Battle of Kursk.*

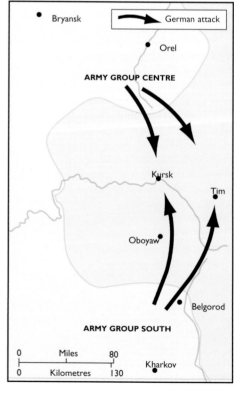

▶ *The German attack plan at Kursk. The Red Army obstructed the German assault routes with mines and antitank guns.*

▲ The aftermath of a bombing raid on Hamburg, one of many cities to be targeted by the British and Americans.

▶ The German Tank Assault Badge, awarded to drivers, radio operators, gunners and commanders after combat.

I need a magnet around which to gather the people together." Meanwhile, German forces in Italy take over the country and disarm Italian troops.

JULY 29

AIR WAR, *GERMANY*

Goebbels is active in visiting bomb-damaged areas of Germany and sees for himself the horrifying extent of the destruction meted out by Allied air attacks. He writes in his diary this day following one of the heaviest single raids on Hamburg:"1000 bombers, *Gauleiter* Kaumann spoke of a catastrophe

▼ Propaganda Minister Goebbels visiting the victims of Allied bombing in Essen. He toured bombed cities tirelessly.

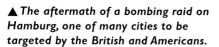

▲ Waffen-SS troops of the Das Reich Division take part in Germany's last great offensive on the Eastern Front: Kursk.

the extent of which blunts the imagination. A city of one million people has been devastated in a manner unknown before in history; problems almost impossible to solve; food for a million people shelter, clothing, 800,000 homeless people wandering the devastated streets."

AUGUST 4

EASTERN FRONT, *UKRAINE*

The Red Army recaptures Orel. The Germans are in general retreat in the East.

▼ Men and vehicles pour ashore during Operation Husky, the Allied invasion of Sicily in July.

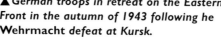

SEPTEMBER 12

MEDITERRANEAN, *ITALY*

Mussolini is rescued from imprisonment by a raiding squad under German commando leader Otto Skorzeny and installed as head of a new government in Northern Italy by the Germans. Earlier, on the 9th, the Allies landed on the Italian mainland at Messina, Calabria and Salerno, south of Naples.

Italy had surrendered on the 8th, but German troops under Field Marshal Albert Kesselring, already commander in southern Europe, occupied Rome and moved south.

▼ *Following the rescue of Mussolini (in black coat), he poses for photographs with his rescuers. Skorzeny is to his right.*

▲ *German troops in retreat on the Eastern Front in the autumn of 1943 following he Wehrmacht defeat at Kursk.*

Rommel was transferred to northwest Europe. Many disbanded Italian soldiers took to the hills to form partisan units.

GERMANY, *RESISTANCE*

The "Solf tea-party" resistance group, mostly German diplomats, is broken up by Gestapo.

SEPTEMBER 26

SEA WAR, *NORWAY*

British midget submarines known as X-craft launch a successful attack on the German battleship *Tirpitz* as she lays at anchor in Alten Fjord in Norway.

OCTOBER 13

POLITICS, *ITALY*

Italy declares war on Germany. Hitler orders a line to be held south of Rome.

GERMANY, *RESISTANCE*

Claus von Stauffenberg takes over the planning for the 1944 anti-Hitler coup.

▼ *The Tiger tank could defeat any Soviet tank in 1943, but the panzer divisions never had enough to regain the initiative.*

▲ *The Scharnhorst test-fires some of its guns prior to setting sail on her fateful journey in December.*

OCTOBER 17

SEA WAR, *PACIFIC*

The last German auxiliary cruiser *Michel* is sunk by the American submarine *Tarpon*.

NOVEMBER 6

EASTERN FRONT, *UKRAINE*

The Soviets recapture Kiev.

DECEMBER 26

SEA WAR, *ATLANTIC*

Admiral Dönitz told Hitler on December 19 that the *Scharnhorst* would attack a convoy soon if the circumstances were favourable. However, the circumstances were far from favourable, for the convoy they chose to attack this day in the Battle of the North Cape were covered by the flagship of the British Home Fleet, the battleship HMS *Duke of York*, and a strong force of cruisers and destroyers. The British had decoded the orders to the *Scharnhorst* and so she ran into a hot reception. The cruisers with the convoys damaged her radar and fire control, but she was still a formidable adversary. While her attention was distracted in a gun-duel with the *Sheffield* and *Norfolk*, the *Duke of York* approached unobserved to within 11km (6.8 miles) before opening fire. The *Scharnhorst*'s aim was not good, and she scored only two minor hits on the *Duke of York*, whereas she herself was hit repeatedly. She was attacked by four destroyers, which hit her with four torpedoes, slowing her down for the *Duke of York*. Finally the cruiser *Jamaica* torpedoed the *Scharnhorst*, which sunk with the loss of her entire crew, except for 36 men.

The year 1943 ended badly for the Germans. The qualitative improvement in the Red Army was matched by a marked

▼ *A Panther in Russia. The supply of the new Tiger and Panther tanks did not offset German manpower shortages in the East.*

▲ *A Tiger sheds a track during the German withdrawal in the East in the second half of 1943.*

increase in the supply of materiel from beyond the Urals. Tanks and artillery became increasingly available to Soviet commanders, and problems of mobility were largely overcome by the supply of American trucks. On the German side, the year's end saw serious shortages of manpower which could not be disguised by fielding divisions at half-strength.

1944

The Third Reich suffered a series of crippling blows in 1944. Having lost the initiative on the Eastern Front in 1943, the Red Army destroyed Army Group Centre in June 1944 when it launched Operation Bagration. In addition, the Western Allies finally landed in France on June 6, thereby opening the Second Front. Only in Italy did the German Army have any degree of success in slowing the Allied advance.

JANUARY 14

EASTERN FRONT, *LENINGRAD*

The siege of Leningrad is lifted. The German blockade and siege has claimed around one million Leningraders, mostly from starvation, exposure, disease, and shelling from German artillery. Sparse food and fuel supplies reached the city by barge in the summer and by truck and ice-borne sled in winter across

Lake Ladoga. These supplies kept the city's arms factories operating and its inhabitants barely alive, while one million more of its children, sick, and elderly were evacuated.

JANUARY 15

SEA WAR, *ATLANTIC*

U-377, commanded by *Oberleutnant zur See* Gerhard Kluth, is sunk by an acoustic

torpedo fired from *U-972*, commanded by *Oberleutnant zur See* Klaus König, who was to suffer a similar fate later in the month.

JANUARY 21

ITALY, *ANZIO*

The Allies land at Anzio, south of Rome, by means of an Anglo-American amphibious

▼ *Men and equipment pour ashore following the amphibious landings at Anzio, south of Rome, in January.*

▲ *German troops in Rome. Following the Italian capitulation to the Allies, the Germans took control of the country.*

assault. The Anglo-American armies in Italy, which had invaded a year earlier, are stalemated on the Gustav Line, the key point of which is Monte Cassino. General Mark Clark, commanding the US VI Corps, plans to mount an assault from the sea, at Anzio, to break the Gustav Line by linking up with the British attack due to strike in the centre, particularly the Abbey of Monte Cassino. It is hoped that the Anzio assault, by cutting the German Tenth Army's lines of communication, will oblige Kesselring to order the evacuation of the Gustav Line and allow the Anzio and Cassino attackers to link up, march on Rome and thus break the German hold on Italy.

▼ *The Allied plan to bypass the German defence line by landing at Anzio was sound, but relied on speed to succeed.*

▲ *The key to the Gustav Line was the hilltop monastery at Monte Cassino, seen here following bombing and shelling.*

▼ *German paratroopers during the defence of Monte Cassino. The Germans retreated from Cassino in good order.*

▲ *A German 88mm Flak gun deployed for action against Allied tanks on the Gustav Line. It was a fearsome tank killer.*

The Cassino attack quickly succeeds in attracting the German reserves. But the American General Lucas, though he gets his Anglo-American force easily ashore at Anzio, fails to profit from the temporary weakness around his bridgehead by pressing an advance from it. As a result, the Germans are able to rush forces to contain the bridgehead.

JANUARY 30

ITALY, *ANZIO*
When Lucas attempts a breakout from the Anzio bridgehead, he finds the Germans are very organized opposite him. He is obliged thereafter to conduct a static defence.

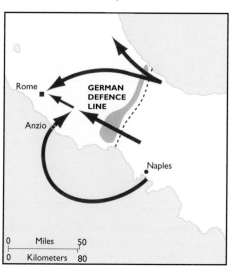

Rome
GERMAN
DEFENCE
LINE
Anzio
Naples

| 0 | Miles | 50 |
| 0 | Kilometers | 80 |

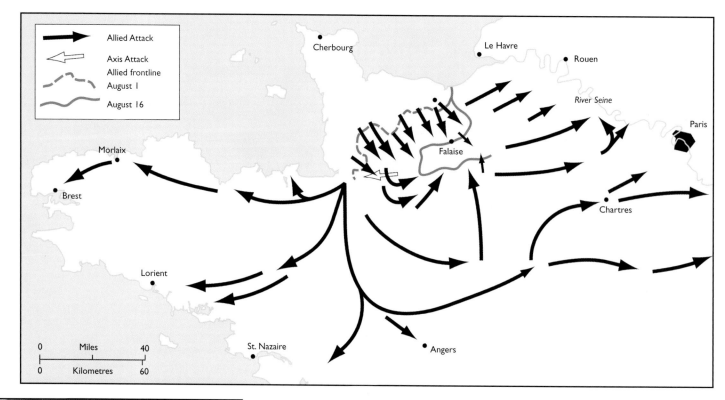

▲ The Germans attempted to contain the Allied bridgehead after D-Day, but lacked the resources to do so.

◄ The battleship *Tirpitz* holed up in Kaa Fjord in July 1944. Note the antisubmarine net around the ship.

FEBRUARY 15

ITALY, *ANZIO*

The Germans, having gathered enough strength, attack and penetrate deeply into General Lucas' positions at the Anzio bridgehead. They are halted only by a desperate US counterattack on February 19. The Germans then seal the bridgehead and contain it. A general Allied offensive on May 11 permitted General Truscott, who had succeeded Lucas, to break out on May 23.

FEBRUARY 26

EASTERN FRONT, *BALTIC*

Germany's Army Group North loses Porkhov in the face of the Red Army offensive. Three German divisions are wiped out and another 17 badly mauled. Elsewhere on the Eastern Front Nikopol, with its manganese-ore mines, was abandoned on the 8th; and Krivoi Rog was lost before the end of the month.

MARCH 19

POLITICS, *HUNGARY*

As Soviet forces reach the Carpathians, Hitler orders the occupation of Hungary.

▲ The Defence Medal, instituted for work on Germany's fortifications, principally the Siegfried Line in the autumn of 1944.

APRIL 5

SEA WAR, *NORWAY*

The British mount a large-scale air attack on the *Tirpitz* moored in Kaa Fjord.

MAY 9

EASTERN FRONT, *CRIMEA*

The Crimea is cleared and Sevastopol recaptured by the Soviets. The Germans

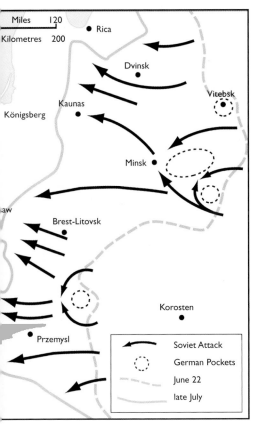

lose 100,000 men. Hitler dismisses Manstein to show where he places the blame for Germany's failures on the Eastern Front.

JUNE

GERMANY, *ESPIONAGE*

The *Abwehr*, the German military intelligence organization, is closed and absorbed into the SD under Walter Schhellenberg. Admiral Canaris, head of the *Abwehr*, is dismissed on suspicion of being part of the anti-Hitler resistance, though nothing has been proved. In fact, Canaris was a member of the Resistance.

◀ *The Soviet frontline during Operation Bagration. Launched in June, it destroyed Germany's Army Group Centre.*

▼ *Red Army troops in the attack during Operation Bagration. The offensive took the Soviets to the gates of Warsaw.*

▲ *One of the Vergeltungwaffen (Reprisal Weapons) that Hitler believed would turn the tide of war: a V-1 rocket.*

JUNE 6

WESTERN FRONT, *NORMANDY*

Operation "Overlord", the D-Day Anglo-American landings, commences. The invasion begins before dawn with units of the US 82nd and 101st Airborne Divisions making night landings near the town of Sainte-Mère-Église, while British commando units capture key bridges and knock out Nazi communications. In the morning, the assault troops of the combined Allied armies land at five beaches along the Normandy coast codenamed Utah, Omaha, Gold, Juno and Sword. While four beaches

JUNE 11

are taken easily and quickly, the forces landing at "Bloody Omaha" encounter stiff German resistance. By nightfall, sizeable beachheads have been secured on all five landing areas, and the final campaign to defeat Germany is underway.

JUNE 11

SEA WAR, *ATLANTIC*

The last remaining supply U-boat, *U-490*, is sunk.

JUNE 12

SEA WAR, *GERMANY*

The first electro-boat, *U-2321*, is commissioned. It is a Type XXIII, a small coastal submarine carrying two torpedoes.

JUNE 23

EASTERN FRONT, *BELORUSSIA*

Soviets launch their summer offensive, codenamed Bagration, concentrating on the White Russian fronts. The Red Army has

assembled 1,254,000 men, 2175 tanks, 1355 assault guns and 24,000 artillery pieces for the assault. Facing these forces is Army Group Centre, which has 500,000 men to defend 1120km (700 miles) of front. The Soviets smash through the German lines, advancing 240km (150 miles) in a week.

June was a bad month for the Third Reich. In addition to the landings in Normandy

▼ *German panzers make their way to the front in France, July 1944. The last vehicle in the column is a Panzer V Panther.*

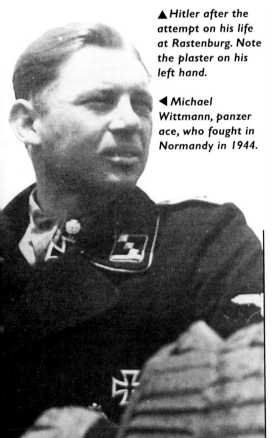

▲ *Hitler after the attempt on his life at Rastenburg. Note the plaster on his left hand.*

◄ *Michael Wittmann, panzer ace, who fought in Normandy in 1944.*

▲ *Though the Germans lacked air cover in Normandy, they made skillful use of camouflage. This is an 88mm gun.*

and Bagration, the Allies captured Rome on the 5th and partisan strength in northern Italy reached 100,000. Also this month the Germans began V-I attacks on Great Britain.

JUNE 27

SEA WAR, *GERMANY*
The first large Type XXI electro-submarine is commissioned: *U-2501*.

JULY 20

EASTERN FRONT, *BELORUSSIA*
Minsk falls; Army Group Centre is virtually destroyed. Total German losses exceed 200,000. Vilna falls and Soviet forces approach the East Prussian frontier.

The catalogue of German disasters continue as the Red Army continues its advance: Lvov falls to Koniev's army at the month's end.

GERMANY, *RESISTANCE*
Hitler moves to his East Prussian head-quarters at Rastenburg. An unsuccessful attempt is made to assassinate Hitler by Colonel Count Claus Schenk von Stauffen-berg at the Wolf's Lair at Rastenburg, Hitler's headquarters in the East.

Stauffenberg had been drawn into the circle of military conspirators against Hitler but also quickly formed the opinion that they lacked resolution. Thus it was that he took it upon himself, as someone with access to Hitler's conferences but so disabled as to escape body search, to smuggle a bomb into the Führer's

conference room. Hitler and the other 24 occupants of the room suffer varying degrees of wounds, the most serious being the loss of life of Colonel Brant and Herr Berger, who die immediately, and *Generalleutnant* Schmundt and General Korten, dying subsequently from wounds they have received. The remaining 20 suffer superficial wounds and shock, save for General Buhle and *Generalmajor* Scherff, who are more seriously injured. Unfortunately, though Stauffenberg makes good his escape from the Rastenburg headquarters, the Berlin conspirators fail to act with resolution during his return flight to the city, and by the time he has arrived, they have lost irretrievable time. By the evening the coup has foundered and General Fromm, head of the Home Army, who hoped thereby to remove the evidence of his own complicity, shot Stauffenberg, with others, in the courtyard of the War Ministry.

The assassination attempt, codenamed Valkyrie, had failed, but coup signals had been sent out. The German command in Paris started to take over from the Nazis until news of the failure came through. Coup plotters and large numbers of suspects, including Canaris and Oster, were rounded up. General Ludwig Beck and

▲ *The special Wound Badge issued by Hitler following the July Bomb Plot. This particular one was awarded to Jodl.*

▼ *Roland Freisler (centre), head of the People's Court where most of the anti-Hitler conspirators were tried.*

others committed suicide. From July until April 1945 trials and executions of suspects continued.

WESTERN FRONT, *NORMANDY*
The American, British and Canadian forces have consolidated their D-Day beachheads and link up. For the loss of 5000 men killed, 750,000 have now been put ashore. The Americans to the west, on the Allied right wing, have cleared the peninsula south of Cherbourg. The British, holding the centre, face the city of Caen, and the Canadians on the Allied left have borne the heaviest weight of the German panzer attacks. In the air the Allies have complete superiority and are able to attack German army ground targets at will. Field Marshal von Rundstedt is dismissed when he expresses pessimism over the battle's outcome. The US First Army, with over 350,000 men and 1000 tanks, starts its advance south, while the British Second Army and the Canadian Army attack Caen. Field Marshal Rommel, German commander, is injured in a car crash and replaced by Field Marshal von Kluge.

Some 14 British and Canadian divisions are holding 14 German divisions and are engaged in heavy fighting for Caen. General Omar Bradley on the other wing has 15 US divisions facing a mixture of German units amounting to nine divisions. At the end of the month the Americans move out of the

◀ *To crush the Warsaw Jews the Germans used their most unsavoury characters, such as SS leader Oskar Dirlewanger, seen here.*

▼ *A German antitank gun in action in the Warsaw Ghetto. The destruction attests to the ferocity of the fighting.*

peninsula and reach Brittany, while the Canadians and British take Caen and slowly push the Germans back.

AUGUST 1

POLAND, *RESISTANCE*
The Polish resistance – the "Home Army" – in Warsaw rises as the Soviets approach. Commanded by General Tadeusz Bór-Komorowski, the Warsaw corps of 50,000 troops attacks the relatively weak German force and within three days gains control of

▲ *Poorly armed soldiers of the Polish Home Army. They fought with a courage and tenacity borne of desperation.*

most of the city. The Germans send in reinforcements and force the Poles into a defensive position, bombarding them with air and artillery attacks for the next 63 days. Meanwhile, the Red Army, which had been detained during the first days of the insurrection by a German assault, occupies a position at Praga, a suburb across the Vistula from Warsaw, and remains idle. In addition, the Soviet government refuses to allow the Western Allies to use Soviet airbases to airlift supplies to the beleaguered Poles. Without Allied support, the Home Army is split into small, disconnected units. It was forced to surrender when its supplies gave out (October 2). Bór-Komorowski and his forces

▲ When fighting "sub-humans" the Germans ignored the rules of war. These are hostages hanged in the Warsaw Uprising.

were taken prisoner, and the Germans then systematically deported the remainder of the city's population and destroyed the city block by block.

AUGUST 19

EASTERN FRONT, *BALTIC*
Russian troops surround 55 German divisions on the Baltic coast. The Red Army enters Bucharest. On August 23 Romania sues for peace. Hitler's Eastern Front is crumbling.

▲ Field Marshal Walther Model (with monocle), the German commander in the West. He committed suicide in April 1945.

WESTERN FRONT, *FRANCE*
By this time the Allies have landed 1.5 million soldiers and 300,000 vehicles. Now, 36 Allied divisions, each stronger and more liberally equipped that those of their opponents, now face the 20 German divisions. The British and Canadians advance south; US divisions sweep south

and turn east at great speed, threatening to surround the German forces. Kluge directs his army to move to the attack in obedience to Hitler's orders but is recalled to Paris to answer for his part in the "July Bomb Plot". Kluge commits suicide. Hitler replaces him with the general already in the frontline, Hausser, and gives command in the West to Field Marshal Model. German

◄ A Panther outside Warsaw in August 1944. The Soviets made little effort to aid the Warsaw Jews in the ghetto.

▼ *The German Auxiliary Cruisers Badge. These vessels sailed the oceans as part of the Kriegmarine's war.*

▲ *German paratroopers hitch a ride during the opening days of Hitler's gamble in the West, the Ardennes Offensive.*

▲ *US troops stand on "dragon's teeth" antitank defences on the Siegfried Line. Note the bullet holes in the concrete.*

forces. The French II Corps advances on Marseilles. On the last day of August Patton's Third Army reaches the Meuse.

AUGUST 20

NAZI PARTY, *AWARDS*

To commemorate the attempt on his life at the Wolf's Lair at Rastenburg on July 20, 1944, and his escape, Hitler introduces a special Wound Badge, which he awards to 24 recipients, or dependents in the case of the dead. He declines to award himself one of these medals.

The Recipients are:

KEITEL, Wilhelm *Generalfeldmarschall*
JODL, Alfred *Generaloberst*
WARLIMONT, Walter *General der Artillerie*
von PUTTKAMER, Jesko *Konteradmiral*

ASSMANN, Heinz *Kapitän Z See*
von BELOW, Nicolaus *Oberst*
VOSS, Hans-Erich *Konteradmiral*
GÜNSCHE, Otto *SS-Hauptsturmführer*
FEGELEIN, Hermann *SS-Gruppenführer*
HEUSINGER, Adolf *Generalleutnant*
BORGMAN, G. *Oberstleutnant*
BODENSCHATZ, Karl *General der Flieger*
BUHLE, Walter *General der Infanterie*
SCHERFF, Walter *Generalmajor*
KORTEN, Gunter *General der Flieger*
BRANT, Heinz *Oberst*
BERGER, Civilian
SCHMUNDT, Rudolf *Generalleutnant*

▼ *The bridge at Arnhem, scene of fierce fighting between the British and Germans during Operation Market Garden.*

forces are badly mauled in the Falaise Pocket, and afterwards the Americans advance 80km (50 miles) a day. In Paris the French resistance takes over part of the city, and within days the Free French 2nd Armoured Division, accompanied by US units, liberates the city. In the south of France, US forces land and move north against little opposition. Aix-en-Provence is taken by US

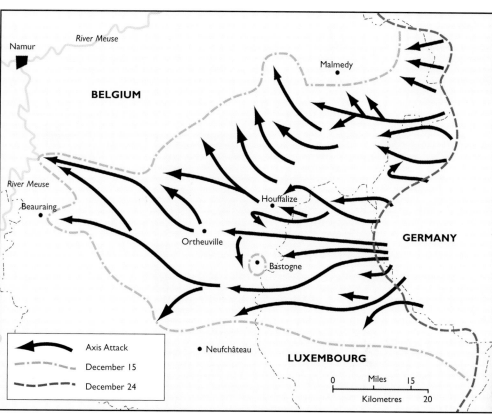

▶ The Ardennes Offensive caught the Allies by surprise, but by the end of December it had run out of momentum.

von JOHN, *Oberstleutnant*
BÜCHS, G. *Major*
HAGAN
WEIZENEGGER, *Oberstleutnant*
HEWELL, Walter, Civilian
von SCHIMANSKI, *Hauptmann*

SEPTEMBER 17

WESTERN FRONT, *HOLLAND*

Operation Market Garden, Montgomery's plan for an armoured and airborne thrust through Holland, begins. General Eisenhower, supreme commander of the Allied forces, has taken over from Montgomery as commander of the Allied ground forces and decides to advance on a broad front towards the Rhine, notwithstanding Market Garden. Field Marshal von Rundstedt is given back command in the West. Allied forces now have a complete front from the Channel to Switzerland and move towards the German West Wall, the "Siegfried" line. France is almost totally liberated.

NOVEMBER 12

SEA WAR, *NORWAY*

The *Tirpitz* sinks at her anchorage, off

▶ German King Tiger tanks. Used during the Ardennes Offensive, many ran out of fuel and had to be abandoned.

Haakoy Island, when a force of Lancaster bombers surprise her without any defending fighters in the air. In perfect visibility the bombers hit her with three "Tallboys" and she capsizes.

DECEMBER 16

WESTERN FRONT, *ARDENNES*

The Ardennes Offensive is launched, Hitler's gamble to reach Antwerp and split the Allied armies in the West. The attack is made in the hilly and wooded Ardennes region of southern Belgium. While Allied aircraft are hampered by bad weather, Rundstedt's Fifth and Sixth Panzer Armies launch two parallel attacks. The Fifth Army, under General Hasso von Manteuffel, bypasses Bastogne (which is held throughout the offensive by the US 101st Airborne Division), and has advanced by December 24 to within four miles (six kilometres) of the Meuse River. Germany's last reserves of men and tanks have been committed to the offensive.

1945

With the failure of the Ardennes Offensive, defeat for Nazi Germany was only a matter of weeks. As her cities were pounded into rubble by fleets of Allied bombers, the Red Army closed in on Berlin for the final battle against National Socialism. Hitler decided to stay in his capital and committed suicide rather than risk capture by the Soviets. Behind him he left a country in ruins, and a people saddled with the great shame of being part of his horrific Final Solution, the evidence of which were found by Allied troops as they liberated the concentration camps.

JANUARY 3

WESTERN FRONT, *ARDENNES*

The final German attack against Bastogne is defeated. Hitler's last offensive in the West has been stopped. The Allies regroup and launch a counterattack. By the 16th the US First and Third Armies have linked up at Houffalize.

JANUARY 27

EASTERN FRONT, *POLAND*

The Soviets liberate Auschwitz, the Third Reich's main death camp. The centre of a rail network, the first camp, Auschwitz I, was reserved throughout its history for political prisoners. In October 1941, work began on Auschwitz II, or Birkenau, located outside the nearby village of Brzezinka. There the SS later developed a huge concentration camp and extermination

▼ *Tired German troops are driven towards the front to meet the next Soviet offensive in early 1945. Few, if any, will return.*

▲ German prisoners, glad to be out of the war, help a wounded comrade in the village of Hemmeres in February.

▲ US C-47 transport aircraft drop supplies to the besieged garrison of Bastogne during the Ardennes Offensive.

complex that included some 300 prison barracks; four large *Badeanstalten* (bathhouses), in which prisoners were gassed to death; *Leichenkeller* (corpse cellars), in which their bodies were stored; and *Einäscherungsöfen* (cremating ovens). Another camp (Buna-Monowitz), near the village of Dwory, later called Auschwitz III, became a slave-labour camp in May 1942.

Newly arrived prisoners at the death camp were divided in a process known as

Selektion. The young and the able-bodied were sent to work; young children and their mothers and the old and infirm were sent directly to the gas chambers. Thousands of prisoners were also selected by the camp doctor, Josef Mengele, for medical experiments, which were mostly sadistic. Experiments involving the killing of twins, for example, were meant to provide information that would supposedly lead to the rapid expansion of the "Aryan race".

Subject to harsh conditions – including inadequate shelter and sanitation – given minimal food, and worked to exhaustion, those who could no longer work faced transport back to Birkenau for gassing.

Between 1.1 and 1.5 million people died at Auschwitz; 90 percent of them were Jews, though other victims included a large number of Gypsies.

▼ Dresden being bombed on February 14. Over 50,000 people were killed in the firestorm caused by the bombing.

◄ The town of St Hubert, Belgium, following its evacuation by German troops after the failure of the Ardennes attack.

▲ *The bridge over the Rhine at Remagen, which was captured by US troops after demolition charges failed to go off.*

▼ *A veteran of the Grossdeutschland Division (left) instructs a young recruit in the use of a Panzerfaust antitank rocket.*

Russian army groups, both north and south of Warsaw, break through and take the city crossing the river Oder within 160km (100 miles) of Berlin. They reach the Baltic at Danzig and overrun industrial Silesia, seizing the last possible coal supplies of the Third Reich. The Soviet offensive in the East causes Hitler to move armoured forces from the West, including "Sepp" Dietrich's Sixth SS Panzer Army.

WESTERN FRONT, *FRANCE*
German losses in France since D-Day amount to 1.5 million men, over half of whom are prisoners of war.

FEBRUARY 14

EASTERN FRONT, *EAST PRUSSIA*
The *Kriegsmarine* evacuates German troops from Baltic ports, Danzig and East Prussia who have been trapped by the advance of the Red Army.

AIR WAR, *GERMANY*
Some 805 Royal Air Force (RAF) bombers attack the city of Dresden during the night. The raid causes a massive firestorm that kills 50,000 people. Then the Americans bomb the city during the day.

WESTERN FRONT, *THE RHINE*

The First Canadian Army, on the Allied left flank, attacks down the west bank of the Rhine, drawing the last German reserves on the Western Front.

MARCH 3

WESTERN FRONT, *FRANCE*

Patton's Third Army approaches the Rhine. His VIII and XII Corps make good progress.

MARCH 6

EASTERN FRONT, *HUNGARY*

Spearheaded by Dietrich's Sixth SS Panzer Army, Hitler launches Operation Spring Awakening to secure the oilfields at Nagykanizsa and retake Budapest. However, the offensive soon bogs down in the face of poor weather and Red Army resistance. Then the Third Ukrainian Front counterattacks and drives the Germans back.

MARCH 7

WESTERN FRONT, *GERMANY*

Hitler has given orders that not a single Rhine bridge must fall intact into Allied hands. What every Allied commander dreams of, a reconnaissance patrol of the US First Army achieves. The unit discovers a basically undamaged bridge across the Rhine at Remagen near Bonn.

Second Lieutenant Emmet J. Burrows appeared out of the woods above Remagen to find disorganized German troops fleeing across the Ludendorff railway bridge. Soon, a platoon of US tanks was charging down to the bridge. As it approached, a German engineer, *Hauptmann* W. Bratke, detonated charges on the bridge which created a small crater. The American pushed on, shelling the Germans on the east bank. One shell knocked out the engineer responsible for firing the demolition charge. When he came to and turned the key, nothing happened. He tried again and still the detonators failed. US troops, led by Sergeant A. Drabik of Holland, Ohio, raced onto the bridge amid a hail of gunfire. Then a powerful explosion lifted the bridge up; it settled back and, incredibly, was still standing. In less than 24 hours more than 8000 troops with tanks and self-propelled guns had crossed the Rhine.

MARCH 19

GERMANY, *ECONOMY*

Hitler issues the so-called "Nero Decree", ordering the destruction of Germany's bridges, industrial plants and railway lines.

◀ *Defeat in the West: dead Hitler Youth. The Führer was determined to fight to the last German boy.*

▼ *The last photograph of Adolf Hitler, taken outside the bunker as he decorates a Hitler Youth member.*

▼ *Defeat in the East: a knocked-out German antitank gun and Panzer IV tanks on the outskirts of Berlin.*

The order is ignored by Albert Speer, who is now thinking of post-war Germany.

MARCH 22

WESTERN FRONT, *GERMANY*

Montgomery's Twenty-First Army Group crosses the Rhine to the north, then moves across north Germany towards Hamburg.

APRIL 2

WESTERN FRONT, *GERMANY*

The US First and Third Armies link up and complete the encirclement of the industrial Ruhr region.

APRIL 13

EASTERN FRONT, *AUSTRIA*

Vienna is taken by the Red Army. With Anglo-American forces driving east, Hitler's

▶ *Field Marshal Montgomery (right) negotiates the enemy surrender at the Twenty-First Army Group's headquarters.*

▼ *The Battle of Berlin. The black arrows depict Red Army attacks, which cut through German defences in five days.*

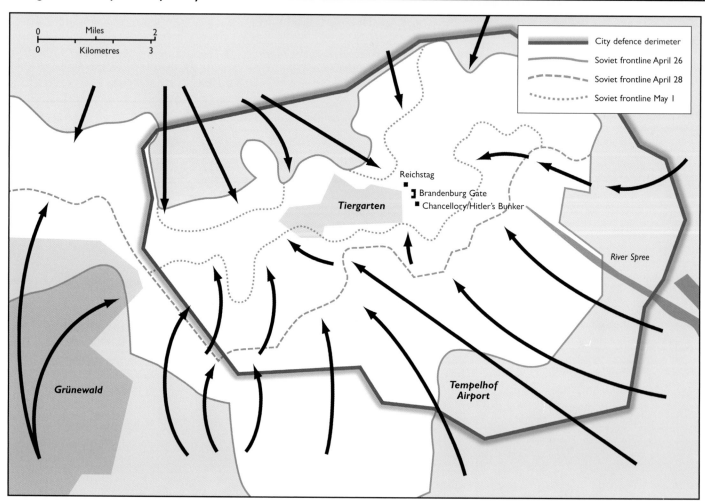

0 — Miles — 2	
0 — Kilometres — 3	

City defence derimeter
Soviet frontline April 26
Soviet frontline April 28
Soviet frontline May 1

Reichstag
Brandenburg Gate
Chancellory/Hitler's Bunker
Tiergarten
River Spree
Grünewald
Tempelhof Airport

General Karl Wolff, governor of north Italy, negotiates with US agent Allen Dulles of the Office of Strategic Service (OSS) in Switzerland with a view to saving Italy's industry from unnecessary destruction. As a result of these negotiations, Kesselring surrenders German forces in Italy on May 2.

APRIL 30

NAZI PARTY, *BERLIN*
As Berlin is engulfed in explosives and fires, Hitler, having first married his mistress Eva Braun, commits suicide. Before he does so he dictates his political testament. In it he states: "I die with a happy heart, aware of the immeasurable deeds and achievements of our soldiers at the front, our women at

◀ *After the battle Berliners come out of their cellars to survey the damage. The first thing they met was choking smoke.*

◀ *Berlin, May 1945. This once-proud city lay in ruins, while an overpowering stench of dead flesh hung over its streets.*

Third Reich is crumbling rapidly. During this month American and Soviet troops meet on the Elbe at Torgau, and the British liberate Belsen.

APRIL 26

EASTERN FRONT, *GERMANY*
The Red Army assault on Berlin begins. Hitler is in the city, having decided to stay in his capital. He issues orders to non-existent armies to come to the city's relief. By the 27th German forces in Berlin have been restricted to an area 16km (10 miles) long by 5km (three miles) wide.

In Italy Mussolini tries to escape to Switzerland but is captured and shot by partisans on the 28th. Also in Italy, SS

▼ *A German prisoner reads a US forces newspaper heralding Hitler's death.*

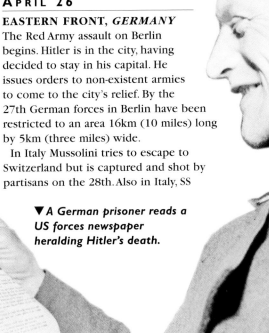

MAY 1

▲ With the war over the perpetrators of atrocities were arrested. This is Auschwitz guard Irma Grese, who was hanged in 1946.

home, the achievements of our farmers and workers and the work, unique in history, of our youth who bear my name." Eva Braun takes poison to be with her new husband in death. Grand Admiral Karl Dönitz becomes Head of State.

MAY 1

NAZI PARTY, *BERLIN*

Dönitz issues the following declaration to all members of the German armed forces still fighting the Allies: "I expect discipline and obedience. Chaos and ruin can be prevented only by the swift and unreserved execution of my orders. Anyone who, at this juncture, fails in his duty and condemns German women and children to slavery and death, is

▶ The V-2 was a supersonic rocket that had a range of 360km (225 miles). It came too late to save Hitler's Reich.

a traitor and a coward. The oath of allegiance which you took to the Führer now binds each and every one of you to me, whom he himself appointed as his successor." But Dönitz realizes that further resistance is useless.

MAY 4

WESTERN FRONT, *GERMANY*

Admiral Friedeburg, head of the *Kriegsmarine*, is authorized by Dönitz to negotiate a separate but partial surrender to Montgomery of all German forces in northern Germany to take effect from 08:00 hours on the morning of May 5. The German delegation signs the surrender document at 18:30 hours in Montgomery's headquarters at Lüneburg Heath just south

▼ German troops sought the Western Allies to surrender to, such as these paratroopers, to avoid Soviet retribution.

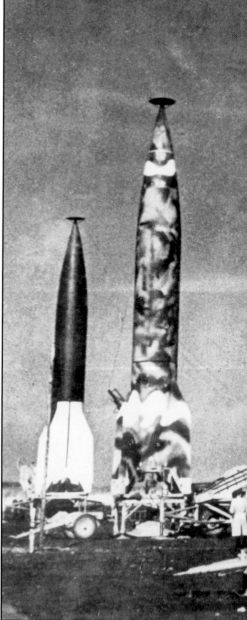

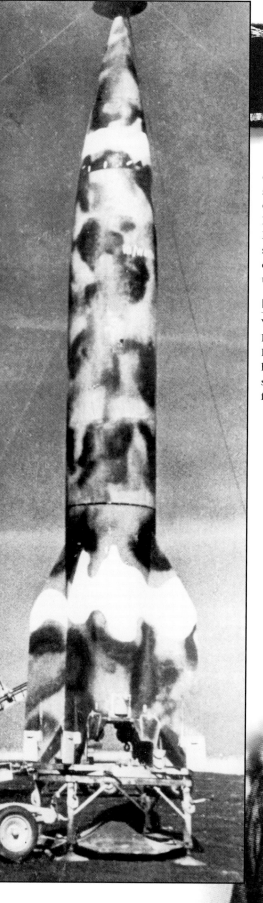

of Hamburg. This partial surrender includes all German forces in Holland, northwest Germany, including the Friesian Islands and Heligoland and all other islands, to Montgomery. This is also to include all naval ships in these areas. These forces are to lay down their arms and surrender unconditionally.

MAY 5

WESTERN FRONT, *GERMANY*
Friedeburg and Jodl are instructed by Dönitz to fly to General Eisenhower's headquarters at Rheims to negotiate the surrender of all remaining German armed forces in southern Germany and France.

▲ *The German people had spent 12 years following their Führer. Their reward was misery, military defeat and shame.*

MAY 10

WESTERN FRONT, *CHANNEL ISLANDS*
The Channel Islands, due to their isolated positions, do not officially surrender until today.

EASTERN FRONT, *CZECHOSLOVAKIA*
Prague is liberated by the Red Army as German troops lay down their arms. World War II in Europe is over, Germany is in ruins and 500,000 of her civilians alone have died in six years of war.

◀ *The banality of evil. This is Josef Kramer, commandant of Belsen. When the camp was liberated there were 13,000 unburied corpses lying on the ground. When the British arrived Kramer took them on a tour of the camp. He was hanged in November 1945.*

CONCLUSION

Adolf Hitler's Legacy

Hitler's European war was just as much a personal creation as the empire that the Führer built. Thus, it was with the nature of Hitler himself that world society had to deal after he came to power in 1933.

Nazism was first and foremost a conspiracy to win political power in Germany, yet it never evolved a coherent political philosophy of its own, merely borrowing social theories available in Germany or elsewhere. Nazism was in fact the creation of a band of men drawn together by a self-appointed leader who fired their frustrated national pride and personal ambitions. Without the individual magnetism of Hitler there would have been no Nazi Party, or at least not one capable of seizing power, and no Third Reich of the quite special kind. To his followers, Hitler had the historical personal greatness of

Caesar or Napoleon. Hitler certainly did possess certain attributes of personal greatness, but without the capacity to fulfil them. He was destitute of human quality; he lacked reliability or any recognizable moral standard. He refused to listen to advice, preferring to accept his intuition, which was to grow increasingly unsound from 1941 onwards. His stamina was derived from his monstrous egotism, the blind self-confidence that made him believe himself a man of destiny, chosen by an act of providence to lead the Nordic world.

Hitler may have believed himself to be unique, but his actions and traits shared certain similarities to other great dictators. To compare Hitler with Napoleon, for example, one can detect a similarity stemming from the nationalism born in

them and stemming from the revolutionary times they lived through.

The revolution that Hitler lived through had as its bloody overture the carnage of World War I. The alliances in Europe made World War I inevitable. When it erupted, it brought with it patriotism, nationalism and a sense of righting old wrongs. But four years of brutal warfare brewed a heady cocktail of barbarism on a scale never before witnessed, fuelled by mass industrial production that could deliver armaments on a scale that was previously unthinkable. Technology fed upon itself, inventing ever-more horrific methods of destruction. For the participants it was seared into their minds and in some cases it totally

▼ *German service chiefs salute their Führer. All military personal took an oath of personal allegiance to Hitler.*

dehumanized them. With the ending of the war they returned to alien worlds. This brought bitter dissatisfaction, and men with time on their hands proved fertile ground for the new political thinking, on one hand communism and the other fascism. The flowering of both creeds would inevitably give rise to intense antagonism.

In Germany there sprang up the *Freikorps*, groups of ex-soldiers who were loyal to the officers who led them, and very little else. They looked with disdain on Germany's Weimar government, which in their eyes had meekly caved in to the dictates of the Treaty of Versailles and had therefore been an accomplice to Germany's humiliation.

It was easy enough for Hitler and his Bavarian party to recruit *Freikorps* members, promising as he did to right Germany's wrongs and to win back her place in the sun. But the path was long and hard for the Nazis, for the German people did not embrace Nazism overnight. It took Hitler 14 years to gain power, and one can argue that he only did so because the world

▲ *The Japanese ambassador is welcomed to Japan. The Berlin–Tokyo Axis was an alliance in name only.*

slump of 1929 made a desperate people more willing to listen to his simple solutions for Germany's ills. He was also aided by Germany's conservative élite, who believed that they could use Hitler to preserve their age-old status quo.

But Hitler had a separate agenda, one that was dominated by two concepts: race and space. Race was at the centre of his world view, and thus dictated the internal and external policies of the Third Reich once he had taken power in 1933. Hitler firmly believed in the racial superiority of the Aryan-Nordic race, whom he believed to be the founder and maintainer of civilization. The Jews, on the other hand, were destroyers of civilization. This anti-Semitism was by no means unique to him: many

▼ *"Ayran brothers": members of the Volunteer Labour Service for Flanders march out of camp into the fields.*

▲ *Norwegian RAD girls, part of the Nordic race that Hitler believed should have living space in the East.*

Europeans in the nineteenth and twentieth centuries had also believed this to be the case. Thus one can see this racial view in the laws introduced in Germany from the early 1935s.

Gradually Jews had their rights stripped away from them. Thus the 1935 Nuremberg Laws denied citizenship to German Jews, and slowly anti-Semitism was given a legal and state-sanctioned framework. It was the first step on the road to the Final Solution, in which the Nazis tried to exterminate European Jewry altogether.

Hitler and the Nazi hierarchy dreamed of a racially pure Germany, and so "racially pure" organizations were established, such as Heinrich Himmler's SS, whose members had to prove Aryan ancestry back to the eighteenth century.

Of course an Aryan "master race" by definition meant that other races were necessarily *Untermenschen* (sub-humans), an idea that was to have horrific consequences concerning Germany policy towards the conquered peoples of Eastern Europe and the Soviet Union.

Hitler's view towards Japan was curious. As they were Asiatics they did not fit into his racial scheme of things. Indeed, he once remarked to Ribbentrop: "One day the showdown with the yellow race will come." However, in the short term they were useful because they kept the British and Americans tied down in the Far East (though both Hitler and Goebbels had mixed feelings about the white man being defeated by the yellow race). Thus the Berlin–Tokyo axis was never anything more than a facade, one that neither party had much faith in. The real test came at the end

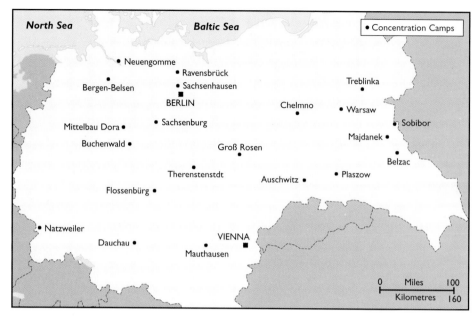

▲ *The Nazi concentration camp system, designed for the systematic destruction of European Jewry and other "undesirables".*

of 1941, when German armies stood before the gates of Moscow. The Japanese had no intention of attacking the Soviet Union in the Far East, a fact Stalin became aware of through his spy network in Japan, thus freeing up valuable reserves that he could ship from Siberia to the Eastern Front. Indeed, one can argue that the Japanese got more out of the axis than Germany, for Hitler's declaration of war on the United States brought him absolutely no benefits. The Japanese thus failed to aid Nazi Germany at a crucial time during the war on the Eastern Front.

The second concept that dominated Hitler's ideology was *Lebensraum* (Living Space). If the German race was to survive and grow strong, it needed space; space for industrial and agricultural output and space in which to raise future generations of "racially pure" Germans. And, like German leaders before him, Hitler looked to the East to fulfil his requirements. That the East was already populated by Slavs was of little consequence. The Slavs fulfiled no other purpose but to serve Germany, that or be eradicated. Above all, there should be no race mixing. Instead, the German race would become one of "pure blood". In this way Germany would remain strong and would not decay.

▶ *Warsaw Ghetto Jews being rounded up for transportation to a concentration camp. Hitler described them as "chaff".*

Space and race therefore defined Adolf Hitler and the Third Reich, and all that took place between 1933 and 1945 had to be placed within the quest for these two aims. Thus, the union with Austria and Czechoslovakia brought ethnic Germans back into the Reich. Having brought all his "children" back into the fold, Hitler then needed his living space. Thus he attacked Poland in September 1939. That Great Britain and France declared war on him in support of Poland was a great surprise, but did not deflect him from his plan. The defeat of these two countries in 1940 postponed his attack on the Soviet Union, but did not cancel it.

Hitler had always planned to attack the Soviet Union. To him it was a place full of Jews and other "undesirables". Moreover, it

was the birthplace of Bolshevism, which he regarded as a "social criminality" that had to be eradicated. It was in the war against the Soviet Union that the concepts of space and race were fused into one, with the result that the war on the Eastern Front became a Nazi ideological crusade.

Seen in this context, some of the more inexplicable military decisions taken in the East are more easily understood. Hitler refused to retreat from Stalingrad because the city's name was that of the leader of the Soviet Union. Similarly, the Führer refused to sanction a withdrawal to a more defensible line following the failure of the attack against Moscow at the end of 1941 for no other reason that he refused to retreat in the face of "sub-humans".

It was therefore ironic that the "sub-human" Soviets should be the main agents in the destruction of the Third Reich, capturing Berlin itself in May 1945. With the fall of the Third Reich, that lasted but 12 turbulent years, not the 1000 Hitler boasted of, what did it leave? Certainly a new form of brutality that had never been witnessed on this scale. Atrocities had been committed before in war and will be in the future, but the systematic murder of millions of people in government-run camps heralded a new chapter in man's inhumanity to man.

In 1945 Germany was in ruins; indeed, never before had a nation been laid so low. However, Germany rose from the ruins, and became a state that today has one of the most democratic constitutions in the world. A nation that previously thrived on militarism now regards its armed forces in a defensive capacity only. This is an achievement that is given too little credit.

In Europe, the destruction of the Third Reich resulted in a continent that was divided for 50 years. As the Cold War developed, former allies became enemies and enemies became allies in weeks. The triploar world of fascism, communism and democracy was reduced to a bipolar stand-off between communism and democracy. The North Atlantic Treaty Organization (NATO) was created in 1949 in answer to the Soviet threat in Europe. Stalin, for his part, was determiined that never again would the Soviet Union be attacked from the West, and set about creating a buffer zone of satellite states in Eastern Europe. And to make sure they remained in the Soviet cam he left one million Red Army troops to garrison Eastern Europe. The

◀ *Erich von dem Bach-Zelewski, the SS general responsible for atrocities in Russia.*

▲ *The consequences of Nazi racial ideology: the corpses of Jews at Belsen concentration camp.*

Warsaw Pact (which was created in 1955 and comprised the USSR and the states of Eastern Europe), though, was a paper tiger, an alliance that created an enormous economic strain on the USSR's finances and was only held together by Soviet coercion. It eventually collapsed, bringing down the Soviet Union with it.

For ordinary Germans, what were the benefits of living in the Third Reich? If you were a Jew you were singled out for persecution and, ultimately, extinction. The Jews were blamed for Germany's troubles, and thereby public opinion was aroused against them and their fate at the hands of the military and the police was condoned.

Nazi Germany was a totalitarian state where the police operated without the constraints of laws and regulations. Their actions were unpredictable and directed by the whim of Hitler. The Weimar constitution was never actually abrogated under Hitler, but an enabling act passed by the *Reichstag* in 1933 permitted him to amend the constitution at will, in effect nullify it. The role of lawmaker became vested in one man. Hitler did not allow change to become predictable, thus increasing the sense of terror among the people and repressing any dissent. Organizations like the Gestapo were everywhere, and its network of informers ensured that dissent and resistance were crushed.

In a positive light it can be stated that German advances in technology and medicine during the Third Reich were to revolutionize the world. The terror weapons of the V-1 and V-2 were eventually to place man on the moon. In the social field, the NSDAP made it possible for the ordinary person to indulge in sports, like tennis, ridding and gliding, that had until then been the preserve of the privileged classes. The arts and theatre were also thrown open. The provision of holidays through the "Strength through Joy" movement laid the ground for Butlins Holiday Camps in Great Britain and the package holiday enjoyed by millions today. (the camping sites on the Adriatic for the old Auto Union are still in operation).

And yet, in the final analysis, these benefits are insignificant when put beside the price the German people paid for Hitler's dreams. Over 10 million German service personnel were killed, wounded or posted as missing in World War II, while 500,000 were killed on the home front. The concentration camps murdered an estimated six million Jews in the name of Nazi racial doctrine, while millions of non-Germans died fighting one of the most evil regimes in world history. The Soviet Union, for example, lost an estimated 20 million killed in a war that really was one of national survival.

Hitler, and thus the Third Reich, rejected liberalism and democracy, the rule of law, human rights, and all movements of international cooperation and peace. He stressed instead instinct, the subordination of the individual to the state, and the necessity of blind and unswerving obedience to Nazi ideology. The result was horror on a grand scale.

▼ *One of the more brutal Nazi governors was Arthur Seyss-Inquart, Reichskommissar for the Netherlands.*

INTERWAR YEARS

The treaties that ended World War I did not bring worldwide peace – various nations fought against each other or were torn apart by civil war. Also, the Treaty of Versailles left two dangerous legacies: a bitter, impoverished Germany and an Eastern Europe made up of small, politically-fragmented states. Interwar politicians, particularly nationalists and other rightwingers, began to exploit the situation created by Versailles. Their aggressiveness and opportunism, coupled with the political inertia of those who might have opposed them, led to World War II.

JANUARY 4, 1919

EASTERN FRONT, *LATVIA*
As part of the ongoing civil war in Russia, Bolshevik forces capture Riga in an attempt to reincorporate the former Russian province. They establish a government, but it is short-lived. With backing from Britain and France, German and Latvian troops evict the invaders. However, the Germans try to take over Riga until forced to return home by their backers on July 3.

JANUARY 18, 1919

POLITICS, *INTERNATIONAL*
Various victorious leaders assemble in Paris to discuss the terms on which peace should be agreed with the defeated Central Powers. Among

▼ *The World War I peacemakers gather – from left to right: Italy's Vittorio Orlando, Britain's David Lloyd George, France's Georges Clemenceau, and Woodrow Wilson of the United States.*

▲ *British troops and local police pictured in Dublin at the height of the Anglo-Irish Civil War, 1919–21.*

those present are President Woodrow Wilson of the United States, British Prime Minister Lloyd George, French Prime Minister Georges Clemenceau, and the prime minister of Italy, Vittorio Emanuele Orlando.

JANUARY 21, 1919

IRELAND, *CIVIL WAR*
Sinn Fein ("Ourselves Alone"), an Irish nationalist group, declares Ireland independent, sparking a rebellion against the British. There is fighting between Catholic nationalists and local Protestants, who favor maintaining links with Britain. The British deploy 100,000 troops and paramilitaries.

FEBRUARY 3, 1919

RUSSIA, *CIVIL WAR*
Revolutionary Bolshevik forces occupy Kiev as the first part of an advance that will see them evict the French troops occupying the Black Sea port of Odessa on December 18. The French have been supplying anti-Bolshevik "White" Russians.

▶ *Members of a rightwing Freikorps unit on the streets of Berlin during the early days of the Weimar Republic.*

FEBRUARY 11, 1919

POLITICS, *GERMANY*
Social Democrat Friedrich Ebert is elected the first president of the new republic. Ebert, a moderate socialist, will attempt to unite the various political factions within Germany from the seat of his government, the town of Weimar. Although his coalition is initially popular, it soon has to call on rightwing military bodies known as Freikorps to deal with pro-Russian

revolutionaries in Germany. However, the Freikorps dislike Ebert's regime only marginally less than they do the revolutionaries because of its contacts with Russia. In March 1920 one Freikorps unit stages a coup in Berlin. This rebellion, known as the "Kapp Putsch" after a rightwing politician, is defeated, but the violence continues.

MARCH 21, 1919

POLITICS, *HUNGARY*
President Mihály Károlyi resigns and a pro-Russian leader, Béla Kun, who has been in exile in Russia, is installed.

MARCH 28, 1919

POLITICS, *HUNGARY*
The pro-Russian regime of Béla Kun initiates a war with Czechoslovakia by invading Slovakia, which has a large Hungarian minority.

APRIL 10, 1919

POLITICS, *ROMANIA*
Romanian troops invade Hungary to forestall any Hungarian attempts to take over Transylvania, which has a large ethnic Hungarian population and has been occupied by Romania since the end of World War I.

APRIL 13, 1919

POLITICS, *INDIA*
Against a background of growing friction between Muslims and Hindus and the campaign of civil disobedience by supporters of former lawyer Mahatma Gandhi, British troops commanded by General Reginald Dyer commit a major

191

KEY MOMENTS

TREATY OF VERSAILLES

The treaty was signed at the Palace of Versailles, France, on June 28, 1919, and its provisions came into force on January 20 the following year. The victors of World War I, led by Britain, France, Italy, and the United States, had formulated the treaty's provisions at the Paris Peace Conference in early 1919. None of the defeated nations had any input into its contents.

The severity of the treaty came as a shock to the Germans present at Versailles. Germany had agreed an armistice in 1918 on the tacit understanding that any subsequent peace treaty would be based on US President Woodrow Wilson's 14-Point Peace Program. Although a number of the Versailles provisions reflected the spirit of Wilson's program, they also revealed the desire of some of the victors, chiefly Britain and France, to punish Germany for the war.

Germany lost some 10 percent of its prewar territory and population. This included surrendering Alsace and Lorraine to France, and having the Saarland placed under the supervision of the League of Nations until 1935. In the east, Germany was to give up West Prussia and Posen to Poland and a slice of territory that allowed Poland access to the Baltic. This, known as the "Polish Corridor," divided East Prussia from the rest of Germany. Danzig on the Baltic was made a free city. After a local vote part of Upper Silesia was also transferred to Polish control. Germany also lost its overseas possessions, which became territories administered by the victors.

Most galling of all to the German delegates was the demand that Germany accept a war guilt clause. Practically, this meant that Germany was burdened with huge reparations to pay for the damage suffered by the victors during World War I. The treaty also allowed the victors to take action if Germany defaulted on payments.

Germany's military power was curtailed. Its army was restricted to 100,000 men, the General Staff abolished, and the manufacture of aircraft, armored vehicles, gas, and submarines prohibited. All of Germany west of the Rhine and a zone 30 miles (48 km) east of it were to be demilitarized.

Many of the clauses of the treaty were modified during the interwar years, usually in Germany's favor, or were only halfheartedly imposed. Nevertheless, the "dictated" peace left many Germans resentful of their country's impoverishment, a situation that was exploited by rightwing politicians.

atrocity at Amritsar in the Punjab. Dyer has been ordered to restore order following a riot in which several Europeans have been killed. His troops open fire on civilians, killing 379 and wounding 1208. Dyer avoids major official censure.

MAY 7, 1919

POLITICS, *INTERNATIONAL*
Various representatives gather at the Palace of Versailles, France, to finalize the peace treaty with Germany.

MAY 15, 1919

MIDDLE EAST, *TURKEY*
A Greek force lands at Smyrna on the coast of Asia Minor, as Turkey descends into civil strife and the victors of World War I squabble over what peace settlements to impose on the country. The Greeks, long-standing enemies of the Turks, commit various atrocities against civilians, prompting patriotic Turkish elements under Mustafa Kemal to form a new nationalist government. Kemal will establish his main base at Ankara in central Turkey.

JUNE 22, 1919

MIDDLE EAST, *TURKEY*
With formal backing from various allies, chiefly Britain, Greek forces in Turkish Asia Minor embark on a military campaign to crush the nationalists led by Mustafa Kemal. The Turks, who are riven by political infighting, do not offer any significant resistance to the Greeks at the outset.

▲ *Germany's delegates attend Versailles, including General Hans von Seeckt (above, II), World War I veteran and later the first commander of his country's much-reduced interwar army.*

JUNE 28, 1919

POLITICS, *INTERNATIONAL*
The Treaty of Versailles, created by the World War I victors and imposed on defeated Germany, is signed in

the Hall of Mirrors at the Palace of Versailles, France. The treaty's provisions shock the German delegation.

JULY 21, 1919

POLITICS, *GERMANY*

Many of the German High Seas Fleet's warships that surrendered and sailed into British waters in November 1918 are scuttled by their crews at Scapa Flow in the Orkneys.

AUGUST 1, 1919

POLITICS, *HUNGARY*

Pro-Russian President Béla Kun flees Budapest in the face of growing unrest and the approach of invading Romanians. His replacement is World War I hero Admiral Miklós Horthy.

SEPTEMBER 2, 1919

RUSSIA, *CIVIL WAR*

"White" Russians under General Anton Denikin drive into Bolshevik Russia, capturing Kiev. The "White" General Peter Wrangel's Caucasian Army has already captured Tsaritsin on June 17, but fails to meet up with Admiral Alexander Kolchak's Volunteer Army, which has been pushed back through the Urals. Wrangel retreats.

SEPTEMBER 10, 1919

POLITICS, *INTERNATIONAL*

The Austrians sign the Treaty of St.

Germain at Versailles. Austria surrenders a large percentage of its German-speaking population as various territories are redistributed to Italy, Czechoslovakia, Yugoslavia, and Romania. Its army is reduced to 30,000 men and *Anschluss* ("Union") with Germany is forbidden.

SEPTEMBER 12, 1919

POLITICS, *ITALY*

Italian Nationalist Gabriele d'Annunzio takes control of the former Austro-Hungarian port of Fiume, which has a large Italian population but is also claimed by Yugoslavia. The Italian government disowns d'Annunzio and the rival claims are settled by the Treaty of Rapallo on November 12. Outraged by the perceived weakness of his own government, d'Annunzio declares war. However, his coup fails.

OCTOBER 24, 1919

RUSSIA, *CIVIL WAR*

"White" General Peter Krasnov's Don Army, advancing on Voronezh, is counterattacked by the Red Army and retreats. Exploiting the victory, the Red Army strikes westward, recapturing Kiev on December 17. The "Whites" retreat to the Black Sea.

OCTOBER 25, 1919

POLITICS, *GREECE*

King Alexander dies and is replaced by his father Constantine, who had been deposed in World War I.

DECEMBER 8, 1919

POLITICS, *POLAND*

The victors of World War I attempt to settle territorial disputes between Poland and Russia by demarcating a new border. This is known as the "Curzon Line" and follows the Bug River. However, it is unacceptable to the Polish government, which is

intent on taking over former Polish territories to the east of the river – a move likely to provoke war.

FEBRUARY 7, 1920

RUSSIA, *CIVIL WAR*

Captured "White" Russian Admiral Alexander Kolchak is executed by the Bolsheviks. His execution marks the end of serious opposition to the Bolsheviks in Siberia. The Bolsheviks now turn to deal with the "Whites" in the Ukraine.

MARCH 27, 1920

RUSSIA, *CIVIL WAR*

The defeated "White" forces on the Black Sea escape surrender to the Red Army thanks to an evacuation carried out by British warships. This leaves just General Peter Wrangel's forces in the Crimea opposing the Bolsheviks. He launches an offensive northward in June but is forced to retreat back into the Crimea by early November.

APRIL 25, 1920

EASTERN FRONT, *POLAND*

Polish forces under General Jósef Pilsudski launch an ambitious pre-emptive strike into

◀ *Pro-Bolshevik troops, part of the Red Army commanded by Leon Trotsky, head off to battle "White" Russian forces.*

▶ *General Jósef Pilsudski, head of the Polish government and armed forces.*

the Russian-controlled Ukraine. Both Poland and Russia have claims to each other's territory. The complex Polish operation stalls in early May as the Russians plan a counterattack.

APRIL 23, 1920

POLITICS, *TURKEY*

A provisional nationalist government headed by World War I hero Mustafa Kemal is proclaimed in Ankara.

MAY 15, 1920

EASTERN FRONT, *RUSSIA*

Russian forces in the Ukraine under Marshal Mikhail Tukhachevski and General Semën Budënny counterattack General Jósef Pilsudski's Polish forces. Pilsudski's army is in danger of being surrounded and is pushed into headlong retreat. Warsaw, the Polish capital, is under threat by August.

JUNE 4, 1920

POLITICS, *INTERNATIONAL*

The Hungarians sign the Treaty of Trianon in France. It confirms that Hungary will lose two-thirds of its former territories. Among those benefiting from Trianon are Romania, Poland, Czechoslovakia, Austria, and the Kingdom of Serbs, Croats, and Slovenes (later Yugoslavia), which gains Croatia and Slavonia. Hungary's armed forces are restricted to just 35,000 men.

AUGUST 14, 1920

POLITICS, *CZECHOSLOVAKIA*

The government signs what becomes

▲ *Lenin addresses soldiers of the Red Army as they prepare to fight against the Poles. Leon Trotsky, their commander, stands on the right of the podium.*

▶ *"White" Russian forces pose with the bodies of dead Red Army troops.*

known as the Little Entente with Yugoslavia, chiefly to prevent Hungary taking back the lands given to both of the former at the Treaty of Trianon. A similar arrangement is reached with Romania on April 23, 1921.

AUGUST 16–25, 1920

EASTERN FRONT, *POLAND*

Polish forces launch a counterattack against the Russian armies arrayed around Warsaw. The attack smashes through the Russian center, forcing the two wings to retreat eastward and to the north. Russian casualties total 150,000 men; those of the Poles 50,000. The Poles pursue the mauled Russians eastward, and they are fighting on Russian soil by the middle of September.

AUGUST 20, 1920

POLITICS, *TURKEY*

Turkey accepts the Treaty of Sèvres, which effectively signals the end of the old Turkish Empire. The country gives up its provinces in the Middle East and North Africa, and grants independence to Armenia. It also has to surrender most of its European possessions and accept a Greek garrison in both Thrace and on the fringes of Asia

Minor. Italian troops occupy parts of the south coast of Asia Minor.

The Greek presence will spark the outbreak of a war that will rage until 1922. Turkish opposition to the occupiers is led by Mustafa Kemal, who does not accept the treaty.

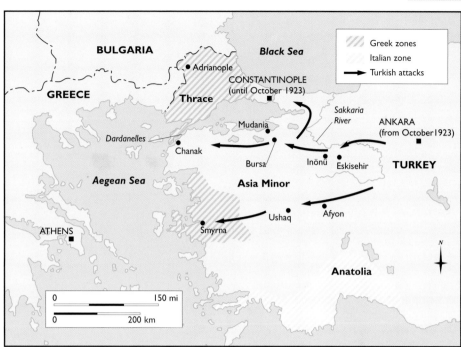

▲ *The course of the war between Greece and Turkey in Asia Minor, 1920–22. Both sides committed frequent atrocities.*

1920. The Poles have saved their country from occupation by Russia's Bolshevik regime, but a legacy of bitterness between the two Eastern European neighbors remains.

OCTOBER 14, 1920

POLITICS, *FINLAND*
The Finns finally win independence from Russia in the Treaty of Dorpat.

NOVEMBER 14, 1920

RUSSIA, *CIVIL WAR*
General Peter Wrangel's "White" forces are evacuated from the Crimea and transferred to Constantinople by British warships. This marks the end of effective opposition to the Bolsheviks.

OCTOBER 12, 1920

POLITICS, *RUSSIA*
The authorities agree an armistice with the Poles, who have inflicted a number of defeats on them over the previous months. The armistice is ratified by the Treaty of Riga signed on March 18,

MARCH 23, 1921

MIDDLE EAST, *TURKEY*
The Greeks renew their offensive deeper into Asia Minor, which had begun in January but was halted at the First Battle of Inönü. The Second Battle of Inönü on March 28-30 initially goes well for the Greeks, but the Turks finally defeat a succession of offensives.

JUNE 16–17, 1921

MIDDLE EAST, *TURKEY*
As part of their continuing attempts to secure territory in Asia Minor, the Greeks under King Constantine launch an offensive toward Afyon. Despite suffering high casualties in the intense fighting, the Turks are able to withdraw to the east. The Greek advance halts at the Sakkaria River due to exhaustion and supply shortages.

AUGUST 24– SEPTEMBER 6, 1921

MIDDLE EAST, TURKEY
The Battle of Sakkaria, part of the ongoing Greek-Turkish War, takes place. After several days of bitter fighting the Greeks under King Constantine are forced to retreat.

◄ *Red Army troops with one of the armored trains that allowed them to move across Russia to counter threats.*

195

The Turkish nationalists under Mustafa Kemal do not pursue closely. Kemal wishes to build up his military forces and strengthen his diplomatic relations with various foreign powers before launching an all-out offensive.

NOVEMBER 12, 1921

POLITICS, *INTERNATIONAL*

Several of the world's leading powers meet in Washington. They make several treaties designed to prevent any future war. The Four-Power Act is signed on December 13. It agrees that Britain, France, Japan, and the United States will be consulted over any problems arising in the Pacific between any two of the signatories to the act. An attached document states that they will respect each signatory's right to its colonial possessions and mandated territories in the region.

A further agreement, the Five-Power Naval Limitation Treaty, is signed by Britain, France, Italy, Japan, and the United States, on February 6, 1922. The signatories agree to scrap a large number of warships and set the relative strengths of the battleships in their fleets. They also are to cut back their shipbuilding programs for the next 10 years.

A final document, the Nine-Power Pact, agrees to respect China's territorial integrity. Aside from the five states already mentioned above, it is signed by Belgium, China, the Netherlands, and Portugal.

▲ A British warship at Constantinople. The Turkish capital was occupied from March 1920 until October 1923.

▼ British delegates at the Washington Conference, which attempted to limit the post-World War I naval race and reduce friction between the world's leading powers.

DECEMBER 6, 1921

POLITICS, *IRELAND*

The British grant dominion status to southern Ireland, but six counties in the north with a Protestant majority keep their links with Britain. Many in southern Ireland, though agreeing the compromise, believe that the northern counties should be part of an Irish state and demand total independence.

AUGUST 18, 1922

MIDDLE EAST, *TURKEY*

Turkish nationalists under Mustafa Kemal launch a major offensive against the Greek forces occupying the coastal fringe of Asia Minor. The Greeks are compelled to fall back. The Greek armies collapse, allowing the Turks to capture Smyrna on September 11. Its fall destroys the Greek presence in Asia Minor. Kemal next turns his attention toward Constantinople, which is occupied by foreign powers.

OCTOBER 3–11, 1922

POLITICS, *TURKEY*

Turkish nationalists led by Mustafa Kemal and the various foreign powers occupying Constantinople agree the Convention of Mudania. This promises to restore Thrace and the city of Adrianople to Turkey, and to make the Dardanelles neutral. Kemal takes the opportunity to announce the end of the Turkish sultanate, and the ruling sultan goes into exile on November 1.

▶ *French troops occupy the Rhineland following Germany's default in paying war reparations. They stayed until 1925.*

▼ *Italian fascist leader Benito Mussolini (second from right) and some of his supporters, known as "Blackshirts."*

OCTOBER 28, 1922

POLITICS, *ITALY*

Rightwing fascist leader Benito Mussolini leads his followers, the "Blackshirts," on what becomes known as the "March on Rome." Mussolini forces the government and king to give him dictatorial powers on November 28 and he initiates a reign of terror against leftwing opponents, which lasts from 1923 to 1925.

DECEMBER 30, 1922

POLITICS, *SOVIET UNION*

The Union of Soviet Socialist Republics comes into existence following the communist victory in the Russian Civil War. It initially comprises four soviet federated republics – the Russian, the Transcaucasian, the Ukrainian, and the Belorussian.

JANUARY 10, 1923

POLITICS, *UNITED STATES*

President Warren Harding withdraws the last detachments of US troops based in Europe.

JANUARY 11, 1923

POLITICS, *EUROPE*

French and Belgian troops march into the Ruhr, Germany's industrial heart. They are allowed to do so because of Germany's default on paying the war

JULY 24, 1923

reparations imposed by the Treaty of Versailles. The occupation forces remain until August 1925, by which time Germany has paid the outstanding reparations chiefly due to the US-sponsored Dawes Plan. This was able to reorganize Germany's parlous financial affairs in part due to large loans from the United States.

JULY 24, 1923

POLITICS, *TURKEY*

Following seven months of discussions the Treaty of Lausanne is agreed. It effectively repeals much of the Treaty of Sèvres, which was imposed on Turkey in 1919. Under the provisions agreed at Lausanne, Turkey regains much of Thrace from Greece and confirms that it will end all claims in the Middle East and elsewhere. The treaty is a triumph for Mustafa Kemal, the nationalist, who is proclaimed the first president of the new Turkish republic on October 29.

NOVEMBER 8–11, 1923

POLITICS, *GERMANY*

Extreme rightwingers of the National Socialist German Workers' Party (Nazis) under Adolf Hitler stage a coup

▼ **Armed supports of the Adolf Hitler's National Socialist German Workers' Party in Munich during their coup attempt.**

in Munich. They intend to overthrow the Bavarian government. However, the coup, known as the "Munich Putsch," ends in farce. Hitler is tried for treason and sentenced to five years in prison. However, he serves just nine months, spending the time writing a personal political testament, *Mein Kampf* ("My Struggle"). On his release Hitler continues his political career.

JANUARY 21, 1924

POLITICS, *CHINA*

Nationalist leader Sun Yat-sen chairs a conference of leading figures in the Kuomintang (National People's Party) at Canton. The discussions center on liberating the country from the various warlords who run its provinces as personal fiefdoms with no regard for central authority. To further their cause the Nationalists establish a military academy under the command of General Chiang Kai-shek.

POLITICS, *SOVIET UNION*

The death of leader Lenin sparks a political struggle as several former Bolshevik comrades vie for power. The turmoil continues until the second half of 1926 when Joseph Stalin emerges as the new leader.

NOVEMBER 26, 1924

POLITICS, *MONGOLIA*

Mongolian communists, who have

▲ *Delegates at Locarno sign the various treaties designed to maintain security in Western Europe after World War I.*

received support from the Soviet Union, announce the formation of the Mongolian People's Republic, which becomes a puppet of the Soviet Union.

APRIL 26, 1925

POLITICS, *GERMANY*

World War I hero Marshal Paul von Hindenburg is elected president.

JUNE 17, 1925

POLITICS, *INTERNATIONAL*

The League of Nations in Geneva, intent on controlling any arms race, attempts to limit the international arms trade. The Geneva Protocol prohibits the use of poison gas.

OCTOBER 5–16, 1925

POLITICS, *INTERNATIONAL*

Various nations meet under the aegis of the League of Nations. The discussions center on creating a framework that can help to provide a degree of security in Europe. Those present at the meeting, known as the Locarno Conference, agree several points. Belgium, Britain, France, and Germany are to mutually guarantee the frontiers between France and Germany and Belgium and Germany. Any disputes between Germany and Poland and Germany and Czechoslovakia are to go to arbitration, as well as any disputes

JUNE 20–AUGUST 4, 1927

POLITICS, *INTERNATIONAL*
Britain, Japan, and the United States, their representatives meeting in Geneva, fail to agree a formula to establish the ratio of cruisers, destroyers, and submarines in their respective fleets.

AUGUST 1, 1927

POLITICS, *CHINA*
Communist elements within the Nationalist armed forces rebel in Nanchang. Although they are defeated, the rising marks the beginning of civil war. Other communist uprisings occur throughout the year, most notably in the province of Hunan where communist leader Mao Zhe-dong organizes a revolt of local peasants. However, Nationalists crush the communist-led resistance in Hunan.

SEPTEMBER 18, 1927

POLITICS, *GERMANY*
President Paul von Hindenburg rejects German responsibility for World War I, thereby denying a key part of the Treaty of Versailles.

NOVEMBER 22, 1927

POLITICS, *ITALY*
The government agrees the Second Treaty of Tirana with Albania. Under its provisions Albania becomes an Italian protectorate.

---

involving Germany and Belgium and Germany and France. Mutual assistance treaties are signed between France and Poland and also France and Czechoslovakia to prevent attack by Germany. However, France continues to build the Maginot Line defenses along its border with Germany.

MARCH 26, 1926

FAR EAST AND PACIFIC, *CHINA*
Chinese Nationalist forces under General Chiang Kai-shek capture the city of Nanking. This action is part of an ongoing offensive by the Nationalists, who are trying to unite the country and wrest power from the warlords who run the greater number of China's provinces.

APRIL 12, 1926

FAR EAST AND PACIFIC, *CHINA*
Chiang Kai-shek's Nationalist forces seize Shanghai in a move to prevent perceived subversion by both Chinese communists and leftwingers in the Kuomintang's national government. Following the action, which is denounced by the communists and leftwingers, Chiang establishes his own government in Nanking.

MAY 10, 1926

POLITICS, *UNITED STATES*
US Marines land in Nicaragua to stop a revolt. The United States will maintain a military commitment in the Central American country until 1933.

MAY 12–14, 1926

POLITICS, *POLAND*
The government is overthrown and a dictatorship headed by Marshal Jósef Pilsudski takes power.

NOVEMBER 27, 1926

POLITICS, *ITALY*
The government signs the Treaty of Tirana with Albania in which both agree to respect the territorial integrity of the other.

JANUARY 31, 1927

POLITICS, *INTERNATIONAL*
The Inter-Allied Military Control Commission, which had been created by the World War I victors to ensure Germany's compliance with the Treaty of Versailles' provisions, is dissolved. None of its members is willing to use troops to enforce Versailles, despite Germany's frequent flouting of its clauses. The League of Nations takes over its administration.

▶ *President Hindenburg rejected German responsibility for World War I.*

APRIL 12, 1928

APRIL 12, 1928

POLITICS, *CHINA*
Nationalist troops under Chiang Kai-shek launch an offensive against various warlords. The warlords are forced to accept Nationalist authority.

AUGUST 2, 1928

POLITICS, *ETHIOPIA*
The government signs the 20-Year Friendship Pact with Italy. Ethiopia gains trading rights in exchange for allowing Italian engineers to construct roads in Ethiopia.

FEBRUARY 6, 1929

POLITICS, *GERMANY*
The government accepts the Kellogg–Briand Pact, which has been under discussion since August 1928. Those signing renounce aggressive war. Also among the signatories are Britain, France, Italy, Japan, and the United States.

FEBRUARY 9, 1929

POLITICS, *SOVIET UNION*
Along with Estonia, Latvia, Poland, and Romania, Soviet delegates sign a pact rejecting aggressive war. It is named after the Soviet Union's chief negotiator, Maksim Litvinov.

OCTOBER 24, 1929

ECONOMICS, *INTERNATIONAL*
The US stock market crashes, heralding a period of worldwide economic failure, which becomes known as the "Great Depression." Among those badly hit is Germany, where inflation soars and unemployment rises to 25 percent of the work force by 1932. The insecurity prompts many Germans to support Adolf Hitler.

JULY 28, 1930

POLITICS, *CHINA*
Chinese communist forces capture Chang-sha in central China. The opposing Nationalists retake the city and initiate a series of "bandit suppression" campaigns. These are attempts to wipe out the communists. By 1934 the campaigns are successful, forcing communists under Mao Zhe-dong to retreat to safe havens. The trek, which becomes known as the "Long March," covers some 6000 miles (9600 km) and ends in 1935.

APRIL 14, 1931

POLITICS, *SPAIN*
In a near-bloodless coup initiated by the country's pro-democratic bodies, King Alfonso XIII is deposed and Republican leader Alcalá Zamora is made head of the new government. He is named president on December 10. However, the country is far from stable.

◀ *Chinese communists pictured on the "Long March," 1934–35.*

SEPTEMBER 19, 1931

POLITICS, *CHINA*
The Japanese engineer an incident on the border between Manchuria, much of which they effectively control, and China. They claim that the Chinese Nationalists are planning to blow up key bridges along the railroad that links the Japanese bases at Port Arthur and Mukden. Chinese troops are forced to retreat from the area and the Japanese then continue their offensive. By February 1932 all of Manchuria is under their control.

FEBRUARY 18, 1932

POLITICS, *JAPAN*
The government announces the creation of the puppet state of Manchukuo, formerly Manchuria, which they have taken control of during the previous months. Former Chinese Emperor Pu-Yi is made nominal leader of state but is no more than a figurehead.

JUNE 16, 1932

POLITICS, *GERMANY*
Chancellor Franz von Papen ends the ban on the activities of members of the Nazi Party's SA (*Sturmabteilung* – "Storm Detachment"). Known as

and the United States sign an agreement to scrap certain types of warships by 1933. However, a clause allows any of the signatories to increase the tonnage of any particular type of vessel in their fleet if its national needs require it. The provisions of the London Naval Conference are to run until 1936.

JANUARY 30, 1933

POLITICS, *GERMANY*

Adolf Hitler, leader of the Nazi Party, becomes chancellor at the second time of asking following the resignation of Franz von Papen on November 17, 1932. Hitler refused the post the previous November as he was denied absolute power.

Hitler had already tried to gain power through another route by attempting to become president in November 1932. However, he was beaten by the incumbent, Paul von Hindenburg, polling just 36.9 percent of the vote on the second ballot.

FEBRUARY 27, 1933

POLITICS, *GERMANY*

The Reichstag (German parliament) building in Berlin is destroyed in a mysterious arson attack. A communist sympathizer is arrested and Chancellor Adolf Hitler uses the incident to warn

▲ *Members of Hitler's "Brownshirts" attend the funeral of a comrade killed in political streetfighting with communists.*

"Brownshirts," they have been responsible in the past for considerable political violence. With the ban lifted, SA-inspired streetfighting rises.

JULY 25, 1932

POLITICS, *SOVIET UNION*

The authorities sign nonaggression pacts with Estonia, Latvia, Finland, and Poland. A similar agreement is reached with France the following November.

AUGUST 10, 1932

POLITICS, *SPAIN*

Republican President Alcalá Zamora, already facing growing calls for autonomy in some provinces, is faced by a rightwing revolt in Seville led by General José Sanjurjo. The revolt is quickly defeated, but the political violence continues.

NOVEMBER 8, 1932

POLITICS, *UNITED STATES*

Democratic contender Franklin Delano Roosevelt wins the presidential election in a landslide victory over incumbent Republican Herbert Hoover.

Roosevelt, who suffers from the debilitating impact of childhood polio, will prove to be one of his country's greatest leaders. He will serve as president for an unprecedented four terms, create policies designed to drag the United States out of the economic and social misery engendered by the worldwide Great Depression, and lead his country for most of its involvement in World War II.

NOVEMBER 17, 1932

POLITICS, *GERMANY*

The chancellor, Franz von Papen, resigns amid growing political unrest.

JANUARY 21– APRIL 22, 1933

POLITICS, *INTERNATIONAL*

Representatives of Britain, France, Italy, Japan, and the United States meet in London in an attempt to establish limits to their fleets. It is agreed to curb submarine tonnage and aircraft carriers. Britain, Japan,

▶ *US President Franklin D. Roosevelt was elected for the first of his four terms in office in 1932.*

NOVEMBER 17, 1933

POLITICS, *UNITED STATES*
The administration recognizes the legitimacy of the Soviet Union.

JANUARY 26, 1934

POLITICS, *GERMANY*
The government signs a nonaggression agreement with Poland. Its central tenet is that each should accept the territorial rights of the other for the next 10 years.

FEBRUARY 8–9, 1934

POLITICS, *BALKANS*
Greece, Romania, Turkey, and Yugoslavia agree a pact in which each is pledged to consult the other signatories if its security is threatened. However, Bulgaria rejects the pact.

MARCH 17, 1934

POLITICS, *ITALY*
Officials from Italy, Hungary, and Austria meet in Rome and agree to establish closer economic ties and create a rightwing power bloc to

▲ *The Reichstag (German parliament) after the mysterious and controversial arson attack in February 1933.*

of a plot to take over the country. President Paul von Hindenburg outlaws communists and suspends various constitutional freedoms.

MARCH 5, 1933

POLITICS, *GERMANY*
Adolf Hitler's Nazi Party secures 43.9 percent of the popular vote in national elections, which have been marred by violence and intimidation by Nazi paramilitaries. On the 23rd the Reichstag passes a bill granting Hitler wide-ranging powers.

SEPTEMBER 15, 1933

POLITICS, *GREECE*
The administration signs a 10-year nonaggression pact with Turkey.

OCTOBER 14, 1933

POLITICS, *GERMANY*
The government resigns its seat in the League of Nations after disagreeing with plans to curb the expansion of armed forces and the growth of armaments production.

▶ *A large poster exhorts ordinary Germans to vote for Nazi Party leader Adolf Hitler in 1933.*

counter France's increasingly close ties with Czechoslovakia, Romania, and Yugoslavia. The latter three, known as the Little Entente powers, had already established various mutually-beneficial defensive agreements in 1920–21 to block German and Hungarian ambitions along the Danube River.

JUNE 30, 1934

POLITICS, *GERMANY*

More than 70 members of the Nazi Party are murdered in a purge ordered by Adolf Hitler, who believes they are a threat to his absolute authority. The action is known as "The Night of the Long Knives." Chief among those killed in the purge is Ernst Röhm, head of the Nazi Party's "Brownshirts."

JULY 25, 1934

POLITICS, *AUSTRIA*

Local Nazis assassinate Prime Minister Engelbert Dollfuss in an attempted coup. Although Chancellor Adolf Hitler denies all knowledge of the putsch, German troops are preparing to intervene. However, Hitler is forced to back down when both Italy and Yugoslavia mobilize their own forces.

AUGUST 2, 1934

POLITICS, *GERMANY*

President Paul von Hindenburg dies, allowing his chancellor, Adolf Hitler, to assume dictatorial powers by combining the posts of chancellor and president. The German people are permitted to vote on the matter – 90 percent are in favor. It also makes Hitler the supreme commander of all of the country's armed forces. Hitler receives the title of Führer ("leader") of the German Third Reich.

SEPTEMBER 18, 1934

POLITICS, *SOVIET UNION*

Joins the League of Nations.

OCTOBER 6, 1934

POLITICS, *SPAIN*

The government puts down leftwing revolts in the provinces of Asturias and Catalonia. There are reports that its troops have committed atrocities.

DECEMBER 5, 1934

EAST AFRICA, *ETHIOPIA*

Ethiopian and Italian forces clash over disputed territory on the border of Italian Somaliland. The League of Nations is unable to identify the instigator of the aggression.

▲ *The body of Prime Minister Engelbert Dollfuss lies in state following his assassination by Austrian Nazis.*

DECEMBER 19, 1934

POLITICS, *JAPAN*

The government rejects the Washington and London Naval Treaties, giving, as is required, two years' notice that it will no longer abide by the Washington Treaty and that it will not renew the London Treaty when it ends in 1936. The decision is sparked by Britain and the United States rejecting Japan's demands that it has parity with their fleets. Although Britain, France, Italy, Japan, and the United States will attend the Five-Power Naval Conference in December 1935, it also ends in failure when Japan's representatives walk out of the discussions.

MARCH 16, 1935

POLITICS, *GERMANY*

Hitler rejects the disarmament terms of the Treaty of Versailles, claiming that other nations are rearming. He embarks on a rearmaments program and reintroduces conscription.

MAY 2, 1935

POLITICS, *FRANCE*

Alarmed at Germany's announcement of a rearmaments program, the authorities agree an alliance with Russia. France begins rearming the next year.

MAY 16, 1935

POLITICS, *SOVIET UNION*

The authorities sign an alliance with Czechoslovakia to curb German expansionism into Eastern Europe.

JUNE 18, 1935

POLITICS, *GERMANY*

The government signs a naval agreement with Britain. Germany's fleet, excluding submarines, will have a tonnage no more that 35 percent of Britain's. The French authorities are outraged by the pact.

JULY 25, 1935

POLITICS, *SOVIET UNION*

Delegates attending the Third International agree to support those democracies arrayed against Europe's rightwing dictatorships, marking a major shift in the foreign policy of the Soviet Union.

OCTOBER 3, 1935

KEY PERSONALITIES

GENERAL FRANCISCO FRANCO

Franco (1892–1975) was the dictator of Spain from the end of the Spanish Civil War (1936–39) until his death. Pro-monarchy and opposed to anti-Catholics, he was a careerist who entered the Toledo Infantry Academy in 1907 and whose abilities were recognized. By 1926 he was commanding the Spanish Foreign Legion, which defeated an Arab uprising in Spanish Morocco.

Franco fell out of favor following the overthrow of the monarchy and the election of a republican government in April 1931. He was sent to the Balearic Islands, returning in 1935 to suppress a leftwing revolt at the behest of the rightwing government of the time. However, Spain's volatile politics led to the election of a leftwing government and Franco was effectively exiled to the Canary Islands.

In 1936 Franco joined forces with other generals to launch a coup against the government, an act that sparked the civil war. Franco was made the rebels' chief of staff and by the end of the year he and his generals controlled roughly 50 percent of the country. At the end of the war Franco was the leader of the Nationalists and instigated a brutal campaign to crush all support for the former leftwing regime.

Although pro-Axis during World War II, Franco steadfastly refused to go to war in support of Germany and Italy, although Spanish workers were sent to Germany and a division of volunteers fought on the Eastern Front. As the war turned against the Axis, he became strictly neutral.

After 1945 Franco reorganized the Spanish government, concentrating even more power in his own hands, and made himself regent for the monarchy. His limited and short-lived political reforms in the 1950s did little to satisfy the aspirations of Spain's ethnic groups in the Basque country and in Catalonia. In his final years he ensured that the monarchy would continue after his death.

▲ Italian marines march in triumph through the streets of Addis Ababa, the Ethiopian capital, after its capitulation.

OCTOBER 3, 1935

EAST AFRICA, *ETHIOPIA*
Italian forces invade, although there has been no formal declaration of war. The military adventure is part of Italian dictator Benito Mussolini's plan to create an Italian empire in northern and eastern Africa. Four days later the League of Nations declares Italy the aggressor, and imposes sanctions the following month. The Italian offensive continues, despite fierce resistance from the Ethiopians.

NOVEMBER 12, 1935

POLITICS, *GERMANY*
The Saarland, which as part of the Treaty of Versailles settlement has been administered by the League of Nations, votes to return to direct German political control.

FEBRUARY 16, 1936

POLITICS, *SPAIN*
National elections lead to the formation of a new leftwing government headed by Manuel Azãna.

MARCH 7, 1936

POLITICS, *GERMANY*
Adolf Hitler renounces the Locarno Pact signed in 1925. It had been designed to guarantee territorial security in Europe, particularly in relation to Germany and its neighbors. Simultaneously, German forces reoccupy the Rhineland. Britain does not support the French government, which is ready to intervene, and the reoccupation goes unchallenged.

MAY 5, 1936

EAST AFRICA, *ETHIOPIA*
Invading Italian forces capture the capital, Addis Ababa, forcing Emperor Haile Selassie to flee his country. Four days later Italy formally annexes Ethiopia. Together with Eritrea and Italian Somaliland, it comprises Italian East Africa.

JUNE 18, 1936

SPAIN, *CIVIL WAR*
Twelve military garrisons on the Spanish mainland and five in Spanish Morocco rebel against Manuel Azãna's Republican government. General Francisco Franco, exiled in the Canary Islands, flies to Spanish Morocco and takes charge of the rebelling garrison

at Melilla. Meanwhile, anti-government troops, known as Nationalists, are flown from Spanish Morocco and establish bases at Algeciras and La Linea on the mainland. In northern Spain antigovernment forces are centered on Burgos.

AUGUST 15, 1936

SPAIN, *CIVIL WAR*
Nationalist rebels capture Badajoz from forces loyal to the Republican government.
They continue their advance toward Madrid, the capital, relieving the Nationalist troops under siege at Toledo on September 28. As the fighting intensifies, the Nationalists receive military aid from Germany and Italy; the Republicans are supplied by the

▶ **Italian guns are turned on their former owners during the Spanish Civil War.**

Soviet Union. Various foreign volunteers flock to both sides, but the bulk fight with the Republicans in units known as International Brigades.

AUGUST 26, 1936

POLITICS, *EGYPT*
The authorities enter into an agreement with Britain, which grants the country full independence. Britain is allowed to maintain a military presence along the Suez Canal and keep its naval base at Alexandria.

SEPTEMBER 4, 1936

POLITICS, *SPAIN*
The leftwing Popular Front government is formed under the leadership of Francisco Largo Cabellero in an attempt to unite the various political groups opposing the rebelling Nationalists, who appoint General Francisco Franco the chief of their rival Spanish state in October.

OCTOBER 27, 1936

POLITICS, *GERMANY*
Germany reaches an agreement with Italy. Italy agrees not to oppose the planned German take-over of Austria, while Germany pledges to recognize the legitimacy of Italy's conquest of Ethiopia. The arrangement marks the beginning of even closer ties between Nazi Germany and fascist Italy, the so-called Rome–Berlin Axis.

NOVEMBER 6, 1936

SPAIN, *CIVIL WAR*
Nationalist forces lay siege to Madrid but are unable to capture the capital. The fighting continues into 1937.

NOVEMBER 18, 1936

POLITICS, *SPAIN*
The authority of General Francisco Franco's Nationalist government is recognized by Germany and Italy.

NOVEMBER 25, 1936

POLITICS, *GERMANY*
The government signs what becomes known as the Anti-Comintern Pact with Japan. It is to reinforce the existing German–Italian power bloc, which opposes the French and Russian alliance.

MARCH 18, 1937

SPAIN, *CIVIL WAR*
Italian troops fighting for the Nationalist rebels are defeated at the Battle of Brihuega by forces loyal to the Republican government. The Nationalists call off their attempts to surround Madrid and push into northern Spain instead, capturing Bilbao in April.

MARCH 25, 1937

POLITICS, *ITALY*
The authorities sign an agreement with Yugoslavia, which guarantees the two countries' existing borders.

APRIL 25, 1937

SPAIN, *CIVIL WAR*
German aircraft, part of the Condor Legion which is fighting for the Nationalists, bomb the town of Guernica in the north. In what is considered an atrocity by many, some 1600 civilians are killed and nearly 900 wounded – one-third of the town's total population.

◄ *Japanese troops extricate their trucks from mud during their push into northeastern China.*

MAY 17, 1937

POLITICS, *SPAIN*
The Popular Front coalition government of Francisco Largo Cabellero falls following political infighting between the various leftwing groups within the government. Juan Negrín is named the new leader.

JUNE 18, 1937

SPAIN, *CIVIL WAR*
Nationalist rebels capture the northern port of Bilbao from forces loyal to the Republican government. The Nationalist continue their attacks and by the end of the year will control all of northern Spain.

JULY 7, 1937

FAR EAST AND PACIFIC, *CHINA*
Japanese forces clash with Chinese units near the Marco Polo Bridge to the northeast of Beijing. The incident is engineered by the Japanese and heralds a full-scale invasion of China. The Chinese forces opposing the Japanese consist of some two million poorly-trained Nationalists under General Chiang Kai-shek and some 150,000 communist guerrillas. Relations between the Nationalist and communist forces are strained. The Japanese have a front-line strength of 300,000 men supported by 150,000 local troops. Some two million reserves are also available from Japan itself. Japan's air force and navy are incomparably superior to those of the Chinese.

The initial Japanese attacks are overwhelmingly successful. Beijing falls on the 28th and Tientsin the following day. Despite increasing Chinese resistance and problems of resupply, the Japanese capture most of China north of the Yellow River by the end of the year. Chief among the Japanese victories, which are often accompanied by atrocities against civilians, is the capture of Shanghai in early November.

OCTOBER 13, 1937

POLITICS, *GERMANY*
Adolf Hitler offers a guarantee that Belgium's borders will be respected with the key proviso that Belgium does not take any military action against Germany.

NOVEMBER 5, 1937

POLITICS, *GERMANY*
Adolf Hitler meets with his senior military commanders and foreign minister. The discussions, held in great secrecy, center on his plans for gaining *Lebensraum* ("living room") for the German people. He expects Austria, Czechoslovakia, Poland, and the Soviet Union to be seized by force between 1938 and 1943.

NOVEMBER 28, 1937

SPAIN, *CIVIL WAR*
Nationalist leader General Francisco Franco orders a naval blockade of Spain to prevent supplies from reaching the Republican government.

DECEMBER 11, 1937

POLITICS, *ITALY*
The government announces its withdrawal from the League of Nations.

DECEMBER 13, 1937

FAR EAST AND PACIFIC, *CHINA*
Japanese forces capture the city of

▼ *German forces occupy Austria, a gamble by Adolf Hitler that was unopposed by the international community.*

the country is now held by the Nationalists, who are preparing for a final offensive.

JULY 11, 1938

FAR EAST AND PACIFIC, *CHINA*
Fighting breaks out between the Soviet Union and Japan, which is occupying Manchuria and Korea, over a disputed border. Japanese attacks are beaten off by mid-August but tension remains.

In May the fighting flares up again. This time it occurs along a river, which the Japanese claim to be the true border between Manchuria and Soviet-occupied Mongolia. The Soviet response is to occupy the disputed territory lying between the river and Nomonhan, but Japanese attacks force the invaders back. However, a Soviet counteroffensive led by General Georgi Zhukov pushes the Japanese back and beats off several counter-attacks over the following months.

SEPTEMBER 15, 1938

POLITICS, *CHINA*
The fighting between Soviet and Japanese forces over a disputed border ends with a cease-fire.

POLITICS, *GERMANY*
Hitler demands that Czechoslovakia gives up its province of Sudetenland,

Nanking. Its fall is followed by several weeks of slaughter and looting by the Japanese. An estimated 42,000 civilians are killed. However, the horror of Nanking stiffens Chinese resolve against the Japanese, whose plans to take over China suffer a series of military setbacks.

MARCH 12, 1938

POLITICS, *GERMANY*
Hitler orders the take-over of Austria, where some six million Germans live. The operation is completed the next day. Italian dictator Benito Mussolini backs Hitler's political gamble of *Anschluss* ("Union") with Austria.

APRIL 15, 1938

SPAIN, *CIVIL WAR*
Nationalist forces reach the port of Vinaroz on the coast of Valencia in the east, effectively isolating Catalonia to the north from other Republican-held areas of the country.

JUNE 24, 1938

SPAIN, *CIVIL WAR*
Republican forces launch an offensive along the line of the Ebro River in an attempt to restore communications between isolated Catalonia and the other parts of the country held by their troops. The main attack is halted after just seven days, but the fighting continues into November, when the Republicans withdraw. More than half

▲ *The Soviet Union's General Georgi Zhukov (in peaked cap) holds a field briefing during the brief border war with the Japanese.*

▼ *The course of the Spanish Civil War, fought during 1936–39.*

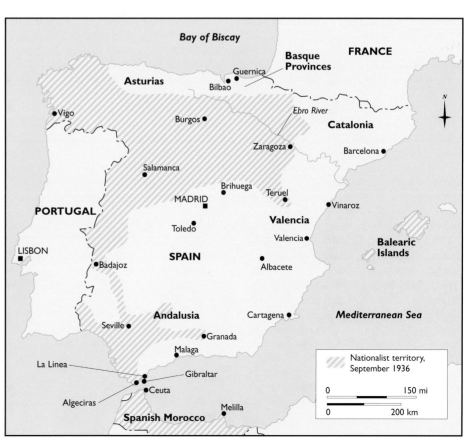

Nationalist territory, September 1936

▲ Bewildered Czech nationals look on as the German armed forces occupy the Sudetenland in 1938.

which contains some three million German-speakers. Hitler's propaganda machine has been demanding its return over the preceding two years. British Prime Minister Neville Chamberlain attends conferences with Hitler to negotiate an acceptable compromise on two occasions but returns to Britain without securing any agreement.

SEPTEMBER 29, 1938

POLITICS, *GERMANY*
Adolf Hitler, accompanied by Foreign Minister Joachim von Ribbentrop, meets with several European statesmen at Munich. Among those present are Italian dictator Benito Mussolini, his foreign minister, Count Ciano, British Prime Minister Neville Chamberlain and Edouard Daladier, France's prime minister.

Both Britain and France's leaders are painfully aware of their military weakness and believe that by acceding to Hitler's claims on Czechoslovakia they can secure a long-lasting peace in Europe. Hitler, who indicates this is his last territorial demand in Europe, is effectively given a free hand and the Sudetenland is incorporated into Germany. The Czech leaders are not invited to the meeting.

OCTOBER 21, 1938

FAR EAST AND PACIFIC, *CHINA*
Following amphibious landings near British-controlled Hong Kong, Japanese forces capture Canton from the Chinese. The fall of the port is a temporary boost to Japanese morale, which has suffered in the previous months because of their inability to deliver a knockout blow against the Chinese Nationalists and communists attempting to prevent the takeover of their country.

▶ *Chamberlain and Hitler during the discussions over the Sudetenland.*

Nevertheless, the Japanese no longer hold out any hopes of conquering China quickly; they settle on a new strategy designed to wear down the Chinese. However, although the Japanese have captured China's major ports, the Chinese wage a guerrilla war and are still able to receive supplies from two directions. One is via a railroad that runs from Haiphong, a port in French-controlled Indochina, while the other is a road that begins in Burma, which is administered by the British. The latter, later known as the "Burma Road," will have an important role to play in World War II.

NOVEMBER 2, 1938

POLITICS, *HUNGARY*
Germany grants the country a large part of former Czech territory for the support it offered during the annexation of the Sudetenland.

NOVEMBER 9–10, 1938

POLITICS, *GERMANY*
Adolf Hitler's supporters launch attacks on Germany's Jewish community and their property, particularly synagogues. The events become known as *Kristallnacht* ("Crystal Night") because of the shards of window glass that litter the roads and sidewalks outside Jewish properties.

Kristallnacht marks an intensification in the persecution of

▲ *A synagogue burns following the Nazi attacks on Kristallnacht, which marked an escalation in anti-Jewish violence.*

Germany's Jews, who have already lost their legal rights as citizens. Since 1933 roughly half of Germany's 500,000-strong Jewish community has fled the country.

NOVEMBER 30, 1938

POLITICS, *ITALY*
Friction between Italy and France rises as the former demands that the latter surrenders Corsica and Tunisia.

DECEMBER 6, 1938

POLITICS, *FRANCE*
The government agrees a pact with Germany. It guarantees the integrity of their existing borders.

DECEMBER 23, 1938

SPAIN, *CIVIL WAR*
Nationalists forces launch an offensive to capture Catalonia, which has been effectively cut off from the rest of Republican-held Spain since April

1937. Republican morale begins to collapse in the face of the onslaught.

JANUARY 12, 1939

POLITICS, *UNITED STATES*
President Franklin D. Roosevelt requests Congress to approve a defense budget of $552 million, marking a significant rise in military spending.

JANUARY 26, 1939

SPAIN, *CIVIL WAR*
Barcelona, the Republican-held capital of Catalonia, is captured by the Nationalists.

▶ *Nationalist howitzers prepare to open fire on Republican positions in the battle for Catalonia, early 1939.*

FEBRUARY 27, 1939

POLITICS, *SPAIN*
The authority of the Nationalist regime of General Francisco Franco is recognized by Britain and France.

MARCH 5, 1939

POLITICS, *SPAIN*
The factions within the leftwing coalition government of Republican Juan Negrín disagree over the future of the war. Negrín is for fighting on despite the increasingly hopeless position; others favor an end to the war. Negrín is overthrown and replaced by Colonel Sigismundo Casado.

MARCH 10, 1939

POLITICS, *GERMANY*
Adolf Hitler begins the annexation of Bohemia and Moravia, both part of Czechoslovakia with sizeable German populations. The operation, which is in direct violation of the Munich Agreement, is completed by the 16th. Czechoslovakia ceases to exist, with only Slovakia remaining nominally independent. Hungary cooperates with Germany and gains Ruthenia.

MARCH 23, 1939

POLITICS, *GERMANY*
Adolf Hitler orders the annexation of Memel, Lithuania, and demands the return of the "Polish Corridor" and Danzig from Poland. His actions spark intense defensive negotiations between Britain and the Soviet Union over the following months.

MARCH 28, 1939

SPAIN, *CIVIL WAR*
Nationalist troops enter

▲ *Some of the German troops fighting for the Nationalists during the Spanish Civil War (right) march through Madrid, 1939.*

the capital, Madrid, thereby ending the fighting. Over the following weeks the various Republican forces surrender.

The civil war has cost the lives of some 300,000 Spaniards, perhaps a third killed in reprisals and atrocities by both Nationalists and Republicans. Nationalist leader General Francisco Franco sets out to eradicate those with strong Republican sympathies and an estimated 300,000 are killed in the subsequent purges.

MARCH 31, 1939

POLITICS, *BRITAIN*
The British government guarantees to aid Poland if the latter country is the victim of any external aggression. The arrangement is a last-ditch attempt to prevent Hitler from taking over the country, but Britain is ill-prepared to offer any immediate military aid to Poland. Similar pledges are later made to Greece and Romania. The French also give the same assurances.

APRIL 7, 1939

BALKANS, *ALBANIA*
Italian forces invade and quickly conquer the country. The attack is part of Mussolini's aim to create an Italian empire stretching along the Mediterranean coast.

APRIL 11, 1939

POLITICS, *HUNGARY*
The authorities withdraw from the League of Nations.

APRIL 13, 1939

POLITICS, *ROMANIA*
The country's independence is guaranteed by Britain and France. However, the value of the agreement is soon undermined when the Romanian government agrees closer economic ties with Germany.

APRIL 28, 1939

POLITICS, *GERMANY*
Adolf Hitler rejects Germany's 1934 nonaggression pact with Poland and the Anglo-German Naval Agreement signed in 1935.

MAY 3, 1939

POLITICS, *SOVIET UNION*
Maksim Litvinov, who is considered to be supportive of the Western democracies, is replaced as foreign minister by Vyacheslav Molotov. Although the Soviet Union continues to discuss alliances against Germany with Britain and France, Molotov does not trust their motives and the discussions stall without any formal or informal arrangements being made by any of the parties involved.

MAY 22, 1939

POLITICS, *ITALY*
The government agrees closer military ties with Germany. The strengthened alliance between the two becomes known as the "Pact of Steel."

MAY 23, 1939

POLITICS, *GERMANY*

Adolf Hitler orders his military high command to begin planning the invasion of Poland. Over the following months there are "border incidents" between Germany and Poland. These are usually instigated by German troops. They heighten tension between the two countries and one such event will be used to justify the German invasion in September.

AUGUST 22, 1939

POLITICS, *GERMANY*

Adolf Hitler gives his final approval for the invasion of Poland, and German forces move to their war stations along Poland's western border. The Germans plan to use a strategy of combining tanks, fast-moving troops, and aircraft to crush Polish resistance within a matter of a few weeks.

◄ *Adolf Hitler (far left), Hermann Goering, head of the Luftwaffe (sixth from right), and various military figures greet the Italian delegation during the "Pact of Steel" discussions, May 1939.*

▲ *Hitler's foreign minister, Joachim von Ribbentrop (center, standing), announces the signing of the nonaggression pact over Poland with the Soviet Union.*

AUGUST 23, 1939

POLITICS, *GERMANY*

Foreign Minister Joachim von Ribbentrop signs a nonaggression pact with the Soviet Union's foreign minister, Vyacheslav Molotov, in Moscow. The Soviet Union agrees not to oppose the German invasion of Poland and both countries agree to divide Poland between them. Eastern Europe is split between the two states' exclusive spheres of influence.

The Soviet leadership believes the agreement will give them time to reorganize their military forces, whose officer corps has been decimated by purges instigated by Joseph Stalin.

POLITICS, *JAPAN*

The government withdraws from the Anti-Comintern Pact with Germany and Italy following the former's recent surprise alliance with the Soviet Union concerning the immediate fate of Poland.

WORLD WAR II
Day by Day

INTRODUCTION

World War I, "The War to End All Wars," was to create many of the conditions that would lead to the outbreak of an even more destructive conflict – World War II. At the end of World War I Germany was in dire straits: its population was near starvation and devoid of hope, and its army and navy were in disarray. The Treaty of Versailles of June 1919 added to Germany's woes as it removed its overseas possessions, implemented the occupation of part of the Rhineland to ensure Germany complied with provisions of the treaty, and imposed huge reparations for the damage inflicted on France and other countries during World War I.

The fact that Germany was almost bankrupt meant that it was extremely unlikely Germany would be able to pay, even less so when the world slump of 1921 arose. The next year German defaulted on reparations payments for the second year running. In retaliation, France, showing amazing shortsightedness, occupied the Ruhr, the center of German industry. This not only reduced the already slim chances of Germany paying any reparations, but also increased hostility between the two countries.

The stoppage of the Ruhr industries had a calamitous impact on the German currency, which plummeted in value. Overnight, savings were wiped out, leaving millions penniless and destitute, their careers, hopes, and finances totally destroyed.

ADOLF HITLER

In such an atmosphere people desperately searched for answers. They found them in the vitriolic oratory of an

▼ *A Nuremberg rally. Each one was designed to increase support for both Hitler and Nazism.*

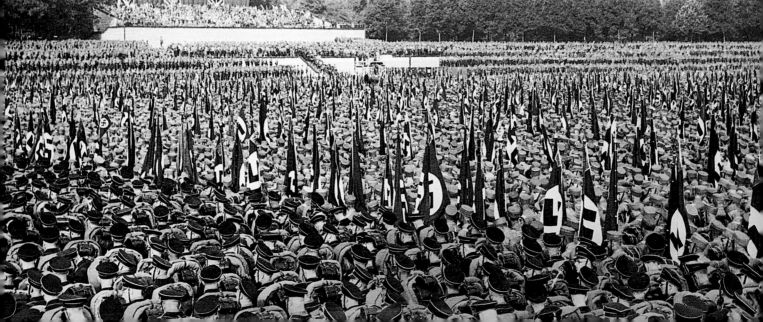

▶ *German dictator Adolf Hitler, who was obsessed with the creation of German "living space" in Eastern Europe.*

ex-soldier named Adolf Hitler, who belonged to the *Nationalsozialistische Deutsche Arbeiterpartei* (National Socialist German Workers' Party, or Nazi Party for short). The failure of Germany's Weimar government to cope with war debts and inflation made Hitler's claim that an alternative was needed seem sensible.

Notwithstanding his failure in the ludicrous 1923 Munich Beer Hall

▲ *The 1936 Berlin Olympic Games, which provided Hitler with an opportunity to present Nazism on a world stage.*

Putsch, the Nazi Party's membership continued to grow in the 1920s. The 1929 worldwide economic slump played into the Nazis' hands, for Hitler was able to blame the financial crisis on unpatriotic Jews and the conspiracies of communists – views that found receptive ears. In 1932 Hitler polled 36.9 percent of the vote, and after ingratiating himself with the World War I hero President Paul von Hindenburg, the latter invited the Nazi leader to become chancellor in 1933.

Once in power Hitler was able to establish a dictatorship. He created jobs by expelling Jews, by insisting that women should stay at home and produce offspring, and by sending young men to labor camps (not to be confused with concentration camps). But there was a heavy price to be paid: the abolition of trade unions, and the persecution of Jews and communists. Hitler also renounced the Treaty of Versailles, began rearming, and reoccupied the Rhineland.

EXPANDING THE REICH

Having consolidated his position within Germany, Hitler now looked for *Lebensraum* ("living space") beyond its borders. His ambitions were helped by the peace treaties that followed World War I. For example, he wished to bring Czechoslovakia's Sudeten Germans back into the fold, while at the same time coveting Czechoslovakia's armaments industry.

As Austria and Czechoslovakia were absorbed into the Third Reich, the Western democracies dithered. Indeed, in both Britain and France there was a belief that the terms imposed on Germany by the Treaty of

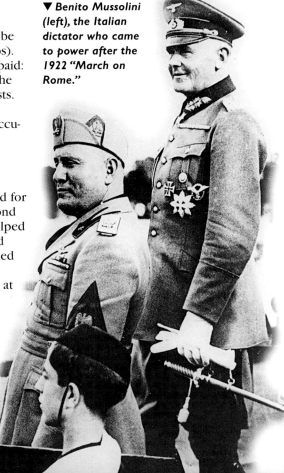

▼ *Benito Mussolini (left), the Italian dictator who came to power after the 1922 "March on Rome."*

KEY MOMENTS

APPEASEMENT

Appeasement has, since the end of World War II, been equated with cowardice and is held in contempt by some. In the 1930s, however, appeasement as believed in by British Prime Minister Neville Chamberlain and French leaders such as Edouard Daladier encapsulated reasonable steps that might be taken to prevent Hitler taking the law into his own hands. It was also the manifestation of a very real desire to avoid another general European war and its many associated horrors.

Appeasement had its roots in the growing feeling in the early 1930s in Britain and France that the terms of the Treaty of Versailles had been harsh on Germany. Seen in this light, Adolf Hitler's demands for a rearmed Germany and the restoration of "German" territories appeared reasonable. Thus by agreeing to these essentially "just" demands, Chamberlain believed he could lay the foundations for a lasting peace.

Unfortunately, appeasement relied on the goodwill of both parties to be a success. Thus after the Munich talks in September 1938, Chamberlain and Daladier agreed to Hitler's demands for the incorporation into the Third Reich of German-speaking Czechoslovak Sudetenland. Chamberlain proclaimed the agreement heralded "peace with honor." For his part Hitler had expected a confrontation over the issue, and Britain and France's failure to stand up to him encouraged more brinkmanship. He occupied the rest of Czechoslovakia in March 1939, signaling the end of appeasement. This guaranteed that both Britain and France would fight to defend Poland.

Versailles had been harsh, and that by appeasing Hitler by assenting to his "just" demands, a basis for a lasting European peace could be laid.

But they were both mistaken. The belief that the Munich agreement of September 1938, whereby the Sudetenland was ceded to Germany, would lead to "peace in our time" was also wrong. This was confirmed in March 1939 when Germany occupied the rest of Czechoslovakia.

MUSSOLINI'S ITALY

World War II had, for all practical purposes, begun; the more so because Hitler had similarly belligerent allies in Europe and the Far East. In Italy, for example, Benito Mussolini fancied himself as a twentieth-century Caesar. His fascist regime had achieved some notable results in the country, such as the drainage and cultivation of marshes, the construction of factories and roads, the balancing of the budget, and, probably his greatest achievement, making the trains run on time. His regime built up the army, navy, and air force, and glorified war, while Mussolini himself talked of the Mediterranean as being *Mare Nostrum* ("Our Sea").

Mussolini realized that his armed forces required modern equipment, and so he picked his opponents carefully. His attack against Ethiopia (then Abyssinia) was regarded with disgust

by other European nations, as Italian warplanes dropped bombs and poison gas on spear-armed tribesmen. Nevertheless, the war confirmed the impotence of the League of Nations, which could not rally any of its members to take effective action.

THE AXIS ALLIANCE

In the Far East, Japan flexed its muscles. Having defeated Russia in 1904–05, it went on to annex Korea

▼ *Danzig, on the Baltic at the mouth of the Vistula River, was designated a "free city" by the League of Nations. Hitler demanded its return to Germany, along with the so-called "Polish Corridor."*

◀ *Italian light tanks pictured during the Spanish Civil War. Both Italian and German units participated in the conflict, picking up valuable battle experience.*

Poland now became the focus of Hitler's attention. Recreated after World War I, it had been given access to the sea via a corridor of land which reached the Baltic at Danzig. It had been formerly German territory, and Hitler was determined it would be again. Danzig was, in theory, a "free city" administered by the United Nations, but in reality the Nazis had gained control of the city in 1934 and did largely what they liked. Hitler ranted that it and the strip of land that divided Germany and East Prussia should be returned to the Reich.

Few people in the West knew or cared very much what the "Polish Corridor" was – some believed it to be an underground tunnel – but in March 1939 Britain and France took the fateful step of pledging themselves to the defense of Poland, which neither of them was in a military position to do. When German armies entered Poland on September 1, 1939, they had no choice but to declare war two days later. World War II had begun, little more than two decades after the end of the first great conflict.

and overrun the whole of Manchuria, which was renamed Manchukuo. When the League of Nations protested, Japan simply resigned its membership. In 1936 it signed the anticommunist Anti-Comintern Pact with Germany and Italy. Japan was now part of the Rome-Berlin-Tokyo Axis, which was seemingly further strengthened when Hitler and Joseph Stalin, the Soviet

leader, signed a nonaggression pact on August 23, 1939, in which a secret clause divided up a conquered Poland between the two dictators (Stalin did not want German troops on the frontier of the Soviet Union itself).

▼ *The fruits of Nazi Germany's rearmament program – Hitler inspects a new warship at Kiel.*

After months of diplomatic wrangling and "appeasement" bargaining, war erupted when Germany invaded Poland. Germany's Blitzkrieg offensive, which plunged Europe into conflict, heralded a new and dramatic style of modern warfare. Although there was no Allied advance into Germany in Western Europe, fighting flared up on the Eastern Front between the Soviet Union and neighboring Finland.

SEPTEMBER 1

EASTERN FRONT, *POLAND*

A German force of 53 divisions, supported by 1600 aircraft, crosses the German and Slovak borders into Poland in a pincer movement. Plan White, directed by General Walther von Brauchitsch, aims to totally paralyze Poland's 24 divisions by swift encirclement, thus cutting their lines of supply and communication. While Poland mobilizes its full strength, its forces in action, lacking both air and armored support, are largely placed on the country's borders. They are quickly overrun, and reinforcements often arrive too late to halt the German attacks.

SEPTEMBER 2

POLITICS, *ALLIES*

Ultimatums are delivered by Britain and France to Germany demanding its immediate withdrawal from Poland.

SEPTEMBER 3

POLITICS, *ALLIES*

Britain and France declare war on Nazi Germany after their ultimatums regarding the invasion of Poland expire. Australia and New Zealand also declare war. British Prime Minister Neville Chamberlain forms a war cabinet, which includes prominent antiappeasers First Lord of the Admiralty Winston Churchill and Secretary for the Dominions Anthony Eden.

▲ The German invasion of Poland began in September with air and ground attacks that quickly paralyzed the Polish forces.

◀ German troops tear down border posts as they advance into Poland.

▲ *French citizens cheer their soldiers after mobilization orders are issued in 1939.*

SEA WAR, *ATLANTIC*
The liner *Athenia* is sunk by the *U-30* after being mistaken for a British auxiliary cruiser, claiming 112 lives.

SEPTEMBER 4

AIR WAR, *GERMANY*
Britain's Royal Air Force (RAF) Bomber Command launches its first attacks against Nazi warships in the Heligoland Bight off northwest Germany, but the government will not authorize raids on targets within Germany.

SEPTEMBER 5

POLITICS, *SOUTH AFRICA*
Prime Minister Jan Christiaan Smuts declares war on Nazi Germany following the formation of a new cabinet after political disagreements over joining the conflict.
POLITICS, *UNITED STATES*
The authorities officially proclaim their neutrality.

SEPTEMBER 6

EASTERN FRONT, *POLAND*
The Polish government and high command leave Warsaw and order

▶ *German troops make a hasty river crossing during the invasion of Poland.*

their forces to withdraw to the line of the Narew, Vistula, and San Rivers. Nazi troops make a dramatic advance that reaches beyond Lódz. They also seize Cracow in the south.

SEPTEMBER 7

WESTERN FRONT, *GERMANY*
France begins minor skirmishes across the border with Germany near Saarbrücken.

SEA WAR, *ATLANTIC*
Britain's first convoys sail across the Atlantic. The system is already operating on Britain's east coast to protect merchant ships from U-boat attacks.

SEPTEMBER 8

EASTERN FRONT, *POLAND*
The German Tenth Army led by General Walter von Reichenau reaches the outskirts of Warsaw, the capital.

▲ *Polish lancers head for the front.*

General Wilhelm List's Fourteenth Army reaches the San River around Przemysl, while General Heinz Guderian's tank corps reaches the Bug River to the east of Warsaw.

SEPTEMBER 9

EASTERN FRONT, *POLAND*
A Polish counterattack is launched by 10 divisions, which gather around Kutno under General Tadeuz Kutrzeba. The attack over the Bzura River against Germany's Eighth Army is the most effective Polish offensive of the campaign, but only achieves short-term success.

▼ *A grief-striken Polish girl finds her sister has been killed during a German air attack on Warsaw.*

SEPTEMBER 10

POLITICS, *CANADA*
The government declares war on Germany.

WESTERN FRONT, *FRANCE*
Major elements of the British Expeditionary Force, led by General Lord Gort, begin to land in France. Some 160,000 men and 24,000 vehicles arrive throughout the course of September.

SEPTEMBER 13

POLITICS, *FRANCE*
Prime Minister Edouard Daladier forms a war cabinet and takes additional responsibility for foreign affairs.

SEPTEMBER 16–27

EASTERN FRONT, *POLAND*
Warsaw's defenders are encircled but refuse to surrender until the 27th. Elements of Germany's Fourteenth Army west of Lvov are still locked in battle, while other units advance to join General Heinz Guderian's units in action along the Bug River.

SEPTEMBER 17

SEA WAR, *ATLANTIC*
The British aircraft carrier *Courageous* is sunk by *U-29* during an antisubmarine patrol off southwest Ireland. The aircraft carrier *Ark Royal* has managed to escape a similar attack just three days beforehand. The naval authorities act quickly and withdraw Britain's aircraft carriers from such duties to preserve these valuable vessels for other maritime roles.

◄ Polish forces surrendering to a German officer. Despite Poland's fighting spirit, its armies were decisively defeated by Germany's Blitzkrieg attack.

formed and many fighters escape to join the Allies. Poland is split into two zones of occupation divided by the Bug River. Germany has lost 10,572 troops and the Soviet Union has 734 men killed in the campaign. Around 50,000 Poles are killed and 750,000 captured.

SEPTEMBER 21

POLITICS, *ROMANIA*

A local fascist group, the "Iron Guard," assassinates Romanian Prime Minister Armand Calinescu.

SEPTEMBER 27

POLITICS, *GERMANY*

Adolf Hitler's senior commanders are told of his plans for a western offensive at the earliest opportunity. This announcement is met with hostility by the military, who resent Hitler assuming direct control over strategic planning and also feel unprepared for this undertaking. His plan for invading the Low Countries, formulated as Plan Yellow on October 19, is constantly aborted due to bad weather. The plan is also modified and its objectives widened before the actual offensive in 1940.

▼ The British aircraft carrier **Courageous** *was sunk in September 1940 by a U-boat during an antisubmarine patrol. British aircraft carriers were quickly withdrawn from such duties.*

SEPTEMBER 17–30

EASTERN FRONT, *POLAND*

In accordance with a secret clause in their 1939 pact with Germany, the Red Army invades. Little resistance is encountered on Poland's eastern border as the Polish Army is fighting for its life to the west.

SEPTEMBER 18–30

POLITICS, *POLAND*

The Polish government and high command flee to Romania, only to be interned. A government-in-exile is

STRATEGY & TACTICS

BLITZKRIEG

Blitzkrieg ("lightning war") aimed to inflict a total defeat on an enemy through a single, powerful offensive. This was to be achieved by speed, firepower, and mobility. General Heinz Guderian's book *Achtung! Panzer!* (1933) articulated the strategy, which aimed to avoid the costly and indecisive trench warfare of 1914–18.

Germany exploited the developments in tanks, mobile artillery, and aircraft in its first Blitzkrieg, the attack on Poland. Blitzkrieg always avoided strong resistance in order to sustain the momentum of the assault, which concentrated on an enemy's rear areas to break his lines of supply and communication. Once this was achieved, less-mobile forces could annihilate isolated pockets of resistance.

Blitzkrieg not only required new technology; it also needed commanders with the tactical vision and flexibility to exploit opportunities and overcome obstacles in order to sustain an attack's momentum.

The Allies, having failed to appreciate the lessons of the Blitzkrieg strike on Poland, were equally stunned by the 1940 attacks against France and the Low Countries. Germany's formidable strategy, therefore, inflicted another major defeat.

A German Heinkel He 111 attacks Warsaw during the invasion of Poland. Aircraft were a vital component of the Blitzkrieg and acted as mobile artillery for the advancing land forces during an offensive.

KEY PERSONALITIES

ADOLF HITLER

Adolf Hitler (1889–1945), the founder and leader of Nazi Germany, was born in Austria. His experiences as a failed artist in Vienna and decorated soldier in World War I helped shape his extremist political ambitions, which led to the Nazi Party's foundation.

He exploited Weimar Germany's political turbulence and social unrest to maneuver himself into power in 1933. Violence and intimidation secured his position as dictator. His Nazism fused nationalism with racism and created powerful expansionist ambitions. Hitler articulated the dream of creating an empire by destroying Germany's supposed racial and ideological enemies. His desire to realize his expansionist ambitions plunged Europe into diplomatic chaos and, ultimately, war.

Hitler's political skills centered upon his opportunistic character and mastery of propaganda. However, as Führer ("leader") Hitler also became Germany's military master. In this capacity Hitler's boldness and confidence were demonstrated in Germany's early Blitzkrieg successes.

By 1941 Hitler's skills were in decline, and his stubbornness and lack of strategic vision exacerbated the military problems. He became isolated from reality and refused to admit the war was lost.

Hitler survived an assassination attempt in 1944 but finally took his own life in 1945. Hitler's empire was finally crushed, but the destruction it wrought left the world remolded by the bloodiest war in history.

▶ *Soviet forces in Finland dismantle antitank obstacles along the Mannerheim Line in the Karelian Isthmus.*

SEPTEMBER 29

POLITICS, *SOVIET UNION*
After occupying Poland, the Soviet Union concentrates on extending its control over the Baltic Sea region to safeguard against any German threat. During the next few weeks it gains bases and signs "mutual assistance" agreements with Lithuania, Latvia, and Estonia. Finland, however, will not agree to the Soviet Union's territorial demands and mobilizes its armed forces in October as political dialogue fails to resolve the crisis.

OCTOBER 14

SEA WAR, *NORTH SEA*
The British battleship *Royal Oak* is sunk, with 786 lives lost, after *U-47* passes through antisubmarine defenses at Scapa Flow in the Orkneys, where the Home Fleet is anchored. Defenses are improved at the base after this dramatic attack.

NOVEMBER 4

POLITICS, *UNITED STATES*
Changes to the Neutrality Act permit belligerent states to purchase arms from private suppliers on a "cash-and-carry" basis, whereby they have to pay for any weapons and then transport them using their own vessels. Given Britain's command of the Atlantic sea-lanes, this act is clearly intended to benefit the Allied nations.

NOVEMBER 26

POLITICS, *FINLAND*
Criticism of Finland in the Soviet press and a faked border incident further sours Soviet–Finnish relations. Joseph Stalin, the Soviet leader, subsequently withdraws from the nonaggression pact with Finland and breaks off relations. Finland, lacking allies or arms, fails to anticipate the attack, believing talks will avert a conflict.

NOVEMBER 30

EASTERN FRONT, *FINLAND*
A Soviet force of over 600,000 men, backed by air and naval power, attacks Finland in support of Otto Kuusinen's newly-proclaimed Finnish People's Government, which is sponsored by the Soviet Union. As aircraft bomb the capital, Helsinki, Field Marshal Karl von Mannerheim leads the nation's defense with a mainly reservist

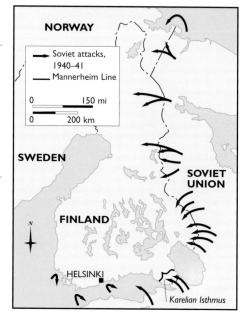

▲ *The Soviet invasion of Finland comprised land, air, and amphibious attacks.*

force, inferior in both numbers and arms. The main Soviet thrust through the Karelian Isthmus is obstructed by the Mannerheim Line, a 1914–18 system of fortifications that runs through rugged terrain and forest.

Other Soviet forces attack eastern and northern Finland, and also launch failed amphibious assaults on the southern coast. As the campaign progresses, highly-motivated Finnish troops exploit their familiarity with the terrain and use their ability to ski through snow-covered areas to launch hit-and-run raids on Red Army units bogged down by the weather.

DECEMBER 2

POLITICS, *FINLAND*
The League of Nations is asked by Finland to intervene in its conflict

with the Soviet Union. The League eventually agrees, but the Soviet Union opposes its involvement and is expelled from the organization on December 14.

DECEMBER 7

EASTERN FRONT, FINLAND
The Soviet 163rd Division approaches Suomussali village in eastern Finland. Halted by freezing conditions, its troops are targeted by the Finnish 9th Division, which severs its supply lines. The Soviet 44th Division, sent as a relief force, is blocked by Finnish attacks and both Red Army units attempt a breakout. By the end of the year these divisions have been forced to

capitulate, after having 27,500 men killed by enemy action or the freezing temperatures. The Finns achieve similar successes in other engagements during the "Winter War."

DECEMBER 16

EASTERN FRONT, FINLAND
After advancing to the Mannerheim Line, the Soviet Seventh Army begins a major offensive. To compensate for their lack of armor and artillery, innovative sabotage techniques and improvised explosive devices ("Molotov Cocktails," named after the Soviet foreign minister) are used by Finnish ski-troops to destroy enemy tanks. The fighting will continue until February 11, 1940.

DECEMBER 13

SEA WAR, ATLANTIC
The British heavy cruiser *Exeter*, with light cruisers *Ajax* and *Achilles*, engage the German pocket battleship *Graf Spee* at the mouth of the Plate River, off Uruguay. The British vessels sustain severe damage as they maneuver to prevent *Graf Spee* delivering concentrated fire on a single vessel.
  Graf Spee, itself damaged, withdraws to neutral Uruguay for repairs. *Ajax* and *Achilles* are later joined by the heavy cruiser *Cumberland* to await *Graf Spee*'s emergence from Montevideo port. The *Graf Spee*, however, is scuttled by its crew on the 17th.

DECEMBER 23

POLITICS, CANADA
The first Canadian troops, some 7500 men, arrive in Britain.

▲ Marshal Karl von Mannerheim led Finland's determined defense against the Soviet attack on his country.

▼ Germany's pocket battleship **Graf Spee** is scuttled after being trapped by the Royal Navy in neutral Uruguay.

1940

The German Army conquered much of Western Europe in 1940 in a series of spectacular Blitzkrieg victories. German armor and aircraft attacked and defeated a succession of Allied armies in Scandinavia, France, and the Low Countries. Germany's defeat in an aerial battle over Britain, however, saved that nation from any invasion. Britain's survival now depended on North American aid. Meanwhile, the war widened, with Italian offensives in Africa and the Balkans.

JANUARY 7–FEBRUARY 17

EASTERN FRONT, *FINLAND*
General Semyon Timoshenko assumes command of the Soviet invasion forces in the Karelian Isthmus and initiates a training program to improve service cooperation. After reorganizing and reequipping, his forces begin a determined attack on the Mannerheim Line on the 12th. The Finns complete a withdrawal to a secondary zone of defense on the line by February 17. Secret peace negotiations have already begun in late January.

JANUARY 10

WESTERN FRONT, *BELGIUM*
A lost German plane carrying two army officers lands at Mechelen.

▶ *Finnish officers discuss the battle against the Soviet invaders.*

Captured documents read by the Allies reveal an invasion plan for the 17th. For this reason, and because of poor weather, Adolf Hitler postpones the invasion until the spring.

JANUARY 14

POLITICS, *JAPAN*
Admiral Mitsumasa Yonai forms a new government in Japan after the resignation of Prime Minister Nobuyuki Abe's cabinet. Yonai's government, however, provokes opposition from the prowar military hierarchy.

FEBRUARY 5

POLITICS, *ALLIES*
The Allied Supreme War Council decides to intervene in Norway and Finland. This vague and indecisive policy relies on the cooperation of neutral Norway and Sweden. The main motivation is the Allied desire to deny Germany access to Swedish iron ore supplies, which pass through the ice-free port of Narvik in Norway.

FEBRUARY 16

SEA WAR, *NORTH SEA*
The British destroyer *Cossack* violates Norway's neutrality to rescue 299 British merchant seamen aboard the German transport *Altmark*. Germany accelerates its invasion preparations, believing that Britain is planning more military actions in Norway.

FEBRUARY 24

POLITICS, *GERMANY*
Plans for the invasion of Western Europe are revised. The main focus of

◀ *The British destroyer Cossack, which sailed into Norwegian waters to rescue 299 British sailors imprisoned on a German vessel.*

▼ *The British destroyer* **Glowworm** *sinks after ramming the German heavy cruiser* **Admiral Hipper.**

the offensive is changed to the Ardennes region after a suggestion by General Erich von Manstein. The bulk of the German Army's armored units are allocated to this radical plan.

MARCH 11

EASTERN FRONT, *FINLAND*
The Treaty of Moscow between Finland and the Soviet Union is agreed after the Red Army makes hard-won gains. Although Allied help to the nation is negligible, the Finnish Army has not capitulated. Finland retains its independence but has to surrender the Karelian Isthmus and Hangö – 10 percent of its territory. Campaign losses: 200,000 Soviet troops and 25,000 Finns.

MARCH 20

POLITICS, *FRANCE*
Prime Minister Edouard Daladier resigns after criticism of his failure to take the initiative to support Finland and thereby redirect the war away from France. Paul Reynaud succeeds Daladier on March 21.

MARCH 28

POLITICS, *ALLIES*
Britain and France agree not to make any separate peace treaties. From April 5 they plan to mine Norwegian waters to force Nazi ships carrying Swedish iron ore into the open seas and expose them to naval attack. The minelaying is deferred to April 8. This is too late to prevent the Nazi invasion planned for the 9th.

APRIL 8

SEA WAR, *NORTH SEA*
The British destroyer *Glowworm* intercepts part of the German invasion fleet

◀ *Edouard Daladier, France's premier to March 1940.*

bound for Norway. It is sunk after ramming the heavy cruiser *Admiral Hipper*, but a British submarine then sinks the transport *Rio de Janiero*. However, Royal Navy vessels deployed in the North Sea have not received sufficient information about the German invading force and are unable to intercept it.

APRIL 9

WESTERN FRONT, *NORWAY/DENMARK*
A German invasion force, including surface ships, U-boats, and 1000 aircraft, attacks Denmark and Norway. Denmark is overrun immediately. The first ever airborne assault is made on Oslo and Stavanger airports in Norway, while ships land troops at six locations. Norway's six divisions have no tanks or effective artillery, while its coastal defenses and navy are generally inferior.

However, in Oslo Fiord, shore guns sink the German cruiser *Blücher*, claiming 1600 lives. This enables King Haakon to escape northward with his

APRIL 10–13

▶ *Germany's Blitzkrieg on Norway and Denmark began with combined airborne and amphibious landings.*

government. The British battlecruiser *Rodney* engages the battlecruisers *Scharnhorst* and *Gneisenau*, damaging the latter. The cruiser *Karlsruhe* is later sunk off Kristiansand by a British submarine.

APRIL 10–13

SEA WAR, *NORWAY*

Five British destroyers launch a surprise attack on 10 German destroyers and shore batteries to the west of Narvik. During short and confused engagements each side loses two destroyers, while eight German merchant vessels and an ammunition carrier are also sunk. The cruiser *Königsberg* becomes the first vessel to be sunk by dive-bombing during a British air attack on Bergen.

Subsequent air attacks on the *Gneisenau*, *Scharnhorst*, and *Admiral Hipper* by the British on the 12th fail. A British battleship and nine destroyers succeed in sinking eight German destroyers, plus a U-boat, by aerial attack in the Second Battle of Narvik on April 13.

APRIL 10–30

WESTERN FRONT, *NORWAY*

After securing their initial objectives, the Germans begin their conquest of Norway. Major General Carl Otto Ruge, Norway's new commander-in-chief, leads a stubborn defense around Lake Mjösa and the Glomma Valley.

APRIL 14–19

WESTERN FRONT, *NORWAY*

An Allied expeditionary force of over 10,000 British, French, and Polish

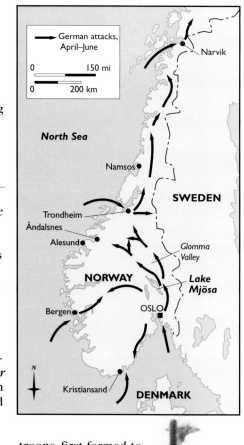

troops, first formed to assist Finland, lands at Namsos, Alesund, and Narvik. Its objective is to recapture Trondheim to secure a base in Norway, but its units

▼ *German infantry arrive in Oslo, the Norwegian capital.*

coordination with the Norwegian forces is poor, but the Germans in the area eventually withdraw at the end of April.

MAY 7–10

POLITICS, *BRITAIN*

Prime Minister Neville Chamberlain is severely criticized over the Norwegian

▲ *Norwegian ski-troops were especially useful in disrupting German lines of communication.*

▼ *French mountain soldiers arriving in Norway to help repel the Nazi invasion. The Allies sent a force of British, French, and Polish troops to help the country.*

▲ *The German cruiser Königsberg sinks after a British air attack.*

are ill-prepared for the campaign. There has been little liaison with the Norwegians. The various Allied units lack cohesion, training in arctic warfare, key supplies, air cover, and anti-aircraft weaponry.

APRIL 20–30

WESTERN FRONT, *NORWAY*

German troops defend Trondheim and wait for the arrival of more forces. German aircraft launch determined attacks against the Allies. British and French troops eventually evacuate Namsos and Åndalsnes on May 1–2.

APRIL 24

WESTERN FRONT, *NORWAY*

An Allied offensive on Narvik begins with a naval bombardment. Allied

campaign during a House of Commons debate. Chamberlain resigns after a significant fall in government support in a vote of confidence and the opposition Labour Party's refusal to serve under him in a coalition. Winston Churchill replaces him and forms a coalition government.

MAY 8

POLITICS, *SOVIET UNION*
General Semyon Timoshenko replaces Marshal Kliment Voroshilov as the Soviet commissar for defense.

MAY 10

WESTERN FRONT, *LUXEMBOURG/ HOLLAND/BELGIUM*
The Germany's Army Group A, under General Gerd von Rundstedt, and Group B, commanded by General Fedor von Bock, invade after preliminary air attacks. Successful airborne landings are made against Belgium's key frontier fortress of Eben Emael,

◀ *British premier Neville Chamberlain, the appeasement advocate, who resigned after failing to save Finland and Norway.*

▼ *German troops crossing the Maas River during the invasion of Holland.*

and in Holland, to dislocate resistance. General Ritter von Leeb's Army Group C covers France's Maginot Line, the line of subterranean forts and other defensive positions running along its border with Germany.

In accordance with Allied planning, the left flank of the British and French line moves into Belgium. This decision facilitates Rundstedt's surprise Ardennes advance, which eventually divides the Allied armies in Belgium from those in France. The Allied armies advancing into Belgium up to the Dyle and Meuse Rivers above Namur, a position known as the Dyle Plan Line, are hampered by poor coordination with Dutch and Belgian forces.

MAY 11–15

WESTERN FRONT, *HOLLAND/BELGIUM*
Dutch resistance to the German attack crumbles, despite opening the flood gates and mining the Rhine River to obstruct the enemy. German forces begin to approach the Allied Dyle Line, while Belgian defenders are driven back from the Albert Canal.

Queen Wilhelmina of the Netherlands escapes with the Dutch government to Britain on May 13. The city of Rotterdam is bombed before a cease-fire is declared on the 14th, and the Dutch Army capitulates the next day.

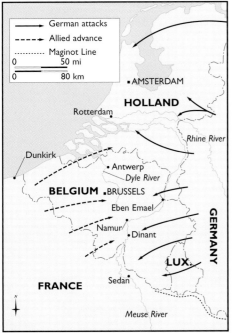

▲ A six-inch (15-cm) howitzer in action with the French Second Army during the desperate fight to save France in 1940.

◀ Germany's offensive, which began on May 10, lured the Allies into the Low Countries, while a surprise attack went into France through the Ardennes.

and Second Armies, which then mount a futile response.

MAY 15–20

WESTERN FRONT, *BELGIUM*
Germany's Sixth and Eighteenth Armies force the Allies to withdraw from the Dyle Plan Line to the Scheldt

MAY 12–14

WESTERN FRONT, *FRANCE*
German forces reach the Meuse River, the crossing of which is critical for the advance into France. Dive-bombers pound French positions and inflatable rafts are used to establish bridgeheads at Sedan and Dinant on the 13th. Despite Allied air attacks, German armor advances westward rapidly, opening a 50-mile (75-km) gap in the Allied line. This drives a wedge between the French Ninth

KEY PERSONALITIES

PRIME MINISTER SIR WINSTON CHURCHILL

Winston Spencer Churchill (1874–1965), soldier, journalist, and statesman, had held ministerial offices but was relegated to the margins of political life in Britain during the 1930s for his anti-appeasement stance. He was propelled into power, however, as prime minister in 1940 as the Nazis appeared close to total victory. Churchill reversed the fortunes of the nation by dismissing any sign of defeatism.

The bold but often impatient prime minister constantly urged his military commanders to take offensive action. Churchill forged a coalition of Allied nations, but it was the solid support he secured from the United States that was critical to Britain's survival.

A series of international conferences enabled Churchill and other Allied leaders to decide on the strategic direction of the war. Despite Churchill's anticommunist stance, he created a working alliance with the Soviet Union, although he correctly predicted that postwar Europe would be divided along political lines.

In domestic politics he secured the loyalty and cooperation of the House of Commons during the period of coalition government. Winston Churchill's mastery of propaganda, eccentricity, and powerful oratory helped galvanize the British people and secured their cooperation during the war years. Despite Churchill's popularity as Britain's war leader, he lost the 1945 election as many felt that a new premier was needed for the challenges of postwar Britain. Nevertheless, Churchill remains one of the twentieth century's most significant figures.

MAY 15

Line, west of Brussels, and the Dendre River. French forces have been forced to fall back from Holland, while the Belgians continue fighting between Antwerp and Brussels, finally retreating to the Escaut Canal and then to the Lys River, which is reached on the 20th.

MAY 15

AIR WAR, *GERMANY*

Britain launches its first strategic air attack on Germany with 99 aircraft hitting oil plants and railroad marshaling yards in the Ruhr region.

MAY 16–20

WESTERN FRONT, *FRANCE*

The French General Reserve and units south of the German forces are ordered to form the Sixth Army to bolster the vulnerable Allied lines, but this fails to halt the German advance. Brigadier General Charles de Gaulle's 4th Armored Division attempts to counterattack around Laon–Montcornet on May 17–19 but fails.

German tanks reach Cambrai on May 18, and finally the sea at Abbeville two days later. It now becomes critical for the Allies to cut the "corridor" made by the panzers or risk the isolation of their armies to the north from the forces in the south. The dismissal of General Maurice Gamelin, the Allied commander-in-chief, and the appointment of Maxime Weygand as his successor on the 19th further delays military decision-making, which reduces the potential for any action.

MAY 21–28

WESTERN FRONT, *FRANCE*

British tanks battle with the 7th Panzer Division at Arras until May 23. General Heinz Guderian moves toward Boulogne and Calais unaffected by the Allied "Weygand Plan," which attempts to split the tank spearhead from troops and supplies in the German "corridor." Boulogne and Calais capitulate after the naval evacuation of Allied troops.

Eager to preserve his panzers for taking Paris, Hitler halts General Gerd von Rundstedt's armor at Gravelines and allows the air force to attack the Allied "pocket" centering on

▲ *British troops surrender in Calais after trying to defend the port against attacking German armor and aircraft.*

▼ *General Maurice Gamelin, commander of the Allied armies in France, failed to halt the German Blitzkrieg.*

Dunkirk. British aircraft, however, resist the attacks, enabling the Allies to prepare for an evacuation.

MAY 25–28

WESTERN FRONT, *BELGIUM*

King Leopold of Belgium's forces are left surrounded as the Allies

Paris condemns King Leopold's surrender and assumes his powers.

MAY 26

WESTERN FRONT, *FRANCE/BELGIUM*

Operation Dynamo, the evacuation of Allied forces from the Dunkirk area, begins. A defensive perimeter established on the Aa, Scarpe, and Yser "canal line" covers the withdrawal, while an assorted rescue flotilla of pleasure boats, commercial craft, and naval vessels crosses and recrosses the English Channel.

MAY 31

POLITICS, *UNITED STATES*

President Franklin D. Roosevelt launches a "billion-dollar defense program" to bolster the armed forces.

JUNE 1–9

WESTERN FRONT, *NORWAY*

After Britain and France reveal to the Norwegians that they are to begin an evacuation, troops begin to withdraw

▼ *Plumes of smoke rise from Dunkirk's port area as troops sail back to Britain.*

withdraw to Dunkirk. Resistance seems futile and he decides to surrender on the 28th. Belgium has lost 7550 men killed. The surrender leaves the left flank of the Allied line increasingly vulnerable, and there is no hope of holding out in Belgium. The exiled Belgium government in

KEY MOMENTS

THE BATTLE OF FRANCE

Germany's sensational seizure of France and the Low Countries was the pinnacle of Blitzkrieg strategy and secured Adolf Hitler's mastery of Western Europe. The invasion that began on May 10 first struck the Low Countries, which had relied on their neutrality to save them, and were in no condition to resist the invaders.

As British and French forces rushed into Belgium in response to Germany's diversionary attack, the Nazis launched their main assault by advancing through the Ardennes forest. The Allies had dismissed this area as being unsuitable for any tank advances, which allowed the German units to move straight through against minimal opposition. This gateway into France enabled the fast-moving armored columns to advance into the Allied rear and disable communications. As the panzers raced westward to the sea, the Allied armies in the north were effectively isolated from potential reinforcements in the south. The Allies were unable to match Germany's effective exploitation of armor and aircraft or develop a credible strategy to counterattack the invaders.

As British, Belgian, and French forces completed the evacuation from Dunkirk, Germany launched the final phase of the offensive to complete the conquest. The Maginot Line, on which France's security had been entrusted, but had been completely bypassed by German forces, was eventually surrounded and penetrated.

As France's politicians floundered, the nation's high command attempted to regroup its faltering armies but resistance crumbled in the face of well-orchestrated German attacks that captured Paris on June 14. French and German officials signed an armistice agreement on June 22.

A French soldier surrenders to the German invaders.

▲ *Wounded troops return to Britain after being rescued from Dunkirk.*

on June 4. King Haakon and his government leave for Britain on the 7th, and 24,500 troops are evacuated. The king finally orders the Norwegians to stop fighting on June 9, after losing 1335 men in the campaign. Entire Allied losses include 5600 men, one carrier, two cruisers, nine destroyers plus other smaller craft, and 100 aircraft. German loses total 3692 men, 19 warships, and 242 aircraft.

JUNE 3–4

WESTERN FRONT, *FRANCE*
Operation Dynamo ends. The remarkable operation has rescued

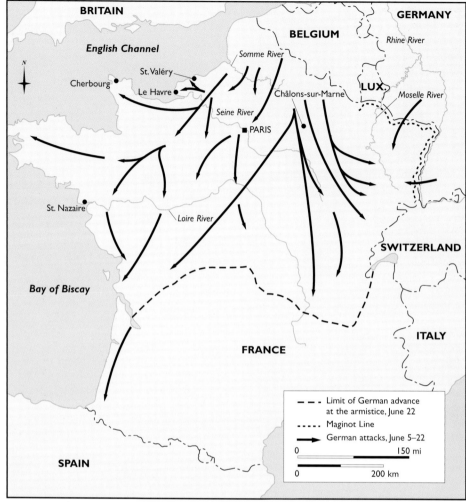

Limit of German advance
at the armistice, June 22

Maginot Line

German attacks, June 5–22

0   150 mi

0   200 km

▲ *German motorized units make rapid progress during the Battle of France.*

▲ *Germany's conquest of France followed the Blitzkrieg principle. Armored thrusts bypassed the Maginot Line and other defensive positions. The Allied forces were then quickly isolated and defeated by air and ground attacks.*

338,226 men – two-thirds of them British – from the beaches of Dunkirk, although 243 vessels and 106 aircraft have been destroyed. General Lord Gort, the British Expeditionary Force's commander, leaves Lieutenant General Sir Harold Alexander in command after being evacuated on May 31. The Germans occupy Dunkirk on June 4 and capture 40,000 French troops.

JUNE 5–12

WESTERN FRONT, *FRANCE*
A German force of 119 divisions opens Operation Red, the conquest of France, with General Fedor von Bock's Army Group B attacking along the Somme River to reach the Seine River west of

▶ *Triumphant German troops parade through Paris after conquering France.*

Paris by June 9. General Gerd von Rundstedt's Army Group A, moving toward the Moselle River in front of the Maginot Line, launches an offensive east of Paris. Rundstedt's tanks, reinforced by Army Group B panzers, overcome resistance from the French Fourth Army to break through at Châlons-sur-Marne on the 12th.

France's response, the Weygand Line, stretching along the Somme and Aisne Rivers, aims to protect Paris and the interior. Some of France's 65 divisions fight determined actions, but many units lack manpower and equipment. Air attacks and logistical problems also undermine General Maxime Weygand's vulnerable forces.

JUNE 8

SEA WAR, *NORTH SEA*
The German battlecruisers *Scharnhorst* and *Gneisenau* sink three empty vessels while hunting for convoys from Norway. They then sink the British carrier *Glorious* and two destroyers. These losses are blamed on the British failure to provide sufficient naval escorts for the Norway convoys.

JUNE 10

WESTERN FRONT, *FRANCE*
Some 11,000 British and other

French troops begin to evacuate from St. Valéry and Le Havre to Britain.

JUNE 10–11

POLITICS, *ITALY*
Italy declares war on France and Britain. Benito Mussolini, eager to capitalize on France's collapse, enters the war despite previous assertions that his nation will not have the capability to fight alongside Germany until 1942. Canada declares war on Italy on the 10th, as do Australia, New Zealand, and South Africa the following day.

JUNE 12–14

SEA WAR, *MEDITERRANEAN*
Britain launches a naval bombardment against the Italian base of Tobruk, Libya, on the 12th. The French Navy bombards the ports of

Genoa and Vado on the 14th. British air raids are also made on Turin and Genoa. Libyan and East African airfields are raided.

JUNE 13

POLITICS, *UNITED STATES*
President Franklin D. Roosevelt signs a $1.3 billion navy bill to improve the service. Shipments of arms also leave the country in response to Winston Churchill's request to Roosevelt for surplus weapons.

JUNE 13–25

WESTERN FRONT, *FRANCE*
Paris is declared an "open city" in order to save it from destruction and all French forces withdraw south of the capital, leaving the Maginot Line isolated. German troops enter Paris on June 14 as thousands flee the capital. Germany's Army Group C, deployed from the Maginot Line to the Swiss border, breaks through French

▼ *The German battlecruisers* Scharnhorst *(foreground) and* Gneisenau, *which attacked Allied ships evacuating troops from Norway in June 1940.*

◄ *French representatives sign articles of surrender in the railroad carriage in which Germany signed the 1918 documents.*

After Italy's armistice with France on the 24th, a cease-fire occurs on all fronts. French casualties since May 10 total more than 85,000 men, the British lose 3475 men, and German losses reach 27,074.

While Pétain's regime will collaborate with Nazi Germany, the French Army officer Brigadier General Charles de Gaulle begins broadcasting his opposition from London on the 18th with pledges to liberate the country.

JUNE 20

POLITICS, *UNITED STATES*
Democratic President Franklin D. Roosevelt appoints two anti-isolationist

defenses. German forces advance in all directions, crossing the Rhine and Loire Rivers. All of the coastal ports between Cherbourg and St. Nazaire are soon captured.

JUNE 15–25

WESTERN FRONT, *FRANCE*
The evacuation of the remaining Allied troops in northwest France begins. Operation Ariel extends this to the Biscay ports from the 16th. Some 214,000 troops are saved during the evacuation, although 3000 perish when the liner *Lancastria* is sunk on the 17th.

JUNE 16–24

POLITICS, *FRANCE*
Prime Minister Paul Reynaud fails to motivate his government to continue fighting and releases France from its agreement with Britain not to make any separate peace. France rejects a British idea to create a union between the countries.

Reynaud, after losing support, resigns and Marshal Henri-Philippe Pétain replaces him. Pétain requests Germany's armistice terms on the 17th, and the signing takes place at Compiègne, site of the World War I armistice agreement, on the 22nd. Under the terms Germany occupies two-thirds of France, including the Channel and Atlantic coastlines. The south, which becomes known as Vichy France, will have a nominal French administration and keep its colonies.

▶ *German troops enter Rouen during the offensive to conquer France.*

▲ *Italian bombers on their way to strike Allied targets. Italy's poor performance in France, North Africa, and Greece contrasted sharply with propaganda about the nation's military prowess.*

Republicans to his cabinet. Henry Stimson becomes secretary for war and Frank Knox is appointed secretary for the navy.

JUNE 20–21

WESTERN FRONT, *FRANCE*
Benito Mussolini launches attacks along the south coast. Offensives are also made along the Franco-Italian border. Italy also bombs the strategically-important island of Malta.

JUNE 26

POLITICS, *ROMANIA*
The government agrees to the Soviet occupation of Bessarabia and northern Bukovina, although Romanian troops attempt to halt the Red Army when it enters the country.

JUNE 30

WESTERN FRONT, *CHANNEL ISLANDS*
Germany invades the Channel Islands. This is the only British territory occupied during hostilities.

JULY 1

SEA WAR, *ATLANTIC*
The "Happy Time" begins for U-boat crews as their operational range is increased now that they have bases in French ports. This lasts until October. U-boat crews inflict serious losses on Allied convoys.

▶ *A German officer speaks to a British police officer in the Channel Islands, the only part of Britain occupied in the war.*

JULY 3–7

JULY 3–7

SEA WAR, *MEDITERRANEAN*

Britain, fearing that France's navy will be seized by Germany, sends two battleships, a battlecruiser, and a carrier (Force H) to neutralize French vessels at Oran and Mers-el-Kebir, Algeria. After negotiations fail, the British sink one battleship and damage two. In Britain, two French battleships, nine destroyers, and other craft are acquired with minimal force. French naval forces in Alexandria, Egypt, are disarmed on the 7th.

JULY 9–19

SEA WAR, *MEDITERRANEAN*

At the Battle of Punta Stilo, the British Mediterranean Fleet tries to separate the Italian Fleet from its base at Taranto in southern Italy. An Italian battleship and cruiser suffer damage, and Italian aircraft hit a British cruiser. On the 19th, the Australian light cruiser *Sydney* and four destroyers engage two Italian light cruisers. The Italians lose a cruiser and the *Sydney* is damaged.

JULY 10

AIR WAR, *BRITAIN*

The Battle of Britain begins. Hermann Goering, the Nazi air force chief, orders attacks on shipping and ports in the English Channel. The movement of Allied vessels in the Channel is soon restricted as a result of British naval and aircraft losses.

▲ *Barges being prepared for Operation Sealion, Germany's planned invasion of Britain that was to begin in the fall of 1940.*

▼ *British pilots rush to their Hurricanes during the Battle of Britain. The Nazis failed to destroy Britain's fighter capability in the aerial war over southern England.*

JULY 16–22

POLITICS, *GERMANY*

Adolf Hitler's Directive No. 16 reveals his military plan to invade Britain, code-named Operation Sealion. This requires control of the English Channel for transporting the invasion force and the destruction of Britain's fighter

▲ *Allied vessels under German air attack in the English Channel.*

▶ *Hermann Goering (right), the Nazi air chief, with Adolf Hitler (left).*

capability to ensure a safe crossing. The air force is made responsible for destroying the strength of the RAF and Royal Navy. Hitler's plans are further advanced after his final peace offer is rejected by the British on the 22nd.

JULY 18

POLITICS, *BRITAIN*
British Prime Minister Winston Churchill agrees to close the Burma Road to disrupt supplies to the Chinese in order to avoid a confrontation with the Japanese. The onset of the monsoon season means that the supply line would be disrupted anyway. The British will reopen the aid route in October.

JULY 21

POLITICS, *SOVIET UNION*
The authorities formally annex Lithuania, Latvia, and Estonia.

JULY 22

ESPIONAGE, *BRITAIN*
Britain establishes the Special Operations Executive (SOE) to secretly give support to resistance groups across Nazi-occupied Europe.

JULY 25

POLITICS, *UNITED STATES*
The United States introduces licensing to restrict the export of oil and metal products outside the Americas and to Britain. This measure is particularly directed toward Japan, which is heavily dependent upon imports of these

▼ *Peasants on the Burma Road, a key supply route to China during the war. Britain temporarily closed it to avoid a rift with the Japanese.*

resources. As a consequence, Japanese strategic planning devotes greater attention to the resources of the Dutch East Indies and Malaysia to relieve their raw material shortages.

AUGUST 1

POLITICS, *GERMANY*
Hitler issues Directive No. 17, which states that preparations for the invasion of England are to be complete by September 15, ready for an invasion between the 19th and 26th.

▲ *Air Chief Marshal Sir Hugh Dowding led the RAF's fighters to victory in the Battle of Britain.*

▼ *A German Heinkel bomber over the East End of London during the Luftwaffe's air offensive on Britain.*

AUGUST 2

SEA WAR, *MEDITERRANEAN*
A British naval force attacks the Italian naval base on the island of Sardinia.

AUGUST 3–19

AFRICA, *BRITISH SOMALILAND*
Italian forces, superior in manpower and artillery, attack the 1475-strong garrison in British Somaliland from neighboring Ethiopia.

AUGUST 5

POLITICS, *GERMANY*
General Franz Halder, the chief-of-staff, inspects the first plans for the invasion of the Soviet Union. He proposes a two-pronged offensive, principally

▲ *German pilots discuss their daring dog-fight tactics during the Battle of Britain.*

directed against Moscow, and a secondary attack on Kiev.

AUGUST 13–17

AIR WAR, *BRITAIN*
"Eagle Day" heralds a four-day German air offensive designed to destroy Britain's Fighter Command with raids on airfields and industrial targets. Hermann Goering, head of the Luftwaffe, postpones the early raids, however, and the later attacks are inconclusive.

AUGUST 15

AIR WAR, *BRITAIN*
Three German air fleets totaling 900 fighters and 1300 bombers launch massed daylight and night attacks on British airfields and ports to lure RAF fighters into combat. Air Chief Marshal Sir Hugh Dowding's 650 operational fighters, aided by effective radar defenses,

KEY MOMENTS

THE BATTLE OF BRITAIN

The Battle of Britain was Germany's attempt to achieve air superiority over the skies of southern England. With this achieved, it could then control the English Channel for the crossing of the invasion force, which was being prepared on the continent.

Germany's air force commander, Hermann Goering, assembled 2800 aircraft against Britain's 700 fighters. Widespread German attacks on ports, shipping, and airfields lured British fighters into action and inflicted heavy losses.

Britain's fate rested upon the bravery, determination, and skill of its fighter pilots. These men were drawn from the British Empire, North America, Czechoslovakia, Poland, and other Allied nations. The performance of the Hurricane and Spitfire fighters they flew also played a key role.

Crucially, a centralized command-and-control structure and radar network also enabled fighters to be effectively concentrated to meet enemy attacks. Germany's gravest strategical error was the decision, from September 7 onward, to concentrate on the

bombing of British cities, despite eroding the capability of Fighter Command by widespread and incessant raids across southern England. This change in strategy enabled the RAF to concentrate its fighters and inflict heavier losses on the Luftwaffe. The RAF also benefitted from longer flying time as it operated over its own territory. In addition, crews who baled out were able to resume fighting, unlike their opponents who parachuted into captivity.

On October 31, after 114 days of aerial combat, Germany conceded defeat, having lost 1733 aircraft and 3893 men. The RAF, at a cost of 828 aircraft and 1007 men, had effectively saved Britain from invasion.

▼ *Hurricane fighters helped Britain defeat Germany's air offensive in 1940.*

are able to concentrate effectively to intercept the attackers in the coming days.

AUGUST 17

POLITICS, *GERMANY*
A total blockade of the British Isles is declared. Any Allied or neutral vessels found in British waters will be attacked on sight.

AUGUST 17–18

SEA WAR, *MEDITERRANEAN*
British naval vessels bombard Bardia and Fort Capuzzo, Libya, and shoot down 12 Italian bombers sent to attack them.

AUGUST 24–25

AIR WAR, *BRITAIN*
The Luftwaffe inflicts serious losses on the RAF during attacks on its main air bases in southeast England, straining the resources of Fighter Command to breaking point in a few days. London has also been bombed.

AUGUST 26–29

AIR WAR, *GERMANY*
The RAF launches a night raid with 81 aircraft on Berlin following a similar raid on London. Raids also take place against Düsseldorf, Essen, and other cities. The raids contribute toward a critical change in Germany's strategy, as aircraft are redirected to make retaliatory raids on London. This move relieves the pressure on Fighter Command's air bases.

SEPTEMBER 2

POLITICS, *BRITAIN*
Britain and the United States ratify a deal whereby 50 old destroyers, needed for convoy duties, are handed to

◄ *Police and rescue workers frantically clear debris after a German air raid on London. The Nazi bombing offensive quickly spread to other cities in Britain.*

bridgeheads on the south coast of England for an invasion force of nine divisions and 250 tanks.

SEPTEMBER 7–30
AIR WAR, *BRITAIN*
Full-scale bombing raids on London – the "Blitz" – begin with 500 bombers and 600 fighters. The RAF is initially surprised by the new German tactics, but adapts and concentrates its weakened forces against this threat. The bombing reaches its greatest intensity on the 15th, but the Luftwaffe is now

◀ *Civilians prepare to spend the night safe from the bombing by sheltering in one of London's underground stations.*

suffering heavy losses, especially during its daylight raids on English cities, which are largely abandoned by the 30th. Bomber Command raids in France and the Low Countries destroy a tenth of the Nazi invasion barges on the 14th–15th.

SEPTEMBER 13–18
AFRICA, *EGYPT*
An Italian force of 250,000 men under Marshal Rodolfo Graziani advances from Libya into neighboring Egypt against the British Western Desert

▼ *Bomb damage to St. Paul's Cathedral. Nazi raids tore the City of London apart but failed to destroy public morale.*

Britain in exchange for bases in the Caribbean and Bermuda. Such exchanges will accustom the US public to aiding the Allied war effort.

SEPTEMBER 3
POLITICS, *GERMANY*
The Operation Sealion landings are postponed from September 15 to the 21st. Two airborne divisions will be used to establish three

▼ *Charles de Gaulle, the leader of the Free French forces based in Britain, opposed the puppet Vichy French regime.*

▶ *Italian forces invade Egypt from Libya. The offensive was later shattered by a British counterattack.*

Force of two divisions under General Sir Richard O'Connor. Graziani establishes fortified camps along a 50-mile (75-km) front, while the British remain 75 miles (120km) to the east. British plans to attack Graziani are delayed as units are redirected to Crete and Greece, where an Italian invasion is feared.

SEPTEMBER 15

POLITICS, *CANADA*
Men aged between 21 and 24 are to be conscripted.
POLITICS, *SOVIET UNION*
Men aged between 19 and 20 are to be conscripted.

SEPTEMBER 16–17

SEA WAR, *MEDITERRANEAN*
The British carrier *Illustrious* and battleship *Valiant* sink two Italian destroyers and two cargo ships at Benghazi, Libya.
HOME FRONT, *BRITAIN*
The Selective Service Bill permits the conscription of men aged between 21 and 35.

SEPTEMBER 17

POLITICS, *GERMANY*
Adolf Hitler decides to suspend Operation Sealion after Germany's failure to achieve aerial supremacy over southern England, while the General Staff in-spects further plans for the invasion of the Soviet Union. General Friedrich von Paulus, deputy chief of the Army General Staff, suggests offensives

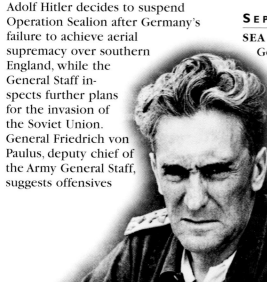

toward Leningrad, Kiev, and Moscow, with the latter being the main thrust.

SEPTEMBER 20–22

SEA WAR, *ATLANTIC*
German U-boats launch their first successful "Wolf Pack" operation, sinking 12 ships. In this tactic some 15–20 U-boats are de-ployed across the approaches to Britain. When a U-boat finds a convoy, it tracks the vessels and awaits the gathering of the entire "Wolf Pack" for a combined attack.

◀ *Marshal Rodolfo Graziani, the commander of Italian forces in Libya, who was responsible for the attack against British, Indian, and Australian forces in Egypt.*

SEPTEMBER 21

POLITICS, *AUSTRALIA*
Prime Minister Robert Menzies wins another general election for the United Australia Party, although Labor remains the largest individual party.

SEPTEMBER 22

FAR EAST, *INDOCHINA*
Japanese forces enter the French colony after the powerless Vichy French authorities finally agree to the occupation. Some Vichy French resist the Japanese, who aim to prevent China obtaining supplies through the country.

SEPTEMBER 23–25

SEA WAR, *AFRICA*
A British and Free French expedition, code-named Menace, attempts to occupy Dakar, French West Africa, with naval forces, including the British aircraft carrier *Ark Royal*, and 7900 troops. The Free French commander Charles de Gaulle fails to reach any agreement with the Vichy authorities, whose warships open fire. The Vichy French lose a destroyer and two submarines. Prime Minister Winston

DECISIVE WEAPONS

RADAR

Radar uses synchronized radio transmitters and receivers that emit radio waves and process their reflections for display. This is especially useful for detecting aircraft. Although the United States and Germany had been working on this technology since the beginning of the century, it was Britain that first established a series of radar stations in 1938 in response to the threat of German bomber raids. The stations acted as a warning system to alert fighter aircraft to the presence of approaching bombers. This was critical in the Battle of Britain as the overstretched RAF was able to concentrate its fighter forces to repel enemy attacks. Axis aircraft could be detected over 70 miles (112km) from the stations in southeast England. Sector stations (as seen above) recorded the information from the various radar sites under their control and scrambled fighters to intercept the threat.

As the accuracy of ground-based radar increased, target range and direction information provided firing data for anti-aircraft guns. Eventually, guns received a stream of accurate information as radars "locked on" and automatically tracked the targets.

Aircraft radar, introduced in 1941, initially enabled nightfighters to locate targets and eventually aided bomber navigation. U-boats that surfaced in darkness for safety could also be detected by aircraft, which then illuminated the submarines with lights before attacking them. Ground-based radar also helped bomber crews hit targets by precisely tracking and relaying information to the aircraft. In the war at sea, radar was used to detect enemy aircraft and also directed gunfire, which could be effectively employed even in complete darkness with the new technology.

Churchill cancels Operation Menace after a Free French landing fails and British vessels suffer damage from Vichy French forces.

SEPTEMBER 24–25

AIR WAR, *MEDITERRANEAN*
Vichy France launches ineffective air raids on Gibraltar in retaliation for the British attack on Dakar.

SEPTEMBER 25

POLITICS, *NORWAY*
Nazi sympathizer Vidkun Quisling, who proclaimed himself Norway's leader following the German invasion, becomes head of the government. In reality Quisling remains a German puppet with limited authority.

SEPTEMBER 27

POLITICS, *AXIS*
Germany, Italy, and Japan agree a military, political, and economic alliance that pledges each country to fight any state that declares war on an Axis nation. The Tripartite Pact specifically aims to deter intervention by the United States in Europe or Asia.

▼ *Greek troops send letters home during the war against the Italian invasion. Italy's invasion, which was launched in October 1940, met fierce Greek resistance.*

OCTOBER 7

BALKANS, *ROMANIA*
German forces enter Romania on the pretext of helping to train the army of the fascist Iron Guard government. Germany's principal motive is to occupy the Ploesti oil fields.

OCTOBER 9

POLITICS, *BRITAIN*
Winston Churchill succeeds Neville Chamberlain, the former prime minister, as Conservative Party leader. Churchill was initially an unpopular figure in the party but his war leadership has gone a long way to reverse this.

OCTOBER 12

POLITICS, *GERMANY*
Hitler postpones Operation Sealion until spring 1941.

OCTOBER 15

POLITICS, *ITALY*
The Italian war council decides to invade Greece. Italy plans not to tell its Axis partner Germany about the operation, which is scheduled to commence at the end of October.

OCTOBER 16–19

POLITICS, *JAPAN*
The Dutch East Indies agrees to supply 40 percent of its oil production to

Japan for six months despite British attempts to obstruct this.

OCTOBER 18

POLITICS, *VICHY FRANCE*
The puppet Vichy regime introduces anti-Semitic laws.

OCTOBER 28

BALKANS, *GREECE*
Italy issues an ultimatum to Greece demanding the right to occupy the country for the war's duration. Before the ultimatum expires, eight divisions, led by General Sabasiano Visconti-Prasca, attack from Albania. Italy hopes for a rapid advance to rival Germany's conquests, but mountainous terrain and the absence of maps for commanders hamper the invasion. The winter weather limits air support and thousands die of cold. Greek forces, under General

▶ *Franklin D. Roosevelt was elected for a third term as US president in 1940. He prepared the nation for war and aided the Allies by expanding economic output.*

▲ *Greek troops carry brandy to the front. The ill-prepared Italian invaders lacked proper clothing and supplies to sustain their campaign during the freezing winter months in the mountains.*

Alexander Papagos, the commander-in-chief, mount stiff resistance.

OCTOBER 30–31

MEDITERRANEAN, *CRETE*
British forces occupy the Greek island.

NOVEMBER 5

POLITICS, *UNITED STATES*
President Franklin D. Roosevelt is elected for an unprecedented third term.
SEA WAR, *ATLANTIC*
The German pocket battleship *Admiral Scheer* attacks a British convoy of 37 ships escorted by the armed merchant cruiser *Jervis Bay*, which fights to save the convoy. The battleship rams and sinks *Jervis Bay*, but only five other vessels are lost. Eastbound convoys are suspended until the 17th while the Allies search for the *Admiral Scheer*.

"IL DUCE" BENITO MUSSOLINI

Benito Mussolini, journalist, soldier, and politician, exploited the instability of inter-war Italy to become the dictator of a fascist state. After rising to power in 1922, he suppressed opposition and promised the nation that a new Roman Empire would arise. Mussolini presented himself as a tough alternative to previous liberal statesmen and a patriotic enemy of communism. Fascist propaganda hid his regime's economic instability, and the conquest of Ethiopia (1935–36) and Albania (1939) attempted to divert public attention away from domestic problems.

Mussolini established close relations with Adolf Hitler, but insisted that Italy would not be ready to enter into war until 1942. After the defeat of France in June 1940, however, he was keen to capitalize on Germany's conquests and declared war on the Allies. Military blunders in France, North Africa, and Greece left Italy dependent on German military assistance. Mussolini, physically and mentally weakened, faced growing public apathy and political threats as his country faltered.

In July 1943, Mussolini was overthrown by the Fascist Grand Council. The new regime agreed to an armistice with the Allies in September. Mussolini, now imprisoned, was then rescued by the Germans. Axis-controlled Italy remained under Berlin's direction but Hitler was benevolent toward Europe's first fascist leader. Italian partisans shot Mussolini in April 1945.

November 10

▲ *Marshal Pietro Badoglio, the Italian commander-in-chief, who resigned after the failure of the invasion of Greece.*

November 10

POLITICS, *ITALY*
General Ubaldo Soddu replaces General Sabasiano Visconti-Prasca as the Italian commander-in-chief in Albania.

November 11–12

SEA WAR, *MEDITERRANEAN*
At the Battle of Taranto British torpedo aircraft from the carrier *Illustrious* destroy three Italian battleships and damage two vessels during the raid on the Italian base. *Illustrious* loses only two aircraft. When the fleet leaves for Naples and Genoa, three British cruisers sink four vessels in the Strait of Otranto. This air attack on a fleet in harbor is closely studied by other navies, especially the Japanese.

November 14–22

BALKANS, *GREECE*
Greece launches a major counter-attack and 3400 British troops, plus air support, arrive from Alexandria, Egypt. When Greek forces finally enter Koritza they capture 2000 Italians and drive almost all the invaders back into Albania by December.

November 14

AIR WAR, *BRITAIN*
Germany sends 449 bombers to bomb the city of Coventry. The raid kills 500 civilians, leaves thousands homeless, and shocks the British public.

November 18

TECHNOLOGY, *BRITAIN*
British "Air-to-Surface-Vessel" radar

▲ *A German reconnaissance photograph of Coventry, the English city devastated by an air attack in November 1940.*

▶ *A Polish Jew in the Warsaw ghetto, which was created in November 1940.*

fitted to a Sunderland flying boat locates its first U-boat during a patrol in the Atlantic.

November 20

POLITICS, *HUNGARY*
Hungary joins the Axis powers. Since the Italian invasion of Greece, the Germans have been attempting to secure their food and oil supplies from the Balkans by pressing the countries of the region to join the Tripartite Pact.

November 23

POLITICS, *ROMANIA*
Prime Minister General Ion Antonescu leads Romania into the Axis alliance.

November 26

FINAL SOLUTION, *POLAND*
The Nazis begin creating a ghetto in Warsaw for the Jews, who will eventually be kept there in intolerable conditions.

DECEMBER 18

POLITICS, *GERMANY*
Adolf Hitler issues his plan for invading the Soviet Union, code-named Operation Barbarossa. His Directive No. 21 retains a three-pronged offensive but the weight of the invasion plan has now shifted northward to Leningrad and the Baltic area, where Army Groups North and Center are to annihilate the enemy forces, before attacking and occupying Moscow.

DECEMBER 29

POLITICS, *UNITED STATES*
In President Franklin D. Roosevelt's "fireside chat" broadcast, he describes how the United States must become the "arsenal of democracy" by giving maximum assistance to Britain in its fight against the Axis powers.

◀ *General Sir Archibald Wavell (right), the British commander-in-chief in North Africa who repelled Italy's attack on Egypt in December 1940.*

▼ *British, Indian, and Australian troops in Egypt halted the Italian offensive despite the numerical superiority of the invaders. This success was only reversed after the arrival of German forces.*

NOVEMBER 30

POLITICS, *JAPAN*
Japan officially recognizes the puppet government of President Wang Ching-wei in China.

DECEMBER 6

POLITICS, *ITALY*
Marshal Pietro Badoglio, Italy's commander-in-chief, resigns.

DECEMBER 9–11

AFRICA, *EGYPT*
General Sir Archibald Wavell, the commander-in-chief in the Middle East and North Africa, launches the first British offensive in the Western Desert. Major General Sir Richard O'Connor's Western Desert Force of 31,000 British and Commonwealth troops, supported by aircraft and long-range naval gunfire, is ordered to attack the fortified camps that have been established by the Italians in Egypt. Sidi Barrani is captured on the 10th and 34,000 Italians are taken prisoner as they retreat rapidly from Egypt. It is a famous victory in the face of overwhelming odds.

The Allies continued fighting in North Africa, where they now faced General Erwin Rommel's Afrika Korps, and the war in the Balkans intensified with Germany conquering Yugoslavia and Greece. In the Mediterranean and Atlantic, the Allies fought a bitter campaign to defend their vital sea-lanes. The Axis powers' declarations of war on the Soviet Union and the United States proved a critical turning point. Germany undertook a bitter campaign on the Eastern Front, while Japan had to safeguard its conquests in the Pacific. The Axis powers had to face the might of the Soviet Union and the United States.

JANUARY 2

POLITICS, *UNITED STATES*
President Franklin D. Roosevelt announces a program to produce 200 freighters, called "Liberty" ships, to support the Allied Atlantic convoys.

JANUARY 3–15

AFRICA, *LIBYA*
General Sir Archibald Wavell's Middle East Force, renamed XIII Corps, with air and naval support, resumes its offensive into Cyrenaica. In Australia's first land action of the war, the Australian 6th Division leads the attack to capture Bardia, just across Libya's border with Egypt, on the 15th. Some 70,000 Italians, plus large amounts of equipment, are captured.

JANUARY 7–22

AFRICA, *LIBYA*
After the British 7th Armored Brigade encircles Tobruk, the Australian 6th Division leads

◀ Italian troops in Tobruk. Allied and Axis forces battled for control of the strategically-important port.

▶ Admiral Ernest King led the US Atlantic Fleet in 1941 and rose to become a key naval commander during the war.

the assault against the Italian defenders of the port, who eventually capitulate on the 22nd. Some 30,000 Italians, as well as port facilities, and vital supplies of fuel, food, and water, are seized. Major General Sir Richard O'Connor immediately sends forces farther west along the coast to capture the port of Benghazi.

JANUARY 19

AFRICA, *ERITREA*
British forces in the Sudan, led by General William Platt, begin attacking Italian forces, heralding the start of General Sir Archibald Wavell's campaign against Italian East Africa.

JANUARY 24

AFRICA, *LIBYA*
The British 4th Armored Brigade engages Italian tanks near Mechili. The Italian forces in Libya are now divided,

with units inland positioned around Mechili, and other forces on the coast around Derna. They do not support each other and both face encirclement.

JANUARY 29

AFRICA, *ITALIAN SOMALILAND*
British forces based in Kenya led by General Sir Alan Cunningham begin attacking the Italian colony's garrison in the next stage of their campaign against Italian East Africa.

POLITICS, *UNITED STATES*
A significant advance in Anglo-US cooperation begins with staff talks in Washington. A decision, code-named ABC1, is eventually made that places Germany's defeat as the principal Allied aim in the event of the US declaring war. These talks lead to a US mission in March to visit potential sites for military bases in Britain.

FEBRUARY 1

POLITICS, *UNITED STATES*
Major organizational changes to the US Navy lead to it being divided into three fleets: Atlantic, Asiatic, and Pacific. Admiral Ernest King is to lead the new Atlantic Fleet, and US naval forces will be strengthened in this vital war theater.

SEA WAR, *ATLANTIC*
The German heavy cruiser *Admiral Hipper*, operating from Brest in France, embarks on a series of highly-destructive raids on Atlantic convoys that last until April.

▼ A column of British tanks prepares for action against Axis forces in Libya.

SEA WAR, *ATLANTIC*
The German battlecruisers *Scharnhorst* and *Gneisenau* embark on commerce-destroying raids in the Atlantic. They succeed in dispersing

▼ *Prince George of Greece and Princess Bonaparte speak to Greek troops wounded while fighting the Italian invaders.*

numerous convoys and sink 22 ships before returning to the safety of French waters on March 22.

FEBRUARY 5–7

AFRICA, *LIBYA*
The Italians fail in their final attempt to escape encirclement at Beda Fomm, south of Benghazi, and surrender to the British 7th Armored Division. Meanwhile, the Australian 6th Division, advancing along the coastal roads, forces troops in Benghazi to surrender on the 7th.

This ends a two-month campaign in which the British have inflicted a complete defeat on a stronger enemy by executing a carefully-planned offensive using highly-trained troops backed by air and naval support.

FEBRUARY 14

POLITICS, *BULGARIA*
Bulgaria grants Germany access to its border with Greece. This move enables Germany to increase its power in the Balkans and provides a route for forces earmarked to invade Greece.

POLITICS, *SOVIET UNION*
General Georgi Zhukov is appointed chief of the General Staff and deputy commissar for defense. He has previously commanded the Red Army forces fighting against the Japanese in Mongolia in the summer of 1939.

AFRICA, *LIBYA*
In response to Adolf Hitler's offer to send an armored division to ensure that the Italians will not withdraw in Libya, the first detachments of General

▲ *Italian troops in action near Benghazi during the major British offensive into Cyrenaica, Libya.*

Erwin Rommel's Afrika Korps disembark at Tripoli.

FEBRUARY 19–23

POLITICS, *ALLIES*
A meeting of political and military leaders in Cairo, Egypt, decides to deploy forces to Greece. The Greek and British authorities subsequently agree to send 100,000 British troops to bolster the country's defenses.

FEBRUARY 25

AFRICA, *ITALIAN SOMALILAND*
British-led East and West African troops advance into Mogadishu, the capital. The defeated Italians begin evacuating the colony.

MARCH 1

POLITICS, *BULGARIA*
Bulgaria joins the Axis powers.
AFRICA, *LIBYA*
Free French forces from Chad seize the Italian air base and garrison at Kufra Oasis in the southeast after a 22-day siege.

▶ *General Erwin Rommel, the audacious commander of the German Afrika Korps, outlining his strategy for winning a battle against the British in North Africa.*

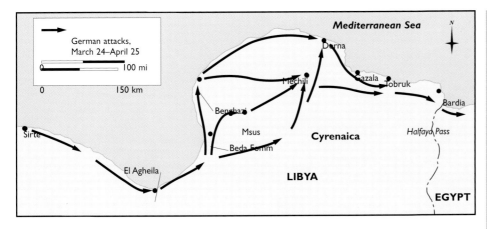

LEND-LEASE

Following the fall of France in June 1940, US President Franklin D. Roosevelt pursued a policy of supplying Britain with the military equipment it required to carry on the fight against Nazi Germany. As dependence on these imports increased, in December 1940 the British prime minister, Winston Churchill, proposed an arrangement whereby the Allied nations could obtain essential US goods and equipment but would repay the United States after the war.

In March 1941 Congress passed the Lend-Lease Act and gave Roosevelt wide-ranging powers to supply goods and services to "any country whose defense the president deems vital to the defense of the United States." Almost $13 billion had been allocated to the Lend-Lease arrangement by November 1941.

Although Britain now had the opportunity to increase the amount of US imports, its own war production had been increasing during this period. Food and oil from the United States, however, was still crucial to its survival.

Lend-Lease was terminated by President Harry S. Truman on August 24, 1945, although Britain was still under contract to receive large quantities of US goods for which it had to pay in dollars.

Britain was not the only beneficiary of the act. The British Commonwealth, the Soviet Union, and other Allied nations also became recipients of US aid in this manner to help their respective war efforts.

MARCH 4

WESTERN FRONT, *NORWAY*

A joint British and Norwegian commando raid and naval assault on the Lofoten Islands destroys fish-oil plants used in the production of explosives, captures 215 Germans, rescues 300 Norwegians, and sinks 10 ships.

MARCH 5

BALKANS, *GREECE*

The first contingent of British troops sails from Egypt. By April 2 some 58,000 troops will have been sent to help defend the country.

MARCH 9–25

BALKANS, *GREECE*

Italy launches a spring offensive between the Devoli and Vijosë Rivers in northwest Greece to counter the reverses it has suffered. Mussolini himself travels to Albania to supervise the deployment of

▲ *General Erwin Rommel's first offensive in the desert drove the British from Libya and threatened to seize Egypt.*

12 divisions for the attack. Greek intelligence and defensive preparations ensure that the poorly-planned Italian attacks from Albania are rebuffed.

MARCH 11

POLITICS, *UNITED STATES*

President Franklin D. Roosevelt signs the Lend-Lease Act that allows Britain to obtain supplies without having to immediately pay for them in cash. For the remainder of 1941, however, Britain is able to pay. The bill grants the president greater powers to supply military equipment to any nation he considers important to US security.

MARCH 24

AFRICA, *LIBYA*

General Erwin Rommel begins his first offensive in Libya by driving the British from El Agheila. He now begins a counteroffensive similar to the original attack by the British. While the 21st Panzer

US shipbuilding dramatically increased to provide vessels for the Atlantic convoys that sailed to Britain.

MARCH 25

Division races across the desert toward Tobruk, Italian forces take the longer coastal route.

MARCH 25

POLITICS, *YUGOSLAVIA*
Yugoslavia joins the Axis powers by signing the Tripartite Pact.

MARCH 27–30

POLITICS, *YUGOSLAVIA*
A coup by air force officers deposes Prince Paul's pro-Axis administration. King Peter II takes nominal charge of the country and General Dusan Simovic becomes head of government. The events alarm the Axis powers, chiefly Germany.

Adolf Hitler responds to the overthrow of Prince Paul by issuing Directive No. 25, the order for the invasion of Yugoslavia, which will commence alongside the attack on Greece, codenamed Operation Marita. Hitler approves of the army's proposals for the invasions, both of which are scheduled to begin on April 6.

MARCH 27

AFRICA, *ERITREA*
The Battle of Keren, in northeast Eritrea, ends with Italian forces being forced to retreat toward the capital Asmara. The Italians lose 3000 men compared to British fatalities of 536. Asmara falls five days later.

MARCH 28–29

SEA WAR, *AEGEAN*
The Italian fleet sails into the Aegean Sea to disrupt British convoys to Greece. A British force led by Admiral Henry Pridham-Wippell engages some Italian cruisers in a long-range bombardment. The Italians retire, fearing the presence of more enemy vessels.

▲ *British trucks carrying troops at the Battle of Keren during the campaign against the Italians in Eritrea.*

▼ *The Italian battleship* Vittorio Veneto *fires a salvo against the British in the Aegean Sea during the Battle of Cape Matapan. Torpedo-bombers hit the vessel during the action.*

KEY PERSONALITIES

FIELD MARSHAL ERWIN ROMMEL

Erwin Rommel (1891–1944) was a decorated World War I officer who commanded Hitler's bodyguard and was responsible for the Führer's personal safety during the Polish campaign. He then took command of the 7th Panzer Division for the 1940 invasion of France. His speedy advance across the Meuse River and drive to the English Channel earned him a reputation as a daring tank commander.

Following the failed Italian campaign in North Africa, he was sent there to lead the Afrika Korps in 1941. Rommel became a master of desert warfare tactics with his ability to exploit opportunities, employ unorthodox methods, and deploy his armored forces to maximum effect. After recapturing Tobruk in 1942, he pushed the Allies back to El Alamein in Egypt. The "Desert Fox" was promoted to field marshal, having led the Afrika Korps to a string of victories.

Rommel was forced to retreat into Tunisia after the British victory at El Alamein in November 1942 and the Allied Torch landings. He left North Africa in 1943. Rommel's next major appointment was in France, where he was tasked with establishing the anti-invasion program he had proposed to Hitler. He commanded Army Group B after the Allied landings in June 1944. Rommel was badly wounded during an air attack and returned to Germany. After being implicated in the failed July assassination attempt on Adolf Hitler, Rommel took poison to avoid a trial and the threatened reprisals against his family.

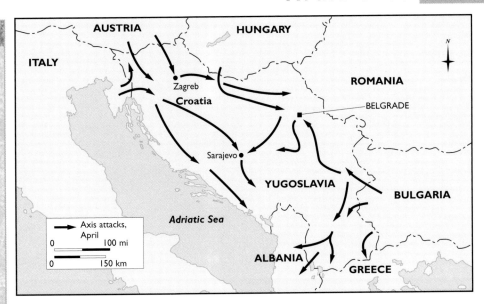

▲ *After Italy failed to seize Greece in 1940, the Germans conquered the Balkans with a successful campaign in 1941.*

Their fears are realized when the main British force, led by Admiral Sir Andrew Cunningham, sends two torpedo-bombers from the carrier *Formidable* to attack the Italian naval vessels. They damage the battleship *Vittorio Veneto* and cripple the cruiser *Pola*. Three British battleships then engage two cruisers sent to cover the *Pola*. The Battle of Cape Matapan claims five Italian ships sunk and 3000 men killed. The British lose just one aircraft in the action.

MARCH 30

POLITICS, UNITED STATES
The authorities confiscate 65 Axis ships, which are immediately taken into "protective custody."

APRIL 1–18

POLITICS, IRAQ
Nationalist politician Rashid Ali and army officers hostile to Britain depose Regent Faisal and form a pro-Axis

▼ *Prisoners-of-war captured during the invasion of Greece pass a variety of German armored vehicles.*

regime in Iraq. British troops begin arriving in Iraq on the 18th to safeguard access to key oil supplies.

APRIL 4

AFRICA, LIBYA
General Erwin Rommel's Axis troops are advancing across Libya in three groups. A predominantly Italian force on the coast takes Benghazi. Another group inland is advancing to Msus, while farther south a third force is also heading toward the same objective.

APRIL 6–15

BALKANS, YUGOSLAVIA/GREECE
Thirty-three German divisions, with Italian and Hungarian support, invade Yugoslavia from the north, east, and southeast. Aerial bombing centering on Belgrade dislocates the nation's military command and communication structure, and further undermines the ineffective mobilization of its 640,000-strong army. Major cities are quickly

251

▲ *German tanks crossing the desert during General Erwin Rommel's first offensive in the desert war.*

seized, including Zagreb, Belgrade, and Sarajevo, between the 10th and 15th.

In Greece, German forces attack the Greek Second Army on the fortified Metaxas Line along the country's northern border with Bulgaria. Air raids on Piraeus port destroy a British ammunition ship, which explodes and sinks 13 vessels. The Second Army, cut off after German forces reach the sea at Salonika on the 9th, soon surrenders. The British, after initially occupying positions between Mount Olympus and Salonika, are quickly forced back to a new defensive line just north of the mountain following the collapse of Greek forces on their left flank.

APRIL 6–9

AFRICA, *ETHIOPIA/ERITREA*
British General Sir Alan Cunningham, after an impressive advance of over 1000 miles (1600 km) from Kenya, captures Addis Ababa, Ethiopia's capital, and then continues to harass the retreating Italian forces. Allied

▲ *Italian troops were often unprepared for crossing freezing, mountainous terrain during the invasion of Greece.*

◄ *Following the conquest of Yugoslavia by Axis forces, Italian troops march into the province of Slovenia.*

forces in Eritrea then seize the port of Massawa on the 9th and capture 17 Axis merchant vessels and other assorted craft in the harbor.

APRIL 7

AFRICA, *LIBYA*
General Erwin Rommel captures Derna, along with British Generals Philip Neame and Sir Richard O'Connor, during his advance toward Tobruk.

APRIL 10

POLITICS, *YUGOSLAVIA*
The Ustachi political group in the province of Croatia declares the formation of an independent republic separate from Yugoslavia.

SEA WAR, *GREENLAND*
The United States begins occupying Greenland to prevent the Danish colony falling into German hands. Valuable weather-observation points for Britain are situated in Greenland.

APRIL 10-13

AFRICA, *LIBYA*
General Erwin Rommel begins the siege of Tobruk. The Allies, who repulse his first attacks, are determined to hold Tobruk as it is the only major port between Sfax in Tunisia and Alexandria in Egypt, a distance of 1000 miles (1600 km). It is therefore a strategic base for forces fighting in North Africa. Tobruk comes under constant air and ground attack, its caves providing the only real shelter, while the sea-lane to Egypt is to be its only lifeline.

APRIL 13

POLITICS, *SOVIET UNION/JAPAN*
A five-year nonaggression pact between the Soviet Union and Japan is signed, which enables the Red Army to move units from Siberia to bolster its forces preparing to meet any future German attack.

▼ *An Australian gun crew defending Tobruk. The besieged garrison and the ships supplying the defenders came under constant Axis attack.*

APRIL 17

POLITICS, *YUGOSLAVIA*
Yugoslavia signs an armistice with Germany. The country is now under military administration except for the Croatian puppet state. Immediately, guerrilla forces emerge to resist the Nazi occupation.

APRIL 18-21

BALKANS, *GREECE*
Greek positions are quickly collapsing as the German invaders advance. The British have fallen back from Mount Olympus to Thermopylae. A British evacuation appears inevitable as reinforcements from Egypt are canceled on the 18th. King George assumes temporary charge of the government after the premier, Alexander Koryzis, commits suicide. A British evacuation is finalized after General Alexander Papagos, the Greek commander-in-chief, realizing the situation is hopeless, recommends a withdrawal on the 21st. Greek forces fighting in Albania surrender on the 20th.

▼ *Yugoslavian soldiers surrender to the conquering Axis forces. Although the country was occupied, partisan forces carried on fighting to liberate the nation.*

APRIL 21–30

AIR WAR, BRITAIN
Two raids on the nights of the 21st–22nd and 29th–30th against Plymouth by 640 bombers claim 750 lives and leave 30,000 homeless.

APRIL 21–27

BALKANS, GREECE
British forces leave their lines around Thermopylae on the 24th after Greek forces in Thrace capitulate. The British evacuation operation now begins, and some 43,000 men are rescued by the Royal Navy from ports and beaches in eastern Greece, while under constant German air attack. Two destroyers and four transport ships are lost.

A German attack by paratroopers at Corinth on the 26th and an advance to Patras pose a threat to the British evacuation. German forces occupy Athens on the 27th, but the Greek government has already left for Crete. Campaign dead: Greek 15,700; Italian 13,755; German 1518; and British 900.

APRIL 25

POLITICS, GERMANY
Adolf Hitler issues Directive No. 28, ordering the airborne invasion of Crete, code-named Operation Mercury.

APRIL 30

AFRICA, LIBYA
The most intense Axis attack on Tobruk to date commences but meets determined resistance from

▲ *German parachutists engaged in street fighting with the Allies in Corinth during the invasion of Greece.*

▲ *Ethiopian fighters in action against Italian troops during the British campaign to destroy Mussolini's East African empire.*

the defenders. Four days later Axis forces secure a salient on the southwestern area of the defensive perimeter. Both sides then dig in for a lengthy campaign, with the garrison entirely dependent on supplies carried by the Royal Navy. German submarines, torpedo-boats, and medium and dive-bombers constantly threaten the supply vessels, which are especially vulnerable when unloading.

MAY 1–17

MIDDLE EAST, IRAQ
Iraqi forces, totaling four divisions, commence attacks on British troops, which intensify in the following days. British forces are soon bolstered by reinforcements. Germany supports the Iraqis by launching air attacks.

MAY 3–19

AFRICA, ETHIOPIA
At the Battle of Amba Alagi in the mountains of northern Ethiopia, the Italians make their last major stand against the Allies in defense of their East African empire. The surrender of the Duke of Aosta and 7000 troops heralds an Allied victory in East Africa. Some 230, 000 Italians have been killed or captured. The Allied victory safeguards the Suez Canal from any potential threat from East Africa and also secures control of the Red Sea for Allied shipping.

MAY 5

POLITICS, ETHIOPIA
Emperor Haile Selassie returns to Ethiopia after being exiled for five years by the Italians.

MAY 6–12

SEA WAR, MEDITERRANEAN
Operation Tiger, the first Gibraltar-to-Egypt convoy for many months, transports supplies intended for a British desert offensive. Two convoys also sail from Egypt to Gibraltar. The entire Mediterranean Fleet supports

▶ A British servicewoman shelters under a table in case an air raid occurs while she has a rest. Work carried on throughout the "Blitz" regardless of the dangers.

the convoy of five transports. They suffer attacks from Italian aircraft on the 8th. One transport, carrying 57 tanks, sinks after striking a mine. The convoy, however, delivers 238 tanks and 43 Hurricane fighters.

MAY 10

POLITICS, *BRITAIN*
Rudolf Hess, deputy leader of Germany, flies to Scotland on a strange mission to ask Britain to allow Germany a "free hand" in Europe in return for the Nazis leaving the British Empire intact. Hess flies to Scotland to see the Duke of Hamilton, whom he believes to be the leader of the antiwar party in Britain. Germany does not authorize his actions and the British imprison him. Martin Bormann, national party organizer, replaces Hess and becomes a key confidant of
Adolf Hitler.

◀ Rudolf Hess, the Nazi who tried to make peace with the British.

MAY 10–11

AIR WAR, *BRITAIN*
In the climax to the "Blitz," London is attacked by 507 bombers. This will be the last major German air raid for three years. The aerial bombing of Britain now affects Liverpool, Bristol, Belfast, and several other cities. Since September 1940, 39,678 people have been killed and 46,119 injured by Luftwaffe raids. Civil defense, fire, police, and medical organizations help the population to cope with the attacks. Infrastructure is quickly repaired and shelters provide some protection for people. The population in general remains resilient in the face of the onslaught, despite the dislocation and the strains caused by the bombing.

MAY 15–16

AFRICA, *EGYPT*
Operation Brevity, the first British operation against the Afrika Korps, attempts to throw the Axis forces back from the Egyptian frontier. Halfaya Pass and Sollum are recaptured in the operation.

MAY 20–22

MEDITERRANEAN, *CRETE*
A German force of 23,000 men, supported by 600 aircraft, attacks Crete. The German

plan is to launch an airborne assault that can then be reinforced by a seaborne force. After preparatory air attacks, the Germans launch the first major airborne operation in history.

Paratroops come under attack while landing and meet determined resistance from the 42,000 British, New Zealand, Australian, and Greek troops stationed on the island. After an Allied battalion commander holding Máleme airfield mistakenly withdraws, the Germans gain a footing for

▼ German mountain troops en route to Crete, where many would die in the bitter battle to seize the island.

MAY 23–27

▼ *The German battleship* Bismarck *fires a salvo at the British battleship* Hood. *The* Hood *was sunk during the fierce battle in the Denmark Straits.*

reinforcements to be landed. While the Germans are able to land some troops by glider and parachute, around 5000 men are lost on vessels sailing from Greece that are intercepted by British ships. The British Mediterranean Fleet in Cretan waters is subjected to massive German air attacks on the 22nd, forcing it to withdraw its ships off northern Crete.

MAY 23–27

SEA WAR, *ATLANTIC*
Two British cruisers, *Norfolk* and *Suffolk*, assisted by radar, find the German battleship *Bismarck* and cruiser *Prinz Eugen* in the Denmark Straits between Iceland and Greenland. However, the two Germans ships sink the battlecruiser *Hood* and damage the battleship *Prince of Wales*, which have been sent to engage them. *Bismarck*'s oil tanks, however, are hit and begin leaking. That night, a torpedo-bomber hits the ship but does little damage.

The German vessels make for Brest and the British lose radar contact

▶ *Bernard Freyberg, the New Zealander who led the Allied defense of Crete.*

for several hours. Aircraft from the carrier *Ark Royal* disable *Bismarck*'s steering with a torpedo on the 26th and other ships encircle her. Shelling from the battleships *Rodney* and *King George V* leave the *Bismarck* a shattered and burning wreck.

MAY 27

POLITICS, *UNITED STATES*
President Franklin D. Roosevelt declares that "an unlimited national emergency now exists." The government assumes wide-ranging powers over the economy and pledges to resist any act of aggression from Germany.

MAY 28–31

MEDITERRANEAN, *CRETE*
Major General Bernard Freyberg, the New Zealand commander responsible for defending Crete, decides the island cannot be saved as the German offensive intensifies. His forces are already retreating toward

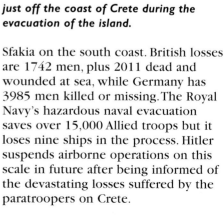

▲ *British and Commonwealth soldiers just off the coast of Crete during the evacuation of the island.*

Sfakia on the south coast. British losses are 1742 men, plus 2011 dead and wounded at sea, while Germany has 3985 men killed or missing. The Royal Navy's hazardous naval evacuation saves over 15,000 Allied troops but it loses nine ships in the process. Hitler suspends airborne operations on this scale in future after being informed of the devastating losses suffered by the paratroopers on Crete.

MAY 30

POLITICS, *IRAQ*
Iraq signs an armistice with Britain whereby the country agrees not to assist the Axis nations. It also agrees not to obstruct the stationing of British forces in Iraq. A pro-Allied government is subsequently installed.

MAY 31

AIR WAR, *EIRE*
The Luftwaffe mistakenly bombs the capital, Dublin, killing 28 people.

JUNE 8–21

MIDDLE EAST, *SYRIA*
An Allied force of 20,000 Free French, British, and Commonwealth troops, under General Sir Henry M. Wilson, invades Syria from Palestine and Iraq amid fears of increasing German influence in the country. They face 45,000 Vichy French troops under General Henri Dentz, plus naval forces that engage the Allies on the 9th.

In subsequent days the Allies encircle enemy units and use heavy artillery to overcome resistance. Vichy forces abandon the capital, Damascus, to the Allies on the 21st.

JUNE 13

FINAL SOLUTION, *VICHY FRANCE*
Over 12,000 Jews have been "interned" in concentration camps after being accused of disrupting relations between Vichy France and Germany. The Vichy authorities are increasingly persecuting Jews and passing legislation to deny them property rights.

JUNE 15–17

AFRICA, *LIBYA*
General Sir Archibald Wavell launches Operation Battleaxe to relieve Tobruk and break the German hold on

▶ *A soldier writes a defiant message outside a military post in Tobruk.*

▼ *A British truck pulls an antiaircraft gun across a dusty track in Syria during the Allied invasion of the country.*

Cyrenaica. An armored and infantry division crosses the Egyptian–Libyan border around Halfaya Pass, Fort Capuzzo, and Hafid Ridge. The new British tanks brought to strengthen the 7th Armored Division have suffered mechanical problems and their crews have had inadequate training. The understrength Allied divisions suffer heavily against the experienced German armor and antitank guns. Wavell halts Operation Battleaxe after losing 90 of his 190 tanks.

JUNE 17

POLITICS, *GERMANY*

Adolf Hitler decides to launch Operation Barbarossa, the invasion of the Soviet Union, on June 22. He has an extreme hatred of the Slav people and the communism that rules them. Hitler aims to enslave the "inferior" Slav peoples, exploit their resources, and occupy their lands as part of his *Lebensraum* ("living space") policy for the Aryan race.

▶ *An Italian mine-thrower crew in action during the desert campaign in Libya and Egypt against British and Commonwealth forces.*

JUNE 22

EASTERN FRONT, *SOVIET UNION*

Germany launches Operation Barbarossa, the invasion of the Soviet Union, with three million men divided into three army groups along a 2000-mile (3200-km) front. Hitler aims to achieve a speedy victory to destroy the Red Army before the summer ends and the Soviets can mobilize their immense resources. Army Group North, under Field Marshal Wilhelm Ritter von Leeb, strikes toward the Baltic and Leningrad. Army Group Center, under Field Marshal Fedor von Bock, aims to take Smolensk and then Moscow, and destroy communications. Army Group South, under General Gerd von Rundstedt, advances toward the Ukraine and the Caucasus.

Soviet forces are caught by surprise and lose a series of battles along the

▲ *Soviet soldiers surrendering to the invading German forces. Red Army units were often quickly encircled and destroyed by German tank formations.*

frontier. German air attacks quickly destroy 1800 Soviet aircraft on the ground. German forces make rapid progress in the north and center but meet stiffening resistance in the south.

JUNE 26–29

POLITICS, *FINLAND*

Finland declares war on the Soviet Union and launches an attack on the 29th. The Finns aim to recapture the territory lost to the Soviets during the Russo-Finnish War. When they finally achieve this objective, Adolf Hitler asks Marshal Karl von Mannerheim, the Finnish leader, to help Germany besiege Leningrad, but he refuses.

JUNE 26–30

EASTERN FRONT, *SOVIET UNION*

The fortress at Brest-Litovsk is taken after fierce resistance, while the important crossing of the Bug River by Army Group Center begins on the 26th. This group's initial objective is Minsk. The fast-moving panzers encircle Red Army units at Bialystok, Novogrudok, and Volkovysk, leaving them open to destruction by follow-on infantry forces. Unimaginative Soviet linear defensive tactics and weak divisions are proving vulnerable to rapid German panzer advances, especially on the flanks. In addition, Germany's total aerial superiority has led to heavy Red Army losses.

JUNE 27

POLITICS, *HUNGARY*
The government declares war on the Soviet Union.

JUNE 29

POLITICS, *SOVIET UNION*
Joseph Stalin assumes control of the federation's Defense Ministry and appoints a five-man council of defense.

▲ *A German tank drives among ruins during the invasion of the Soviet Union in the summer of 1941.*

◄ *Triumphant German troops aboard a Soviet train. Logistics were an essential element for both sides on the Eastern Front.*

JULY 1

POLITICS, *BRITAIN*
General Sir Claude Auchinleck replaces General Sir Archibald Wavell as the commander of British Middle East forces. Wavell's Middle East Command has achieved considerable success against numerically-superior Italian forces, despite supply shortages. However, subsequent commitments in Greece, Iraq, and Syria have overstretched his forces. Nevertheless, Prime Minister Winston Churchill wants a decisive offensive in the Western Desert and Wavell's failure to achieve this has led to his transfer.

JULY 1–11

EASTERN FRONT,
BELORUSSIA/UKRAINE
The German advance continues. Army Group North crosses the Dvina River. Army Group Center moves across the Berezina River and efforts now center on bridging the Dniepr River in order to prevent the Soviets forming any defensive line that would obstruct the Moscow advance. Army Group South overcomes Soviet fortifications on the Stalin Line and moves forward on July 10. The panzer divisions are just 10 miles (16 km) from Kiev, the Soviet Union's third-largest city, by the 11th.

Such armored units, however, are unsuitable for urban fighting and risk suffering heavy losses, especially as Kiev is strongly defended. General Gerd von Rundstedt plans to lure the Soviet units into the open steppes with the threat of encirclement. Once exposed, they might be annihilated.

JULY 3

AFRICA, *ETHIOPIA*
Italian resistance ends in the south after 7000 men surrender.

◄ *Italian troops surrender during the campaign by Allied troops to liberate Ethiopia.*

JULY 4

JOSEPH STALIN

Joseph Stalin (1879–1953), the leader of the Soviet Union, had supported the 1917 Bolshevik Revolution and then proceeded to rise through the Communist Party's ranks. After the death of Lenin in 1924, he established a dictatorship by destroying all political opposition. The development of industry and agriculture was then achieved at enormous human cost, but it made Stalin's Soviet Union a formidable power.

As Europe moved closer to war in the 1930s, Stalin feared that a German attack on the Soviet Union was inevitable and delayed this with a nonaggression pact with Hitler in 1939. His occupation of half of Poland, Finland, and the Baltic states followed, but proper preparations for the impending German attack were not implemented. Stalin was stunned by Hitler's invasion in June 1941, and it was not until the fall that he properly mobilized the human and economic resources of the Soviet Union to mount an effective defense. Stalin controlled both civil and military affairs as Chairman of the People's Commissars. In both realms he displayed a grim determination to maximize the Soviet war effort and finally stood firm when Germany reached the gates of Moscow. He even exploited nationalist sentiments to maintain morale among Russians, appealing for a "holy war" to defend "Mother Russia."

At the great conferences held by the Allies, Stalin was a forceful negotiator who constantly demanded the establishment of a "Second Front" in Europe to relieve the Soviet Union and additional supplies for his war effort. As the war progressed, Stalin often bypassed the decisions of these meetings concerning the political profile of postwar Europe, and the Allies looked nervously on as Stalin maneuvered to create a series of communist "buffer states" around the Soviet Union.

JULY 4

POLITICS, *YUGOSLAVIA*

Joseph Broz, known as "Tito," emerges as the leader of the Yugoslavian resistance movement, although the government-in-exile does not support him. Tito, a communist, has popular support and proposes a Yugoslavian federation that overrides ethnic and national differences.

JULY 7

SEA WAR, *ICELAND*

US troops garrison the country to protect shipping from U-boat attacks.

JULY 10

POLITICS, *SOVIET UNION*

Joseph Stalin, in an attempt to halt the advancing Germans, appoints a number of "commander-in-chiefs of direction" in three command areas (fronts – groups of armies). These are Marshal Semën Budënny (South and Southwest Front), Marshal Semyon Timoshenko (Central West Front), and Marshal Kliment Voroshilov (Northwest Front).

▲ *Vichy French soldiers are marched into captivity after the surrender of Syria.*

JULY 12

POLITICS, *ALLIES*

Britain and the Soviet Union sign a Mutual Assistance Pact, which includes a declaration that neither will make a separate peace with the Axis powers.

AIR WAR, *SOVIET UNION*

Moscow suffers its first air raid. The bombing then intensifies with three large-scale attacks this month and 73 minor raids that last until the end of the year.

JULY 14

MIDDLE EAST, *SYRIA*

General Henri Dentz defies the Vichy French authorities and surrenders Syria to the Allies. British forces begin occupying the colony and pro-Allied administrations are formed in

◀ *Kliment Voroshilov, the Red Army commander of the Northwest Front.*

Syria and neighboring Lebanon. The Allies have sustained about 2500 casualties in the campaign, while the Vichy French forces have suffered some 3500 casualties defending their colonies in the region.

JULY 16

EASTERN FRONT, *SOVIET UNION*
Following the crossing of the Dniepr and Dvina Rivers, the encirclement of Smolensk by Germany's Army Group Center commences. The city falls after 300,000 Red Army troops and 3200 tanks are trapped in the vicinity of the city but, despite this, the surrounded Soviet forces are not finally defeated until August.

JULY 18

POLITICS, *CZECHOSLOVAKIA*
Britain recognizes the Czech government-in-exile led by Edouard Beneš. The Czechs also make a mutual assistance agreement with the Soviet Union and promise to form an army.

▶ *Edouard Beneš, the leader of the Czech government-in-exile during the war.*

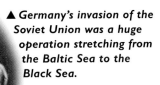

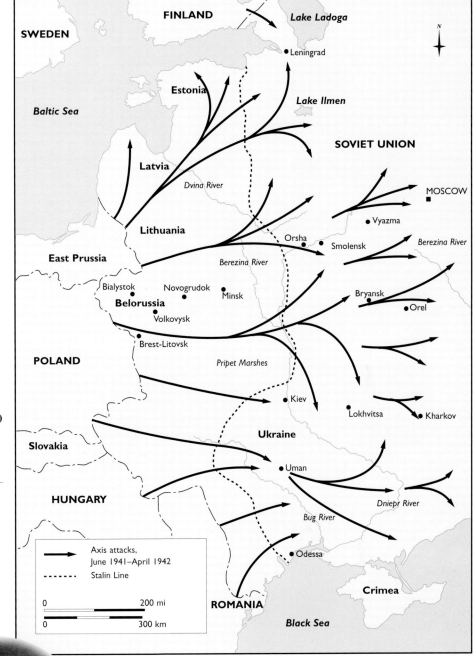

▲ *Germany's invasion of the Soviet Union was a huge operation stretching from the Baltic Sea to the Black Sea.*

JULY 19–29

EASTERN FRONT, *SOVIET UNION*
General Heinz Guderian's 2nd Panzer Group, plus supporting infantry, leading the advance toward Moscow, receives orders to swing south and help tackle the Soviet Fifth Army, which is situated in the Pripet Marshes. This Soviet force vastly outnumbers the opposing German units and poses a serious threat to Field Marshal Walther von Reichenau's southern operations. Army Group Center's remaining panzer unit, the 3rd Panzer Group, is assigned to assist Army Group North take Leningrad. Guderian and other

▲ *Japanese industrial power relied on fuel and raw material imports. The nation's moves to war thus accelerated after vital imports of US oil ceased.*

◀ *Soviet fighters surrender during the German encirclement of Red Army forces in the Ukraine.*

commanders are hostile to this decision and attempt to persuade Adolf Hitler not to halt the Moscow advance, but to no avail.

JULY 21

SEA WAR, *MEDITERRANEAN*
Operation Substance, the British transportation of supplies from Gibraltar to Malta, begins. Besieged Malta, a naval base, occupies a key location across the short sea and air route between North Africa and Italy.

JULY 22

EASTERN FRONT, *BALTIC*
Germany's Army Group North halts west of Lake Ilmen, south of the city

▶ *Reinhard Heydrich, the infamous head of the SS secret police and architect of the "Final Solution" to destroy the entire Jewish population of Europe.*

of Leningrad. Troops and equipment along the entire front are suffering from the rigors of the advance and stronger Soviet resistance. During such rest periods the Soviets reinforce their lines, especially those in front of Moscow and Leningrad. The resources needed to take these two cities will be immense.

JULY 24

EASTERN FRONT, *UKRAINE*
Hitler orders Army Group South in the Ukraine to close the pocket around the concentration of Soviet forces based on Uman. They seal it 15 days later, isolating three Soviet armies from Red Army forces around Kiev. This leaves the Soviet South and South-west Fronts seriously weakened, and Odessa is now only accessible by sea. The Germans trap some 100,000 men and 317 tanks in the pocket.

JULY 26–29

POLITICS,
BRITAIN/UNITED STATES
Britain and the United States freeze Japanese assets in their countries. Japan retaliates likewise against both. Holland freezes Japanese assets in the Dutch East Indies on the 29th. As a consequence, much of Japan's foreign trade is lost.

JULY 31

POLITICS, *GERMANY*
Reinhard Heydrich, Germany's

▶ *General Heinz Guderian, the talented armored warfare tactician, inspecting his men on the Eastern Front.*

security chief and head of the SS secret police, receives orders to begin creating a draft plan for the complete destruction of the Jews, which becomes known as the "Final Solution." Heydrich will become the infamous administrator of the state apparatus that persecutes and murders millions of people.

AFRICA, *LIBYA*
General Ludwig Cruewell takes command of the Afrika Korps and General Erwin Rommel takes charge of Panzer Group Africa (one infantry and two panzer divisions).

AUGUST 1

POLITICS, *UNITED STATES*
The United States bans the export of oil except to the British Empire and western hemisphere states. Japan, which is entirely dependent on oil imports, is severely affected by this and has to choose between changing its foreign policy or seizing oil by force.

AUGUST 5

POLITICS, *VICHY FRANCE*
Admiral Jean François Darlan assumes responsibility for Vichy-controlled North Africa.

EASTERN FRONT, *UKRAINE*
Romanian and German forces begin a 73-day siege of Odessa. The Soviet high command sends reinforcements to try to help form a line on the east bank of Dniepr River. Meanwhile,

troops delay the Germans on the west bank while industrial resources are destroyed or removed to beyond the Ural Mountains, where Soviet industry is being relocated.

AUGUST 6

POLITICS, *POLAND*
Lieutenant General Wladyslaw Anders is appointed to form a Polish army in the Soviet Union. Anders eventually forms an army but will lack the supplies to fight, while the Soviets will not permit the Poles to serve on the Eastern Front.

AUGUST 12

POLITICS, *GERMANY*
Adolf Hitler's Directive No. 34 outlines revisions to Operation Barbarossa, with the advance on Moscow being halted while the advance to Leningrad is resumed. The southern wheatlands and industries of the Ukraine have also become a higher priority than the Soviet capital.

AFRICA, *LIBYA*
Australian troops, at the request of their government, leave Tobruk; 6000 Poles relieve them.

AUGUST 14

POLITICS,
BRITAIN/UNITED STATES
A meeting between Winston Churchill and Franklin D. Roosevelt in Canada produces the Atlantic Charter. This

AUGUST 18

asserts liberal policies that articulate their intentions not to acquire any territories or change national borders without the support of the populations concerned. People are also to be granted self-determination regarding how they are governed, and equal access is to be given to economic resources. The United States also secretly guarantees to defend any British possessions and to commence search-and-destroy patrols to support Atlantic convoys.

AUGUST 18

EASTERN FRONT, *UKRAINE*
Soviet forces in the Ukraine begin withdrawing across the strategically-important Dniepr River to form a defensive line farther north – the Bryansk front – leaving the Thirty-fifth Army in Kiev.

Hitler plans to trap and then destroy the bulk of the Red Army before it retreats across the Dniepr. To achieve this the Germans have to make wide encirclements to trap Soviet units. This move, however, creates large gaps through which Red Army troops can escape east.

▶ *British forces move into Iran to safeguard oil supplies inside the country.*

AUGUST 21

SEA WAR, *ARCTIC*
The first trial convoy to the Soviet Union from Britain transports vital supplies to the Russian port of Archangel. The Arctic convoy reaches its destination on the 31st.

AUGUST 23

EASTERN FRONT, *UKRAINE*
The German 2nd Panzer Group and 2nd Army Group strike southward aiming to link up with Army Group South to the east of Kiev.

AUGUST 25

MIDDLE EAST, *IRAN*
Soviet and British forces begin occupying Iran following fears that Germans are operating in the country. Allied forces seize vital oil installations and encounter little resistance.

AUGUST 30

EASTERN FRONT, *UKRAINE*
The Soviet Union launches a counter-attack with the Twenty-first Army

north of Kiev, but it fails and risks defeat by the 2nd Panzergruppe.

SEPTEMBER 1

EASTERN FRONT, *BALTIC*
German forces near Leningrad are now within artillery range of the city. Soon, the city's rail and road approaches are cut off and a bitter siege commences that lasts until early 1944. Leningrad is a key industrial center and is used by the Soviet Baltic Fleet, which potentially threatens vital Swedish iron ore shipments to Germany.

SEPTEMBER 3

FINAL SOLUTION, *POLAND*
Experiments using Zyclon-B gas chambers to slaughter Jews and others deemed "undesirable" by the Nazis are carried out in Auschwitz concentration camp, Poland. The experiments are a success, and will lead to the widespread use of the gas.

SEPTEMBER 4

SEA WAR, *ATLANTIC*
A U-boat mistakes the US destroyer *Greer* for a British vessel and attacks it. This is presented as an act of aggression and US warships are ordered to "shoot on sight" in waters integral to national defense.

SEPTEMBER 6

FINAL SOLUTION, *GERMANY*
Restrictions on Jews are reinforced with an order requiring them to wear a Star of David badge. Their freedom of movement is also restricted.

◀ *The British cruiser* Sheffield *sailing with an Arctic convoy of merchant ships taking vital supplies to the Soviet Union.*

OCTOBER 6–15

EASTERN FRONT, *UKRAINE*
Germany's Second Army and Second Panzer Army encircle three Soviet armies north and south of Bryansk on the 6th. Soviet forces begin evacuating 35,000 troops by sea from the besieged port of Odessa on the 15th.

OCTOBER 7–20

EASTERN FRONT, *SOVIET UNION*
After fierce fighting, six Soviet armies are encircled around Vyazma by the 14th. German forces elsewhere cover great distances, but the onset of heavy rains on the 8th severely limits mobility as the roads to Moscow become quagmires. Until the 20th, the Second Panzer Army also has to reduce the Bryansk pocket. The encirclements at Vyazma and Bryansk trap 673,000 troops and 1242 tanks, but also preoccupy the advancing forces, giving the Red Army time to establish new defensive positions.

OCTOBER 16

POLITICS, *JAPAN*
General Hideki Tojo, defense minister and

◄ *Japanese war leader General Hideki Tojo.*

SEPTEMBER 15

EASTERN FRONT, *UKRAINE*
Guderian's 2nd Panzer Group links up with Army Group South at Lokhvitsa, 100 miles (160 km) east of Kiev, trapping four Soviet armies. This seals the fate of the Soviet Southwest Front and its 500,000 men.

SEPTEMBER 17–19

EASTERN FRONT, *UKRAINE*
Soviet forces begin a fighting withdrawal from Kiev, having been delayed in abandoning the city by Joseph Stalin's insistence on holding it. This delay enables the Germans to cut off their escape routes. The Germans seize Kiev on the 19th, killing or capturing 665,000 men after 40 days of bloody combat. This seals the fate of the western Ukraine.

SEPTEMBER 24

SEA WAR, *MEDITERRANEAN*
The first U-boat enters the Mediterranean (half the entire U-boat force will be operating there later in the year). The Operation Halberd convoy leaves Gibraltar bound for Malta. During the six-day trip, Italian warships attempt to intercept the convoy, but an Italian submarine is sunk. The British bombard Pantellaria, an Italian island situated between Sicily and Tunisia.

SEPTEMBER 29

FINAL SOLUTION, *UKRAINE*
Nazi troops kill 33,771 Jews in Kiev.

SEPTEMBER 30

EASTERN FRONT, *UKRAINE*
The 1st Panzer Group begins the offensive against the southern Ukraine

from the Dniepr and Samara Rivers, and immediately severs a vital Soviet rail line. The advance toward Rostov moves behind three Soviet armies. General Erich von Manstein's Eleventh Army then advances to trap 106,000 Soviet troops and 212 tanks between the two German forces on October 6 in a classic encirclement operation. One Soviet force, the weakened Twelfth Army, retreats northeastward.

EASTERN FRONT, *SOVIET UNION*
Operation Typhoon, the attack on Moscow, officially begins. Germany's Army Group Center's 73 divisions face 85 Soviet divisions plus 10–15 in reserve. General Heinz Guderian's Second Panzer Group thrusts toward Bryansk and Orel. Two days later, the 3rd and 4th Panzer Groups move to encircle Soviet forces around Vyazma.

leader of the militarist faction within Japan, replaces the more moderate Prince Fumimaro Konoye as prime minister. Konoye's attempts to satisfy the prowar military hierarchy and reach some form of settlement with the United States has failed. His

▲ *Female fighters march through Moscow. Thousands of Soviet women helped defend the city from attack.*

▼ *Soviet infantry in their winter clothing. German troops often lacked the kit needed for the freezing temperatures.*

successor exerts authoritarian control over the War and Home Affairs Ministries. This change signals the political ascendancy of the prowar faction in Japan and is a step closer to conflict with the United States and the Allies.

OCTOBER 19

EASTERN FRONT, *SOVIET UNION*
Joseph Stalin declares a state of siege

in Moscow. The Soviet Union is now in the process of mounting an enormous defensive operation. Reinforcements are arriving from northern and southern regions, and a formidable series of defensive lines are now being built by Moscow's citizens, who are also ready to fight in them. General Georgi Zhukov is to command the West Front responsible for defending Moscow.

Across the entire Eastern Front the Soviets are preparing strong defensive positions and mobilizing the entire population to support the war. Soviet resistance is fierce, and atrocities become commonplace on both sides. Agricultural and industrial resources are destroyed if they cannot be prevented from falling into German hands – a deliberate scorched earth policy.

OCTOBER 20–25

EASTERN FRONT, *SOVIET UNION*
Germany halts the original Typhoon offensive and sets more limited objectives, reflecting the deteriorating weather and strengthening Soviet

resistance. The Ukraine offensive has delayed the advance on Moscow. The Germans are now racing to beat the winter weather and the mobilization of Soviet men and equipment.

OCTOBER 24

EASTERN FRONT, *UKRAINE*
The German Sixteenth Army enters Kharkov, the Soviet Union's

fourth-largest city. Unlike the siege of Kiev, Joseph Stalin does not order a costly defense of the city. The Soviets' ill-equipped soldiers of the Southwest Front around Kharkov escape by making a gradual withdrawal.

OCTOBER 31

SEA WAR, *ATLANTIC*
The US destroyer *Reuben James*, part of an escort group accompanying a British convoy, is sunk by a U-boat, claiming 100 lives.

NOVEMBER 1

EASTERN FRONT, *UKRAINE*
Germany launches an offensive on Rostov, at the mouth of the Don River. The Soviet Ninth Army's deep and flexible defensive lines, together with the winter weather, obstruct the encirclement. A frontal assault from the coast on the 17th is then counter-balanced by the Soviet Thirty-seventh

► *A muddy German motorcyclist on the Eastern Front in the fall of 1941.*

◄ *The British aircraft carrier* Ark Royal, *which was hit by torpedoes and then sank after a fire broke out.*

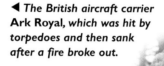

Army's attack north of the city. The Germans capture Rostov on the 21st but the Soviets recapture it within eight days. General Gerd von Rundstedt then resigns after defying Hitler's orders concerning a tactical withdrawal from the city.

NOVEMBER 6

POLITICS, *UNITED STATES*
A loan of US $1 billion is made to the Soviet Union for Lend-Lease purchases.

NOVEMBER 13

SEA WAR, *MEDITERRANEAN*
Two U-boats attack the British carriers *Argus* and *Ark Royal* en route to Gibraltar after flying off fighters to Malta. *Ark Royal* is badly hit. The carrier sails to within

NOVEMBER 15

25 miles (40 km) of Gibraltar when a fire breaks out and the ship sinks along with 70 aircraft.

NOVEMBER 15

EASTERN FRONT, *SOVIET UNION*

The strength, mobility, morale, and logistical support of the German forces on the Eastern Front are severely affected by fierce winter weather. By the 27th, the panzer spearheads are only 20 miles (32 km) from Moscow, but the second phase of the advance is soon halted by Soviet counterattacks and freezing temperatures. Red Army troops, many newly equipped with the superb T-34 tank and Katyusha multiple rocket-launchers, are also properly clothed for winter operations. They are reinforced by partisan volunteers, whose hatred of the enemy is increased by Nazi atrocities against Soviet civilians.

NOVEMBER 18–26

AFRICA, *LIBYA*

The British Eighth Army in Egypt, under General Sir Alan Cunningham, launches Operation Crusader to relieve Tobruk by striking into Cyrenaica. British light tanks suffer serious losses (exacerbated by mechanical and tactical shortcomings) in various

▲ Japanese Zero fighters take off from the carrier Akagi to escort bombers bound for Pearl Harbor US naval base.

▼ South African troops use a grenade to clear Germans from a building during Operation Crusader, the attempt to relieve Tobruk in North Africa.

engagements with the Germans around Sidi Rezegh, southeast of Tobruk, from the 19th to the 23rd. On the 22nd, the Tobruk garrison attacks besieging Italian units in order to link up with the Eighth Army advancing to relieve it. General Erwin Rommel then strikes at the Allied flank but sustains heavy losses. He eventually retreats, relieving the pressure on Tobruk, although the fighting continues. On the 26th, General Neil Ritchie relieves Cunningham.

NOVEMBER 26

SEA WAR, *PACIFIC*

The Japanese First Air Fleet of six aircraft carriers, two battleships, three cruisers, nine destroyers, three submarines, and eight tankers leaves the Kurile Islands on a mission to destroy the US Pacific Fleet at Pearl Harbor, Hawaii. The carrier force,

under Admiral Chuichi Nagumo, sails 3400 miles (5440 km) and remains undetected by maintaining strict secrecy and radio silence. Japan's war aims are to destroy US naval power in the region, their only real threat, and then to seize territories in the Pacific and Far East. By establishing their "Greater East Asian Co-Prosperity Sphere," they can then obtain their economic resources and establish a defensive perimeter to repel attacks.

A series of diplomatic exchanges between Japanese and US officials has proved unsuccessful, and war appears inevitable. The United States mistakenly believes that Japan will launch its first offensive against the Philippines, Borneo, or the Malay Peninsula – Hawaii is not thought to be a likely target. Japan will thus take the US Pacific Fleet completely by surprise when its forces attack the naval base.

▼ *US Navy warships ablaze after the surprise Japanese air strike on Pearl Harbor, Oahu Island, Hawaii, in December 1941.*

NOVEMBER 27–28

AFRICA, *ETHIOPIA*
After an Allied attack on the city of Gondar, northwest Ethiopia, General Nasi, the local Italian commander, orders the surrender of 20,000 troops. Ethiopia's liberation by the Allies is complete.

NOVEMBER 30

SEA WAR, *ATLANTIC*
The first successful attack using Air-to-Surface-Vessel radar is made by a British bomber, which sinks *U-206* in the Bay of Biscay.

DECEMBER 6

POLITICS, *BRITAIN*
Britain declares war on Finland, Hungary, and Romania.

DECEMBER 7

AIR WAR, *PACIFIC*
A Japanese force of six carriers launches two

▲ President Franklin D. Roosevelt stands before the US Congress and asks for a declaration of war against Japan in 1941.

▲ Thousands of German troops perished as winter set in and Soviet resistance hardened on the Eastern Front at the end of 1941. Many more would die during Hitler's war in the Soviet Union.

▼ A German supply column smashed by the Soviets. Supply problems became critical with the onset of winter.

strikes on the US Pacific Fleet at Pearl Harbor on Oahu Island, Hawaii. Over 183 Japanese aircraft destroy six battleships and 188 aircraft, damage or sink 10 other vessels, and kill 2000 servicemen. The Japanese lose 29 aircraft. Five midget submarines are lost during a failed underwater attack. A planned third strike, intended to

destroy totally the harbor and oil reserves, is not launched for fear that the valuable Japanese aircraft carriers might be attacked by the remainder of the US Pacific Fleet. Japan then declares war on the United States and the British Commonwealth.

Despite information from Allied codebreaking operations, diplomatic

▶ *Australian troops in Tobruk take shelter in a cave during one of the frequent air attacks upon the besieged garrison.*

sources, and other warnings, the raid is a tactical surprise. The failure to take appropriate precautions at the base, exacerbated by failures in interservice cooperation, is severely criticized. Despite the attack's success, the US Pacific Fleet's aircraft carriers are at sea and thus survive, while the fleet itself is quickly repaired. In the United States there is outrage over the attack and popular support for declaring war.

DECEMBER 8

EASTERN FRONT, *SOVIET UNION*
Adolf Hitler reluctantly agrees to issue Directive No. 39, which suspends the advance on Moscow for the duration of the winter. Army Group Center begins withdrawing to less exposed positions farther west, much to Hitler's anger.

POLITICS, *ALLIES*
The United States, Britain, Australia, New Zealand, Holland, the Free French, several South American states, and Yugoslavia declare war on Japan in response to Pearl Harbor. China declares war on the Axis states.

DECEMBER 8

▶ British and Commonwealth troops occupying defensive positions around the perimeter of the key port of Tobruk. The besieged garrison was finally relieved in December 1941 after the Axis forces under Rommel withdrew.

AFRICA, *LIBYA*

General Erwin Rommel finally decides to withdraw his greatly-weakened units from around Tobruk. He falls back to Gazala by the 11th and then withdraws toward El Agheila on the 16th. The naval operation to sustain Tobruk, finally ended on the 10th, has evacuated 34,000 troops, 7000 casualties, and 7000 prisoners. Around 34,000 tons (34,544 metric tonnes) of supplies have been brought in. Some 27 Allied vessels have been sunk.

▼ Afrika Korps motorcyclists speed across the desert. Germany's forces attempted to drive the British and Commonwealth forces from Libya and then strike Egypt.

▲ *US troops in the Philippines prepare to meet the Japanese invaders who landed on the islands in December 1941.*

◄ *A Filipino family flees from their home following a Japanese bombardment. Thousands of civilians were affected by the fighting in the islands.*

PACIFIC, *PHILIPPINES*
Japanese air attacks destroy 100 US aircraft at Clark Field, while a small force lands on Luzon Island to build an airfield. General Douglas MacArthur, commanding the 130,000-strong US and Filipino force in the Philippines, had intended that US aircraft would strike the invading Japanese force as his troops are not capable of stopping any landing. On the 10th, Luzon is invaded and Guam Island quickly falls. The Japanese forces also attack Wake Island and capture it on the 24th – after two invasion attempts.

▲ *Japanese troops wade ashore during the invasion of the Malayan Peninsula.*

FAR EAST, *HONG KONG*

The Japanese 38th Division attacks the 12,000-strong Hong Kong garrison. After the garrison refuses the Japanese surrender demand on the 13th, it faces an intense attack followed by amphibious assaults. Hong Kong finally surrenders on the 25th.

FAR EAST, *MALAYA/THAILAND*

A Japanese force of 100,000 troops (the 5th and 18th Divisions), under General Tomoyuki Yamashita, begins landing on the northeast coast of Malaya and in Thailand after initial air attacks. Japanese units quickly move southward down both sides of the Malayan Peninsula. British forces are mainly stationed in the south, having anticipated an attack nearer Singapore. Japanese aircraft soon destroy most of the British aircraft. British reluctance to move into neutral Thailand before a Japanese attack enables General Yamashita to complete his landings. British forces finally advance into Thailand on the 10th but cannot halt the Japanese invasion. Well-equipped and experienced Japanese troops continue pushing southward, many by bicycle.

DECEMBER 10

SEA WAR, *FAR EAST*

About 90 Japanese aircraft sink the British battleship *Prince of Wales* and the battlecruiser *Repulse* while they are attempting to intercept Japanese warships off Malaya. The attack claims 730 lives and leaves the Allies without a single battleship in the theater.

DECEMBER 11

POLITICS, *AXIS*

Germany and Italy declare war on the United States. The United States then declares war on the two Axis states. Romania declares war on the United

274

States on the 12th. Germany's declaration now confirms US participation in the European war.

DECEMBER 13

SEA WAR, *MEDITERRANEAN*
Three British and one Dutch destroyer sink the Italian fast cruisers *Alberico da Barbiano* and *Alberto di Giussano* off Sicily. The Italian warships are carrying fuel to North Africa, and the attack claims 900 lives. Off Messina, the British submarine *Urge* sinks two Italian transports and damages the battleship *Vittorio Veneto*, which is carrying supplies to Libya.

DECEMBER 14

SEA WAR, *ATLANTIC*
A British convoy of 32 ships, including the aircraft carrier *Audacity*, leaves Gibraltar for Britain. *Audacity* is the first British escort carrier introduced to provide Allied convoys with constant air cover by intercepting enemy bombers or U-boat "Wolf Packs" when they are beyond the operational range of land-based aircraft. During the voyage, the convoy suffers attacks from 12 U-boats, but destroys five of them. The convoy loses *Audacity*, a

▲ A British soldier is led into captivity by Japanese troops during the invasion of Malaya in December 1941.

▼ British troops prepare defenses in Hong Kong. Despite such measures, the colony was quickly overwhelmed.

DECEMBER 16

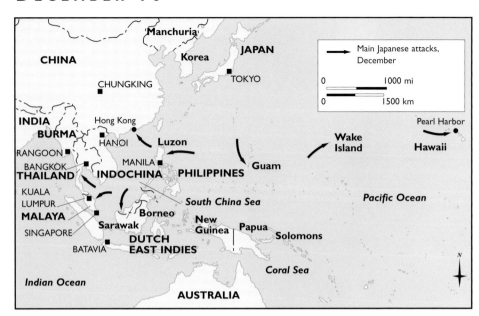

▲ *Japan launched a series of attacks across Southeast Asia in 1941 to seize strategic bases and economic resources.*

destroyer, and two merchant ships, before it reaches Britain on the 23rd.

DECEMBER 16

FAR EAST, *BORNEO*
The Japanese 19th Division makes three landings along the coast of

Borneo. The British and Dutch forces defending the island set oil installations ablaze before retreating.

DECEMBER 17

POLITICS, *UNITED STATES*
Admiral Chester Nimitz replaces Admiral Husband Kimmel as commander of the Pacific Fleet following the attack on Pearl Harbor on December 7.

DECEMBER 18–19

SEA WAR, *MEDITERRANEAN*
The Royal Navy's Force K, operating from Malta, runs into a minefield off Tripoli. The cruiser *Neptune* and destroyer *Kandahar* are both sunk, while the remaining two cruisers are damaged. An Italian "human torpedo" attack upon the British Mediterranean Fleet in Alexandria, Egypt, sinks the battleships *Queen Elizabeth* and

Valiant. However, both vessels sink upright in shallow waters and are eventually repaired. Nevertheless, these losses severely reduce British naval power in the Mediterranean.

The "human torpedo," a midget submarine driven by two operators, is designed to enter defended harbors and clamp its warhead onto a ship's hull. The British soon develop their own version called "Chariot."

▲ *An Italian "human torpedo." These craft were used to great effect against British vessels in the Mediterranean.*

▶ *Allied convoys became increasingly vulnerable as naval forces were seriously overstretched and losses mounted.*

▼ *The British battleship* Queen Elizabeth *(front), which was sunk by an Italian "human torpedo" in Egypt.*

▲ *Adolf Hitler (center) discusses strategy with Field Marshal Walther von Brauchitsch (left) and General Franz Halder (right).*

DECEMBER 19

POLITICS, *GERMANY*

Adolf Hitler appoints himself as commander-in-chief of the army following Field Marshal Walter von Brauchitsch's resignation on the 7th. Brauchitsch resigned following a heart attack brought on by the strain of Soviet counterattacks. He was already under pressure to resign. His authority had been increasingly undermined by Hitler dominating strategic planning.

Hitler successfully keeps the Eastern Front armies in defensive positions during the winter. He develops an increasing skepticism toward the competence of his army commanders. Parallel to this is the expansion of the Waffen SS, seen by Hitler as being politically-reliable troops.

POLITICS, *UNITED STATES*

An amendment to the Selective Service Act requires all men aged 18–64 to register, and for men aged 20–44 to be liable for conscription.

DECEMBER 20–26

POLITICS, *UNITED STATES*

Admiral Ernest King becomes chief of naval operations.

PACIFIC, *PHILIPPINES*

Japanese forces invade Mindanao, the most southerly island, and Jolo. The islands offer Japan the chance to gain naval and air bases. The main invasion of Luzon commences on the 22nd. General Douglas MacArthur decides not to defend Manila, the capital, but declares it an open city in order to withdraw his forces westward to the Bataan Peninsula.

DECEMBER 22

POLITICS, *ALLIES*

US President Franklin D. Roosevelt and British Prime Minister Winston Churchill meet at the Arcadia Conference, Washington. Talks between the

▶ *African-American conscripts doing their war service with the US Army.*

▲ *Manila, the Philippines' capital, just after it was abandoned by the US and Filipino forces.*

respective political and military delegations reaffirm the "Germany First" strategic priority and establish the Combined Chiefs-of-Staff to direct Allied military action. They also agree to build up US forces in Britain in preparation for future military action against Nazi Germany and in order to continue the aerial bombing of Nazi-occupied Europe.

DECEMBER 26-28

SEA WAR, *NORTH SEA*
Britain launches Operation Archery, a commando attack against Lofoten Island, off Norway. The first force of 260 troops succeeds in destroying a fish-oil plant.

On December 27, a second landing by a further 600 troops successfully attacks fish-oil plants and radio facilities. The raids reinforce Hitler's fears that Britain is planning to invade the whole of Norway.

KEY PERSONALITIES

PRESIDENT FRANKLIN D. ROOSEVELT

Franklin D. Roosevelt, US president from 1933 to 1945, was the only person to be elected for three terms. He trained as a lawyer and subsequently pursued a political career in the Democratic Party, despite being stricken with polio. Roosevelt's peacetime administration, which began in 1932, generated popular support with its "New Deal" program to establish social and economic reconstruction during the Great Depression of the 1930s.

Once war broke out in 1939, he worked to overcome American "isolationism" and generate support for the Allied cause. Roosevelt was responsible for transforming the United States into the "arsenal of democracy" by expanding the economic capacity of the nation in order to sustain the Allies with war supplies and build up US military capability. A series of economic agreements were made with Allied states, while trade restrictions were imposed on Axis powers. Roosevelt also put the nation on a firm war-footing with military service legislation that provided the manpower for the expanding armed forces.

When the United States entered the war in 1941, Roosevelt ignored his critics and made the key decision to maintain the "Germany First" strategy rather than devoting greater effort to defeating Japan. He also took the crucial decision to demand the unconditional surrender of Japan and Germany. Roosevelt also rejected proposals by US commanders to invade Europe in 1942, and followed British plans to attack North Africa, Sicily, and Italy first.

Roosevelt adopted a conciliatory manner in inter-Allied relations, urging diplomacy between Britain and the Soviet Union to overcome the distrust that existed between these politically divergent states. This popular war leader died on April 12, 1945, three weeks before the end of the fighting in Europe.

1942

Japan's territorial conquests appeared to signal its triumph over Europe's colonial powers in the Far East. The United States, however, was now on the offensive and won crucial strategic victories at sea over the Japanese. These had serious repercussions for Japan's ability to sustain both its domestic and overseas power. In North Africa and on the Eastern Front, Axis offensives, although initially successful, were halted and then defeated by a series of Allied counterattacks. Control of the sea-lanes continued to be a crucial factor in the war.

JANUARY 1

POLITICS, *ALLIES*
At the Arcadia Conference in Washington, 26 Allied countries sign the United Nations Declaration, pledging to follow the Atlantic Charter principles. These include an agreement to direct their "full resources" against the three Axis nations and not to make any separate peace agreements or treaties. This is a key development in the formation of the United Nations Organization.

JANUARY 2–9

PACIFIC, *PHILIPPINES*
US and Filipino forces under General Douglas MacArthur prepare defensive positions on the Bataan Peninsula and the island of Corregidor as Manila falls. MacArthur realizes that Japan has air and sea superiority. He also knows that no reinforcements will be sent. His troops begin a desperate resistance against Japanese attacks across the mountainous peninsula, which begin on the 9th. For several months the 80,000 troops will resist the Japanese, despite suffering from tropical diseases and being short of supplies.

JANUARY 3

POLITICS, *ALLIES*
Following the Arcadia Conference, British General Sir Archibald Wavell takes charge of the new American, British, Dutch, and Australian (ABDA) command. He is responsible for holding the southwest Pacific. Chinese Nationalist leader Chiang Kai-shek is made commander-in-chief of the Allied forces in his country.

JANUARY 5

EASTERN FRONT, *SOVIET UNION*
Joseph Stalin orders a general offensive against the German invaders, despite warnings from General Georgi Zhukov, the Western Front commander, that the Soviet Union lacks the resources for

◀ *A Japanese tank charges through a Philippines plantation as part of the relentless Japanese offensive to capture the islands from the Americans.*

▲ *Chiang Kai-shek took charge of Allied forces in China in January 1942.*

an attack on four fronts (Leningrad, Moscow, Ukraine, and Crimea). Zhukov advocates a concentrated attack against Army Group Center, which is threatening Moscow. However, the general offensive initially makes considerable inroads and captures trains, food, and munitions. German forces offer stiff resistance and are ordered to hold their positions. They set up defensive areas ("Hedgehogs") that frustrate the Red Army's attacks.

JANUARY 5–12

FAR EAST, *MALAYA*

Following the recent landing of Japanese troops on the northeast coast, British, Indian, and Australian forces are now retreating southward toward Singapore, unable to mount any meaningful defense against the Japanese. The British have underestimated the Japanese, who are well trained and equipped. Kuala Lumpur, the capital, falls to the Japanese on the 12th.

JANUARY 9–21

EASTERN FRONT, *SOVIET UNION*

The Battle of the Valdai Hills begins in the Moscow sector. During the 12-day battle Soviet troops make a 75-mile (120-km) penetration of the German lines that captures nine towns between Smolensk and Lake Ilmen.

JANUARY 10–11

FAR EAST, *DUTCH EAST INDIES*

A Japanese force, under General Tomoyuki Yamashita and Admiral Takahashi, begins attacking the Dutch East Indies to secure the oil assets of this island-chain. The Japanese Eastern Force lands on Celebes and Amboina before taking Bali, Timor, and east Java. The Central Force lands at Tarakan and

▶ *A Japanese tank crosses an improvised bridge during the invasion of Burma.*

▼ *Japanese troops occupy Kuala Lumpur, the capital of Malaya, following the hasty retreat of British forces from the city.*

aims to take Borneo. The Western Force moves from Indochina to attack Sumatra and Java. The remaining Allied troops under ABDA command in the region, including local forces of doubtful loyalty, attempt to resist the Japanese onslaught.

JANUARY 12

POLITICS, *YUGOSLAVIA*

General Dusan Simovic resigns as prime minister of the Yugoslavian government-in-exile. Professor Yovanovic replaces him.

AFRICA, *LIBYA*

General Erwin Rommel agrees to a plan proposed by his officers to counterattack the Allies. British naval strength in the Mediterranean has been eroded, which has enabled new German supplies to arrive. At the same time, Allied forces have suffered the departure of the 7th Armored Brigade plus two Australian divisions, which have been sent to the Far East.

JANUARY 12–31

FAR EAST, *BURMA*

The Japanese Fifteenth Army's two reinforced divisions, plus air support, move northwestward into Burma from neighboring Thailand. A small group under Burmese nationalist Aung Sang

supports Japan and encourages uprisings. British, Burmese, and Indian troops around the town of Moulmein unsuccessfully engage the invaders and withdraw. Already in the previous month the Japanese have taken a key

▼ *Japanese offensives to conquer Burma drove the Allies back to the Indian and Chinese borders by May 1942.*

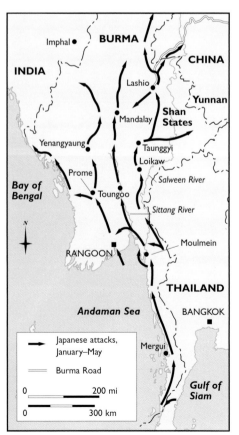

southern air base at Mergui, forming part of the air route between India and Malaya, which they have now blocked. Such airfields are then used for bombing missions. Burma has the only viable supply route to sustain the Chinese fight against Japan. The Allied possession of Burma also keeps India's northeast region secure from attack.

JANUARY 13

POLITICS, *ALLIES*
At a London meeting, the Allies agree to punish Axis leaders responsible for war crimes.

SEA WAR, *ATLANTIC*
Germany's U-boats launch attacks, code-named Operation Drum Roll, on shipping off the east coast of the United States. Approximately 20 ships are sunk in the first month of operations as a result of the US Navy's failure to take proper antisubmarine measures, despite British warnings. U-boats begin hunting in the Caribbean the following month.

JANUARY 16–19

POLITICS, *GERMANY*
Field Marshal Walther von Reichenau, commander of the German Army Group South on the Eastern Front, dies in a plane crash. Field Marshal Fedor von Bock replaces him on the 19th. Adolf Hitler removes Field Marshal Wilhelm von Leeb and replaces him

▶ *Field Marshal Wilhelm von Leeb, one of the commanders whom Adolf Hitler blamed for failures on the Eastern Front.*

▲ *A female Soviet sniper in the Caucasus. Women made a valuable contribution to the Soviet war machine.*

with General George von Küchler as Army Group North's commander. Since December, the Führer has removed over 30 senior officers, including two army group and two panzer group commanders, due to his impatience with their constant appeals to make withdrawals in the face of Soviet offensives.

POLITICS, *UNITED STATES*
Donald Nelson becomes head of the new centralized War Production Board.

JANUARY 17

AFRICA, *LIBYA*
The Axis garrison of Halfaya, besieged throughout the British Operation Crusader, finally falls and 5500 Germans and Italians are captured.

SEA WAR, *ARCTIC*
U-boats make their first attack on an Allied Arctic convoy. *U-454* sinks the destroyer *Matabele* and a merchant ship from convoy PQ-8.

JANUARY 18–27

EASTERN FRONT, *UKRAINE*
Soviet South and Southwest Front forces, under Marshal Semyon Timoshenko, make an attack aiming to cross the Donets River and then swing south toward the Sea of Azov to trap units of the German Sixth and Seventeenth Armies. The Donets River is crossed by the 24th, but the Soviet advance is halted by the 27th.

JANUARY 20

FINAL SOLUTION, *GERMANY*
At the Wannsee Conference, Berlin, deputy head of the SS Reinhard Heydrich reveals his plans for the "Final Solution" to the so-called "Jewish problem." Heydrich receives permission to begin deporting all Jews in German-controlled areas to Eastern Europe to face either forced labor or

▲ *Concentration camp prisoners receive rations from an SS officer in a carefully-staged propaganda photograph.*

extermination. The killing of Jews in Eastern Europe is already common-place. Execution by shooting, however, is proving inefficient and a strain for the troops engaged. A more efficient way of killing using poison gas will soon become widespread.

SEA WAR, *PACIFIC*
In Japan's ongoing offensive against Allied possessions in the Far East, four carriers begin air strikes on Rabaul, New Britain (soon to become a major Japanese naval base), and two submarines shell Midway Island. US and Australian warships sink a Japanese submarine off Darwin. Japanese amphibious landings are made on Borneo, New Ireland, and the Solomons on the 23rd.

JANUARY 21–29

AFRICA, *LIBYA*
General Erwin Rommel begins his second desert offensive in North Africa, moving from El Aghelia to Agedabia on the 22nd. The British Eighth Army is caught unawares and the Germans capitalize on

JANUARY 22

this by driving it back. Benghazi falls on the 29th.

JANUARY 22

EASTERN FRONT, *SOVIET UNION*
The besieged city of Leningrad evacuates 440,000 citizens over 50 days. Thousands are dying of starvation, typhus, and other diseases due to inadequate supplies reaching the city and the German shelling and bombing.

JANUARY 23–24

PACIFIC, *PHILIPPINES*
US and Filipino forces on Bataan begin withdrawing to a line running from Bagac in the east to Orion in the west.

SEA WAR, *FAR EAST*
At the Battle of Macassar Strait, four US destroyers, Dutch bombers, and a submarine attack a Japanese convoy off Borneo. Four Japanese transports are lost.

JANUARY 25

POLITICS, *THAILAND*
The government declares war on Britain and the United States.

▲ Desert fighters from Germany's Afrika Korps make use of a captured truck during Rommel's second offensive against the British Eighth Army.

▼T-34 tanks in Leningrad. Thousands of people were evacuated to escape the hardships of the besieged city.

JANUARY 26

WESTERN FRONT, *BRITAIN*
The first US troop convoy of the war reaches Britain.

SEA WAR, *FAR EAST*
Several Japanese troopships off Malaya are struck by 68 British aircraft, of which 13 are lost. That night, the British increase their attacks. The destroyer *Thanet* and the Australian destroyer

Vampire are sunk while attacking the Japanese convoy.

JANUARY 29

POLITICS, *UNITED STATES*
Major General Millard Harmon succeeds General Carl Spaatz as United States Army Air Force chief-of-staff. Spaatz takes over the Air Force Combat Command.

JANUARY 30

FAR EAST, *SINGAPORE*
Retreating British and Commonwealth troops cross the Johore Strait, separating Singapore from the mainland, and partly destroy the connecting causeway. They abandon the rest of the Malayan Peninsula, where mobile Japanese units have constantly outwitted them. Singapore is designed to repel a naval attack. Its great guns have no suitable shells for bombarding land forces as the British believe that a land invasion through dense jungle is impossible, although the RAF has asked for more aircraft to meet a land attack from the north.

FEBRUARY 1

POLITICS, *NORWAY*
Nazi collaborator Vidkun Quisling becomes prime minister, although he will be controlled by Berlin.
SEA WAR, *ATLANTIC*
Germany adopts a new radio code for

▼ *Filipino troops prepare to fight alongside US forces in Bataan.*

▲ *Japanese troops cautiously scale a hill during their advance to Singapore. The British were shocked that the Japanese could move through dense jungle.*

U-boat communications in the Atlantic. Although the British are unable to crack the code until the end of the year, the detection of U-boats is made easier by photoreconnaissance and radio direction-finding technology.
SEA WAR, *PACIFIC*
The US Navy carriers *Enterprise* and *Yorktown*, together with the cruisers *Northampton* and *Salt Lake City*, attack the Marshall and Gilbert Islands.

FEBRUARY 4

AFRICA, *LIBYA*
Axis forces have overextended their lines of communication and a stalemate is developing in the desert. Allied forces are establishing a fortified line from

Gazala on the coast to Bir Hacheim farther inland. Both sides are building up their forces for a new offensive.
FAR EAST, *SINGAPORE*
Britain rejects Japanese demands for Singapore to surrender. Reinforcements are being sent to help defend the base, which is believed to be impregnable.

FEBRUARY 5

POLITICS, *UNITED STATES*
The US government declares war on Thailand.

FEBRUARY 8

▶ *Victorious Japanese soldiers celebrate their conquest of Singapore. The British had totally underestimated the military capability of the Japanese Army.*

FEBRUARY 8

POLITICS, *PHILIPPINES*
President Manuel Quezon proposes to the United States that his country should become independent, that both Japanese and US forces should withdraw, and Filipino units be disbanded. The United States rejects the proposal.

FEBRUARY 8–14

FAR EAST, *SINGAPORE*
Two Japanese divisions, supported by artillery and air bombardment, land on the northwest of the island, quickly followed by a third. Repairs to the Johore causeway enable tanks and 30,000 troops to advance, while in the air the Japanese achieve supremacy. Confused orders often result in the defenders making unnecessary withdrawals and much equipment is lost. Lieutenant General Arthur Percival, the Singapore commander, is forced to surrender on February 14 as the water supply for Singapore's residents and the 85,000-strong garrison is cut. Japan has fewer than 10,000 casualties in Malaya. British and Commonwealth forces have lost 138,000 men, and thousands more will die in captivity. The campaign is one of Britain's greatest defeats.

FEBRUARY 10

SEA WAR, *ATLANTIC*
Britain offers the United States 34 antisubmarine vessels with crews to battle the U-boats.

FEBRUARY 11–12

SEA WAR, *NORTH SEA*
The German battlecruisers *Gneisenau* and *Scharnhorst*, and the heavy cruiser *Prinz Eugen*, supported by destroyers and air cover, leave Brest and sail through the English Channel. RAF and Royal Navy strikes against the German ships are total failures, and 42 aircraft are downed. During the "Channel Dash" to the North Sea, both battlecruisers hit mines and need repairs. British operations to contain the threat of these

▼ *Lieutenant General Sir Arthur Percival's surrender of Singapore was a military disaster.*

commerce-raiders are easier while the vessels are in port. *Gneisenau* subsequently has to be rebuilt after being hit during an air raid against Kiel on February 26, but the project is never completed before the war's end.

FEBRUARY 13

POLITICS, *GERMANY*
Adolf Hitler finally abandons the invasion of Britain, Operation Sealion.

FEBRUARY 14

AIR WAR, *GERMANY*
Britain issues the "Area Bombing Directive," which outlines the strategic objectives of RAF Bomber Command. Bombing will now aim to destroy the psychological will of the German people as well as the country's war industry. Air raids will now aim to destroy residential areas to erode civilian morale.

FEBRUARY 18–23

FAR EAST, *BURMA*
Japanese forces are in constant pursuit of British forces. At the Battle of the Sittang River, the

British are withdrawing across a single bridge over the river when Japanese troops make a sudden crossing elsewhere. The British quickly blow up the bridge, losing much of their equipment with their forces only partially across; those left behind have to use boats. The Sittang River is the only major physical obstacle in the path of the Japanese forces moving toward Rangoon, the capital.

FEBRUARY 19

POLITICS, *UNITED STATES*
The virtually unknown General Dwight D. Eisenhower becomes head of the US Army General Staff War Plans Division. In this capacity he will advocate the intensification of Operation Bolero, the buildup of US forces in Britain, and press for the development of Operation Sledgehammer, a cross-Channel invasion of Europe from Britain.

◀ *General Dwight D. Eisenhower, who became a key figure in US strategic planning and commanded the North African landings in 1942.*

▼ *The German heavy cruiser Prinz Eugen, one of the commerce-raiders that evaded the British and sailed from France into the North Sea.*

KEY PERSONALITIES

AIR CHIEF MARSHAL SIR ARTHUR HARRIS

Arthur Harris (1892–1984) served as British Deputy Chief of Air Staff (1940–41) before taking charge of Bomber Command in 1942. He believed precision bombing was ineffective and favored area bombing against Germany, and he secured Prime Minister Winston Churchill's support to expand Bomber Command's size. Great bomber fleets therefore saturated districts with high explosives and incendiaries to destroy both industry and public morale.

The determination and inspiration shown by Harris encouraged his aircrews to undertake hazardous bombing missions. Raids increased in intensity, more night attacks were flown to avoid hazardous daylight missions, and photoreconnaissance improved bombing accuracy. Despite Harris's initiatives, though, there is still doubt over the success of his strategy.

The impact on Germany's civilians and economy have led some to question the morality of "Bomber" Harris's strategy. Harris himself, however, defended his strategy, claiming it saved many British lives by shortening the war.

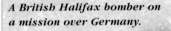

A British Halifax bomber on a mission over Germany.

▲ *Scenes of devastation in Darwin after a Japanese air attack on the port. This attack on the Australian mainland shocked the population.*

SEA WAR, *FAR EAST*
At the Battle of Lombok Strait, east of Bali, Dutch and US vessels fight several actions with the Japanese. A Dutch cruiser and a destroyer are sunk, while one Japanese destroyer is damaged.

AIR WAR, *AUSTRALIA*
Japanese carrier aircraft and land-based bombers attack Darwin, northern Australia. The raid sinks or damages 16 vessels, claims 172 lives, and causes widespread panic.

HOME FRONT, *UNITED STATES*
President Franklin D. Roosevelt signs Executive Order 9066 giving the secretary of war powers to exclude persons from military areas. This legislation is directed at the nation's Japanese-American population, which has faced growing public hostility since Pearl Harbor. The US Army subsequently removes 11,000 Japanese-Americans from the Pacific coast to camps in Arkansas and Texas for the war's duration (there are fears that they may aid a Japanese attack on the West Coast, which is regarded by many as a real possibility). Not a single Japanese-American, however, is convicted of spying for Tokyo during the war. Others go on to serve with distinction in the US armed forces, winning many awards for gallantry.

FEBRUARY 20

POLITICS, *VICHY FRANCE*
Political leaders of the Third Republic are tried by the Vichy Supreme Court, charged with being responsible for France's humiliating 1940 defeat. Former premiers Léon Blum, Paul Reynaud, and Edouard Daladier all defend their records with great skill. The trial, which quickly becomes a public joke, is never completed.

FEBRUARY 22

POLITICS, *BRITAIN*
Air Chief Marshal Sir Arthur Harris takes over Bomber Command.

FEBRUARY 23

POLITICS, *ALLIES*
Britain, Australia, the United States, and New Zealand ratify the Mutual Aid Agreement.

◀ The British Avro Lancaster bomber entered operational service in 1942.

FEBRUARY 24

SEA WAR, *PACIFIC*
The US aircraft carrier *Enterprise* leads a task force to attack the Japanese on Wake Island.

FEBRUARY 25

POLITICS, *ALLIES*
ABDA is disbanded and its commander, British General Sir Archibald Wavell, becomes commander-in-chief in India.

HOME FRONT, *UNITED STATES*
An air raid scare in Los Angeles results in a heavy antiaircraft barrage being fired.

FEBRUARY 27–29

SEA WAR, *FAR EAST*
Under the command of Dutch Rear Admiral Karel Doorman, five cruisers and nine destroyers from four Allied nations engage a Japanese force of four cruisers and 13 destroyers in the Java Sea. Following an inconclusive opening engagement, the Japanese inflict severe losses using their faster "Long Lance" torpedoes. Five Allied cruisers and five destroyers are sunk. Doorman is killed. Japan loses two transports, one cruiser is sunk, and six destroyers are damaged.

FEBRUARY 28

WESTERN FRONT, *FRANCE*
A British parachute assault destroys a German radar station at Bruneval near Le Havre. The force then escapes by sea with captured equipment.

MARCH 1–7

SEA WAR, *FAR EAST*
Two Japanese task forces, including four aircraft carriers, inflict serious losses on Allied shipping while sailing to Java in the Dutch East Indies. The Japanese surround the Allies and sink nine warships and 10 merchant vessels with close-range fire.

MARCH 2

POLITICS, *AUSTRALIA*
All Australian adult civilians become liable for war service.

MARCH 3

AIR WAR, *GERMANY*
The British Lancaster bomber undertakes its first operation by dropping mines in the Heligoland Bight in the North Sea.

MARCH 5

POLITICS, *BRITAIN*
General Sir Alan Brooke replaces Admiral Sir Dudley Pound as chairman of the Chiefs-of-Staff Committee responsible for the daily running of the war and future planning. Britain also extends conscription to men aged 41–45.

MARCH 5–7

FAR EAST, *BURMA*
Lieutenant General Sir Harold Alexander replaces Lieutenant General Thomas Hutton as British commander

◀ Chinese troops crossing the Sittang River during the campaign to save their vital supply road through Burma.

in Burma. Two British divisions have been trying to resist Japanese advances toward Rangoon. Its port is the main point of entry for British supplies and troops. Alexander, however, evacuates Rangoon after realizing his dispersed forces cannot hold it. He himself narrowly escapes before the Japanese seize it on the 7th.

MARCH 9

POLITICS, *UNITED STATES*

Admiral Harold Stark replaces Vice Admiral Robert Ghormley as US naval commander in European waters. Admiral Ernest King assumes Stark's position as Chief of Naval Operations on the 26th.

FAR EAST, *DUTCH EAST INDIES*

Japan gains possession of its "Southern Resources Area" with the surrender of Allied

combatants in the Dutch East Indies. The capture of this resource-rich area and Malaya allows Japan to consider offensives against India and Australia.

MARCH 11

PACIFIC, *PHILIPPINES*

General Douglas MacArthur leaves his Far East command to become commander-in-chief of US forces in Australia. On leaving, he famously declares: "I shall return!"

FAR EAST, *BURMA*

US General Joseph Stilwell assumes command of the Chinese Fifth and Sixth Armies around the eastern Shan States and city of Mandalay. Their aim is to protect the Burma Road into China. The Allied ground forces are supported by one RAF squadron and up to 30 "Flying Tiger" aircraft flown by an all-volunteer force of US pilots. They face over 200 enemy aircraft.

MARCH 12

PACIFIC, *NEW CALEDONIA*

US Forces, including the first operational deployment of "Seabee" engineers, begin establishing a base in Noumea on New Caledonia in the southwest Pacific.

MARCH 13–30

FAR EAST, *BURMA*

Lieutenant General Sir Harold Alexander forms an Allied line below the central towns of Prome, Toungoo,

◀ *General Douglas MacArthur, the US commander in the Philippines, who directed the defense of the islands.*

and Loikaw near the Salween River and then eastward. Major General William Slim assumes command of the Burma Corps, the main elements of the British forces there on March 19. Japanese attacks begin on the 21st, directed at Chinese forces at Toungoo and the British at Prome.

MARCH 14

POLITICS, *AUSTRALIA*

Large numbers of US troops begin arriving in Australia.

MARCH 22–23

SEA WAR, *MEDITERRANEAN*

A superior Italian force engages a British convoy sailing from Alexandria to Malta. A relatively small escort of five light cruisers and 17 destroyers initially resists an attack led by the battleship *Littorio* at the Battle of Sirte. A storm, however, results in the loss of two Italian destroyers. The convoy subsequently faces air attacks and only 5000 of the original 25,000 tons (25,400 metric tonnes) of supplies arrive. British naval losses and commitments in the Mediterranean have reduced the number of ships available for convoy escorts.

MARCH 27

POLITICS, *BRITAIN*

Admiral Sir James Somerville assumes command of the Far East Fleet in Ceylon (modern Sri Lanka).

POLITICS, *AUSTRALIA*

Australian General Sir Thomas Blamey becomes commander-in-chief of the Australian forces and commander

◀ *Japanese troops pass a destroyed railroad bridge as they enter Burma from neighboring Thailand.*

main fleet, though, which is at sea. A British air attack against the Japanese force fails. Over several days, Japanese aircraft destroy the carrier *Hermes*, two heavy cruisers, an Australian destroyer, and several merchant ships.

APRIL 3-9

PACIFIC, *PHILIPPINES*
Japan launches its final offensive on Bataan, beginning with air and artillery bombardments. The US line is penetrated on the 4th. Major General Jonathan Wainright, commanding the US and Filipino forces, cannot mount an effective counterattack with his decimated units. Following the surrender on the 9th, some 78,000 US and Filipino troops are forced to make a 65-mile (104-km) march without sustenance, and are constantly beaten. Many die along the way. Wainright escapes with 2000 men to Corregidor Island off Bataan.

APRIL 10-23

FAR EAST, *BURMA*
Japan begins an offensive after reinforcements arrive. Lieutenant General

▲ *Japanese troops establish control in the Dutch East Indies following their conquest of the resource-rich islands.*

▼ *US troops captured by the Japanese following the capitulation of US and Filipino forces on Bataan, the Philippines.*

of Allied Land Forces in Australia, under the supreme command of US General Douglas MacArthur.

MARCH 28-29

AIR WAR, *GERMANY*
RAF bombers, including the new Lancaster, attack Lübeck on the Baltic coast. The raid on the historic, timber-built houses of the town signals a change in Bomber Command's strategy, which is now concentrating on the civilian population.

SEA WAR, *BAY OF BISCAY*
Britain's Combined Operations launches an operation to destroy the St. Nazaire dry-dock in France with a force of 611 men. The objective is to prevent the German battleship *Tirpitz* (currently in Norway) being able to use the only dock large enough to enable it to mount commerce-destroying operations in the Atlantic. An old destroyer, *Campbeltown*, is filled with explosives and destroys the lock gates after ramming them. A commando force attacks St. Nazaire's dock facilities, but 144 men die and over half are captured.

MARCH 29

POLITICS, *BRITAIN/INDIA*
Britain announces its proposals to grant India semi-independent status when the war ends.

APRIL 2-8

SEA WAR, *FAR EAST*
Japan's First Air Fleet attacks British air and sea bases in Trincomalee and Colombo, Ceylon. It fails to hit the

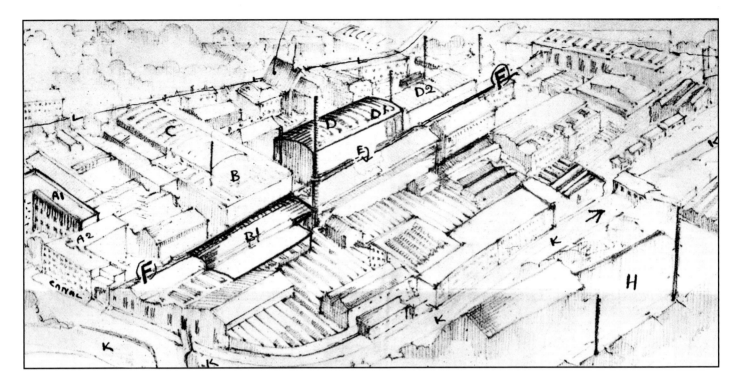

▲ *A hand-drawn plan of the Augsburg diesel engine factory prepared for crew briefings before the raid to destroy it.*

▶ *James Doolittle, the pilot who led the first US air attack on Tokyo, presents awards to other airmen of the US Army Air Force.*

William Slim fails to prevent the Japanese advancing on the oil fields at Yenangyaung in the south and sets large amounts of crude oil ablaze. The Chinese Sixty-fifth Army enters Burma to bolster the faltering defense against the Japanese. Around the central towns of Loikaw and Taunggyi, the Japanese 56th Division overwhelms the Chinese Sixth Army by the 23rd.

APRIL 17

AIR WAR, *GERMANY*
The RAF launch one of the war's most hazardous bomber raids, attacking a diesel engine factory in Augsburg. Seven of the 12 Lancaster bombers assigned to the daylight attack are lost and the other five sustain damage.

APRIL 18

POLITICS, *VICHY FRANCE*
Pierre Laval returns to head the government; Henri-Philippe Pétain continues as head of state. Laval is eager to enhance Franco-German relations and undermines the more hesitant approach advocated by Pétain.

AIR WAR, *JAPAN*
Lieutenant Colonel James Doolittle leads 16 B-25 bombers, launched from the aircraft carrier *Hornet,* on a daring mission to strike targets in Japan, including the capital Tokyo. The damage inflicted by the daylight raid is secondary to the impact on Japan's leaders, who are alarmed that US aircraft can strike at the heart of their homeland. This reinforces a decision to seek a decisive engagement to destroy US naval power in the Pacific.

APRIL 23

SEA WAR, *ATLANTIC*
The first "milch cow" submarine (*U-459*) delivers fuel and supplies to Germany's U-boats. This supply vessel doubles the operational range of the U-boats, which are no longer restricted by having to return to base for refueling.

APRIL 24

AIR WAR, *BRITAIN*
Germany bombs Exeter at the start of an air campaign against historic towns

and cities, following the British attack on Lübeck. Hitler has ordered raids against every English city featured in the famous Baedeker tourist books.

APRIL 29

FAR EAST, *BURMA*

The Japanese cut the Burma Road after seizing the town of Lashio, where the route ends. Chinese Nationalists are now almost wholly dependent on supply by air. The Japanese, being reinforced through the port at Rangoon, are advancing up the river valleys and plan to encircle the Allies in the Mandalay area. The Allies will then have to fight with their backs to the Irrawaddy River. The Burma Corps aims to fall back to India, whose defense is the main priority. Rapid Japanese advances, however, force the British to make a hurried (and potentially disastrous) retreat rather than an organized withdrawal.

APRIL 30

POLITICS, *SOVIET UNION*

Premier Joseph Stalin declares that the USSR has no territorial ambitions except to wrest its own lost lands from Nazi control.

▲ *A U-boat in port. The "milch cow" supply submarines enabled U-boats to receive supplies at sea and thereby operate for long periods away from base.*

▼ *The German bombing of Bath damaged many fine buildings. This was one of the targets in the "Baedeker Raids" on historic English towns and cities.*

MAY 1

FAR EAST, *BURMA*
The city of Mandalay falls to the Japanese. The Allies are now retreating, with the Chinese Sixth Army heading for the Chinese province of Yunnan. Units of the Fifth and Sixty-sixth Armies withdraw to Yunnan or northern Burma. General Joseph Stilwell leads a 100-strong group on a 400-mile (600-km) journey to Imphal, India. Heavy rain hampers the Allied retreat.

▲ *General Joseph Stilwell (right), the US commander of Chinese forces, leads his staff on a epic journey from Burma to India to escape the advancing Japanese troops.*

HOME FRONT, *SOVIET UNION*
A six-month evacuation commences, which is intended to move the besieged citizens of Leningrad to safety across Lake Ladoga. Around 448,700 people are taken out of the city.

MAY 2

SEA WAR, *PACIFIC*
Japan deploys a large carrier force to surprise the US Pacific Fleet in the Coral Sea as part of its plan to establish greater control of the Solomon Islands. A key aim is to seize Port Moresby on the southwest Pacific

▼ *The Japanese Navy's forces gather for the battle against the US Pacific Fleet in the Coral Sea.*

▲ *Major General Jonathan Wainright broadcasts the surrender of US and Filipino forces on Corregidor, the Philippines.*

island of Papua New Guinea, which would facilitate bomber attacks on Australia and help sever its communications with the United States. The Japanese have a Carrier Striking Force containing the carriers *Shokaku* and *Zuikaku* under Vice Admiral Takeo Takagi. They also have a Covering Group that includes the carrier *Shoho,* plus four heavy cruisers under Rear Admiral Aritomo Goto. There is also the Port Moresby Invasion Group and a support force. US codebreaking enables Admiral Chester Nimitz, the US Pacific Fleet commander, to prepare his forces. He deliberately withdraws from Tulagi in the Solomons before a Japanese attack in order to reinforce their belief that only one US carrier is operating in the area.

MAY 3

SEA WAR, *PACIFIC*
US Rear Admiral Frank Fletcher's Task Force 17, including the

▶ *British Royal Marines prepare to land on Madagascar in the Indian Ocean.*

carrier *Yorktown*, damages a Japanese destroyer, three minesweepers, and five aircraft off Tulagi during the Coral Sea engagement.

MAY 5–7

AFRICA, *MADAGASCAR*
Britain launches Operation Ironclad, the invasion of Vichy French Madagascar, with a battleship and two aircraft carriers carrying a landing force. The occupation is intended to deny Axis forces access to the island. An armed Vichy merchant cruiser and submarine are lost. A British

vessel is mined. The Diego Suarez naval base surrenders on the 7th.

MAY 5–10

PACIFIC, *PHILIPPINES*
US and Filipino forces on Corregidor finally surrender after a Japanese landing on the island. Some 12,495 US and Filipino troops (including Major Generals Jonathan Wainright and Edward King) are captured. The Philippines campaign has claimed 140,000 US and Filipino lives, plus 4000 Japanese dead.

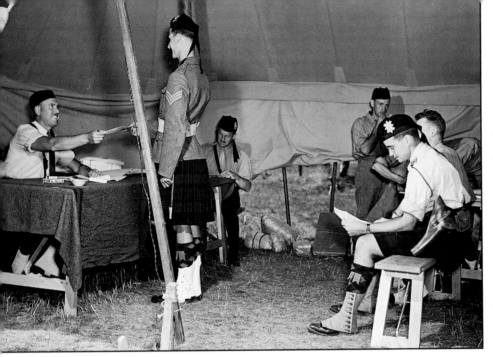

Canadian troops in Ontario. Thousands of men became liable for military service after full conscription was introduced.

US destroyer *Sims*, and the tanker *Neosho* (which is mistaken for a carrier) is scuttled. US forces successfully destroy the *Shoho* and 21 aircraft that attempt to engage the US carriers.

MAY 8

SEA WAR, *PACIFIC*

US aircraft damage the *Shokaku*, while *Zuikaku*'s aircraft losses are very serious in the Battle of the Coral Sea. Japanese aircraft hit the *Lexington*, which is later scuttled, and damage the *Yorktown*. This is the first ever battle fought exclusively with carrier aircraft. The US Navy loses a carrier but repairs to the *Yorktown* are speedy. Japan loses a smaller carrier while the other two Coral Sea carriers will be unfit for action in the approaching battle at Midway. Large numbers of Japanese aircraft and experienced pilots have also been lost. The abandonment of the Port Moresby landing is the first major blow to Japanese expansionism.

MAY 8–15

EASTERN FRONT, *CRIMEA*

The German Eleventh Army launches its attack against the Soviet Crimean Front. The Soviets resume their attempt to surround German units against the Sea of Azov in a battle around Kharkov. Germany's Eleventh Army captures the Crimean Kerch Peninsula on the 15th and continues to fight along the Donets River.

MAY 11

POLITICS, *CANADA*

Full conscription is introduced following a referendum on the issue, the only significant opposition being in Quebec province.

FAR EAST, *BURMA*

British and Commonwealth troops fight a last, bitter battle at Kalewa before the remaining forces in Burma finally enter the border region with

MAY 6–7

SEA WAR, *PACIFIC*

Although the opposing Japanese and US carrier groups are only 70 miles (112 km) apart, their reconnaissance flights fail to locate each other. Australian and US cruisers in Task Force 44, under British Rear Admiral Sir John Crace, are then sent to find the Port Moresby Invasion Group. Although poor weather prevents an attack, the unfolding battle leads the group to turn back to its Rabaul base on the 7th. Japanese aircraft sink the

▲ A German armored unit during Rommel's offensive against the British Eighth Army in Libya during 1942.

▼ US sailors abandon the Lexington during the Battle of the Coral Sea.

India and eventually reach Imphal. Japan now has control over some 80 percent of Burma.

SEA WAR, *MEDITERRANEAN*
A special German bomber force locates and sinks the British destroyers *Kipling, Lively,* and *Jackal* to the west of Alexandria, Egypt.

MAY 14

ESPIONAGE, *UNITED STATES*
US codebreakers deciphering Japanese radio messages obtain their first intelligence about the impending Japanese operation to destroy the US Pacific Fleet in the central Pacific Ocean by drawing into battle around Midway.

MAY 15

FAR EAST, *INDIA*
British and Commonwealth forces retreating from Burma begin to arrive in India. Some 13,463 British, Indian, and Burmese troops have been killed in the Burma campaign thus far.

The 95,000-strong Chinese force has been decimated, while Japan has suffered an estimated 5000–8000 casualties to date.

MAY 18

POLITICS, *BRITAIN*
Admiral Harwood assumes command of the British Mediterranean Fleet.

MAY 22

POLITICS, *MEXICO*
The Mexican government declares war on Germany, Italy, and Japan.

MAY 25

POLITICS, *AUSTRALIA*
Three people are arrested for conspiring to establish a fascist government to negotiate peace terms with Japan.

MAY 26–31

AFRICA, *LIBYA*
General Erwin Rommel attacks the Gazala Line in Libya. Italian armor strikes at Bir Hacheim, 40 miles (60 km) from the coast,

▲ *A view of the Germany city of Cologne after the British "1000 Bomber" raid.*

but is repulsed by Free French troops. Axis tanks try to outflank the Allied lines beyond Bir Hacheim. Although the British Eighth Army has 850 tanks (plus 150 in reserve), the Axis forces deploy their 630 tanks more effectively, and their antitank guns present a serious threat. British armor and aircraft engage Axis tanks at the Knightsbridge crossroads, behind the Gazala Line. Axis armor suffers serious fuel problems until the Italians penetrate the Gazala Line to bring up fresh supplies on the 31st.

MAY 27

HOME FRONT, *CZECHOSLOVAKIA*
British-trained Czech agents attack Reinhard Heydrich, the deputy chief of the SS, who has been appointed deputy governor of occupied Czechoslovakia. Heydrich is traveling in an open-top car without an escort when the agents strike.

MAY 30

AIR WAR, *GERMANY*
Britain launches its first "1000 Bomber" raid. The target is Cologne. Over 59,000 people are made homeless. The British lose 40 aircraft.

MAY 31

AIR WAR, *GERMANY*
British Mosquito bombers, constructed from wood, make the first of many raids over Germany.

the US base at Midway and then destroy the US Pacific Fleet commanded by Admiral Chester Nimitz. Japan deploys 165 vessels, including eight carriers, but they are too widely dispersed to provide mutual support. US code-breakers are able to warn the Pacific Fleet, which then converges to repel the Midway attack and is not diverted by a raid on the Aleutian Islands. The US Navy has a smaller force but has managed to gather three carriers.

The reconnaissance operation by Japan's 29 large cruiser submarines fails to establish the movements of the Pacific Fleet. Nagumo has no idea of US deployments when he first strikes Midway. Japan's I Carrier Striking Force

◀ *US dive-bombers in action against the Japanese during the decisive Battle of Midway.*

June 1

AIR WAR, *GERMANY*
Britain launches a "1000 Bomber" raid against Essen and the Ruhr industrial area.

June 4

SEA WAR, *PACIFIC*
The Battle of Midway begins. Japan's Admiral Chuichi Nagumo aims to seize

▼ *A German woman collects water from a street tap. Water, gas, and electricity supplies were all disrupted by bombing.*

▲ *The Japanese cruiser* **Mogami** *after sustaining an attack by US aircraft during the Battle of Midway.*

is decimated by US aircraft and three heavy carriers are lost. Japan's fourth carrier, *Hiryu*, then cripples the US carrier *Yorktown* before herself being fatally hit. Japan's attempt to destroy the enemy with its superior forces by luring it into a surface battle has failed. The loss of half of its carrier strength, plus 275 aircraft, puts Japan on the defensive in the Pacific.

JUNE 7

EASTERN FRONT, *UKRAINE*
The siege of Sebastopol intensifies with massive assaults by Germany's Eleventh Army. Sebastopol is under heavy shelling from German siege artillery, which includes the *Dora* gun, the world's largest mortar. The Soviet defenders continue to hold out, despite the intense bombardment.

JUNE 10

HOME FRONT, *CZECHOSLOVAKIA*
Reinhard Heydrich, the deputy governor of occupied Czechoslovakia and architect of the Nazi genocide program, dies after an attack by Czech agents on May 27. In retaliation, over 1000 Czechs accused of anti-Nazi activities are murdered, 3000 Czech Jews are deported for extermination,

◀ *An aerial photograph of the Japanese carrier* **Hiryu** *during the Battle of Midway. The ship was set ablaze by a US air attack and subsequently scuttled.*

and 150 Berlin Jews are killed. The Czech village of Lidice is leveled. Its men are executed; its women and children are sent to concentration camps.

JUNE 10–13

AFRICA, *LIBYA*

Axis forces have created a fortified area ("the Cauldron") inside the Allied lines. Following the Free French withdrawal from Bir Hacheim on the 10th–11th, Axis armor advances east from the Cauldron to threaten the entire Eighth Army. British commander General Neil Ritchie orders a withdrawal on the 13th.

▼ *Soviet reinforcements being sent to Sebastopol. Despite fierce resistance, the port was captured by the Germans.*

JUNE 18

POLITICS, *ALLIES*

At the Second Washington Conference in the United States, British Prime Minister Winston Churchill and US President Franklin D. Roosevelt try to agree a strategy in Europe for 1942–43. Conditions appear unsuitable for a "Second Front" in France, so Churchill proposes a North African invasion. In July, Roosevelt accepts that Europe cannot yet be attacked and agrees to Churchill's North African option, later code-named Operation Torch. Cooperation in nuclear research is also agreed on.

▲ *British troops surrender to the Afrika Korps after the fall of Tobruk.*

AIR WAR, *GERMANY*

Britain launches a "1000 Bomber" raid on Bremen.

JUNE 21

AFRICA, *LIBYA*

Following the Allied withdrawal into Egypt, the Tobruk garrison suddenly falls following German land and air attacks. Some 30,000 men, rations, and fuel are seized. Newly-promoted Field Marshal Erwin Rommel continues chasing the retreating Allies, taking

Mersa Matruh on the 28th. General Sir Claude Auchinleck, British Middle East commander, takes personal charge of the Eighth Army and establishes a fortified line. This runs inland for 40 miles (64 km) from El Alamein on the coast to the impassable Quattara Depression. Rommel fails to penetrate the position, and the front stabilizes as his lines of supply in the Mediterranean are being strained by British air and sea attacks, assisted by intelligence from codebreaking.

JUNE 25

POLITICS, *UNITED STATES*
Major General Dwight D. Eisenhower assumes command of US forces in Europe.

JUNE 28

EASTERN FRONT, *UKRAINE*
Germany launches its summer offensive, with its Army Group South attacking east from Kursk toward Voronezh, which falls nine days later.

JULY 4–10

EASTERN FRONT, *CRIMEA*
The siege of Sebastopol ends with the Germans capturing 90,000 troops.
SEA WAR, *ARCTIC*
British Admiral of the Fleet Sir Dudley Pound gives a disastrous order for the PQ-17 convoy to disperse after air and U-boat attacks. The escorts therefore withdraw, leaving the convoy's isolated merchant ships vulnerable. PQ-17 loses 23 vessels out of 33 and enormous amounts of supplies during renewed German attacks.

JULY 13

EASTERN FRONT, *CAUCASUS*
Adolf Hitler orders simultaneous attacks on Stalingrad and the Caucasus, despite the strain this causes to his armies. Army Group B's advance toward Stalingrad is slowed after Hitler redeploys the Fourth Panzer Army to Army Group A's Caucasus drive. He believes Army Group A will not be able to cross the Don River without reinforcements. Field Marshal Fedor von Bock, leading Army Group B, is later dismissed for opposing this. The divergence of the two groups creates a gap through which Soviet forces are able to escape.

▲ *A British vessel from the PQ-17 Arctic convoy sinks after being torpedoed by a U-boat. The decision to scatter the convoy led to it suffering severe losses.*

JULY 21

POLITICS, *UNITED STATES*
Admiral William Leahy becomes the president's personal chief-of-staff. In this role he is closely involved in key military decisions.

JULY 23

EASTERN FRONT, *UKRAINE*
The city of Rostov is taken by

AUGUST 1

Germany's Army Group A, which then crosses the Don River and makes a broad advance into the Caucasus.

AUGUST 1

EASTERN FRONT, *UKRAINE*
Adolf Hitler moves the Fourth Panzer Army back to Stalingrad to accelerate the German advance. The Eleventh Army receives similar orders. This seriously strains the Caucasus advance.

AUGUST 7–21

PACIFIC, *SOLOMONS*
The US 1st Marine Division lands on Guadalcanal Island to overwhelm the 2200 Japanese garrison and capture the partly-built airfield that would enable bombers to strike Allied sea-lanes. Tulagi is also taken. US naval forces are subjected to air attacks and eventually withdraw. The Marines suffer supply shortages but are later relieved by air and sea. Japan sinks four cruisers on the 9th and starts landing forces by night to harass the Marines. US forces destroy the first major Japanese attacks on the Tenaru River on the 9th. Fighting now centers on the airstrip known as Henderson Field.

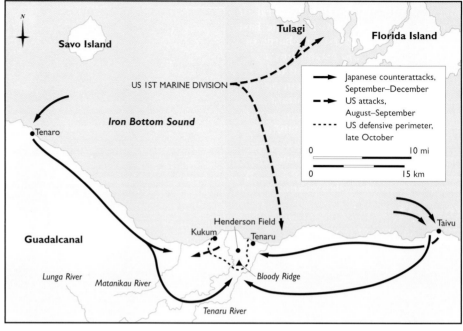

AUGUST 9

SEA WAR, *PACIFIC*
At the Battle of Savo Island, between Guadalcanal and Tulagi, the US Navy suffers one of its most serious defeats. A Japanese cruiser squadron, aiming to attack transports unloading off Guadalcanal, surprises five US and Australian cruisers. Superior night-fighting and gunnery skills enable the Japanese to sink four cruisers and damage the remaining one. The Japanese retire, fearing an air attack, while the US transports withdraw leaving the troops on Guadalcanal with serious supply problems.

AUGUST 10–15

SEA WAR, *MEDITERRANEAN*
Operation Pedestal, a 14-ship, Gibraltar-to-Malta

▼ *A German soldier leaps into action near Stalingrad.*

▲ *The fighting on Guadalcanal was among the most savage of the Pacific War, especially near Henderson Field.*

convoy, is devastated by enemy surface vessel, U-boat, and air attacks. Only four vessels reach Malta, but they enable the besieged island to survive.

AUGUST 12

POLITICS, *ALLIES*
Winston Churchill meets Joseph Stalin for the first time in talks that focus mainly on the decision to delay forming a "Second Front" in Europe.

AUGUST 13

POLITICS, *BRITAIN*
Lieutenant General Bernard Montgomery replaces General Neil Ritchie as Eighth Army commander. General Sir Harold Alexander replaces General Sir Claude Auchinleck as Middle East commander on the 18th.

AUGUST 17

AIR WAR, *FRANCE*
The first wholly US bomber raid over Europe strikes targets in France.

AUGUST 19

WESTERN FRONT, *FRANCE*
A force of 5000 Canadian, 1000 British, and 50 US troops attacks the port of Dieppe. It is a "reconnaissance in force" to gain experience and intelligence for landing a force on the continent. The assault is disastrous. Allied losses include almost 4000 men killed or captured.

▲ *American ground crew prepare an aircraft for action during US offensives against the Japanese on Guadalcanal.*

AUGUST 19–24

EASTERN FRONT, *SOVIET UNION*
Determined drives toward Stalingrad by Germany's Army Group B eventually reach the Volga River. Fierce resistance by the Soviet forces begins within a 30-mile (45-km) range of the city of Stalingrad.

AUGUST 22

POLITICS, *BRAZIL*
The government declares war on Germany and Italy.

AUGUST 22–25

SEA WAR, *PACIFIC*
In the Battle of the Eastern Solomons, Admiral Frank Fletcher's three-carrier task force engages a Japanese convoy bound for Guadalcanal, plus three other carriers operating in two separate groups. The Japanese light carrier *Ryujo*, a destroyer, plus 90 aircraft are lost. The US carrier *Enterprise* is damaged and 17 US aircraft downed.

AUGUST 23

AIR WAR, *SOVIET UNION*
A raid by 600 German bombers on Stalingrad claims thousands of lives.

AUGUST 30

AFRICA, *EGYPT*
Germany's tanks try to outflank the Allied line at El Alamein, but meet dense minefields and fierce resistance. The offense disintegrates under air attack and supply problems.

SEPTEMBER 2

FINAL SOLUTION, *POLAND*
The Nazis are "clearing" the Jewish Warsaw Ghetto. Over 50,000 Jews have been killed by poison gas or sent to concentration camps. The SS (*Schutzstaffel* – protection squad), a fanatical Nazi military and security organization, is chiefly responsible for Nazi persecution of the Jews and others deemed to be ideological or racial enemies of the Third Reich.

SEPTEMBER 9

POLITICS, *GERMANY*
Adolf Hitler dismisses Field Marshal Wilhelm List, commander of Army Group A laying siege to Stalingrad, for criticizing his Eastern Front strategy. General Paul von Kleist replaces him.

SEPTEMBER 12

SEA WAR, *ATLANTIC*
The liner *Laconia*, carrying 1800 Italian prisoners and Allied service

DECISIVE WEAPONS

CONVOYS

Convoys provided protective escorts for merchant vessels against enemy surface, submerged, or air attack. Allied convoys, often containing over 50 vessels, sailed in columns and weaved their way across the sea-lanes. In the Atlantic and Arctic, the atrocious weather reduced visibility, froze the crews, and created great waves that left vessels vulnerable to collision.

The main threat to Allied convoys were the U-boats, which inflicted critical losses on shipping. Antisubmarine measures gradually improved, however, with enhanced air and sea coordination, new tactics, and scientific innovations. Shipbuilding was also increased to replace lost vessels. The interception of German radio transmissions, centimetric radar, escort carriers, U-boat-detection technology (asdic and sonar), improved depth-charges, and launchers all helped protect convoys.

Germany's campaign to destroy Allied control of the Atlantic sea-lanes was especially critical as Britain came to rely upon North American aid. In the North Atlantic alone, some 2232 vessels were sunk, but the destruction of 785 U-boats secured Allied command of the sea-lanes.

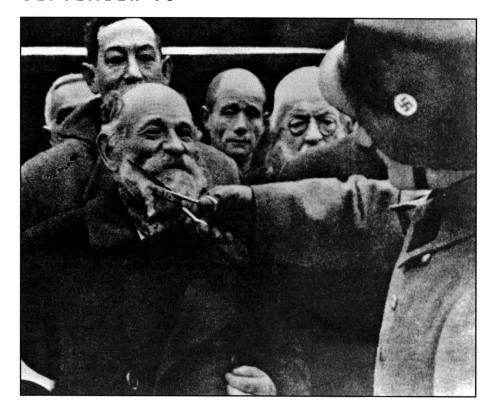

families, is sunk by *U-156*. A US bomber attacks *U-156* while it tries to aid the survivors. As a result, German navy chief Admiral Karl Doenitz instructs *U-156* to cancel the rescue. In future, no lifesaving attempts will be made by U-boats after an attack.

SEPTEMBER 13

PACIFIC, *SOLOMONS*
At the Battle of Bloody Ridge, 6000 Japanese try to seize Henderson Field, Guadalcanal, but are repulsed.

SEPTEMBER 15

SEA WAR, *PACIFIC*
Two Japanese submarines intercept a carrier force escorting troop transports to Guadalcanal. The US carrier *Wasp* and a destroyer are lost, but the troop transports arrive safely.

SEPTEMBER 24

POLITICS, *GERMANY*
General Franz Halder, chief of the General Staff, is replaced by General Kurt Zeitzler. Halder has made the mistake of criticizing Adolf Hitler's Eastern Front strategy, which demands that German troops should not retreat.

OCTOBER 18

POLITICS, *UNITED STATES*
Vice Admiral William Halsey replaces Vice Admiral Robert Ghormley as South Pacific Area commander.

▲ *A German soldier removes the beard of a Jewish man inside the Warsaw Ghetto. The abuse and terrorizing of Jews across Europe was Nazi policy.*

OCTOBER 22

AIR WAR, *ITALY*
Britain launches a series of raids on the industrial areas around Turin, Milan, and Genoa.

OCTOBER 23

AFRICA, *EGYPT*
The Battle of El Alamein begins. General Bernard Montgomery's carefully-prepared attack by 195,000 Allied troops against 104,000 Axis men begins with an enormous artillery bombardment and numerous deception measures. Massive mine-clearance operations enable Allied armor formations to push forward and leave the infantry to widen the gaps. Field Marshal Erwin Rommel is in Germany, but immediately returns after the temporary commander, General Georg Stumme, dies suddenly. First reports confirm that the Allies have made an excellent start, although Axis resistance is fierce.

OCTOBER 26

SEA WAR, *PACIFIC*
At the Battle of Santa Cruz, Japanese carriers approach Guadalcanal and fatally damage the US carrier *Hornet*

KEY PERSONALITIES

FIELD MARSHAL SIR BERNARD MONTGOMERY

Bernard Montgomery (1887–1976) began World War II leading a British division to France in 1939. After Dunkirk, he became a corps commander before Prime Minister Winston Churchill appointed him to lead the Eighth Army in the Western Desert.

Montgomery, exploiting the arrival of more men and supplies, halted Germany's drive into Egypt in 1942. Using careful planning and his ability to inspire confidence in his men, Montgomery inflicted the first British defeat on the German Army at El Alamein. This raised public morale and bolstered his reputation. After the landing of Allied armies in North Africa he helped secure the defeat of Axis forces in the desert.

After commanding the British Eighth Army in the 1943 invasions of Sicily and Italy, he was recalled to Britain in January 1944. Montgomery now had the task of helping prepare the enormous operation to invade northwest Europe. During the June 1944 D-Day landings he was commander of ground forces under US General Dwight D. Eisenhower's supreme command. From August, he became 21st Army Group commander. His relationship with US commanders was not always harmonious. He particularly disagreed with Eisenhower over the strategy for defeating Germany, favoring an all-out thrust rather than the more cautious "broad front" plan that was adopted. At the Battle of the Bulge in December 1944 Montgomery temporarily commanded two US armies, but then returned to 21st Army Group for the Rhine crossings to seal the defeat of Germany in 1945.

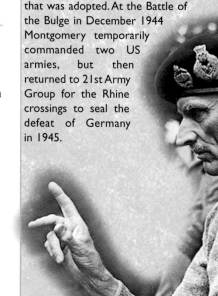

(leaving the US Pacific Fleet with one carrier). The Japanese cruiser *Yura* is sunk and the carrier *Shokaku* rendered ineffective by aircraft strikes.

NOVEMBER 2–24

AFRICA, *EGYPT/LIBYA*
Field Marshal Erwin Rommel, severely lacking supplies, decides to withdraw from El Alamein. He delays this for 48 hours, after Adolf Hitler's order to stand firm, but then continues following further Allied attacks. The Allies push him back to Tobruk, Benghazi, and then El Agheila by the 24th. Germany and Italy have lost 59,000 men killed, wounded, or captured. The Allies have suffered 13,000 killed, wounded, or missing. General Bernard Montgomery's victory saves the Suez Canal and raises Allied morale. Alamein is the first major defeat of German forces during the war.

NOVEMBER 5

AFRICA, *MADAGASCAR*
Vichy French forces in control of the island surrender.

NOVEMBER 8–11

AFRICA, *MOROCCO/ALGERIA*
Three Allied Task Forces, including five carriers, land 34,000 US troops near Casablanca, 39,000 US and British

▶ *Gurkhas of the British Eighth Army go on the attack during the Battle of El Alamein.*

▲ *A Japanese bomber in action against US warships during the Battle of Santa Cruz.*

troops near Oran (accompanied by a parachute assault), and 33,000 troops near Algiers. US General Dwight D. Eisenhower, the supreme commander, aims to seize Vichy French North Africa as a springboard for future operations to clear the whole of North Africa of Axis forces. Admiral Jean François Darlan, Vichy commissioner in Africa, causes

diplomatic turbulence by arranging a cease-fire and agreeing to support the Allies. The surprise invasion is a product of successful interservice planning, and Rommel is now fighting on two fronts.

NOVEMBER 11

WESTERN FRONT, *VICHY FRANCE*
German and Italian forces occupy Vichy France to prevent an Allied invasion from the former Vichy French territories in North Africa.

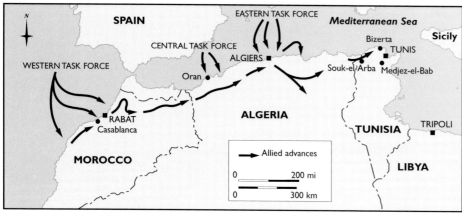

NOVEMBER 12–14

PACIFIC, *SOLOMONS*
A US cruiser-destroyer squadron inflicts serious losses on a Japanese naval force of 18 warships attempting to bombard Guadalcanal's Henderson Field, and also lands 11,000 troops.

NOVEMBER 17–28

AFRICA, *TUNISIA*
British paratroopers land at Souk-el-Arba and join a limited Allied advance toward Bizerta. Thousands of German reinforcements are arriving daily, and the Allies are not yet ready for a large offensive. By the 28th, they are within 20 miles (32 km) of Tunis but are halted by Axis counterattacks. Allied reinforcements from Algiers are slowed by rain and mud. A stalemate develops across much of Tunisia.

NOVEMBER 19

EASTERN FRONT, *UKRAINE*
General Georgi Zhukov launches a Soviet counteroffensive at Stalingrad with 10 armies, 900 tanks, and 1100 aircraft, to be carried out along a front of 260 miles (416 km). Soviet forces

▲ *The Allied landings in North Africa precipitated the surrender of the Vichy French forces stationed there.*

▶ *German troops trapped outside Stalingrad search the skies for the arrival of supplies being brought by aircraft.*

north and south of Stalingrad are to trap the Germans in a pincer movement. The attack is made during the frost, which assists tank mobility. It also coincides with the Allied North African landings, which divert Germany's attention. Allied supplies have equipped the Soviet forces for the advance. The German front buckles.

NOVEMBER 25

EASTERN FRONT, *UKRAINE*
The airlift to supply the German Sixth Army trapped around Stalingrad commences with 320 aircraft. The operation, which eventually requires 500 aircraft, lasts until February 1943.

NOVEMBER 27

SEA WAR, *MEDITERRANEAN*
Vichy French naval forces in Toulon are scuttled with the loss of 72

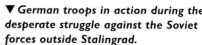

▼ *German troops in action during the desperate struggle against the Soviet forces outside Stalingrad.*

for postwar Britain that aim to provide a state pension and health care for everyone. This reflects aspirations for social justice to tackle society's problems.

DECEMBER 2

TECHNOLOGY, *UNITED STATES*
The first successful controlled nuclear "chain reaction" is made. It is a key step in making an atomic bomb. In this reaction, neutrons from the splitting of uranium atoms split other uranium atoms, releasing enormous energy rapidly in the form of a massive explosion.

DECEMBER 6–9

AFRICA, *TUNISIA*
Two German tank columns try to retake Medjez-el-Bab, 35 miles (40 km) southwest of Tunis. However, Allied armor and aircraft block one column as it advances, while artillery fire stops the second.

▼ A German Junkers Ju 52 transport aircraft is refueled during the airlift that attempted to sustain the trapped Army inside the city of Stalingrad.

DECEMBER 9

POLITICS, *UNITED STATES*
General Alexander Patch succeeds Lieutenant General Alexander Vandegrift as commander of operations on Guadalcanal. The 1st Marine Division is replaced by the US XIV Corps.

DECEMBER 10

PACIFIC, *SOLOMONS*
The Japanese are establishing a well-defended front some six miles (9 km) west of Henderson Field, Guadalcanal. Japan has a 20,000-strong force, however, while there are 58,000 US troops who are better equipped and supplied on the island. Japanese prospects are poor.

DECEMBER 11

SEA WAR, *FRANCE*
A British commando force of 10 men canoes up the Gironde River and disables six vessels in Bordeaux harbor with mines in a daring raid.

DECEMBER 19

EASTERN FRONT, *UKRAINE*
Field Marshal Erich von Manstein's attempt to relieve the German Sixth

vessels, including three battleships, before the Germans can seize them.

NOVEMBER 30

SEA WAR, *PACIFIC*
At the Battle of Tassafaronga, five US heavy cruisers and seven destroyers attack a Japanese convoy of eight destroyers bound for Guadalcanal. Japan loses one destroyer; the US four cruisers.

DECEMBER 1

POLITICS, *BRITAIN*
A report by Liberal economist Sir William Beveridge outlines proposals

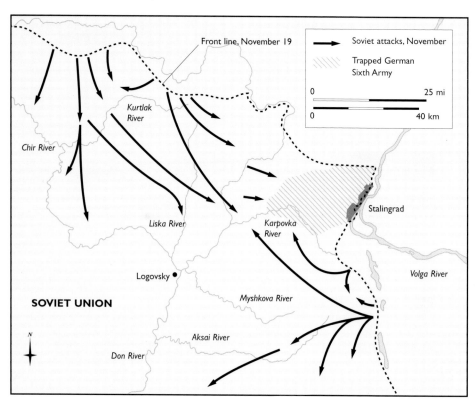

▲ The Red Army completely surrounded the German Sixth Army outside Stalingrad. A German counteroffensive failed to break the Soviet grip.

▼ Soviet troops battle their way forward in the ruins of Stalingrad as the Red Army tightens its grip on the city. The damaged buildings indicate the savage fighting.

▲ Dead Japanese troops lying in a river bed on Guadalcanal. Thousands of Japanese soldiers died on the island.

Army with an attack by Army Group Don (13 divisions formed from Army Group A in the north) advances to within 35 miles (56 km) of Stalingrad in the face of heavy resistance. Despite Manstein's pleas for General Friedrich von Paulus' Sixth Army to launch a break-out, Adolf Hitler orders him not to retreat, but fuel shortages limit

any possible action anyway. The year ends with Soviet offensives pushing the German relief force westward. In Stalingrad, German troops are suffering severe hardships, chiefly due to the weather and supply shortages.

DECEMBER 24

POLITICS, *VICHY FRANCE*
Admiral Jean François Darlan, high commissioner in North Africa, is shot dead by a young Frenchman who accuses him of betraying the Vichy regime.

DECEMBER 30–31

SEA WAR, *ARCTIC*
At the Battle of the Barents Sea, the German pocket battleship *Lützow*, heavy cruiser *Admiral Hipper*, and six destroyers attempt to destroy the Allied Arctic convoy JW-51B. Although outnumbered, the British use superior tactics and exploit the German caution arising from orders not to sustain serious damage. Germany has one destroyer sunk, while the British also lose a destroyer and have one badly damaged. The battle outrages Adolf Hitler, who believes that the German

▲ *Henri-Philippe Pétain (left) with Admiral François Darlan, who ordered Vichy French forces in North Africa to surrender after the Allied invasion.*

fleet is tying down a huge amount of manpower and resources for very little result. Indeed, the Battle of the Barents Sea will lead to the end of significant sorties by major German surface vessels for the rest of the war.

1943

Allied successes in Papua New Guinea and the Solomon Islands, together with hard-won British and Chinese advances in Burma, forced the Japanese onto the defensive in the Pacific and Far East. Allied forces also triumphed in North Africa and went on to invade Italy, triggering the fall of Mussolini, while in the Soviet Union the clash of armor at Kursk resulted in a key German defeat.

JANUARY 1–3

EASTERN FRONT, *CAUCASUS*
Soviet troops launch offensives to encircle the German forces in the north of the region. Since August 1942 the Germans have been attempting to conquer the resource-rich area and reach the oil supplies of the Near and Middle East. The Soviet South Front moves toward Rostov and the Terek River, from where the Germans withdraw on the 3rd.

JANUARY 2

PACIFIC, *PAPUA NEW GUINEA*
US forces meet stubborn Japanese resistance after assaulting Buna on the east coast.

JANUARY 3

SEA WAR, *MEDITERRANEAN*
British Chariot "human torpedoes" damage the Italian cruiser *Ulpio* and a tanker in Palermo harbor, Sicily.

JANUARY 3–9

SEA WAR, *ATLANTIC*
U-boats destroy seven of nine tankers,

▼ *US Marine Corps pilots scramble to attack Japanese forces on Guadalcanal.*

POLITICS, *CHINA*
The Japanese puppet government declares war on both Britain and the United States.

JANUARY 10

EASTERN FRONT, *CAUCASUS*
Soviet attacks from the north, south, and east of Stalingrad split Germany's Sixth Army into pockets and isolate them from any sort of relief. Axis forces across southern Russia are under intense pressure.

JANUARY 10–31

PACIFIC, *GUADALCANAL*
A force of 50,000 US troops launches a westward offensive to destroy strong Japanese jungle positions. A disease-ridden and starving force of 15,000 Japanese troops mounts fierce resistance and fights a rearguard action at Tassafaronga Point. The Japanese have decided to evacuate Guadalcanal.

JANUARY 13

PACIFIC, *PAPUA NEW GUINEA*
The Japanese in New Guinea finally lose control of the Kokoda Trail – a major route across the Owen Stanley Range to Port Moresby, which they intended to use as an air base. Fighting between General Douglas MacArthur's Australian and US troops and the Japanese has been going on since March 1942.

carrying 100,000 tons (90,720 metric tonnes) of oil in the TM-1 convoy, which is sailing from the Caribbean to the Mediterranean.

JANUARY 5

AFRICA, *TUNISIA*
The US Fifth Army is formed under Lieutenant General Mark Clark. Allied forces form a line from Cape Serrat on the Mediterranean to Gafsa in the south. A stalemate arises in Tunisia until Field Marshal Erwin Rommel's offensive in February.

JANUARY 6

POLITICS, *GERMANY*
Admiral Erich Raeder resigns as commander-in-chief of naval forces following the blunders made at the Battle of the Barents Sea in December. Admiral Karl Doenitz replaces him.

JANUARY 6–9

SEA WAR, *PACIFIC*
At the Battle of Huon Gulf, the Allies gather aircraft from across the south-west Pacific to launch repeated attacks on Japanese convoys carrying troops to Papua New Guinea. Three transports and some 80 Japanese aircraft are lost. Allied casualties during the action are comparatively light.

▲ *A German U-boat undergoes routine maintenance while on the lookout for Allied shipping in the Mediterranean.*

▼ *Admiral Karl Doenitz (third from left), replaced Erich Raeder as commander-in-chief of German naval forces.*

JANUARY 14–23

POLITICS, *ALLIES*

British Prime Minister Winston Churchill and US President Franklin D. Roosevelt meet at Casablanca, Morocco. The conference highlights differences between them regarding the defeat of Hitler.

The British want to keep fighting in the Mediterranean before the main attack on Europe via the English Channel. They propose invasions of Sicily and Italy as a means of drawing German reserves away from France and the Low Countries, which will precipitate the fall of Mussolini; and establishing air bases in Italy, from where German armaments factories and Romanian oil-producing facilities can be bombed.

The Americans believe this will only dissipate resources for the cross-Channel invasion, and tie down forces in a sideshow. They believe the quickest way to defeat Hitler is an invasion of northern France. However, as a cross-Channel invasion is not possible in 1943, they grudgingly accept the invasion of Sicily (though no invasion of Italy is planned).

A further source of disagreement is Roosevelt's "unconditional surrender" call. Churchill wants to split the Axis by treating Italy differently, but is persuaded to go along with the US view after considering that a more lenient treatment of Italy will only antagonize Greece and Yugoslavia.

▲ *Jewish fighters reinforce a strongpoint in the Warsaw Ghetto at the beginning of their uprising against the Germans.*

JANUARY 15–22

AFRICA, *LIBYA*

The British Eighth Army attacks Field Marshal Erwin Rommel's forces at Buerat and pursues them to the Homs and Tarhuna area, approximately 100 miles (150 km) from Tripoli, the capital. British forces reach Homs on the 19th, and Rommel resumes his retreat toward Tunisia. Although Rommel has been ordered to defend Tripoli, he decides to save his troops and abandons the city on the 22nd to make a stand around Mareth.

▼ *Prime Minister Churchill and President Roosevelt at the Casablanca Conference, where differences of strategy arose between Great Britain and the United States.*

JANUARY 16–17

EASTERN FRONT, *CAUCASUS*
The Soviet Fifty-sixth Army begins an attack to take the town of Krasnador. Southern Front forces are halted by German resistance between the northern Donets and Manych Rivers.

JANUARY 18

EASTERN FRONT, *POLAND*
Jewish fighters in the Warsaw Ghetto begin attacking German troops. Resistance was triggered by the resumption of deportations to extermination camps, which has been suspended since October 1942.

JANUARY 21

PACIFIC, *PAPUA NEW GUINEA*
After capturing Sanananda in New Guinea, the Allies prepare to advance northwestward to clear the Japanese from Salamua and Lae. Allied control of the sea and air around Papua New Guinea will force the Japanese finally to abandon the island.

JANUARY 29

PACIFIC, *PAPUA NEW GUINEA*
Allied troops force the Japanese to withdraw from Wau at the start of the Bulldog Track, the second route used by the Japanese for their offensive against Port Moresby.

JANUARY 30

AIR WAR, *GERMANY*
In the escalating Allied air offensive, British bombers make the first daylight bombing raid over Berlin.

KEY PERSONALITIES

GENERAL DOUGLAS MACARTHUR

Douglas MacArthur (1880–1964) was appointed commander of US troops in the Far East in July 1941. After the Japanese declared war in December, he directed the defense of the Philippines from the islands. He finally left for Australia in March 1942 to assume command of the whole of the Southwest Pacific theater.

MacArthur then led a campaign to free Papua New Guinea before commanding the Pacific "island-hopping" operations that finally reached the Philippines in October 1944. In April 1945, MacArthur became commander of the US Army in the Pacific and then Supreme Allied Commander for the occupation of Japan. In this role he accepted the Japanese surrender.

This flamboyant general always appeared to achieve his objectives yet maintain low casualty rates. His self-publicity has, however, led some historians to scrutinize the claims he made about his campaigns.

FEBRUARY 1–9

PACIFIC, *GUADALCANAL*
Japanese Navy warships evacuate 13,000 troops in night operations from the island. Their abandonment of Guadalcanal marks the first major land defeat of Japan. The Japanese have lost 10,000 men killed; the Americans some 1600.

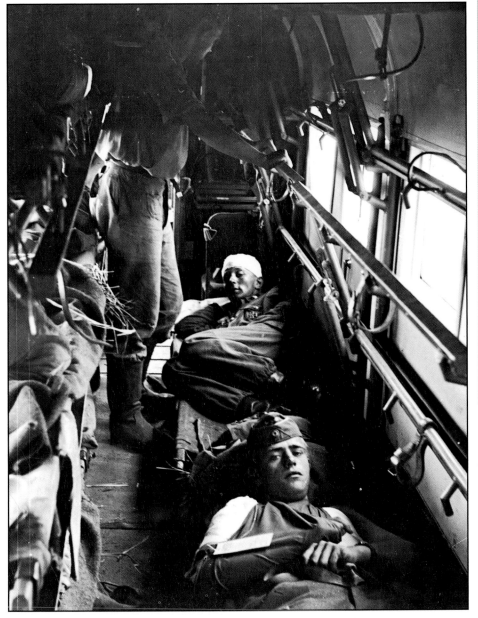

◀ *Some of the lucky ones: German casualties evacuated out of Stalingrad before the defeat of the Sixth Army.*

313

FEBRUARY 2

▶ *British Avro Lancaster heavy bombers were used against German U-boats in the Bay of Biscay.*

FEBRUARY 2

EASTERN FRONT, *CAUCASUS*
The siege of Stalingrad ends: Field Marshal Friedrich von Paulus and 93,000 German troops surrender. The Sixth Army has finally collapsed under the strain of supply shortages and constant attacks masterminded by Marshal Georgi Zhukov.

FEBRUARY 4

AIR WAR, *FRANCE*
British and US bombers launch Operation Gondola with a series of raids aimed at destroying U-boats in the Bay of Biscay. Bombers use immensely powerful searchlights to illuminate submarines during attacks.

▼ *Some of Orde Wingate's Chindits who operated behind Japanese lines in Burma in February 1943.*

FEBRUARY 8

EASTERN FRONT, *UKRAINE*
In their continuing offensive Soviet forces take the city of Kursk, which will be the site of a major battle.

FEBRUARY 9

SEA WAR, *MEDITERRANEAN*
An Axis convoy carrying reinforcements to Tunisia leaves Italy. Malta-based Allied aircraft sink 10 vessels between February 9 and March 22. Minefields and British submarines also destroy several of the ships.

FEBRUARY 12–14

EASTERN FRONT, *CAUCASUS*
The Soviets capture Krasnodar on the 12th and Rostov on the Don River two days later.

FEBRUARY 14–22

AFRICA, *TUNISIA*
Field Marshal Erwin Rommel launches an attack northwest from his fortified zone at Mareth to break through Allied forces between the Axis front and Bône on the coast. In the Battle of Kasserine Pass his forces strike the US II Corps and cause panic among the ranks.

US forces are 100 miles (160 km) from Gabès, a key part of Germany's Mareth Line because of its crossroads, port, and airfield. German troops exploit poor US command, land and air coordination, unit dispositions, and the inexperience of some troops. Attacks reach Thala until they lose momentum and Rommel orders a withdrawal. He loses 2000 men; the Americans 10,000.

FEBRUARY 15

EASTERN FRONT, *UKRAINE*
Kharkov and other cities are liberated as Soviet forces reoccupy territory held by the Germans. Stalin has begun to think of total victory in 1943.

FEBRUARY 16–21

HOME FRONT, *GERMANY*

Student demonstrations against Hitler's regime take place in Munich. Protests in other university cities in Germany and Austria then occur. Hans and Sophie Scholl, leaders of the anti-Nazi White Rose student group at the University of Munich, are beheaded on the 21st.

FEBRUARY 18

FAR EAST, *BURMA*

Brigadier Orde Wingate launches the first British Chindit mission. This 3000-strong, long-range penetration force aims to operate behind Japanese lines and disrupt communications. The Chindits are to be supplied by air. The six-week mission has limited military success but Prime Minister Winston Churchill is impressed by Wingate's unorthodox methods. As a result, further Chindit operations in Burma will be sanctioned.

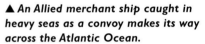

▲ *An Allied merchant ship caught in heavy seas as a convoy makes its way across the Atlantic Ocean.*

FEBRUARY 18-27

EASTERN FRONT, *UKRAINE*

Field Marshal Erich von Manstein, commander of Army Group Don, launches a counteroffensive against the Red Army to crush the enemy thrust to the Dniepr River. Using four panzer corps, he isolates three Soviet armies, inflicting severe losses on the Red Army.

FEBRUARY 20–25

SEA WAR, *ATLANTIC*

During U-boat attacks, Allied convoy ON-166 loses 15 of its 49 ships. Only one German submarine is sunk.

FEBRUARY 21

PACIFIC, *SOLOMONS*

US forces land on Russell Island. This is their first move in the campaign to capture the island chain. The operation, code-named Cartwheel, eventually aims to seal off the key Japanese air and sea base at Rabaul in New Britain. The US Pacific commanders Admiral Chester Nimitz and General Douglas MacArthur have devised an "island-hopping" strategy whereby certain

◄ *Letters from home bring a smile to the faces of these two German soldiers of Army Group Don on the Eastern Front.*

315

selected islands are retaken, while heavily-defended Japanese positions are bypassed. Allied aircraft and sea power will then isolate these strong-points, preventing them from being a threat. They will "wither on the vine."

FEBRUARY 23–24

SEA WAR, *ATLANTIC*
Seven tankers from the UC-1 Allied convoy are sunk by a U-boat group.

FEBRUARY 26–28

AFRICA, *TUNISIA*
Colonel General Jürgen von Arnim's Fifth Tank Army in northeast Tunisia finally launches a counterattack from

the Mareth Line that should have been made during the previous series of attacks. It is unsuccessful.

FEBRUARY 28

POLITICS, *GERMANY*
General Heinz Guderian is appointed "Inspector-General of Armored Troops" and is given wide-ranging powers to strengthen Germany's tank arm.
WESTERN FRONT, *NORWAY*
Nine Norwegian paratroopers from Great Britain sabotage the Norsk Hydro power station where "heavy water" is made for atomic research.

MARCH 2–5

SEA WAR, *PACIFIC*
At the Battle of the Bismarck Sea eight Japanese transports and eight destroyers are attacked while sailing from Rabaul to Lae in New Guinea. US

◄ *German troops and armor await orders to advance against Kharkov in February 1943.*

nine, south of the Mareth Line. They attack across a broad front but fail to concentrate and are decisively thrown back. Field Marshal Rommel, whose morale and health are both deteriorating, leaves North Africa.

MARCH 6–20

SEA WAR, *ATLANTIC*
Two Atlantic convoys (HX-229 and SC-122) fight a running battle with 20 U-boats of a "Wolf Pack" in the Atlantic.

KEY PERSONALITIES

ADMIRAL CHESTER NIMITZ

Admiral Chester Nimitz (1885–1966) was appointed commander of the US Pacific Fleet just after the Pearl Harbor attack in December 1941. From April 1942, he was made commander of all naval, sea, and air forces in the Pacific Ocean Area.

Aided by US codebreaking efforts, he was able to anticipate and defeat Japanese plans at the Battles of the Coral Sea in May and Midway in June. These actions secured US naval superiority in the Pacific by inflicting decisive defeats on Japan's carrier capability. Nimitz then went on to lead a series of strikes against the Japanese Navy and supported the "island-hopping" operations to establish Allied control over the Pacific region. He was a strong advocate of this amphibious strategy, which pushed the Japanese back across the ocean to Japan. He was made a Fleet Admiral in 1944 and was present at the Japanese surrender in 1945. One of his strengths was being able to achieve his goals without antagonizing his colleagues.

▲ *Kharkov's battle-scarred Red Square following Manstein's brilliant capture of the city in March 1943.*

and Australian aircraft and torpedo-boats sink all the transports and four destroyers. The Allies lose six aircraft; the Japanese 25. This is the last Japanese attempt to reinforce their presence in New Guinea.

MARCH 5

AIR WAR, *GERMANY*
The British launch a four-month offensive against the Ruhr industrial area. A force of 367 bombers strikes the Krupp Works at Essen in the first attack; 14 aircraft are lost.

MARCH 6–9

AFRICA, *TUNISIA*
The Germans attempt to disrupt General Bernard Montgomery's preparations for a final offensive at Mede-

Although 21 ships are sunk, only one U-boat is lost. The Allies cannot afford such attrition.

MARCH 13

HOME FRONT, *GERMANY*
An unsuccessful assassination attempt is made on Adolf Hitler by army officers. They place a bomb in his aircraft but it fails to explode.

MARCH 14

EASTERN FRONT, *UKRAINE*
After his spearheads reached the Donets River, Manstein's forces have trapped and destroyed the Soviet Third Tank Army. In all, the Red Army has abandoned nearly 6,000 square miles (9,600 sq km) of newly-won ground in the face of Manstein's brilliant armored counteroffensive, which has stabilized the German front in southern Russia. Manstein has averted a total Axis collapse.

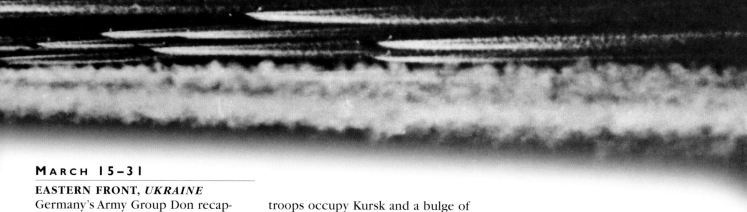

MARCH 15–31

EASTERN FRONT, *UKRAINE*

Germany's Army Group Don recaptures Kharkov, and Belgorod three days later. By the end of the month the Soviet Voronezh Front is back on the east bank of the northern Donets. The final phase of Manstein's offensive – a combined attack with Army Group Center's Second Panzer Army heading south from Orel toward Kursk – is halted by the spring thaw.

This victory encourages the German high command to launch Operation Citadel, an ambitious plan to destroy the Soviet Central and Voronezh Fronts in the Kursk salient to the north of Kharkov. Over 500,000 Red Army

▼ *Italian troops on the Mareth Line.*

troops occupy Kursk and a bulge of land stretching 100 miles (160 km) westward from the Soviet line.

MARCH 20–28

AFRICA, *TUNISIA*

Allied forces under General Bernard Montgomery launch a carefully-planned attack against the Mareth Line. The line's principal defenses along the banks of the Wadi Zigzaou are penetrated on the 21st–22nd but the 15th Panzer Division successfully counterattacks. Montgomery, however, develops an outflanking move into a major offensive, and by the 26th the Axis forces have retreated northward to the El Hamma Plain. The weakened German forces fall back to Wadi Akarit by the 28th, while many of their Italians allies surrender.

MARCH 26

SEA WAR, *PACIFIC*

At the Battle of the Kommandorsky Islands in the Bering Sea, two US cruisers and four destroyers engage four Japanese cruisers and five destroyers. The Japanese abandon the action just before they can exploit their numerical superiority. Both sides have a cruiser badly damaged.

MARCH 27

AFRICA, *TUNISIA*

General Sir Harold Alexander sends the US 34th Infantry Division to seize the Foundouk Pass but heavy artillery fire halts its advance.

MARCH 30

SEA WAR, *ARCTIC*

Britain suspends the Arctic convoys to the Soviet Union because it cannot provide enough escorts to guard against the increasing number of German warships in Norway.

APRIL 5–6

AFRICA, *TUNISIA*

The British Eighth Army attacks the Wadi Akarit Line, a defensive position situated across the route into Tunisia. The line cannot be outflanked. While

▲ *Trailing vapor, US B-17s Flying Fortresses bomb the German city of Dresden in daylight.*

the assault is successful, the British fail to exploit their breakthrough and Axis forces are able to regroup.

APRIL 7–10

AFRICA, *TUNISIA*

The British IX Corps, which includes the US 34th Infantry Division, attacks the Foundouk Pass but the Axis forces

▼ *Members of the Polish Commission look at evidence of the Katyn Forest massacre.*

hold the area until they can successfully disengage the bulk of their units from the fighting.

APRIL 7–13

AIR WAR, *SOLOMONS*
Over 180 Japanese aircraft begin Operation I by attacking Allied shipping off Guadalcanal. On the 11th, the Japanese attack ships off New Guinea and raid Port Moresby airfield on the 12th, and British at Milne Bay the following day. They sink a destroyer, one corvette, one tanker, two cargo ships, and destroy some 20 aircraft. The massive aerial operation against shipping and airfields, however, does not achieve the scale of success that the Japanese anticipated.

APRIL 8

POLITICS, *JAPAN*
General Kawbe succeeds General Iida as commander of Japanese forces operating in Burma.

APRIL 10–12

AFRICA, *TUNISIA*
British troops enter Sfax, one of the ports vital for reducing the long supply lines from Tripoli, and finally halt at Enfidaville, southeast of Tunis. Axis forces are now established in their final defensive line running from Cape Serrat on the Mediterranean to Enfidaville. Defeat for the Axis forces is inevitable. Allied sea and air control denies them any reinforcements. They are determined to fight on, however, in order to delay the Allied plan to invade Italy until the fall, when deteriorating weather is likely to disrupt any Allied landings.

APRIL 12

HOME FRONT, *POLAND*
The German authorities announce that they have found a mass grave in Katyn Forest. They claim that it contains the bodies of some 10,000 Polish officers executed by the Soviet secret police in 1939. The Soviets claim that this is deliberate German propaganda aimed at discrediting them. Subsequent investigations reveal the Soviets were indeed responsible for the massacre of 4500 officers at Katyn Forest.

APRIL 17

AIR WAR, *GERMANY*
The US 8th Army Air Force attacks Bremen's aircraft factories from its bases in eastern England. It is one of its largest raids to date. Sixteen of the 115 B-17 Flying Fortress bombers from the raid are lost.

▶ *A Jewish fighter surrenders in the Warsaw Ghetto as the SS fights its way through the city street by street.*

319

APRIL 18

▲ Admiral Minichi Koga, commander of the Japanese Combined Fleet.

APRIL 18

AIR WAR, *TUNISIA*
An operation by 100 German transport aircraft to fly supplies to the Axis forces in North Africa suffers a devastating attack by US fighters. Over half the transport aircraft and 10 fighters are shot down.

APRIL 19–22

AFRICA, *TUNISIA*
General Bernard Montgomery, eager for his Eighth Army to seal victory in Tunisia, launches an offensive toward Enfidaville. The attack gains little ground and casualties are heavy.

APRIL 19

EASTERN FRONT, *POLAND*
The destruction of the Warsaw Ghetto begins with German SS troops making a large-scale attack. The Jewish fighters construct a network of hiding places and fight with small-arms or improvised weapons. Up to 310,000 Jews have already been deported from the ghetto, to be executed or imprisoned in labor camps.

APRIL 21

POLITICS, *JAPAN*
Admiral Minichi Koga succeeds Admiral Isoroku Yamamoto as commander-in-chief of the Combined Fleet. US codebreakers had learned that Yamamoto was visiting bases in the southwest Pacific and aircraft were deployed to intercept the fleet. The admiral was killed after his aircraft was destroyed by US fighters on the 18th.

APRIL 22

AFRICA, *TUNISIA*
The British First Army and US II Corps prepare to breach the series

▼ Guns and vehicles of the British Royal Artillery Regiment on the road to Tunis during the last phase of the war in Africa.

of interlocking strongpoints across the high ground above the approaches to Tunis. The First Army attacks between Medjez-el-Bab and Bou Arada while the US II Corps farther north strikes toward Mateur and Bizerta. The main thrust is made by the First Army's V Corps along a direct line toward Tunis from Medjez-el-Bab. To achieve this, they have to capture two major Axis positions on the high ground at Peter's Corner and Longstop Hill along the Medjerda River.

APRIL 26–30

AFRICA, *TUNISIA*
The First Army's V Corps captures Longstop Hill and reaches Djebel Bou Aoukaz. From April 28–30 the Germans counterattack and take Djebel Bou Aoukaz. Meanwhile, the US II Corps fights a bitter battle to capture Hill 609. The First Army's advance is being blocked by protracted engagements against strong Axis positions. To achieve a breakthrough across the Medjerda Valley, the Eighth Army sends two divisions and a brigade to bolster the offensive.

APRIL 28

SEA WAR, *ATLANTIC*
The Allied convoy ONS-5 begins a seven-day running battle against 51 U-boats. The convoy achieves considerable success despite the limited air

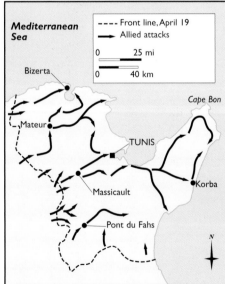

▲ The final Allied victory in Tunisia brought an end to the North African campaign. Total Axis losses were 620,000 men, a third of them German. The Third Reich could not afford such wastage.

support it receives. Seven U-boats are sunk and 17 damaged. The convoy loses 13 of its 42 ships.

APRIL 30

ESPIONAGE, *BRITAIN*

The British release a corpse, dressed as an officer and carrying false documents, into the Mediterranean Sea as part of a deception operation to divert German attention from Allied plans to invade Sicily. The corpse is recovered by the Germans, who find the false documents containing details of an Allied attack on Greece and Sardinia. As a result German reinforcements are sent to these areas.

MAY 3

POLITICS, *UNITED STATES*

General Frank Andrews, US commander in the European theater, is killed in an air crash. General Jacob Devers is named as his replacement.

MAY 5–7

AFRICA, *TUNISIA*

Reinforcements sent by the Eighth Army help the First Army recapture Djebel Bou Aoukaz and enable the British 7th Armored Division to advance into open "tank country." General Sir Harold Alexander can now exploit the numerical and material superiority of his armies against the

Axis forces defending Tunis. Massicault is reached on the 6th, and tanks enter Tunis on the 7th. The US III Corps reaches Bizerta the same day. The Axis forces in North Africa are facing imminent defeat, with no chance of escaping the Allies.

MAY 11–29

PACIFIC, *ALEUTIANS*

A US 12,000-man amphibious force attacks Attu Island, one of Japan's fortified positions in the northern Pacific. During the bitter offensive, only 29 of the 2500 Japanese survive. US forces sustain 561 fatalities and have 1136 men wounded.

▲ *Water gushes from the damaged Möhne dam following the successful raid by the British Royal Air Force.*

MAY 12–25

POLITICS, *ALLIES*

The Allied Trident Conference is held in Washington. Churchill and Roosevelt reinforce the "Germany First" strategy by agreeing to intensify bombing raids in Europe. A date is set for the cross-Channel invasion (May 1, 1944) and Britain urges that the Sicilian attack is extended to the Italian mainland. The British feel that the United States is committing increasing resources to the Pacific at the expense of European military operations.

MAY 13

AFRICA, *TUNISIA*

Axis forces officially surrender. Some 620,000 casualties and prisoners have been sustained by Germany and Italy. Allied campaign losses: French 20,000; British 19,000; and US 18,500.

MAY 16–17

AIR WAR, *GERMANY*

The dams on the Möhne and Eder Rivers are attacked by 19 British Lancaster aircraft, which are carrying

◀ *A happy Eisenhower (center) and General Montgomery after the Allied victory in Africa.*

◀ A German fireman struggles to douse the flames after a heavy British raid on Dortmund in late May.

MAY 23–29

AIR WAR, GERMANY

A massive British raid is made on Dortmund. Another offensive against Wuppertal on the 29th kills 2450 people. British bombers are intensifying their large-scale night attacks against industrial centers.

MAY 26

BALKANS, YUGOSLAVIA

An Axis force of 120,000 men attacks 16,000 communist partisans in Montenegro. A British military mission arrives on the 27th to meet partisan leader Joseph Tito, who confirms their intelligence reports that the rival Chetnik resistance group now supports the Axis forces. Since the fall of 1941, Tito has led a full-scale campaign in the province of Serbia but has since endured several major attacks from the Axis occupiers. Partisan forces have been preserved by withdrawing to the mountains and are now to be strengthened by large quantities of Allied aid.

JUNE 1–11

AIR WAR, ITALY

A round-the-clock naval and air bombardment of Pantellaria Island forces it to surrender on the 11th. Italian propaganda had falsely hailed it as an impregnable fortress and, consequently, the Allies had considered it an obstacle blocking their plans to invade Sicily and the mainland.

specially-designed "bouncing bombs." The dams generate electricity and supply water to the Ruhr region. The squadron led by Wing Commander Guy Gibson loses eight aircraft. The raid causes some disruption to industry, and boosts morale in Great Britain. German casualties are high, particularly among forced foreign workers.

MAY 16

HOME FRONT, POLAND

The Warsaw Ghetto uprising ends. Some 14,000 Jews have been killed, 22,000 sent to concentration camps, and 20,000 to labor camps.

MAY 22

SEA WAR, ATLANTIC

Admiral Karl Doenitz suspends patrols in the northern Atlantic. Some 56 submarines have been destroyed since April alone in a campaign of attrition the Germans cannot afford.

▶ Communist partisans on the move in Montenegro as an Axis force of 120,000 men launches a campaign to wipe them out. The offensive failed.

Escalating losses of both vessels and experienced crews force him to redeploy his remaining forces to less hazardous Caribbean waters and the Azores. Improved tactics, radar, code-breaking, air cover, and the increased building of escorts have combined to strengthen convoy defenses.

◄ *Operation Pointblank in action: the ruins of a German fighter factory after being bombed by the Allies.*

Claude Auchinleck succeeds him as commander-in-chief of India although a new East Asia Command will reduce his importance. Churchill has made these appointments as he has lost confidence in their capabilities and wishes to limit their military roles.

JUNE 20–24

AIR WAR, *GERMANY/ITALY*
The Allies launch their first "shuttle" raid. British bombers attack Friedrichshafen in Germany and then fly on to refuel in North Africa. On their return flight to Britain, they attack La Spezia naval base in Italy.

JUNE 21

PACIFIC, *SOLOMONS*
US forces begin an offensive against the New Georgia Island group. Munda airfield is the first major objective. The Solomon offensives are aided by vital reconnaissance information provided by Allied "coastwatchers" based on these little-known islands and equipped with high-powered radios. New Georgia airfields sustain air and sea bombardments while US warships mine the surrounding seas to destroy ships bringing reinforcements and supplies.

JULY 5

POLITICS, *POLAND*
General Wladyslaw Raczkiewicz, prime minister

JUNE 3

POLITICS, *FREE FRENCH*
Rival leaders General Charles de Gaulle and General Henri Giraud agree to share the presidency of the Committee of National Liberation.

JUNE 10

AIR WAR, *GERMANY*
Operation Pointblank is launched. The offensive by British and US bomber forces will last until the 1944 cross-Channel invasion. US strategy concentrates on daylight precision raids to destroy Germany's aircraft industry and its air force. British attacks focus on

night saturation bombing to undermine Germany's economy and civilian morale. Aircrews are assisted by the "Pathfinder" system, whereby targets are fixed by radar and marked by flares.

JUNE 18

POLITICS, *BRITAIN*
Field Marshal Sir Archibald Wavell becomes Viceroy of India. General Sir

▶ *The blazing hull of a Japanese ship hit by US aircraft off the Solomon Islands.*

JULY 5-6

▶ *Both sides lost heavily at Kursk. This Soviet tank crew fell foul of a German antitank gun and panzergrenadiers.*

of the Polish government-in-exile, is killed in an air crash. His deputy, Stanislaw Mikolajczyk, replaces him.

JULY 5-6

PACIFIC, *SOLOMONS*
The US 43rd Infantry Division leads the main landing on New Georgia. That night US and Japanese destroyers clash at the Battle of Kula Gulf. One Japanese destroyer is sunk.

JULY 6

EASTERN FRONT, *UKRAINE*
Soviet intelligence has uncovered the plans for the offensive by 900,000 German troops against Kursk. The Germans believe that a victory on the Eastern Front will bolster domestic morale and preserve the Axis coalition, while also demonstrating to the Allies that the Nazis can still achieve victory.

From March to July, they gather 900,000 troops but the Red Army succeeds in establishing numerical superiority in men (1.3 million) and equipment. Consequently, German units are exposed to aerial and land bombardment while the Red Army prepares for the attack.

The German Army Group Center's Ninth Army, south of Orel, and Field Marshal Erich von Manstein's Fourth Panzer Army, north of Kharkov, open Operation Citadel with an offensive

against the salient. The Ninth Army under Field Marshal Gunther von Kluge only penetrates six miles (9 km) and loses 250,000 men. Over 6000 German and Soviet tanks and assault guns take part in the war's greatest armored battle. Special attention is given by the Soviets to antitank guns and obstacles. The Germans deploy 200 aircraft for the operation and the Soviets 2400.

JULY 6-9

EASTERN FRONT, *UKRAINE*
Increasing numbers of German troops reinforce the Kursk offensive but the

▼ *Polish President Wladyslaw Raczkiewicz, seen here reviewing sailors, was killed in a plane crash on July 5.*

Red Army stands firm. The Soviets counter the Germans with a deep defensive network while heavily-armed antitank units deliver concentrated fire against German armor. The Soviets quickly gain air superiority and fighters provide valuable tactical support. These measures combine to prevent the German attacks penetrating the Soviet defenses.

JULY 7-13

PACIFIC, *PAPUA NEW GUINEA*
The Japanese strongpoint at Mumbo, 10 miles (16 km) inland from Salamaua, is seized by the Australians. US and Australian forces are battling to dislodge the Japanese from the high ground they have retreated to.

▼ *The Royal Navy brings troops ashore as Allied units push farther inland on Sicily.*

Allied reinforcements are to be landed in order to clear the Japanese from northeast New Guinea.

JULY 9

MEDITERRANEAN, *SICILY*

Chaotic US and British airborne landings begin the attack on Sicily. Preparatory bomber attacks have already hit air bases on Sicily, Sardinia, and on the mainland. Mussolini expects the Allied attack to be against Sardinia. The main strategic objectives are to clear the Mediterranean sea-lanes, divert Axis forces from the Eastern Front, and possibly apply pressure on Italy to accelerate its capitulation.

JULY 10

MEDITERRANEAN, *SICILY*

An invasion fleet of 2500 vessels carries General Bernard Montgomery's Eighth Army and General George Patton's Seventh Army

▲ *German armored personnel carriers and assault guns (note armored skirts) rumble forward at the Battle of Kursk.*

to southern Sicily. The Italians are surprised as they did not expect an attack during stormy weather. The Allies will eventually land 160,000 men to fight General Guzzoni's Sixth Army (230,000 Italian and 40,000 German troops). Landings are assisted by a new amphibious truck – the DUKW.

JULY 11–12

MEDITERRANEAN, *SICILY*

The German *Hermann Goering* Panzer Division almost reaches US forces on the coast near Gela and Licata but the counterattack is obstructed by US paratroopers. General Sir Harold Alexander, overall commander of the operation, expects the Eighth Army to advance up the east coast toward the key bases at

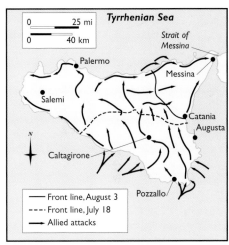

▲ *The Allied invasion of Sicily involved the largest seaborne assault mounted to date. During the initial assault seven divisions, one armored combat team, two commandos, and an assault brigade were put ashore against an enemy almost equal in numbers.*

Catania and Messina. The less experienced Seventh Army is to protect the British flank and rear.

JULY 12–13

EASTERN FRONT, *UKRAINE*

At Kursk, the Soviets launch a counteroffensive around Prokhorovka and an enormous tank battle develops. Field Marshal von Manstein's Fourth Panzer Army advances 25 miles (40 km) but loses 10,000 men and 350 tanks. Farther north, the Soviet Bryansk and West Fronts begin an offensive around Orel. Adolf Hitler calls off Operation

JULY 15–23

Citadel on the 13th. The last major German offensive on the Eastern Front has been a costly failure with the loss of over 550 tanks and 500,000 men killed, wounded, or missing. It is a major disaster for Germany, not least because the carefully-gathered strategic armored reserves have been wiped out in the fighting.

KEY PERSONALITIES

FIELD MARSHAL ERICH VON MANSTEIN

Erich von Manstein (1887–1973) was chief of staff to General Gerd von Rundstedt in 1939 before being demoted for challenging the high command's strategy for the invasion of France in 1940. He advocated a surprise thrust through the Ardennes, and when Hitler adopted this plan, his fortunes changed. Manstein led an infantry corps with distinction during the invasion of France and then took command of an armored Corps, which he led at the start of Operation Barbarossa.

By September 1941, he had risen to command the Eleventh Army on the Eastern Front. His conquest of the Crimea earned him a reputation as a top field commander and he became a field marshal in 1942. Manstein's use of armor to seize Kharkov in February 1943, when he yielded ground in the face of Soviet numerical superiority before counterattacking with his panzer corps when the enemy was suffering attrition and at the end of his supply lines, was the greatest German counteroffensive of the war.

His appreciation of the need for a flexible defensive strategy brought him into conflict with Hitler. The Führer's narrow strategic view of the Eastern Front was based on holding ground. The field marshal's plans were thus considered an abandonment of Germany's front. As a result of this conflict over strategy, Manstein was dismissed in 1944.

▲ Troops of the British Eighth Army in Catania, Sicily, in July 1943. Palermo, the capital, fell at the end of the month.

SEA WAR, *PACIFIC*

At the Battle of Kolombangara, off New Georgia, a Japanese squadron led by Admiral Izaki engages three US light cruisers and 10 destroyers. One US destroyer is sunk and one New Zealand and two US cruisers are damaged. The Japanese lose a cruiser.

JULY 15–23

MEDITERRANEAN, *SICILY*

The US Seventh Army advances westward aiming to seize the capital Palermo with an armored thrust.

JULY 17

EASTERN FRONT, *UKRAINE*

The Soviet Voronezh Front, just to the south of Kursk, and the Steppe Front, to the west of Kharkov, begin pursuing the German forces, which are now retreating in some confusion.

JULY 17–18

MEDITERRANEAN, *SICILY*

The British Eighth Army strikes northward toward the Axis stronghold at Catania but meets determined resistance from the *Hermann Goering* Division on the plain beneath Mount Etna. The British therefore decide to go around Catania toward Mount Etna, while the US Seventh Army moves along the north coast toward Messina.

JULY 19

POLITICS, *AXIS*

Benito Mussolini and Adolf Hitler meet at Fletre in northern Italy. The Italian dictator fails to tell Hitler that his country is to cease fighting and instead endorses the proposal for Germany to assume military control in Italy. The first major Allied air raid is made on the Italian capital, Rome, by US bombers on the same day.

JULY 23

MEDITERRANEAN, *SICILY*

The US Seventh Army enters Palermo and the west coast ports of Trapani and Marsala.

JULY 23–24

EASTERN FRONT, *UKRAINE*

The German armies have now withdrawn to the lines held at the start of Operation Citadel at Kursk.

JULY 23–30

MEDITERRANEAN, *SICILY*

The Allies drive to Messina while German forces try to save the Sicilian bridgehead and the airfields around Catania. US forces move along the north coast and Highway 120 inland.

JULY 24

POLITICS, *ITALY*

The Fascist Grand Council, the key constitutional body for debating government and party decisions, meets for the first time since 1939. Dino Grandi, former minister of justice, proposes that military authority should be given to the king and not Mussolini. His motion is approved.

JULY 24–AUGUST 2

AIR WAR, *GERMANY*

A series of massive British raids are made on Hamburg. The attacks are made over four nights and last until August 2. The dropping of foil strips to confuse German radar equipment (the "Window" system) helps the bombers. Around 50,000 people are killed and 800,000 are made homeless. The attack on the 27th–28th creates a firestorm, which blazes so intensely that the flames suck oxygen from the area nearby. This creates a "hurricane" effect that feeds the flames, which travel at great speed.

JULY 25

POLITICS, *ITALY*

The king of Italy relieves Benito Mussolini of his office. Mussolini is arrested and Marshal Pietro Badoglio forms a new government that lasts only six weeks. The government deters Germany from occupying the entire country by promising to fight on. Badoglio hopes, however, that the

Allies will land and occupy most of Italy quickly and therefore confine any fighting to the north.

JULY 26

EASTERN FRONT, *UKRAINE*

The German high command orders forces around Orel to withdraw to the previously-prepared Hagen Line, just to the east of Bryansk.

AUGUST 1

AIR WAR, *ROMANIA*

A US force of 178 bombers make a 1000-mile (1500-km) flight from Libya to attack the Ploesti oil fields, which provide essential supplies to Axis forces. The low-level attack is met by fierce antiaircraft fire and 54 aircraft are lost. Damage to the oil fields is

superficial but increases Hitler's fears over the area's susceptibility to air raids or ground attack.

AUGUST 2

EASTERN FRONT, *UKRAINE*

Adolf Hitler orders Field Marshal Erich von Manstein to hold the line firmly around Kharkov. Hitler is keen to prevent the Eastern Front being pushed farther westward by the likely Soviet summer offensive. However, German forces in the region lack the manpower, tanks, and artillery to halt the Red Army permanently.

▼ *The aftermath of the raids on the city of Hamburg. The bombing and firestorms killed an estimated 50,000 people.*

AUGUST 3

AUGUST 3

POLITICS, *ITALY*
The Italian regime puts out peace-feelers to the Allies. In reply, the Allies lay down the following conditions for an armistice: the handing over of the fleet; all Italian territories to be made available to the Allies for military operations; Allied prisoners in Italy to be freed and not be allowed to fall into German hands; and the disarming of all ground and air forces.

AUGUST 3–16

MEDITERRANEAN, *SICILY*
Italian forces withdraw from Sicily. Catania surrenders to the British on the 5th.

AUGUST 4–11

EASTERN FRONT, *UKRAINE*
Red Army units retake Orel and Belgorod by the 5th. The Voronezh and Steppe Fronts are near Kharkov.

AUGUST 5–22

PACIFIC, *SOLOMONS*
US forces capture the important Munda airfield on New Georgia Island. Japanese resistance on the island disintegrates and the defenders are not to be reinforced. A sea evacuation is made from the north of the island to neighboring Kolombangara on the 22nd.

AUGUST 6

MEDITERRANEAN, *ITALY*
German reinforcements begin arriving in Italy. Hitler orders four operations: the rescue of Mussolini from imprisonment by the new Italian government, the formation of a strong Italian defense line, the revival of fascism, and the seizure of the Italian fleet. Hitler also wishes to occupy as much of Italy as possible, using it as a bastion to keep the war as far away from Germany as possible.

AUGUST 6–7

SEA WAR, *PACIFIC*
Four Japanese destroyers carrying troops and supplies to Kolombangara in New Georgia fight a night action against six US destroyers at the Battle of Vela Gulf. Torpedo strikes sink three Japanese destroyers and claim 1210 lives. No US vessels are damaged.

AUGUST 8–17

MEDITERRANEAN, *SICILY*
US forces advancing along the coast are assisted by amphibious landings east of San Stefano. British, Canadian, and Free French Moroccan troops

▼ *US bombers on their way to hit the Romanian Ploesti oil fields at the beginning of August.*

▲ *The Quebec Conference, where a British plan for a cross-Channel invasion of Europe in mid-1944 was agreed.*

have fought a series of bitter actions to overcome determined German resistance to the southwest of Mount Etna. The Germans finally start withdrawing on the 11th and evacuate 100,000 Axis troops before US forces enter Messina on the 17th.

Around 10,000 Germans have been killed or captured during the campaign. The Italians have lost 132,000 men, mainly prisoners. The British and US forces have suffered 7000 fatalities and 15,000 men have been wounded. The capture of Sicily means the Allies have a springboard for the invasion of Italy.

AUGUST 13-24

POLITICS, *ALLIES*
British Prime Minister Winston Churchill and US President Franklin D. Roosevelt attend the First Quebec Conference in Canada. Britain reaffirms US control over the Pacific theater, where it is intensifying operations. Further Chindit operations are proposed for Burma and aid to Chiang-Kai-shek in China will continue. Vice Admiral Lord Louis Mountbatten takes charge of Southeast Asia Command.

Fighting in Italy will intensify to capitalize on Mussolini's downfall. They adopt British General Sir Frederick Morgan's plan for the cross-Channel invasion, Operation Overlord, scheduled for May 1, 1944. Floating artificial ports (Mulberry Harbors) are to be built in Britain and towed to the French beaches. The supreme commander for the invasion will be a US senior general.

AUGUST 15

PACIFIC, *ALEUTIANS*
A US and Canadian amphibious assault on Kiska Island finds that the Japanese garrison has been evacuated.

AUGUST 17-18

AIR WAR, *GERMANY*
The rocket research center at Peenemünde on the Baltic Sea is attacked by 597 British bombers. The center has been developing a remote-controlled, pulse-jet-powered "Flying Bomb" (V1) and a faster, liquid-fuel model (V2) as terror weapons to undermine the morale of enemy populations. The raid kills 732 people and delays V2 testing. The British lose 40 aircraft. A raid by 230 US bombers is made on ball-bearing works at Schweinfurt and Regensburg. Around 20 percent of the bombers are destroyed.

AUGUST 19

PACIFIC, *PAPUA NEW GUINEA*
Allied forces finally take the Japanese strongpoint of Mount Tambu. Japanese troops are now wedged between Salamaua and the Francisco River.

AUGUST 22-23

EASTERN FRONT, *UKRAINE*
Kharkov is retaken by the Red Army. The Soviets now seriously threaten the southern area of the German front in Ukraine and are well placed for advancing to the Dniepr River. The Soviets have

won victories at Kursk, Orel, and Kharkov by exhausting the enemy with fierce defensive actions followed by decisive counterattacks.

AUGUST 26

EASTERN FRONT, *UKRAINE*
Soviet forces begin their offensive to seize the eastern Ukraine and cross the Dniepr River. The river forms a key part of the German defenses established to halt Red Army advances.

AUGUST 28

POLITICS, *DENMARK*
The Danish government resigns after refusing a German demand for the repression of "saboteurs." The Danish authorities have tried to avoid collaboration with Germany. Martial law is declared on the 29th, the army is disarmed but many Danish warships are scuttled or sent to Sweden before the Germans can seize them.

SEPTEMBER 3

MEDITERRANEAN, *ITALY*
General Bernard Montgomery's Eighth Army crosses from Sicily to seize a bridgehead in Calabria. The British encounter little opposition as the Germans in southern Italy have orders to withdraw.

SEPTEMBER 4-5

PACIFIC, *PAPUA NEW GUINEA*
An Allied offensive is launched to capture the major settlement and airfield at Lae. Amphibious landings are made

▶ *Red Army artillery pounds German units outside Kharkov in the Soviet advance to the Dniepr River.*

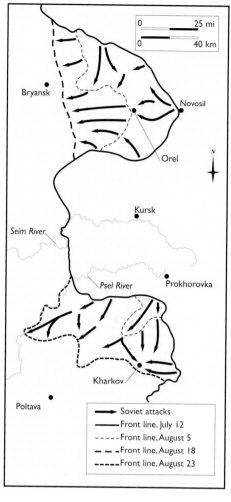

━▶	Soviet attacks
───	Front line, July 12
-----	Front line, August 5
─ ─ ─	Front line, August 18
-------	Front line, August 23

▲ *The Red Army quickly recaptured Kharkov following the collapse of Germany's Citadel attack.*

STRATEGY & TACTICS

STRATEGIC BOMBING

Strategic bombing – air offensives against an enemy's industrial centers and population – using fleets of bombers had been considered a war-winning formula by its prewar proponents. After Germany began its first major raids against Britain in 1940, however, its limitations were exposed.

Although attacks were highly destructive, they failed to paralyze the economy or undermine morale; indeed, the opposite seemed the case as the population steeled itself for the onslaught. The effect of Allied raids on Germany met with similar results, especially as they sustained heavy losses during daylight raids, in which they were easily targeted, and were forced to make less-accurate night raids. Britain's answer was to use saturation bombing to destroy homes and factories across wide areas.

US bombers began operations over Europe in 1942 and were primarily trained for daylight, high-level precision attacks. They soon found that enemy fighters and poor weather seriously undermined the effectiveness of their missions. Fighter, flak, and radar defenses combined to make bomber raids increasingly hazardous. The Allies countered this with a series of technological innovations to enhance navigation and bomb aiming. The defensive firepower of bombers and fighter escort cover was also improved. Nevertheless, aircrew losses were often heavy and Britain's Bomber Command lost 55,573 men while the US 8th Army Air Force (based in Britain) had 43,742 airmen killed.

While the Allied bombing of Germany's oil industry and transport system did play a key role toward the end of the war, the bombers were never capable of completely defeating the enemy alone as its prewar proponents had often predicted (Germany industrial output actually increased during the Allied bomber offensive).

Raids against Japan began in 1944. Although the attacks against 65 cities succeeded in undermining the faltering economy, the nation did not capitulate until the nuclear strikes in 1945. Although the earlier bombing raids did not force Japan to surrender, they did reduce whole cities to ashes and killed many thousands.

The questionable impact such raids had on the economic and psychological capacity of a population to continue fighting, and the moral concerns over civilian deaths, subsequently led many to question this method of waging war.

▶ Free French troops catch their first glimpse of Corsica as they arrive off the island on an Allied troopship.

around 20 miles (30 km) east of Lae on the 4th. US paratroopers land at Nadzeb on the 5th and begin securing the Markham River valley.

SEPTEMBER 8

POLITICS, ITALY
The surrender of Italy is officially announced by the Allies. German forces take over the north of the country and occupy coastal defenses in anticipation of a major Allied invasion. They disarm Italian ground units but the navy succeeds in sending 24 warships to Malta.

SEPTEMBER 9

MEDITERRANEAN, ITALY
Lieutenant General Mark Clark's US Fifth Army, plus the British X Corps, lands in the Gulf of Salerno.

SEPTEMBER 10–11

MEDITERRANEAN, SARDINIA/CORSICA
The Germans withdraws 25,000 men from Sardinia to Italy, via Corsica. A 7000-strong French and US force leaves Algeria to occupy Corsica at the beginning of October.

SEPTEMBER 11–15

PACIFIC, PAPUA NEW GUINEA
Salamaua is captured on the 11th and Lae four days later. These victories deny the Japanese a key port and airfield. The Japanese are now left occupying the Finschhafen fort. The fort has to be taken to clear the peninsula, which is adjacent to the sea approaches to New Britain – the next Allied objective.

SEPTEMBER 12

POLITICS, ITALY
German airborne troops led by Lieutenant Colonel Otto Skorzeny rescue Mussolini from imprisonment in Gran Sasso in the Abruzzi Mountains. Mussolini, however, will now be under Germany's control.

SEPTEMBER 12–18

MEDITERRANEAN, ITALY
German forces fiercely counterattack the Allies around Salerno and threaten the entire bridgehead. Only massive aerial and artillery support saves the besieged Allied units.

SEPTEMBER 15

MEDITERRANEAN, AEGEAN SEA
British forces land on the island of Kos in the Dodecanese. The islands, off southwest Turkey, are a potential approach to southeast Europe and a base for air operations against German communications and oil resources in Romania. A victory here might also persuade Turkey to support the Allied cause as the threat of German air raids from Rhodes would be eliminated. Kos is to be a springboard for an assault against the German stronghold on Rhodes. By the end of September,

▲ German troops on their way to the Dodecanese following the landing of British forces on the islands.

▼ Jubilant German paratroopers photographed after their rescue of Mussolini from the Gran Sasso hotel.

British forces make contact with cooperative Italian troops on most of the neighboring islands.

SEPTEMBER 17

EASTERN FRONT, *SOVIET UNION*
The Red Army capture Bryansk.

SEPTEMBER 19–23

SEA WAR, *ATLANTIC*
The German U-boat packs resume operations against Allied convoys. They are now equipped with electronic monitoring devices, improved anti-aircraft guns, and acoustic torpedoes. Twenty U-boats inflict serious losses on warships and merchant vessels in convoys ON-202 and ONS-28 from the 18th to the 23rd.

SEPTEMBER 21

SEA WAR, *FAR EAST*
Australian commandos sink two Japanese transports after canoeing into Singapore harbor.

SEPTEMBER 22

EASTERN FRONT, *CRIMEA*
The Soviet Thirteenth Army crosses

the Dniepr River south of Kiev and bridgeheads gradually emerge along it.
PACIFIC, *PAPUA NEW GUINEA*
Allied land and seaborne offensives begin against the Japanese on the Huon Peninsula.
SEA WAR, *ARCTIC*
A raid by British midget submarines to destroy the German battle squadron at Altenfiord in Norway cripples the battleship *Tirpitz*. The submarines, however, are unable to attack the battlecruiser *Scharnhorst* as it is at sea, and the pocket battleship *Lützow* could not be found. The three midget submarines involved in the attack on the *Tirpitz* are sunk.

SEPTEMBER 22–23

MEDITERRANEAN, *ITALY*
The Eighth Army's 78th Division lands at Bari. British forces then advance to seize Foggia and its valuable airfield five days later.

SEPTEMBER 23

POLITICS, *ITALY*
Benito Mussolini announces the formation of the Italian Social Republic in

September 25

northwest Italy. Germany, however, is given control of some northern areas by this "republic."

SEPTEMBER 25

EASTERN FRONT, *SOVIET UNION*
The Soviets recapture Smolensk in their continuing offensive. Germany's Army Group Center is now falling back in some disarray.

OCTOBER 1–8

MEDITERRANEAN, *ITALY*
British troops enter Naples on the 1st, and the US Fifth Army advances northward. Its move north is stopped on the 8th at the Volturno River; all the bridges have been destroyed by the retreating Germans.

OCTOBER 2–11

MEDITERRANEAN, *ITALY*
British commandos land at Termoli on the 2nd and a British brigade arrives nearby on the next night. German forces counterattack but fall back as the British take control of the town by the 11th.

OCTOBER 3–4

MEDITERRANEAN, *AEGEAN SEA*
A force of 1200 German paratroopers capture Kos. Around 900 Allied and 3000 Italian troops are made prisoner. The Germans shoot 90 Italian officers for fighting against their former ally.

OCTOBER 6

MEDITERRANEAN, *AEGEAN*
A German convoy bound for Leros is attacked by two British cruisers and two destroyers. Seven German transports and one escort are sunk. British vessels are also making hazardous sailings without adequate air cover to reinforce their troops on Leros.

OCTOBER 9

EASTERN FRONT, *CAUCASUS*
The Red Army reaches the Kerch Strait. This completes the liberation of the north Caucasus.

▼ *A German sailor struggles to keep his footing on a U-boat during an operation in the Atlantic Ocean.*

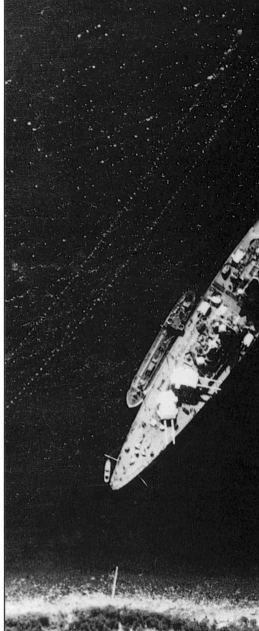

OCTOBER 10–23

EASTERN FRONT, *UKRAINE*
Strong Red Army units continue to strengthen and expand their Dniepr bridgeheads and destroy fiercely defended German positions around Zaporozhye and Melitopol.

OCTOBER 12–22

MEDITERRANEAN, *ITALY*
US forces makes slow progress across the Volturno River and through the mountain terrain in the face of increasingly bad weather. The British Eighth Army begins advancing north across the Trigno River on the 22nd. Field Marshal Albert Kesselring, the German commander-in-chief of Italy since September, has created a strong defensive system along the Garigliano and Sangro Rivers. It is known as the Gustav Line.

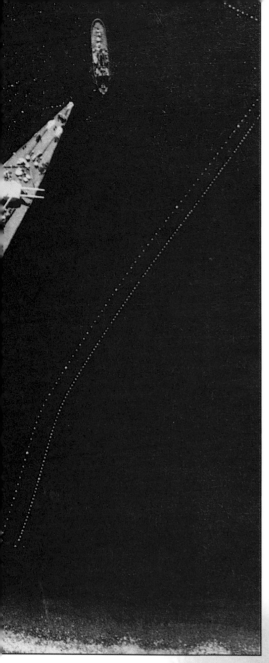

OCTOBER 13

POLITICS, *ITALY*

Marshal Pietro Badoglio's government, which has some power in southern Italy, declares war on Germany.

OCTOBER 14

AIR WAR, *GERMANY*

A second raid is made on the Schweinfurt ball-bearings complex by 291 US B-17 Flying Fortress bombers. Sixty aircraft are lost and 140 damaged for little gain. Following this operation, the US 8th Army Air Force halts unescorted daylight raids due to the high losses it has sustained. Daylight bombing raids will be given escorts of long-range fighter aircraft.

▲ *Disarmed Italian troops pictured at an internment camp in Bozzano following the German occupation of their country in late September.*

OCTOBER 19

POLITICS, *ALLIES*

Representatives from the main Allied nations attend the Second Moscow Conference in the Soviet Union. Agreements are reached over security for postwar China, the punishment of war criminals, and the establishment of advisory councils to consider the fate of Italy and Europe as a whole.

OCTOBER 21

POLITICS, *BRITAIN*

Admiral John Cunningham is appointed commander of British naval forces in the Mediterranean after Admiral Andrew Cunningham becomes the First Sea Lord.

▲ *The German battleship* **Tirpitz** *was attacked by British submarines on September 22.*

▼ *A British mortar fires on German positions during the fighting north of Naples in early October.*

◀ *Japanese antiaircraft troops watch for enemy warplanes following the US invasion of the Solomon Islands.*

island is of strategic importance as it offers the Allies airfield sites that can be used for operations against the Japanese base at Rabaul. The island is defended by 40,000 troops and 20,000 sailors. Most of these are concentrated in the south but US forces land farther west at Empress Augusta Bay, where there are fewer defenders.

NOVEMBER 1–2

SEA WAR, *PACIFIC*
A Japanese force of three heavy cruisers, one light cruiser, and six destroyers attempts to disrupt the Bougainville landings at Empress Augusta Bay. A lack of radar and over-complicated maneuvers enable US Task Force 39 to sink a light cruiser and a destroyer. Two heavy cruisers and a destroyer are damaged. Only one of Task Force 39's 12 vessels is damaged by the Japanese.

NOVEMBER 5–11

SEA WAR, *PACIFIC*
US Rear Admiral Frederick C. Sherman's Task Force 38, including the heavy carrier *Saratoga* and light

OCTOBER 25

FAR EAST, *BURMA*
The Burma to Siam rail link is completed by Allied POWs and indigenous forced labor. This Japanese project to build a track through dense jungle forests is achieved at tremendous human cost. A fifth of the 61,000 Allied prisoners on the project die as a result of accidents, abuse, disease, and starvation. This is the largest of Japan's many projects across Asia. The Japanese captors show complete indifference to the sufferings of their captives.

OCTOBER 27–28

PACIFIC, *SOLOMONS*
Landings are made on the Treasury Islands and Choiseul by US and New Zealand forces. These are diversionary

raids for the main Bougainville attack. It succeeds in drawing attention to the Shortland Islands and bases around Buin, southern Bougainville, rather than the US landing area farther west.

OCTOBER 30

EASTERN FRONT, *UKRAINE*
Soviet units reach the northern Crimea and have virtually cleared the Germans from the left bank of the Dniepr.

NOVEMBER 1

PACIFIC, *SOLOMONS*
US forces land on Bougainville; their final objective in the campaign. The

▶ *American troops pose for a photograph in a captured Japanese command post in the Solomons.*

▲ An American Hellcat takes off from the carrier USS Essex during Admiral Frederick Sherman's attack on Rabaul.

carrier *Princeton*, attacks Rabaul. A surprise attack by 97 aircraft damages eight cruisers and destroyers commanded by Vice Admiral Takeo Kurita. A second air attack by 183 aircraft, launched from the heavy carriers *Bunker Hill* and *Essex*, plus the light carrier *Independence*, hits Rabaul on the 11th. One light cruiser and a destroyer are sunk; five other destroyers and light cruisers are damaged. The Japanese also lose more than 55 aircraft during the raid and their counterattack.

NOVEMBER 6

EASTERN FRONT, *UKRAINE*

The Soviets recapture Kiev. The Seventeenth Army is trapped in the Crimea

as Adolf Hitler orders the region not to be left. Two bridgeheads – at Kiev and southwest of Kremenchug – have been created by the Red Army for the offensive to liberate the western Ukraine.

NOVEMBER 10

MEDITERRANEAN, *AEGEAN SEA*

The island of Kos is now under German control and British destroyers shell the craft anchored in the harbor. Despite the attack, the Germans sail for Leros on the 12th. Shore batteries and infantry counterattacks attempt to halt the invaders. Strong air support

▼ The US conquest of the Solomons was a superb example of amphibious warfare operations conducted on a vast scale.

NOVEMBER 15

and an airborne assault help the Germans to stabilize their positions.

NOVEMBER 15

MEDITERRANEAN, *ITALY*
The Supreme Allied Commander in the Mediterranean, General Sir Harold Alexander, orders the Fifteenth Army Group, comprising the US fifth and Eighth Armies, to rest and reform after fighting against determined German delaying tactics. The war in Italy is proving to be very attritional.

SEA WAR, *ARCTIC*
Britain resumes its Arctic convoys.

NOVEMBER 16

MEDITERRANEAN, *AEGEAN SEA*
Germany completes the capture of Leros and defeats the British attempt to seize the Dodecanese. Poor planning and enemy air superiority have led to the failure of the operation. Britain sustains more than 4800 casualties, and loses 20 vessels and 115 aircraft. Germany has 12 merchant ships and 20 landing craft sunk, and suffers 4000 casualties during the short campaign.

▼ *An American soldier fires his Thompson submachine gun against a Japanese position on Cibik Ridge, Bougainville.*

NOVEMBER 18–26

PACIFIC, *SOLOMONS*
At the Battle of Piva Forks on Bougainville, the Japanese desperately try to hold a key strongpoint known as Cibik Ridge, but US troops finally capture the heavily-fortified position.

NOVEMBER 18

AIR WAR, *GERMANY*
A five-month British bomber offensive on Berlin begins. Over 6100 people are killed, 18,400 injured, and vast areas of the city are destroyed. Fifty diversionary raids are made on other cities.

NOVEMBER 20–23

PACIFIC, *GILBERTS*
US Task Force 53 lands 18,600 troops on Tarawa and Betio following several days of preparatory bombardment. Tarawa's network of bunkers, containing some 4800 Japanese defenders, manages to escape destruction.

The landings are hampered by this determined garrison and also because amphibious craft are grounded on the reef around the islands, which means the troops have to wade ashore. This makes them easy targets to hit.

Over 1000 US troops are killed before the island is captured on the 23rd. Of the garrison, only 110 Japanese soldiers survive. Nearby Makin Island is captured by the US 27th Infantry Division during the same operation.

▲ *Following the resumption of Arctic convoys, a depth-charge explodes near a U-boat closing in for an attack.*

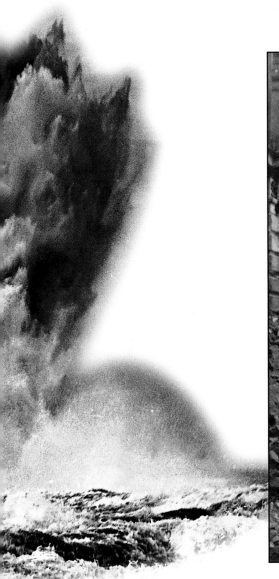

▲ *Bomb damage in Berlin – a familiar sight to those who suffered the RAF's five-month campaign against the city.*

◄ *The Lancaster was an integral part of RAF Bomber Command's arsenal used against the German capital.*

NOVEMBER 20–24

MEDITERRANEAN, *ITALY*
The Allies resume the offensive toward Rome but halt at the defenses of the Gustav Line. The British establish a small bridgehead across the Sangro River by the 24th.

NOVEMBER 22–26

POLITICS, *ALLIES*
British Prime Minister Winston Churchill, US President Franklin D. Roosevelt, and China's Chiang Kai-shek meet in Cairo, Egypt. They mainly consider postwar planning for China and Burma. A second conference, between December 4–7, draws up a schedule for the Pacific "island-hopping" campaign.

337

NOVEMBER 24

SEA WAR, *PACIFIC*
A Japanese submarine sinks the US escort carrier *Liscombe Bay* off Makin Island, claiming 644 lives.

NOVEMBER 25

SEA WAR, *PACIFIC*
At the Battle of Cape St. George, a Japanese destroyer-transport force is attacked by five US destroyers after landing troops at Buka, next to Bougainville. The Japanese lose three vessels during the last surface action in the Solomons.

NOVEMBER 28

POLITICS, *ALLIES*
British Prime Minister Winston Churchill, US President Franklin D. Roosevelt, and the Soviet leader Joseph Stalin meet in Tehran, Iran. Top priority is given to Operation Overlord, the cross-Channel invasion of German-occupied Europe, and a landing in southern France, Operation Anvil, in May 1944. The Soviets have been lobbying for the opening of the Second Front for some time.

DECEMBER 9–26

PACIFIC, SOLOMONS
US advances on Bougainville ensure that air bases can now be opened and missions launched.

DECEMBER 20

PACIFIC, *PAPUA NEW GUINEA*
The Allies achieve supremacy on the Huon Peninsula, although Japanese resistance persists.

DECEMBER 24–29

POLITICS, *ALLIES*
The commanders for the liberation of Europe are announced: General Dwight D. Eisenhower, Supreme Allied Commander; Air Chief Marshal Sir Arthur Tedder, Deputy Supreme Commander; General

Sir Henry Maitland Wilson, Supreme Allied Commander, Mediterranean; Admiral Sir Bertram Ramsay, Allied Naval Commander-in-Chief; Air Chief Marshal Sir Trafford Leigh Mallory, Allied Air Commander-in-Chief; and General Sir Bernard Montgomery, Commander-in-Chief of British Armies.

DECEMBER 25

PACIFIC, *SOLOMONS*
Allied forces land on New Britain and begin advancing to isolate the base of Rabaul from the west.

▲ Chiang Kai-shek (seated, extreme left), Roosevelt and Churchill at the Cairo Conference in November 1943.

▼ A Sherman searches out the enemy during the Allied drive to Rome in November.

DECEMBER 26

SEA WAR, *ARCTIC*

At the Battle of the North Cape, the German battleship *Scharnhorst* is sunk during an ill-planned operation against convoys JW-55B and RA-55A, which are escorted by the British Home Fleet's battle squadron. The battleship first has its radar and fire control damaged. A running battle follows until the *Scharnhorst* begins to lose speed and is finally sunk by torpedo strikes. Only 36 of *Scharnhorst*'s 1800-strong crew survive.

▲ *Australian troops in typical jungle terrain near Lae, Papua New Guinea, during an offensive against the Japanese.*

▼ *The British battleship HMS Duke of York, photographed after participating in the sinking of the Scharnhorst.*

1944

In the Pacific, Japanese defeats at the Battle of the Philippine Sea and around the Mariana Islands, plus losses in Burma, signaled the growing might of the Allies. In Europe, Axis forces suffered reverses and withdrawals in Italy, France, and on the Eastern Front, as the Allies invaded northern France and the Red Army virtually wiped out Army Group Center.

JANUARY 2

POLITICS, *FREE FRENCH*
General Jean de Lattre de Tassigny is appointed commander-in-chief of Free French forces in North Africa.

PACIFIC, *PAPUA NEW GUINEA*
Troops of the US Sixth Army land at Saidor on the north coast of New Guinea as part of Operation Dexterity, cutting off Japanese rearguard forces from their main base at Madang, only 55 miles (88 km) away. The loss of Saidor, a major supply depot, means

▼ *US troops follow a Sherman tank during mopping-up operations on the northern coast of New Guinea.*

◄ *Lancasters over Germany in early January. At this time the RAF was suffering losses of up to 10 percent per month.*

EASTERN FRONT, *UKRAINE*

As part of the Red Army's plan to recover the western Ukraine and the Crimea, General Ivan S. Konev's 2nd Ukrainian Front launches an offensive toward Kirovgrad. Despite desperate German resistance, the town falls on the 8th.

JANUARY 9

FAR EAST, *BURMA*

As part of the Allied attempt to break into Burma, the British XV Corps takes the Burmese town of Maungdaw.

JANUARY 10

EASTERN FRONT, *UKRAINE*

General Rodion Y. Malinovsky's 3rd Ukrainian Front launches an offensive toward Apostolovo, but the attack is halted after six days in the face of fierce German resistance.

JANUARY 11

POLITICS, *ITALY*

Count Galeazzo Ciano, the former Italian foreign secretary and Mussolini's son-in-law, is executed by firing squad in Verona. His "crime" was to have voted with other fascists to oust Mussolini in July 1943. Ciano and his wife had been lured to Bavaria in August 1943 following a report that their children were in danger. Having been promised safe passage to Spain, they were handed over to Italy's puppet fascist government.

JANUARY 12–14

ITALY, *CASSINO*

At Cassino, General Alphonse Juin's colonial troops of the French Expeditionary Corps cross the Rapido River on the Fifth Army's

northern sector. Although they fail to take Monte Santa Croce, their success fills the headquarters of the Fifth Army with renewed optimism.

JANUARY 14–27

EASTERN FRONT, *LENINGRAD*

The Soviet Second Shock Army attacks from the Oranienbaum bridgehead, and the Fifty-ninth Army attacks toward Novgorod, in an attempt to break the German blockade of the city. The next day the Forty-second Army attacks from the Pulkovo Heights. On the 19th, the three armies link up near Krasnoe, and two days later German forces in the Petergof and Streina area are wiped out. Fighting continues as the Germans try to stop the Red Army onslaught, but on the 27th a salute of 324 guns announces the end of the German blockade of Leningrad. Some 830,000 civilians have died during the long siege.

JANUARY 17

ITALY, *GUSTAV LINE*

The Allied attempt to break through the Gustav Line – a frontal assault combined with a seaborne hook to the German rear at Anzio – begins. The British X Corps attacks across the Garigliano River and strikes northwest toward the Aurunci Mountains and the Liri Valley. In response, the German commander, General Heinrich von Vietinghoff, transfers two armored divisions to counter this new threat.

that 20,000 Japanese soldiers are now sandwiched between Australian and US forces. Their only escape route is through dense jungle.

JANUARY 3

AIR WAR, *GERMANY*

In a large-scale air raid on Berlin, the RAF loses 27 Lancasters out of 383 aircraft committed, plus 168 crew members. The damage to the German capital is negligible.

JANUARY 4

ESPIONAGE, *EUROPE*

Operation Carpetbagger – regular airborne supply drops to resistance groups in the Netherlands, Belgium, France, and Italy – begins.

JANUARY 5

POLITICS, *POLAND*

The Polish government-in-exile has authorized the Polish underground movement to cooperate with the Red Army only in the event of a resumption of Polish–Soviet relations (the Soviet Union has not yet recognized the London-based Polish government-in-exile).

▶ *Algerian troops of General Alphonse Juin's French Expeditionary Corps in action at Monte Cassino, Italy, in the middle of January.*

JANUARY 20

Rome is open. However, although by the evening Lucas has nearly 50,000 men and 3000 vehicles ashore, he orders his forces to dig in to repel any enemy counterattacks. He thus misses the opportunity to strike inland from the beachhead.

JANUARY 24

ITALY, *CASSINO/ANZIO*

At Anzio, Allied patrols venturing inland are halted by increasing German resistance. At Cassino, the US 34th Division finally establishes bridgeheads across the Rapido River to allow the armor to cross. At the other end of the Allied line, French troops make further gains.

JANUARY 26

POLITICS, *ARGENTINA*

Argentina has severed relations with Germany and Japan following the

▲ *German paratroopers on their way to attack the Allied bridgehead at Anzio, which had been contained by late January.*

JANUARY 20

ITALY, *GUSTAV LINE*

As part of the Allied attack on the Gustav Line, the US II Corps attempts to cross the Rapido River to clear a path for the US 1st Armored Division. The German defenses are strong and the Americans suffer heavy losses.

JANUARY 22

ITALY, *ANZIO*

Troops of the Allied VI Corps make an amphibious landing at Anzio, behind the German lines. Commanded by US General John Lucas, the initial attack is almost unopposed and the road to

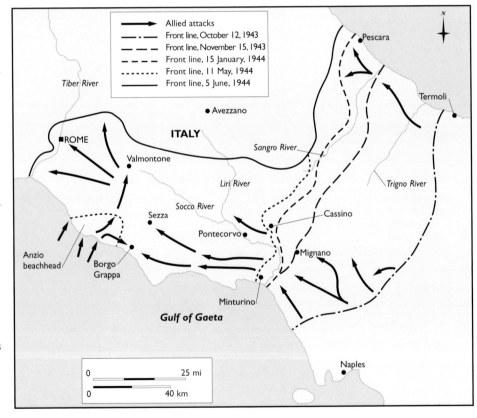

▲ *The campaign to break through the German defenses to reach Anzio was both long and costly.*

◄ *A US Marine signals unit in shattered buildings on Kwajalein Atoll, the Marshall Islands, which fell after four days of fighting.*

uncovering of a vast Axis spy network in the country.

PACIFIC, *PAPUA NEW GUINEA*

Following several days of fighting, the Australian 18th Brigade takes the key Japanese position of Kankiryo Saddle.

JANUARY 30

PACIFIC, *MARSHALLS*

The American conquest of the Marshall Islands, Operation Flintlock,

begins with an amphibious assault against Majuro Atoll. The strategy is to concentrate on key islands and their air bases. Once these have been taken, enemy garrisons on lesser islets will be starved into submission. The landing on Majuro was made on one of the atoll's islands, which was undefended.

FEBRUARY 1–4

PACIFIC, *MARSHALLS*

The amphibious assault against the islands of Kwajalein Atoll is launched. Some 40,000 US Marines and infantry land on the islands of Roi, Namur, and Kwajalein. Japanese resistance is fanatical. It takes the Americans two days to secure Roi and Namur at a cost of 737 killed and wounded; four days to conquer Kwajalein for the loss of 372 killed and wounded. Total Japanese losses are 11,612 men killed.

FEBRUARY 4

ITALY, *CASSINO/ANZIO*

Allied attacks edge closer to Monte Cassino, but then fierce German counterattacks stop the advance in its tracks. At Anzio, the Germans, located on the high ground, contain the Allied bridgehead, which now holds more than 70,000 men and 18,000 vehicles.

FEBRUARY 4–24

FAR EAST, *BURMA*

The Japanese launch Operation Ha-Go with their 55th Division, designed to cut off the forward troops of the Allied

▲ *General Joseph Stilwell (right), whose troops were advancing on Myitkyina in early February 1944, with Chinese allies.*

XV Corps and force the Allies back to the Indian border. Initial Japanese attacks are successful and push Allied troops back to a defensive position near Sinzweya called the "Admin Box." The Japanese ring around the position is not broken until the 25th, when the 123rd Brigade fights its way through the Ngakyedauk Pass and reaches the "Admin Box." The failure of Ha-Go is a watershed in the Burma campaign, as Japanese enveloping tactics have failed to produce the expected results.

FEBRUARY 5

FAR EAST, *BURMA*

The 16th Brigade of Orde Wingate's Chindits begins to move south from Ledo, India, toward Indaw in northern Burma. Its mission is threefold: to aid General Joseph Stilwell's advance on Myitkyina by drawing off enemy forces; to create a favourable situation for the Yunnan armies; and to inflict the maximum amount of damage and loss on the Japanese in northern Burma.

FEBRUARY 12

SEA WAR, *FAR EAST*

The Japanese submarine *I-27* sinks the British troopship *Khedive Ismail* with the loss of many lives. The submarine is then sunk by the destroyers *Petard* and *Paladin*.

KEY PERSONALITIES

MARSHAL JOSIP BROZ TITO LEADER OF YUGOSLAVIA

Tito (1892–1980) was nearly 50 years old when World War II broke out. Having seen service in the Russian Revolution and Spanish Civil War, he quickly organized resistance when the Germans invaded Yugoslavia in March 1941. By the fall of that year, he was waging a full-scale guerrilla campaign in Serbia, capturing a number of towns, including Uzice, where he set up an arms factory and printing facilities. He disagreed with the rival Chetnik resistance group and defeated them, but was then driven out of Serbia by the Germans in the first of seven major Axis offensives against the Yugoslavian partisans.

His tactics on the ground consisted of fighting as long as possible, then withdrawing into the hills with his forces, all the while maintaining tight communication and organization as he did so. In May 1943 he was attacked by forces six times greater than his own, lost a quarter of his strength and half his equipment, but still managed to keep his forces together.

In late 1942 Tito began receiving aid from the Western Allies, and the withdrawal of Italy from the war gave him Croatia and vast quantities of Italian weapons. By 1944 he had an army of 250,000 men and women, and on October 20 he took Belgrade. He became the symbol of the country's unity, and was able to establish a postwar communist government.

FEBRUARY 16–17

ITALY, *CASSINO*
The US 34th Division makes a last attempt to capture the German-held monastery. Its attack is halted, however, and the unit is replaced by the 4th Indian and New Zealand Divisions of the British Eighth Army.

FEBRUARY 16–19

ITALY, *ANZIO*
With massive artillery support, 10 German divisions attack the Anzio beachhead in an attempt to wipe it out. By the morning of the 17th, the Germans have created a wedge one mile (1.6 km) deep in the Allied line. However, that afternoon aircraft from the entire Italian front bomb and strafe the German units in an effort to save the beachhead. Allied air attacks, supported by artillery on the ground, eventually force the Germans to retire on the 19th.

FEBRUARY 18–22

PACIFIC, *MARSHALLS*
US forces complete their conquest of

▲ *American Dauntless dive-bombers returning from a strike against Japanese targets in the Marshall Islands.*

the islands with the seizure of Eniwetok Atoll. This combined army and Marine operation is a bloody affair, with 3400 Japanese defenders dying, along with 254 US Marines and 94 army personnel being killed. The Marshalls are the first Japanese prewar territories to fall to the Allies so far in the war.

FEBRUARY 26

EASTERN FRONT, *BALTIC*
The Red Army captures Porkhov and regroups on the Novorzhev and Pustoshka line. In the course of a six-week campaign the Volkhov, Leningrad, and 2nd Baltic Fronts have

inflicted a shattering defeat on Germany's Army Group North. They have wiped out three German divisions, routed another 17, and captured 189 tanks and 1800 artillery pieces. In addition, units of local partisans have killed over 21,500 German troops, destroyed 300 bridges, and derailed 136 military trains during a series of wide-ranging attacks.

FEBRUARY 29

PACIFIC, *ADMIRALTIES*
As part of their strategy for isolating the Japanese base at Rabaul, American forces land on the islands, a staging

▼ *A mortar of the US 34th Division shells German-held positions around Cassino.*

KEY PERSONALITIES

GENERAL GEORGE S. PATTON

Something of an innovator in the US Army, Patton (1885–1945) had seen service in World War I and was a firm believer in the tenets of armored warfare. He was given command of the US II Corps in the Torch landings in November 1942, and was then ordered to lead the US Seventh Army in the invasion of Sicily. However, the controversial hitting of shell-shocked soldiers in a field hospital resulted in public censure.

During the campaign in France he led the US Third Army, using it to achieve quick advances to Lorraine and the German frontier. However, he strongly disagreed with Eisenhower's policy of sharing vital military supplies between US forces and Montgomery's British and Commonwealth units. Patton believed that if he had been given more supplies he could have ended the war in 1944. Instead, he fought a bitter battle of attrition on the border and intervened decisively in the Battle of the Bulge. In 1945 he conducted a masterful crossing of the Rhine, which was followed by a whirlwind advance into Czechoslovakia. Patton, the founder of the armored tradition in the US Army, was killed in an motor vehicle accident in December 1945.

post through which the Japanese can reach Rabaul. The fall of the Admiralties will secure the southwest Pacific for the Allies.

MARCH 1

FAR EAST, *BURMA*
The Chindits' 16th Brigade crosses the Chindwin River, as Chinese forces and Merrill's Marauders (a US commando force) under General Joseph Stilwell, advance toward Myitkyina.

MARCH 2

POLITICS, *ALLIES*
The Allies cut off all aid to Turkey due to its government's reluctance to help their war effort.

MARCH 5–11

FAR EAST, *BURMA*
Brigadier Mike Calvert's 77th Brigade of the Chindits begins landing by glider at two selected points code-named "Broadway" and "Piccadilly" in the Kaukkwe Valley, northern Burma. During the first lift, 61 gliders are used, although only 35 reach their target. By the 11th, the whole of Calvert's brigade has been flown in.

MARCH 7

HOME FRONT, *GERMANY*
Members of the Nazi organization for women are making house-to-house calls to recruit females between the ages of 17 and 45 to work "in the service of the community." This is to bolster Germany's depleted labor force.

▼ *Chinese infantry under the overall command of General Joseph Stilwell crossing the Chindwin River in March.*

▲ *Anxious German troops wait for action as the Red Army attacks Army Group North on the Eastern Front.*

MARCH 7–8

FAR EAST, *BURMA/INDIA*
Operation U-Go, the Japanese offensive to drive the Allies back into India by destroying their bases at Imphal and Kohima, begins with moves to sever the Tiddim to Imphal road. The Japanese 33rd Division has orders to cut off the 17th Indian Division at Tiddim and force the British to commit their reserves to rescue it, while the

March 8

▲ Japanese troops on the attack between Homalin and Thaungdut in their efforts to cut the Imphal to Kohima road.

▼ For German workers in 1944 it was a never-ending task of laying new railroad tracks after Allied air raids, in this case after an US 8th Army Air Force attack.

31st and 15th Divisions are to cross the Chindwin farther north and fall on Imphal and Kohima.

March 8

AIR WAR, *GERMANY*

The US 8th Army Air Force launches a massive daylight precision raid on the Erker ball-bearing works, Berlin. A total of 590 aircraft mount the raid. There are 75 direct hits on the target, but the Americans lose 37 aircraft. This is the third US raid on Berlin under the escort of P-51 Mustang fighters. It results in the halting of ball-bearing production for some time.

March 11

EASTERN FRONT, *UKRAINE*

General Rodion Malinovsky's 2nd Ukrainian Front reaches the Bug River, brushing aside resistance from the German Eighth Army. The Germans hope to halt the Red Army on this great water barrier.

March 11–12

FAR EAST, *BURMA*

In the Arakan, northern Burma, the Allies recapture Buthidaung and then surround and capture the Japanese fortress at Razabil.

March 15–16

FAR EAST, *BURMA/INDIA*

The Japanese 15th and 31st Divisions cross the Chindwin River between Homalin and Thaungdut and move forward with the intention of cutting the Imphal to Kohima road.

◄ *US B-25 medium bombers on their way to pound German units dug in amid the ruins of Monte Cassino.*

MARCH 18

EASTERN FRONT, *UKRAINE*
The Soviet 2nd Ukrainian Front has reached the Dniester River and seized a large bridgehead at Mogilev Podolsky. This has split the German Army Group South's front in two and has put the Red Army in a position to advance to the Romanian frontier.

MARCH 19

POLITICS, *HUNGARY*
With the Red Army rapidly approaching the Balkans, Hitler has sent troops to occupy the country. Admiral Miklós Horthy, the regent, has been ordered to appoint a pro-Nazi premier, allow the German Army to take over the transport system, and give the SS a free hand in deporting Hungarian Jews to concentration camps.

ITALY, *CASSINO*
A German counterattack against Peak 193 is unsuccessful but has loosened the Allied stranglehold. A New Zealand armored assault against the monastery is destroyed.

MARCH 20-22

ITALY, *CASSINO*
Despite further frontal attacks by New Zealand troops under General Harold Alexander, the German defenders, veterans of the 1st Parachute Division, remain in and around the monastery and repulse all efforts to dislodge

◄ *The remains of the monastery of Monte Cassino.*

MARCH 15-17

ITALY, *CASSINO*
Allied aircraft launch a massive raid against the unoccupied monastery of Monte Cassino (which is later criticized by the Vatican). The New Zealand 2nd Division then launches an assault that takes Peak 193. During the evening the 4th Indian Division attacks and captures Peak 165. All Allied attacks on the 16th are frustrated, but on the 17th a breakthrough by the New Zealanders takes Cassino railroad station. They fail, though, to complete the encirclement of the town itself.

▲ *Waiting for the next Japanese attack: a British machine-gun position at Imphal in late March 1944.*

▲ *Major General Orde Wingate, the brilliant Chindit commander, who was killed in an air crash at Imphal.*

them. On the 22nd, therefore, Alexander halts all frontal assaults.

MARCH 24

FAR EAST, *BURMA*
Major General Orde Wingate, the commander of the Chindits, is killed in a plane crash. A charismatic and controversial figure, Winston Churchill has called him a "man of genius and audacity" following the success of his long-range penetration missions in Burma.

MARCH 28

EASTERN FRONT, *UKRAINE*
As the Germans retreat in haste from the waters of the southern Bug River, Nikolayev falls to the Red Army. The 3rd Ukrainian Front is now developing an assault toward the port of Odessa.

MARCH 29

FAR EAST, *INDIA*
The Japanese 20th Division establishes itself on the Shenam Saddle near

Imphal. Japanese forces have cut the Imphal to Kohima road and begun the siege of Imphal.

MARCH 30

POLITICS, *GERMANY*
Hitler, outraged at the Soviet victories in the Ukraine, has dismissed two of his field marshals – Erich von Manstein and Paul von Kleist – for disregarding his "stand fast" orders. In addition, the Nazi leader believes that the army in the Ukraine has put up weak resistance against the Soviets.

FAR EAST, *BURMA*
The Chindits' 16th Brigade, commanded by Brigadier Bernard Fergusson, retreats following its failure to take the main Japanese supply base at Indaw.

MARCH 30-31

AIR WAR, *GERMANY*
A night raid by the RAF against Nuremberg results in little damage to the city but substantial losses are inflicted on the aircraft involved. The RAF loses 95 out of the

attacking force of 795 bombers, with a further 71 damaged.

APRIL 3

AIR WAR, *NORWAY*

The German battleship *Tirpitz* has been damaged in Altenfiord, Norway, by Royal Navy aircraft flown from the British carriers *Victorious* and *Furious. Tirpitz* has been hit 14 times, which means that it will not sail again for several months.

APRIL 4–13

FAR EAST, *INDIA*

The first stage of the Imphal battle has ended. The Japanese have failed to destroy the Allied defense line. The British IV Corps, now concentrated around Imphal, can turn its attention to the destruction of the Japanese. By April 13, the Japanese have been ejected from Nungshigum, one of the hills commanding the Imphal plain, and their 15th Division is being harried down the road to Ukhrul.

APRIL 5

EASTERN FRONT, *UKRAINE*

The Soviet 3rd Ukrainian Front captures Razdelnaya station and cuts the local German forces in two, one of which is forced to withdraw toward Odessa and the other toward Tiraspol.

APRIL 6–11

FAR EAST, *BURMA*

Japanese forces attack the Chindit fortified position at "White City," which is subsequently evacuated.

APRIL 8

EASTERN FRONT, *CRIMEA*

General Fedor I. Tolbukhin's 4th Ukrainian Front (470,000 men, 6000 field guns and mortars, 560 tanks and self-propelled guns, and 1250 combat aircraft) begins the liberation of the

▲ *General Fedor Tolbukhin, whose 4th Ukrainian Front liberated the Crimea and captured Sebastopol in April.*

peninsula. The German and Romanian forces defending the region as part of the Seventeenth Army can muster only 200,000 men, 3600 field guns and mortars, 200 tanks and self-propelled guns, and 150 aircraft.

APRIL 9

EASTERN FRONT, *UKRAINE*

The Soviet 3rd Ukrainian Front reaches the outskirts of Odessa.

APRIL 12

POLITICS, *ROMANIA*

In reply to a Romanian mission regarding the conditions for an armistice between Romania and the Soviet Union, Moscow demands that Romania break with the Germans, that its forces fight alongside the Red Army, and insists on the restoration of the Romanian and Soviet border. It also calls for reparations for damage inflicted on the Soviet Union by Romania, freedom of movement through the country for Soviet and other Allied forces, and the repatriation

◄ *A Swordfish torpedo-bomber returns to HMS* Victorious, *which took part in an attack on the German battleship* Tirpitz.

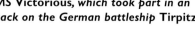

APRIL 15

of Soviet prisoners. The Romanians reject these conditions and remain with the Axis.

APRIL 15

AIR WAR, *EUROPE*

The US 8th Army Air Force and RAF Bomber Command decide to switch bombing from German urban centers to railroads in Belgium and France to prepare for the forthcoming Allied invasion by preventing German reinforcements reaching the front.

A force of 448 Flying Fortresses and Liberators of the US 15th Army Air Force, escorted by 150 Mustang fighters, also attacks the oil fields at Ploesti and the Romanian capital, Bucharest. During the night the RAF bombs the railroad lines at Turnu Severin in Romania.

▲ *A US A-20 bomber hits an important rail junction at Busigny in northern France.*

APRIL 22

PACIFIC, *PAPUA NEW GUINEA*

General Douglas MacArthur, leading a 52,000-strong Allied invasion force, makes an amphibious landing in Hollandia, northern New Guinea. Hollandia will be the base for the next phase of MacArthur's Operation Cartwheel, which is

designed to drive the Japanese from northwest New Guinea.

MAY 3

POLITICS, *JAPAN*

Admiral Soemu Toyoda is appointed commander-in-chief of the Japanese Combined Fleet. He replaces Admiral Mineichi Koga, who has been killed in a plane crash on March 31.

MAY 9

EASTERN FRONT, *CRIMEA*

The Soviet 4th Ukrainian Front liberates the port of Sebastopol. It is a crushing defeat for the German defenders, who have lost 100,000 men killed and captured during the fighting.

◄ *Admiral Soemu Toyoda, the new commander-in-chief of the Japanese Combined Fleet.*

◄ *Mopping up the last pockets of Japanese resistance on the Admiralty Islands – both tedious and dangerous.*

MAY 19

HOME FRONT, *GERMANY*

Following their recapture after a mass breakout from Stalag Luft III near Sagan, Silesia, 50 Allied airmen are shot by the Gestapo. Only three of the escaped prisoners – two Norwegians and a Dutchman – reach England.

MAY 23–31

ITALY, *ANZIO*

Troops of the US VI Corps begin the breakout from the Anzio beachhead in the face of stubborn German resistance. The linkup with troops of the US II Corps occurs on the 25th, four months after the original Anzio landing. Steady gains are made by the Allies, although taking the Adolf Hitler Line, which runs from Terracina on the coast along the Foni to Pico road to Pontecorvo and across the Liri Valley through Aquino and Piedmonte to Monte Cairo, does result in heavy Allied losses. Once again the Germans have proved adept at defense.

▼ *Infantry of the British 4th Division pick their way through shattered streets during the advance to the Rapido River in Italy.*

MAY 11–18

ITALY, *CASSINO*

The Allied 15th Army Group begins its offensive to outflank the monastery. On the 12th, the French Expeditionary Corps takes Monte Faito, but the Polish 5th Division fails to capture Colle Sant'Angelo. On the 13th, the French open the way to Rome, while the US II Corps takes Santa Maria Infante, and the British 4th Division begins to enlarge its bridgehead across the Rapido River.

On the 17th, the Germans evacuate the monastery at Monte Cassino because of the deep breakthroughs by the French Expeditionary Corps and the US II Corps. The next day, the Polish 12th Podolski Regiment storms the ruins of Monte Cassino.

MAY 18

PACIFIC, *ADMIRALTIES*

The last pockets of Japanese resistance on the islands have been crushed. This effectively isolates the main Japanese bases at Rabaul and Kavieng in the southwest Pacific.

On the 25th, the US Fifth Army attacks toward Rome, but is held by the Germans, who have had time to dig in around Valmontone along the Caesar Line. It is not until the night of May 30 – when Major General Fred L. Walker's US 36th Division moves silently up Monte Artemisio and breaks the Valmontone defenses – that the final defensive line barring the entrance to Rome is cut.

MAY 25

BALKANS, *YUGOSLAVIA*
The Germans launch an air, glider, and mortar attack on the partisan headquarters at Divar, in which Marshal Tito narrowly escapes capture. The attack is believed to have been the plan of SS Major Otto Skorzeny, the officer who rescued Mussolini.

▼ *German paratroopers in Rome on the eve of their evacuation of the city in early June.*

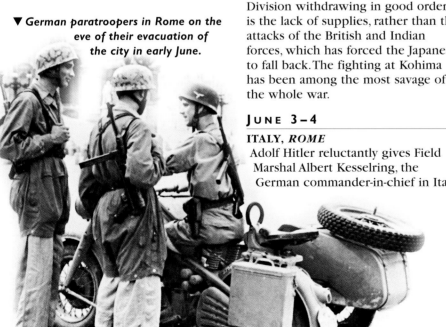

▲ *Soldiers of the US 4th Infantry Division wade ashore under fire at Utah Beach on D-Day, the invasion of northern France.*

MAY 29

PACIFIC, *PAPUA NEW GUINEA*
The first tank battle of the Pacific campaign is fought on Biak Island, off New Guinea, between the Japanese and Americans. It is a US victory.

JUNE 1

FAR EAST, *BURMA*
Brigadier Mike Calvert, commander of the Chindits' 77th Brigade, reaches Lakum near Mogaung.

JUNE 3

FAR EAST, *INDIA*
The 64-day Battle of Kohima ends with the remnants of the Japanese 31st Division withdrawing in good order. It is the lack of supplies, rather than the attacks of the British and Indian forces, which has forced the Japanese to fall back. The fighting at Kohima has been among the most savage of the whole war.

JUNE 3–4

ITALY, *ROME*
Adolf Hitler reluctantly gives Field Marshal Albert Kesselring, the German commander-in-chief in Italy,

permission to abandon Rome. Covered by expert rearguard actions of IV Parachute Corps, the German Fourteenth Army pulls back across the Tiber River. US troops enter the city on the 5th – the first Axis capital to be captured.

JUNE 6

WESTERN FRONT, *FRANCE*

The Allies launch the greatest amphibious operation in history. The statistics for the invasion force are staggering: 50,000 men for the initial assault; over two million men to be shipped to France in all, comprising a total of 39 divisions; 139 major warships used in the assault, with a further 221 smaller combat vessels; over 1000 minesweepers and auxiliary vessels; 4000 landing craft; 805 merchant ships; 59 blockships; 300 miscellaneous small craft; and 11,000 aircraft, including fighters, bombers, transports, and gliders. In addition, the invasion force has the support of over 100,000 members of the French Resistance, who launch hit-and-run attacks on German targets.

D-Day, the Allied invasion of Normandy, code-named Operation Overlord, begins with the assault of three airborne divisions – the US 82nd and 101st on the right flank of the US forces, and the British 6th Airborne on

▲ *German prisoners are led away after their surrender on D-Day.*

◄ *British Horsa gliders litter the fields northeast of Caen on the morning of D-Day – 6 June 1944.*

▼ *After consolidating their beachhead, the Allies built up their forces for the liberation of France. Air superiority, which restricted the movement of German forces, greatly aided their efforts.*

the left flank of the British – while seaborne forces land on five beaches. Utah Beach is the target of the US 4th Infantry Division (part of the US VII Corps); Omaha Beach is the target of the US 1st Infantry Division (part of the US V Corps); Gold Beach is the landing site of the British 50th Infantry Division (part of the British XXX Corps); Juno is the target for the Canadian 3rd Infantry Division (part of the British I Corps); and the British 3rd

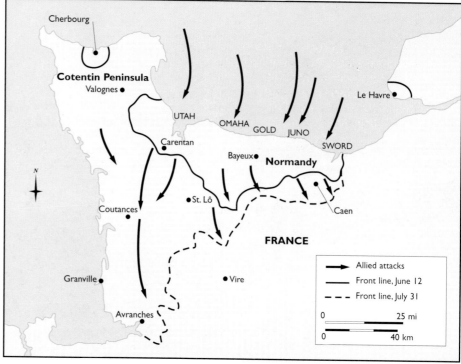

Map legend:
- Allied attacks
- Front line, June 12
- Front line, July 31

Map labels: Cherbourg, Cotentin Peninsula, Valognes, UTAH, OMAHA, GOLD, JUNO, SWORD, Le Havre, Carentan, Bayeux, Normandy, Caen, St. Lô, Coutances, FRANCE, Granville, Vire, Avranches

0 — 25 mi
0 — 40 km

DECISIVE WEAPONS

RESISTANCE

Within those countries and regions overrun by the Germans and Japanese in Word War II, there were those among the various populations who were determined to oppose the occupiers in some way, often at great risk to themselves and their families. This resistance could be active or passive. Passive resistance involved demonstrations, industrial strikes, and slowdowns, the production of underground newspapers and leaflets, and wall slogans. Active resistance involved gathering intelligence, assisting escaped Allied prisoners of war and shot-down aircrews, sabotage, and armed action against occupation forces.

Throughout Europe and the Far East, resistance was never the preserve of any particular political grouping or social class; rather it encompassed a complete cross-section of each country's society.

The dangers of fighting back against occupiers were ever present, and resistance movements were under constant threat from enemy intelligence, collaborators, and informers, with torture and death the usual price of being caught. Ownership of a carrier pigeon, for example, warranted death by firing squad in Europe. In addition, there was often infighting between various resistance groups. In Yugoslavia, the Chetniks and Tito's forces fought each other as well as the Axis occupiers. Nevertheless, with outside help (which was often crucial in keeping the various units going), resistance groups in Europe and the Far East aided the general Allied war effort against the Axis powers.

Jubilant members of the French Resistance near Paris in August 1944, with the Germans in full retreat.

▲ *American troops march through bomb-damaged Carentan, the first French city to fall to the invaders after D-Day.*

Infantry Division (also part of the British I Corps) is tasked with seizing Sword Beach.

The initial parachute and seaborne landings have mixed results: on Utah resistance is slight and the troops are off the beach by 1200 hours; on Omaha the lack of specialized armor means the Germans can pin down the troops on the beach, with great slaughter; on Gold and Juno the specialized armor of the British and Canadians allow the troops to get off the beaches quickly, and by the afternoon they are probing inland toward Bayeux and Caen; and on Sword the troops are able to link up with airborne units that have been dropped farther inland.

This is fortunate, for it is between Juno and Sword that the Germans make their one major counterattack, comprising a battlegroup of the 21st Panzer Division. However, it is defeated. By the end of the day, at a

▼ *US Marines under fire on the island of Saipan, Marianas, on June 23, 1944. Japanese resistance was, as usual, very fierce.*

cost of 2500 dead, the Allies have a toehold in German-occupied Europe.

JUNE 9-10

EASTERN FRONT, *FINLAND*
The Soviets, in an effort to drive the Finns back to the 1940 frontier and compel them to make peace, launch a major offensive with two armies. The offensive is preceded by a sustained barrage from 5500 guns and 880 rocket-launchers. The attack shatters the Finnish front and, on the 10th, Marshal Karl von Mannerheim, Finland's military leader, orders a retreat to a stronger defensive line.

JUNE 10

WESTERN FRONT, *FRANCE*
The 2nd SS Panzer Division *Das Reich*, moving from its base at Toulouse

to Normandy, has been the constant target of members of the French Resistance. In retaliation, the small town of Oradour-sur-Glane is chosen as the target for a brutal reprisal, one intended to be a lesson to the people of France. The men of the village are herded into barns, the women and children into the church, and the whole town is set on fire. Those who flee are machine-gunned. In total, 642 people are killed, with only 10 able to feign death and escape.

JUNE 11

PACIFIC, *MARIANAS*
US Task Force 58 begins a heavy bombardment of Saipan, Tinian, Guam, Rota, and Pagan prior to an assault on the islands, the occupation of which will allow the US forces operating in the area to

▲ *A Japanese ship under American air attack during the Battle of the Philippine Sea, which fatally wrecked Japanese naval air strength in the Pacific.*

sever the lines of communication to Japan's units operating in the southern Pacific.

JUNE 13

WESTERN FRONT, *FRANCE*
Lieutenant Michael Wittmann, company commander of the SS 501st Heavy Tank Battalion, destroys 27 tanks and armoured vehicles of the British 4th Country of London Yeomanry in a tank battle around the village of Villers-Bocage, Normandy.
PACIFIC, *JAPAN*
The Japanese Combined Fleet is alerted to prepare for Operation A-Go, which is intended to lure the US Pacific Fleet to one of two battle areas – either the Palaus or the Western Carolines – where it can be destroyed. These areas are chosen because they are within range of the greatest possible number of Japanese island air bases, thereby counterbalancing US aircraft carrier superiority.

JUNE 15

PACIFIC, *MARIANAS*
The US Northern Attack Force arrives off Saipan. In response, the Japanese Combined Fleet is ordered to gather. On the island itself, landings are conducted on the west coast by the US 2nd and 4th Marine Divisions.
AIR WAR, *JAPAN*
The iron and steel works at Yahata on the mainland is bombed by B-29s of the US 20th Army Air Force, which is operating from bases in China.

JUNE 16

FAR EAST, *BURMA*
The 22nd Division, part of Lieutenant General Joseph Stilwell's Chinese force, has taken Kamaing, the first of his three objectives – the others being Mogaung and Myitkyina.

JUNE 18

WESTERN FRONT, *FRANCE*
US forces reach the west coast of the Cotentin Peninsula, Normandy, trapping the German garrison in Cherbourg. Hitler has ordered the garrison to fight to the death.
PACIFIC, *MARIANAS*
The warships of US Task Force 58 rendezvous west of Saipan.

JUNE 19–21

PACIFIC, *PHILIPPINE SEA*

On hearing of the US assault on Saipan, the Japanese Combined Fleet, under Admiral Jisaburo Ozawa, puts to sea immediately with five heavy and four light carriers, five battleships, 11 heavy and two light cruisers, and 28 destroyers. The US 5th Fleet, under Admiral Marc Mitscher's tactical command, numbers seven heavy and eight light carriers, eight heavy and 13 light cruisers, and 69 destroyers. Aircraft on either side total 573 Japanese (including 100 based on Guam, Rota, and Yap) and 956 American.

Ozawa's search planes locate the 5th Fleet at daybreak, 300 miles (480 km) from his advance element of four light carriers and 500 miles (800 km) from his main body. Ozawa launches an attack in four waves, while Mitscher, on discovering the enemy aircraft, sends out his interceptors.

Disaster strikes Ozawa immediately, for US submarines sink the carriers *Taiho* and *Shokaku*, and US fighters shoot down many of his aircraft. In the Battle of the Philippine Sea, nicknamed the "Great Marianas Turkey Shoot" by the Americans, the Japanese lose 346 aircraft and two carriers. US losses are 30 aircraft and slight damage to a battleship. Meanwhile, Mitscher's bombers neutralize the Japanese airfields on Guam and Rota.

On the 20th, Mitscher launches 216 aircraft, which sink another carrier and two oil tankers, and seriously damage several other vessels. While the Americans lose 20 aircraft, Ozawa loses another 65, although many US aircraft are forced to ditch into the sea.

Ozawa's costly battle deals a crippling blow to the Japanese naval air arm, not least through the loss of 460 trained combat pilots.

JUNE 20

ITALY, *UMBRIA*

The British XXX Corps opens its attack on the Albert Line, one of a series of German rearguard positions in northern Italy, south of Lake Trasimeno on either side of Chiusi. The fighting is hard; the Germans give ground grudgingly.

JUNE 22

POLITICS, *GERMANY*

Foreign Minister Joachim von Ribbentrop visits Helsinki to try to tie Finland more tightly to Germany.

FAR EAST, *INDIA*

The British 2nd Division reach the defenders of Imphal, but Japanese resistance continues.

▲ *The Red Army liberates another town in Belorussia and its soldiers are welcomed by grateful civilians.*

JUNE 22–26

FAR EAST, *BURMA*

The Chindits' 77th Brigade begins attacking Mogaung from the southeast. Following bitter fighting, it finally falls on the 26th.

JUNE 23

EASTERN FRONT, *BELORUSSIA*

The Red Army launches its Belorussian offensive. Four fronts – 1st Baltic, 1st, 2nd, and 3rd Belorussian, comprising

▼ *Allied troops in the ruins of Valognes during the drive against Cherbourg, which fell on June 29, 1944.*

1.2 million men in all – attack the German divisions of Army Group Center. The Soviets have a four-to-one superiority in tanks and aircraft.

JUNE 26

WESTERN FRONT, *FRANCE*
The British launch Operation Epsom, a drive west of Caen. Troops and tanks of the 15th, 43rd, and 11th Armored Divisions make good initial progress, but are then halted following very heavy losses.

JUNE 29

WESTERN FRONT, *FRANCE*
The port of Cherbourg finally surrenders to forces of the US VII Corps. The cost to the US has been 22,000 casualties, while 39,000 Germans are taken prisoner.

JUNE 30

TECHNOLOGY, *GERMANY*
The Germans have formed the first operational unit equipped with Messerschmitt Me 262 jet fighters.

▲ *Paratroopers belonging to the US 503rd Parachute Infantry Regiment land on Kamirir airstrip, Noemfoor, July 2, 1944.*

The unit will be deployed to France in the near future.

AIR WAR, *BRITAIN*
To date, 2000 German V1 "Flying Bombs" have been launched against England, mostly against London. In response, the British have increased the number of anti-aircraft guns, fighter aircraft, and barrage balloons.

JULY 2

ITALY, *TUSCANY*
The British XIII Corps takes the town of Foiano, northwest of Lake Trasimeno, thereby completing the breakthrough of the German Albert Line.

JULY 4

EASTERN FRONT, *BALTIC*
The Red Army offensive to clear the Baltic states begins. Three Soviet Fronts – 1st, 2nd, and 3rd Baltic – are to be used. The Baltic states are of major importance to Germany, as they are a major source of food and enable the Germans to blockade the Russian fleet and keep supply lanes to Sweden and Finland open.

JULY 7–9

PACIFIC, *MARIANAS*
The Japanese commander on Saipan, General Yoshitsugu Saito, launches a

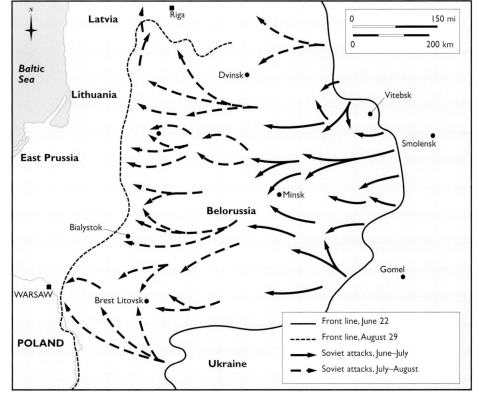

◀ *The Soviet offensive in Belorussia in mid-1944 shattered Army Group Center under a deluge of tanks and men.*

JULY 8

mass charge against the US 27th Infantry Division at Makunsho. Despite losing hundreds of men to US gunfire, the Japanese crash through the American lines. However, they soon lose their momentum and fail. Saito commits suicide and the island is declared secure on the 9th. At least 8000 Japanese defenders and civilians have committed suicide rather than surrender.

JULY 8

POLITICS, *HUNGARY*
With the Red Army fast approaching, Hungary's leader, Admiral Miklós Horthy, orders a halt to the deportation of Hungarian Jews to Auschwitz concentration camp.

JULY 11

POLITICS, *UNITED STATES*
President Franklin D. Roosevelt announces he will run for an unprecedented fourth term in the White House.

EASTERN FRONT, *BELORUSSIA*
The Minsk area falls to the Red Army. The Germans have lost over 70,000 men killed and 35,000 taken prisoner, and their Fourth Army has ceased to exist.

▶ *Same task, different island – flushing out Japanese defenders on Tinian, one of the Mariana Islands, with a pack howitzer.*

▲ *Admiral Miklós Horthy (center), regent of Hungary, who halted the deportation of Hungarian Jews to Auschwitz.*

JULY 15

EASTERN FRONT, *FINLAND*
The battle for the Karelian Isthmus ends with a defensive victory for Finland. Three Soviet armies make excellent early progress, but are unable to achieve the objectives laid down in their orders of June 21. The Soviet military leadership orders its troops in Finland to go over to the defensive on the 11th.

JULY 17

EASTERN FRONT, *UKRAINE*
Units of the Soviet First Guards Tank Army cross the Bug River into Poland.

JULY 18

FAR EAST, *BURMA*
The Japanese high command calls off Operation U-Go.

JULY 18–22

WESTERN FRONT, *FRANCE*
In the face of fanatical resistance, US troops enter St. Lô. The German 352nd Division is destroyed in the process. On the eastern sector of the front, the British and Canadians launch Operation Goodwood, a drive east of Caen to provoke heavier German concentrations in the area. The aim is to wear down German armor to such an extent that it is of no further value to them. The Allies lose over 100 Sherman tanks in the assault. By the 22nd, however, the British have cleared southern Caen.

JULY 19–21

PACIFIC, *MARIANAS*
US battleships begin the pre-invasion bombardment of Asan and Agat beaches on Guam, the most important island in the Marianas group. Two days later, troops of the 3rd Marine Division and 77th Infantry Division begin landing on the island. The Japanese fight back hard.

JULY 20

POLITICS, *GERMANY*

An attempt is made by German officers to assassinate Adolf Hitler. Count Schenk von Stauffenberg, chief-of-staff to General Friedrich Fromm, plants a bomb near Hitler in a conference room at the Nazi leader's East Prussian headquarters at Rastenburg. The bomb explodes at 1242 hours, after von Stauffenberg has left. The bomb fails to kill Hitler and the conspiracy falls apart. Josef Goebbels, Nazi minister for propaganda, acts quickly to convince the Berlin garrison that Hitler is still alive by linking them by telephone. Fromm, to allay suspicions of his involvement in the plot, has von Stauffenberg shot in the evening.

The failure of the plot results in the arrest, torture, and execution of dozens of suspects in the following months. Field Marshal Erwin Rommel is among the most notable of those senior military figures aware of the conspiracy.

JULY 21

POLITICS, *POLAND*

The Soviet-backed Polish Committee of National Liberation is formed.

JULY 23

ITALY, *TUSCANY*

After taking the vital port of Livorno on the 19th, the US 34th Division enters the town of Pisa.

JULY 25

WESTERN FRONT, *FRANCE*

Operation Cobra, the Allied breakout from Normandy, begins. Following a massive aerial bombardment, three infantry divisions of General J. Lawton Collins' US VII Corps open a breach in the German line between Marigny and St. Gilles, allowing the armor to get through. Within five days, the US spearhead reaches Avranches, turning the west flank of the German front.

JULY 25–29

PACIFIC, *MARIANAS*

A Japanese counterattack against the US 3rd Marine Division on Guam is defeated. The Japanese lose 19,500 dead, while US fatalities number 1744. On the 24th, the US 4th Marine Division lands on the island of Tinian.

JULY 27–30

EASTERN FRONT, *UKRAINE*

The Soviet 1st Ukrainian Front liberates Lvov, and goes on to establish

▲ *Hitler shows Mussolini his bomb-damaged conference room following the July assassination attempt.*

▼ *Field Marshal Erwin von Witzleben. Involved in the plot to kill Hitler, he was hanged with piano wire at Ploetzenzee.*

several bridgeheads on the Vistula River by the 30th.

JULY 30

WESTERN FRONT, *FRANCE*

Avranches falls to the US VIII Corps.

AUGUST 1

EASTERN FRONT, *POLAND*

The Warsaw uprising begins. Under the command of Lieutenant General Tadeusz Bor-Komorowski, 38,000 soldiers of the Polish Home Army battle with about the same number of German troops stationed in and around the city. Although the two sides are equal in number, the Germans are superior in weapons and can also call on tank and air support. The uprising is designed to free the city from German control and give the Polish government-in-exile in London some influence over the fate of Poland when the Red Army enters the city.

PACIFIC, *MARIANAS*

The battle for the island of Tinian ends. The entire Japanese garrison of 9000 men has been wiped out.

AUGUST 2

EASTERN FRONT, *POLAND*

The left wing of the Soviet 1st Belorussian Front establishes two bridgeheads across the Vistula River south of Warsaw.

AUGUST 3

FAR EAST, *BURMA*

The Japanese withdraw from Myitkyina following an 11-week blockade by Allied forces.

AUGUST 4

POLITICS, *FINLAND*
Marshal Karl von Mannerheim succeeds Rysto Ryti as president of the country. Mannerheim makes it clear to the Germans that he is not bound by Ryti's promises to them.

AUGUST 8

POLITICS, *GERMANY*
Eight German officers, including Field Marshal Erwin von Witzleben, are hanged at the Ploetzenzee prison in Berlin for their part in the July Bomb Plot against Hitler. They are hanged by piano wire, their last moments recorded on film for Adolf Hitler's amusement. All the condemned go to their deaths with dignity, despite their callous treatment.

AUGUST 10

PACIFIC, *MARIANAS*
Organized Japanese resistance on Guam ends, although it is 1960 before the last Japanese soldier on the island surrenders.

▲ *US forces in Paris after its liberation. The German commander of the city chose to ignore Hitler's order to destroy it.*

▶ *General Mark Clark, commander of the US Fifth Army that took Rome.*

AUGUST 11

WESTERN FRONT, *FRANCE*
Operation Totalize, the Canadian First Army's offensive toward Falaise, is called off after failing to meet its main objectives.

AUGUST 15

POLITICS, *SOVIET UNION*
Moscow announces that the Polish Committee of National Liberation is the official body representing the Polish nation and that de facto all negotiations with the émigré government in London are at an end.

WESTERN FRONT, *FRANCE*
Units from the US VI Corps and the French II Corps, together with paratrooper support, launch the Allied invasion of southern France, code-named Operation Anvil.

EASTERN FRONT, *UKRAINE*
The Soviet 4th Ukrainian Front, attacking to seize the passes across the Carpathian Mountains, makes some progress but fails to capture the passes themselves.

AUGUST 19

WESTERN FRONT, *FRANCE*
Allied units have closed the Falaise pocket two weeks after the Canadian First Army launched Operation Totalize to cut off the encircled German troops. Some 30,000 German soldiers escape from the pocket across the Seine River, but an estimated 50,000 are captured and another 10,000 killed. In the pocket, which has been continually strafed and bombed by Allied aircraft, are hundreds of destroyed and abandoned German vehicles. Canadian, British, and Polish forces coming from the north link up with the US First Army driving from Argentan.

AUGUST 23

POLITICS, *ROMANIA*
King Michael orders his forces to cease fighting the Allies and has his pro-Axis premier, Marshal Ion Antonescu, dismissed. He announces that the armistice terms have been accepted.

▲ *Members of the Polish Home Army march to battle as German forces squeeze the Polish-held areas in Warsaw.*

WESTERN FRONT, *FRANCE*
The US 36th Division takes Grenoble. General Dwight D. Eisenhower, Supreme Commander of the Allied Expeditionary Force, overrules General Bernard Montgomery, commander of the 21st Army Group, regarding the latter's plea for a concentrated thrust through the Low Countries into northern Germany. Eisenhower decides that after the capture of Antwerp – a port vital to the Allies – there will be an American assault toward the Saar by General George Patton's US Third Army.

AUGUST 25

POLITICS, *ROMANIA*
The former member of the Axis power bloc declares war on Germany.
WESTERN FRONT, *FRANCE*
The commander of the German garrison of Paris, General Dietrich von Choltitz, surrenders the city to Lieutenant Henri Karcher of the French 2nd Armored Division. Choltitz, who has 5000 men, 50 artillery pieces, and a company of tanks under his command, had been ordered by Hitler to ensure that "Paris [does] not fall into the hands of the enemy except as a heap of ruins." Some 500 Resistance members and 127 other civilians are killed in the fighting for the city.

AUGUST 25–26

WESTERN FRONT, *FRANCE*
The British XII and XXX Corps cross the Seine River.
ITALY, *ADRIATIC SECTOR*
The Allied assault on the Gothic Line begins. The German defense line is 200 miles (320 km) long and runs from the valley of the Magra River, south of La Spezia on the west coast, through the Apuan Mountains and the Apennines, ending in the valley of the Foglia River, and reaching the east coast between Pesaro and Cattolica. The assault is conducted by three corps – the British V, Canadian I, and Polish –

▼ *Reconnaissance vehicles of the British Guards Armored Division in Belgium during the Allied advance on Brussels.*

of the Eighth Army. The plan is to seize the Gemmano-Coriano Ridge complex, thereby unlocking the coastal "gate" and allowing Allied armor to break out to the plains of the Po Valley. However, German resistance is fierce.

AUGUST 27

FAR EAST, *BURMA*
The last of the Chindits are evacuated to India.

AUGUST 28

EASTERN FRONT, *POLAND*
The Polish Home Army continues to fight in Warsaw, but German air attacks and artillery fire are so heavy that the Poles have been forced into the sewers. Soviet leader Stalin has refused to help the freedom fighters, and so the Red Army awaits the outcome on the far side of the Vistula River.

AUGUST 30

EASTERN FRONT, *SLOVAKIA*
Elements of the armed forces and partisans in the Nazi puppet state stage an uprising against their German over-lords as the Red Army approaches the country's eastern border.

AUGUST 31

WESTERN FRONT, *FRANCE*
The US Third Army spearheads an advance toward the Meuse River as the British XXX Corps secures all the main bridges over the Somme near Amiens.

SEPTEMBER 1–3

WESTERN FRONT, *FRANCE/BELGIUM*
The British Guards and 11th Armored Divisions, both part of the British XXX

SEPTEMBER 2

Corps, reach Arras and Aubigny. The Canadian II Corps, part of the Canadian First Army, liberates Dieppe.

On the 2nd, XXX Corps is instructed to slow its advance and await a projected paratroop drop. With the cancellation of the drop, the advance resumes again. The 32nd and 5th Brigades of the Guards Armored Division begin a race for Brussels, which is won by the 32nd Brigade on the 3rd. On the same day, the British XII Corps is bogged down in fighting around the town of Béthune.

SEPTEMBER 2

POLITICS, *FINLAND*
Finland accepts the preliminary conditions for a peace treaty with the Soviet Union and breaks off diplomatic relations with Germany. The Soviet Union then agrees to an armistice.

EASTERN FRONT, *BULGARIA*
The Red Army reaches the Bulgarian border.

SEPTEMBER 3

WESTERN FRONT, *FRANCE/BELGIUM*
The US First Army takes Tournai and three German corps are crushed. The British Second Army liberates Brussels.

SEPTEMBER 4

WESTERN FRONT, *BELGIUM*
The British Second Army liberates the port of Antwerp.

ITALY, *ADRIATIC SECTOR*
The British Eighth Army fails to breach the Gemmano–Coriano Ridge on the Gothic Line. The ridge is the pivot point of the German Tenth Army's second line of defense, and as such it is strongly held, particularly by anti-tank weapons. An attack by the British 2nd Armored Brigade, for example, is defeated easily, with the British losing over half their tanks.

▼ *British Eighth Army artillery shells German strongpoints on the Gothic Line in Italy. But the initial assaults failed.*

▲ *Those Allied troops who liberated Brussels experienced something akin to a Roman triumph on the streets of the city.*

SEPTEMBER 5

WESTERN FRONT, *FRANCE*
US Third Army spearheads cross the Meuse River. General Karl von Rundstedt is made Commander-in-Chief West by Hitler with orders to counterattack the Allies and split their armies apart. However, his resources for such an undertaking are scant.

EASTERN FRONT, *BULGARIA*
After declaring war on the country, Red Army units invade rapidly and reach Turnu Severin. The Soviet Union's leadership is planning to occupy the entire Balkans.

SEPTEMBER 8

POLITICS, *BULGARIA*
Bulgaria declares war on Germany.

AIR WAR, *MANCHURIA*
China-based B-29 Superfortress bombers make their first daylight raid against Japanese industrial targets at Anshan.

SEPTEMBER 8–13

WESTERN FRONT, *BELGIUM/HOLLAND*
The British 50th Division crosses the Albert Canal at Gheel. On the 10th, the British Guards Armored Division advances to De Groot.

Three days later, the British 15th Division crosses the Meuse–Escaut Canal.

SEPTEMBER 8–25

EASTERN FRONT, *SLOVAKIA*

The Soviet 1st and 4th Ukrainian Fronts begin their attacks on the Dukla Pass, the key to the Carpathian Mountain barrier separating the Red Army from eastern Slovakia. It will take the Soviets until the end of November to clear the Carpathians.

SEPTEMBER 10–14

EASTERN FRONT, *POLAND*

Despite Stalin's refusal to aid the hard-pressed Warsaw insurgents, units of Marshal Konstantin Rokossovsky's 1st Belorussian Front attack Praga, the east bank quarter of the city. Fighting is savage, and it is not until the 14th that the area is freed from German control.

SEPTEMBER 15

EASTERN FRONT, *POLAND*

Units of the Soviet-raised First Polish Army cross the Vistula River and seize bridgeheads in Warsaw.

AIR WAR, *NORWAY*

Lancasters from 9 and 617 Squadrons of the RAF attack Germany's only remaining battleship – the *Tirpitz* – in Altenfiord. However, little damage is done, chiefly due to the effectiveness of the German smokescreens.

▲ *British paratroopers in action near Arnhem. The enemy is close, as indicated by the acute angle of the mortar tube.*

▼ *Allied vehicles rumble across the bridge at Nijmegen, Holland, during the disastrous Operation Market Garden.*

SEPTEMBER 17

WESTERN FRONT, *HOLLAND*

Operation Market Garden, General Bernard Montgomery's plan for an armored and airborne thrust across Holland to outflank the German defenses, begins. The British 1st Airborne Division lands near Arnhem, the US 101st Airborne Division near Eindhoven, the US 82nd Airborne Division near Grave and Nijmegen, while the British XXX Corps advances from the Dutch border. The 82nd lands without difficulty and takes the Maas and Maas–Waal Canal bridges, but then encounters heavy resistance at Nijmegen. The 101st Division also takes its bridges, but the British paratroopers discover their way to Arnhem is blocked by German units. Only one battalion, under Lieutenant Colonel John Frost, manages to reach the bridge, where it is quickly cut off.

SEPTEMBER 19–21

WESTERN FRONT, *HOLLAND*

Forward elements of the British XXX Corps reach US paratroopers at Eindhoven, but at Arnhem all attempts to break through to the troops fail. On the 20th, the bridge at Nijmegen is captured by a combined force drawn from the US 82nd Airborne Division and the British XXX Corps. The next day, the British troops at Arnhem are

Canadian II Corps; its garrison of 20,000 men is taken into captivity.

SEPTEMBER 22–25

WESTERN FRONT, *HOLLAND*
Outside Arnhem, the British XXX Corps' advance is slowed by German resistance. The Polish Brigade drops south of the Neder Rijn near Driel. On the 23rd, attempts by the Poles and advance troops of XXX Corps to cross the river are driven back, and so the evacuation of the surviving paratroopers begins two days later, leaving 2500 of their dead comrades behind.

SEPTEMBER 23

AIR WAR, *GERMANY*
The RAF makes a night precision raid on the Dortmund to Ems Canal, the inland waterway that links the Ruhr with other industrial centers. A total of 141 aircraft are involved, the canal is breached, and a section drained. The RAF loses 14 bombers.

SEPTEMBER 23–30

WESTERN FRONT, *FRANCE*
The Canadian 3rd Division invests the port of Calais, which is defended by

▲ *A PIAT antitank weapon waits for enemy armor on the outskirts of Arnhem as the Germans close in on the British.*

overwhelmed. The remainder form a defensive perimeter on the northern bank of the Neder Rijn, around the village of Oosterbeek.

SEPTEMBER 21

POLITICS, *YUGOSLAVIA*
The partisan chief Marshal Tito meets the Soviet leader Joseph Stalin. They reach agreement on the "temporary entry of the Red Army into Yugoslavia."

ITALY, *ADRIATIC SECTOR*
The Eighth Army takes Rimini after a week of heavy fighting. Since the beginning of its offensive against the Gothic Line, it has lost 14,000 men killed, wounded, and

missing, plus 200 tanks. The Italian campaign has not lived up to being the "soft underbelly of Europe." A more accurate description would be "tough old gut."

SEPTEMBER 22

WESTERN FRONT, *FRANCE*
Boulogne surrenders to the

▼ *Sherman tanks of the British Eighth Army on the move near Rimini during the grim battle of attrition against the Gothic Line.*

▲ *Beaten but defiant, these British paratroopers are led into captivity at the end of Market Garden – 2500 of their comrades were killed in the operation.*

7500 men. Following heavy artillery and bomber attacks, and the use of specialized armor, Calais surrenders on the 30th.

OCTOBER 2

EASTERN FRONT, *POLAND*

After a bitter two-month battle, the last Poles in Warsaw surrender. The Germans evacuate the entire remaining population and begin the systematic destruction of anything left standing. Polish deaths number 150,000, while the German commander, SS General Erich von dem Bach-Zelewski, claims he has lost 26,000 men.

OCTOBER 3

AIR WAR, *BRITAIN*

The German bombardment of Britain with V2 long-range heavy rockets has resumed from new launch sites dotted across Holland.

▶ *A British paratrooper in cover on the outskirts of Oosterbeek. The failure of XXX Corps to cross the Neder Rijn doomed the airborne operation.*

OCTOBER 4

MEDITERRANEAN, *GREECE*

Determined to prevent a communist takeover in Greece, Winston Churchill launches Operation Manna. British troops land at Patrai in the Peloponnese as German forces pull back.

OCTOBER 9

WESTERN FRONT, *BELGIUM*

Although the Allies captured Antwerp on September 4, they have not been able to use the great port because there are German units on both sides of the Scheldt estuary. Therefore, the Canadian First Army commences operations to eradicate the enemy presence in this area.

PACIFIC, *IWO JIMA*

Admiral Chester W. Nimitz, commander of all Allied forces in the Central Pacific, informs Lieutenant General Holland M. "Howling Mad" Smith, one of the leading exponents of amphibious warfare and commander of all US Marines in the Pacific, that the island of Iwo Jima will be his next target and that Smith will lead

▲ Landing craft and vehicles of the Canadian First Army engaged in clearing the Scheldt estuary near Antwerp.

▼ A German V2 rocket is readied for launch from a site in Holland. The only way to reduce the damage caused by these weapons was to bomb their launch sites and their construction factories.

the invasion with three US Marine divisions. The island is within bombing range of the Japanese mainland.

OCTOBER 10-29

EASTERN FRONT, *HUNGARY*

A massive tank battle rages around Drebrecan between two panzer divisions of Germany's Army Group Southern Ukraine, commanded by General Johannes Friessneer. The German forces have cut off three Soviet tank corps of Marshal Rodion Malinovsky's 2nd Ukrainian Front. The Soviets lose many tanks in the initial German attacks, but fresh Soviet units tip the scales against the Germans, who do not have the forces to fight attritional battles. Farther south, the German Army Group E leaves Greece.

OCTOBER 11-19

BALKANS, *YUGOSLAVIA*

The Red Army joins with the Yugoslavian First Army in the drive to Belgrade, which is abandoned by the Germans on the 19th.

OCTOBER 14

POLITICS, *GERMANY*

Field Marshal Erwin Rommel commits suicide with poison. Implicated in the July assassination plot against Hitler, he has killed himself, under pressure, to save his family from arrest. He is to be given a state funeral as part of the charade to maintain the illusion that he was an uncompromising Nazi.

▲ *A knocked-out Joseph Stalin tank at Drebrecan, the site of a massive tank battle and a German defeat.*

▼ *General Douglas MacArthur (second from left) wades ashore in the Philippines, keeping his promise "I shall return."*

OCTOBER 20

BALKANS, *YUGOSLAVIA*

The 1st Proletarian Division of Marshal Tito's Army of Liberation captures Belgrade.

PACIFIC, *PHILIPPINES*

As the US Sixth Army lands on Leyte Island, General Douglas MacArthur wades ashore and keeps a promise he made two years earlier: "I shall return." By the evening 10,000 US troops are dug in around Leyte's capital, Tacloban, and Dulag to the south.

OCTOBER 21

WESTERN FRONT, *GERMANY*

The city of Aachen surrenders to US forces following a 10-day siege.

OCTOBER 23-26

PACIFIC, *PHILIPPINES*

Following the US landings on Leyte, the Japanese put in motion their Sho Plan, in which a part of the Combined Fleet is used to decoy the US carrier force while the remainder concentrates against the landing area and attempts to destroy the amphibious armada. The resulting naval battle of Leyte Gulf has four phases: the Battle of the Sibuyan Sea, the Battle of the Surigao Strait, the Battle of Samar, and

DECISIVE WEAPONS

KAMIKAZE

Kamikaze, meaning "Divine Wind," was a suicide tactic employed by the Japanese military to destroy US military shipping by crashing explosive-filled aircraft into vessels. The cult of the kamikazes was influenced by the Bushido code of conduct based on spiritualism under the influence of Buddhism, which emphasized both bravery and conscience.

The Battle of Leyte Gulf in October 1944 saw the beginning of the Kamikaze Corps, and at the end of the war Japan had over 5000 aircraft ready for suicide missions. Kamikaze pilots endeavored to hit the deck of their target to cause maximum damage (against carriers the best point of aim was the central elevator). The overall military effect of the kamikazes was limited: during the Okinawa battles, for example, of the 1900 suicide sorties made, only 14 percent were effective.

The damaged hangar of USS Sangamon following a kamikaze attack by just one aircraft.

the Battle of Cape Engano. The result is that the Japanese Combined Fleet is finished as a fighting force, not least because its losses in trained pilots are irreplaceable. It loses 500 aircraft, four carriers, three battleships, six heavy and four light cruisers, 11 destroyers, and a submarine, while every other ship engaged is damaged. US losses are 200 aircraft, one light carrier, two escort carriers, two destroyers, and one destroyer-escort.

OCTOBER 31
EASTERN FRONT, *BALTIC*
The Soviet 1st Baltic Front isolates the remnants of Army Group North in the Courland Peninsula.

NOVEMBER 7
ESPIONAGE, *JAPAN*
The Japanese hang the spy Richard Sorge at Sugamo Prison, Tokyo. He has been working for eight years as the Tokyo correspondent for a German newspaper, and during this time has sent the Soviet Union detailed information concerning German and Japanese plans, including the attack on the Soviet Union in 1941.

NOVEMBER 8
WESTERN FRONT, *BELGIUM*
The Canadian First Army completes the clearing of the Scheldt estuary. It takes 41,000 prisoners during the operation at a cost of 12,873 men killed, wounded, and missing.

NOVEMBER 9
WESTERN FRONT, *FRANCE*
General George Patton's US Third Army (500,000 men and 500 tanks) crosses the Moselle River on a broad front toward the heart of the Reich.

▲ *The US Navy bombards the island of Iwo Jima to soften up the defenses prior to an amphibious landing.*

NOVEMBER 11–12
PACIFIC, *IWO JIMA*
The US Navy bombards the Japanese-held island for the first time.

NOVEMBER 12
AIR WAR, *NORWAY*
RAF Lancaster bombers from 9 and 617 Squadrons sink the German battleship *Tirpitz* in Altenfiord, killing 1100 of its crew when the ship capsizes.

NOVEMBER 24
AIR WAR, *JAPAN*
American B-29 Superfortress bombers mount their first raid against Tokyo from the Mariana Islands.

DECEMBER 4
FAR EAST, *BURMA*
General William Slim, commander of the British Fourteenth Army, begins the destruction of Japanese forces in Burma. The British IV and XXXIII Corps begin the offensive, heading for the Japanese airfields at Yeu and Shwebo. The Japanese Fifteenth Army, commanded by General Shihachi

Katamura, is in a weakened state following its reverses during the fighting at Kohima and Imphal.

DECEMBER 5–7

PACIFIC, *PHILIPPINES*
The final US offensive on Leyte begins with a drive by the X Corps into the northern Ormoc Valley, with simultaneous assaults by the XIV Corps in central and southwestern Leyte. On the 7th, the 77th Division lands virtually unopposed below Ormoc. Japanese forces are pressed into the Ormoc Valley, and are under intense artillery and aerial attack.

HOME FRONT, *GERMANY*
The Nazi women's leader, Gertrud Scholtz-Klink, appeals for all women over 18 to volunteer for service in the army and air force to release men for the front.

DECEMBER 8

PACIFIC, *IWO JIMA*
The US Air Force begins a 72-day bombardment of Iwo Jima, the longest and heaviest of the Pacific war, to pave the way for an amphibious assault.

DECEMBER 15

PACIFIC, *PHILIPPINES*
As part of General Douglas MacArthur's second phase of the invasion of the Philippines, the US 24th Division lands on the island of Mindoro.

FAR EAST, *BURMA*
The British 19th and 36th Divisions meet at Indaw, and set up a continuous front against the Japanese in northern Burma.

▲ *After spending most of the war in Norwegian coastal waters, the Tirpitz was finally sunk on November 12.*

▶ *British troops of IV Corps move against the Japanese Fifteenth Army after Kohima and Imphal.*

MEDITERRANEAN, *GREECE*
British tanks and armored cars have lifted the siege of Kifissia RAF base by ELAS rebels (the National Liberation Army – the military wing of the country's communist party).

AIR WAR, *BELGIUM*
The first jet bomber operation takes

▲ *A barrage of rockets is unleashed against enemy beach defenses as the first wave of US assault units heads for Mindoro Island in the Philippines.*

DECEMBER 16–22

WESTERN FRONT, *ARDENNES*
Hitler launches Operation Watch on the Rhine, his attempt to break through the US VIII Corps on the Ardennes front, reach the Meuse River, and capture Antwerp, thereby splitting the Allies in two. The German units – 200,000 men – form Army Group B under the overall command of Field Marshal Gerd von Rundstedt. This force comprises the Sixth SS Panzer Army, Fifth Panzer Army, and Seventh Army. US forces total 80,000 men.

Surprise is total and there is dense cloud and fog, which negates Allied air superiority, but the Germans fail to take the towns of St. Vith and Bastogne immediately, which narrows their attack front. On the 17th, troops of SS Lieutenant Colonel Joachim Peiper's battlegroup murder 71 American prisoners of war at Malmédy in Belgium, leaving their bodies in a field.

By the 22nd, the Americans, having lost 8000 of 22,000 men at St. Vith, pull back from the town, but the men of the 28th Infantry, 10th, and 101st Airborne Divisions continue to hold out stubbornly in Bastogne against one infantry and two panzer divisions. On the same day the Germans mount their last attempt to reach the Meuse.

As part of their sabotage operations, the Germans are using English-speaking commandos dressed in US uniforms to spread confusion, especially at road junctions and on bridges. However, measures have been taken to defeat these infiltrators, many of whom are later shot as spies.

south of the German "bulge" into the Ardennes. The US Third Army's 4th Armored Division relieves Bastogne as Hitler is informed by his generals that Antwerp can no longer be reached by his forces. The only hope of salvaging any sort of victory in the Ardennes is to swing the Fifth and Sixth Panzer Armies north to cross the Meuse west of Liège and come in behind Aachen. However, this presupposes the capture of Bastogne and an attack from the north to link with the panzers – both are increasingly unlikely.

DECEMBER 30

WESTERN FRONT, *ARDENNES*
At Bastogne, General George Patton, his forces swollen to six divisions, resumes his attack northeast toward Houffalize. At the same time, General Hasso von Manteuffel, commander of the German Fifth Panzer Army, launches another major attempt to cut the corridor into Bastogne and take the town. The fighting is intense, but Patton's forces stand firm and defeat the German attack.

DECEMBER 31

POLITICS, *HUNGARY*
The Provisional National Government of Hungary, set up under Soviet control in the city of Drebrecan, declares war on Germany.

▲ *Aided by secrecy and poor weather, the initial assaults of the German Ardennes offensive met with success.*

▼ *Abandoned German Panther and Panzer IV tanks in the Ardennes in late December. Shortages of fuel, stubborn defense, and Allied air attacks contributed to the failure of the offensive.*

place when twin-engined German Arado 234B bombers raid a factory and marshaling yards. The raid is led by Captain Dieter Lukesch.

DECEMBER 26

WESTERN FRONT, *ARDENNES*
The US First and Third Armies launch counterattacks against the north and

1945

In this final year of the war, Germany and Japan were defeated by a relentless tide of aircraft, tanks, ships, and men. Their cities were devastated by fleets of bombers, their armies were encircled and then annihilated, and their merchant and naval fleets were either sunk or trapped in port. There was no match for the economic might of the United States and the numerical superiority of the Soviet Union. Atomic bombs finally ended the war against Japan.

JANUARY 1

EASTERN FRONT, *CZECHOSLOVAKIA*
The Soviet 2nd and 4th Ukrainian Fronts begin an offensive against the German Army Group Center in Czechoslovakia. The German-held area contains the last foreign industrial resources under the control of the Third Reich. The Soviet fronts between them have 853,000 men, 9986 guns, 590 tanks, and 1400 combat aircraft. German forces total 550,000 men, 5000 guns, and 700 combat aircraft. Despite German fortifications and resistance, the Red Army makes good progress.

JANUARY 1–21

WESTERN FRONT, *FRANCE*
In a follow up to the attack in the Ardennes sector, General Johannes von Blaskowitz's Army Group G attacks the US Seventh Army in Alsace and Lorraine, forming the so-called Colmar Pocket. The Americans retreat, although General Dwight D. Eisenhower, commander-in-chief of Allied forces in Europe, orders Strasbourg to be held after the leader of the Free French, General Charles de Gaulle, expresses concern that the loss of the city would affect French morale. The fighting

► *Chinese soldiers of the Northern Combat Area Command march to the front in northern Burma.*

▲ *US troops and vehicles in Bastogne, which resisted all German assaults in December 1944 and January 1945.*

▼ *The US 7th Fleet prior to the assault on Luzon. The Consolidated Catalinas are from the Air-Sea Rescue Squadron.*

JANUARY 3–4

PACIFIC, *RYUKYUS*
The US 3rd Fleet attacks Japanese targets on Formosa, destroying 100 enemy aircraft.

JANUARY 3–16

WESTERN FRONT, *ARDENNES*
The last German attack against Bastogne is defeated. The Allied counterattack begins: on the northern flank the US First Army attacks the northern sector of the "bulge," while the southern sector is assaulted by the US Third Army. In the "bulge" itself, Hitler orders a German withdrawal to Houffalize on the 8th. However, in the face of overwhelming Allied superiority in men and hardware the Germans are forced to retreat farther east, and the US First and Third Armies link up at Houffalize on the 16th.

JANUARY 4

FAR EAST, *BURMA*
Units of General William Slim's British Fourteenth Army make an unopposed landing on the island of Akyab, securing the port and the airfield.

JANUARY 4–6

PACIFIC, *PHILIPPINES*
Prior to the landings on Luzon, the Japanese launch a series of kamikaze attacks on ships of the US 7th Fleet. Over 1000 Americans and Australians are killed in the suicide attacks, a minesweeper is sunk, and more than 30 other vessels are damaged.

JANUARY 5

AIR WAR, *BELGIUM/HOLLAND*
The Luftwaffe launches Operation Bodenplatte in support of the

is bitter. It costs the US 15,600 casualties, and the Germans, 25,000.

JANUARY 1–27

FAR EAST, *BURMA*
The Chinese units of Lieutenant General Daniel Sultan's Northern Combat Area Command and Marshal Wei Lihuang's Y Force link up in northern Burma in the face of significant resistance from the Japanese 56th Division.

JANUARY 2

TECHNOLOGY, *UNITED STATES*
An American Sikorsky helicopter is used in convoy escort duties for the first time.

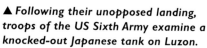

▲ *Following their unopposed landing, troops of the US Sixth Army examine a knocked-out Japanese tank on Luzon.*

Ardennes offensive with 1035 fighters and bombers attacking Allied airfields in Belgium and southern Holland. The Germans destroy 156 Allied aircraft but lose 277 of their own, losses the Luftwaffe cannot make good. It is the last major German air attack.

JANUARY 7

EASTERN FRONT, *HUNGARY*
German forces capture Esztergom, northwest of Budapest, a Nazi National Redoubt, in their attempt to relieve the garrison in the capital.

JANUARY 9

PACIFIC, *PHILIPPINES*
Preceded by a heavy bombardment, units of the US Sixth Army, commanded by Lieutenant General Walter Krueger, make unopposed amphibious landings on Luzon.

JANUARY 10–FEBRUARY 10

EASTERN FRONT,
CZECHOSLOVAKIA
With the Red Army on their soil, Czech partisans begin to attack German units and supply lines.

JANUARY 12–17

EASTERN FRONT, *POLAND*
The Red Army begins its Vistula–Oder offensive. Soviet forces total over two million men: Marshal Georgi Zhukov's 1st Belorussian Front, Marshal Ivan Konev's 1st Ukrainian Front, and General Ivan Petrov's 4th Ukrainian Front. In addition, Marshal Konstantin Rokossovsky's 2nd Belorussian Front and General Ivan Chernyakhovsky's 3rd Belorussian Front are providing tactical and strategic cooperation. The Soviets make excellent progress, and by the 17th, Zhukov's Second Guards Tank Army has reached Sochaczew. To the north, the 1st Baltic, 2nd Belorussian, and 3rd Belorussian Fronts launch an offensive into East Prussia on the 13th.

JANUARY 14

FAR EAST, *BURMA*
The 19th Division, part of Lieutenant General William Slim's British Fourteenth Army, crosses the Irrawaddy River at Kyaukmyaung but is then violently attacked by Japanese troops holding the line of the waterway. Forced back by hordes of infantry with fixed bayonets, the division manages to hold the bridgehead in the face of the fierce onslaught.

JANUARY 15–26

WESTERN FRONT, *GERMANY*
After the containment of the German Ardennes offensive, the Allies launch a large counterattack against the Germans. In the north, Field Marshal Bernard Montgomery's British 21st Army Group presses into the Roermond area, while farther south General Omar Bradley's US 12th Army Group approaches the upper Roer River.

JANUARY 16

FAR EAST, *BURMA*
In the north of the country, General Daniel Sultan's Chinese New First Army occupies Namhkan. The last Japanese positions threatening the Burma Road have been eradicated.

JANUARY 18–27

EASTERN FRONT, *HUNGARY*
The German IV SS Panzer Corps launches an

▶ *One of the hundreds of Japanese soldiers killed in and around the Irrawaddy River, Burma.*

MARSHAL GEORGI ZHUKOV

Georgi Zhukov (1896–1974) was born into a peasant family and conscripted into the Imperial Russian Army in 1915. After fighting in World War I, he joined the Red Army in October 1918. He studied at the Frunze Military Academy (1928–31), and in 1938 was appointed deputy commander of the Belorussian Military District. Apparently earmarked for execution in the Stalinist purges, he escaped with his life due to an administrative error.

Zhukov's generalship skills first came to the fore in 1939, when he led the Soviet 1st Army Group to a decisive victory over the Japanese at the Khalka River (the so-called "Nomonhan Incident" over a disputed frontier in Manchuria). Following the German invasion of the Soviet Union in June 1941, Zhukov held a variety of staff positions and field commands, repulsing the enemy from Moscow in late 1941, having a hand in the great Soviet victories at Stalingrad and Kursk, and capturing Berlin in 1945. The victory at Stalingrad was particularly impressive, as the German Sixth Army had more men than Zhukov's forces. He used his units to achieve a crushing superiority over weaker Romanian armies along the front on both flanks of the Sixth Army. Once they had been smashed, he cut off the German forces in the Stalingrad area.

Zhukov was a forceful commander who possessed outstanding tactical and strategic ability – qualities that made his superiors view him as a potential threat. The fact that as a general he never lost a single battle is testament to his attributes as a military leader.

offensive to relieve Budapest. In the face of Soviet resistance, it reaches the Vali River on the 22nd, only 15 miles (24 km) southwest of the city. However, the momentum of the attack had been halted by the 25th, and two days later the Red Army counterattacks with 12 rifle divisions and strong armored support, effectively ending the German Budapest relief operation.

JANUARY 18–FEBRUARY 3

FAR EAST, *BURMA*
A vicious battle develops at Namh-pakka between the Japanese 56th Division, which is

▲ *As the Red Army steamroller gathers momentum, Estonian coastguards fire a salute to welcome the Soviets.*

retreating to Lashio, and the American Mars Brigade.

JANUARY 19

EASTERN FRONT, *POLAND*
Following heavy fighting, units of the 1st Ukrainian Front liberate Cracow, the former capital of Poland. The German Third and Fourth Panzer Armies are now isolated in East Prussia, and the German front is falling apart in the face of immense pressure.

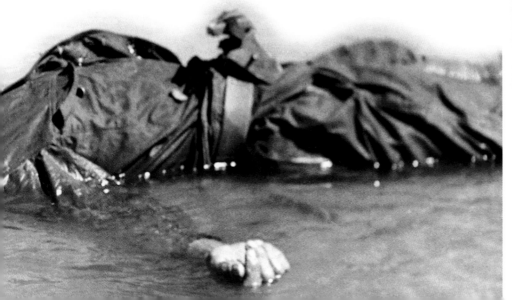

JANUARY 21

JANUARY 21

FAR EAST, *BURMA*
The island of Ramree is invaded by the British 71st Brigade. Japanese resistance is virtually non-existent, although it stiffens as Allied troops push farther inland. The island is not cleared until the middle of February, by which time General William Slim has an invaluable base for future long-range operations against Rangoon.

JANUARY 23

EASTERN FRONT, *EAST PRUSSIA*
The Soviet 2nd Belorussian Front cuts all road and rail crossings across the Vistula River, isolating German units on the east bank.

EASTERN FRONT, *POLAND*
The Soviet Second Guards Tank Army, part of the 1st Belorussian Front, storms the fortified town of Bromberg, an important strongpoint in the German Poznan Line.

JANUARY 27

EASTERN FRONT, *POLAND*
The Red Army liberates the Nazi death camp at Auschwitz. The SS has evacuated the camp nine days previously, taking 20,000 weak inmates with them. Those left number a few hundred disease-ridden inmates in the camp's hospital block.

FAR EAST, *BURMA*
Units of the Allied Y Force, pushing across the Shweli River at Wanting,

▼ *British troops carry a wounded comrade to a dressing station near Myitson, Burma.*

reopen the Burma Road supply route into China.

JANUARY 28

WESTERN FRONT, *ARDENNES*
The last vestiges of the German "bulge" in the Ardennes are wiped out. The total cost to the Germans in manpower for their Ardennes offensive has been 100,000 killed, wounded, and captured. The Americans have lost 81,000 killed, wounded, or captured, and the British 1400. Both sides have lost heavily in hardware – up to 800 tanks on each side. The Germans have also lost around 1000 aircraft.

▲ *German prisoners taken during the Ardennes offensive. The Wehrmacht lost over 100,000 men and 800 precious tanks.*

However, whereas the Americans can make good their losses in just a few weeks, for the Germans the military losses are irreplaceable.

JANUARY 28–FEBRUARY 1

WESTERN FRONT, *ARDENNES*
Two corps of General Courtney Hodges' US First Army and one from General George Patton's US Third Army try to penetrate the German defenses

northeast of St. Vith, which lies astride the Losheim Gap. Snow and ice inhibit progress, and the Germans manage to fight back hard, thereby slowing the rate of the US advance.

▼ *As fighting rages in and around Manila, the capital of the Philippines, refugees pour out of the city. This bridge was built by US engineers.*

JANUARY 29

PACIFIC, *PHILIPPINES*
Major General Charles Hall's US XI Corps lands unopposed on the west coast of Luzon just to the north of the Bataan Peninsula.

JANUARY 30

EASTERN FRONT, *GERMANY*
The left wing of the 1st Ukrainian Front has reached the Oder River and some of its units have set up bridge-heads on the west bank. This ends one of the greatest strategic operations of the whole war.

The Red Army has advanced 355 miles (568 km), liberated all of Poland and a large part of Czechoslovakia, reached the Oder on a broad front, and is only 100 miles (160 km) from Berlin. In its offensive, it has inflicted losses of 500,000 dead, wounded, or captured on the Germans, and captured 1300 aircraft, 1400 tanks, and over 14,000 guns of all calibers.

JANUARY 31

PACIFIC, *PHILIPPINES*
Elements of the US 11th Airborne Division go ashore at Nasugbu Bay against light Japanese resistance. The US troops land just 50 miles (80 km) southwest of the capital Manila, which is their ultimate objective.

▲ *The destruction in Manila after the city fell to the US XIV Corps. The whole of the Japanese garrison was wiped out.*

JANUARY 31–FEBRUARY 21

FAR EAST, *BURMA*
The British 36th Division effects a crossing of the Shweli River at Myitson following a savage battle against the Japanese. The division's success threatens the Japanese northern approaches to the Mandalay Plain.

FEBRUARY 1

EASTERN FRONT, *EAST PRUSSIA*
The trapped German Fourth Army attempts to reach German-held Elbing but is halted by a Soviet counterattack.

FEBRUARY 3–MARCH 3

PACIFIC, *PHILIPPINES*
The US XIV Corps begins its attack against Manila, which is defended by 17,000 Japanese troops under Rear Admiral Sanji Iwabuchi. The garrison, after destroying the city (the "Rape of Manila"), is wiped out. US casualties total 1000 dead and 5500 wounded; 100,000 Filipino citizens are killed.

FEBRUARY 4–11

POLITICS, *ALLIES*
Marshal Joseph Stalin, President Franklin D. Roosevelt, and Prime

▲ *The "Big Three" at the Yalta Conference, where the postwar division of Germany and Austria was agreed.*

Minister Winston Churchill meet at the Yalta Conference in the Crimea to discuss postwar Europe. The "Big Three" decide that Germany will be divided into four zones, administered by Britain, France, the United States, and the Soviet Union. An Allied Control Commission will be set up in Berlin, and Austria will also be divided into four zones. The capital, Vienna, will be in the Soviet zone and will also have a four-power administration. The Soviet Union will declare war on Japan two months after the war in Europe has ended, while changes to Poland's borders will allow the Soviet Union to annex former Polish areas.

FEBRUARY 5

WESTERN FRONT, *FRANCE*
The German bridgehead on the west bank of the Rhine, south of Strasbourg around the town of Colmar – the Colmar Pocket – is split by units of the French First Army attacking from the south and elements of the US Seventh Army advancing from the north. The elimination of the pocket is essential to the crossing of the Rhine.

FEBRUARY 8–24

EASTERN FRONT, *GERMANY*
Marshal Ivan Konev's 1st Ukrainian Front begins its offensive to disrupt German plans and establish an impregnable defense line along the southern Oder. By the 24th his forces have advanced 75 miles (120 km) and seized Lower Silesia, in addition to freeing 91,300 Soviet citizens and 22,500 other foreigners from German imprisonment.

FEBRUARY 9

WESTERN FRONT, *FRANCE*
Following Allied pressure against the Colmar Pocket, Field Marshal Gerd von Rundstedt, German commander-in-chief in the West, convinces Hitler to pull back the Nineteenth Army across the Rhine. The west bank of the river south of Strasbourg is now free of German troops.

FEBRUARY 10

EASTERN FRONT, *POLAND*
The Soviet 2nd Belorussian Front launches an offensive in the region of Grudziadz and Sepolno but runs into determined resistance from the German Second Army. Soviet progress is very slow.

◀ *German rockets scream through the air as the Second Army tries to halt the Soviet 2nd Belorussian Front in Poland.*

▼ *Women help clear rubble from the ruins of the Catholic cathedral in Dresden after the Allied air raids against the city.*

suburbs. The bombing triggers the worst firestorm of the war, in which at least 50,000 people are killed. The raid is controversial, as the city has negligible strategic value, is virtually undefended, and is crammed with refugees. The next morning, the city is bombed again by 400 aircraft of the US 8th Army Air Force.

FEBRUARY 14

EASTERN FRONT, *EAST PRUSSIA*

As a result of the Red Army's advance, over half of the 2.3 million population of East Prussia have fled west. Some have been taken out by boat, although most have walked or made their way by horse and wagon. Thousands have died from either cold or exhaustion, or in Soviet air and artillery attacks.

FEBRUARY 16–28

PACIFIC, *PHILIPPINES*

US forces begin to clear the Japanese from the entrance to Manila Bay, Luzon. The peninsula of Bataan falls relatively easily, though Corregidor proves a harder nut to crack. The assault begins on the 16th with a battalion of US paratroopers dropping on the southwest heights of the island. Simultaneously, an amphibious assault by a battalion of infantry takes place on the southern shore. By the evening of the 26th, almost the whole island is in US hands. It is declared secure on the 28th. The Japanese garrison refuses to surrender, and is virtually wiped out in the fighting.

FEBRUARY 11

EASTERN FRONT, *HUNGARY*

The trapped Axis garrison in Budapest attempts to break through the Soviet lines. However, of the nearly 30,000 Germans and Hungarians, fewer than 700 are able to escape.

▲ *Boeing B-17 Flying Fortress bombers of the US 8th Army Air Force unleash death and destruction on Dresden.*

▼ *American paratroopers in action on Corregidor during the operations to clear the entrance to Manila Bay.*

FEBRUARY 13–14

AIR WAR, *GERMANY*

The RAF mounts a night raid on Dresden. The 805 bombers inflict massive damage on the city's old town and inner

FEBRUARY 16

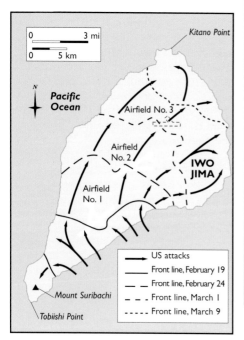

▲ The conquest of Iwo Jima was a tough battle, especially the agonizing drive to the north against a fanatical enemy.

FEBRUARY 16

PACIFIC, *IWO JIMA*

The US Navy begins a three-day concentrated bombardment of Iwo Jima. The island has to be taken for four reasons: the unescorted US bombers flying from the Marianas to Japan are suffering heavy losses, and, therefore, airfields closer to Japan are needed for fighter escorts; Iwo Jima has two air bases and is only three hours' flying time from Tokyo; Iwo

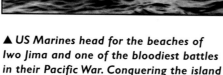

▲ US Marines head for the beaches of Iwo Jima and one of the bloodiest battles in their Pacific War. Conquering the island required the destruction of the garrison.

Jima is prewar Japanese territory, whose loss would be a severe blow to the homeland; and it is a key link in the air defenses of the Marianas.

FEBRUARY 17

PACIFIC, *IWO JIMA*

Under the command of Lieutenant General Holland M. Smith, the US 4th and 5th Marine Divisions land. Resistance is at first light, but then the attackers are hit by intense artillery and small-arms fire from the 21,000-man Japanese garrison. However, despite casualties, the Americans have 30,000 men on the island by the end of the day.

FEBRUARY 21

WESTERN FRONT, *GERMANY*

The Canadian First Army takes Goch, which ends Operation Veritable, an offensive from the Nijmegen area between the Rhine and the Maas Rivers.

FAR EAST, *BURMA*

General William Slim's British Fourteenth Army begins the reconquest of

▶ Troops of Slim's army wade across the Irrawaddy in the drive toward Mandalay.

◀ Lieutenant General Holland M. Smith, who commanded the US forces on Iwo Jima.

central Burma. Breaking out of the Irrawaddy bridgeheads, columns are directed to Mandalay, Burma's second city, and the important rail and road communications center at Meiktila.

In northern Burma, the British 36th Division breaks through Japanese positions at Myitson after a vicious three-week battle. Japanese forces are now on the retreat in the area.

FEBRUARY 23

WESTERN FRONT, *GERMANY*

The US First and Ninth Armies launch Operation Grenade, the crossing of the Roer River, and head to the Rhine. Preceded by a barrage from over 1000

that only those states that declare war before March 1 will be invited to a conference in San Francisco on the proposed postwar United Nations.

WESTERN FRONT, *GERMANY*
The US First Army begins its drive to the Rhine River, spearheaded by the VII Corps.

PACIFIC, *PHILIPPINES*
A regiment of the US 41st Division captures the island of Palawan.

MARCH 1

EASTERN FRONT, *GERMANY*
Marshal Georgi Zhukov's 1st Belorussian Front begins an offensive to destroy the German Third Panzer Army – which has 203,000 men, 700 tanks, 2500 guns, and 100 coastal artillery and fixed anti-aircraft guns – as part of the Red Army's effort to secure its flanks prior to the assault on Berlin itself.

MARCH 3

WESTERN FRONT, *FRANCE*
In snow and freezing rain, General George Patton unleashes his US Third Army over the Kyll River toward the

▼ *General George Patton's US Third Army on the move toward the Rhine River at the beginning of March.*

guns, four infantry divisions cross the river in the face of sporadic resistance. German reserves have been committed to halt Operation Veritable farther north. By the end of the day, 28 infantry battalions have crossed the river.

PACIFIC, *IWO JIMA*
US Marines raise the American flag on the summit of Mount Suribachi in the south of the island. The US Marines now have to turn north to clear the rest of the island.

FEBRUARY 25

PACIFIC, *IWO JIMA*
As the fighting on Iwo Jima becomes more intense, the US 3rd Marine Division is committed to the battle.

FEBRUARY 28

POLITICS, *SAUDI ARABIA*
Following the example of Syria on the 26th, Saudi Arabia declares war on Germany. The rush to join the Allies in part stems from the announcement

MARCH 4

Rhine. The attack is spearheaded by the VIII and XII Corps, which make good progress.

EASTERN FRONT, *GERMANY*
In an effort to try to recapture the lost defenses on the Oder River, the German Fourth Panzer Army counterattacks from the Lauban area toward Glogau. However, strong Soviet entrenched positions stop the attack in its tracks.

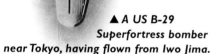

▲ A US B-29 *Superfortress bomber near Tokyo, having flown from Iwo Jima.*

FAR EAST, *BURMA*
General David Cowan's 17th Indian Division and 255th Indian Tank Brigade take the communications center of Meiktila after heavy fighting.

MARCH 4

PACIFIC, *IWO JIMA*
The first US B-29 Superfortress bomber lands on the island.

MARCH 6

EASTERN FRONT, *HUNGARY*
The Germans launch Operation Spring Awakening, designed to secure the Nagykanizsa oil fields, retake Budapest, and win a prestigious victory on the Eastern Front. The Sixth SS Panzer and Second Panzer Armies make good initial progress despite very poor weather conditions.

MARCH 7

POLITICS, *YUGOSLAVIA*
Marshal Tito forms a provisional government in which he accepts representatives of the former royalist government-in-exile. This is a temporary measure, as he intends to retain full control of the government for the Communist Party, which he believes the population will accept without question as a result of partisan successes during the war.

WESTERN FRONT, *GERMANY*
Units of the US First Army capture the Ludendorff bridge over the Rhine River at Remagen. The bridge, having withstood bombs, demolition, heavy usage, and artillery shells, collapses into the river 10 days later.

MARCH 10

WESTERN FRONT, *GERMANY*
Field Marshal Bernard Montgomery's 21st Army Group completes the conquest of the area west of the Rhine River. The group has lost 22,934 casualties, although the Germans have suffered casualties totaling 90,000 men defending the area immediately west of the Ruhr.

AIR WAR, *JAPAN*
The first American fire raid on Japan, against Tokyo, burns out over 16 square miles (25.6 sq km) of the city and kills 100,000 people.

MARCH 14

WESTERN FRONT, *GERMANY*
General George Patton's US Third Army crosses the lower Moselle River to cut behind the German Siegfried Line defensive system.

MARCH 16

EASTERN FRONT, *HUNGARY*
Marshal Fedor Tolbukhin's 3rd Ukrainian Front commences the Red Army's counterattack against Operation Spring Awakening on the front between Lake Velencei and Bicske. The German IV SS Panzer Corps holds in the face of overwhelming superiority in tanks and men, but the Hungarian Third Army on the left collapses.

PACIFIC, *IWO JIMA*
The island of Iwo Jima is declared secure by the Americans following 26 days of combat. They have lost 6821 soldiers and sailors dead, while of the 21,000 Japanese garrison, only 1083 are taken prisoner. The rest have been killed or have committed suicide.

▲ *Paratroopers of the British 6th Airborne Division dropping on the east bank of the Rhine on 23 March, 1945.*

▼ *The Rhine was a formidable barrier, but crossing it was largely a logistical rather than a military problem for the Allies.*

MARCH 17–19

FAR EAST, *BURMA*
The battle for Mandalay begins. The main Japanese garrison is situated in Fort Dufferin, which is pounded incessantly by British artillery. Following an intensive aerial bombardment, the

Japanese evacuate the fort on the 19th – Mandalay is in British hands.

MARCH 18

PACIFIC, *PHILIPPINES*
In the island-hopping campaign in the theater, the US 40th Division lands on Panay, secures it, and then moves on to clear nearby Guimaras Island.

MARCH 20

EASTERN FRONT, *GERMANY*
Units of the 1st Belorussian Front storm Altdamm. There are now no German positions on the east bank of the northern Oder River.

MARCH 22–31

WESTERN FRONT, *GERMANY*
The Allied crossings of the Rhine River begin. The 5th Division of the US Third Army crosses the Rhine near Nierstein and Oppenheim and establishes bridgeheads on the east bank. By the end of the 23rd, the whole of the division is over the river. German resistance is negligible.

Field Marshal Bernard Montgomery's 21st Army Group (1.25 million men) begins crossing the river on the 23rd, when the British 51st (Highland)

▼ *Prisoners taken by the Allies in their Rhine operations. Many Germans were now offering only token resistance.*

▲ *The US II Amphibious Corps pours ashore on Okinawa. By the end of the first day, 50,000 troops had been landed.*

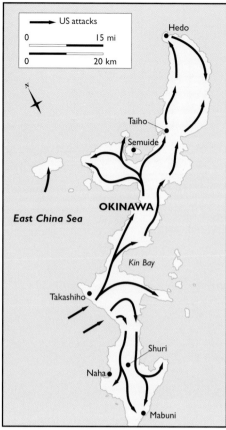

▲ *After the initial US Army and Marine thrust across Okinawa, the 6th Marine Division cleared the north of the island.*

Division and the Canadian 3rd Division cross near Rees and Emmerich. On the 24th, the US 87th Division crosses at Boppard and the 89th at St. Goer, while farther north the British 6th and the US 17th Airborne Divisions land east of the Rhine and link up with advancing British forces.

German units, exhausted and depleted by the fierce battles west of the river, are only able to offer token resistance. By the end of the month the Algerian 3rd Division of General de Lattre de Tassigny's French First Army has crossed the river – every Allied army now has troops on the east bank of the Rhine.

MARCH 24

FAR EAST, *BURMA*
The Allied Chinese New First Army links up with the Chinese 50th Division near Hsipaw, thus bringing the campaign in northern Burma to an end.

MARCH 25–28

EASTERN FRONT, *HUNGARY*
The Soviet 2nd Ukrainian Front starts its attack across the Hron River and along the north bank of the Danube. Hungarian troops begin deserting their German allies in droves, while German commanders report a loss of confidence among their own men. By the

28th, the Red Army has reached the Austrian border in the Köszeg–Szombathely area.

MARCH 30

EASTERN FRONT, *POLAND*
Danzig is captured by the Red Army, along with 10,000 German prisoners and 45 submarines in the harbor.

APRIL 1

PACIFIC, *OKINAWA*
Operation Iceberg, the US invasion of the island, commences. Admiral Chester W. Nimitz, commander-in-chief Pacific Fleet and Pacific Ocean areas, has assigned Vice Admiral Richmond Turner as commander of the amphibious forces and Vice Admiral Marc Mitscher as commander of the fast carrier forces. The US Tenth Army is led by Lieutenant General Simon B. Buckner, and comprises 183,000 men.

The island, only 325 miles (520 km) from Japan, has two airfields on the western side and two partially-protected bays on the east coast – an excellent springboard for the proposed invasion of the Japanese mainland.

The amphibious landing by the US II Amphibious Corps and XXIV Corps is virtually unopposed. The Japanese commander, Major General Mitsuru

▶ *The conquest of islands close to Japan meant US fighters, such as these Mustangs, could escort the bombers on their missions to the Japanese homelands.*

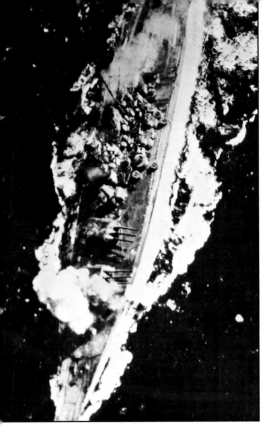

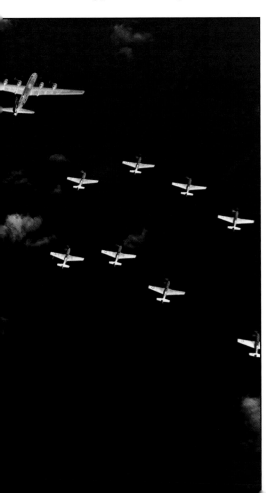

◄ *The Japanese battleship* Yamato *under air attack. Its sinking signaled the end of the Japanese surface fleet.*

encirclement of the economically-important Ruhr region.

APRIL 4

WESTERN FRONT, *HOLLAND*

Field Marshal Bernard Montgomery's 21st Army Group begins its offensive to liberate Holland and sweep across northern Germany. As food stocks in Holland are low, this operation is important as the Dutch postwar political attitude toward the Allies will depend on the speed of liberation.

APRIL 5

POLITICS, *CZECHOSLOVAKIA*

At Kosice, the National Front government of Czechs and Slovaks announces its program and proclaims the democratic principles of the Czech Republic. Stating that the liberation of the country is the first priority, it calls on the population to undertake a broad and active struggle against the Germans.

APRIL 7

SEA WAR, *PACIFIC*

The *Yamato*, the world's largest battleship, is sunk at sea by US warplanes while making its way to attack US forces on Okinawa. The battleship is on a suicide mission, with just enough fuel to reach the island.

AIR WAR, *JAPAN*

Some 108 P-51s take off from Iwo Jima to escort B-29 bombers heading for Japan. They are the first US land-based fighters to reach mainland Japan.

Ushijima, has withdrawn his 80,000 men behind Shuri, where he has built a major defensive line.

APRIL 2–3

WESTERN FRONT, *GERMANY*

Units of the US First and Third Armies meet at Lippstadt to complete the

APRIL 9

PACIFIC, *OKINAWA*

The US XXIV Corps begins to attack the Shuri defenses on Okinawa. Japanese resistance is heavy and the Americans can make no headway.

APRIL 9–10

ITALY, *ARGENTA GAP*

The final campaign in Italy begins as the US Fifth and British Eighth Armies commence their fight for control of the Po Valley. The plan of Field Marshal Harold Alexander, commander-in-chief of Allied forces in Italy, is for the Eighth Army to attack westward through the Argenta Gap, while the Fifth Army strikes north, west of Bologna, thereby trapping German Army Group C between the two.

On the night of April 9, after a massive aerial bombardment and five artillery bombardments, the offensive opens with the Indian 8th and New Zealand 2nd Divisions attacking toward Lugo across the Senino River. By dawn on the 10th, Allied tanks are crossing the Senino River over three bridges, with Allied aircraft overhead providing effective support to the operation.

APRIL 10

FAR EAST, *BURMA*

General William Slim's British Fourteenth Army commences an offensive to capture Rangoon. It is a race against time to take the city before the monsoons begin in mid-May. He must

▼ *The funeral procession of US President Franklin D. Roosevelt, who died with victory in Europe a matter of days away.*

DECISIVE WEAPONS

ATOMIC BOMBS

The science behind the atomic bomb is relatively simple: a neutral neutron particle hits the nucleus of a uranium atom, which splits into two fragments: a krypton atom and a Barium atom. The reaction also releases an enormous burst of energy. One or two fresh neutrons are released, some of which find other nuclear targets and repeat the process. Each splitting or "fission" causes more – the chain reaction. A rapid chain reaction becomes a nuclear explosion. However, uranium has several isotopes, and the trick is to find a way of isolating the uranium isotope U-235, which has the highest energy factor for the development of nuclear power.

The atomic bomb dropped on Hiroshima, "Little Boy," was a "gun-type" weapon, shooting a piece of subcritical U-235 into another, cup-shaped piece to create the supercritical mass – and the nuclear explosion. The bomb used against Nagasaki – "Fat Man" – used the implosion method, with a ring of 64 detonators shooting segments of plutonium together to obtain the supercritical mass. The costs were huge: the Manhattan Project, the secret US project led by J. Robert Oppenheimer that developed the atomic bomb, cost the US government $2 billion.

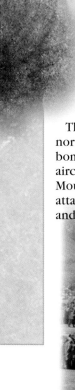

also stop the Japanese forming a defensive line north of Rangoon and halting his advance.

APRIL 11

WESTERN FRONT, *GERMANY*
The US Ninth Army arrives at the Elbe River near Magdeburg. An increasing number of German towns are surrendering without a fight, while Hitler's armies fighting in western Germany are disintegrating.

APRIL 12

POLITICS, *UNITED STATES*
President Franklin D. Roosevelt dies of a cerebral haemorrhage in Warm Springs, Georgia. Vice President Harry S. Truman takes over the position of president, and one of his first decisions is to cancel a plan to launch old, pilotless aircraft packed with explosives against industrial targets in Germany following Prime Minister Winston Churchill's concern that it may provoke retaliation against London.

APRIL 13

EASTERN FRONT, *AUSTRIA*
The Red Army liberates Vienna.

APRIL 14

POLITICS, *ALLIES*
General Dwight D. Eisenhower, Supreme Commander of Allied Armies in the West, informs the Combined Chiefs-of-Staff that the Allied thrust against Berlin takes second place to the securing of the northern (Norway and Denmark) and southern (south Germany and Austria) Allied flanks. The British chiefs-of-staff are dissatisfied, but acknowledge Eisenhower's reasoning, and approve his plans on the 18th.

ITALY, *ARGENTA GAP*
The offensive by the US Fifth Army in northern Italy begins. Preceded by a bombardment by 500 ground-attack aircraft, the US 1st Armored, US 10th Mountain, and Brazilian 1st Divisions attack between Vergato and Montese, and make good progress.

APRIL 16

EASTERN FRONT, *GERMANY*
The Soviet offensive to capture Berlin commences. The Soviet plan has three parts: a breakthrough on the Oder and Neisse Rivers; the fragmentation and isolation of German units in and around Berlin; and the annihilation of said units, capture of the city, and an advance to the Elbe River.

The Red Army forces involved are the 2nd Belorussian and 1st Ukrainian Fronts, the Long Range Force, the Dniepr Flotilla, and two Polish armies – a total of 2.5 million men, 41,600 guns and mortars, 6250 tanks and self-propelled guns, and 7500 combat aircraft. German forces consist of the Third Panzer and Ninth Armies of Army Group Vistula; the Fourth Panzer and Seventeenth Armies of Army Group Center; a host of *Volkssturm* ("home guard"), security and police detachments in Berlin itself; and a reserve of eight divisions – a total of

▼ *US Private Paul Drop stands guard over thousands of German prisoners taken in the Ruhr Pocket in April 1945.*

▲ The Hohenzollern Bridge over the Rhine River near Cologne, demolished by retreating German forces in April 1945.

▲ A US truck races past the corpse of a German soldier during the Allied drive to liberate Holland.

▼ The taking of Berlin, Hitler's capital, was the climax of the Red Army's war.

one million men, 10,400 guns and mortars, 1500 tanks or assault guns, and 3300 combat aircraft.

ITALY, *ARGENTA GAP*
The 78th and 56th Divisions of the British Eighth Army overcome the Fossa Marina, a canal running northeast from Argenta into

Lake Comacchio, with a combination of land and amphibious assaults. The German line has been fractured, and the Allies are through the Argenta Gap.

APRIL 17

PACIFIC, *PHILIPPINES*
Elements of the US X Corps land on Mindanao.

APRIL 18

WESTERN FRONT, *GERMANY*
All German resistance in the Ruhr industrial area ceases; 370,000 prisoners fall into Allied hands.

WESTERN FRONT, *HOLLAND*
The Canadian I Corps, encountering sporadic resistance, has reached Harderwijk, thus isolating German forces in the west of the country.

APRIL 20

WESTERN FRONT, *GERMANY*
Nuremberg, the shrine of National Socialism in southern Germany, falls to the US Third Army after a five-day battle. The city had been defended by two German divisions, Luftwaffe and

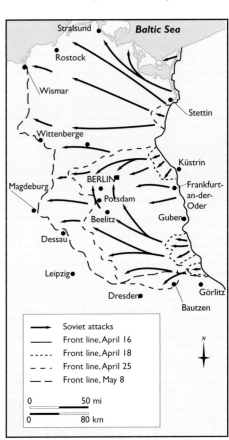

Stralsund

Baltic Sea

Rostock

Wismar

Wittenberge

Stettin

Küstrin

Magdeburg

BERLIN

Frankfurt-an-der-Oder

Potsdam

Beelitz

Guben

Dessau

Leipzig

Dresden

Görlitz

Bautzen

→ Soviet attacks
— Front line, April 16
---- Front line, April 18
-·-· Front line, April 25
-- Front line, May 8

0   50 mi
0   80 km

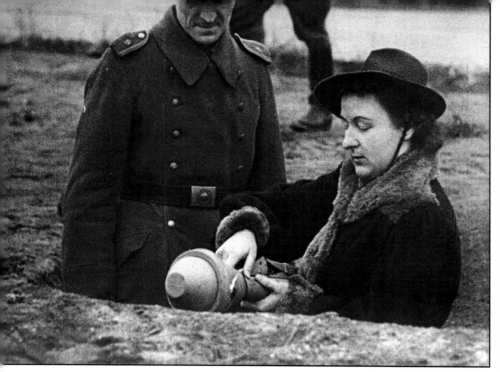

Volkssturm battalions, and ringed by anti-aircraft guns, and the German commander had vowed to Hitler that he and his men would fight to the bitter end.

EASTERN FRONT, *GERMANY*
Marshal Georgi Zhukov's 1st Belorussian Front has smashed German resistance on the Oder River and is advancing toward Berlin. The Soviet troops have had to overcome three defensive belts, each consisting of two or three layers of troops.

APRIL 22

EASTERN FRONT, *GERMANY*
The Soviet high command has ordered Marshals Georgi Zhukov and Ivan Konev to complete the encirclement of German forces in the forests southeast of Berlin by April 24 to prevent them breaking through to the city to increase the strength of its garrison. This move will also close the Red Army ring to the west of Berlin to prevent the escape of enemy units from the capital of the Third Reich. Adolf Hitler, spurning a chance to flee to Bavaria, decides to stay in the city and supervise its defense.

ITALY, *ARGENTA GAP*
The South African 6th Armored and British 6th Armored Divisions meet at Finale, north of the Reno River. The Germans are in headlong retreat from the Argenta Gap toward the Po River, leaving most of their guns, tanks, and transport behind.

▲ *The last reserves: a Berlin woman learns how to use an antitank weapon in the final days of the war.*

▶ *Soviet troops close in on "Fortress Berlin." German resistance alternated between the fanatical and token.*

APRIL 23

WESTERN FRONT, *GERMANY*
The last German defenders in the Harz Mountains are captured. Farther north, the British Second Army enters the outskirts of Hamburg.

APRIL 25–27

EASTERN FRONT, *GERMANY*
Marshal Georgi Zhukov's 1st Belorussian Front and Marshal Ivan Konev's 1st Ukrainian Front complete the encirclement of Berlin, trapping its defenders. The assault on the

▶ *As the Battle of Berlin rages, British troops mop up the last pockets of resistance in north Germany.*

city begins on the 26th, preceded by heavy air strikes and artillery bombardments, with attacks from all sides simultaneously. By the 27th, "Fortress Berlin" has been reduced to an east-to-west belt 10 miles (16 km) long by three miles (5 km) wide. German forces within the city are affected by widespread desertions and suicides.

APRIL 28

POLITICS, *HOLLAND*

The first meeting between Allied and German representatives takes place in western Holland. The Reichskommissar for the Netherlands, Artur von Seyss-Inquart, has offered the Allies the freedom to import food and coal into German-occupied western Holland to alleviate the plight of the civilian population if they will halt their forces to the east. This leads to a cessation of hostilities and saves the country from the ravages of further fighting.

POLITICS, *ITALY*

Mussolini's puppet fascist state collapses along with German resistance in the north of the country. Attempting to flee to Austria, Il Duce and his mistress Claretta Petacci are captured by partisans. On the orders of the Committee of National Liberation, Walter Audisio, a communist member of the Volunteer Freedom Corps, shoots them both. Their mutilated bodies are later hung up in the Piazzale Loreto, Milan.

EASTERN FRONT, *GERMANY*

Soviet troops begin the assault on the Reichstag by attacking across the Moltke Bridge. The Germans launch furious counterattacks, and at the strongpoints of the Ministry of the Interior (defended by SS troops) and the Kroll Opera resistance is fierce.

APRIL 29

POLITICS, *GERMANY*

Adolf Hitler, now confined to the "Führerbunker" behind the Reichs Chancellery, orders Colonel General Ritter von Greim to leave Berlin and arrest Heinrich Himmler, head of the SS, for his attempts to seek peace with the Allies. Greim had been appointed commander-in-chief of the Luftwaffe on the 23rd following Hermann Goering's attempt to negotiate with the Allies on his behalf. Hitler publishes his "Political Testament," in which he blames international Jewry for the outbreak of the war. He nominates Admiral Karl Doenitz as his successor, and marries his long-time mistress, Eva Braun.

POLITICS, *ITALY*

As a result of behind-the-scenes dealings between Karl Wolff, senior commander of the SS and police in Italy, and Allen Dulles, head of the American Office of Strategic Services (OSS) in Switzerland, Wolff and General Heinrich von Vietinghoff, German commander-in-chief in Italy, sign the instrument of unconditional surrender in northern Italy, to come into affect on May 2. The Swiss, the Allies, and many Germans and Italians in Italy have been concerned about a drawn-out campaign in Hitler's "Alpine Fortress," and the probable destruction of north Italy's industry as a result of Hitler's scorched earth policy.

▼ *Soviet rocket-launchers blast German positions in Potsdam railroad station in the final days of the Battle of Berlin.*

▲ *Hitler and his mistress Eva Braun, whom he married in Berlin just prior to their mutual suicide at the end of April.*

EASTERN FRONT, *GERMANY*

The trapped German force around Frankfurt-an-der-Oder attempts to break out of its pocket to reach Berlin. This results in three days of savage fighting in which it is annihilated. Of its original strength of 200,000 men, 60,000 are killed, and 120,000 taken prisoner. Only small groups succeed in slipping through Soviet lines.

HOME FRONT, *HOLLAND*

The RAF begins dropping food supplies to alleviate the plight of the country's starving civilians.

APRIL 30

POLITICS, *GERMANY*

Adolf Hitler and Eva Braun commit suicide in the Führerbunker in Berlin. Hitler shoots himself, while Braun takes poison. Their bodies are later cremated by the SS.

MAY I

POLITICS, *GERMANY*

General Krebs, chief of the General Staff of the Army High Command, initiates cease-fire negotiations with the Soviets on behalf of the Nazi leadership in Berlin (Martin Bormann, Nazi Party Minister, and Josef Goebbels, Reichskommissar for Defense of the Capital). The Soviets demand unconditional surrender and the fighting in the capital and elsewhere continues.

FAR EAST, *BURMA*

In the early hours, the 2nd Gurkha Parachute Battalion makes an airborne drop to secure Elephant Point, southeast of Rangoon, to enable Allied amphibious forces to enter the Rangoon River unopposed from the sea. After a brief fight the site is secured.

MAY 2

WESTERN FRONT, *GERMANY*

The British 6th Airborne Division of the 21st Army Group moves into Wismar, just in time to prevent the Red Army entering Schleswig-Holstein.

EASTERN FRONT, *GERMANY*

Following a savage three-day battle, in which half the 5000-strong garrison has been killed, the Reichstag in Berlin falls to the Red Army and the Hammer and Sickle is raised above the shell-scarred parliament building.

General Helmuth Weidling, commandant of Berlin, surrenders the city and its remaining troops to Marshal Georgi Zhukov. Taking the city has cost the Soviets 300,000 men killed, wounded, or missing, over 2000

▶ *The Hammer and Sickle flies over Berlin, signaling the fall of the city to the Red Army and the end of the Third Reich.*

tanks and self-propelled guns, and over 500 aircraft. The Germans have lost one million men killed, wounded, or taken prisoner.

FAR EAST, *BURMA*

The Indian 20th Division captures the town of Prome, thus severing the Japanese line of retreat from the Arakan. In the south, the Indian 26th Division makes an amphibious landing along the Rangoon River.

MAY 3

FAR EAST, *BURMA*

Following 38 months of Japanese occupation, Rangoon falls to the Allies without a fight. The city's infrastructure is in tatters, with buildings extensively damaged by bombing.

MAY 3–4

POLITICS, *GERMANY*

The whole of the northwest of the country is under British control. Admiral Karl Doenitz sends Admiral Hans von Friedeburg to Field Marshal Bernard Montgomery's headquarters at Lüneburg to discuss surrender terms. On the 4th, the German delegation signs the instrument of surrender – covering German forces in

Holland, northwest Germany, the German islands, Schleswig-Holstein, and Denmark – to come into effect at 0800 hours on May 5.

MAY 4–5

POLITICS, *DENMARK*

Some 20,000 members of the Danish Resistance movement, organized under the central leadership of the Freedom Council, come out of hiding and take over the key points in the country. Soon, they are in control of Denmark. The first Allies arrive on the 5th.

MAY 5

EASTERN FRONT, *CZECHOSLOVAKIA*

With the Red Army getting nearer, Czech nationalists begin the Prague uprising. By the end of the day, there are 2000 barricades in the city, and all the important bridges over the Vltava River have been seized. Field Marshal Ferdinand Schörner, commander of the German Army Group Center, has ordered units to the city to crush the rebellion.

MAY 7

POLITICS, *GERMANY*

General Alfred Jodl, acting on behalf of the German government, signs the act of surrender to the Allies of all German forces

realizing that the situation is hopeless, commits ritual suicide in the early hours of the morning in a cave near Mabuni. The 82-day battle, which has seen the extensive use of Japanese kamikaze attacks, has claimed the lives of 110,000 Japanese military personnel. US Navy losses amount to 9731, of whom 4907 are killed, while the Tenth Army has suffered 7613 men killed or missing, and 31,807 wounded. There have also been over 26,000 noncombatant casualties, mostly Japanese civilians, many of whom have committed suicide.

JULY 3–11

FAR EAST, *BURMA*

The remnants of the Japanese Thirty-third Army – 6000 men – attack Allied positions at Waw from the Pegu Yomas. The aim is to threaten and, if possible, to cut the British Twelfth Army's rail and road links to Rangoon, and also draw some of its units away from the center, thus making possible the movement of the Japanese Twenty-eighth Army east between Toungoo and Nyaunglebin. However, in the face

still in the field. Hostilities are to cease by midnight on May 8 at the latest. In Norway the German garrison of 350,000 men capitulates to the Allies. The German Army Group South surrenders to the US Third Army in Austria.

MAY 9–10

EASTERN FRONT, *CZECHOSLOVAKIA*

Prague is liberated by the Red Army with the help of the partisans. By the evening, Soviet troops have sealed off all avenues of escape west for Army Group Center. German troops, seeing the hopelessness of their situation, begin to surrender in their thousands. On the 10th, the 1st Ukrainian Front makes contact with the US Third Army on the Chemnitz–Rokycany line.

MAY 15

BALKANS, *YUGOSLAVIA*

The last German troops fighting in the country surrender.

MAY 29

PACIFIC, *OKINAWA*

The US 1st Marine Division takes Shuri after hard fighting. To date the Americans have suffered 20,000 casualties trying to take the Japanese-held island.

JUNE 1

FAR EAST, *BURMA*

Having broken and scattered all Japanese opposition in Burma, General William Slim's British Four-teenth Army is mopping up the 70,000

widely-dispersed enemy troops in the country. The Japanese Twenty-eighth Army, having been forced to retreat east to avoid starvation, has been shattered by the XXXIII Corps at the Kama bridgehead. It is now nothing more than an ill-armed rabble.

JUNE 22

PACIFIC, *OKINAWA*

All Japanese resistance on the island ends. The Japanese commander, Lieutenant General Mitsuru Ushijima,

▼ *Czech nationalists fight German troops in Prague behind one of the 2000 barricades erected by the insurgents.*

of heavy ground and air resistance, all Japanese efforts to take Waw cease by the 11th.

JULY 12

POLITICS, *JAPAN*

War leader Shigenori Togo instructs the Japanese ambassador in Moscow to inform the authorities that the emperor wants the war to cease. To this end, Prince Konoye is to be sent as a special envoy to the Soviet Union, with authority from the emperor to discuss Soviet and Japanese relations, including the future of Japanese-occupied Manchuria. However, Togo has repeatedly stressed that the Allied demand for unconditional surrender leaves his

government with no choice but to continue fighting.

Indeed, the Allies are laying plans to invade the Japanese mainland. Its is proposed that the first landings, code-named Operation Olympic, will take place in November. The second, Operation Coronet, is scheduled for March 1946. The US planners expect to suffer severe casualties. However, neither operation will take place.

JULY 16

TECHNOLOGY, *UNITED STATES*

The world's first atomic bomb is

▼ *The Soviet offensive in Manchuria was a superb example of an all-arms mobile operation on a vast scale.*

▲ *The Japanese city of Hiroshima, devastated by the first use of an atomic bomb in warfare on August 6, 1945.*

exploded at Alamogordo, New Mexico. The secret work to develop the weapon is code-named the Manhattan Project. A specialized bomber unit, the 509th Composite Group, is training to attack Japan with atomic bombs.

JULY 17–AUGUST 2

POLITICS, *ALLIES*

The Potsdam Conference takes place in Germany. The "Big Three" – US President Harry Truman, Soviet leader Marshal Joseph Stalin, and British Prime Minister Clement Attlee (who had defeated Churchill in a general election on July 5) – meet to discuss postwar policy. Japan

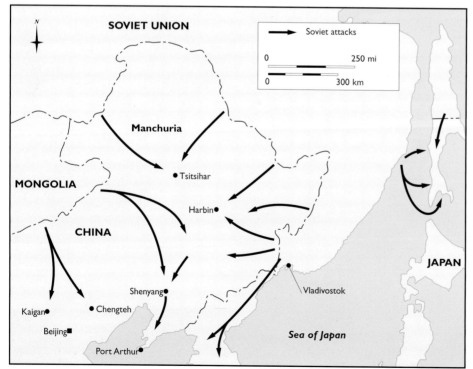

is informed that an immediate surrender would result in the continued existence of its nation, although not its empire. War criminals will be prosecuted and there will be a temporary occupation. The proclamation also makes it clear that continued resistance will lead to the "utter devastation of the Japanese home-land." This is a veiled reference to the use of atomic weapons against Japan.

JULY 19

FAR EAST, *BURMA*

The Japanese Twenty-eighth Army attempts to break out of the Pegu Yomas east across the Sittang River. Forewarned, the Indian 17th Division's guns cut down the Japanese in their hundreds, while many others drown in the river. The breakout is a shambles, and signals the end of the army.

JULY 26

PACIFIC, *PHILIPPINES*

Following an amphibious landing at Sarangani Bay on the 12th, Japanese resistance on Mindanao is overcome.

JULY 28

POLITICS, *JAPAN*

Prime Minister Kantaro Suzuki announces that both he and his cabinet will ignore the recent Allied Potsdam Proclamation.

▼ *Sailors and officials on the deck of the* USS Missouri *witness the Japanese sign surrender documents in Tokyo Bay.*

AUGUST 4

FAR EAST, *BURMA*

The last remnants of the Japanese Twenty-eighth Army are killed. The Allies have lost just 96 men killed.

AUGUST 6

AIR WAR, *JAPAN*

The B-29 Superfortress *Enola Gay* drops an atomic bomb on the Japanese city of Hiroshima, killing 70,000 and injuring the same number.

AUGUST 9

FAR EAST, *MANCHURIA*

A massive Soviet offensive by 1.5 million men begins against the Japanese Kwantung Army. The swiftest campaign in the Red Army's history has begun.

AIR WAR, *JAPAN*

A second US atomic bomb is dropped on Nagasaki, following Tokyo's non-compliance with an ultimatum that further bombs would be dropped unless there was an immediate surrender. The bomb kills 35,000 people and injures a further 60,000.

AUGUST 10

POLITICS, *JAPAN*

Following a conference, during which the emperor voices his support for an immediate acceptance of the Potsdam Proclamation, Japan announces its willingness to surrender unconditionally.

AUGUST 15

POLITICS, *JAPAN*

Emperor Hirohito broadcasts to the Japanese people for the first tine calling on them to respond loyally to his command to surrender.

AUGUST 23

FAR EAST, *MANCHURIA*

The campaign in Manchuria ends in total Soviet victory. The Japanese have lost over 80,000 dead and 594,000 taken prisoner. Soviet losses are 8000 men killed and 22,000 wounded.

SEPTEMBER 2

POLITICS, *ALLIES*

Aboard the battleship *Missouri* in Tokyo Bay, Foreign Minister Mamoru Shigemitsu and General Yoshijiro Umezo sign the Instrument of Surrender. General Douglas MacArthur, Supreme Commander for the Allied Powers, signs on behalf of all the nations at war with Japan. World War II is finally over.

KEY MOMENTS

COUNTING THE COST

World War II was probably the most destructive conflict in the history of mankind. Of the major belligerents, the Soviet Union suffered the most casualties, with an estimated 7.5 million military dead. The Nazis' racial policies and general disregard for the population of the Soviet Union resulted in an estimated 15 million Russian civilian deaths. Germany, having plunged the world into conflict, paid a huge price, its armed forces suffering 2.8 million fatalities and a further 7.2 million wounded. On the home front, a total of 500,000 Germans lost their lives. Japan suffered 1.5 million military dead in the war, and 300,000 civilians died during the US bombing campaign of the Japanese homeland. Italy had 77,000 military deaths and upward of 40,000 civilian fatalities.

The Western Allied nations lost far fewer men than the Soviet Union: the United States 292,000; Great Britain 397,762; and France 210,600. US civilian deaths were negligible, while Great Britain suffered 65,000 civilian deaths; France 108,000.

In total, the military dead during the war is estimated to be 15 million, and civilian deaths are estimated at 34 million, including some six million Jews murdered in the various Nazi extermination camps.

INTRODUCTION

I n the immediate aftermath of World War I, a future conflict between Japan and the United States and European colonial nations seemed an unlikely prospect. Japan had fought on the side of the Allies against Germany's Pacific colonies during the war, and after 1918 was rewarded with territorial acquisitions throughout the Pacific. During the early decades of the twentieth century, Japan had transformed itself into a truly modern industrial society, imitating and improving on Western standards of production and consumption.

The "Second Class" Nation

Despite its contribution to World War I, however, Japan felt – with some justification – that its status in the world was not confirmed. Although Japan had gained some Pacific colonies in the Allied territorial share out, she was also forced to relinquish Chinese regions conquered during the Russo-Japanese War of 1904–5. In Japanese eyes, insult was added to injury in 1922 when the Washington Naval Treaty limited the size of the Japanese Navy to below that of the US and British fleets, despite the fact that the quality and quantity of Japanese shipping could match and even exceed Allied fleets in the Pacific.

To a people with an extremely high concept of respect, the "loss of face" was stinging, particularly amongst the leaders of the Japanese Army whose philosophy retained strong elements of anti-Westernism. Critically, however, the Japanese were aware that their entire

▶ *The Japanese battleship* Kongo *in dry dock at Yokosuka in 1930. On the eve of World War II, the Japanese Imperial Navy had 11 battleships in its inventory.*

industrial revolution was dependent upon US and colonial imports. Almost every vital domestic and industrial product, including food, rubber and most metals, had to be imported, and the United States supplied around 60 percent of Japanese oil. The dependence on the outside world rubbed salt into the Japanese wound, and many felt that Japan had been relegated to a second-class nation within a geographical area in which it should have been dominant.

The Japanese were particularly aggrieved by the fact that what they felt was their natural sphere of influence from which they could obtain the raw materials to run a modern economy was largely occupied by colonial powers: the British in Malaya, the French in Indochina, the US in the Philippines, and above all the Dutch in the oil-rich region of the Dutch East Indies – what is now Indonesia.

▼ *Japanese troops on their way to China in the 1930s. Japan had invaded Manchuria on September 30, 1931.*

The one big area where there was no colonial power was on the Asian mainland: China. In 1931 Japan invaded and occupied Manchuria, a northern province semi-independent of China, and rich in mineral resources, and in 1937 Japan invaded China itself. The war between China and Japan turned into a hugely violent and costly eight-year conflict, in which the Japanese Army in particular demonstrated its utter ruthlessness. At Nanking, for example, between December 1937 and March 1938, the occupying Japanese Army murdered around 400,000 civilians and raped an estimated 80,000 women and girls. Yet the military campaign was as professional as it was cruel, and by the end of 1938 almost all of central and southern China was in Japanese hands.

The Japanese expansion and tales of its atrocities infuriated many in the West. The United States was particularly aggrieved. It had long-standing missionary and trade connections with China, and close associations with the Nationalist leader Chiang Kai-shek. China was also militarily important to the US and

European powers, as "extraterritoriality" agreements permitted the Western nations to establish sovereign commercial settlements on Chinese territory with the accompanying ability to station military units. Relations between the West and Japan plunged further during the late 1930s after US and European warships and troops in the region were attacked in localized incidents.

In 1940 Prince Konoye became the Japanese prime minister, introducing a hardline leadership and rejecting political moderation. His minister of war was Hideki Tojo, and his foreign minister was Yosuke Matsuoka. Both of these ministers were strong advocates of expansion by force. On September 27, 1940, with war already raging across Europe, Matsuoka signed the Tripartite Pact with Germany and Italy. The Tripartite Pact committed the signatories to defend the other countries if they were attacked by any nation other than China, or countries already involved in the European conflict. This commitment essentially aligned Japan with the European Axis powers.

INTRODUCTION

▶ *A meeting of Japan's Greater East Asia Co-Prosperity Sphere. Formally announced in August 1940, it was an attempt by Japan to create a bloc of Asian nations free of influence from Western countries.*

In September 1940 Japanese forces entered northern French Indochina. After defeat by Germany earlier that year, the French were in no position to resist. The Indochina acquisition gave Japan tremendous logistical strength for its war against China and numerous coastal bases to prosecute a naval campaign throughout East Asia. By this time, Japan had already formulated a clear imperialist outlook, looking to establish what it called the "Greater East Asia Co-Prosperity Sphere". This envisaged an East Asia free of colonial influence and united under Japanese hegemony. Japan hoped that the Co-Prosperity Sphere would lead many colonial Asian countries to work, violently or otherwise, towards their independence from British, Dutch and US influence.

In July 1941, the Japanese sent their forces into the south of Indochina. This move, however, drove the United States to retaliate. Japanese assets in the US were seized, and the US placed a ferocious trade embargo on Japan which reduced its oil supplies by 90 percent. The British and the Dutch also imposed their own economic sanctions, and in total Japan's foreign trade was cut by 75 percent.

Minister for War Tojo and the military hawks in the Japanese Government now had a straightforward argument for war. Debate in the Japanese cabinet swung from appeasement through to outright military action, but steadily the latter won out, mainly through Tojo's persuasive representations that Japan would become a "third class nation" if it did not assert itself – the oil embargo, for example, meant that the Japanese fleet would be confined to port by the spring of 1942. Also in 1941, the US had commit-

▼ *From the start of their occupation of China the Japanese used airpower to enforce their rule. This is Chungking under aerial attack. Between 1939 and 1941, 12,000 died in bombing raids on the city.*

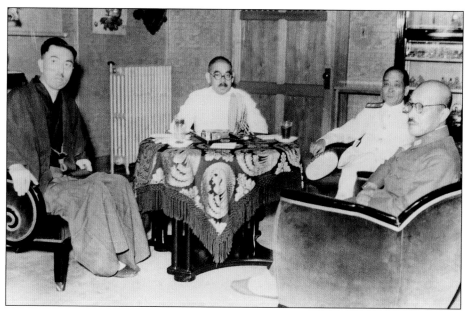

▶ *Prince Konoye (left) became Japanese prime minister in 1940. He resigned in October 1941 after clashing with Tojo.*

ted itself to the Two Ocean Naval Expansion Act, a massive naval building programme which would set a ratio of Japanese to US ships of 3:10 by 1944. If the long-term outlook was bleak, in the short term Tojo also argued that the time was militarily right to launch an attack. In mid-1941 Japan was undeniably the strongest force in the Pacific. The British and Dutch had weak naval forces in the area, and the Japanese Navy had around double the numbers of vessels of all types when compared to the US Pacific Fleet. The Japanese Army had a total manpower of 1,800,000, and was one of the most well-trained and professional forces in the world, specializing in amphibious warfare. Japan's air force numbered well over 2000 aircraft, dwarfing any other air force in the entire East Asian region. Tojo and others argued that although Japan could not compete with US industrial might, a rapid campaign could secure a large expanse of Pacific and Asian territory, which could then be defended at a price too high for the US and Allies to countenance, forcing the Allies to accept Japanese superiority in the East.

In addition, the general world situation in late summer 1941 pushed the Japanese to take a positive view of their prospects if they attacked later that year.

Germany had conquered Western Europe and was engaged in a very successful assault on the Soviet Union. Britain was beleaguered, and the United States was reluctant to commit itself to war. If war was bound to come, as many Japanese believed it would because the Western powers would not give up their colonies in the Far East without a fight, then late 1941 was the time to start it.

On November 5, Emperor Hirohito and the Japanese Government agreed on the course of war should the US not soften its position on the oil embargo by the end of the month. Further debates with

the US during November were fraught, especially as US intelligence had already revealed that Japan's army, navy and air force were making preparations for war. On November 26 the US Secretary of State, Cordell Hull, restated US demands for Japanese withdrawal from Manchuria, China and Indochina and its effective renunciation of the Tripartite Pact. On November 26, 1941, the Japanese Combined Fleet set sail from the Kurile Islands. Its combat destination was Pearl Harbor, Hawaii.

▶ *US Secretary of State Cordell Hull (1871–1955) became convinced that Japan would attack US bases in the Pacific region.*

▲ *Mitsubishi A6M Zero fighters outside their assembly plant in Japan. Over 400 had been built by December 1941.*

1941

NOVEMBER 26

SEA WAR, *PACIFIC OCEAN*

The Japanese First Air Fleet sets sail from the Kurile Islands on a 5440km (3400-mile) journey. Its mission: to destroy the US Pacific Fleet at Pearl Harbor. The Japanese force comprises more than 30 vessels – including six aircraft carriers: the *Akagi, Kagi, Hiryu, Soryu, Zuizaku* and *Shokaku* – and is commanded by Vice-Admiral Chuichi Nagumo.

DECEMBER 6

ATOMIC BOMB, *USA*

President Roosevelt authorizes a secret project known as the Manhattan Engineering District, beginning the development of atomic weaponry under the control of the US Office of Scientific Research and Development. This will eventually be renamed the Manhattan Project.

DECEMBER 7

AIR WAR, *PEARL HARBOR*

The Japanese First Air Fleet launches a massive air assault on the US Pacific Fleet stationed at Pearl Harbor, flying from six carriers positioned 443km (275 miles) north of Hawaii. The first wave begins at 07:55 hours, and US defences are completely unprepared. More than 180 Japanese aircraft attack US warships, sinking six battleships, three cruisers and four other vessels. They damage two other battleships. A total of 188 US mili-

The Japanese, achieving total surprise at Pearl Harbor, went on to complete a series of spectacular victories in the western Pacific at the end of 1941. The British, lacking military resources due to their commitments in the European theatre (and defeats at the hands of the Germans), suffered a series of shattering catastrophes that resulted in the loss of Singapore, Hong Kong and most of Malaysia.

▼ The busy flight deck of the Japanese carrier **Akagi** prior to the attack on Pearl Harbor. In the foreground are Zero fighters, while towards the rear are massed Aichi D3A Val two-seat dive-bombers.

▲ **The attack on Pearl Harbor as seen from a Japanese aircraft. Here, US ships at anchor around Ford Island are under assault. Just visible is a Japanese aircraft pulling up after bombing the USS Oklahoma.**

tary aircraft are destroyed on the ground, and 2403 US military personnel and civilians are killed. More than 1000 US sailors are killed aboard the USS *Arizona* alone, after its magazine explodes. Japanese losses total only 29 aircraft. Most of these are incurred in the second (and final) wave of attack at 08:54 hours, by which

time US defences are more prepared. One Japanese I-class submarine and five midget submarines are also sunk. The final Japanese assaults are completed by 10:00 hours. Importantly, the strike at Pearl Harbor fails to destroy any US aircraft carriers, which are out at sea. Many of the damaged ships are repaired quickly. Furthermore, Nagumo calls off a third strike aimed at destroying Pearl Harbor's oil and shore facilities. Such a raid could have rendered Pearl Harbor inoperable. Instead, it continues to function. Although a stunning short-term tactical success, the attack on Pearl Harbor and the onset of the Pacific War effectively consigns Japan to future destruction.

DECEMBER 8

PACIFIC, *JAPANESE OFFENSIVE*
Japanese forces across the Pacific begin campaigns to secure Allied territories in a Blitzkrieg-style offensive.

◀ **Vice-Admiral Chuichi Nagumo, the commander of the Japanese carrier strike force at Pearl Harbor. A cautious man, he decided against ordering a third air wave.**

KEY MOMENTS

PEARL HARBOR – HOW MUCH DID THE AMERICANS KNOW?

The question of how much the United States knew about the Japanese attack on Pearl Harbor has excited conspiracy theorists and historians alike ever since that fateful day. The more fanciful theories suggest that the US knew an attack was imminent, but allowed it to happen so that the US could enter the war on the Allies' side. They point to the fact that US carriers were not in the harbour when the attack took place, and that the wealth of intelligence pointing to a Japanese attack leading up to December 1941 was impossible to miss. Whilst it was certainly unfortunate that the intelligence collected did not raise the alarm earlier, and the coincidence that the carriers were absent is almost unbelievable, simple intelligence failure seems to be the most likely cause of the surprise.

There were crucial pieces of evidence in the months prior to the attack. US intelligence officials noted that the Japanese carriers had disappeared from their usual moorings. Similarly, in November 1940, low-frequency signals, the kind used by Japan's carriers, were detected northwest of Hawaii but not investigated. Dutch intelligence intercepted an encrypted message sent to the Japanese ambassador in Bangkok suggesting an attack on the Philippines and Hawaii, and the Dutch informed the US, but the warning was dismissed (the US was also aware that the Japanese were telling their diplomatic officials to destroy code books and to prepare for war). Sadly for servicemen who lost their lives at Pearl Harbor, these warnings were missed or mis-read.

▶ *Smoke billows from the torpedo-damaged cruiser USS* Helena *(left) during the Pearl Harbor assault. Her anti-aircraft guns shot down six enemy aircraft.*

LAND WAR, *MALAYA*

Two Japanese divisions (5th and 18th) invade the northern coastlines of Thailand and Malaya, striking south into the Malayan Peninsula. Their objective is the concentration of British troops around Singapore, and the port itself. Singapore is a vital goal for the Japanese offensive, being the Allies' main port for control of the Malacca Strait between Malaya and the Dutch East Indies.

LAND WAR, *HONG KONG*

British forces opposite Hong Kong on the coast of mainland China are put into retreat after an assault by three Japanese regiments.

LAND WAR, *PHILIPPINES*

Japanese infantry units occupy Bataan Island and land several detachments around Vigan and Aparri on the northern coast.

PACIFIC, *WAKE ISLAND*

The Japanese attempt to take the US outpost of Wake Island (an atoll located between Manila and Pearl Harbor), beginning with a large-scale naval and aerial bombardment.

LAND WAR, *BURMA*

The Japanese Fifteenth Army, commanded by Lieutenant-General Shojiro Iida, occupies the Kra isthmus between Prachuab and Nakhon, beginning Japan's Burma offensive. Occupying Burma will protect the Japanese offensive into Malaya on its northerly flank. It will also sever cross-Burma supply routes to Chinese forces in the north, and secure Burmese oil production.

LAND WAR, *THAILAND*

Japanese forces take Bangkok, the Thai capital. The Japanese campaign into Thailand begins on December 8 with Japanese amphibious landings at Singora and Patani. Today, the Thai prime minister, Field Marshal Pibul Songgram, orders the end of resistance against the Japanese. He will ultimately embrace pro-Japanese tendencies.

LAND WAR, *GILBERT ISLANDS*

Japanese troops land on Tarawa and

▼ *One of the five Japanese Type A midget submarines used in the Pearl Harbor attack (this one beached at Oahu).*

KEY MOMENTS

PEARL HARBOR – ACHIEVING COMPLETE SURPRISE

The Japanese assault on Pearl Harbor was planned by Admiral Isoroku Yamamoto (Commander-in-Chief, Imperial Japanese Navy) and commanded by Vice-Admiral Chuichi Nagumo. It was delivered by a strike force of six aircraft carriers, together containing around 450 aircraft, with a defensive/logistical accompaniment of two battleships, two cruisers, several destroyers and eight support vessels. This large body of shipping managed to sail completely undetected from the Kurile Islands north of Japan to attack positions only 443km (275 miles) north of Hawaii. The reasons for the Japanese achieving such complete secrecy have been hotly debated. Total Japanese radio and communications silence clearly assisted free passage, although British Far East Combined Bureau (FECB) intelligence officers informed Washington of a suspicious halt in fleet communications in mid-November. A front of poor weather protected the strike force from aerial observation, and the US strategic focus on the southern and western Pacific meant that the northern Pacific re-

ceived little monitoring. A war warning had been issued to US commanders on December 7. However, the belief was that, barring sabotage, Pearl Harbour was safe. Consequently, no anti-torpedo nets were installed (it was believed at the time that Pearl Harbor was too shallow for torpedo runs); most anti-aircraft ammunition was locked away and accessible only to a duty officer; and US aircraft were assembled in the open in large, closely packed groups. US and British intelligence should have heightened security, but inter-service rivalries and inefficiencies negated its value. Crucially, US agents had deciphered messages to the Japanese Consul General in Honolulu instructing spies to map Pearl Harbour in a grid and plot the ships within the grid. This information was not passed on to Rear-Admiral Kimmel (C-in-C, US Pacific Fleet) – it would probably have energized defensive preparations. The final act of Japanese fortune occurred when the attacking air units themselves were detected 212km (132 miles) off the coast by the Opana Mobile Radar Unit. The signals were interpreted as being those of a friendly flight of Boeing B-17 bombers. There can be no doubt that the US left itself open to a surprise attack.

Makin in the Gilbert Islands, extending their field of conquest to the South Central Pacific.

DECEMBER 10–13

LAND WAR, *MALAYA*
The Japanese 5th and 18th Divisions make important advances down through Malaya. British positions at Betong fall on the 10th, and on the 13th the Japanese take Alor Setar on the northwest coast of Malaya, thereby securing important operational airfields in the north of the country.

LAND WAR, *PHILIPPINES*
The Japanese 16th Division goes ashore in the southeast at Lamon Bay, cutting across the island to Tiaong then

▼ *US battleships under attack at Pearl Harbor. From left to right: USS* **West Virginia** *(badly damaged), USS* **Tennessee** *(damaged) and USS* **Arizona** *(sunk with the loss of over 1100 crew).*

KEY MOMENTS

"DAY OF INFAMY"
The shock of the Japanese attack on Pearl Harbor on December 7, 1941, sent reverberations around the world, and caused a virtual earthquake in the United States. The reaction of the American people went from stunned disbelief to fury. In the confusion of the initial reports, fears of an invasion swept across Los Angeles, thousands of men flooded into the streets armed with pistols and rifles, and the National Guard was ordered out. The next day, shortly before 13:00 hours on December 8, 1941, US President Franklin Delano Roosevelt, in an address to Congress and the Supreme Court, asked Congress to declare war on Imperial Japan.

The famous speech began, "Yesterday, December 7, 1941 – a date that will live in infamy – the United States of America was suddenly and deliberately attacked by naval and air forces of the Empire of Japan." It was received to thunderous applause by Congress, and heartfelt cheers across the nation. Aside from becoming one of the most famous pieces of oratory in American, indeed world, history, the Roosevelt address had the effect of uniting a disunited nation. Prior to Pearl Harbor, the United States had been riven by division over whether American should enter the war. Strikes had been called, and the general feeling across the country was by and large anti-war. The Japanese attack and Roosevelt's speech changed all that, and from that point on the American people, assured by the president that they would achieve "absolute victory", threw their weight behind the national cause with verve, vigour and great patriotism.

DECEMBER 10

heading northwards for Manila. US and Filipino forces in the Luzon interior are threatened with encirclement around the capital.

DECEMBER 10

SEA WAR, *SOUTH CHINA SEA*
The British battleships HMS *Prince of Wales* and HMS *Repulse* are sunk by 88 Japanese aircraft in a two-hour attack in the South China Sea, with the death of 840 seamen. The destruction of the two vessels allows the Japanese to make unhindered amphibious landings along the Malayan coastline. A force of 5000 Japanese troops invades Guam,

▼ *Japanese troops invade Burma in December. The British relied on airpower to defend the country, though they had no bombers in Burma!*

▲ *Sailors of the British battleship HMS Prince of Wales abandon ship following an attack by Japanese aircraft.*

easily overcoming a US garrison of fewer than 400 men.

AIR WAR, *MANILA*
Japanese carrier aircraft destroy around half of the US Far East Air Force in the Philippines, striking the aircraft as they sit on the ground at Clark, Ibu and

Nicholls airfields. The Japanese now exercise almost total air superiority over the Philippines.

DECEMBER 11

PACIFIC, *WAKE ISLAND*
The Japanese attempt a landing on Wake Island, but a tenacious defence repulses it. Despite having suffered three days of constant bombardment, US shore gunners manage to sink two Japanese destroyers and damage a Japanese cruiser.

DECEMBER 16

LAND WAR, *DUTCH EAST INDIES*
The Japanese 19th Division (part of the Japanese Western Force assaulting Burma, Malaya and the western Dutch East Indies) lands on the northern coastline of Borneo, at Miri and Seria on the coast of Sarawak, sending British and Dutch forces into retreat. In advance of the landings, the Allies set fire to oil installations to deprive the Japanese forces of fuel stocks. Conquest of the Dutch East Indies will bring the Japanese vital natural resources, including oil and rubber, consolidate their control of

▼ *Japanese troops in Malaya in early December. The main landings took place on the 8th at Singora and Patani on the northeast coast.*

DECISIVE WEAPONS

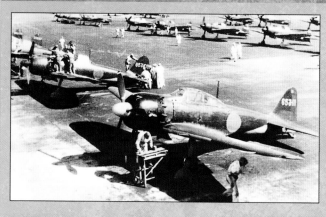

Examples of the Zero version that was built in quantities far greater than any other Japanese aircraft: the A6M5.

MITSUBISHI A6M ZERO

For the first six months of the Pacific War, the Mitsubishi A6M Zeke – otherwise known as the "Zero" – was the best combat aircraft of the theatre. The A6M was designed in 1938, and A6M2 machines were in service aboard carriers by the time of Japan's entry into the war. It combined a highly manoeuvrable airframe with a powerful 708kW (950hp) Nakajima Sakae 12-cylinder radial engine. Its armament of two 20mm cannon and two 7.7mm machine guns gave it a lethal knock-down capability. The most numerous version, the A6M5, had an upgraded Sakae 21 engine which gave it a top speed of 565kmh (351mph). The A6M5 was introduced to counter the new range of US fighters that entered the Pacific War in 1942–43, and ultimately overturned the Zero's superiority. Such aircraft included the Lockheed P-38 Lightning and Grumman F6F

Hellcat. US pilots found the Zero's fatal flaw to be its lack of survivability because of its lightweight frame. Yet the Zero remained a respected aeroplane until the end of the war. Over 10,000 were built in total, many being used for kamikaze attacks.

SPECIFICATIONS:

CREW: one
POWERPLANT: one 820kW (1100hp) Nakajima NK2F Sakae 21 radial piston engine
DIMENSIONS: wing span 11m (36ft); length 9.12m (29.9ft); height 3.51m (11.5ft)
PERFORMANCE: max speed 565kmh (351mph); range 1143km (710 miles); service ceiling 11,740m (38,517ft)
ARMAMENT: two wing-mounted 20mm Type 99 cannon; two 7.7mm Type 97 machine guns (or one 7.7mm and one 13.2mm), both nose-mounted; underwing provision for two 60kg bombs or one 250kg bombs

southwest Pacific seas, and enable them to dominate or invade Australia.

AIR WAR, *BURMA*
The important Allied air base at Victoria Point falls to the Japanese, cutting off aerial resupply of local British forces. Capturing such air bases enables Japanese fighter aircraft to escort bombers on raids into southern Burma, particularly against the Burmese capital Rangoon.

DECEMBER 17

POLITICS, *PACIFIC*
Admiral Husband Kimmel is replaced as commander of the US Pacific Fleet by Rear-Admiral

▶ *Wrecked US aircraft on Wake Island in early December 1941. The Japanese captured the island on the 24th, at a cost of 700 dead. US casualties were 109 killed.*

Chester Nimitz, who is in turn promoted to the rank of Admiral.

DECEMBER 18

POLITICS, *HONG KONG*
The governor of Hong Kong, Sir Mark Young, rejects the third offer from the Japanese for the surrender of the British garrison on the island, despite the fact that the ratio of Japanese to British troops is almost four to one.

DECEMBER 19

LAND WAR, *HONG KONG*
The Japanese 38th Infantry Division crosses from Kowloon Bay to Hong Kong, the 40,000 Japanese soldiers outnumbering the 12,000-strong British garrison.

LAND WAR, *PHILIPPINES*
A Japanese regiment from Palau takes Davao, a major port on Mindanao in the southern Philippines. Davao will be used as a staging post for subsequent Japanese invasions of the Dutch East Indies, and the landing opens another front in the Japanese offensive against the Philippines, which until this point has been concentrated in the north against Luzon.

LAND WAR, *MALAYA*
British forces on Penang, off the northwest coast of Malaya, are forced to abandon the island.

DECEMBER 20

AIR WAR, *CHINA*
Ten Japanese bombers are shot down by the US pilots of the so-called Flying Tiger volunteer force in the Tigers' first engagement.

DECEMBER 21-30

LAND WAR, *MALAYA*
Following further Japanese landings along the western coast of Malaya, and

DECEMBER 22

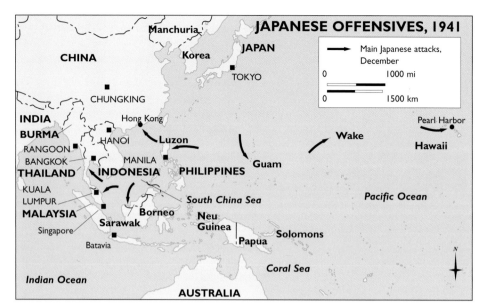

JAPANESE OFFENSIVES, 1941

Main Japanese attacks, December

| 0 | 1000 mi |
| 0 | 1500 km |

▲ Japan's offensives during late 1941 were designed to weaken US strength in the Pacific, giving Tokyo time to seize strategic bases and economic resources.

motivated by the fact that the Japanese have secured four operational airfields, British forces are ordered to withdraw behind the Perak River, a main defensive line in central Malaya, while the 11th Indian Division fights delaying actions. By December 30, the Indian Division itself is in retreat into southern Malaya, and Japanese troops on the east coast of the country have advanced nearly 322km (200 miles) to Kuantan, pushing back the Australian 8th Division.

DECEMBER 22

ALLIES, *POLITICS*
During discussions between US President Franklin D. Roosevelt and British Prime Minister Winston Churchill, the two nations agree on a "Germany First" strategic orientation. The Allied leaders also discuss the establishment of Com-

bined Chiefs of Staff to oversee the Pacific Theatre.

LAND WAR, *PHILIPPINES*
The main Japanese landing in the Philippines takes place at Lingayen Gulf on the western edge of Luzon, as the Japanese 48th Division is landed and begins a southerly advance. With other Japanese forces advancing from the north of the island, the Lingayen Gulf operation threatens to cut off retreating US and Filipino forces around Manila.

DECEMBER 23

LAND WAR, *PHILIPPINES*
Lieutenant-General Douglas MacArthur orders 130,000 US and Filipino troops on Luzon to begin withdrawing into the Bataan Peninsula in an effort to avoid Japanese encirclement of Manila, which MacArthur declares an open city.

▼ Some of the 43,000 troops of General Homma's Fourteenth Army which landed in Lingayen Gulf, Luzon, 240km (150 miles) north of Manila, on December 22.

▲ Japanese Mitsubishi G3M Nell bombers release their bombs over Rangoon on December 24.

DECEMBER 24

LAND WAR, *WAKE ISLAND*
Two weeks of bombardment against Wake Island finally pays dividends for Japan as a Japanese regiment lands successfully and forces the surrender of remaining US forces.

AIR WAR, *RANGOON*
A major Japanese air offensive is launched against the Burmese capital, Rangoon, which is an important British naval and air base.

LAND WAR, *PHILIPPINES*
A Japanese landing force of around 7000 men goes ashore in Lamon Bay on the east coast of Luzon. The landing prevents US and Filipino forces from retreating through the narrow land passage into the far south of Luzon, and traps them around Manila and on the Bataan Peninsula.

DECEMBER 24-31

LAND WAR, *BORNEO*
The Japanese make an amphibious landing along Borneo's coast, moving 644km (400 miles) along to Kuching. By December 31, the British are in general retreat throughout the Dutch East Indies.

DECEMBER 25

LAND WAR, *HONG KONG*
Resistance by the British garrison on Hong Kong proves futile, and on December 25 the governor, Sir Mark Young, formally surrenders the island.

DECEMBER 26

POLITICS, *AUSTRALIA*

Fearing the imminent invasion of his country by the Japanese, Australian Prime Minister John Curtin tells the Allies not to give priority to the European war at the expense of the Pacific theatre.

DECEMBER 28

LAND WAR, *SUMATRA*

Japanese paratroopers are dropped on Sumatra. Japan has been training in air-

▼ *Victorious Japanese troops enter Hong Kong led by General Sakai.*

▲ *A bomb explodes on Hong Kong's Kai Tak aerodrome during the Japanese assault on the British crown colony. Hong Kong surrendered on December 25.*

borne warfare, with German assistance, since 1940; and paratroopers are subsequently used to capture forward air bases throughout the Dutch East Indies.

DECEMBER 31

POLITICS, *PACIFIC*

Admiral Chester Nimitz arrives in the Pacific and assumes command of the US Pacific Fleet.

1942

The year began with Japan continuing its series of victories in the southwest Pacific. The Philippines, Malaya and most of New Guinea fell to the Imperial Army, while Japanese air and naval assets tightened their grip on the Solomons. However, US forces dislodged the Japanese on Guadalcanal, Australian troops pushed back an offensive on New Guinea, and at sea the US won the Battle of Midway.

JANUARY 2

LAND WAR, *PHILIPPINES*
Elements of the Japanese Fourteenth Army enter and occupy Manila while others push up against the Porac Line, the US defensive positions located across the entrance to the Bataan Peninsula. Cavite naval base also falls to the Japanese. An initial attempt to take the Porac Line ends with heavy Japanese casualties, but it forces US and Filipino troops deeper into Bataan.

◀ *Sir Archibald Wavell (third from left), who in January was appointed to head the American-British-Dutch-Australian Command.*

◄ **One of the 60,000 Allied soldiers who surrendered to the Japanese Twenty-Fifth Army, commanded by General Yamashita, during its conquest of Malaya.**

DUTCH EAST INDIES, *BORNEO*
A Japanese landing force occupies Brunei Bay.

JANUARY 3

POLITICS, *WASHINGTON*
The scattered Allied forces in South-East Asia are brought under a unified command named ABDACOM (American-British-Dutch-Australian Command), with the British General Sir Archibald Wavell as Supreme Commander. This attempt at a joint command structure will prove to be difficult in practice, with international and inter-service rivalries reducing efficiency.

POLITICS, *CHINA*
The Chinese Nationalist leader Chiang Kai-shek is made C-in-C of Allied forces in China.

▼ **Japanese soldiers in landing barges approach a burning Manila in early January. On the advice of President Quezon, General MacArthur had declared it an open city on December 25, 1941.**

JANUARY 4–9

LAND WAR, *MALAYA*
The Indian 11th Division is driven back across the Slim River, only 322km (200 miles) from Singapore. The defence of the Malayan capital, Kuala Lumpur, appears futile, so British forces receive orders to fall back to Johor in the far south of the country.

JANUARY 7–23

LAND WAR, *PHILIPPINES*
Some 80,000 US and Filipino troops fall

▲ **Japanese troops enter Kuala Lumpur. During their conquest of Malaya the Japanese never gave British forces time to regroup.**

back to main defensive positions running down either side of Mount Santa Rosa and Mount Nahib, two high-altitude features occupying central-northern Bataan. The positions are held against numerous Japanese assaults until January 23, when I Corps occupying the western defences and II Corps

in the eastern half are forced to pull back to reserve positions some 48km (30 miles) to the south.

JANUARY 8

LAND WAR, *DUTCH EAST INDIES*
The Japanese occupy the capital of British North Borneo, Jesselton.

JANUARY 10–17

LAND WAR, *DUTCH EAST INDIES*
Two massive Japanese task forces, known as Central Force and Eastern Force, make major landings throughout the Dutch East Indies. On January 11, Central Force goes ashore at Tarakan in northeastern Borneo, while Eastern Force lands on the northernmost tip of Celebes. On January 17, Japanese units land and take the coastal town of San-dakan in British North Borneo.

JANUARY 11

LAND WAR, *MALAYA*
The Japanese advance through Malaya continues, with British and Common-wealth forces establishing defensive lines that are subsequently outflanked by Japanese amphibious "jumps" down the western Malayan coastline.

▼ *The aftermath of a Japanese air raid on Singapore. As the Japanese advanced, the stream of people into Singapore turned into a flood. Soon, medical services were on the verge of collapse.*

STRATEGY AND TACTICS

JAPANESE STRATEGY FOR 1942

The Japanese surprise attack on the Ameri-can fleet at Pearl Harbor was designed to cripple the American Pacific Fleet to such an extent that the Greater East Asia Co-Pros-perity Sphere, Japan's innocent-sounding name for her territorial acquisitions, would be beyond the range of US forces after the American carriers had been destroyed. Though the carriers were never found and destroyed, Japanese strategy for 1942 was built upon this same precept: protection. The Japanese high command in Tokyo decided that the Greater East Asia Co-Prosperity Sphere had to be protected by a defensive line extending south and north of the Mar-shall Islands. This meant that certain islands that lay within this perimeter had to be taken and fortified. This included the Philip-pines, where the US had 130,000 men sta-tioned, the key strategic island of Corregi-dor, New Guinea, the Solomon Islands and the Gilbert Islands.

It was also hoped that by achieving six months of steady and overwhelming mili-tary defeats in the Pacific, the US would be forced to negotiate a surrender, or at the very least accept Japan's territorial gains. In the face of an aggressive US counter-strate-gy (the complete opposite of what the Japanese had actually planned and hoped for), the Imperial Japanese Navy sought to devise a plan whereby the US Pacific Fleet could be engaged in battle and sunk, achiev-ing the same aim as was intended at Pearl Harbor. Away from the ocean, Japanese goals included the capture of Singapore (and the whole of the Malaysian Peninsula), and the conquest of Burma.

SEA WAR, *CENTRAL PACIFIC*
The aircraft carrier USS *Saratoga* is hit by a torpedo fired from a Japanese sub-marine 805km (500 miles) southwest of Oahu.

JANUARY 12

LAND WAR, *MALAYA*
The Japanese Twenty-Fifth Army occu-pies the Malayan capital. The capture of the city enables Japanese forces to resupply its units for the subsequent drive into southern Malaya against Johor and Singapore.

JANUARY 15–20

LAND WAR, *BURMA*
The Japanese Fifteenth Army advances northwards from the Kra isthmus and mainland Thailand into Burma. On January 20, it launches its main attack, demolishing the 17th Indian Division and a single Burmese division (both commanded by Lieutenant-General T.J. Hutton) attempting to defend the town of Moulmein.

JANUARY 16

AIR WAR, *SINGAPORE*
In the face of overwhelming Japanese air superiority, almost all British aircraft on Singapore are flown to Sumatra. Although nearly 500 aircraft were com-mitted to the defence of Malaya, most were obsolete types and were use-less against Japanese air units, which enjoyed an aircraft numerical superiority of roughly three to one.

JANUARY 18

POLITICS, *BURMA*
The Burmese prime

▶ *A column of Japanese Type 95 light tanks in Malaya. Highly mobile, the Type 95 stayed in production until 1943.*

▲ Troops of the Japanese Fifteenth Army at the frontier bridge near Moulmein, Burma, at the start of their invasion.

▲ US troops take cover in a slit trench on Bataan during a Japanese air raid. Note the British-style helmets they are wearing.

minister, U Saw, is arrested by the British as he attempts to discuss Burmese independence plans with British officials in Palestine.

JANUARY 19

LAND WAR, *MALAYA*
Allied defensive positions around Muar, only 160km (100 miles) from Singapore, are crushed by the Japanese 5th and 8th Divisions. The Allies lose around 3700 men killed, wounded or captured in the action.

JANUARY 20

AIR WAR, *NEW BRITAIN*
Aircraft from four Japanese carriers begin the bombardment of the port of Rabaul, New Britain.

SEA WAR, *AUSTRALIA*
A Japanese submarine is sunk off the coast of Australia near Darwin by US and Australian warships, heightening Australian fears that they will soon become victims of a Japanese invasion. Two days later, the Japanese prime minister, General Hideki Tojo, delivers a warning to Australia that, "if you continue your resistance, we Japanese will show you no mercy".

JANUARY 20-31

LAND WAR, *SINGAPORE*

Having been driven from mainland Malaya, British and Commonwealth forces under Lieutenant-General Percival cross the Johor Strait bound for

▼ *Two dead Japanese soldiers on Bataan. The Imperial Army suffered heavy losses capturing the peninsula.*

Singapore, the final troops moving to Singapore on the 31st. The Johor causeway across the Strait is badly damaged by British demolition teams to prevent the Japanese making an easy crossing. The island braces itself for the inevitable Japanese onslaught. An air raid against Singapore City on the 20th kills 50 and injures another 150. Southern Singapore is heavily protected from

naval assault by large-calibre coastal guns, but the Japanese will be coming from the opposite direction. An appeal is made for reinforcements of RAF aircraft, as most of the island's remaining RAF planes were evacuated to Sumatra on January 16.

JANUARY 22

LAND WAR, *PHILIPPINES*

The Japanese strengthen their operations in the Philippines by landing reinforcements at Subic Bay in the top western corner of the Bataan Peninsula. In the night, a Japanese battalion makes an amphibious assault down the Bataan coastline and attempts to establish a beachhead on the southern coast of the peninsula

JANUARY 23

LAND WAR, *SOUTHERN PACIFIC*

More than 5000 Japanese troops make amphibious landings on New Britain, New Ireland and Bougainville in the Solomon Islands. Rabaul on the northern tip of New Britain is occupied, and will become one of Japan's most important Pacific naval and aviation bases.

POLITICS, *MANILA*

A puppet government is established in Manila. The Japanese tended to establish such regimes in most of the coun-

▶ *The Burma invasion was intended to secure the flank for the conquest of Malaya, and cut Allied links to China.*

tries they conquered, hoping to create the appearance of encouraging independence from European colonial powers for Southeast Asian states.

LAND WAR, *BORNEO*
A major Japanese landing force is put ashore at Balikpapan on the eastern coast of Borneo.

JANUARY 24

LAND WAR, *SAMOA*
A protective force of US Marines occupies Samoa.

SEA WAR, *BORNEO*
Off the coast of Borneo, a Japanese convoy is mauled by US destroyers and Dutch bombers, with four transport vessels sunk. The convoy was heading to reinforce troop landings at Balikpapan.

JANUARY 24–31

LAND WAR, *DUTCH EAST INDIES*
Japanese units in the Dutch East Indies consolidate their coastal gains with more amphibious advances. On January 24, Western Force moves down to Kuching in southern Sarawak, before making two subsequent leaps down to Pemangkat and Pontianak in Borneo on January 27 and 29 respectively. Meanwhile, Central Force and Eastern Force makes several advances through their respective territories, effectively accomplishing a

coastal encirclement of Allied forces in the Dutch East Indies.

▼ *Lieutenant-General Joseph Stilwell (fourth from left) was appointed to lead US forces in China, India and Burma.*

▲ *The carrier USS Enterprise, which was damaged during a suicide aircraft attack in early February 1942.*

JANUARY 25

▲ Manuel Quezon, the president of the Philippines Commonwealth, formed a government-in-exile in the US when Japan occupied the Philippines in 1942.

▲ US internment: people of Japanese ancestry are interned at the Santa Anita Assembly Center, San Pedro, California.

JANUARY 25

POLITICS, *THAILAND*
The government of Thailand, basing its outlook on undeniable Japanese successes, declares war on Britain and the US.

JANUARY 26

LAND WAR, *PHILIPPINES*
US forces retreat deeper into the Bataan Peninsula and take up a defensive line stretching from Bagac on the west coast to Orion on the east coast. These positions become the main battle lines for the next two months, as the Japanese are unable to prosecute their advance through a combination of combat fatigue, heavy casualties and various tropical diseases.

SEA WAR, *MALAYA*
British and Australian naval and aviation units suffer heavy casualties when attacking a Japanese convoy off the Malayan coast. Thirteen of sixty-eight aircraft are shot down and the Australian destroyer *Vampire* and the British destroyer HMS *Thanet* are sunk during the engagements.

JANUARY 30

LAND WAR, *BURMA*
Moulmein is occupied as the Japanese drive towards Rangoon and forge three

▼ Japanese armour rolls down Orchard Street in Singapore as British resistance collapses.

other lines of advance. During the course of the advance to Moulmein, several major Allied air bases at Tenasserim, Tavoy and Martaban fall into Japanese hands, severing the British India–Burma air lifeline. A mere 35 operational Allied aircraft in Burma face more than 150 Japanese air opponents.

FEBRUARY 1

SEA WAR, *MARSHALL AND GILBERT ISLANDS*
The US carriers USS *Enterprise* and USS *Yorktown* and the cruisers USS *Northampton* and USS *Salt Lake City*

make an aerial and naval bombardment of Japanese positions at Kwajalein, Wotje, Maloelap, Jaluit and Mili in the Marshall Islands, and Makin in the Gilbert Islands, committing a total force of 92 aircraft. During the raid, the carrier USS *Enterprise* is damaged by a suicide aircraft attack, the earliest example of kamikaze air raids in the war. The attack is more likely to have been opportunistic rather than planned, though.

FEBRUARY 2

APPOINTMENTS, *WASHINGTON*
Lieutenant-General Joseph Stilwell becomes commander-in-chief of the US

▲ *Rangoon under threat. Members of a Japanese artillery battalion train their field gun on Rangoon from high ground outside the city.*

forces in the China-Burma-India theatre, and chief of staff to Chiang Kai-shek. Stilwell, who is fluent in Chinese, becomes one of the most successful commanders in the Southeast Asian region.

SEA WAR, *PHILIPPINES*
A Japanese force attempting to land on southwest Bataan behind US lines is defeated at sea by US Navy patrol boats and US aircraft. Several Japanese landings aiming for south Bataan have been defeated over the last week, resulting in the loss of two Japanese battalions.

FEBRUARY 3

AIR WAR, *DUTCH EAST INDIES*
The Dutch naval base at Surabaya on Java is damaged severely by a Japanese air attack.

FEBRUARY 4

AIR WAR, *MADURA STRAIT*
An Allied naval force under the command of Rear-Admiral Doorman, Royal Netherlands Navy, suffers a massive air attack as it attempts to intercept a Japanese invasion fleet heading for Borneo. Three cruisers are damaged: one Dutch and two US.

POLITICS, *SOUTH PACIFIC*
The Australia-New Zealand Naval Command is established and led by US Navy Admiral H.F. Leary.

KEY MOMENTS

BATTLE OF THE JAVA SEA

On the night of February 27, 1942, a large naval element of the Japanese Eastern Force comprising 4 cruisers, 14 destroyers and 41 transport vessels sailing for Java was intercepted by a mixed unit of US, Dutch, British and Australian warships. The Allied force consisted of five cruisers and nine destroyers under the command of Dutch Rear-Admiral Karel Doorman. The subsequent action was inauspicious for the Allies, as they suffered from inferior firepower, no reconnaissance aircraft (Doorman had left seaborne aircraft ashore, mistakenly believing they wouldn't be needed in a night action), no air cover and the inexperience of Doorman himself. Two Allied cruisers and three destroyers were sunk, the British cruiser HMS *Exeter* withdrew owing to battle damage, and Doorman was killed. The Japanese force under the command of Vice-

Admiral Takagi Takeo suffered only one damaged destroyer.

The following night, the remaining two Allied cruisers (the USS *Houston* and Australia's HMAS *Perth*) engaged other Japanese shipping west of Batavia, sinking two vessels and damaging four others, though they were subsequently destroyed themselves by a massive retaliation force of 12 Japanese warships. HMS *Exeter* and two other destroyers were also sunk as they attempted to make an escape from Surabaya to Ceylon on March 1. Four US destroyers were the only Allied survivors of the Battle of Java Sea.

The action showed the perils of makeshift multinational task forces and the importance of clear tactical direction and aerial reconnaissance. In addition, the battle demonstrated the superiority of certain Japanese weapon types, particularly their faster "Long Lance" torpedoes.

FEBRUARY 4–5

▲ *General Douglas MacArthur (second from left), US commander in the Philippines during the Japanese offensive.*

FEBRUARY 4–5

POLITICS, *SINGAPORE*

British commanders on Singapore reject Japanese demands for the colony to surrender. The next day, the British cruise liner *Empress of Asia*, converted to a logistical role, is sunk while attempting to reach Singapore with supplies.

FEBRUARY 5

POLITICS, *US*

The US Government declares war on Thailand.

FEBRUARY 6

LAND WAR, *PHILIPPINES*

US troops mount a counterattack against Japanese reinforcements advancing on Luzon, but make little headway.

FEBRUARY 7–11

LAND WAR, *SINGAPORE*

On the night of February 7, the Japanese Guards Division makes a feint

▼ *The British destroyed anything that might be of use to the Japanese at Rangoon before they evacuated the port.*

attack against the island of Pulau Ubin off Singapore's northeastern coast. The next evening, the Japanese 5th and 18th Divisions cross into Singapore from the opposite direction, striking inland and taking the vital British air base at Tengeh. They are followed the next night by the Guards Division landing on the central-northern coast around Kranji. Having repaired the Johor causeway, the Japanese now pour more than 30,000 troops of the Twenty-Fifth Army, commanded by Lieutenant-General Yamashita, on to the island. These troops are supported by large numbers of armoured vehicles and ground-attack aircraft. The Japanese have

STRATEGY AND TACTICS

US STRATEGY FOR 1942

Though the US had believed that a war against Japan was inevitable long before Pearl Harbor, indeed air bases and other facilities were being constructed on Wake Island and the Marshall Islands in the months leading up to war, the Japanese surprise attack caught the US off guard. Therefore, the initial US strategy for 1942 was at first disorganized and lacking coherence.

The US lacked the manpower or the equipment to hold on to what Pacific territory it had, and had little way of reinforcing the Philippines nor any other islands in the face of Japanese invasion. Thus US strategy was to hold on for as long as possible, whilst US strategists came up with a plan. However, strategic thinking in 1942 was limited by several factors. Firstly, the shock of Pearl Harbor and the destruction of vital

shipping there took its toll. Secondly, superior Japanese planning in the lead-up to 1942 gave them an advantage over the Americans. Lastly, the condition of US unpreparedness could only be improved over a period of time, and not overnight. By the summer of 1942, American strategic planning began to take shape as the US reorganized its Pacific forces. Strategic goals included carrier-based attacks against the Marshall Islands and Wake Island, the daring Doolittle Raid that was designed to boost morale, and the build-up of forces in Australia. After the crucial Battle of Midway, US strategic planners could plan without Japanese carrier craft ever presenting a major threat to US operations in the Pacific. It was this fact that allowed Nimitz and MacArthur to plan aggressive counteroffensives for the second half of 1942.

▲ *The Australian war effort swings into action: soldiers of the Australian Imperial Forces (AIF) at Freemantle in 1942.*

complete air supremacy. Allied forces are squeezed into the southernmost tip of Singapore around Singapore City.

FEBRUARY 8

POLITICS, *PHILIPPINES*

The US Government rejects a proposal from the president of the Philippines, Manuel Quezon, that the Philippines should become entirely independent of both the Japanese and the

US so that the country can declare its neutrality in the war.

FEBRUARY 10-20

LAND WAR, *DUTCH EAST INDIES*

The Japanese Army continues its southward-moving consolidation of the Dutch East Indies. With Borneo and Celebes under Japanese control, the invaders of Western Force land on southern Sumatra on February 14, following up with parachute landings around Palembang to take its oil refinery on the 15th. Timor and Bali are the next to be invaded on the 19th and 20th, the Japanese again using paratroopers for a drop at Kupang, Timor, on February 20.

FEBRUARY 14

POLITICS, *PACIFIC*

Vice-Admiral C.E.L. Helfrich of the Royal Netherlands Navy takes over

as C-in-C Allied Naval Forces, South West Pacific, relieving Admiral T.C. Hart of the US Navy.

FEBRUARY 15

POLITICS, *SINGAPORE*

British and Commonwealth forces suffer the worst defeat in their history when Lieutenant-General Percival finally surrenders the island of Singapore to the Japanese. A total of 62,000 British, Australian and Indian soldiers fall into captivity, many of whom will die from sickness, overwork and malnutrition in Japanese prison camps. The defence of Singapore became futile when Japanese forces took control of the island's reservoirs and severed Singapore City's

▼ *P-40 Warhawk aircraft of the US 16th Fighter Squadron, 51st Fighter Group, lined up on an airfield in Burma prior to a flight to a Chinese air base.*

KEY PERSONALITIES

ADMIRAL E.J. KING

Admiral Ernest J. King was a driving force behind US Navy operations in both the Atlantic and Pacific theatres during World War II. He was born in Ohio in 1878, and under the strict discipline of a tough-minded father King soon developed the aggressive and determined personality that was to distinguish his career. He entered the US Navy during World War I, and rose quickly through the ranks by showing capable leadership. By 1938 he was a temporary vice-admiral, and in February 1941 was appointed C-in-C of the US Atlantic Fleet. In this post he gained additional combat experience and, prior to America's entry into the war, made a significant impact on U-boat operations in the Atlantic. In December 1941, King was again promoted to C-in-C of the US Fleet.

In the Pacific war he showed great aplomb, using amphibious and carrier resources to defeat the Japanese. He excelled in the Pacific by knowing every aspect of naval operations (in the 1930s he had commanded a submarine flotilla and then the Battle Fleet's aircraft carriers). More importantly, he was also instrumental in obtaining sufficient resources to conduct offensive operations against Japan. Despite his strategic excellence, King did not always get his way, and was overruled by Roosevelt on issues such as his proposed invasion of Formosa in 1944 – the president preferred MacArthur's Philippines operation. King was, however, undoubtedly one of the great architects of the Pacific victory. He retired on December 15, 1945.

water supply. Japanese losses amounted to fewer than 2000 killed. The day before the surrender, Japanese troops had killed 150 patients and staff at the Alexandra Military Hospital.

FEBRUARY 19

SEA WAR, *BADOENG STRAIT*
Dutch and US warships engage Japanese Imperial Navy vessels in the Badoeng Strait, east of Bali, the Japanese having just landed an invasion force on the coast. While one Japanese destroyer is damaged, the Dutch lose a cruiser and a destroyer.

HOME FRONT, *UNITED STATES*
Some 11,000 Japanese-Americans are moved from the Pacific coast to camps in Arkansas and Texas under new US

▼ *Soldiers from the Japanese 18th Infantry Division land on the Andaman Islands to score another easy victory.*

Government war powers. Executive Order 9066 enables the war secretary to displace people from military areas, and the Japanese-Americans, already alienated following Pearl Harbor, are the primary victims of this policy. There are fears in the US, mostly unfounded, that Japanese-Americans might provide intelligence for a Japanese attack on the US west coast. Such fears prove groundless, but more than 112,000 people are interned.

AIR WAR, *AUSTRALIA*

Darwin is bombed by Japanese aircraft in an attack that kills 172 people and damages 16 ships.

FEBRUARY 20

POLITICS, *PHILIPPINES*

The leader of the Philippines, President Quezon, and many of his officials are evacuated from Luzon by the submarine USS *Swordfish*.

▲ *Chinese troops retreat in the face of the rapid Japanese advances in Burma at the end of February.*

FEBRUARY 21

LAND WAR, *BURMA*

Allied resistance to the Japanese Army's advance through Burma crumbles at the Sittang River, 160km (100 miles) north of Moulmein. At one point, British forces crossing the river using a single bridge are forced to blow it up with large numbers of men stranded on the other side. Allied losses are heavy, many men drowning when attempting to swim the Sittang. Elements of the Japanese Fifteenth Army are now free to turn west and drive for Rangoon itself, which the British began to evacuate on February 18.

FEBRUARY 23

SEA WAR, *UNITED STATES*

Making a rare attack on the US homeland, the Japanese submarine *I-17* shells an oil refinery at Ellwood, California. In total 17 rounds are fired, inflicting only minor damage to a pier and an oil well derrick.

FEBRUARY 24

SEA WAR, *WAKE ISLAND*

Japanese forces occupying Wake Island are attacked by a US naval task force led by the carrier USS *Enterprise*.

FEBRUARY 25

POLITICS, *ALLIES*

The ABDA Command is disbanded, and its leader, General Sir Archibald Wavell, goes on to become C-in-C of India. ABDA proved to be too complicated for the effective coordination of forces and was unable to overcome national animosities and suspicions.

FEBRUARY 27–28

DUTCH EAST INDIES, *BATTLE OF JAVA SEA*

A combined force of US, Dutch, British and Australian warships is almost entirely destroyed during two nights of battle against powerful naval elements of the Japanese Eastern Force.

MARCH 1–8

SEA WAR, *DUTCH EAST INDIES*

Japanese naval power is proven in ocean manoeuvres when nine Allied warships and ten merchant ships are sunk during close-range naval engagements off the coast of the Dutch East Indies. Losses include the British cruiser HMS *Exeter* and the British destroyer HMS *Stronghold*.

LAND WAR, *DUTCH EAST INDIES*

Japanese troops land on the northern coastline of Java on March 1, occupying the important naval base at Surabaya and pushing south to conclude their conquest of the Dutch East Indies by March 8. The surrender of Allied forces in the region gives the Japanese access to invaluable stocks of natural materials, including oil, rubber, bauxite and rice, and raises the possibility of further Japanese assaults against Australia.

▲ *Admiral Sir James Somerville was created commander of the British Far East Fleet, which operated from Ceylon.*

419

MARCH 3

▶ *US and Filipino troops surrender to the Japanese during the campaign on the Bataan Peninsula in early march.*

MARCH 3

AIR WAR, *AUSTRALIA*
Seventy people are killed and twenty-four aircraft destroyed during a fifteen-minute Japanese air raid at Broome, Western Australia.

HOME FRONT, *US*
All Japanese-American citizens are prohibited from living on the eastern seaboard of the US.

MARCH 4

SEA WAR, *MARCUS ISLAND*
US carrier aircraft from the USS *Enterprise* bomb Japanese positions and installations on Marcus Island. One US aircraft is downed, but a total of 96 bombs cause damage among ammunition dumps, airfields and radio installations.

MARCH 8

LAND WAR, *BURMA*
The British garrison of Rangoon narrowly escapes as the city falls to the Japanese Fifteenth Army. The collapse follows a period of social chaos and internal support for the Japanese from Burmese nationalists. The loss of the Burmese capital results in several British command changes. The commander of the Burma Army, General Thomas Hutton, is replaced by General Harold Alexander.

LAND WAR, *NEW GUINEA*
The battle for New Guinea begins as Japanese invasion forces land two battalions at Lae and Salamaua in the Huon Gulf. Allied air attacks are directed against the Japanese two days later but, at the same time, the Japanese begin preparatory air raids on Port Moresby, the Papuan capital on the southeast coast.

▼ *Victorious Japanese troops celebrate on New Guinea after being landed at Lae in early March.*

MARCH 10

LAND WAR, *NEW GUINEA*

The Japanese consolidate their hold of New Guinea's northern coastline by landing troops at Finschafen at the tip of the Huon Peninsula.

AIR WAR, *NEW GUINEA*

The carriers USS *Enterprise* and USS *Lexington* launch major air raids against Japanese shipping supporting the New Guinea landings. By March 18, the US Navy is reporting two enemy heavy cruisers sunk, one light cruiser and three destroyers probably sunk, one cruiser and one destroyer badly damaged, and five other transport vessels sunk.

ATROCITIES, *FAR EAST*

Anthony Eden, the British foreign secretary, gives a report to a shocked gathering of Members of Parliament in the Houses of Parliament concerning Japanese atrocities in the Far East. The

▼ *Japanese tanks, with air support overhead, close in on Rangoon. In 1942 neither Britain nor the US was prepared to commit significant forces to save Burma. For its part, Japan deployed the Fifteenth Army to take the country.*

▶ *General Jonathan Wainwright began evacuating US troops to Corregidor as the Japanese conquered Bataan.*

report reveals horrific details of torture, murder and rape against Allied prisoners of war and indigenous peoples.

MARCH 12

US COMMAND, *PHILIPPINES*

General Douglas MacArthur is flown out of the beleaguered Bataan Peninsula, and Lieutenant-General Jonathan Wainwright takes over command. MacArthur's parting words are, "I shall return".

LAND WAR, *BURMA*

US General Joseph Stilwell is appointed commander of the Chinese Fifth and Sixth Armies in the China-Burma-India theatre (particularly the eastern Shan States and around Mandalay), with the main objective of keeping the Burma Road open in China. Air support is provided by a volunteer force of around 30 US airmen known as the "Flying Tigers" and an RAF squadron.

SEA WAR, *PACIFIC*

Giving an early indication of how significant submarine warfare will be in the Pacific, a single US submarine sinks three Japanese freighters and one troop ship in Japanese home waters.

MARCH 13–24

▶ *Japanese troops on the outskirts of a Burmese oil field during their triumphant advance in March.*

MARCH 13–24

LAND WAR, *BURMA*

British forces establish a defensive line across from Prome, Toungoo and Loikaw around the Salween River, with Major-General William Slim in command of the Burma Corps, an ill-equipped force of one Indian and one Burmese division.

MARCH 14

HOME FRONT, *AUSTRALIA*

US troops begin to arrive in Australia, the first convoy to arrive disembarking 30,000 American soldiers. Since March 2, all physically fit Australian adult male civilians have been eligible for war service.

MARCH 16–18

AIR WAR, *NEW GUINEA*

Combined US and Australian air units attack Japanese shipping and shore installations around Lae and Salamaua, New Guinea. Two Japanese heavy

cruisers are sunk and 10 other ships are either sunk or damaged. Allied losses are light, only one aircraft being shot down.

MARCH 21

LAND WAR, *PHILIPPINES*

US forces trapped in the Bataan Peninsula begin to occupy the heavily fortified island of Corregidor, 3.2km (2 miles) off the coast. The island features a labyrinth of bomb-proof underground tunnels and food stocks sufficient to feed 10,000 men for six months (the garrison numbers 15,000 Americans and Filipinos). Its strategic position astride Manila Bay makes its occupation a vital war aim for the Japanese.

▼ *Striking back – a US B-25 bomber takes off from the deck of the USS Hornet during the Doolittle Raid against Japan.*

MARCH 21–28

POLITICS, *INDIA*

The British Government announces that post-war India will achieve a semi-independent status from the British Empire. Sir Stafford Cripps, the Lord Privy Seal, visits India and discloses that it will have dominion status following the conflict. The move is a result of pressure put on Winston Churchill by the Labour Party, and also because Indian troops are being so heavily committed as combatants on behalf of the British.

MARCH 22

LAND WAR, *BURMA*

Allied forces abandon the airfield at Magwe, just over 160km (100 miles) east of Akyab. The capture of the airfield allows the Japanese to fly tactical air operations as far as Mandalay.

MARCH 23

LAND WAR, *ANDAMAN ISLANDS*

The Japanese occupy the Andaman Islands in the Bay of Bengal in the face of no resistance.

MARCH 24–30

LAND WAR, *BURMA*

The Chinese Fifth and Sixth Armies engage the Japanese around Taung-gyi in central Burma, but are defeated. British forces to the west at Prome withdraw farther up Burma, as the Chinese defeat and renewed Japanese assaults leave them in danger of being outflanked.

MARCH 26

POLITICS, *WASHINGTON*

Admiral E. J. King takes over from Admiral H. R. Stark as US Chief of Naval Operations, in addition to his role as C-in-C of the US Fleet.

MARCH 27

MILITARY APPOINTMENTS, *BRITAIN*

The Far East Fleet in Ceylon receives a new commander, Admiral Sir James Somerville.

POLITICS, *AUSTRALIA*

Australian forces come under the command of General Sir Thomas Blamey. Supreme command of Allied forces in the theatre is in the hands of MacArthur, who comes to hold Blamey

KEY PERSONALITIES

ADMIRAL ISOROKU YAMAMOTO

As C-in-C of the Combined Fleet from July 1939, Isoroku Yamamoto (1884–1943) was Japan's greatest wartime naval strategist. Born in 1884 in Nagaoka, he joined the naval academy shortly after the turn of the century, gaining combat experience in the Russo-Japanese War of 1904. He went to the US in 1919 to study English, and also to learn about US naval and industrial strengths.

Yamamoto returned to Japan in 1921 and rose quickly through a series of influential positions. Most significantly, he became an expert in the new art of naval aviation warfare, something he later put to devastating effect as architect of the Pearl Harbor attack. However, Yamamoto was not a supporter of Japanese aggression, correctly believing that US industrial power would triumph in a sustained campaign. But once war was inevitable he committed himself to Japanese victory. Pearl Harbor ably demonstrated the forward-thinking and tactical capabilities of Yamamoto, and it fulfiled all his claims for naval aviation being the future of war at sea.

Respect for Yamamoto grew as the initial Japanese Pacific campaign went from victory to victory. He experienced his first criti-

cal defeat at Midway, by which time ULTRA intelligence was giving the US warning of Japanese naval movements. After Midway, Yamamoto's combined fleet remained potent, but increasingly disadvantaged by US technology, intelligence, tactics and numbers. In the end, it was the US mastery of the principles of naval aviation that helped force the Japanese navy into submission. On April 18, 1943, Yamamoto was killed when he flew to inspect bases in the Solomon Islands. The itinerary of his aircraft was intercepted by ULTRA and the admiral was shot down by US fighters.

▲ *Japanese troops at Mandalay railway yard. The British had stocked a series of depots in the Mandalay–Meiktila area, which were captured by the Japanese.*

in little regard. However, Blamey upholds Australia's interests against British and American strategic demands.

M A R C H   30

POLITICS, *PACIFIC*

Meetings between the US and British divide up the operational responsibilities of World War II. The US takes command of the Pacific theatre. Its territorial responsibilities include Australia and New Zealand.

The Pacific theatre is separated into two commands. Admiral Nimitz takes command of the Pacific Ocean Areas, with its sub-divisions of North, Central and South Pacific areas. General MacArthur is the commander of the special Southwest Pacific area. The territories stretching from Singapore westwards to the Mediterranean are under British command.

LAND WAR, *BURMA*

The Japanese occupy Toungou in central Burma after ejecting the Chinese Fifth Army, which held out for a violent 10 days. Toungou provides the Japanese with another useful air base.

M A R C H   31

POLITICS, *INDIA*

The nationalist Indian Congress Party makes demands for immediate independence from the British Empire.

A P R I L   1

LAND WAR, *NEW GUINEA*

Japanese forces assaulting New Guinea mount two more landings: one is at Hollandia on the north coast; the other on the west coast at Sorong.

LAND WAR, *SOLOMON ISLANDS*

The Japanese occupy Buka Island in the Solomon Islands.

SEA WAR, *INDIAN OCEAN*

A Japanese naval raiding group led by the carrier *Ryujo* sets out from Burma to conduct operations against Allied shipping along the Orissa coast. In the next 10 days it will sink 28 Allied merchant vessels.

◀ *General Stilwell (right) and his staff in the Burmese jungle. After rescuing the encircled Chinese garrison at Toungoo, Stilwell and his men retreated to India, travelling on foot.*

▲ *Corregidor under Japanese attack. The island had nine major batteries mounting twenty-five coast artillery weapons, with full support facilities.*

APRIL 6

LAND WAR, *SOLOMON ISLANDS/ ADMIRALTY ISLANDS*

Japanese forces make amphibious landings at Bougainville in the Solomon Islands and also on the Admiralty Islands.

SEA WAR, *CEYLON*

The Japanese Navy launches a major air and sea attack against Colombo harbour. However, the harbour is practically empty of Allied shipping, most of it having been moved to Addu Atoll west of Ceylon two days earlier. The Japanese do find the destroyer USS *Tenedos* and the cruisers HMS *Dorsetshire* and HMS *Cornwall*, however, which are subsequently sunk. Also in the vicinity is the dated British carrier HMS *Hermes* and the destroyer HMAS *Vampire*. Twenty-six Allied aircraft are shot down during the attack.

APRIL 6

AIR WAR, *INDIA*

The east coast of India faces Japanese air attacks at Vizagapatam and Cocanada on April 6. The India Congress Party leader subsequently pledges full military support for the Allied resistance.

APRIL 8

LAND WAR, *PHILIPPINES*

US soldiers are ordered to destroy their equipment in preparation for their surrender to the Japanese.

APRIL 2

AIR WAR, *PACIFIC*

US Army Air Force (USAAF) B-17 Flying Fortress bombers attack the Japanese fleet around the Andaman Islands.

APRIL 2

LAND WAR, *BURMA*

The Japanese Fifteenth Army continues to push back the Allied Burma Army. Two key positions fall to the Japanese today: the town of Prome, located on the Irrawaddy River north of Rangoon; and the vital port island of Akyab. This latter conquest brings the entire territory of the Arakan in western Burma under Japanese control.

APRIL 5–7

LAND WAR, *PHILIPPINES*

On April 5, the Japanese begin a fresh offensive to take enemy positions on Bataan. They are reinforced by the 4th Division, and inflict heavy US casualties after a five-hour bombardment. By April 7, the US I and II Corps are in retreat.

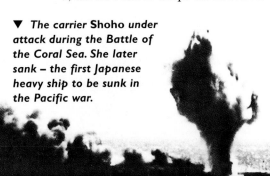

▼ *The carrier Shoho under attack during the Battle of the Coral Sea. She later sank – the first Japanese heavy ship to be sunk in the Pacific war.*

APRIL 9

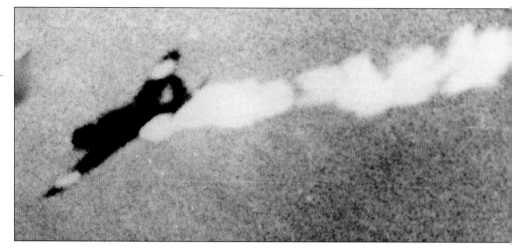

▶ *A Nakajima B5N Kate bomber trails smoke after being hit during the Battle of the Coral Sea.*

APRIL 9

POLITICS, *PHILIPPINES*

The remaining US forces in the Bataan Peninsula finally surrender. Their commander, Major-General Wainwright, has escaped with 2000 men to Corregidor to continue resistance there. The 78,000 US and Filipino troops who fall into Japanese hands on Bataan are subsequently made to walk 104km (65 miles) in the most dreadful conditions. Around one in three men die in what will become known as the "Bataan Death March". On April 10, the Japanese put ashore another 12,000 men on Cebu Island, consolidating their hold over the Philippines.

AIR WAR, *CEYLON*

Eighty-five Japanese carrier aircraft attack Trincomalee harbour, but find no Allied shipping there. Eight Allied aircraft and fifteen Japanese aircraft are shot down in aerial combat. However, a Japanese scout plane spots the carrier HMS *Hermes* and the destroyer HMAS *Vampire*. The subsequent air strike sinks HMS *Hermes* in only 10 minutes after 40 bomb hits, and the *Vampire* goes down after suffering 13 explosions. The Japanese attacks of the last four days have effectively finished the British Pacific Fleet as a significant force in the region.

APRIL 10

POLITICS, *PACIFIC*

The US Pacific Fleet is reorganized into type commands: Battleships (Rear-Admiral W.S. Anderson); Aircraft Carriers (Vice-Admiral W.F. Halsey); Cruisers (Rear-Admiral F.J. Fletcher); Destroyers (Rear-Admiral R.A. Theobald); Service Force (Vice-Admiral W.L. Calhoun); Amphibious Force (Vice-Admiral W. Brown); Submarine Force (Rear-Admiral T. Whiters); and Patrol Wings (Rear-Admiral H.S. McCain).

APRIL 10–16

LAND WAR, *BURMA*

The Japanese continue their northward advance through Burma. The retreating "BurCorps" destroys the oil facilities at Yenangyaung (the largest oil field in the Far East) on April 16 as the unit is pushed up against the Irrawaddy valley. The Chinese Fifth and Sixth Armies are unable to halt the onslaught.

APRIL 12

POLITICS, *INDIA*

Despite the British rejection of Indian proposals for post-war independence, Pandit Nehru, the leader of the Indian Congress Party, pledges to cooperate with the Allies in bringing about the full defeat of Germany and Japan.

APRIL 16

LAND WAR, *PHILIPPINES*

The Philippine island of Panay is invaded by 4000 Japanese troops (41st Infantry Regiment).

APRIL 18

AIR WAR, *JAPAN*

Sixteen US B-25 Mitchell bombers flying from the aircraft carrier USS *Hornet* and led by Colonel James Doolittle strike a major propaganda victory by bombing the Japanese capital, Tokyo. The planes operate at the extremes of range, so fly on to China after the mission rather than return to the carrier. Although the damage inflicted is militarily insignificant, the Japanese Government is shocked. Japanese forces will now go all out to destroy US airpower.

APRIL 19

LAND WAR, *BURMA*

Allied troops fall back to Meiktila, a crucial town in central Burma on the main Rangoon to northern Burma rail route. The capture of Meiktila would be of crucial advantage to Japanese logistics in the Burma campaign.

APRIL 23

LAND WAR, *BURMA*

Troops of the Chinese Expeditionary

▼ *The crew of the USS* **Lexington** *abandons ship during the Battle of the Coral Sea. The destroyer at right is taking off the sick and wounded.*

Force hold off Japanese advances around Twingon, allowing thousands of Allied troops around Yenangyaung to escape the Japanese net.

APRIL 25

LAND WAR, *NEW CALEDONIA*

US troops land on the Free French colony of New Caledonia. The island's capital, Nouméa, becomes a major US naval base.

APRIL 29

LAND WAR, *BURMA*

The Japanese 56th Division pushing through Burma reaches as far north as Lashio, having defeated the Chinese 55th Division. Elements of the Japanese

Army now turn southwest to begin the attack on Mandalay, in support of the 18th Division heading directly up from the south. More worryingly, on April 29, the Japanese cut the Burma Road, thus making Chinese Nationalist forces entirely dependent on air supplies.

APRIL 30

LAND WAR, *BURMA*

General Stilwell, commander of the "BurCorps" in Burma, receives permission to withdraw his troops into India.

SEA WAR, *PACIFIC*

Three of Japan's most formidable carriers – *Shoho*, *Shokaku* and *Zuikaku* – begin to deploy for operations against Port Moresby, New Guinea.

DECISIVE WEAPONS

USS *ENTERPRISE*

The USS *Enterprise* was one of the most influential warships of World War II. A "Yorktown" class aircraft carrier that joined the Pacific Fleet in 1938, the USS *Enterprise* was immediately sent into action following the Japanese attack on Pearl Harbor. The ship made its first successful engagement of the war on December 11, 1941, when its aircraft sank the Japanese submarine *I-170*. The USS *Enterprise*'s defining engagement came in June 1942 during the Battle of Midway. Aircraft flying from the USS *Enterprise*, particularly the redoubtable Douglas SBD Dauntless dive-bomber, sank the Japanese carriers *Kaga* and *Akagi*, assisted in the sinking of the carrier *Hiryu*, and later sank the heavy cruiser *Mikuma*.

After Midway, the USS *Enterprise* was to be found wherever action was thickest, from providing air cover for the Guadalcanal landings to participating in the huge air engagements during the Battle of the

Philippine Sea, known as "The Marianas Turkey Shoot", in June 1944. The USS *Enterprise* suffered critical battle damage. She was hit by three bombs during the Battle of the Eastern Solomon Islands in August 1942, and by another three bombs the following October during the Battle of Santa Cruz. In 1945, Japanese kamikaze attacks nearly destroyed the great ship, and in May she returned to the US for major repairs, sitting out the rest of the war.

SPECIFICATIONS:

CREW: 2919 officers and enlisted men

DIMENSIONS: length 246.7m (810ft); beam 34.75m (114ft); draught 8.84m (29ft)

DISPLACEMENT: 25,908 tonnes (25,500 tons)

SPEED: 33 knots

ARMAMENT: eight 12.7cm AA guns; four quadruple 28mm AA guns; 16 12.7mm Browning machine guns in AA mounts

AIRCRAFT: (1942) 15 torpedo bombers; 37 dive-bombers; 27 fighters

◄ **US Douglas Dauntless dive-bombers at the Battle of Midway. Each aircraft could carry a bomb load of 544kg (1197lb) over a range of 730km (456 miles).**

MAY 1–8

LAND WAR, *BURMA*

The Japanese advance through Burma continues. Mandalay falls to the 18th and 56th Divisions on May 1, while the 33rd Division takes Monywa to the west. The Japanese then drive up the Irrawaddy valley against the Chinese Fifth Army's futile defensive positions around Myitkyina. General Stilwell personally leads the 241km (150-mile) retreat of a group of 100 men and civilians from the River Irrawaddy to Imphal, India.

MAY 3

LAND WAR, *SOLOMON ISLANDS*

Japanese forces land on the island of Tulagi in the Solomons. The island is subsequently turned into a major Japanese seaplane base.

MAY 4–6

SEA WAR, *CORAL SEA*

The Battle of the Coral Sea, the first major carrier battle of the war, is ignited as three US task forces head to intercept a Japanese invasion group from Rabaul bound for Port Moresby. A Japanese covering group, including the carriers *Shoho*, *Zuikaku* and *Shokaku*, is heading around the Solomon Islands in the hope of surprising US naval forces from the rear. The US has been forewarned of Japanese intentions through its ULTRA intelligence, but throughout the 5th and 6th the two carrier forces are unable to locate one another.

MAY 6

LAND WAR, *PHILIPPINES*

The US-held fortress island of Corregidor off the coast of Bataan finally falls after a Japanese landing preceded by a massive bombardment. This brings to an end the Philippines campaign, which has cost the Allies 140,000 lives. With the surrender on May 10, nearly 12,500 US and Filipino soldiers become prisoners of the Japanese.

MAY 6

LAND WAR, *CHINA*

Chinese forces led by General Chiang Kai-shek begin a major offensive along a 640km (400-mile) front against Japanese occupiers in seven major cities, including Shanghai and Nanking.

MAY 7

SEA WAR, *CORAL SEA*

Japanese carrier aircraft attack Allied Task Force 44, the unit of cruisers and destroyers set to intercept the Japanese Invasion Group heading for Port Moresby. However, Task Force 44, commanded by Rear-Admiral Crace of the Royal Navy, manages to turn back the Japanese invasion force. Meanwhile, Japanese carrier aircraft to the south of the Solomon Islands bomb and sink the US destroyer USS *Sims* and the fleet oiler USS *Nesho*. The US carriers have already located the Japanese covering group, and a massive air assault by carrier aircraft from the USS *Lexington* and USS *Yorktown* hits the *Shoho* with 1000lb bombs and seven torpedoes. The *Shoho* sinks at 11:35 hours.

MAY 8

SEA WAR, *CORAL SEA*

US and Japanese carriers exchange major air strikes throughout the day at a range of only 320km (200 miles). The *Shokaku* is badly damaged after bomb hits from US dive-bombers. On the US side, the USS *Yorktown* receives substantial bomb damage while the USS *Lexington* is critically damaged by torpedo and bomb strikes, precipitating huge onboard fires that force the carrier to be abandoned at 17:00 hours (enemy bombs rupture a number of her gasoline tanks; gasoline vapour then seeps out of the bulging tanks). She is later sunk by US ships. Most of the 1200 crew are saved.

LAND WAR, *BURMA*

The Japanese capture Myitkyina, an important rail terminus and air base in northern Burma. In a futile attempt to stem the Japanese Burma offensive, the Chinese Fifth Army had been sent to occupy defensive positions around the town, but was unable to halt the Japanese Fifteenth Army.

MAY 9

SEA WAR, *CORAL SEA*

US and Japanese carrier forces break off contact in the Battle of the Coral Sea. Although the losses of shipping on both sides are roughly equivalent, the Battle of the Coral Sea halts Japanese expansion plans in Papua and the Solomon Islands, and signals the first major Japanese reverse in the war. Japan has also suffered heavy loss of pilots and aircraft.

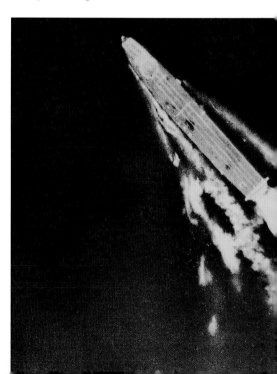

◄ *A photograph taken from a Japanese aircraft of the carrier* **Hiryu** *on fire and disabled at Midway. She was later scuttled.*

STRATEGY AND TACTICS

MIDWAY– THE PLAN

The Japanese plans for the Battle of Midway centred around their efforts to lure the US Pacific Fleet into the open and destroy it. However, as was common in Japanese strategic planning, the operation was over complex, made unjustified assumptions about how US naval forces would react, and failed to concentrate force. Indeed, even the choice of Midway Island was flawed, and deeply unpopular with Imperial Japanese Navy captains. A diversionary force would be sent to the Aleutians to draw off part of the US fleet, whilst the Japanese forces under Admiral Yamamoto would capture Midway. This would force the Americans to try to re-take the island, which would give Yamamoto the opportunity to destroy Nimitz's carriers with his carrier-based aircraft, aided by land-based bombers stationed on the newly captured island. This would leave the west coast of America at the mercy of the Japanese and force the US to negotiate a peace, or so the theory went (a rather bizarre idea that took no account of the vast military and economic resources of the United States). What Yamamoto did not know was that the US Navy was well aware of his plans through communications intercepts, and had devised its own plan to destroy his forces, despite the odds being stacked against the Americans. Nimitz divided his forces into two, Task Force 16 with the carriers *Hornet* and *Enterprise*, and Task Force 17 with the USS *Yorktown*. Putting faith in his forces' ability to strike at extreme ranges, he planned to knock out the Japanese Carrier Striking Force under the command of Admiral Nagumo. It was with this simple plan in mind that Nimitz set sail for Midway.

MAY 12

LAND WAR, *BURMA*
Japan's steady advance through Burma slows substantially under extremely heavy monsoon rains, which turn jungle trails into almost impassable quagmires.

MAY 14

SEA WAR, *PACIFIC*
US intelligence code-breakers obtain details of Japanese plans to destroy the US Pacific Fleet by fighting a decisive carrier engagement around Midway.

MAY 15

ATROCITIES, *CHINA*
In retaliation for the US Doolittle air

◄ *As seen from a US bomber, the Japanese carrier* **Akagi** *takes evasive action at Midway. She was later hit and scuttled.*

raid on Tokyo, Japanese troops kill 100 Chinese families.

MAY 20

LAND WAR, *BURMA*
The Japanese conquest of Burma is completed, with the Japanese having suffered around 7000 casualties against 13,463 British, Indian and Burmese dead. Allied troops are now arriving in Imphal.

MAY 22

SEA WAR, *PACIFIC*
US intelligence reveals Japanese plans for attacks on Midway Island and the Aleutian Islands.

MAY 22

▶ Heavy anti-aircraft fire erupts around Japanese torpedo-bombers as they endeavour to sink US ships at the Battle of Midway in early June.

MAY 22

POLITICS, *MEXICO*
The Mexican Government announces its declaration of war on the Axis powers.

MAY 23

LAND WAR, *BURMA*
Lieutenant-General Stilwell and a small group of men reach safety at Dimapur after a 241km (150-mile) retreat through the Burmese jungle.

MAY 27

SEA WAR, *PEARL HARBOR*
The damaged carrier USS *Yorktown* reaches safety. Navy repair teams restore the carrier (she had been dam-

▼ Midway cost the Japanese four aircraft carriers, a cruiser and 332 aircraft. The US lost one carrier and 137 aircraft.

aged by bombs at the Battle of the Coral Sea) and return her to combat readiness in only four days.

MAY 28–29

LAND WAR, *CHINA*
The Japanese penetrate Yunnan Province using the Burma Road. In Chekiang Province, Japanese forces take the capital, Kinhwa, having suf-

fered heavy losses from Chinese resistance. In one action, the Japanese lost 1500 men in a minefield.

MAY 29

TECHNOLOGY, *AUSTRALIA*
Australia's first home-produced wartime aircraft, the Commonwealth CA-12 Boomerang, makes its first flight. Although designed in only five months,

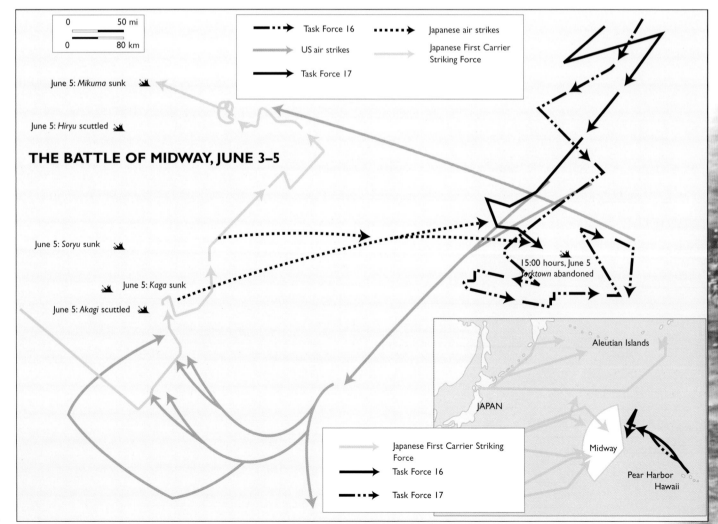

THE BATTLE OF MIDWAY, JUNE 3–5

0 50 mi	
0 80 km	

Task Force 16   Japanese air strikes

US air strikes   Japanese First Carrier Striking Force

Task Force 17

June 5: *Mikuma* sunk

June 5: *Hiryu* scuttled

June 5: *Soryu* sunk

June 5: *Kaga* sunk

June 5: *Akagi* scuttled

15:00 hours, June 5 *Yorktown* abandoned

Aleutian Islands

JAPAN

Midway

Pear Harbor Hawaii

Japanese First Carrier Striking Force

Task Force 16

Task Force 17

the Boomerang proves to be a tough and manoeuvrable fighter.

JUNE 1

SEA WAR, *AUSTRALIA*

Three Japanese midget submarines are sunk during an attack on shipping in Sydney harbour. The Australians lose the logistics vessel HMAS *Kuttabull* and with it 16 sailors. Fears are raised that the attack signals a full-scale Japanese invasion.

AIR WAR, *MIDWAY ISLAND*

Japanese carrier aircraft make a heavy raid against US installations located on Midway Island.

JUNE 2

POLITICS, *CHINA*

The US and China sign a lend-lease agreement. Thereafter US begins channelling large amounts of military equipment through to Chinese forces via Indian ports.

JUNE 3

SEA WAR, *MIDWAY*

The Battle of Midway begins, effectively the turning point in the Pacific War. Almost the entire Japanese Combined Fleet under Admiral Isoroku Yamamoto sets sail with several key objectives, including the capture of the Aleutian Islands and Midway Island with its important air base. By taking these objectives, the Japanese hope to draw the remaining US aircraft carriers into battle, to be destroyed by Vice-Admiral Chuichi Nagumo's First Carrier Striking Force comprising the carriers *Akagi*, *Kaga*, *Hiryu* and *Soryu*. The US face this threat with Task Force 17 commanded by Rear-Admiral Fletcher and containing the carrier USS *Yorktown* (patched up from the Coral Sea action), and Rear-Admiral Spruance's Task Force 16 with the carriers USS *Hornet* and USS *Enterprise*.

From June 3–7, the Japanese occupation of the Aleutian islands of Kiska and Attu is completed successfully, but Admiral Nimitz keeps his Pacific forces concentrated around Midway, having been informed through US intelligence of the Japanese battle plan to divert US warships northwards.

▼ *The Japanese heavy cruiser* Mikuma, *photographed from an SBD aircraft during the afternoon of June 5, 1942, after she had been bombed by US aircraft.*

▲ *Japanese troops on Attu Island during their invasion of the Aleutian Islands, a diversionary move in conjunction with their strike against Midway.*

AIR WAR, *ALASKA*

Dutch harbour in Alaska is attacked by a force of four Japanese bombers and about fifteen Japanese fighters. The raid results in minimal damage to shore installations.

JUNE 4–5

SEA WAR, *MIDWAY*

Japanese carrier aircraft begin a bombardment of Midway Island, although Nagumo does not know the locations of US naval positions and he believes there are no US carriers in the area. An

◀ *A Japanese observation post outside a base for maritime attack aircraft on New Guinea. The post was used to spot the approach of Allied aircraft.*

blistering attack, three Japanese carriers – *Kaga*, *Akagi* and *Soryu* – are sunk in only five minutes.

Remaining Japanese carrier aircraft retaliate and cripple the USS *Yorktown* – the great ship is sunk two days later by a Japanese submarine while under tow. But the US then repeats its success after aircraft from the USS *Enterprise* create a devastating fire aboard the *Hiryu*, which is scuttled the next day.

The Battle of Midway ends with the balance of power dramatically altered in the Pacific theatre, with the Japanese having lost half of its carrier fleet and 275 aircraft. The US and Japanese navies now face each other with virtual parity.

JUNE 5

LAND WAR, *INDIA*

A huge British convoy of men and materials reaches India intact, substantially raising India's defensive capability against the Japanese.

JUNE 5–7

ALEUTIAN ISLANDS, *KISKA*

The Japanese make an unopposed landing on Attu in the Aleutians on June 5, taking Kiska two days later. US forces

▶ *The US war economy gets into full swing: President Roosevelt (left) and magnate Henry Kaiser watch the launch of a new cargo ship.*

initial US attack by aircraft based on Midway Island fails, resulting in heavy losses. Around 09:30 hours, a wave of 150 aircraft from the carriers USS *Enterprise*, USS *Yorktown* and USS *Hornet* roll into action against the Japanese carriers. Again, the attack by the vulnerable Devastator torpedo-bombers is smashed by Japanese Zero fighters. A subsequent flight of US dive-bombers cannot find Nagumo's ships, which have changed course. Finally, at around 10:30 hours, US dive-bombers locate the Japanese carriers, fortuitously catching them when their decks are packed with aircraft, munitions and aviation fuel. In a

will not discover the Japanese military presence on these islands for another five days.

JUNE 8

SEA WAR, *AUSTRALIA*

Japanese submarines shell the Australian cities of Newcastle and Sydney. The bombardment is ineffectual, with little significant material damage and no casualties.

JUNE 21

SEA WAR, *US*

Fort Stevens on the Oregon coast is

shelled by a Japanese submarine. Seventeen shells are fired in total, but they cause no damage.

JUNE 24

POWS, *THAILAND*

Six hundred Allied POWs begin work on what will be a 470km (294-mile) extension to the Singapore–Bangkok railway. The Japanese intend to connect the existing rail line with Rangoon in southern Burma, and are relying on vast numbers of Allied POWs and Asian slave workers to perform the manual labour. This is acceptable under the Geneva Convention, but not the brutal regime they will work under.

▼ *The USS* George F. Elliot *burns off Tulagi after a Japanese air attack.*

▲ *Men of the 1st US Marine Division storm ashore on Guadalcanal in the Solomons. They met little initial resistance.*

JUNE 27

AIR WAR, *WAKE ISLAND*

Japanese positions on Wake Island are bombed by US aircraft.

JULY 4

SEA WAR, *ALEUTIANS*

US submarines torpedo four Japanese destroyers around the Aleutian Islands, three at Kiska and one at Agattu. Three of the destroyers are sunk.

JULY 7–12

LAND WAR, *NEW GUINEA*

Australian troops make a five-day march across the Owen Stanley Mountains in southern Papua. They take up defensive positions along the Kokoda trail, which snakes from coast to coast across southern Papua.

JULY 21

SEA WAR, *ALEUTIAN ISLANDS*

US submarines sink a further three Japanese destroyers around Kiska in the Aleutians.

KEY MOMENTS

BURMA–THAILAND RAILWAY

The Burma–Thailand railway was one of the greatest, and most appalling, engineering feats of World War II. In mid-1942, the Japanese were faced with chronic problems in supplying their forces fighting in Burma, particularly as shipping routes to Rangoon were increasingly interdicted by Allied aircraft, ships and submarines. The solution was to build a railroad extension between Thanbyuzayat in Burma and Nong Pladuk in Thailand, which, when linked to existing rail routes, would provide a logistical lifeline throughout Burma and give better access to shipping supplies running up through the Gulf of Siam.

The main challenge, however, was that the rail route stretched over 321km (200 miles) of mountainous jungle terrain. Tropical temperatures would easily exceed 100 degrees F, humidity approached 100 percent, and tropical diseases (particularly malaria) abounded.

To achieve this feat, the Japanese used 61,000 Allied POWs and more than 270,000 labourers from Japanese-occupied territories. The work was done under the most inhumane conditions. The labourers were forced to work 14-hour days or more on starvation rations, with little water and no medical attention. Beatings, executions and torture were constant, and anyone who fell through illness was likely to be bayoneted or shot on the spot. The railway extension ultimately stretched 420km (240 miles) and cost an estimated 12,000 POW lives and the lives of 90,000 other labourers – an average of 425 deaths for every mile of track laid.

The Burma–Thailand railway did not improve Japanese logistics in Burma as significantly as expected. Allied aerial bombing managed to cut the infamous bridge over the Kwai Yai in 1944; and, by early 1945, the stretch of railway was abandoned in the face of Allied advances.

July 21-29

LAND WAR, *NEW GUINEA*

Units of the Japanese Eighteenth Army land at Buna on the northern coast of Papua in a renewed Japanese attempt to take Port Moresby, following the defeat of the previous invasion force during the Battle of the Coral Sea. Major-General Tomitaro Horii's "South Seas Force" intends to push across the Kokoda trail and take the town. On July 29, the Japanese take Kokoda itself, halfway along the trail, after a shock night attack.

July 30

POLITICS, *US*

The industrial magnate Henry J. Kaiser is "enlisted" by the US Government to galvanize US war production. Kaiser has previously revolutionized production of the US Liberty cargo vessels (nicknamed "American ugly ducklings") using assembly line techniques of construction (one ship could be produced in only 80 hours), and the US Government hopes he can achieve similar results in the production of aircraft, armoured vehicles and warships.

▼ *A US Marine Corps LVT-1 Alligator amphibious assault vehicle hits the beach on Guadalcanal. Each vehicle could accommodate up to 24 soldiers.*

STRATEGY AND TACTICS

JAPANESE STRATEGY ON GUADALCANAL

After the setback at the Battle of Midway in June 1942, the Japanese concentrated their efforts on defence of their territorial gains – what they euphemistically called the Greater East Asia Co-Prosperity Sphere – basically the areas of Asia that gave Japan the raw materials and resources it needed to fight the war. This strategy of defence included building an airfield on Guadalcanal (later renamed Henderson Field by the Americans) as a way of using land-based aircraft in support of carrier-borne units against any US attack.

For the US, the assault on Guadalcanal was a mission of denial rather than of long-term occupancy, preventing the airfield from falling into Japanese hands and allowing it the chance to use its bombers against the US Pacific Fleet. Once entrenched on Guadalcanal, the Japanese planned to use the "Tokyo Express" (essentially a naval supply chain of ships) to keep the island re-supplied and reinforced by sea from the base at Rabaul. When the US attacked the vital shipping routes they fought fiercely to keep these lanes open, resulting in a number of relatively large naval battles off the coast of the Solomon Islands. The overall Japanese strategy once Henderson Field had been seized by the Americans shortly after they landed on August 7, 1942, was to wrest control of the airfield and use it to attack the US fleet, though in this venture they were unsuccessful as the US Marines had secured victory on Guadalcanal by early February 1943. The Japanese lost thousands of troops in futile attacks on the perimeter of the airfield.

July 31

AIR WAR, *SOLOMON ISLANDS*

Japanese airfields on Tulagi and Guadalcanal are bombed by US aircraft.

August 7-8

LAND WAR, *GUADALCANAL*

On August 7, units of the 1st Marine Division land on Guadalcanal in the Solomon Islands. It is the first major US offensive operation of the war, expedited by Japanese construction of an airfield (Henderson Field) on Guadalcanal, and is composed of a 19,000-strong amphibious task force under Rear-Admiral Turner, with operational

▲ *After a heavy naval bombardment (seen here), landings began on Tanambogo, spearheaded by a pair of tanks. By nightfall the island was in US hands.*

command falling to Rear-Admiral Fletcher. The initial landings on Guadalcanal are unopposed, but stiff resistance is encountered during subsequent landings at Tulagi and Gavutu. By August 8, Henderson Field is secured by the Allies, but the Japanese begin a major naval and aerial bombardment of US positions.

AUGUST 8–11

LAND WAR, *NEW GUINEA*
Kokoda is temporarily recaptured from

the Japanese by a mixed force of Australian and Papuan troops, but by August 11 the Allies are driven 8km (5 miles) back towards Port Moresby.

AUGUST 8–9

SEA WAR, *BATTLE OF SAVO ISLAND*
A force of Allied cruisers under Rear-Admiral Crutchley fights a brutal night action north of Savo Island against a Japanese cruiser force attempting to destroy US transport vessels supplying operations on Guadalcanal. The Japanese force, led by Vice-Admiral Mikawa, demonstrates total superiority in night-fighting, sinking four Allied cruisers for no losses in only 90 minutes, killing more than 1000 Allied seamen. The Allied resistance, however, prevents the Japanese attacking the vital logistics shipping; and the day after the battle, a

US submarine sinks the Japanese heavy cruiser *Kako*.

AUGUST 12

LAND WAR, *CHINA*
Japanese forces in central Shantung Province launch a massive new offensive against Chinese Nationalist troops. The Japanese are taking advantage of internecine warfare raging between Communist and Nationalist soldiers.

AUGUST 17

COMMANDO RAID, *GILBERT ISLANDS*
US troops of the 2nd Raider Battalion, US Marine Corps, attack Japanese coastal installations on Makin Island during a night-time raid. The commandos are transported to their objective by the submarines USS *Nautilus* and USS *Argonaut*, with USS *Nautilus* providing offshore gunfire support as the 2nd Raiders go ashore in small landing craft.

AUGUST 18–19

LAND WAR, *NEW GUINEA*
The main pass across the Owen Stanley Mountains is now in the hands of the Japanese Eighteenth Army. On the 19th, troops from the Australian 7th Division begin amphibious reinforcement of Port Moresby.

▼ *A US SBD Dauntless dive-bomber lies wrecked on Henderson Field following a Japanese air attack. The airfield was originally constructed by the Japanese.*

AUGUST 18–22

LAND WAR, *GUADALCANAL*
The Japanese land a regiment at Taivu, 32km (20 miles) east of Henderson Field. The regiment, under Colonel Ichiki, is around 900-men strong and advances westwards and attacks the US perimeter around the air base on August 21–22. All attacks are repulsed, the US having constructed a solid defensive perimeter around Henderson Field since the initial landings. Ichiki's force is decimated on the Tenaru River, and Ichiki himself commits suicide.

AUGUST 20–24

AIR WAR, *GUADALCANAL*
US forces on Guadalcanal receive their first contingent of land-based aircraft (31 fighters) for use from Henderson Field. The aircraft will provide much needed close-support and naval interdiction operations over the coming weeks. On August 24, a Japanese air at-

tack suffers 21 aircraft downed against 3 US losses.

AUGUST 23–25

SEA WAR, *EASTERN SOLOMON ISLANDS*
A Japanese supply convoy, protected by the aircraft carriers *Ryujo*, *Zuizaku* and

▲ *Japanese premier Hideki Tojo (front row, second from left) with his war cabinet in Tokyo. He took over the office of foreign minister in early September.*

Shokaku, attempts a resupply mission to Guadalcanal, but is intercepted by Vice-Admiral Fletcher's Task Force 61,

▲ Australian troops, supported by a US M2A2 light tank, assault a Japanese position on New Guinea. Note how the wartime censor has masked any unit identification markings on the tank.

also containing three carriers (USS *Saratoga*, USS *Wasp* and USS *Enterprise*). On the 24th, US and Japanese carrier aircraft deal mutual blows, the US sinking the *Ryujo* and the Japanese damaging, although not critically, the USS *Enterprise*. The carrier forces separate, but the next day US Marine dive-bombers flying from Henderson Field sink two Japanese transporters (*Jintsu* and *Kinryu Maru*) and the destroyer *Mutsuki*. Japanese supply runs to Guadalcanal are now to be made under more awkward night conditions.

▲ US Marines on the island of Guadalcanal photographed just after they had stormed a Japanese camp. The enemy left in a hurry, leaving their food on the table.

AUGUST 25

LAND WAR, *GILBERT ISLANDS*
Japanese forces occupy Nauru in the Gilbert Islands and Goodenough Island off the coast of New Guinea.

AUGUST 25–26

LAND WAR, *NEW GUINEA*
Milne Bay, in the southeastern corner of Papua, is invaded by a Japanese unit of 1200 men. They are attempting to occupy land suitable for a Japanese forward air base to support the army's drive on Port Moresby. The landing is heavily resisted by Australian troops occupying coastal positions, who kill numerous Japanese and destroy several landing craft.

AUGUST 28

AIR WAR, *SOLOMON ISLANDS*
USAAF aircraft attack a Japanese reinforcement convoy heading for Guadalcanal. The Japanese destroyer *Asagiri* is sunk and two other destroyers are damaged, with the convoy unable to put ashore its troops.

◄ Troops of the US 1st Marine Division with an M1918 155mm howitzer on Guadalcanal. This artillery piece was based on a French World War I design.

437

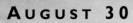

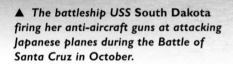

▲ *The battleship USS* South Dakota *firing her anti-aircraft guns at attacking Japanese planes during the Battle of Santa Cruz in October.*

AUGUST 30

LAND WAR, *ALEUTIAN ISLANDS*
US Navy and Army troops occupy Adak in the Aleutian Islands, intending to use it as an air and naval operating base in the North Pacific area.

AUGUST 31

SEA WAR, *SOLOMON ISLANDS*
The carrier USS *Saratoga* is damaged by a torpedo launched from the Japanese submarine *I-25* 418km (260 miles) southeast of Guadalcanal. She is then towed part of the way to Pearl Harbor for repairs.

SEPTEMBER 1

LAND WAR, *GUADALCANAL*
Troops of the Naval Construction Battalion – otherwise known as "Seabees" – are landed on Guadalcanal to assist in developing the US base there. The Seabees are known for ingenious and fast engineering work under combat conditions.

SEPTEMBER 3

POLITICS, *JAPAN*
The Japanese war minister and premier, Hideki Tojo, takes over the office of foreign minister after the resignation of Shigenori Togo. There are now

▼ *Two Japanese aircraft are shot down during the Battle of Santa Cruz. Both had been attempting to attack the US cruiser seen in the background.*

no civilian personnel in the Japanese cabinet.

SEPTEMBER 3–7

LAND WAR, NEW *GUINEA*
The Japanese land 1000 reinforcements at Buna to reinforce the flagging New Guinea campaign. On September 5-7, the Japanese Special Navy Landing

▼ *US Marine Corps pilots race to their Corsair aircraft on Guadalcanal. The first deliveries of this excellent aircraft to combat units began in July 1942.*

◄ *The USS Hornet on fire at the Battle of Santa Cruz. During the engagement she was hit by two kamikaze attacks, seven bombs and two torpedoes in one assault, followed by another assault by torpedo bombers. She later was abandoned and eventually sunk.*

Force is compelled to withdraw from Milne Bay by the violent defence of the Australian 7th Brigade and the 18th Brigade of the Australian 7th Division. The Japanese lose around 1000 men in the action, the first defeat for a Japanese amphibious invasion force.

SEPTEMBER 7/8

LAND WAR, *GUADALCANAL*
A force of Marine Raiders conducts a night-time assault against Japanese positions at Taivu, obtaining intelligence about Japanese campaign plans and inflicting damage on Japanese logistics.

SEPTEMBER 11

AIR WAR, *NEW GUINEA*
The Japanese destroyer *Yayoi* is sunk by a combined force of British and US aircraft flying from Normandy Island, D'Entrecasteaux Islands, off New Guinea.

▶ *The fighting around Henderson Field was particularly savage, with the Japanese launching mass infantry attacks against US positions, to no avail.*

SEPTEMBER 12–14

LAND WAR, *GUADALCANAL*

The 6000-strong Japanese 25th Brigade launches a major attack against Henderson Field around "Bloody Ridge". The US Marines, forewarned by intelligence gathered from Taivu Field, put up a ferocious defence. After two days of fighting and more than 1200 losses, the Japanese commander, General Kawaguchi, orders his men to withdraw.

SEPTEMBER 14–15

LAND WAR, *NEW GUINEA*

By September 14, Japanese forces advancing across the Kokoda trail are only 50km (30 miles) from Port Moresby. The capital, however, is receiving heavy reinforcements in the shape of US infantry.

SEPTEMBER 15

SEA WAR, *GUADALCANAL*

The carrier USS *Wasp* and a US destroyer are sunk by Japanese submarines while running convoy protection duties for transport ships bound for the island of Guadalcanal.

▼ *Smoke rises from a Japanese bomber shot down in the Guadalcanal area, just as its pilot attempted to ram the ship whose rail can be seen in the foreground. The puffs of smoke are from anti-aircraft fire.*

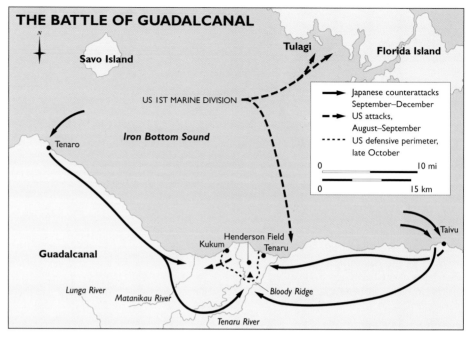

THE BATTLE OF GUADALCANAL

| Japanese counterattacks September–December |
| US attacks, August–September |
| US defensive perimeter, late October |

0 — 10 mi
0 — 15 km

Savo Island · Tulagi · Florida Island · US 1ST MARINE DIVISION · Iron Bottom Sound · Tenaro · Guadalcanal · Kukum · Henderson Field · Tenaru · Taivu · Lunga River · Matanikau River · Bloody Ridge · Tenaru River

SEPTEMBER 18

LAND WAR, *GUADALCANAL*

US forces on Guadalcanal are reinforced by the 7th Marine Regiment.

SEPTEMBER 21

LAND WAR, *BURMA*

Allied forces in Burma attempt to go on the offensive against Japanese units in the Arakan around the Bay of Bengal. The offensive fails, and the 14th Indian Division suffers heavy losses.

SEPTEMBER 23–31

LAND WAR, *NEW GUINEA*

The 7th Australian Division launches a major counteroffensive against the Japanese in the Gona/Buna area of Papua, attacking the Japanese at the very point where they made their initial landings the previous July. The Japanese, now starving and struck with tropical diseases, are forced into retreat from Port Moresby by the Australians, and by the end of the month are driven as far back as Wairopi.

SEPTEMBER 24–27

LAND WAR, *GILBERT ISLANDS*

Japanese forces make three landings throughout the Gilberts, putting troops ashore at Maiana, Beru and Kuria.

SEPTEMBER 27

ALEUTIAN ISLANDS, *ATTU*

The Japanese forces on Attu begin secretly transferring to Kiska to strengthen the garrison there.

OCTOBER 1

SEA WAR, *CHINA*

The Japanese ship *Lisbon Maru* carrying 1816 Allied POWs is torpedoed by the US submarine USS *Grouper* off the coast of China. Japanese seamen close the hatches on the prisoners, and 840 go to the bottom. Many of those who manage to escape

▶ *The cruiser USS Boise arrives at the Philadelphia Navy Yard for repairs following damage suffered at the Battle of Cape Esperance.*

▲ *Japanese troops in retreat on New Guinea following the counterattack by the 7th Australian Division at the end of September, which saved Port Moresby.*

▲ *Sailors from the cruiser USS Boise admire their battle score after service in the Solomons: two heavy cruisers, a light cruiser and three destroyers sunk.*

are machine-gunned on the surface. Japanese prison ships did not display the red cross to signify prisoners aboard, and conditions were so horrifying that more than 22,000 Allied POWs died on Japanese ships during the war.

OCTOBER 3–4

AIR WAR, *GUADALCANAL*

US and Japanese aircraft trade blows over Guadalcanal. On the 3rd, 30 Japanese Zeros attack US positions, but 7 Navy Wildcat fighters manage to shoot down 9 of the attackers while anti-aircraft batteries destroy another 2. In the

night, US Navy and Marine Corps aircraft bomb a Japanese convoy landing troops on Guadalcanal, hitting one cruiser.

OCTOBER 5

AIR WAR, *SOLOMON ISLANDS*

US carrier aircraft strike at a concentration of Japanese ships massing around Shortland Island, south of Bougainville. Six vessels are damaged, and around ten Japanese aircraft are destroyed.

OCTOBER 7–9

LAND WAR, *GUADALCANAL*

US Marine forces at Henderson Field

make westward attacks against nearby Japanese forces, fighting heavy engagements on the Matanikau River. Shortly after the battles, the US Marines receive their first US Army reinforcements in the form of the 164th Infantry Regiment of the Americal Division.

OCTOBER 11–12

SEA WAR, *CAPE ESPERANCE*

A US cruiser force under Rear-Admiral Scott intercepts a Japanese supply convoy, covered by a Japanese cruiser squadron under Rear-Admiral Goto, heading for Guadalcanal between the

OCTOBER 14

East and West Solomon Islands. Despite some inefficient communications and poor tactical manoeuvring by the US ships, US radar provides an advantage and the initial clash sees the Japanese lose the destroyer *Fubuki*, while the cruisers *Furutaka* and *Aoba* are seriously damaged. The Japanese retaliate by crippling the USS *Duncan* and USS *Boise*, but are forced into retreat. The action shows how US advances in shipboard radar might deprive the Japanese of their tactical supremacy in night fighting.

OCTOBER 14

SEA WAR, *GUADALCANAL*

Henderson Field suffers a heavy bombardment from the Japanese battleships *Kongo* and *Haruna* and an assortment of other vessels. US battery fire damages two Japanese destroyers.

OCTOBER 23–26

LAND WAR, *GUADALCANAL*

Henderson Field suffers another major Japanese attack by 20,000 soldiers under the command of General Maruyama. Wave after wave of Japanese troops assault the US Marines' southern positions, concentrated along the Mananikau, Lunga and Tenaru rivers, over the next three days, but each attack is defeated and the offensive collapses with 3500 Japanese casualties.

OCTOBER 25–26

SEA WAR, *SANTA CRUZ*

The Japanese Combined Fleet moves towards Guadalcanal in support of General Maruyama's offensive against the US Marines on the island. US Task Forces 16 and 17, containing the carriers USS *Hornet* and USS *Enterprise*, are sent to intercept the Japanese around Santa Cruz Island. A strike force of US carrier aircraft miss their target on the 25th, and at first light on the 26th both the US and Japanese put flights of attack aircraft into the sky. Over the course of a four-hour battle, the Japanese carriers *Zuiho* and *Shokaku* are badly damaged, while the USS *Enterprise* suffers a smashed flight deck and the USS *Hornet* is destroyed by two torpedo and six bomb strikes and has to be abandoned. The Japanese claim victory in the battle, but have lost more than 100 pilots and aircraft, unacceptably high losses that render many of the carriers almost inoperable.

OCTOBER 30

LAND WAR, *ALEUTIAN ISLANDS*

The Japanese land a second invasion force on the island of Attu in the Aleutian Islands.

▶ The battleship USS **New Jersey** is launched at the Philadelphia Naval Shipyard. It took a year to train her crew before she was ready for duty.

▲ Japanese troops in a firefight with Australians during the retreat from the Port Moresby area. Japanese forces were desperately short of food by this time.

NOVEMBER 1–30

LAND WAR, *GUADALCANAL*

US forces on Guadalcanal continue to pressure Japanese units. On November 3, six US battalions trap a Japanese unit near Point Cruz and kill 300 enemy troops. In addition, the 7th Marines and units of the 164th Infantry Division attack a 1500-strong Japanese force landed as reinforcements near Koli Point, inflicting heavy losses and pushing the Japanese inland. Following these actions, the Japanese abandon their two-front strategy on Guadalcanal. The US keeps receiving reinforcements, including the 2nd Raider Battalion, 8th Marines and 182nd Infantry, so the Japanese have little respite.

NOVEMBER 2

LAND WAR, *NEW GUINEA*

Australian forces in New Guinea retake Kokoda, having pushed the Japanese halfway back across the Kokoda trail.

NOVEMBER 7

AIR WAR, *GUADALCANAL*

US aircraft flying from Henderson Field bomb and damage two Japanese destroyers off the coast of Guadalcanal.

NOVEMBER 11–13

LAND WAR, *NEW GUINEA*

The disease-ravaged and exhausted Japanese suffer another defeat on Papua, losing 600 men in an Australian flanking action at the town of Oivi. Japanese troops on the Kokoda trail are pushed back beyond the Kumusi River, ensuring the safety of Port Moresby. Advancing Australian troops find evidence of cannibalism among the starving Japanese.

NOVEMBER 12–13

SEA WAR, *SOLOMON ISLANDS*

A Japanese convoy of transport ships, supported by 11 destroyers and carrying 13,000 infantry reinforcements, heads for Guadalcanal, while a large force of 18 Japanese warships (including two battleships and two cruisers) under Admiral Tanaka bombards Henderson Field as a covering action. Japanese carriers provide air cover from the northern Solomon Islands. A US force of eight destroyers and five cruisers, commanded by Rear-Admiral Callaghan, moves to intercept, guided by ship-borne radar.

Tanaka's and Callaghan's forces clash in the early hours of the morning around "Ironbottom Sound" between the coast of Guadalcanal and Savo Island. The action is bloody, the Japanese suffering two cruisers sunk and one battleship (the *Hiei*) crippled, while the US loses one cruiser and four destroyers. Almost all vessels participating in the battle are damaged, and Callaghan is killed. The action is broken off, and the Japanese supply convoy is unable to reach Guadalcanal.

NOVEMBER 13

SEA WAR, *SOLOMON ISLANDS*

The crippled battleship *Hiei* is sunk by a US air attack north of Savo Island. Meanwhile, the Japanese attempt once again to run the reinforcements convoy into Guadalcanal.

NOVEMBER 14–15

SEA WAR, *SOLOMON ISLANDS*

US dive-bombers and torpedo aircraft sink six transports and two cruisers of the convoy heading for Guadalcanal. A rescue force of 14 Japanese warships under Admiral Kondo is sent into battle and is met by US Task Force 64 under Admiral Lee, comprising two battleships and four destroyers. They fight around midnight on November 14/15. Task Force 64 loses four warships in quick succession, leaving the battleship USS *Washington* to destroy the Japanese battleship *Kirishima* and one destroyer with its radar-controlled guns. By 00:30 hours, the Japanese are in retreat, and the attempt to reinforce the Japanese Guadalcanal garrison is

▲ *A Japanese machine gunner on Guadalcanal. By the end of the year the Imperial Army had lost over 20,000 dead trying to dislodge US forces from the island.*

▶ *An Australian mortar crew on New Guinea. By the end of 1942, many Australians were sick with malaria and their units were understrength.*

NOVEMBER 17–19

▲ Australian tanks and infantry flush out Japanese troops in pillboxes in the final assault on Buna. In the foreground, a soldier is reloading his rifle.

curtailed, although Japanese destroyers still manage to put ashore around 10,000 men (most rescued from the sunken transports).

NOVEMBER 17–19

LAND WAR, *NEW GUINEA*
The Japanese on the Kokoda trail are forced back into defensive positions in the Buna/Gona area, reinforced by some 1000 extra troops on November 17. A US-led attack against Buna on November 19 is beaten off.

NOVEMBER 24

LAND WAR, *SOLOMON ISLANDS*
The Japanese land troops at Munda Point, New Georgia.

◄ The corpses of Japanese soldiers, shattered ammunition boxes and debris litter a beach near the port of Gona, New Guinea, in late 1942.

NOVEMBER 30

SEA WAR, *SOLOMON ISLANDS*
The Japanese 2nd Destroyer Flotilla under Admiral Tanaka attempts to run a supply convoy to Guadalcanal through Ironbottom Sound under the cover of darkness. A large force of destroyers and cruisers under Rear-Admiral Wright engages the Japanese with gunfire, sinking the destroyer *Takanami*, before losing one cruiser and suffering three badly damaged cruisers by a nimble Japanese torpedo counterattack. Despite the failure of the supply convoy, the action again demonstrates Japanese excellence in naval night-fighting.

DECEMBER 2

LAND WAR, *GUADALCANAL*
US Marines ambush a Japanese patrol around the Lunga River, killing 35 of the 60 enemy soldiers.

DECEMBER 3

AIR WAR, *NEW GEORGIA*
US bombers concentrate attacks on Munda Point in an attempt to prevent the construction of a Japanese air base there.

DECEMBER 7

SEA WAR, *US*
The USS *New Jersey* is launched, the largest battleship in the US Navy

with a displacement of 55, 767 tonnes (54,889 tons), and featuring a main armament of nine 16in guns set in three triple turrets.

DECEMBER 9

LAND WAR, *GUADALCANAL*
Major-General Alexander M. Patch takes over command of the US Guadalcanal forces from General Vandegrift. The 1st US Marine Division begins to leave Guadalcanal as reinforcements arrive. During December, the US forces on Guadalcanal will reach 58,000 men, as opposed to 20,000 poorly equipped Japanese.

LAND WAR, *NEW GUINEA*
Australian troops of the 21st Brigade take Gona, sealing the Japanese entry

point to the Kokoda trail. More than 630 Japanese are killed in the close-quarters battle, while the Australian victory is bought at the heavy price of 530 casualties.

DECEMBER 17–31

LAND WAR, *BURMA*

The 14th Indian Division begins to take the Allied war back into Burma. It crosses the Indian border and advances 241km (150 miles) to positions just north of the Maungdaw–Buthidaung line extending out from the western coast of Burma. The goal of the advance is Akyab, around 96km (60 miles) to the south, but the 14th Indian Division faces nimble Japanese delaying tactics and is eventually halted by the 55th Division. Allied penetration, how-

▼ *Jeeps loaded with military equipment on their way to supply US forces fighting Japanese troops in New Guinea.*

KEY PERSONALITIES

ADMIRAL CHESTER NIMITZ

Admiral Chester W. Nimitz was one of the most gifted naval commanders of World War II. Born in 1885 in Texas, Nimitz first set his sights on a career in the US Army, but owing to a lack of places at West Point he began attendance at the Naval Academy Class in 1905.

Nimitz excelled academically, athletically and in leadership skills. He first took to sea in the USS *Ohio*, before commanding the gunboat USS *Panay* then the USS *Decatur*. Between 1907 and 1918, Nimitz was assigned to service in submarines: he commanded a number of vessels and, for one year, the Atlantic Submarine Flotilla. In 1919, he returned to service on board surface vessels for one year; and, during the 1920s, he occupied more strategic-level roles in the US Navy, including Chief of Staff to the Commander Battle Forces and Chief of Staff to the C-in-C, US Fleet. The late 1920s and 1930s saw Nimitz take various ship and submarine commands, including the heavy cruiser USS *Augusta*, before moving on to naval division commands and also becoming the Chief of the Bureau of Navigation in 1939.

Nimitz's crowning achievement came when he replaced Rear-Admiral Kimmel as

C-in-C of the US Pacific Fleet after the attack on Pearl Harbor, Nimitz being promoted to full admiral. Throughout the Pacific campaign, Nimitz demonstrated an aggressive defensive attitude combined with a deep practical understanding of naval warfare, and an affable personality that made him popular and respected. Nimitz presided over the great naval battles of the Pacific War, and had an excellent grasp of how to support amphibious land campaigns. It is a sign of his capabilities that, in November 1945, he was made Chief of Naval Operations on the retirement of Admiral King.

ever, resumes southwards; and, on December 31, Rathedaung is taken.

DECEMBER 19

LAND WAR, *NEW GUINEA*

Australian troops overwhelm the Japanese defences at Buna, signalling the end of the Japanese campaign in New Guinea.

DECEMBER 26–31

LAND WAR, *GUADALCANAL*

US XIV Corps faces a bloody Christmas battling with desperate Japanese forces on Guadalcanal. Despite being half-starved, stricken with malaria and running out of ammunition, the Japanese on Mount Austen still put up a tenacious defence. However, on December 31, the Japanese imperial general staff orders the abandonment of Guadalcanal.

DECEMBER 27–28

LAND WAR, *NEW GUINEA*

Recognizing the futility of resistance in New Guinea, the Japanese high command orders troops at Napopo and Buna to begin retreating to Giruwa.

1943

LAND WAR, *GUADALCANAL*
The Japanese high command gives the orders for a phased withdrawal of Japanese forces from Guadalcanal. US strength on the island is now around 50,000 troops, with massive air, artillery and naval resources, while Hyakutake's Seventeenth Army consists of fewer than half that number, has limited ammunition and rations, and little hope of resupply. General Patch's XIV Corps pushes outwards from the Lunga perimeter.

▼ Two US soldiers prepare to enter a Japanese dugout on New Guinea, January 3, 1943. Their weapons are M1 Garand semi-automatic rifles.

As the US war economy switched into high gear, more ships and aircraft became available for the Pacific theatre. With resources to hand, the Allies, with the US as the major player, were able to mount sustained offensives in the central and southwest Pacific. The Japanese were forced back in New Guinea and the Solomons, while US forces won hard-fought victories in the Gilbert Islands.

▼ A Japanese Zero fighter, its fuselage riddled with machine-gun rounds, lies wrecked on Guadalcanal in January 1943.

JANUARY 2

LAND WAR, *GUADALCANAL*
US troops attack Japanese positions on Mount Austen, a piece of high ground dominating the landscape between the Lunga and Matanikau rivers. However, the Japanese beat off the attack.

JANUARY 2-13

LAND WAR, *NEW GUINEA*
Allied forces achieve total control over the Kokoda trail, having engaged in fierce fighting along its length for 10 months. The Japanese do not go easily, and a US assault against Buna on January 2 meets heavy resistance: there are 2870 Allied casualties, but the settlement is finally taken.

JANUARY 3-55

AIR/SEA WAR, *NEW GEORGIA*
US fighter and bomber aircraft attack Japanese targets around the New Geor-gia group, concentrating on the Japanese airfield at Munda and several Japanese destroyers anchored off Rendova Island. On the 5th, US surface vessels bombard Munda.

JANUARY 5

LAND WAR, *GUADALCANAL*
US troops manage to capture high-ground positions on Mount Austen, and

▲ Surrounded by tall kunai grass, a US Army sergeant drinks from his canteen during a lull in the fighting around Buna in New Guinea in early January.

see off six enemy counterattacks with 150 Japanese soldiers dead.

JANUARY 6-9

SEA WAR, *HUON GULF*
The US demonstrates its increasing su-premacy in sea power during the Battle

▲ *A photograph taken from a US aircraft shows bombs bursting on a Japanese airfield at Lae on New Guinea.*

STRATEGY AND TACTICS

JAPANESE STRATEGY FOR 1943

By 1943, it was becoming apparent to a number of Japanese commanders that they were fighting a losing battle. After failing to knock out the US carriers at Pearl Harbor, the hope for 1942 had rested on securing a perimeter wide and deep enough to protect its territories. Yamamoto, commander of the Combined Fleet, felt that the qualitative difference in national strength between Japan and the US was patently obvious, and that any prolonged war between the two countries could only end in defeat for Japan. He hoped that the rapid destruction of the main force of the US fleet and the strategy of continually seeking decisive engagements would weaken the morale of both the US Navy and the people, forcing the government to seek peace at the negotiation table.

But, by 1943 the Japanese had suffered a series of serious setbacks, such as the Battle of Midway in mid-June 1942. They therefore set about devising another way of holding back the American tide. They were determined to hold what they could, and this meant vigorously fighting for and reinforcing New Guinea and the neighbouring islands. By using the fortified base at Rabaul, the Japanese hoped to strike at the Americans with air- and sea-based power. Meanwhile, in Burma and on the Indian border, the Japanese went ahead with Operation U-Go, the assault on Imphal, and Operation Ha-Go, a diversionary attack on the Arakan Peninsula. By striking into India, the Japanese planned to take the communication centres of Imphal and Kohima and thus deliver a crippling blow against the British build-up for operations to retake Burma.

of Huon Gulf. Waves of US aircraft attack Japanese supply convoys destined for Papua New Guinea, sinking three Japanese transports and downing eighty Japanese aircraft with few losses.

JANUARY 9

POLITICS, *CHINA*
The Japanese puppet government established in China declares war on the US and Britain. In response, Japan reduces the extent of its claims on Chinese territory and hostility towards Chinese sovereignty.

LAND WAR, *NEW GUINEA*
Troops of the Australian 17th Brigade

are airlifted into Wau, landing under Japanese fire. The landing prevents 2500 Japanese troops from capturing Wau airfield, and fighting continues as the Allies attempt to regain control of the airfield and the surrounding jungle.

JANUARY 12–19

LAND WAR, *ALEUTIAN ISLANDS*
At the northern extremity of the Pacific War, US troops start to claw back Japanese conquests in the freezing Aleutian Islands. On January 12, a US amphibious force deploys 2000 men on the island of Amchitka, losing 14 soldiers after the destroyer USS *Worden* sinks in severe weather. On January 18/19, a force of six US warships bombards Japanese-held Attu Island.

JANUARY 14

LAND WAR, *GUADALCANAL*
In a clear signal of Japanese intentions,

◄ *The heavy cruiser USS Chicago (in the foreground), which was sunk by Japanese aircraft in the Solomon Islands at the end of January.*

▲ *US motor torpedo boats. During the Solomons campaign they operated against Japanese shipping in the "Slot".*

Japanese troops are landed at Cape Esperance on the far northwestern tip of the island to prepare landing zones for evacuation shipping.

SEA WAR, *GUADALCANAL*
US motor torpedo boats make torpedo runs against Japanese destroyers attempting to deliver supplies to army units on Guadalcanal. Three destroyers are hit and the enemy force withdraws.

JANUARY 16–18

LAND WAR, *BURMA*
The Indian 14th Division suffers heavy losses during the continued Allied offensive into the Arakan. A stern Japanese resistance beats off attacks against Rathedaung and Donbaik.

JANUARY 21–30

LAND WAR, *NEW GUINEA*
The Allied advance through New Guinea is now directed towards Salamaua and Lae in the Huon Gulf, driving the Japanese towards New Guinea's western coastline. Victory is now complete in Papua with the fall of Sanananda, though at the cost of more than 7000 US/Australian casualties. An estimated

13,000 Japanese have been killed in the Papuan campaign. In northern New Guinea, 3000 Japanese troops begin a three-pronged offensive against Allied positions around the mining town of Wau in northern Papua, forcing 700 Australian troops into a localized offensive withdrawal. Heavy rains and airlifted reinforcements permit the Allies to stop the Japanese advance by the end of the month.

JANUARY 23

LAND WAR, *GUADALCANAL*
US forces on Guadalcanal take the Japanese base at Kokumbona after a three-day naval bombardment and a final assault. The Japanese are now being driven into the northwestern corner of Guadalcanal as Japanese shipping prepares to evacuate remaining troops.

JANUARY 27

LAND WAR, *GUADALCANAL*
During the US westward advance across Guadalcanal, a major enemy command post is captured, with 37 Japanese soldiers killed and 3 taken prisoner. Significant amounts of arms, ammunition and supplies are also captured.

JANUARY 30

SEA WAR, *SOLOMON ISLANDS*
The heavy cruiser USS *Chicago* of Rear-

GRUMMAN F6F HELLCAT

In early 1943, the Grumman F6F Hellcat carrier-borne fighter began its operational deployment to the Pacific theatre, having first flown in prototype form in June 1942. The Hellcat had the manoeuvrability, power and armament to take on and surpass the best of Japanese aircraft, and its kill rate was formidable – 5156 Japanese aircraft destroyed between 1943 and 1945. Some 480 F6Fs of US Task Force 58 were at the frontline of the slaughter of more than 400 Japanese aircraft during the Battle of the Philippine Sea; and, in total, F6Fs accounted for three-quarters of all Japanese aircraft downed during the war. The F6F was produced in a number of forms, including the radar-equipped F6F-3E and F6F-3N and the F6F-5 fighter-bomber. Total production of F6Fs was 12,275.

SPECIFICATIONS: (F6F-5)

CREW: one
POWERPLANT: one 1419kW (2000hp) Pratt & Whitney R-2800-10W radial piston engine
DIMENSIONS: wingspan 13.05m (42.8ft); length 10.24m (33.6ft); height 3.99m (13ft)
PERFORMANCE: max speed 612kmh (380mph); range 1521km (945 miles); service ceiling 11,396m (37,300ft)
ARMAMENT: two 20mm cannon and four 12.7mm machine guns, wing-mounted (alternatively, six 12.7mm machine guns); underwing provision for two 454kg bombs

Admiral Robert Giffen's Task Force 18 is sunk following an air raid by 31 Japanese G4M bombers 80km (50 miles) north of Rennell Island. Tactical errors by Giffen aggravate the attack, which also damages a US destroyer.

FEBRUARY 1

LAND WAR, *NEW GUINEA*
Australian forces manage to hold off Japanese attempts to take Wau airfield, even though the Japanese advance

FEBRUARY 1-9

comes within 350m (1148ft) of the airfield's centre.

FEBRUARY 1-9

LAND WAR, *GUADALCANAL*
The final 11,000 Japanese troops on Guadalcanal are evacuated from the northern sector of the island around Cape Esperance. Ejecting the Japanese from Guadalcanal is a crucial land victory for the US, giving it a base from which to penetrate Japan's Pacific conquests and providing security for Australia and New Zealand. The Japanese leave more than 20,000 dead on the island.

FEBRUARY 1-3

LAND WAR, *BURMA*
A major British offensive in the Arakan around Donbaik and Rathedaung ends without success, as the Japanese hold on to extremely strong defensive positions in the area.

▼ *A US Marine 155mm howitzer in action on Guadalcanal during the final phase of the campaign to eject the Japanese from the island.*

FEBRUARY 4

AIR WAR, *GUADALCANAL*
US aircraft attack a large force of Japanese destroyers around Guadalcanal. One Japanese destroyer is sunk and four others badly damaged. In aerial combat during the incident, the US loses four torpedo planes, four fighters and two bombers, while twenty-two Japanese aircraft are shot down.

▲ *US Marine Raiders deploy into rubber boats during the seizure of Russell Island. The Japanese evacuated the island before the US Marines arrived.*

FEBRUARY 6

AIR WAR, *NEW GUINEA*
The Allies begin to demonstrate their air superiority over New Guinea when 37 Allied fighters shoot down 26 Japanese aircraft out of a raiding force of 70.

FEBRUARY 7

POLITICS, *CHINA*

The Chinese Nationalist leader Chiang Kai-shek consents to the use of Chinese military forces in the future Burmese campaign. Chiang usually shows interest only in the Chinese theatre, but the promise of US aid has brought concessions.

FEBRUARY 8–15

LAND WAR, *BURMA*

General Orde Wingate leaves Imphal in India to conduct guerrilla warfare behind Japanese lines with the newly formed 77th Indian Brigade, known as the "Chindits". Named after the stone lions seen guarding Buddhist temples, the 3000-strong Chindits are created for deep-penetration incursions into northern Burma, operating in eight self-contained units (known as "Columns") supplied only by air drops. Their mission is to disrupt Japanese communications and tactical deployments, and so open more opportunities for conventional offensives. On February 14/15, the Chindits cross the Chindwin River.

FEBRUARY 10–11

POLITICS, *INDIA*

Mahatma Gandhi, the Indian leader, begins a 21-day hunger strike, having been interned by the British along with all other members of the All-India Congress Party. The action puts considerable pressure on British policy in India,

▼ *Chindits lay explosive charges on a railway bridge deep behind Japanese lines in Burma. The Chindits relied on airdrops for their supplies during operations.*

STRATEGY AND TACTICS

ALLIED STRATEGY FOR 1943

The strategic outlook for 1943 could not have been more different from the previous year. Compared with the position of weakness after Pearl Harbor, the planning for 1943 was aggressive, bold and determined. Operation Cartwheel, the two-pronged assault on the Japanese stronghold at Rabaul on New Britain, began in earnest. This called for large-scale attacks on New Guinea and the Solomon Islands. Within the highest levels of the US command there had been disagreement about what kind of strategy to take (two independent, coordinate commands, one in the Southwest Pacific under General of the Army Douglas MacArthur, and the other in the Central, South, and North Pacific Ocean Areas under Fleet Admiral Chester W. Nimitz, were created early in the war). Except in the South and South-west Pacific, each conducted its own operations with its own ground, air, and naval forces in widely separated areas.

The argument centred on whether to move through the southwest Pacific towards the Philippines (the plan favoured by General MacArthur), or to strike at Formosa through the central Pacific (the method favoured by Admiral Nimitz). It was the endorsement of MacArthur's plan that saw Operation Cartwheel launched.

Meanwhile, on the Asian mainland, Allied plans to strike back at the Japanese forces in Burma and China were formulated and launched. This included a disastrous attack on the Arakan Peninsula as well as the use of the Chindit long-range guerrilla troops to attack the Japanese behind their lines. US strategy also saw immense efforts being put into keeping China in the war.

especially as Indian troops are dying for the Allied cause in places such as Burma and North Africa.

FEBRUARY 12

LAND WAR, *NEW GUINEA*

The Allies initiate the Elkton Plan, the campaign to eject Japanese forces from New Guinea, New Britain and the Solomon Islands and isolate the Japanese base at Rabaul. In response to Allied victories in Papua and Guadalcanal, the Japanese begin pouring reinforcements into New Guinea, including the Eighteenth Army under Lieutenant-General Adachi Hatazo and the Fourth Air Army.

FEBRUARY 17

LAND WAR, *BURMA*

Attacks by the 47th and 55th Indian Brigades against Japanese positions at Donbaik in the Arakan are repulsed.

FEBRUARY 18

LAND WAR, *BURMA*

The Chindits encounter the Japanese in action for the first time as part of "Operation Longcloth". On February 18, the

▼ *General Orde Wingate (left), the commander of the Chindits. The man to his left holds a device used to signal aircraft.*

FEBRUARY 21

▶ *Chinese Nationalist troops repair the damage caused by a landslide on the Burma Road, which ran through treacherous mountain country.*

Southern Group advancing towards Kyaikthin engages in a firefight around Maingnyaung, also cutting the railway line between Mandalay and Myitkyina.

FEBRUARY 21

LAND WAR, *SOLOMON ISLANDS*
A force of US assault battalions takes the diminutive Russell Island to the northwest of Guadalcanal in "Operation Cleanslate". The occupation is the first in a series of US campaigns to reclaim the Solomon Islands, and looks to cut off the Japanese naval and air base at Rabaul, New Britain, in a wider pincer operation called "Operation Cartwheel". Cleanslate is also the first element in General MacArthur and Admiral Nimitz's plan to re-conquer the Pacific by working up from the south and east through Japanese-occupied territory in a systematic island-hopping strategy.

FEBRUARY 22

LAND WAR, *BURMA*
Numbers Three, Seven and Eight Columns of the Northern Group of Chindits advancing towards Naungkan raid a Japanese camp at Sinlamaung.

FEBRUARY 25

HOME FRONT, *NEW ZEALAND*
One New Zealand soldier and 48 Japanese POWs are killed after the POWs make an attempted breakout from their prison camp.

▼ *Two US bombers about to attack a Japanese ship during the Battle of the Bismarck Sea. Moments after this photograph was taken the ship was hit and sunk. Another Japanese ship can be seen burning on the horizon.*

KEY PERSONALITIES

GENERAL DOUGLAS MACARTHUR

General Douglas MacArthur (1880–1964) is probably the defining figure of the US land campaign in the Pacific. MacArthur's associations with the Far East began in 1922 when, as a brigadier-general, he was sent to command the military district of Manila. He returned there in 1935, and the following year the Philippine president, Manuel Quezon, made MacArthur field marshal in the Philippine Army. The next year MacArthur retired from army life, becoming a military adviser in the Philippines. However, in July 1941 President Roosevelt recalled him to the forces, making him a lieutenant-general in command of US forces in the Far East.

In 1942, with the US now at war with Japan, MacArthur became supreme commander of the Southwest Pacific Area. His war record in the Pacific is patchy. His defence of the Philippines in 1941–42 was disastrous, and he subsequently showed a tendency towards costly tactics. However, he later took as his own the idea of island hopping – bypassing heavily defended Japanese positions in favour of taking weaker ones – and used it to good effect, isolating Rabaul and advancing his way towards mainland Japan from the southern Pacific. His most controversial act was insisting on the recapture of the Philippines, opposing the plan of Admiral King (MacArthur was generally at odds with the US Navy) and others to isolate Japan by taking Formosa. MacArthur's strategy won over Roosevelt, who probably felt it politically expedient to support him, and MacArthur executed a brilliant campaign to retake the Philippines in 1944. In April 1945, MacArthur was placed in command of all US Army forces in the Pacific, and in September he presided over the Japanese surrender aboard the USS *Missouri*. He then administered Japan for five years.

FEBRUARY 28

LAND WAR, *BURMA*

Completion of a new Burma Road allows Chinese forces in northern Burma to receive supplies by land rather than by laborious air drops and landings, the Japanese having originally cut the road in early 1942. The road runs 428km (300 miles) from Ledo to southern China, and was constructed by US Army engineers with more than 14,000 indigenous labourers.

MARCH 1

LAND WAR, *NEW GUINEA*

Allied forces make steady progress pushing the Japanese back towards the northern coastline of New Guinea. The main offensive to clear the territory is scheduled for June 1943.

MARCH 2-5

SEA WAR, *BISMARCK SEA*

A Japanese convoy (eight transports and eight destroyers), attempting to reach the Lae-Salamaua area of New Guinea with the 7000 men of the 51st Division, is devastated by 355 US and Australian aircraft and US torpedo

boats, the US having been forewarned of the convoy by ULTRA intelligence. The US attacks begin on the night of March 2 with one transport sunk and two damaged. Thereafter, the Japanese suffer constant waves of aircraft employing dive-bombing, skip-bombing, torpedo runs and strafing attacks with superb accuracy, with US PT boats finishing off crippled survivors on March

▲ *A Japanese Zero fighter burns on the ground at Lae during the Battle of the Bismarck Sea. Japanese losses included 72 aircraft; the Allies lost 4 aircraft.*

5. In total, all the transports and four destroyers are sunk, with 3660 Japanese soldiers killed and only 950 making it to New Guinea.

MARCH 3–6

LAND WAR, *BURMA*

The Chindits continue their incursion deep into Japanese territory. On March 3, the Southern Group crosses the Mu River and once again blows up the Mandalay–Myitkyina railway line. Three days later, the Northern Group attacks rail and bridge systems between Bongyaung and Nankan. Despite these successes, the Chindits are suffering casualties as the Japanese mobilize to take on the guerrilla force. Between March 2 and 4, Four Column and Two Column are dispersed in heavy fighting.

MARCH 4

LAND WAR, *BURMA*

The campaign towards Akyab grinds to a halt in the face of very heavy Japanese resistance.

MARCH 6

SEA WAR, *SOLOMON ISLANDS*

Japanese airfields at Munda and Vila are bombarded by US Navy gunfire. During the action, two Japanese destroyers are also hit and sunk.

MARCH 8–13

LAND WAR, *CHINA*

Japanese forces in China renew their offensive drive against much weakened

▼ *Major-General Claire Chennault (standing, in centre), the commander of the US Fourteenth Army Air Force in China.*

Chinese Nationalist troops. On March 8, the Japanese push across the Yangtse River, although the Chinese repel the invaders by March 13.

MARCH 10

AIR WAR, *CHINA*

To expand Allied air cover for Burmese and eastern Pacific operations, the US Fourteenth Army Air Force is created and stationed in China, commanded by Major-General Claire Chennault.

MARCH 17–18

LAND WAR, *BURMA*

The Japanese launch a major offensive to repel the Allies from the Arakan. The

▲ *The heavy cruiser USS* Salt Lake City *fires her guns during the Battle of the Bering Sea in late March.*

Japanese 55th Division and other units make a two-pronged assault against the Allies; attacking from the front along the Arakan coastline and also swinging against the Allied left flank around Htizwe. Indian troops pull back from Buthidaung and Rathedaung and discontinue attacks on the Japanese at Donbaik.

MARCH 24–31

LAND WAR, *BURMA*

The battered Northern and Southern Groups of the Chindits meet up around Baw, combining forces for an attempt to cut the Mandalay–Lashio railway line. Subsequent fighting results in a defeat for the Chindits as the Japanese mass against them; and, on February 24, General Wingate receives orders to return his forces to India. The Chindits now break up into various groups and begin one of the epic retreats of history, each man marching more than 1600km (1000 miles) through the jungle to return to safety, the Chindits losing 500 men in the process.

MARCH 26

SEA WAR, *BERING SEA*

A US Task Force, consisting of two cruisers and four destroyers under Vice-Admiral Charles McMorris, engages Vice-Admiral Hosogaya Boshiro's escort force of four cruisers

◄ Dropping supplies from a transport aircraft to Chindit forces operating in Burma. By late March, the Japanese had forced the Chindits to retreat to India.

all resources will be directed to Japan's defeat following Germany's downfall. In the meantime, Pacific forces have the immediate strategic goal of isolating Rabaul through a two-pronged offensive through New Guinea and the Solomon Islands. The long-term objectives are a sweep through the Gilbert, Marshall and Mariana Islands, although in March 1943 Pacific commanders agree that resources are not present to accomplish such tasks, or even strike all the way to Rabaul.

MARCH 31

LAND WAR, *NEW GUINEA*
A force of US infantry, commanded by Colonel Archibald MacKechnie, makes an amphibious landing at the mouth of the Waria River.

LAND WAR, *ALEUTIAN ISLANDS*
The US invasion of Attu in the Aleutian Islands is scheduled for May 7. The Aleutians have little tactical significance to the Pacific campaign, apart from drawing US and Japanese forces into the north of the ocean.

APRIL 5

LAND WAR, *BURMA*
The British military disaster in the Arakan continues to unfold. The Japanese have by now pushed the British forces halfway back up the Mayu Peninsula, and today they capture the British brigade headquarters.

and four destroyers in the Bering Sea, about 1600km (1000 miles) south of the Komandorskiye Islands in the north Pacific, as the Japanese attempt to run reinforcements to the Aleutian Islands. The four-hour gun battle results in

▼ At the Casablanca Conference, Allied leaders discussed strategic war plans. Prime Minister Churchill (seated, third from left) and President Roosevelt (seated, fourth from left) reiterated the Germany First policy.

both sides suffering one damaged cruiser, and eventually the Japanese withdraw owing to fuel and ammunition shortages.

MARCH 28

POLITICS, *CASABLANCA*
The strategic priorities of the entire war are fixed at the Casablanca Conference of Allied leaders. The Germany First policy is reiterated, with Pacific commanders given the assurance that

▲ *Lieutenant-General Shojiro Iida, commander of Japanese forces in Burma, who was replaced in early April.*

▲ *The general who replaced Iida – Masakazu Kawabe. His forces were reorganized as the Burma Area Army.*

APRIL 7–13

AIR WAR, *SOLOMON ISLANDS*

The Japanese Air Force launches Operation I, a programme of bombardment against Allied shipping in the Solomon Islands and New Guinea. More than 200 Japanese aircraft attempt to weaken the Allies' grip on their new conquests and reclaim air superiority, attacking US, British and Commonwealth shipping and airfields around Guadalcanal, Port Moresby and Milne. Three Allied transports, one destroyer and one corvette are sunk, as well as seven Allied aircraft destroyed. The Japanese lose 19 aircraft, and the offensive is a disappointment, indicating Japanese problems in making good the loss of well-trained pilots in recent campaigns.

APRIL 8

POLITICS, *JAPAN*

The commander of Japanese forces in Burma, General Iida, is replaced by General Kawabe. With the Allied offensive in the Arakan stalled, and the Chin-

dit incursion into northern Burma reversed, Kawbe takes over the command at a favourable juncture.

APRIL 13

AIR WAR, *ALEUTIAN ISLANDS*

US carrier aircraft launch 10 separate attacks on Kiska in the Aleutians, assaulting the airfield and military barracks.

APRIL 18–21

POLITICS, *JAPAN*

On April 18, the Japanese Commander-in-Chief of the Combined Fleet and the tactician behind the Pearl Harbor attack, Admiral Isoroku Yamamoto, is killed after US Lockheed P-38 Lightning fighters (of the US Army Thirteenth Air Force, 339th Squadron) intercept his aircraft in the southwest Pacific. Allied code breakers alerted Allied commanders in advance that Yamamoto was travelling among key bases, allowing them to prepare an ambush and demonstrate the increasingly vital role ULTRA intelligence is playing in the Allied war effort. Yamamoto's death is a major military and psychological blow to the Japanese (he was considered Japan's greatest military leader).

▼ *Japanese troops advance during the large-scale offensive launched in Hunan Province in early May. In the same month the Chinese Nationalists counterattacked along the Yangtze River.*

▲ *A US pilot rushes to his P-38 Lightning in New Guinea. It was P-38s that shot down the aircraft carrying Yamamoto.*

APRIL 20

POLITICS, *TOKYO*
Mamoru Shigemitsu becomes the new Japanese foreign minister.

APRIL 20-21

AIR WAR, *SOUTH PACIFIC*
On April 20, US aircraft attack the Japanese base on Nauru; the Japanese retaliate the next day by bombing US positions in the Ellice Islands.

APRIL 21

POLITICS, *US*
Increasing evidence of Japanese atrocities against US and Allied POWs leads President Roosevelt to declare that all war criminals will be tried following an Allied victory.

POLITICS, *JAPAN*
Admiral Mineichi Koga takes over command of the Japanese Combined Fleet following the death of Yamamoto.

APRIL 23

AIR WAR, *GILBERT ISLANDS*
US bombers attack the Japanese airfield on Tarawa in the Gilbert Islands.

APRIL 30

LAND WAR, *BURMA*
The survivors of General Wingate's first ill-fated Chindit expedition cross into British India and safety. Emaciated and fatigued, the troops have covered more than 1609km (1000 miles) to reach safety, and the campaign has cost 1000 British lives. A question mark now hangs over the future use of the Chindits.

MAY 2

AIR WAR, *AUSTRALIA*
The Australian port of Darwin is bombed by Japanese aircraft.

MAY 5

LAND WAR, *CHINA*
Japanese forces in central China begin a huge offensive into Hunan Province in an attempt to extend territorial gains and seize additional rice fields. Since 1941, the China conflict has been a mixture of savage localized campaigns by the Japanese, often involving the slaughter of whole village populations, and de facto truces between the Japanese, the Chinese Nationalists under Chiang Kai-shek and the Chinese Communists under Mao Tse Tung. US commanders wanting to station air bases in China have been particularly disappointed by the intermittent Chinese co-existence with the Japanese invaders.

MAY 7-14

LAND WAR, *BURMA*
The Allied offensive into the Arakan

▼ *The Trident Conference in Washington. From left to right: Brigadier-General John Deane, Admiral William Leahy and Admiral Ernest King.*

MAY 8

▲ *A US Navy reconnaissance photograph of A6M2-N floatplane Zeroes in the Aleutians, prior to the US invasion.*

finally collapses. The Japanese retake Maungdaw and Buthidaung, driving the Allies northwards and back to the original start positions of the offensive. The disastrous campaign is a salutary reminder of British offensive limitations in the theatre.

MAY 8

AIR WAR, *SOLOMON ISLANDS*
US Dauntless and Liberator aircraft bomb Japanese shipping and installations throughout the Solomon Islands. Three Japanese destroyers are damaged, one severely. The next stage of Operation Cart-

wheel, the invasion of New Georgia, is planned for the following month, and the US commanders are eager to soften up Japanese naval resources throughout the Solomon Islands.

MAY 11

LAND WAR, *ALEUTIAN ISLANDS*
Following a huge aerial and naval bombardment, a US amphibious force lands 11,000 men of the 7th US Infantry Division on Attu, beginning the land campaign to retake the Aleutian Islands. The US troops go ashore in the northern and southern sectors of Attu's southeastern coastline, and from the outset they

▲ *US bombs drop on Attu in the Aleutians from aircraft of the Eleventh United States Army Air Force.*

encounter a ferocious defence from the 2400-strong Japanese garrison commanded by Colonel Yamazaki Yasuyo.

MAY 12–25

POLITICS, *WASHINGTON*
British Prime Minister Churchill and US President Roosevelt attend the Trident Conference of Allied war leaders in Washington. Despite a unified confirmation of the Germany First strategy, including setting a date for the Allied

invasion of occupied Western Europe, British concerns are raised that the Pacific war is diverting too many resources away from European operations.

MAY 15

SEA WAR, *AUSTRALIA*

The Australian hospital ship HMAS *Centaur* is torpedoed and sunk by a Japanese submarine off the coast of Brisbane, despite being clearly marked as a medical vessel. More than 260 people are killed, with only 63 survivors.

MAY 16

LAND WAR, *ALEUTIAN ISLANDS*

The campaign to take Attu has become a war of attrition, with both sides taking heavy losses. The US land forces commander even states his belief that the island will take six months to liberate, a comment that costs him his job. However, the Japanese are steadily being pushed out of their fortified positions and retreat to Chichagof harbour as the southern and northern US groups combine into a single thrust against them.

MAY 17

ESPIONAGE, *US AND BRITAIN*

The US and Britain arrive at a cooperation agreement in the code-breaking

▼ *Troops of the US 7th Infantry Division land on Attu on May 11. A US-occupied Attu would isolate the Japanese on Kiska between US bases on Attu and Adak, making Kiska easier to capture.*

STRATEGY AND TACTICS

ALLIED INTELLIGENCE

There were two forms of Allied intelligence in the Pacific theatre, known as ULTRA and MAGIC. ULTRA referred to the decryption of military communications, whereas MAGIC related to diplomatic sources. Both were part of the massive Allied code-breaking effort which hit a high spot when the British deciphered German Enigma machine codes. As the war progressed, the British and US intelligence communities began to combine their efforts to decipher Japanese equivalents. On May 17, 1943, the BRUSA (Britain and the United States of America) agreement formed a working intelligence partnership, the US Army overseeing decryption of Japanese military codes and ciphers, while the British concentrated mainly on the European theatre. MAGIC codes – which were produced on the formidable "Purple" coding machine – were actually being broken before December 1941, giving the US an indication of the outbreak of war, but not telling it where the first attack would

come. Such was typical of MAGIC intelligence, and it proved more useful as a general guide to future Japanese intentions than as a script to future Japanese operations.

ULTRA intelligence was much harder to acquire. The Japanese naval code, JN-25, was never fully overcome during the war, but the portions of some messages read gave the US a crucial combat advantage at the battles of the Coral Sea and Midway. Japanese Army codes were not read at all until April 1943, but in 1944 – following the capture of Japanese code books on New Guinea – they were readily deciphered to assist victory in the New Guinea and Marshall Islands campaigns.

The deciphering of Japanese military signals was a cat-and-mouse game that neither side lost entirely during the war. US code breaking was certainly not helped by some caustic inter-service intelligence rivalries, but intelligence did give US forces critical advantages at crucial moments in the Pacific campaign.

war against the Axis. From now on, the two countries will actively share the burden of unravelling the ciphers produced by the German Enigma, the Japanese Purple and the Italian C38M machines. The Allies will share not only technical knowledge, but also the intelligence gleaned, to be known as

ULTRA. US intelligence analysts are to spend more time on Pacific theatre intelligence, while Britain focuses on German and Italian ciphers.

LAND WAR, *ALEUTIAN ISLANDS*

US forces take significant Japanese positions on high ground overlooking Holtz Bay.

MAY 19

▶ *Chinese Red Cross nurses attend to wounded Nationalist soldiers during the Japanese offensive in Hunan Province in mid-May 1943.*

MAY 19

LAND WAR, *ALEUTIAN ISLANDS*
US troops on Attu clear the Sarana Pass on the approaches to Chichagof harbour, where much of the remainder of Attu's Japanese garrison is confined.

MAY 21–24

LAND WAR, *ALEUTIAN ISLANDS*
Attu Village, a key Japanese defensive position, is completely wiped out by a massive US assault supported by ground-attack P-38 Lightning fighter-bombers. Lightnings are playing a key role in the US campaign on Attu, despite the appalling Arctic weather. As well as supporting ground units, they are intercepting and shooting down Japanese bombers in the air. On the 24th, Chichagof Valley is cleared of Japanese troops, often by recourse to hand-to-hand fighting.

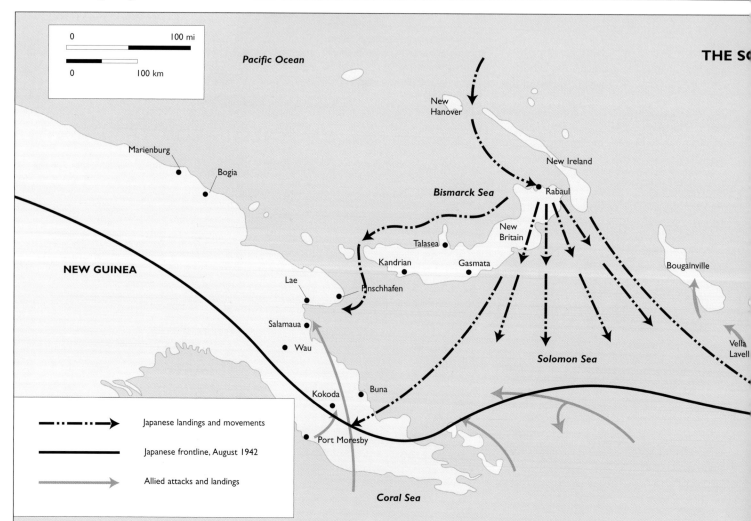

 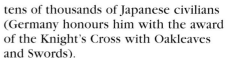
tens of thousands of Japanese civilians (Germany honours him with the award of the Knight's Cross with Oakleaves and Swords).

JUNE 7

AIR WAR, *RUSSELL ISLANDS*
In a major air action around the Russell Islands, South Pacific, US fighter aircraft shoot down 19 Japanese fighters out of a total of 40 attackers.

JUNE 7–16

AIR WAR, *SOLOMON ISLANDS*
Japanese air sorties over the Solomon Islands become increasingly costly in terms of aircraft and pilots. On 7 June, a Japanese air attack against Guadalcanal results in 23 Japanese aircraft lost for only 9 US aircraft destroyed. On June 12, the US kill-to-loss ratio widens, downing 31 Japanese bombers while losing just 6

▼ *A US mortar team in action on Arundel Island, west of New Georgia, in the Solomon Islands.*

MAY 29–30

LAND WAR, *ALEUTIAN ISLANDS*
Japanese troops on Attu launch a final suicidal charge around Chichagof in an attempt to drive US forces from the island. The attack makes some progress, overrunning two US command posts,

▼ *Operation Cartwheel was designed to destroy Japanese power in New Guinea and the Solomon Islands.*

▲ *US B-25 Mitchell bombers drop para-fragmentation bombs on a Japanese airstrip in New Georgia.*

but US firepower proves decisive and Japanese survivors are forced to retreat, whereupon many commit suicide. The Attu campaign costs the Japanese 2351 lives – only 28 soldiers surrender. US losses are also heavy: 561 dead and 1136 wounded.

MAY 31

AIR WAR, *CHINA*
US and Chinese aviators shoot down 20 Japanese fighters in a short aerial combat over Ichang, Hunan Province.

JUNE 5

HOME FRONT, *JAPAN*
Admiral Yamamoto receives a full state funeral in Tokyo. He is mourned by

▼ *An unidentified American seaplane overflies troops landing on Rendova Island in the Solomons in June 1943.*

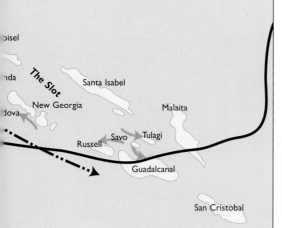

ONS AND NEW GUINEA

JUNE 8

fighters. On June 16, the slaughter reaches unsustainable levels when 107 out of 120 Japanese aircraft attacking Guadalcanal are destroyed.

JUNE 8

POLITICS, *JAPAN*
The Japanese high command gives orders that Kiska, one of the Aleutian Is-

lands, be evacuated. A US blockade of the island, plus the fall of Attu and the strategic irrelevance of the Aleutians, leads the Japanese to abandon this northern Pacific outpost.

JUNE 14

POLITICS, *JAPAN*
The pro-Axis Bengali leader Subhas Chandra Bose is feted by Japanese officials in Tokyo. Bose was forced to flee India in 1939 because of anti-British activities, making his way to Germany by 1941 and then setting off to Japan in February 1943 (he made the journey by German then Japanese submarine).

The Axis countries hope that Bose will be able to mobilize practical Indian resistance to the British war effort.

LAND WAR, *CHINA*
Chinese forces in western Hupeh have now recaptured all territory lost to the Japanese during the recent offensive towards Chungking (the headquarters of Nationalist forces and government). In a two-week push, the Chinese lose more than 70,000 troops.

JUNE 18

POLITICS, *AUSTRALIA*
With the Japanese defence having collapsed in Guadalcanal and Papua, the Australian prime minister, John Curtin, declares that there is no longer the risk of a Japanese invasion of the Australian mainland.

POLITICS, *ALLIES*
The supreme commander of the South West Pacific and C-in-C India, Sir Archibald Wavell, is replaced by Sir Claude Auchinleck following British Prime Minister Churchill's dissatisfaction with progress in the Burma theatre.

▼ *A US mortar team on Rendova fires at Japanese positions on the island. The men are crouching down to avoid the muzzle blast.*

JUNE 20

LAND WAR, *NEW GUINEA*
The US Sixth Army establishes a head-quarters at Milne Bay.

JUNE 21

LAND WAR, *NEW GEORGIA*
The US begins its offensive to retake New Georgia – Operation Toenails. An

▲ *Craft of the 9th Defense Battalion, US Marine Corps, are shelled by Japanese artillery off the island of New Georgia in July 1943.*

air and naval bombardment pounds Japanese positions, while the waters around New Georgia are mined to prevent Japanese reinforcements. Meanwhile, soldiers of the 4th Marine Raider Battalion take Segi Point at the southern tip of New Georgia and begin an advance towards Viru harbour.

JUNE 23

LAND WAR, *SOUTH PACIFIC*
US forces make an unopposed landing on the Troubriand Islands to the southeast of New Guinea.

JUNE 24

POLITICS, *JAPAN*
Subhas Chandra Bose, leader of the Indian National Army, makes a radio broadcast to India, imploring Indian soldiers and civilians to turn against the British.

JUNE 29

SEA WAR, *SOLOMON ISLANDS*
US warships shell Bougainville and Kolombangara in the Solomon Islands.

JUNE 30

LAND WAR, *NEW GEORGIA*
The US 43rd Division has taken the island of Rendova, within artillery range of the New Georgian mainland and the important airfield at Munda. The occupation of Munda is vital to enabling the next

▲ *An Australian infantry officer from the 3rd Division directs fire from a US light tank against Japanese positions at Mumbo in New Guinea.*

"hop" up the Solomon Islands towards Bougainville. Other US landings are made at Wickham, Viru and Segi Point.

JUNE 29/30

LAND WAR, *NEW GUINEA*
A battalion of the US 32nd Division is landed 32km (20 miles) south of Japanese positions at Salamaua. Forces of the Australian 3rd Division are making an overland advance towards Salamaua from Wau, but it will be more than a month before the Japanese are ejected from the town.

JULY 1–7

LAND WAR, *SOLOMON ISLANDS*
The harbour at Viru falls to the US Marines on July 1. The US 43rd Division

JULY 5-6

▶ *Roosevelt (third from left) and Churchill (third from right) with their advisers behind them at the Quebec Conference in August. They decided to bypass the main Japanese base at Rabaul.*

and elements of the 37th Division are landed at Zanana, about 8km (5 miles) east of Munda, on July 2, while US infantry and Marines make a further landing north of Munda at Rice Inlet on July 5. The next few days are an appalling baptism of fire for the inexperienced US troops, who face brutal and jungle-wise Japanese opposition commanded by Major-General Noboru Sasaki – the rate of psychological evacuations rockets. By July 7, the advance on Munda has stalled.

JULY 5-6

SEA WAR, *SOLOMON ISLANDS*

The Battle of Kula Gulf erupts when US warships, acting on ULTRA intelligence, intercept a convoy of Japanese destroyers and transports heading for New Georgia. Despite sinking one Japanese destroyer, the US warships do not stop the convoy and lose one of their own cruisers. The convoy adds a further 850

▼ *General Sir Claude Auchinleck, C-in-C India (centre, in peaked cap), argued that land operations in Burma should be suspended in favour of aiding the Chinese.*

troops to the 10,000-plus already defending the Munda area.

JULY 7-13

LAND WAR, *NEW GUINEA*

Australian troops take the Japanese stronghold at Mumbo on the inland approaches to Salamaua. The action is part of a general Allied campaign pushing the Japanese into the northeastern corner of New Guinea.

JULY 12-13

SEA WAR, *SOLOMON ISLANDS*

A Japanese "Tokyo Express" supply convoy fights a night-time naval en-

gagement with US Task Force 18 off Kolombangara Island. The Japanese once again use their skill in night combat, along with new technologies for detecting US radar signals, and succeed in sinking one Allied destroyer and damaging three cruisers. US warships manage to sink one Japanese vessel – the cruiser *Jintsu*, flagship of Rear-Admiral Tanaka, commander of the Japanese Transport Group. Over the

◀ *When the island of Munda was taken by US forces, the airfield was repaired for use by Allied aircraft, such as this Douglas C-47.*

last week, the Tokyo Express has managed to reinforce the New Guinea garrison with an additional 2000 men.

JULY 15

AIR WAR, *NEW GEORGIA*
Forty-five Japanese aircraft are shot down over Rendova. Such is the superiority of US pilots that only three US aircraft are lost.

JULY 17

AIR WAR, *SOLOMON ISLANDS*
More than 200 Allied aircraft, including Boeing B-17 Flying Fortress four-engined bombers, make a 12-hour attack on Japanese shipping and military positions in and around Bougainville. The action is a major success. Forty-nine Japanese aircraft are shot down, and many others destroyed at the devastated airfield at Kahili. Dauntless dive-bombers and Avenger torpedo-bombers sink seven ships in Buin-Faisi harbour,

▶ *John F. Kennedy, the future president of the United States, seen in his PT boat during World War II in the Pacific.*

including a light cruiser and a destroyer, losing only six aircraft.

JULY 22–30

SEA/AIR WAR, *ALEUTIAN ISLANDS*
US forces continue to pound Japanese positions on Kiska from the sea and air. The US is not aware that Japan is in the process of abandoning Kiska, and it maintains a daily bombardment of the

island, with US aircraft flying constant bombing runs from nearby Adak. The 5200-man Japanese garrison on Kiska is evacuated under cover of fog on July 28; such is the skill of the evacuation that the US is still pounding the island two days later.

JULY 25–31

LAND WAR, *NEW GEORGIA*
US forces begin a new drive to take Munda. Despite the backing of huge firepower, the attack once again stalls after bloody assaults on key features such as Horseshoe Hill, which the US soldiers take, then lose, on July 31. On July 29, the commander of the US 43rd Division, Major-General John Hester, is replaced by the Guadalcanal veteran Major-General John Hodge.

AUGUST 1

SEA WAR, *SOLOMON ISLANDS*
The Japanese destroyer *Amagiri* rams a US Navy fast patrol boat, number *PT-109*. All the crew members are reported missing, including its commander, the future president of the US, John F. Kennedy.
POLITICS, *BURMA*
In an attempt to advance the development of the their Greater East Asia

AUGUST 1–2

Co-Prosperity Sphere, Japan announces that Burma is to be an independent nation led by the nationalist leader Dr Ba Maw. Ba Maw's administration immediately declares war on the Allies.

AUGUST 1–2

POLITICS, *CHINA*

The president of the Chinese National Government, Lin Sen, passes away and is replaced by acting president Chiang Kai-shek.

AUGUST 4

SEA WAR, *SOLOMON ISLANDS*

The US Navy rescues Lieutenant John F. Kennedy and 10 other surviving crew members from *PT-109*. Two crew members die when rammed by the *Amagiri*, and the survivors spend the next three days swimming among minor islands off the Solomons attempting to attract help. Two natives with a canoe take a coconut shell, inscribed with a plea for help, to US naval forces on Rendova, who send a PT boat to rescue the crew.

AUGUST 5

LAND WAR, *SOLOMON ISLANDS*

The vital Japanese base at Munda is finally conquered by US forces of the 43rd Division. It is a major milestone in

▲ *US and Canadian flags fly over Kiska Island following its capture. The barges in the background are bringing in supplies.*

the taking of New Georgia, and US engineers set about making the airfield fit for US aircraft to use as a forward base for the Solomon Islands campaign.

AUGUST 6–7

SEA WAR, *SOLOMON ISLANDS*

A Japanese supply convoy heading for Kolombangara suffers a heavy defeat at the hands of six US destroyers in the Vela Gulf. For no US losses, three Japan-

ese destroyers are sunk and 1210 Japanese troops and sailors killed.

AUGUST 7–15

LAND WAR, *CHINA*

Fighting erupts between Communist and Nationalist Chinese forces in Shantung Province. Taking advantage, the Japanese launch an offensive against the Nationalist LI Corps and are nearly destroyed in the subsequent action.

AUGUST 13

POLITICS, *INDIA*

General Sir Claude Auchinleck, C-in-C India, proposes that there should be no more British offensive land operations in Burma. Instead, he argues, efforts should be concentrated on the air supply of Chinese forces in the north.

AUGUST 13–24

POLITICS, *ALLIES*

Allied leaders, including British Prime Minister Winston Churchill and US President Franklin Roosevelt, attend a war planning conference, codenamed "Quadrant", in Quebec, Canada. Regarding the Pacific theatre, Britain states its intention to re-deploy the Chindits in their insur-

▼ *A US reconnaissance photograph showing the aftermath of an air raid against a Japanese airfield at Lae, New Guinea.*

▲ *US troops make use of a bridge built from felled trees during their advance against Japanese forces in northern New Guinea. Judging by their cloth headgear, the frontline is some way off.*

gency role in Burma. Vice-Admiral Lord Louis Mountbatten becomes the head of the new South East Asia Command (SEAC), with Joseph Stilwell as his deputy. The geographical remit of SEAC is Burma, Malaya, Sumatra, Thailand and French Indochina. SEAC's main objectives are to draw more Japanese away from the Pacific theatre and support Chinese military efforts to the north of the zone. The decision is also made to bypass the fortified port of Rabaul, previously a key objective of Operation Cartwheel.

AUGUST 14

AIR WAR, *SOLOMON ISLANDS*
The air base at Munda, captured from the Japanese, is now in full working order. The base makes the movement of Japanese transport shipping down "the Slot" between the Solomon Islands much more precarious.

DECISIVE WEAPONS

M1 GARAND

The .30in-calibre M1 Garand rifle was the first self-loading rifle issued as a standard firearm to an army. It was actually accepted into military service in 1932, but had a long technical gestation period in which its designer, John C. Garand, refined it into a first-class combat weapon. The M1 was a gas-operated rifle fed by an internal magazine holding eight rounds, refilled by pushing an eight-round clip down through the opened bolt. If anything, the magazine system proved to be the only practical flaw of the M1; the rifle could only be loaded when empty, and the magazine could not be topped up with individual rounds. Also, the empty clip was ejected with an emphatic "ping", signalling to enemy soldiers that the infantryman had to reload. However, in other respects the M1 was a superb weapon. It was extremely rugged, and provided utterly dependable service to US soldiers in all theatres of war. Its semi-automatic action allowed units to generate the heavy firepower so essential in the jungle combat of the Pacific War, and its .30in round had decisive stopping power. The M1 was also accurate, though only in trained hands, explaining why two later sniper versions – the M1C and M1D – never saw large-scale production.

SPECIFICATIONS:

CALIBRE:	0.30in
MAGAZINE CAPACITY:	8 rounds
LENGTH:	1.107m (43.6in)
WEIGHT:	4.313kg (9.5lb)
MUZZLE VELOCITY:	855mps (2805fps)

◀ *Examples of the Garand. One of America's finest military leaders, General George S. Patton, described the M1 Garand as "the greatest battle implement ever devised".*

▲ *US Vought F4U Corsair fighter-bombers ready for take-off prior to a raid against enemy positions on Marcus Island at the beginning of September.*

AUGUST 15

LAND WAR, *ALEUTIAN ISLANDS*
After pounding the island of Kiska for weeks with air and naval bombardment, US and Canadian amphibious troops finally make a landing, but find the island deserted.

LAND WAR, *SOLOMON ISLANDS*
US forces of the 25th Division land on the island of Vella Lavella, north of Kolombangara, against little resistance. The landings bypass the heavy Japanese defences of Kolombangara, with its important airfield. It is the intention to build a new airstrip on Vella Lavella, thus rendering the southerly airfield irrelevant.

AUGUST 17

AIR WAR, *NEW GUINEA*
US aircraft launch a startling raid on the Japanese Fourth Air Army base at Wewak on the northern coast of New Guinea. The attack shocks the Japanese, who believed that US aircraft were outside the combat radius for a raid on Wewak. However, US engineers covertly constructed a forward air base 95km (60 miles) west of Lae, putting Wewak only 640km (400 miles) away from the USAAF aircraft of Lieutenant-General George C. Kenney. The attack by 200 US aircraft results in three-quarters of the Japanese air base being rendered unusable and only 38 Japanese aircraft left operational.

◄ *Destroyed Japanese aircraft on New Guinea. By mid-August, US aircraft were operating from an airfield only 95km (60 miles) west of Lae.*

AUGUST 19

LAND WAR, *NEW GUINEA*
Four Australian divisions and one US division begin a major offensive up through northern New Guinea, enjoying the decline in numbers of Japanese ground-attack aircraft following the air raids of August 17. The Japanese-fortified stronghold on Mount Tambu falls on the 19th.

AUGUST 23

AIR WAR, *CHINA*
Chungking, the home of the Chinese Nationalist Government, is bombed by the Japanese. The city has not been bombed since 1941.

▼ *Soldiers of the 14th New Zealand Brigade come ashore on Vella Lavella Island. The 35th Infantry Regiment, US 25th Division, had originally occupied the island.*

AUGUST 25

LAND WAR, *SOLOMON ISLANDS*
Operation Toenails, the US campaign to take New Georgia, now ends, with all Japanese resistance cleared from the island. The Japanese rearguard survivors are finally evacuated from northern New Georgia to the neighbouring island of Kolombangara on August 22. Reinforcements from the US 25th Division assist the battle-toughened US 43rd Division in finishing the task. The next major American operation in the Solomon Islands chain is an amphibious offensive against Bougainville and Choiseul, planned for October/November.

AUGUST 28

LAND WAR, *ELLICE ISLANDS*
US forces land at Nanomea in the Ellice Islands. The Ellice Islands campaign is the beginning of US penetration into the southeastern corner of Japanese conquests. The Gilbert Islands and the

▲ *A squad of US soldiers from the 25th Division halts during a patrol on Vella Lavella Island.*

SEPTEMBER 1

▶ *US Marines examine the wreckage of a Japanese aircraft abandoned on an airstrip on Kolombangara Island. It appears to have been stripped for spares.*

Marshall Islands are the next objectives in this sector.

SEPTEMBER 1

AIR WAR, *MARCUS ISLAND*
Japanese positions on the mid-Pacific Marcus Island receive an early morning raid by US Navy dive-bombers. US reports state that 85 percent of the island's military installations have been destroyed, including two airstrips severely damaged and seven Japanese aircraft destroyed on the ground. US losses total two fighters and one torpedo-bomber.

SEPTEMBER 4

LAND WAR, *NEW GUINEA*
The Australian 9th Division lands just north of Lae in the Huon Gulf, opening a new front in the advance up New Guinea. The next day, the US 503rd Parachute Regiment is dropped over Nadzab (the first Allied parachute deployment in the Pacific theatre), and the Australian 7th Division is airlifted into the area. While these

forces make an advance on Lae – an important coastal position for the Japanese – farther south the Australian 3rd Division and 17th Brigade strike out from Wau towards Salamaua and Nassau Bay.

▼ *Japanese infantry in New Guinea in September 1943. By this time the initiative in the southwest Pacific had passed to the Allies, specifically the sizeable US forces in the area.*

SEPTEMBER 12–16

LAND WAR, *NEW GUINEA*

The Allies take Salamaua on September 12, and Lae falls four days later. With an important port and airfield now in Allied hands, the New Guinea offensive splits into two lines of advance: one closely following the line of the coastline; the other cutting inland on a northwest bearing towards Kaiapat. The two-pronged offensive threatens to encircle the Japanese in the Huon Peninsula.

SEPTEMBER 13

AIR WAR, *PARAMUSHIRU*

A flight of B-24 Liberator and B-25 Mitchell bombers attacks enemy shipping and ground installations at Paramushiru in the north Pacific. Four enemy vessels are damaged, but ten US aircraft are lost after they are attacked by twenty-five Japanese fighters.

SEPTEMBER 13

POLITICS, *CHINA*

Chiang Kai-shek becomes chairman and president of the National Government of China. Chiang has proved to be a mercurial war leader, and shows little interest in the general Allied war against Japan except when US, British and Commonwealth efforts affect his own campaign. His relationship with General Stilwell, Allied chief-of-staff in the Burma-India-China theatre, is particularly troubled, especially as Stilwell recommends an alliance between the Nationalists and Communists to defeat Japan.

KEY PERSONALITIES

GENERAL SIR WILLIAM SLIM

General Sir William Slim (1891–1970) was an important Allied leader in the Far Eastern war. Slim had long-standing experience of soldiering in the Far East, having moved from the British Army to the Indian Army in 1919 and risen to the rank of brigadier by 1939. This experience was to stand him in good stead with his men, who appreciated both his tough yet personable character, and his ability to talk in Urdu and Gurkhali as well as English.

His first campaigns in World War II were fought in East Africa and Syria, but in March 1942 he was transferred to Burma to oversee the Allied retreat from Rangoon as commander of BurCorps (Slim was by this time ranked lieutenant-general). Burma was to be his battleground for the rest of the war. He led XV Indian Corps during its disastrous campaign into the Arakan, but offset this defeat by steering the Fourteenth Army

to victories in the Arakan and also the crucial defeat of the Japanese offensive at Imphal. In July 1945, Slim rose to the position of C-in-C Allied Land Forces Southeast Asia after the dismissal of General Sir Oliver Leese from the position.

SEPTEMBER 18–19

AIR WAR, *SOUTH PACIFIC*

The US widens its air campaign against Japanese targets in the southeast Pacific, bombing Tarawa, Makin and Apamama Islands in the northern Gilberts, and Nauru Island, west of the Gilbert group. Over 200 land- and carrier-based aircraft participate in the attack, causing severe damage to enemy installations.

SEPTEMBER 19–22

LAND WAR, *NEW GUINEA*

With Japanese forces retreating northwards across the Huon Peninsula towards Sio, the Allies maintain their advance. On the 19th, Kaiapat falls to

▼ *Japanese shipping try to evade US bombs while under aerial assault in Rabaul harbour. The aircraft involved are US B-24 Liberators and B-25 Mitchells.*

Australian forces, and on the 22nd other Australian units make an amphibious landing at positions just north of Finschhafaen, roughly 80km (50 miles) west of Lae on the easterly tip of the peninsula.

SEPTEMBER 20

LAND WAR, *SOLOMON ISLANDS*
New Zealand troops finally clear the island of Vella Lavella of all remaining Japanese opposition. Japanese troops on Vella Lavella numbered around 600, but the greatest threat to the Allies came from air attack.

SEPTEMBER 24

AIR WAR, *SOLOMON ISLANDS*
Allied air operations begin from the new airstrip on Vella Lavella, giving air

▶ A US cruiser bombards enemy positions on Wake Island. Targets on the island included ammunition dumps, fuel stores, aircraft hangers and shore batteries.

◄ *Japanese troops march through a town in the Philippines. Though accorded independent status by Tokyo, the Philippines were still under Japanese occupation.*

cover for the northerly Solomon Islands operations.

SEPTEMBER 26

LAND WAR, *NEW GUINEA*
Japanese troops launch an attack against Australian positions around Finschhafaen, but are unable to dislodge the defenders.

AIR WAR, *NEW GUINEA*
The Japanese airstrips at Wewak are struck once again by US aircraft. More than 60 Japanese aircraft are destroyed on the ground and, offshore, 6 Japanese ships are sunk.

SEPTEMBER 26–27

SEA WAR, *SINGAPORE*
Using canoes for covert night-time deployment, six Australian Special Forces soldiers led by Major Ivan Lyon penetrate Japanese shipping in Singapore harbour and place limpet mines on select vessels. Two Japanese transports are sunk, and a further five are damaged.

OCTOBER 2

LAND WAR, *NEW GUINEA*
Australian forces take Finschhafaen, consolidating Allied positions on the coastline of the Huon Peninsula.

OCTOBER 4

SEA/AIR WAR, *WAKE ISLAND*
The isolated Japanese outpost of Wake Island comes under a heavy naval and aerial bombardment from the large US Navy Task Force 14, commanded by Rear-Admiral Alfred E. Montgomery. B-24 Liberator bombers drop more

▼ *Tightening the stranglehold on Japan. A Japanese merchant ship sinks stern first after being torpedoed by a US submarine.*

than 325 tonnes (320 tons) of bombs. Some 61 Japanese aircraft are destroyed, comprising 30 on the ground and 31 in aerial combat. US forces lose 13 aircraft.

OCTOBER 4

LAND WAR, *NEW GUINEA*
The Australian 7th Division and 21st Brigade advancing northwest up the Huon Peninsula reach Dumpu, only 48km (30 miles) from the northern coast. Japanese forces are now confined along the northern coastline of the peninsula.

OCTOBER 4–6

LAND WAR, *SOLOMON ISLANDS*
The final elements of the Japanese garrison on New Georgia are evacuated

▲ *New Zealand troops unload supplies from Landing Craft Personnel (LCP) amphibious vehicles on Treasury Island following its capture in October.*

from Kolombangara. Japanese forces now have no air base in the central Solomon Islands, and US air superiority is demonstrated by the destruction of 27 Japanese aircraft during the final air battles. The fighting for the Vila airfield region has cost the US nearly 5000 casualties, including 1094 dead. Japanese casualties include 2500 fatalities.

OCTOBER 6

POLITICS, *BURMA*
The Allied Eastern Command receives a new C-in-C, General Sir William Slim,

OCTOBER 12

who also takes command of the newly formed Fourteenth Army.

OCTOBER 12

AIR WAR, *RABAUL*

The crucial Japanese air and naval base at Rabaul is hit by a massive air strike of 349 US bombers. In total, the Allies were to drop 20,913 tonnes (20,584 tons) of bombs on the heavily fortified port.

OCTOBER 15

LAND WAR, *SOLOMON ISLANDS*

Orders are given for "Operation Good-

▲ *US troops land on Bougainville. The absence of enemy shells and small-arms fire suggests that they are reinforcements, landed after the main assault forces.*

time", the next "hop" up through the Solomon Islands. Marines of US Task Force 311 will land on Bougainville at the beginning of November. Possession of the island is a crucial step towards the Allied dominance of the Japanese base at Rabaul.

OCTOBER 18

AIR WAR, *SOLOMON ISLANDS*

The Allies continue preparatory bombardments of Japanese positions around

Bougainville. Today, the Japanese air base at Buin is severely damaged.

OCTOBER 19

SEA WAR, *PACIFIC*

A US Navy communiqué reveals that, since December 7, 1941, US submarines

▼ *The objective of the Allied Solomons campaign was to isolate Rabaul, which made the capture of air bases imperative. This is a US air base in the Russell Islands.*

◀ *US Marines of the 3rd Marine Division clamber down the side of a transport ship into landing craft off Bougainville. The invasion forces consisted of 14,321 troops.*

have sunk or damaged more than 400 Japanese vessels (319 confirmed sinkings). The tally would have been higher had it not have been for defective torpedoes, which often did not explode on hitting a vessel.

OCTOBER 21

POLITICS, *PHILIPPINES*

The Philippines are given independent status by the Japanese Government, although the independence has little real value as the islands remain under Japanese jurisdiction.

OCTOBER 22

AIR WAR, *RABAUL*

The Japanese lose 123 aircraft during another massive US air raid on air facilities around Rabaul.

OCTOBER 25

BURMA, *POWS*

At a cost of 12,000 Allied POWs and 90,000 other slave labourers, the Burma–Thailand rail link is completed. Despite the massive construction project, the railway delivers much less capacity than originally intended.

OCTOBER 27

LAND WAR, *SOLOMON ISLANDS*

"Operation Blissful" is launched, the US 2nd Marine Para Battalion being landed on Choiseul Island, as a diversion away from the main invasion of Bougainville planned for November 1 and codenamed "Cherryblossom". Also today, New Zealand troops capture Treasury Island, just off Bougainville's southern coast. Treasury Island is subsequently used as a build-up point for the Bougainville invasion forces.

POLITICS, *JAPAN*

Emperor Hirohito acknowledges that the war in the Pacific is entering a crucial phase, with the Allies poised to reclaim much of the south Pacific from the Japanese. As early as 1942, Hirohito attempted to persuade the Japanese Government to negotiate a settlement with the Allies, correctly believing that Japan could not sustain a long-term campaign against the US.

NOVEMBER 1

LAND WAR, *SOLOMON ISLANDS*

The US offensive against Bougainville begins with the landing of the 3rd Marine Division, part of I Marine

▼ *A North American B-25 Mitchell bomber swoops low over the harbour at Rabaul during a heavy US air raid.*

NOVEMBER 2

Amphibious Corps, under Lieutenant-General A.A. Vandegrift, at Cape Torokina on the western coastline of the island. The landings go reasonably smoothly, but most of Bougainville's 60,000-strong Japanese garrison is concentrated in the south of the island.

NOVEMBER 2

SEA WAR, *SOLOMON ISLANDS*
A US task force of four light cruisers and eight destroyers battles with four Japanese cruisers and six destroyers around Empress Augusta Bay off Bougainville. The Japanese ships are intending to destroy landing craft and supply vessels supporting the Bougainville landings. The US task force, commanded by Rear-Admiral A.S. Merrill, suffers five ships

▼ *A US cruiser shells Makin Island. The naval bombardment raised a large pall of smoke and dust that obscured the island completely from the assault craft.*

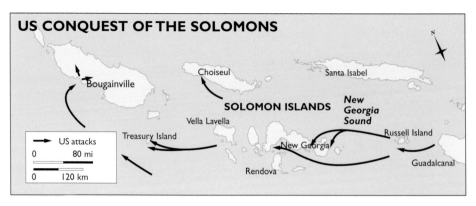

US CONQUEST OF THE SOLOMONS

▲ *During the Solomons campaign US forces displayed a mastery of amphibious warfare techniques.*

badly damaged, but sinks one Japanese light cruiser and a destroyer, and damages two heavy cruisers and two destroyers. The Japanese commander breaks off the attack.

NOVEMBER 5–11

AIR WAR, *RABAUL*
US aircraft from Rear-Admiral Frederick C. Sherman's Task Forces 38 subject Rabaul to six days of intense bombardment. The

US attacks are concentrated against shipping in the attempt to limit naval support available to the Japanese defence of the Solomon Islands. Aircraft from carriers including the USS *Saratoga*, USS *Bunker Hill*, USS *Essex*, USS *Independence* and USS *Princeton* sink two Japanese warships, severely damage 11 other vessels and destroy 55 Japanese aircraft.

NOVEMBER 13

LAND WAR, *SOLOMON ISLANDS*
US troops levels on Bougainville now reach 34,000 men, but the pace of advance through the island's jungle swamps is painfully slow. A priority is

◀ *A flamethrower Sherman tank on Okinawa, April 1945. The US Marines had eight Sherman flame tanks on Okinawa, which were ideal against caves and fortifications.*

▲ *LVTs of the 2nd Marine Division make their way towards Tarawa. The LVTs were used to traverse the reef and Japanese man-made obstacles.*

to establish an airstrip at Torokina to provide the advance with air cover.

NOVEMBER 13–20

AIR/SEA WAR, *GILBERT ISLANDS*
US forces begin the preparatory bombardments of Makin and Tarawa in the Gilbert Islands. The build-up for the US offensive against the Gilbert and Marshall Islands began back in January with the assembly of troops, ships and aircraft in Hawaii, the Fijian Islands and New Hebrides. The force now arraigned against Japanese forces in the Marshall Islands is enormous, and includes eight aircraft carriers and more than 100,000 troops. The first operations, against the Gilbert Islands, are under the overall command of the Commander Central Pacific Force, Vice-Admiral R.A. Spruance.

NOVEMBER 20–23

LAND WAR, *GILBERT ISLANDS*
US troops of the 27th Infantry Division go ashore at Makin, but find the atoll poorly defended and clear it easily over the next three days.

LAND WAR, *GILBERT ISLANDS*
In striking contrast to the operations on Makin, US Marines of the 2nd Marine Di-

DECISIVE WEAPONS

FLAMETHROWERS

Flamethrowers were among the prolific support weapons used by both Japanese and US soldiers during the Pacific war. They were ideal for flushing out enemy troops from fortified jungle and coastal bunkers, working either through burning the troops out or suffocating them as the flames used up all available oxygen around the position. The two basic Japanese flamethrowers were the Type 93 and Type 100, essentially the same weapon with only minor variations. Both types had a three-cylinder configuration (two cylinders for the fuel, one for the compressed-gas propellant), a burn duration of about 10 seconds and a range of around 30m

(99ft). US flamethrowers came in three man-portable versions – the M1, M1A1 and M2-2. All had better performance than the Japanese models, having similar burn durations but ranges of between 35m and 45m (114ft and 148ft). Even more effective were the US tank-mounted flamethrowers. These were usually fitted in place of a bow machine gun or, in light tanks, in place of the main armament. These systems could throw flame 70m (230ft) in a concentrated arc. Tactics included spraying unburned fuel on to a bunker before igniting it all in one explosive fireball and, on Okinawa, pumping the fuel down into caves through a series of pipes before igniting and incinerating the occupants.

vision attacking the atoll of Tarawa face appalling levels of resistance. Although the atoll is cleared by the 23rd, nearly 4500 Japanese are killed and the US Marines lose 1000 dead and 2000 wounded out of a total force of 18,600. Offshore, the US Navy suffers comparable heavy attacks. The light carrier USS *Independence* is damaged by torpedoes, while five other vessels are hit, including the destroyer USS *Frazier* which is rammed by the Japanese submarine *I-35*.

NOVEMBER 22–26

POLITICS, *ALLIES*
Allied war leaders, including the Chinese Nationalist leader Chiang Kai-shek, meet in Cairo, Egypt, to discuss post-war plans for the Far East. Known as the "Sextant Conference", it lasts until the 26th, after which British Prime Minister Churchill and US President Roosevelt fly on to meet with the Soviet leader Joseph Stalin in Tehran, Iran, to discuss overall Allied war strategy.

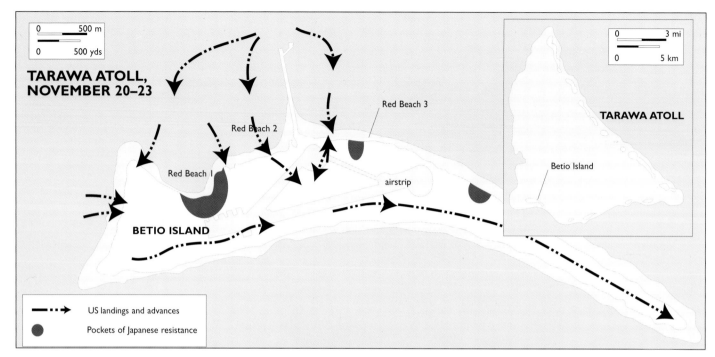

TARAWA ATOLL, NOVEMBER 20–23

Red Beach 3

Red Beach 2

Red Beach 1

airstrip

BETIO ISLAND

TARAWA ATOLL

Betio Island

- - - ▶ US landings and advances

● Pockets of Japanese resistance

▲ *The Americans flew over 1000 sorties against Betio on November 18–19 to soften up the island's defences and to inflict fatalities on the 4500 defenders.*

NOVEMBER 24

SEA WAR, *GILBERT ISLANDS*
The US escort carrier USS *Liscombe Bay* is torpedoed and sunk off Makin Atoll in the Gilbert Islands, with 644 men killed.

NOVEMBER 24–29

INDUSTRY, *USA*
Two new modern aircraft carriers are commissioned in the US, the USS *Wasp* and the USS *Hornet*, both named after US vessels sunk at earlier actions in the war. In 1943 alone, the US commissioned nine new aircraft carriers; the Japanese, suffering from severe industrial shortages, commissioned only two, these being conversions from existing vessels.

NOVEMBER 25

SEA WAR, *CAPE ST GEORGE*
Five US destroyers intercept five Japanese destroyers near Cape St George, off the coast of New Ireland, as the Japanese ships make their way

▼ *Troops of the 2nd Battalion, 155th Infantry Regiment, wade ashore on Yellow Beach Two on Makin Atoll. The assault barge on the right is grounded on the reef.*

▲ *A dead Japanese soldier on Tarawa. Only 17 Japanese and 129 Korean labourers surrendered at Tarawa. The rest of the garrison and construction workers died.*

back from the supply drop at Buka, near Bougainville. The Japanese destroyers *Onami*, *Makinami* and *Yugiri* are sunk, and another destroyer is damaged in the resulting naval action. US forces suffer no sunk or damaged vessels.

DECEMBER 1
POLITICS, ALLIES
After three days of negotiations, the conference of Allied leaders in Tehran finally comes to a close. Most of the

discussions have focused on the Allied invasion of occupied France, with Stalin pushing hard for the opening of a second front to relieve some of the pressure on the Soviet Union.

DECEMBER 1–8
LAND WAR, *NEW GUINEA*
Australian troops continue to make a good overland advance across New Guinea, capturing Huanko on the 1st and Wareo on the 8th, before pushing on towards Wandokai.

▲ *Smashed vehicles and US Marine dead on Tarawa. Some 5000 Marines had stormed the landing beaches of Betio on November 20 – 1500 were dead, wounded or missing by nightfall.*

DECEMBER 1–31
LAND WAR, *BURMA*
Britain's XV Corps builds up forces in northern Burma ready for a renewed offensive down towards Akyab. It is faced by the Japanese Fifteenth Army, which is preparing for an offensive into eastern India.

KEY MOMENTS

THE TARAWA EXPERIENCE

The US operation against Tarawa in the Gilbert Islands in November 1943 was among the bloodiest actions of the entire Pacific war. Tarawa Atoll was a little over 16km (10 miles) long, but the bulk of Japanese defences were concentrated on the islet of Betio, around 3.2km (2 miles) long and 0.8km (0.5 miles) wide. The 4500 Japanese troops on Betio, commanded by Rear-Admiral Shibasaki, had created dense networks of fortified bunkers, trenches and pillboxes, in which they sat out the US Navy's preliminary bombardment of 3048 tonnes (3000 tons) of shells in only two-and-a-half hours (bunkers constructed of sand-packed palm-tree logs proved especially durable).

The first troops of the US 2nd Marine Division went ashore at Betio on November 20, straight into a hail of bullets and shells. Beach reconnaissance had been inaccurate, and many of the "Amtrac" amphibious vehicles grounded on a shallow reef, leaving the occupants to wade ashore under blistering small-arms and artillery fire. On the beach itself, the soft sand made it difficult for the US soldiers to dig in. Radio communications between US units broke down, resulting in 1500 US Marine casualties by the end of the day. However, a beachhead was established through sheer US firepower, and over the next two days the Marines fought their way across Tarawa, the entrenched defenders contesting every metre of ground to the death. A final suicidal charge by the Japanese on the 22nd signified that resistance was finally crumbling,

▲ *A US Marine throws a grenade at a Japanese pillbox from a sandbagged position on Tarawa on November 20.*

and on the 23rd the fighting finally stopped. The fanatical defence of Tarawa shocked US leaders. For this tiny scrap of land, the Japanese had sacrificed nearly 4500 men – only 17 Japanese soldiers surrendered, along with 129 Korean labourers.

DECEMBER 4

▶ *A US Consolidated B-24 Liberator lies smashed on the ground following a Japanese air raid against Allied airfields in Hunan Province, China.*

DECEMBER 4

SEA WAR, *MARSHALL ISLANDS*

Kwajalein and Wotje Atolls in the Marshall Islands are bombed by US aircraft from six carriers, destroying seventy-two Japanese aircraft on the ground and sinking six Japanese transport vessels. In a return attack by the Japanese, the carrier USS *Lexington* is damaged by an aircraft torpedo.

DECEMBER 5–8

AIR WAR, *INDIA*

Using forward air bases in Burma, the Japanese increase the level of air raids on the Indian mainland, attacking Allied air bases and coastal positions. On the 5th, Calcutta port is bombed with 350 people killed, and on the 8th the airfield at Tinsukia is attacked by nearly 70 Japanese warplanes.

DECEMBER 9

AIR WAR, *BOUGAINVILLE*

US engineers on Bougainville bring the airstrip at Torokina, on the island's central-west coast, up to full operational capacity (though it is still shelled by enemy artillery). The air base is used to provide air cover for Allied troops advancing across Bougainville, but is also only 241km (150 miles) from Rabaul, New Britain, well within the operational radius of even fighter aircraft.

▼ *The "Big Three" in December at the Tehran Conference (seated, from left to right): Joseph Stalin, Franklin D. Roosevelt and Winston Churchill.*

LAND WAR, *CHINA*

With Japanese forces increasingly over-stretched in the Pacific theatre, Chinese Nationalist forces make significant gains within their own country. In a major urban battle which costs the Nationalists more troops than the Japanese, Chinese troops reclaim the important city of Changteh, previously held on two occasions by the enemy.

▲ *The US airstrip at Torokina, Bougainville, which achieved operational status in early December and provided air cover for US forces on the island.*

DECEMBER 11

POLITICS, *INDIA*

Air Chief Marshal Sir Richard Edmund Charles Peirse (1892–1970) becomes overall commander of Allied air units, including USAAF forces, within South East Asia Command (SEAC). The air units will now be operating under a new entity, the Eastern Air Command.

AIR WAR, *CHINA*

Forty USAAF and Chinese aircraft are destroyed in a surprise night attack against Allied airfields in Hunan Province, China. The Japanese are hoping to sever the highly efficient air supply services relied on by Chinese Nationalist troops assaulting the city of Kung-an.

DECEMBER 15

LAND WAR, *NEW BRITAIN*

US Army troops of the 112th Cavalry Division are landed on Arawa Peninsula in southern New Britain. The landings are intended as a diversion from the forthcoming main landings on New Britain at Cape Gloucester on the other side of the island. The army soldiers subsequently occupy the airfield at Arawa, and then dig in to face heavy Japanese attacks over the next few weeks. Though determined, the attacks are all repulsed.

KEY PERSONALITIES

GENERAL JOSEPH STILWELL

General Joseph Stilwell (1883–1946) – known to many as "Vinegar Joe" because of his aggressive and difficult personality – rose to command all US and Chinese forces in the China-Burma-India theatre. As a young man he graduated from West Point in 1904, before serving in the Philippines and as an intelligence officer (with the rank of colonel) in France during World War I. Stilwell's suitability for the Asian post came from four military tours of China in the 1920s and 1930s, during which time he learnt to speak Chinese (he also spoke French and Spanish) and gained a genuine understanding of Chinese culture. General George Marshall, the US Army Chief of Staff, noted Stilwell's qualities and gave him command of the 7th Infantry Division in 1940, then III Corps. In 1942, Stilwell returned to China as a lieutenant-general, and commanded two Chinese armies in Burma. He personally headed the retreat of Chinese soldiers and Burmese refugees across 225km (140 miles) of jungle from Burma to India, refusing to take the aircraft provided to him and his staff. Stilwell

subsequently became Chiang Kai-shek's Allied chief of staff, and he invested much effort into turning the Chinese Army into an effective fighting force and organizing the flow of US aid. During 1944, Stilwell's Chinese soldiers had significant success in northern Burma, retaking Myitkyina in August. Stilwell was promoted to general but, two months later, Chiang Kai-shek had him recalled to the US for political reasons.

ALLIES, *SOLOMON ISLANDS*

A US naval operating base is established in the Treasury Islands. The Solomon Islands are now effectively within US control, and US commanders are planning the final operations to encircle Rabaul.

DECEMBER 18

AIR WAR, *CHINA*

Japanese aircraft bomb targets in the southern Chinese province of Yunnan. Southern China is mainly in Nationalist hands, with the Allies using the territory to establish air bases. The Japanese

481

DECEMBER 24

▶ *A transport ship loaded with supplies for the US 1st Marine Division's landing at Cape Gloucester. The ship is part of the Seventh Amphibious Force.*

are planning a major offensive into northern India for 1944, so need to gain a stronger hold over the southern Chinese states that border Burma and India.

POLITICS, *CHINA*

US General Joseph Stilwell takes command of all Chinese troops operating in the India/northern Burma region.

DECEMBER 24

SEA WAR, *SOLOMON ISLANDS*

A US Task Force of three cruisers and four destroyers under Rear-Admiral A.S. Merrill conducts a heavy bombardment of Japanese positions in the Buka-Bunis area of northern Bougainville.

LAND WAR, *BURMA*

In northern Burma, Chinese and US forces in Joseph Stilwell's Northern Combat Area Command push forward through the Hukawng Valley as part of an offensive aimed at retaking Myitkyina. The town has a vital airfield and needs be taken to establish an Allied overland supply route between India and China.

DECEMBER 25

LAND WAR, *CHINA*

Chinese troops recapture the city of Kung-an in northern Hunan Province after weeks of costly and bitter fighting.

DECEMBER 26–29

LAND WAR, *NEW BRITAIN*

The US 1st Marine Division under Major-General W.H. Rupertus, comprising the 1st, 5th and 7th Marine Infantry Regiments and the 11th Marine

KEY PERSONALITIES

HIDEKI TOJO

Hideki Tojo (1885–1948) was the political power behind the Pacific war. The son of a Japanese Army general, he entered the military and quickly rose through the ranks. Political rather than operational appointments beckoned. Within the army he served as the chief of police affairs and chief of staff before becoming the vice minister of war then finally minister of war in 1941, the same year he became Japanese prime minister. Tojo took Japan to war in December of that year by giving the order to attack Pearl Harbor, and he advocated a strategy of total military and economic warfare on the Allies, which helped make the Pacific war the merciless fight it became. After the Japanese defeat on Saipan in July 1944, he was forced to resign; he made a failed attempt at suicide after the final Japanese surrender. In 1948,

he was condemned to death for war crimes by the International Military Tribunal in Tokyo, and hanged.

STRATEGY AND TACTICS

THE TOKYO EXPRESS

"Tokyo Express" was the Allied nickname for the Japanese supply convoys running between Rabaul in New Britain and the Solomon Islands. The Japanese ships usually travelled via the Slot, the narrow stretch of water south of Bougainville that attracted violent naval battles. In early 1943, the Japanese had naval and air superiority over the northern parts of the Solomon sea lanes, but entered more dangerous waters farther south where US carriers were within striking distance. Most of the convoys were part of Rear-Admiral Raizo Tanaka's Transport Group, and featured powerful escorts of cruisers and destroyers, which inflicted significant losses on US shipping. However, in 1943–44, the balance of power tilted towards the Allies as they steadily reclaimed territory in the Solomon Islands. Radar, ULTRA intelligence and coastwatchers – indigenous people trained to provide intelligence on Japanese shipping movements along the coastlines – meant Japanese ships could rarely move undetected (picture

shows Japanese ships under attack). Increased US air superiority and more effective US submarine patrols also meant that the levels of attrition among transport vessels became appalling. The interdiction of the Tokyo Express was an important factor in strangling Japanese resistance throughout the Solomons.

◄ *Troops of the US 1st Marine Division wade ashore at Cape Gloucester. The amphibious landing took place following a heavy bombardment and bombing by naval gunfire and aircraft.*

Artillery Regiment, is landed at Cape Gloucester in New Britain by the 7th Amphibious Force. The action opens the land campaign to take New Britain and isolate the vital Japanese naval and air facilities at Rabaul in the north. Japanese aircraft attempt to repel the invasion fleet, sinking the destroyer USS *Brownson* and damaging three other destroyers and a landing ship. On the 29th, the US troops advance out to seize Cape Gloucester airfield, which will give the Allies air control over the vital corridor between New Britain and New Guinea. Japanese efforts to retake the airfield are unsuccessful.

DECEMBER 31

LAND WAR, *BOUGAINVILLE*
The year ends with the US having established strong positions on Bougainville, despite determined Japanese opposition in the island's interior. Empress Augusta Bay is now a fully operational US Navy base with three airstrips on land.

1944

This was the year when the Allies won substantial victories against the Japanese. The Imperial Navy was effectively destroyed at the Philippine Sea and Leyte Gulf, while US forces landed on the Gilbert and Marshall Islands and the Philippines during their march across the central Pacific. The Japanese were also defeated in Burma, and from airfields in the Philippines B-29s began to bomb Japan itself.

▼ *The final moments of a Japanese cargo ship, as seen through the periscope of the US submarine that torpedoed her.*

JANUARY 1

AIR WAR, *NEW IRELAND*
US aircraft from Rear-Admiral F.C. Sherman's carrier task force bomb a Japanese convoy of transports, destroying several cruisers off Kavieng in New Ireland.

JANUARY 2

LAND WAR, *NEW GUINEA*
Troops of the 126th Regiment, US 32nd Division, launch "Operation Dexterity", a large-scale landing at Saidor on the northeastern coast of New Guinea. The invasion is roughly at the midway point between the Allied advances on New Guinea from the west and east, and severs Japanese rearguard forces from their main base 88km (55 miles) farther up the coastline at Madang. However, Japanese troops of the 20th and 51st Divisions escape entrapment; around 20,000 Japanese soldiers are now forced into the jungle-covered interior of the Huon Peninsula.

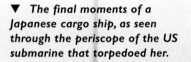

◄ *By 1944 US submarines were taking a heavy toll of Japanese shipping. These submariners display a flag that shows their vessel has sunk 13 Japanese ships.*

JANUARY 6–9

LAND WAR, *NEW BRITAIN*

US troops at Cape Gloucester on the northern edge of southern New Britain begin an advance to the Aogiri River, taking the Aogiri ridge after three days of heavy fighting.

JANUARY 9

LAND WAR, *BURMA*

The British Fourteenth Army, part of XV Corps, takes the port of Maungdaw on the Bay of Bengal, having advanced 32km (20 miles) from around Bawli Bazar near the Indian border. The offensive is part of a renewed Allied attempt to take Akyab, and Maungdaw is an important supply port for the Japanese. Despite the success, the Allied troops have

▼ *A group of US Marine Raiders pose in front of a Japanese dugout they have just knocked out on Cape Totkina, Bougainville, January 1944.*

an exposed left flank, against which huge Japanese forces are massing.

JANUARY 11

SEA WAR, *SOLOMON ISLANDS*

The Japanese cruiser *Kuma* is sunk by the British submarine HMS *Tally Ho*. By 1944, Allied submarines are tightening the stranglehold on Japanese shipping travelling to and from the mainland. On January 8 alone, a US Navy communiqué states that US submarines have sunk 10 Japanese vessels, including an oil tanker.

▲ *A US bomber peels away after dropping its ordnance on the Mu River Bridge, Burma. One bomb has fallen wide, but a second bomb is in midair over the bridge.*

AIR WAR, *MARSHALL ISLANDS*

US B-24 Liberator aircraft make a low-level attack on Japanese shipping around Kwajalein Atoll, sinking two vessels and damaging four others. The raid is just one of the many taking

JANUARY 13–22

▶ *US Marines on Namur Island, February 2. Note how artillery and small-arms fire has stripped the trees of their foliage.*

place around the Marshall Islands during January as the US prepares for a land offensive there.

JANUARY 13–22

LAND WAR, *BURMA*
Stilwell's Chinese troops maintain a solid advance. By January 30, the Chinese 22nd Division has taken Taro, 160km (100 miles) to the northwest of Myitkyina.

JANUARY 15

LAND WAR, *NEW GUINEA*
Australian troops finally take Sio. There is now a gap of only 80km (50 miles) between Australian troops at Sio and US forces at Saidor, and the Japanese

defence of the Huon Peninsula is in complete disarray.

JANUARY 16

LAND WAR, *NEW GUINEA*
Australian forces take over the Finis-terre range in the north of the Huon Peninsula.

JANUARY 16–17

LAND WAR, *NEW BRITAIN*
Japan launches a series of counter-attacks against US forces in southern New Britain but, by the 17th, the Allies have consolidated Arawe and are securing their hold on the southern parts of the island.

JANUARY 22–26

LAND WAR, *NEW GUINEA*
Australian troops of the 18th Brigade capture the Kankiryo Saddle, an important Japanese position crossing the western tip of the mountainous Finis-terre range. The capture of the position puts the Australians only 32km (20 miles) from the coast.

LAND WAR, *MARSHALL ISLANDS*
"Operation Flintlock", the US invasion of the Marshall Islands, starts to roll as the invasion forces set sail.

JANUARY 24

AIR WAR, *RABAUL*
A 200-aircraft raid launched from US carrier groups destroys 83 Japanese aeroplanes. Japan is suffering unsustainable aviation losses in the Pacific, both of aircraft and pilots, and the US is coming to rely more and more on achieving theatre air supremacy.

JANUARY 29

AIR WAR, *MARSHALL ISLANDS*
US carrier aircraft begin a systematic one-week campaign against Japanese airpower and shipping around the Marshall Islands.

◀ *A US patrol on New Britain. The lead soldier carries a Thompson submachine gun equipped with a 50-round drum magazine.*

JANUARY 31

LAND WAR, *MARSHALL ISLANDS*
Operation Flintlock begins with landings on Majuro Atoll and Kwajalein Atoll by US Army and Marine Corps troops. The attack is supported by large numbers of US land-based and carrier-based aircraft. The Majuro landing proceeds smoothly, putting the troops ashore on an undefended island. By contrast, Japanese forces on Kwajalein Atoll resist ferociously, and US casualties are heavy.

▲ *A B-25 Mitchell medium bomber of the Seventh US Army Air Force strikes Japanese targets on Wotje Island.*

FEBRUARY 1–7

LAND WAR, *MARSHALL ISLANDS*
The US expands its invasion of the Marshall Islands by landing Marines on Roi and Namur Islands. The two islands take two days to occupy and cost US forces 737 casualties. On Kwajalein Atoll, the battle results in 372 US casualties but, by the 7th, the island is declared secure. The Japanese lose 11,612 soldiers during the 8-day battle in the Marshall Islands.

FEBRUARY 4

LAND WAR, BURMA
The Japanese 55th Division, commanded by Lieutenant-General Hanaya Tadashi, counterattacks the advancing forces of Lieutenant-General Christison's British XV Corps in Operation Ha-Go. British and Commonwealth troops have a tremendously exposed left flank and an extremely vulnerable supply and administrative centre near Sinzweya, about 10km (6 miles) from the Burmese coastline, subsequently known as "Admin Box" because of its 1000m (3280ft) square layout.

FEBRUARY 5

LAND WAR, NORTHERN BURMA
General Wingate's Long Range Penetration (LRP) unit – the Chindits – crosses the Indian border into northern Burma. The 3000-strong unit, reformed and retrained after its earlier disastrous mission, is now under General

◀ *A Douglas Dauntless dive-bomber waits to take off during the air bombardment phase of Operation Flintlock.*

▲ *Two members of the 1st Punjab Regiment, 7th Indian Division, in northern Burma in early February.*

Stilwell's strategic command, though Wingate remains its immediate leader. The Chindits' mission is to support Stilwell's drive towards Myitkyina on the right flank, drawing Japanese troops away from advancing Chinese forces and cutting supply and communication links.

FEBRUARY 10

LAND WAR, *MARSHALL ISLANDS*
US forces begin mopping up remaining resistance throughout the Marshall Islands. On this day, US Marines are landed on Arno Atoll.

FEBRUARY 12

LAND WAR, *BURMA*
The 17th Indian Division at Sinzweya is cut off from Allied forces by a Japanese encirclement operation. There then be-

▼ *Military supplies are offloaded on Eniwetok Atoll following the US invasion on February 17.*

gins one of the greatest Allied defensive operations of the Far Eastern war. Troops inside the Box come to rely entirely on air supply, which provides them with sufficient ammunition and food to beat off numerous and increasingly desperate attacks.

LAND WAR, *NEW GUINEA*
The Australian 8th Brigade and 5th Division meet up with US troops at Saidor, having advanced around 80km (50 miles) from Sio. Now only 96km (60 miles) of the northern coastline of the Huon Peninsula remains in Japanese hands.

FEBRUARY 15

SEA WAR, *SOLOMON ISLANDS*
Ships of the US Third Amphibious Force land the 3rd New Zealand Division on Green Island, a small outcrop of land roughly halfway between Bougainville and New Ireland.

FEBRUARY 16

SEA WAR, *CENTRAL PACIFIC*
The Japanese light cruiser *Agano* is sunk by the US submarine USS *Skate*.

FEBRUARY 17

AIR WAR, *CAROLINE ISLANDS*
The US takes the war to the Caroline

▲ *Chindits, Burmese farmers and US air personnel at a Chindit base in Burma. The aircraft in the background is a C-47.*

Islands, which offer vital air and naval facilities in the central Pacific area between New Guinea and the Mariana Islands. Today, US Naval Task Force 58, which includes nine carriers and six battleships, makes a major attack on

Truk Atoll, a harbour for the Japanese Combined Fleet. US carrier aircraft sink two cruisers and three destroyers, and for the first time make a radar-guided night operation. More than 260 Japanese aircraft are also destroyed in the raid.

FEBRUARY 17–22

LAND WAR, *MARSHALL ISLANDS*
US Marines and US Army infantry are landed on Eniwetok Atoll, in the far northwest of the Marshall Islands. The first landings by units of the 22nd Marine Battalion proceed smoothly at Engebi, but subsequent landings by more Marines and troops from the 106th Regiment meet heavy resistance from 2000

Japanese defenders, all of whom are killed in the subsequent action.

FEBRUARY 19

AIR WAR, *RABAUL*
Allied air superiority over Rabaul forces the Japanese to give up aviation defence of the important base. From now on, it will rely on anti-aircraft guns.

FEBRUARY 23

SEA WAR, *MARIANA ISLANDS*
Having secured the Marshall Islands, US Pacific forces begin preparatory bombardments of the Mariana Islands, which include the islands of Saipan, Tinian, Rota and Guam. Aircraft from Rear-Admiral M.A. Mitscher's fast carrier task force attack all four islands. The mission to take the Marianas is known as "Operation Forager", and capture of the most northerly island, Saipan, will give the US a bomber base for strikes on the Japanese homeland.

FEBRUARY 24

LAND WAR, *BURMA*
The siege of the Admin Box is finally broken after Allied troops dislodge Japanese forces from the Ngakyedauk Pass, the overland approach route from the Burmese coast at Wabyin to Sinzweya. Elements of the Japanese Army's 55th Division are now cut off in western Burma.

▼ *Two members of the US 22nd Marine Regimental Combat Team, commanded by Colonel John T. Walker, on the beach at Eniwetok, February 22.*

FEBRUARY 21

▶ *Personnel of the 5318th Provisional Unit on the ground at Landing Zone Broadway, Burma, preparing an airstrip for Orde Wingate's Chindits.*

FEBRUARY 21

LAND WAR, *BURMA*

The US 5307th Provisional Regiment – codenamed "Galahad" but popularly known as "Merrill's Marauders" – assembles at Sharaw Ga in northern Burma to provide tactical flanking operations in support of Allied forces advancing down towards Myitkyina. The 5307th Regiment is a US equivalent of the Chindits, and has actually trained with Chindit units. Its nickname comes from the name of its commander, Brigadier-General Frank D. Merrill, although much of the practical leadership of the regiment is handled by his second-in-command, Colonel Charles Hunter.

FEBRUARY 29

LAND WAR, *ADMIRALTY ISLANDS*

The US 1st Cavalry Division invades Los Negros in the Admiralty Islands group. Though the operation was originally a reconnaissance-in-force, the landing is quickly exploited and the US piles in more forces. Capture of the Admiralty chain will provide northerly air bases for strikes against New Britain and New Ireland.

MARCH 1–4

LAND WAR, *ADMIRALTY ISLANDS*

Japanese forces on the Admiralty Islands make two major attacks to eject the US troops from Los Negros; both are beaten back, resulting in heavy Japanese casualties. On the 4th, US reinforcements are landed on Los Negros.

MARCH 3–7

SEA WAR, *ADMIRALTY ISLANDS*

A large Allied task force under Rear-Admiral V.A.C. Crutchley, British Royal Navy, pounds Japanese shore positions on Hauwei and Norilo Islands. The task force includes two US cruisers and four US destroyers.

MARCH 5–7

LAND WAR, *BURMA*

Chinese troops of the 22nd and 38th Divisions capture Maingkwan in the Hukawng Valley. On their left flank, the US troops of Merrill's Marauders cross the Tanai River and take Walabaum, only 97km (60 miles) from Myitkyina. The battle for Walabaum is ferocious, with troops of the Japanese 18th Division making suicidal bayonet charges, while US and Chinese troops often go without food for 24-hour periods. But losses among the Allied soldiers are relatively light.

MARCH 5

LAND WAR, *BURMA*

Chindit forces in northern Burma begin "Operation Thursday". The 77 and 111 LRP Brigades, about 9000 men, are deployed by glider in an area between Indaw and Myitkyina, and establish landing strips for future operational air supply. More Chindit brigades will be flown in over the next three weeks. The purpose of Operation Thursday is to harass Japanese forces to the south of Chinese and

◀ *The guns of USS Phoenix open fire on Japanese positions on Los Negros in the Admiralty Islands on February 29, 1944.*

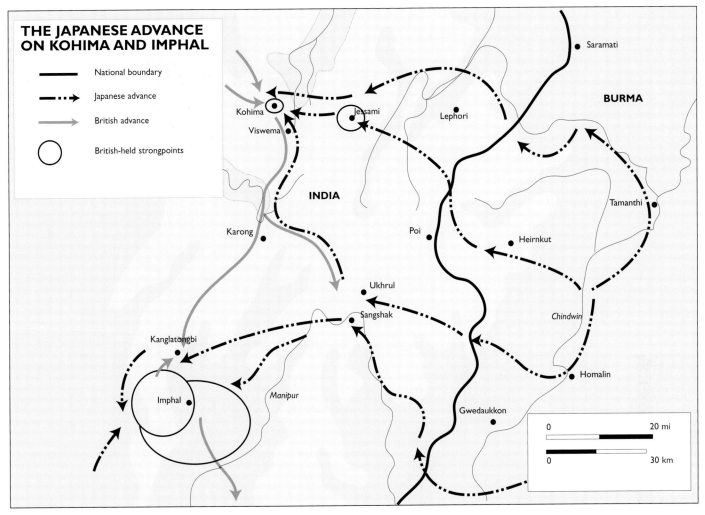

THE JAPANESE ADVANCE ON KOHIMA AND IMPHAL

— National boundary

–▶ Japanese advance

→ British advance

◯ British-held strongpoints

BURMA

INDIA

Saramati · Lephori · Tamanthi · Heirnkut · Poi · Ukhrul · Sangshak · Chindwin · Homalin · Gwedaukkon · Manipur · Imphal · Kanglatongbi · Karong · Viswema · Kohima · Jessami

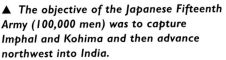

0 — 20 mi
0 — 30 km

US operations against Myitkyina, and cut the flow of Japanese supplies and communications heading north.

▼ *Newly arrived British reinforcements wait for orders at the Imphal airstrip.*

MARCH 7

LAND WAR, *BURMA/INDIA*
The Japanese Fifteenth Army, commanded by Lieutenant-General Renya Mutaguchi, begins "Operation U-Go" in central Burma. U-Go is a Japanese at-

▲ *The objective of the Japanese Fifteenth Army (100,000 men) was to capture Imphal and Kohima and then advance northwest into India.*

tempt to spoil any Allied offensive moves in central Burma by crossing into India, pushing Allied forces out of Burma in the process, cutting the Assam–Burma railway used for supplying Stilwell's Myitkyina offensive, and also occupying Imphal and Kohima and the flat territory between (an ideal launch point for an Allied offensive). The first part of the offensive involves the Japanese 33rd Division advancing out and cutting the Tiddim–Imphal Road, a major Allied supply route to Imphal, and trapping the 17th Indian Division based between Tiddim and Tongzang.

MARCH 11–12

LAND WAR, *BURMA*
While the Allies in central Burma fall back under the onslaught of Operation U-Go, in the Arakan the Allies make progress by recapturing Buthidaung and the Japanese fortress at Razabil.

MARCH 13

LAND WAR, *BURMA*
The Japanese 33rd Division reaches Witok on the approaches to the Shenan Saddle.

MARCH 13

LAND WAR, *BURMA*
Forces from the Japanese Fifteenth Army attack "Broadway", one of the main Allied landing strips in the Chindits' area of operations.

MARCH 15

LAND WAR, *ADMIRALTY ISLANDS*
Troops of the US 1st Cavalry Division land on Manus, the largest island of the Admiralty chain. By taking the Admiralty Islands, the US will further isolate Japanese forces in New Britain and New Guinea.

MARCH 15–16

LAND WAR, *BURMA/INDIA*
The second part of the U-Go offensive is launched. From start positions to the east of Imphal, the Japanese 15th Division begins an advance westwards, aiming to cut the Imphal–Kohima road, cross around the north of the city and make an encirclement of Allied positions by meeting with the Japanese 33rd Division advancing from the south. Meanwhile, farther to the north, the Japanese 31st Division begins a three-pronged assault towards Kohima.

MARCH 16

SEA WAR, *JAPAN*
The Japanese destroyer *Shirakumo* is sunk by the submarine USS *Tautog* off the coast of Japan.

LAND WAR, *BURMA*
Chindit troops cut the Mandalay–Myitkyina rail link just north of the vital Japanese supply base at Indaw, thereby making Japanese resupply of the retreating 18th Division extremely difficult. However, Japanese progress in the Imphal offensive means that many

▶ *Douglas SBD Dauntless carrier-based dive-bombers return from an air strike in the Marshall Islands.*

Allied troops are now being redirected away from the Myitkyina offensive.

MARCH 18–19

SEA WAR, *PACIFIC*
A US task group that includes one aircraft carrier and two battleships bombards Mili Island in the Marshall Islands from air and sea. One US ship is damaged in the engagement, the battleship USS *Missouri*, which is hit by a shell from a Japanese coastal gun. On the 18th, US destroyers also begin a two-day bombardment of Japanese positions at Wewak on the northern coastline of New Guinea.

MARCH 20

SEA/LAND WAR, *BISMARCK SEA*
The US 4th Marine Division makes an unopposed landing on Emirau, the most easterly of the St Matthias Group of Islands just north of New Ireland. Emirau contains an airstrip useful for strikes against Japanese naval bases at Kavieng in New Ireland and Rabaul in New Britain.

MARCH 23–24

LAND WAR, *BURMA*
The 14th LRP Brigade lands at

▶ *On the airstrip at the Chindit base of Broadway, a working party takes a break during repairs to the runway. In the background is a smashed glider.*

"Aberdeen" landing zone near Manhton in support of Chindit operations.

▲ *Vice-Admiral Minechi Koga, the C-in-C of the Japanese Combined Fleet, who died in an air crash at the end of March.*

MARCH 25

ALLIES, LEADERS
Major-General Orde Wingate, leader of the Chindits and pioneer of irregular warfare, is killed in an air crash over Burma. He is succeeded by Major-General W. Letaigne.

MARCH 25–29

LAND WAR, *ADMIRALTY ISLANDS*
US forces consolidate their hold over the Admiralty Islands. Resistance on Manus finally crumbles on the 25th;

four days later, the US occupies Pityilu Island to the north of Manus.

MARCH 29

LAND WAR, *INDIA*
The Japanese 15th Division cuts the Imphal–Kohima road near Kanglatong-bi. Meanwhile, in the south, the 33rd Division has ousted the 17th Indian Division from positions around Maw and Sittang and is besieging it on the Shenan Saddle, southeast of Imphal.

MARCH 30

LAND WAR, *BURMA*
Chindit operations south of Myitkyina begin to falter, the British troops being exhausted. The 16th Brigade is forced to retreat by the Japanese 53rd Division after its attempt to take the Japanese supply base at Indaw ends in failure.

MARCH 31

LEADERS, *JAPAN*
Vice-Admiral Minechi Koga, the C-in-C of the Japanese Combined Fleet from April 1943 (after Yamamoto's death), is killed in an air crash. Though a well-liked man, Koga did not have the offensive instinct of Yamamoto, or the same grasp of carrier air power.

APRIL 1

AIR WAR, *CAROLINE ISLANDS*
Three US Navy carrier groups launch a series of massive air strikes throughout

KEY PERSONALITIES

ORDE WINGATE

Orde Wingate (1903-44) was one of the great pioneers of the British Army. His formation and leadership of the Chindits in Burma were accompanied by important tactical innovations, including techniques of irregular warfare and effective use of air supply/support in tropical terrain.

Wingate was born in Naini Tal, India, on February 26, 1903. His father was an army officer, and Wingate followed him by taking a commission in the Royal Artillery in 1923. An active military career followed, including five years in the Sudan Defence Force (1928-33), working as an intelligence and combat officer in Palestine (1936) and, with the outbreak of World War II, leading units against Italian forces in Abyssinia. Wingate's next assignment was a posting to India along with a promotion to the rank of brigadier. It was in late 1942 that Wingate's commander, General Archibald Wavell, gave Wingate permission to form the Chindits, a group dedicated to insurgency style warfare that entered the Burma campaign in February 1943. Although the Chindits' first mission was essentially a failure, Wingate remained enthused by the idea of long-range

penetration, and personally presented the idea to British Prime Minister Churchill and US President Roosevelt.

It was during the Chindits' second, more auspicious, action in March 1944 that Wingate was killed. He was deeply mourned by his men, who always gave him their absolute loyalty. Wingate was undoubtedly a complex man – difficult, intelligent, ruthless and prone to severe depression. Yet he left an important military legacy relevant to any military student today.

▲ *Japanese troops attack a Stuart light tank during their advance in Burma. The Stuart was armed with a 37mm main gun.*

the Caroline Islands. Although the US loses 20 aircraft in the raids, the Japanese casualties are considerably higher: 150 aircraft destroyed and 6 warships (including 2 destroyers) and 105,664 tonnes (104,000 tons) of merchant shipping sunk.

APRIL 5–6

LAND WAR, *INDIA*
The Japanese 31st Division isolates Kohima: the 138th Regiment moves from the

north; the 58th and 124th Regiments attack from the south and west. Allied forces at Kohima are now trapped in a pocket less than 16km (10 miles) across. On the 6th, the Japanese 58th Regiment succeeds in driving through Naga Village at the northern end of Kohima and up the Imphal–Kohima road to take key positions around the centre of the settlement, but a dogged defence by the Royal West Kents stops the attack in its tracks.

APRIL 6

LAND WAR, *INDIA*
Operation U-Go completes its final objectives as the Japanese 33rd and 15th

Divisions cut off Imphal. The Allied defensive circle around Imphal is roughly 32km (20 miles) across, and contains the following IV Corps units: 17th Indian Light Division; 50th Parachute Brigade; 5th Indian Division; 23rd Indian Division; 254th Tank Brigade. Despite having been thoroughly routed, the Allied forces have made a professional retreat and conserved much of their strength and organization. Both Imphal and Kohima garrisons are now entirely dependent on air supply to maintain the defence, and their aim is to hang on until Britain's XXXIII Corps reaches them and breaks the siege.

APRIL 6–11

LAND WAR, *BURMA*
The Japanese Army's 53rd Division takes the supply base known as "White City" in the south of the Chindits' area of operations.

APRIL 7

LAND WAR, *INDIA*
To consolidate its gains around Kohima, the Japanese 138th Regiment encircles the

◀ *Japanese infantry move towards Kohima in Burma past two abandoned British Bren Gun Carriers of the Fourteenth Army.*

 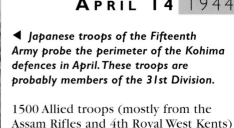
◄ *Japanese troops of the Fifteenth Army probe the perimeter of the Kohima defences in April. These troops are probably members of the 31st Division.*

1500 Allied troops (mostly from the Assam Rifles and 4th Royal West Kents) beats back the Japanese, who also suffer heavy casualties from 3.74in howitzer fire from Jotsoma.

APRIL 14

LAND WAR, *INDIA*
Allied XXXIII Corps begins its relief operations around Kohima. The 5th Brigade, 2nd Division, smashes the Japanese road block at Zubza and also breaks the Japanese grip around the 161st Indian Brigade at Jotsoma. The Jotsoma position is useful for the Allies as an ideal location for bringing

161st Indian Brigade around Jotsoma to the west of Kohima, then establishes a road block at Zubza, cutting the main Dimapur–Kohima road. In Kohima itself, the Japanese take the key defensive points known as the F.S.D. and Kuki Piquet after an intense overnight artillery bombardment.

APRIL 9

LAND WAR, *BURMA*
The Chindits in northern Burma receive glider-borne reinforcements.

APRIL 12

LAND WAR, *ADMIRALTY ISLANDS*
Pak Island is taken by US troops.

APRIL 13

LAND WAR, *INDIA*
The Japanese start to suffer serious setbacks in the U-Go offensive. Allied troops have today pushed the Japanese off Nung-shigum Hill on the Imphal plain, allowing them to intensify attacks on the

Japanese 15th Division. In Kohima, Japanese forces push into the centre of the settlement, throwing themselves at positions reaching from GPT Ridge in the south to the "Tennis Court" in the north around the district commissioner's residence. A tenacious defence by

▼ *A column of troops from the Japanese Fifteenth Army makes its way towards north-east India. By early July 1944, this 100,000-man force had suffered very heavy losses.*

APRIL 18

artillery fire down on the Japanese around Kohima.

APRIL 18

LAND WAR, *BURMA*
The Chindits finally occupy the Japanese supply base at Indaw. The occupation cuts a vital Japanese rail link between Myitkyina and southern Burma.

LAND WAR, *INDIA*
The beleaguered Allied garrison at Kohima is finally relieved by the 5th Brigade of XXXIII Corps. The fighting does not abate, however. Both the Japanese and the British are attempting encirclement and flanking manoeuvres against each other, and severe battles are raging in the hilly and jungle-covered terrain surrounding Kohima.

APRIL 19

SEA WAR, *DUTCH EAST INDIES*
An Allied naval force commanded by Admiral J.F. Somerville of the Royal Navy, and including the US carrier *Saratoga* and the British carrier HMS *Illustrious*, bombs and shells enemy positions around Sabang, Sumatra, as a diversion from imminent US operations in New Guinea.

APRIL 21–22

LAND WAR, *NEW GUINEA*
The US extends its operations by making major landings on the northern coastline of New Guinea. On the 21st/22nd, a US naval Task Force under Vice-Admiral M.A. Mitscher delivers a massive preliminary bombardment against Japanese positions at Sarmi, Sawar, Wadke Island and Hollandia before US Army troops are landed at Aitape, Tanahmerah Bay and Hollandia. The attack comes as Allied troops finalize their hold over the Huon Peninsula farther to the south. The Japanese on New Guinea are increasingly running out of space to retreat or evacuate.

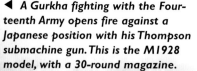
◄ *A Gurkha fighting with the Fourteenth Army opens fire against a Japanese position with his Thompson submachine gun. This is the M1928 model, with a 30-round magazine.*

APRIL 17

STRATEGY, *JAPAN*
Japan attempts to reinvigorate its strategic policy towards China. Although already over-stretched in the Pacific and Burma, the Japanese Army is committed to a major offensive in China – Ichi-Go – which has the objective of occupying southern China, thus providing open land routes to Japanese forces in Malaya and Thailand, while also crushing US air bases in Honan and Kwangsi provinces.

APRIL 22

LAND WAR, *MARSHALL ISLANDS*
The US brings the Marshall Islands under full control by occupying the island of Ungelap. The capture of the Marshall Islands enables US forces in the central Pacific to begin their swing northwards up through the Mariana Islands towards the Japanese homeland.

APRIL 24

STRATEGY, *US*
Based on the fanaticism of Japanese resistance throughout the Pacific so far, Allied war leaders agree that the Japanese homeland will need to be invaded and occupied to secure Japan's final surrender.

APRIL 24–26

LAND WAR, *NEW GUINEA*
Australian soldiers of the 15th Brigade advance northwards out of the Huon Peninsula and take Madang and Alexishafen.

◀ *Japanese troops, either of the 15th or 31st Divisions, wait to cross a river in Burma as part of the U-Go offensive.*

downpours of rain from the 27th complicate movement. In central Kohima, a stubborn Allied resistance around features such as Garrison Hill is devastating Japanese forces, and on the 27th the British retake the important road junction around the district commissioner's bungalow. The Japanese and British settle into entrenched positions less than 22m (72ft) apart around the Tennis Court, and begin an horrific two-week, close-quarter battle.

APRIL 29–30

SEA/AIR WAR, *CAROLINE ISLANDS*
The Japanese base at Truk is bombed by aircraft from 12 US carriers, destroying ships, oil stores, ammunition dumps and 93 Japanese aircraft.

MAY 1

SEA/AIR WAR, *CAROLINE ISLANDS*
A large US battleship and carrier group bombards Ponape Island.

▲ *Admiral Soemu Toyoda, who in early May became Commander-in-Chief of the Japanese Combined Fleet. In 1945, Toyoda favoured continuing the war despite the dropping of atomic bombs on Japan.*

APRIL 26–27

LAND WAR, *INDIA*
The Allied XXXIII Corps begins a major pincer action to take Kohima. From the north, the 5th Brigade begins attacking the Japanese right flank; from the south, the 4th Brigade begins to hook upwards towards GPT Ridge. Torrential

▼ *Chindits about to board a C-47 transport aircraft at one of their strongholds in Burma, probably Broadway.*

MAY 4

LAND WAR, *MARSHALL ISLANDS*

A US naval base and naval air facility is established on Majuro Atoll, providing another logistics centre for US operations in the central Pacific. Just six days

▼ *A US air raid on the Japanese base at Rabaul. By mid-May it was effectively isolated. It would be left "to wither on the vine" until the end of the war.*

later, another US naval base is opened on Eniwetok. Five days later, naval air bases are established at Ebeye and Roi-namur, Kwajalein Atoll. The air bases are used for the next few weeks to hit remaining Japanese installations in the Marshalls.

MAY 4–13

LAND WAR, *INDIA*

The British 4th Brigade retakes GPT Ridge to the south of Kohima. On May

▲ *A US Coast Guard LST (Landing Ship, Tank), loaded with supplies and part of a large flotilla, makes its way to New Guinea. Note the anti-aircraft guns.*

4–7, Allied troops of the 6th and 33rd Brigades attacking Japanese positions between Jail Hill and the Tennis Court experience less success, and are beaten off with heavy casualties. A second attempt on 11–13th finally ejects the Japanese from these positions.

MAY 5

POLITICS, *JAPAN*

Following the death of Admiral Koga, the C-in-C of the Japanese Combined Fleet, on March 31, Admiral Soemu Toyoda is sworn in as his replacement.

LAND WAR, *INDIA*

The British Fourteenth Army begins extensive counterattacks in the Imphal area. Throughout April and into early May, IV Corps has been defending the long perimeter around Imphal, with fighting particularly heavy around the Shenan Saddle, Torbung and Mapao Ridge. Both sides are increasingly exhausted and are running out of basic foodstuffs.

MAY 6

LAND WAR, *BURMA*

Chinese troops are now fighting the Japanese at Ritpong, only 48km (30 miles) from Myitkyina.

eating grass and roots, he acts according to his humanity.

MAY 17

LAND WAR, *NORTHERN BURMA*
A combined force of Chindits, US soldiers of the 5307th Regiment and Chinese troops of the 30th and 38th Divisions attempt to take Myitkyina after their advance through Burma of more than 241km (150 miles). The attack is blunted against strong Japanese defences on the outskirts.

MAY 17

LAND WAR, *NEW GUINEA*
More US Army troops (41st and 6th Divisions) are landed on northern New Guinea, this time in the Wadke-Toem area, 320km (200 miles) west of Hollandia.

AIR WAR, *DUTCH EAST INDIES*
Carrier aircraft of the British Eastern Fleet destroy enemy oil installations at Surabaya and also sink 10 Japanese naval vessels.

MAY 18

LAND WAR, *ADMIRALTY ISLANDS*
Remaining Japanese resistance in the Admiralties is finally extinguished, leaving the fortified Japanese bases at Kavieng (New Ireland) and Rabaul

MAY 7

LAND WAR, *INDIA*
Fourteenth Army counterattacks around Imphal lose force and peter out in the face of ferocious Japanese resistance.

MAY 11

STRATEGY, *MARIANA ISLANDS*
Vice-Admiral Jisaburo Ozawa takes charge of the Japanese naval defence of the Mariana Islands. The defensive operation is codenamed A-Go.

▼ *Chinese troops, kitted out in American uniforms and shouldering US rifles, march down a road in northern Burma on their way to engage Japanese forces. A US P-40 fighter flies overhead.*

▲ *US troops come ashore on New Guinea as part of the American build-up on the island. The Japanese fought a tenacious rearguard campaign throughout 1944.*

MAY 15–31

LAND WAR, *INDIA*
Just south of Naga village, the 33rd Brigade makes repeated attempts to capture Hunter's Hill and Gun Spur. All attacks are initially repulsed. However, the Japanese are steadily pushed back from Kohima during subsequent days; and on May 31, Lieutenant-General Sato Kotoku orders his 31st Division to withdraw. The withdrawal is against official orders but, having lost around 6000 men, and with the survivors reduced to

49

▲ *Gurkhas and members of the West Yorkshire Regiment advance against Japanese troops at Kohima. The tank at left is an M3 Grant.*

(New Britain) entirely surrounded by Allied forces. They will remain this way until the end of the war, escaping invasion owing to the US policy of avoiding Japanese strongholds if they can be bypassed and isolated instead. The Japanese have lost 3280 men killed, while the US Admiralties campaign results in 326 dead and 1189 wounded.

MAY 17–18

LAND WAR, *BURMA*

US and Chinese troops battle hard to take Myitkyina. On the 17th, the Chinese 150th Regiment/50th Division captures Myitkyina airstrip, with the railway station falling the next day. However, severe exhaustion among Allied troops, particularly the US Marauders, means they make limited progress elsewhere and they dig in and wait for the Chinese 38th Division to arrive.

MAY 19

POLITICS, *US*

James Forrestal is appointed Secretary of the Navy, having been under-secretary since June 1940 under James Knox. Forrestal will prove himself a tough and capable naval administrator, and even experience combat by landing under fire on Iwo Jima when visiting US forces in April 1945.

MAY 19–20

SEA/AIR WAR, *MARCUS ISLAND*

US carrier aircraft conduct a two-day bombardment of Marcus Island.

MAY 28

LAND WAR, *NEW GUINEA*

Men of the US 158th, 162nd and 186th Infantry Regiments land on Biak off northwestern New Guinea. Although the landing is unopposed, the US advance towards an airstrip near Mokmer turns into a ferocious firefight after Japanese troops spring a huge machine-gun, artillery and mortar ambush from cliff-side positions.

▼ *Troops of the 2nd Battalion, 6th Marine Regiment, on the outskirts of Garapan on the island of Saipan.*

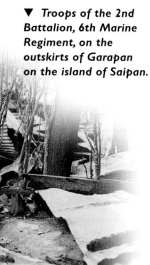

JUNE 6

AIR WAR, *NEW GUINEA*

Two US light cruisers are damaged after a Japanese bombing attack off Biak.

JUNE 7

LAND WAR, *NEW GUINEA*

The Japanese Mokmer airfield on Biak, off the coast of New Guinea, is secured by US troops.

JUNE 8

SEA WAR, *NEW GUINEA*

Five Japanese destroyers are intercepted and turned back by an Allied naval force as they attempt a supply run to beleaguered Japanese troops on Biak Island. The destroyer *Harusame* is sunk.

JUNE 9

SEA WAR, *PACIFIC*

Two Japanese destroyers are sunk by US submarines off the Bonin Islands and in the Celebes Sea. Although a good day of hunting, such sinkings are now unexceptional as US submarines inflict a grievous toll on Japanese merchant and military shipping.

JUNE 12

POLITICS, *CHINA*

In a dramatic political reversal, the Chinese Communist leader Mao Tse Tung makes a public announcement of his support for Chiang Kai-

▶ *The 16in guns of USS Iowa open fire against Japanese defences on Tinian. Her main armament was nine 16in guns.*

▲ *A Japanese Type 96 light tank lies abandoned near Mokmer airstrip, on Biak Island, following a firefight with US forces which landed on the island.*

shek's Nationalist forces. However, such declarations have been made before, and the Communists still jealously guard their own territorial areas in northern China.

JUNE 12–14

AIR/SEA WAR, *MARIANA ISLANDS*

US Task Force 58 begins a huge three-day bombardment of Japanese positions on Saipan and Tinian, while US aircraft add their own firepower and damage or destroy around 200 Japanese aircraft. The battleship USS *California* and the destroyer USS *Braine* are damaged by Japanese coastal guns on the Marianas.

JUNE 14

LAND WAR, *NEW GUINEA*

General Douglas MacArthur replaces the commander of US forces on

MAY 29

SEA WAR, *NEW IRELAND*

US destroyers bombard the northern coastline of New Ireland. However, there will be no invasion – New Ireland will be bypassed in favour of Emirau Island and Hollandia.

LAND WAR, *NEW GUINEA*

US and Japanese tanks engage each other on Biak Island off the coast of New Guinea. The action, the first tank battle in the Pacific theatre, results in a Japanese defeat.

JUNE 1–3

LAND WAR, *INDIA*

The Japanese 31st Division at Kohima begins to withdraw, signalling the final end of the U-Go offensive into India. The collapse begins on June 1 when the 7th Indian Division overruns Japanese positions in Naga village before the 5th Brigade outflanks the Japanese around Aradura Spur on June 3. Although the Japanese have been militarily defeated, lack of supplies is also a major catalyst for the withdrawal.

JUNE 15

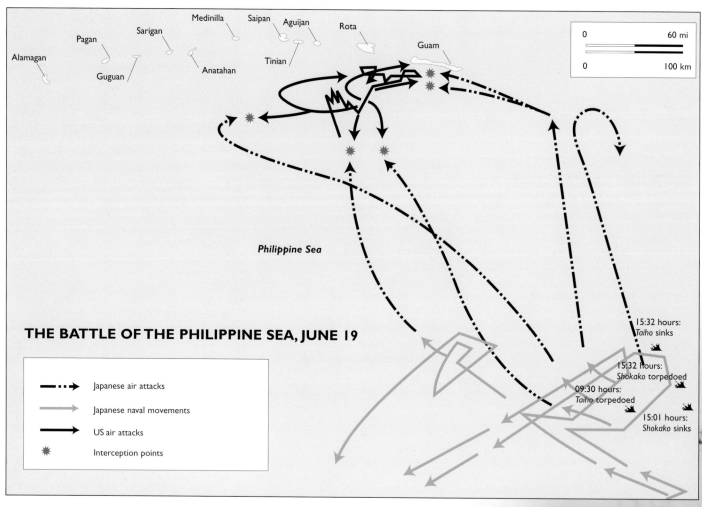

Alamagan
Pagan
Guguan
Sarigan
Medinilla
Anatahan
Saipan
Tinian
Aguijan
Rota
Guam

0 ____ 60 mi
0 ____ 100 km

Philippine Sea

THE BATTLE OF THE PHILIPPINE SEA, JUNE 19

— ∙ ∙ → Japanese air attacks

——→ Japanese naval movements

——→ US air attacks

✳ Interception points

15:32 hours: *Taiho* sinks

15:32 hours: *Shokako* torpedoed

09:30 hours: *Taiho* torpedoed

15:01 hours: *Shokako* sinks

▲ At the Battle of the Philippine Sea, Ozawa had nine carriers and 473 aircraft. The US fleet under Mitscher had 15 carriers and 902 aircraft.

Biak with Lieutenant-General Eichelberger. The change of command galvanizes the Biak offensive, which has ground to a halt against vicious Japanese resistance in the caves and hills of the island.

JUNE 15

LAND WAR, *MARIANA ISLANDS*

The US invasion of the Mariana Islands – Operation Forager – begins with landings on Saipan. While US reserve regiments make a feint against Mucho Point about halfway down the west coast of Saipan, the US 2nd Marine Division and 4th Marine Division put ashore farther down the coast around Charan Kanoa on eight individual beaches. They meet heavy Japanese fire, suffering 4000 casualties in the first 48 hours, but manage to establish beachheads. However, the bulk of Lieutenant-General Saito Yoshitsugo's 32,000-strong garrison has been

relatively untouched by the US preliminary bombardment.

AIR WAR, *PACIFIC*

US carrier aircraft bombard Japanese positions on Iwo Jima in the Volcano Islands and Chichi Jima and Haha Jima in the Bonin Islands. Iwo Jima is also bombed the next day.

AIR WAR, *CHINA*

Industrial facilities on the Japanese mainland at Yahata are

▼ Ships of the US Fifth Fleet in the Philippine Sea in June. These are some of the seven battleships that Mitscher had for the battle, plus 21 cruisers and 69 destroyers.

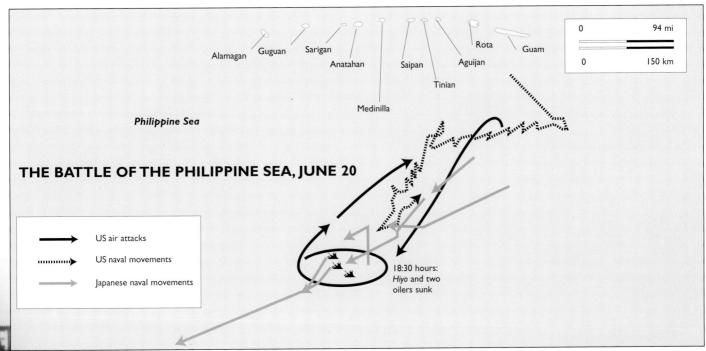

THE BATTLE OF THE PHILIPPINE SEA, JUNE 20

Philippine Sea

Alamagan Guguan Sarigan Anatahan Medinilla Saipan Tinian Aguijan Rota Guam

→	US air attacks
┄┄►	US naval movements
→	Japanese naval movements

18:30 hours: *Hiyo* and two oilers sunk

0   94 mi
0   150 km

▲ *On June 20, US aircraft intercepted the Japanese fleet at the limit of their range. Only 17 aircraft were lost in combat; 82 more ran out of fuel when returning.*

bombed by a flight of 47 Boeing B-29 Superfortress bombers flying from bases in southern China.

JUNE 16

SEA WAR, *MARIANA ISLANDS*
As US troops fight ashore on Saipan, a force of US battleships, cruisers and destroyers under Rear-Admiral W.L. Ainsworth pounds Japanese coastal positions on Guam.

SEA WAR, *PHILIPPINE SEA*
Intelligence from US submarines indicates two large Japanese naval forces (First Mobile Fleet and a Southern Force) making a refuelling rendezvous east of the Philippines, before setting sail in the direction of the Mariana Islands. The combined force totals seven battleships, nine aircraft carriers (four of them light carriers), thirteen cruisers and twenty-eight destroyers. Its objective is to crush naval support of the Marianas landings. The full force of Mitscher's Task Force 58 begins redirecting itself to meet this threat.

▲ *Saipan was the first island conquered by the Americans that had a large number of Japanese civilians on it. Here, the inhabitants of a village are evacuated.*

JUNE 17–18

LAND WAR, *MARIANA ISLANDS*
Japanese resistance on Saipan is so heavy that the reserve 27th Infantry Division is landed to assist Marine operations. On the 18th, Aslito airfield in the south of the island is captured, and the US Marines begin to move northwards.

JUNE 18

SEA WAR, *PHILIPPINE SEA*
All US task groups rendezvous around 320km (200 miles) east of Saipan and

JUNE 19

▶ *Curtiss Helldivers on their way to attack Japanese ships during the Battle of the Philippine Sea.*

sail out to face the Japanese naval force heading its way. The Japanese are heavily outnumbered by US Task Force 58, which includes seven battleships, fourteen carriers (seven heavy), twenty-one cruisers and sixty-nine destroyers. The scene is set for the Battle of the Philippine Sea.

LAND WAR, *CHINA*
The Japanese offensive to take western and southern China makes good progress, with the Japanese Eleventh Army taking the cities of Chuchow and Changsa.

JUNE 19

SEA WAR, *PHILIPPINE SEA*
The Battle of the Philippine Sea. Japanese carriers launch their first air strikes against US forces at 08:30 hours, but these are intercepted by US aircraft and more than 200 Japanese planes are shot down. US submarines also begin to attack the Japanese. At 09:05 hours, the carrier *Taiho* is torpedoed by the USS *Albacore*, and the *Shokaku* is torpedoed at 12:20 hours. Both carriers sink by 16:30 hours. At 14:00 hours, surviving Japanese carriers launch a second strike, which goes off course towards Guam and is once again slaughtered by US fighters – more than 100 aircraft are destroyed. By 16:00 hours, the Japan-

ese fleet is withdrawing, but is attacked constantly by US aircraft. The first day of the battle is over. As well as losing two carriers, the Japanese have lost 346 aircraft in what US pilots subsequently dub "The Great Marianas Turkey Shoot".

◀ *A Japanese aircraft in flames, probably a Yukosuka P1Y1, passes over a US escort carrier during the invasion of Saipan.*

▲ *A Japanese aircraft plunges into the sea off Saipan on June 18. The ship in the foreground is the aircraft carrier USS Kitkun Bay, which had a complement of 18 fighters and 12 torpedo-bombers.*

JUNE 20

SEA WAR, *PHILIPPINE SEA*

US Task Force 58 continues its pursuit of Japanese forces retreating through the Philippine Sea. At 16:24 hours, a major US air strike (210 aircraft) is launched, which begins its attack at 18:44 hours at extreme range. The Japanese carrier *Hiyo* is hit by two air-launched torpedoes and sinks, and bombs damage the carriers *Zuikaku* and *Chiyoda*. Two oil tankers are also sunk. The US suffers seven ships damaged. However, 80 US carrier aircraft are destroyed when attempting night landings or from getting lost and having to ditch at sea. The Battle of the Philippine Sea is a major victory for the US; for the Japanese, a hideous defeat marking the decline of its navy.

JUNE 22

LAND WAR, *INDIA*

As the Japanese U-Go offensive unravels in India, the British 2nd Division from Kohima and the 5th Indian Division from the IV Corps area around Imphal finally meet up on the Imphal–Kohima road at Milestone 107. In total, the Japanese siege at Imphal lasted 88 days.

JUNE 26

LAND WAR, *BURMA*

The town of Mogaung falls to a combined force of the 77th LRP Brigade

STRATEGY AND TACTICS

AMPHIBIOUS WARFARE IN THE PACIFIC

Although naval infantry, such as the British Royal Marines and the US Marines, had elementary amphibious skills at the beginning of World War II, it was the Japanese who truly pioneered amphibious tactics. From experience in China in the late 1930s, and from their opening campaigns of World War II, the Japanese developed a systematic doctrine for amphibious campaigns, including the establishment of naval and air superiority in the area of landing; detailed intelligence concerning landing sites and enemy defences; and systematic disembarkation of troops, ammunition and supplies. They were also capable of night-time amphibious landings, with soldiers and equipment daubed in luminous paint to aid identification.

Yet, despite Japanese capabilities, the undeniable master of amphibious warfare in World War II was the US. American amphibious landings worked in three parts. An amphibious force was responsible for landing troops on the beaches and maintaining the flow of relevant logistics. Preparatory and support bombardments were provided by a force of warships surrounding the landing zone; farther out at sea, fleet carriers and other capital ships provided air and sea cover for the landing operations – and also interdicted Japanese reinforcement convoys.

By late 1944, the US had made amphibious landings a fine art, having learnt painful lessons about issues such as beach reconnaissance and the effectiveness of naval bombardments at Tarawa and Saipan. General MacArthur employed amphibious warfare nimbly at a tactical level, using simultaneous multiple landings to trap Japanese troops (see New Guinea, April 1944; and Leyte, October 1944) or bypassing heavily defended Japanese positions by leapfrogging down a coastline. The Japanese learnt equally painful lessons about US amphibious superiority, and at Okinawa in April 1945 they did not make a costly defence of the beaches but withdrew into the interior where they inflicted massive casualties on the US. The lesson came too late, however, and US amphibious tactics took the Allies to the very doorstep of the Japanese homelands.

US Marines in an LVT2 Water Buffalo amphibious vehicle off Tinian.

and the Chinese 38th Division. These forces then turn eastwards to make the 48km (30-mile) drive towards Myitkyina, which US and Chinese forces are already laying siege to.

LAND WAR, *CHINA*

Japanese forces capture Hengyang airfield in southern China, having cut through the Chinese Tenth Army with some ease (Chinese forces were generally second rate). The US needs to hold on to its Chinese air bases for planned B-29 Superfortress air strikes against targets in the Japanese homeland.

JUNE 28

LAND WAR, *MARIANA ISLANDS*

US troops reach Nafutan Point, Saipan's southeastern tip. It has taken them nearly two weeks to cover 6km (4 miles).

JULY 1-31

LAND WAR, *BURMA*

The British Fourteenth Army, capitalizing on its victories at Imphal and Kohima, pushes the Japanese Fifteenth Army back into Burma across the Kabaw Valley. The Japanese make command

JULY 1

▶ *A US Marine peers into a cave in search of Japanese defenders on Saipan. Note the M1911 semi-automatic pistol in his hand – ideal for close-range work.*

changes, with General Hoyotaro Kimura becoming commander of the Burma Area Army, and leadership of the Fifteenth Army passing to Lieutenant-General Shihachi Katamura. Tactically, the Japanese hope that the Allies will over-extend themselves during their advance, and leave themselves open to flanking counterattacks.

JULY 1

LAND WAR, *MARIANA ISLANDS*
The US 2nd and 4th Marine Divisions and the 27th Infantry Division advance up Saipan against heavy Japanese resistance, pushing forward 0.6km (1 mile) in some sectors and bringing right flank troops to within 9km (5.5 miles) of the northern tip of the island. On the left flank of the advance, US troops have seized the heights overlooking Tanapag harbour.

JULY 2

LAND WAR, *DUTCH EAST INDIES*
US troops are landed at Noemfoor Island, off the coast of New Guinea.
AIR WAR, *IWO JIMA*
US carrier aircraft attack Japanese forces on Iwo Jima, shooting down 16

▼ *Dead Japanese litter a beach near Tanapag, Saipan, following a disastrous counterattack on July 9. Thereafter Japanese resistance collapsed.*

Japanese aircraft and destroying 29 on the ground.

JULY 4

AIR WAR, *BONIN ISLANDS/IWO JIMA*
US carrier-based aircraft have a good day hunting Japanese shipping around the Bonin Islands and Iwo Jima. Backed

by a bombardment from US cruisers and destroyers, they help sink four destroyers and several transport vessels.

JULY 7

LAND WAR, *MARIANA ISLANDS*
Having been squeezed into the northern tip of Saipan, the remaining Japanese

forces mount a large counterattack around Makunsha. The attack is repulsed (an estimated 1500 dead) by the massive firepower of the 4th Marine Division and the 27th Infantry Division, despite the Japanese troops breaking through the US lines at points. Yesterday, the Japanese commanders of the Saipan defence, General Yoshitsugo Saito and Admiral Chichi Nagumo, committed suicide.

SEA WAR, *PACIFIC/SOUTH CHINA SEA*

US submarines sink two Japanese destroyers, one around the Kurile Islands and the other in the South China Sea.

JULY 8

AIR WAR, *JAPAN*

Yahata iron and steel works and several

▼ US troops of the 503rd Parachute Infantry Regiment land on Kamiri airstrip, Noemfoor Island, on July 2. The island was secured by the end of August 1944.

other key military industrial targets are hit by the second B-29 raid in three weeks, the US bombers utilizing air bases in China.

JULY 9

LAND WAR, *MARIANA ISLANDS*

Japanese resistance eventually collapses on Saipan. The final death toll is high on both sides: 3126 US soldiers killed and 27,000 Japanese (including 8000 suicides), horrific casualty figures for an island only 16km (10 miles) long. The next objective for the 2nd and 4th Marine Divisions is Tinian.

JULY 11

POLITICS, *US*

President Franklin D. Roosevelt states his intention to run for an unprecedented fourth term as president.

JULY 14

LAND/SEA WAR, *NEW GUINEA*

Warships bombard Japanese positions around Aitape, providing aid to Allied troops advancing along New Guinea's northern coastline. Heavy fighting, including a large Japanese counterattack on the Wewak River, has slowed the advance.

JULY 18

POLITICS, *JAPAN*

General Hideki Tojo, the Japanese prime minister and chief of staff,

▼ Truck-mounted US Marine rocket launchers on Saipan. Rocket-launcher units were usually deployed just behind frontline troops on the battlefield.

▲ US Marines use a flamethrower to clear a cave on Saipan. Note how the soldier operating the flamethrower has turned his face away from the heat.

resigns along with the whole of his cabinet. A group of former premiers engineered the resignation by asking the emperor to form a new government. The move marks increasing desperation among Japanese politicians as they face defeat by the US. General Kuniaki Koiso and Admiral Mitsumasa Yonai will form the new cabinet, and separate the commands of the army that Tojo had previously held in one office.

STRATEGY AND TACTICS

THE STRATEGIC DEBATE

In July 1944, US military leaders, the joint chiefs of staff and the US president met to debate strategic options for complete victory in the Pacific. Those present divided themselves roughly into two camps. General MacArthur advocated the Philippines as the principal objective following the campaign in New Guinea, whereas Admiral King (chief of the US Navy) wanted to bypass the Philippines and cut straight to the island of Formosa, south of the Japanese mainland. By taking Formosa, King contended, Japan would be isolated from its resources in the Dutch East Indies. Also, Formosa would be an excellent jumping-off point in the final invasion of Japan, and would avoid any wasteful slaughter in the Philippine jungles. MacArthur's plan had a strong ethical dimension to it; he believed that the US was under a "moral obligation" to return to the Philippines and liberate its inhabitants. Militarily, he argued that it would not be advisable to leave a large Japanese presence in the rear for a strike towards Formosa.

The other key figure in the debate was Admiral Halsey. He wanted to develop the central Pacific campaign by capturing Okinawa in the Ryukyu chain, part of Japanese territory itself, and use this as the launch pad for the invasion of the mainland.

The momentum was towards MacArthur and Halsey's plan, and the president and the joint chiefs of staff gave their assent. Formosa would be bypassed.

JULY 19

SEA/AIR WAR, *MARIANA ISLANDS*
US Navy ships and aircraft begin their pre-landing bombardment of Guam, focusing on the Asan and Agat beaches.

JULY 21

LAND WAR, *MARIANA ISLANDS*
The US 3rd Marine Division, 1st Marine Brigade and 77th Army Division are landed on the western coast of Guam, before beginning a slow advance northwards.

JULY 24–25

LAND WAR, *MARIANA ISLANDS*
The US 4th Marine Division lands on northern Tinian while the 2nd Marine Division makes a feint attack off the southern coast around Sunhanon

▼ *US Marines advance north on the island of Guam. The vehicle on the left is an M4 Sherman medium tank.*

▲ *The Japanese cabinet that resigned on July 18 in response to a group of former premiers asking the emperor to form a new government. Tojo is second from left.*

harbour. Japanese resistance is typically ferocious; on the 25th, the 2nd Marine Division moves up the coastline to support the 4th Marines' action.

JULY 25–29

LAND WAR, *MARIANA ISLANDS*
Japanese forces on Guam launch a massive counterattack against the US 3rd Marine Division, but suffer appallingly with nearly 20,000 dead (the US loses 1744 men). On the 29th, the Orote Peninsula, which contains Guam's main airfield at the southern end of the US advance, is occupied.

JULY 26–31

STRATEGY, *US*
Top military chiefs, including General

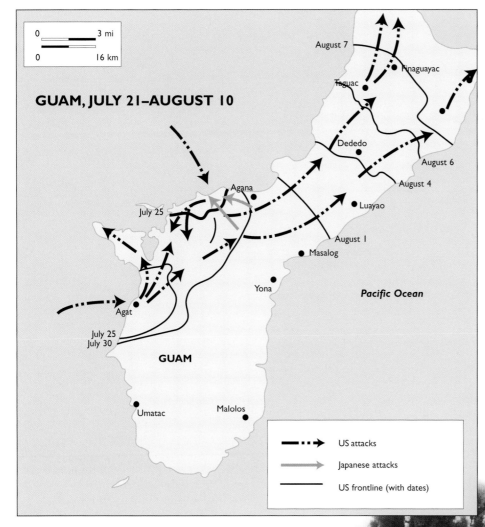

GUAM, JULY 21–AUGUST 10

0 — 3 mi
0 — 16 km

August 7
Finaguayac
Taguac
Dededo
Agana
August 6
July 25
August 4
Luayao
August 1
Masalog
Yona
Pacific Ocean
Agat
July 25
July 30
GUAM
Umatac
Malolos

▪▪▪▶ US attacks

▶ Japanese attacks

— US frontline (with dates)

◀ *The conquest of Guam cost the Americans 1744 dead. Most of the Japanese garrison was wiped out, though some held out in the jungle until 1972.*

aviators with an air base suitable for long-range bombing missions against the Japanese homeland.

LAND WAR, *MARIANA ISLANDS*
US troops maintain a strong advance into Guam, occupying the towns of Utana, Pado, Pulan and Matte while US aircraft soften up Japanese resistance in the north of the island. Fighting is heavy, however, and to this date the US has already suffered 1022 dead and 4926 wounded. By August 2, half the island is in US possession.

AUGUST 3

LAND WAR, *BURMA*
The Japanese withdraw from Myitkyina, allowing British, US and Chinese forces to occupy the town, which sits at the head of a vital rail link running down into southern Burma. The capture of the town after an 11-week blockade is a vindication of General Stilwell and General Wingate's views on long-range penetration operations, although the two men had a frequently difficult relationship.

AUGUST 3–4

SEA WAR, *PACIFIC*
Strikes by US carrier aircraft and warships around the Bonin and Volcano Islands inflict heavy punishment on Japanese shipping. In a two-day onslaught, at least five destroyers, one cruiser, five cargo vessels and twelve other vessels are sunk.

AUGUST 5

LAND WAR, *MARIANA ISLANDS*
Fighting on Guam intensifies as US Marines and infantry push about 5km (3 miles) up the island against fanatical Japanese resistance.

MacArthur, Admiral King, Admiral Nimitz and Admiral Halsey, debate future military strategy for the Pacific war during a conference at Pearl Harbor. President Roosevelt is also present, and sides with MacArthur and Halsey, who argue that the Philippines should be taken before assaulting the Japanese homeland.

AUGUST 1

LAND WAR, *MARIANA ISLANDS*
Final Japanese resistance on Tinian crumbles after a well-executed but difficult US campaign, during which 9000 Japanese have been killed. Such was the excellence of the operation that Lieutenant-General Holland Smith later classes it as the finest amphibious operation of the Pacific war. Tinian provides US

▶ *A Japanese ammunition dump explodes on Tinian after being hit by a US bomb. US Marines have left their foxholes to watch the display.*

By this point in the fighting, the Japanese have lost more than 8100 men. Some 22,000 civilians are sheltering behind US lines.

AUSTRALIA, POWS
Japanese prisoners of war attempt a mass breakout from the Coworra POW camp, Sydney. Three

▼ *Chinese-crewed Stuart light tanks of a composite Chinese-American reconnaissance force move down a road in Burma in the aftermath of the Japanese withdrawal from Myitkyina.*

Australian guards are killed and 334 Japanese manage to escape, but Australian machine-gun fire kills 234 inmates and wounds 108 others.

AUGUST 8

SEA WAR, PHILIPPINES
The Japanese escort carrier *Oraka* is sunk by the submarine USS *Rasher* off the coast of northwest Luzon.

AUGUST 10

LAND WAR, MARIANA ISLANDS
Significant Japanese resistance on Guam collapses. Pockets of Japan-

▲ *Two US B-24 Liberators on their way to bomb Haha Jima in the Bonin Islands. The B-24 could carry up to 3629kg (8000lb) of bombs up to a range of over 3200km (2000 miles).*

ese soldiers continue the fight in isolation, one determined individual surrendering only in 1972. More than 10,000 Japanese soldiers have been killed compared with 1744 US troops. The occupation of Guam brings the Marianas campaign to a close. Now the island will be transformed into a bomber base for an offensive against the Japanese homeland by B-29 Superfortresses.

AUGUST 17–20

LAND WAR, NEW GUINEA
The US crushes resistance on Noemfoor and Biak Islands off the coast of New Guinea. While US paratroopers take over Noemfoor Island, other US troops make an amphibious landing at Wardo Bay on Biak to overcome final Japanese resistance. The Biak engagement alone has cost the Japanese Army 4700 dead.

AUGUST 22–24

SEA WAR, PHILIPPINES
US Marines prosecute a hard campaign against Japanese shipping around the Philippines. On the 22nd, Japan loses three frigates to US torpedoes with the destroyer *Asakaze* being sunk by the USS *Haddo* the next day. Retaliation comes on the 24th when the USS

▶ *Mopping up on Tinian. A US 75mm Pack Howitzer M8, lashed to rocks and crewed by Marines, opens fire on a cave containing Japanese soldiers.*

Harder is sunk off the coast of Luzon by Japanese depth charges.

AUGUST 27

LAND WAR, *BURMA*

Having undertaken several months of exhausting operations in northern Burma, the final groups of Chindits are evacuated to India.

AUGUST 31

AIR WAR, *BONIN/VOLCANO ISLANDS*

US carrier aircraft begin an intensive three-day bombing campaign against the Bonin and Volcano Islands. Japanese positions on these islands will suffer months of relentless bombardment.

SEPTEMBER 1

LAND WAR, *PHILIPPINES*

The US submarine *Narwhal* lands men and supplies on the eastern coast of Luzon in the Philippines, beginning the build-up of troops and logistics ready for the main Philippines offensive.

AIR WAR, *BONIN/VOLCANO ISLANDS*

The Japanese suffer heavy losses of material during the US navy's latest bombing offensive against the Bonin and Volcano Islands. A US Navy communiqué lists the damage as including around 50 Japanese aircraft destroyed either on the ground or in air combat; around 15 ships sunk; and extensive damage to shore installations, hangers and ammunition and fuel dumps.

SEPTEMBER 2

SEA WAR, *WAKE ISLAND*

A US naval task group consisting of one aircraft carrier, three cruisers and three destroyers bombards Japanese positions on Wake Island. The island is one of the most isolated outposts of the

▼ *Two M4 Shermans burn after being hit by Japanese anti-tank rounds on Guam. These are M4A1 versions of the Sherman, armed with a 75mm main gun and three machine guns.*

DECISIVE WEAPONS

THE US TORPEDO SCANDAL

For well over a year, the US Navy's submarine campaign against Japanese shipping in the Pacific was dogged by problems with its primary armament, the Mark XIV torpedo. There were two main problems: the depth-control mechanism of the torpedo was malfunctioning and directed the torpedo too far beneath its target (it ran at about 3–4m/10–12ft below set depth). Also, the torpedoes were equipped with the Mk VI magnetic influence exploder mechanism, an unreliable proximity detonator designed to explode the torpedo underneath a ship rather than on contact. The Germans had already abandoned magnetic detonators, finding that they were affected by magnetic variations at different longitudes and latitudes. US submarines would engage Japanese ships with spreads of four or five torpedoes at close range in good conditions, and none would explode despite being on target. No decision was taken until July 24, 1943, when Admiral Lockwood, a severe critic of the Mk XIV torpedo, finally ordered the deactivation of the Mk VI magnetic detonator and switched to contact detonators.

Unfortunately, problems continued. US submarines began reporting that, although the torpedoes were now striking the targets, many were

A US Tench class submarine on patrol in the Pacific.

failing to detonate. In a landmark incident, the submarine USS *Tinosa* fired 14 torpedoes at the Japanese tanker *Tonan Maru 3*, hitting the ship with at least half of them, none of which exploded. Subsequent tests found the detonator mechanism had a 70 percent failure rate if the torpedo struck at a 90-degree angle. Only when this problem was resolved in mid-1943 did US torpedoes become effective weapons.

Japanese Empire, and will be bypassed by the main US advance across the Pacific towards the Philippines and the Ryukyu Islands.

SEPTEMBER 6-8

AIR WAR, *CAROLINE ISLANDS*

A massive naval force, including 16 aircraft carriers and numerous cruisers and destroyers, attacks the Caroline Islands. Targets on Yap, Ulithi and the Palau Islands are struck. Although most of the Carolines are bypassed, the US hopes to establish a naval anchorage on Ulithi Atoll.

SEPTEMBER 8-11

AIR WAR, *PHILIPPINES*

US carrier aircraft from Vice-Admiral Mitscher's fast carrier task force make a three-day bombing attack against Japanese industrial, naval and aviation targets around Mindanao. Airfields at Del Monte, Valencia, Cagayan, Buayan and Davao are

targeted; and, on the first day of the attack, 60 Japanese aircraft are destroyed.

SEPTEMBER 11-16

POLITICS, *ALLIES*

US President Roosevelt and British Prime Minister Churchill meet together for their eighth war summit, known as the Octagon Conference. Although much of the discussion centres on the European theatre, the two leaders also establish grounds for Anglo-American cooperation in the production of the atomic bomb after the war. They also agree that the atomic bomb may be used operationally against Japan, following a warning.

SEPTEMBER 15

LAND WAR, *PALAU ISLANDS*

The 1st Marine Division under Major-General W.H. Rupertus is landed at

▶ *A US destroyer squadron in the Solomons. By mid-1944, US submarines and surface combatants were inflicting major losses on Japanese merchant shipping.*

Peleliu in the Palau Islands, as the US begins its operation to take the most westerly point in the Carolines. For the central Pacific forces, the Palau Islands are the last major island land mass before the Philippines. Taking the islands will provide a jumping-off point for landings on the east coast of the Philippines, as well as giving vital air bases to support Philippine operations. By nightfall on the 15th, the Marines have consolidated the beachhead and captured the airfield at the southern end of the island.

LAND WAR, *DUTCH EAST INDIES*

US troops are landed at Morotai in the eastern territories of the Dutch East Indies. Resistance is light, although the island is strategically important as it sits astride the entrance to the Celebes Sea, off the southern coast of the Philippines, and is a useful starting point for further operations into the Dutch East Indies.

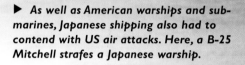

▶ As well as American warships and submarines, Japanese shipping also had to contend with US air attacks. Here, a B-25 Mitchell strafes a Japanese warship.

SEPTEMBER 16

SEA WAR, *SOUTH CHINA SEA*
The Japanese escort carrier *Unyo* is sunk in the South China Sea by the submarine USS *Barb*. Although the US surface fleet has no presence in the South China Sea, US submarines are effectively interdicting Japanese supply convoys running between the Dutch East Indies and Japanese forces in Southeast Asia.

LAND WAR, *CAROLINE ISLANDS*
US Army troops of the 81st Infantry Division go ashore on Angaur Island, the southernmost of the Palau Islands. They establish a beachhead and advance inland against light resistance.

SEPTEMBER 17

LAND WAR, *CAROLINE ISLANDS*
US Marines advancing up Peleliu experience heavy opposition. Japanese forces lay down withering fire from mortars and artillery. Many of these weapons are subsequently destroyed by accurate aerial close-support strikes and naval counter-battery fire. US progress is steady, with the Marines capturing Asias and killing, to date, nearly 6000 Japanese soldiers.

SEPTEMBER 19

SEA WAR, *PACIFIC*
A typical US Navy communiqué (No 554) from this period reports 29 enemy cargo vessels sunk on this date.

LAND WAR, *CAROLINE ISLANDS*
US Marines capture Ngardololok and flush out most Japanese resistance on the eastern coast of Peleliu. They also take Peleliu airfield, capturing 77 fighter aircraft, 36 bombers and 4 transport planes, although most are badly damaged. However, the Japanese are deeply embedded in fortified positions and are well armed, and the advance is painfully slow. US estimates now put the Japanese death toll on Peleliu at 8792. On Angaur Island, most organized Japanese resistance has now collapsed, with 600 Japanese killed.

SEPTEMBER 20–24

AIR WAR, *PHILIPPINES*
Japanese aviators suffer terribly during a massive US air raid against Japanese ships and installations at Manila Bay, Subic Bay, Clark Field, Nichols Field and Cavite Naval Base. The US reports (on

SEPTEMBER 23

the 24th) 169 Japanese aircraft shot down in aerial combat, and a further 188 destroyed on the ground. In addition, more than 50 Japanese transport and cargo vessels are sunk and a further 46 damaged.

SEPTEMBER 23

LAND WAR, *CAROLINE ISLANDS*

US Army troops are landed at Ulithi Atoll in the Carolines as part of the first stage of converting the atoll into a US naval base. The island was abandoned by the Japanese in August.

SEPTEMBER 29

SEA WAR, *PHILIPPINES*

The submarine USS *Narwhal*, always active in the waters of the Philippine Islands, picks up 81 Allied prisoners of war following the sinking of the Japanese vessel *Shinyo Maru*. More than 2000 Allied prisoners went down on the ship.

SEPTEMBER 30

LAND WAR, *PALAU ISLANDS*

Peleliu falls under US control, the US 1st Marine Division having fought metre by metre into the northernmost extremities of the island. Casualties have been appalling on both sides.
Almost all of the 10,600 Japanese soldiers, commanded by Colonel Nakasawa Kunio, have been killed, although 150 become POWs. The Marines have lost 1252 killed and 5274 wounded, a high toll for an island only 18km (11 miles) square. However, intense fighting continues in several pockets around the island, particularly on the aptly named "Bloody Nose Ridge" where Japanese survivors refuse to surrender.

▼ *The US invasion of Peleliu. To the left can be seen small amphibious vessels carrying US Marines, while in the centre the battleship USS* Pennsylvania *shells enemy positions.*

▲ *The US 1st Marine Division heads for Peleliu. The plan was to land on the western beaches, three regiments abreast.*

OCTOBER 2

STRATEGY, *BURMA*

Lord Louis Mountbatten, the supreme commander of SEAC, gives orders for an Allied offensive in Burma against Mandalay. Mountbatten has maintained pressure on the Japanese Fifteenth Army after its defeat in the Imphal offensive by ordering the campaign to continue during the monsoon season.

OCTOBER 4

LAND WAR, *PALAU ISLANDS*

US Marines and infantry battle to remove the final pockets of Japanese resistance in the Palau Islands. Although the islands were effectively secured in late September, the mopping-up operations have been costly. Between September 25 and October 5, 336 US soldiers have been killed and 1707 wounded. The Japanese death toll on Peleliu and Angaur has been put at 2755 in the same period.

OCTOBER 6

POLITICS, *CHINA*

General Joseph Stilwell is removed from his post as chief of staff to the

▲ *Two Sherman tanks assist the Marine advance on Peleliu. Taking the island cost 6526 US casualties, including 1252 killed.*

Chinese Nationalist leader Chiang Kaishek. Relations between the two men had been frequently difficult, and suggestions by President Roosevelt that Stilwell take charge of all Chinese forces in the war were received badly by Chiang. Stilwell maintains control over Chinese troops in Burma and southern Yunnan Province.

OCTOBER 9

AIR WAR, *RYUKYU ISLANDS*

US carrier aircraft take the war close to the Japanese mainland in a major air attack against naval and shore in-

stallations in the Ryukyu Islands. In an attack that achieves complete surprise, 75 Japanese aircraft are destroyed on the ground and 14 shot down. Thirty-eight ships are either sunk or damaged.

STRATEGY, *PACIFIC*

Admiral Nimitz informs Lieutenant-General Holland M. Smith, the US Marine Corps commander in the Pacific, that his next target will be the island of Iwo Jima. Meanwhile, US forces in the Philippines move into the Lingayen Gulf.

SEA WAR, *PACIFIC*

US Navy surface vessels conduct a 15-hour bombardment of enemy shore installations on Marcus Island. The attack is the first surface ship bombardment directed at the island, which offers the

▶ *The reason for the US assault to capture Peleliu – the island's airstrip. The craters were caused by US naval gunfire.*

US a forward base in the western Pacific less than 1600km (1000 miles) from the Japanese mainland.

OCTOBER 10

LAND WAR, *PALAU ISLANDS*

The 1st Marine Division steadily flushes out Japanese defenders from Bloody Nose Ridge. Many of the Japanese are killed today when US fire detonates an ammunition dump held within the ridge's cave system.

AIR WAR, *NORTH BORNEO*

The oil refineries at Balikpapen are devastated by a US raid by B-24 bombers. Oil is one of Japan's most

threatened raw materials. Prior to the war it imported nearly 80 percent of its oil supplies, around 60 percent of that coming from the US. The Balikpapen refinery alone produces 40 percent of Japan's oil imports at this stage of the war.

OCTOBER 10–15

AIR WAR, *FORMOSA*

The US continues to demonstrate its air superiority in a massive five-day air campaign against the island of Formosa. During one action on the 13th, 124 Japanese fighters are shot down in a massive aerial dogfight. More than 95 further aircraft are destroyed on the ground. US losses are 22 aircraft. The total Japanese losses in the Formosa-Ryukyus-Luzon area at the end of the five days are 350 aircraft destroyed on the ground and 596 shot down. In addition, more than 70 Japanese cargo, oiler and escort ships are sunk.

◀ *Marines on the beach at Peleliu. It soon became apparent that the naval bombardment had not eliminated the enemy's heavy weapons positions.*

OCTOBER 15

AIR WAR, *MANILA BAY*

The Japanese attempt to break the US build-up against the Philippines. A large air strike is launched against a carrier task force in Manila Bay, but does insignificant damage while losing 30 aircraft to US fighters and anti-aircraft fire.

▼ *General Walter Krueger, the commander of the US Sixth Army.*

▲ *A Curtiss Helldiver, its arrestor hook down prior to a carrier landing, returns from a bombing mission against the island of Formosa in October.*

OCTOBER 20

LAND WAR, *PHILIPPINES*

The US invasion of the Philippines begins in earnest with X and XXIV Corps of the US Sixth Army under General Krueger. Troops go ashore along a 40km (25-mile) stretch of east Leyte coastline between Dulag and Tacloban, and initially experience only light opposition by soldiers of the Japanese Thirty-Fifth Army that occupies Leyte. On a strategic level, the landing at

Leyte threatens to split Japan's Philippine garrison in half, isolating Japanese forces on Mindanao in the south from those occupying Luzon.

OCTOBER 21

LAND WAR, *PALAU ISLANDS*

Final Japanese resistance on Angaur collapses, with 1300 Japanese military

▼ *The Japanese airfield at Karenko, Formosa, is hit by US bombs. This was one of the targets in a five-day campaign that destroyed 946 Japanese aircraft.*

KEY PERSONALITIES

LORD LOUIS MOUNTBATTEN

Lord Louis Mountbatten (1900–79) was appointed C-in-C SEAC in August 1943 during the Quebec Conference, at the same time being promoted to admiral (the youngest in the history of the Royal Navy). Mountbatten was known for his vanity and desire for power, which at times led to poor military judgement. Other military leaders frequently overrode his operational decisions in the Far East, but he certainly made significant improvements to British campaigning in Burma. The three cornerstones of his Burma policy were morale, monsoon and malaria. He raised Allied morale in Burma mainly through capitalizing on the victories at Imphal and Kohima, promoting the idea that Japanese invincibility was a myth. "Monsoon" refers to his policy of maintaining the Allied campaign through the five-month monsoon season to enforce the Japanese collapse. As a corollary, he created the Medical Advisory Division to tackle tropical diseases such as malaria, which cost the Allies 120 men for every single battle casualty. By 1945, only 13 percent of Allied casualties were illness related.

Such policies aided the British victory in Burma, and Mountbatten had further distinguishing moments in the Pacific war. He knew about the planned use of the atomic bomb in 1945, and received the surrender of more than 600,000 Japanese troops at Singapore on September 12, 1945. When taking the Japanese surrender, he insisted on Japanese officers giving up their swords to induce loss of face.

dead on the small island. US losses are 264 fatalities.

LAND WAR, *PHILIPPINES*

Japanese resistance to the Leyte landings starts to thicken with an intensive Japanese counterattack. It is beaten off with 600 Japanese killed, but 21,500 Japanese soldiers remain on Leyte, most of them taking up positions inland. In total, there are 225,000 Japanese soldiers in the Philippines under the command of General Yamashita.

OCTOBER 22

SEA WAR, *LEYTE GULF*

The whole Japanese Combined Fleet sets sail in "Operation Sho", an attempt to crush the Allied landings in the southern Philippines. The operation is divided into two strikes approaching from opposite directions. From the west, sailing from British North Borneo, is the First Striking Force under Vice-Admiral Kurita. This itself is split into two parts. Kurita's own unit (known to the US as "Centre Force") consists of five battleships, twelve cruisers and fifteen destroyers, and is sailing to the northeast where it intends to move through the Subuyan Sea and attack the US Seventh Fleet from the north. At the same time, a second group ("Southern Force") under Vice-Admiral Nishimura and Vice-Admiral Shima, consisting of two battleships, four cruisers and eight destroyers, intends to attack the Leyte landings from the south through the Surigao Strait.

As these two forces sail from Borneo, approaching the Philippines from the north is the Carrier Decoy Force under Ozawa, featuring four carriers, two battleships, four cruisers and eight destroyers. Its mission is to draw the US Third Fleet away from Leyte so

◄ *US troops land at Tacloban in the Philippines. The US amphibious force for the invasion was very large, comprising 738 ships of the US Navy's Third Fleet.*

▲ A deck hand rushes to release the arrestor hook of a Grumman Avenger that has just landed on a US aircraft carrier at the Battle of Leyte Gulf.

that Kurita's vessels can destroy the American landings.

The scene is set for the Battle of Leyte Gulf. The name "Sho" given to the Japanese operation means "victory", a testimony to the importance of the action for the battle-scarred Japanese Imperial Navy.

▼ The 14in guns of the USS Pennsylvania open fire against enemy positions at Leyte Gulf. During the naval battle the ship fired a total of 866 14in rounds.

OCTOBER 23

SEA WAR, *LEYTE GULF*
Operation Sho suffers its first casualties and loses the element of surprise. Two US submarines off Palawan Island spot the ships of Kurita's First Striking Force and sink the cruisers *Atago* and *Maya*. The Japanese positions are reported to the US carrier units of Task Force 38, US Third Fleet, which set sail to intercept Japanese vessels in the Sibuyan Sea.

OCTOBER 24

SEA WAR, *LEYTE GULF*
The Battle of Leyte Gulf begins in earnest. Vice-Admiral Mitscher's carrier aircraft launch a massive air assault on Kurita's Centre Force and Nishimura/Shima's Southern Force, while Japanese aircraft reply with their own strikes against US shipping around the Philippines. The US suffers numerous ships damaged, including the light carrier USS *Princeton* (she later sinks

▲ The Japanese battleship **Nagato** (foreground) and a cruiser under air attack at Leyte Gulf. **Nagato** survived the battle, and indeed the war.

following magazine fires), the light cruiser USS *Birmingham* and five destroyers. Japanese losses, however, are more severe. The massive battleship *Musashi* – the largest warship ever built, and sister ship of the mighty *Yamato* – is bombed and torpedoed to the bottom of the ocean, although it takes 19 torpedoes and 17 bombs to do so. Other losses include the destroyer *Wakaba*. Towards the end of the day, Kurita's Centre Force turns northwards as if retreating, but later switches back and heads for the San Bernardino Strait, north of Leyte.

OCTOBER 24–25

SEA WAR, *LEYTE GULF*
The Japanese Southern Force is engaged in the night by the warships of Task Group 77. A

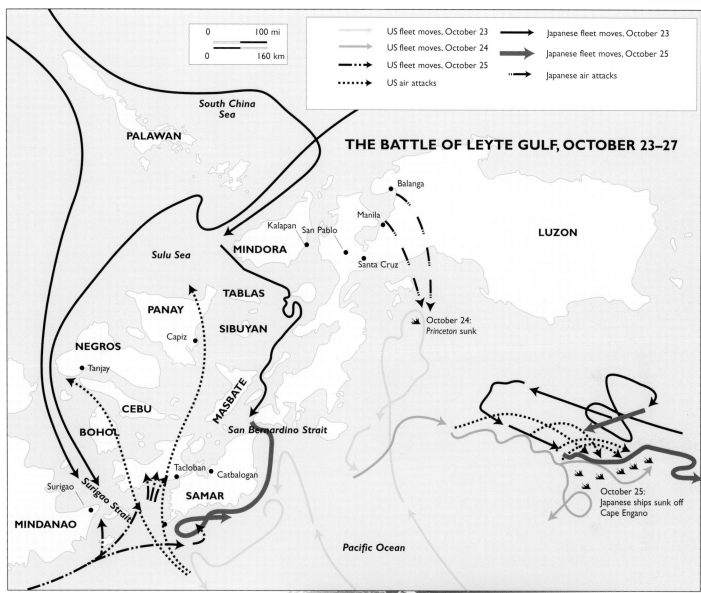

THE BATTLE OF LEYTE GULF, OCTOBER 23–27

Legend:
- US fleet moves, October 23
- US fleet moves, October 24
- US fleet moves, October 25
- US air attacks
- Japanese fleet moves, October 23
- Japanese fleet moves, October 25
- Japanese air attacks

October 24: *Princeton* sunk

October 25: Japanese ships sunk off Cape Engano

Map labels: South China Sea, PALAWAN, Sulu Sea, MINDORA, TABLAS, PANAY, Capiz, SIBUYAN, NEGROS, Tanjay, MASBATE, CEBU, San Bernardino Strait, BOHOL, Tacloban, Catbalogan, SAMAR, Surigao, Surigao Strait, MINDANAO, Pacific Ocean, Kalapan, San Pablo, Santa Cruz, Manila, Balanga, LUZON

▲ The Battle of Leyte Gulf was the last great naval engagement of the Pacific war, and signalled the end of the Japanese Navy's effectiveness.

masterful torpedo run by US destroyers in the early hours of the 25th, followed by a huge gun barrage from cruisers and battleships, devastates Nishimura's entire force (two battleships, one heavy cruiser and four destroyers) in less than two hours, only one destroyer surviving. Shima's unit suffers two cruisers sunk and a battleship damaged, and begins to retreat.

OCTOBER 25

SEA WAR, *LEYTE GULF*

US Task Force 38 heads northwards to intercept Ozawa's carrier force, believing the Japanese Centre and Southern Forces to be in retreat. However,

▶ The Japanese carrier Zuiho under attack during the battle off Cape Engano on October 25.

OCTOBER 26

Kurita's Centre Force has turned back and attacks a US escort carrier group known as TG 77.4.3. "Taffy 3", under Rear-Admiral Sprague, is heavily out-numbered and outgunned by the Japanese force, which includes four battleships. Despite suffering severe damage, including three destroyers and two escort carriers sunk (the USS *St Lo* is sunk later that day by a suicide air-craft in a kamikaze strike), most of TG 77.4.3 manages to escape. Carrier aircraft sink the Japanese cruisers *Kumano*, *Chokai* and *Chikuma*. Kurita withdraws, believing he is engaging the bulk of Task Force 38 – which is actually heading north.

Task Force 38 finds and engages Ozawa's Carrier Decoy Force with overwhelming airpower around first light on the morning of the 25th. The Japanese carriers are chronically de-pleted of aircraft, and in a day of relent-less bombardment all four carriers are sunk (*Zuikaku*, *Zuiho*, *Chitose* and *Chiyoda*) plus five other warships.

OCTOBER 26

SEA WAR, *LEYTE GULF*
The Battle of Leyte Gulf ends in a mas-sive US victory. Several more Japanese cruisers and destroyers are sunk today by pursuing US aircraft. The final tally of Japanese shipping sunk is four air-craft carriers, three battleships, ten cruisers, eleven destroyers and one submarine, with most other Japanese ships severely damaged. In addition, 10,000 sailors and 500 aircraft are also lost. The Battle of Leyte Gulf marks the undeniable collapse of Japanese naval power in the Pacific. From this point on, the suicide air strikes that had their inauguration over Leyte Gulf become an increasing feature of a desperate Japanese military that can no longer oppose the mighty US Navy.

OCTOBER 31

AIR WAR, *PACIFIC*
US Navy communiqué No 170 makes an assessment of Japanese air losses be-tween August 30, 1944 and today's date. The report is compiled by the Third and Seventh Carrier Fleets. Be-tween the two dates, the US lost 300 aircraft, but the Japanese suffered a cat-astrophic 2594 aircraft losses – 1462 shot down and 1132 destroyed on the ground. Even allowing for some pilot exaggeration, it is clear that the Japan-ese Air Force is utterly outclassed and outnumbered in the Pacific war.

STRATEGY AND TACTICS

AERIAL KAMIKAZE ATTACKS
On October 19, 1944, Vice-Admiral Onishi Takijino ordered the formation of a kamikaze force to intercept Allied shipping around the Philippines, officially termed Tokubetsu Koge-ki Tai (Special Attack Group). The term kamikaze literally means "divine wind", refer-ring to the typhoons that destroyed Kublai Khan's fleets in 1274 and 1281, saving Japan from a Mongol invasion. Kamikaze pilots were all volunteers, usually very young, who were given the most rudimentary flying training and piloted old or battle-repaired aircraft, usually with only enough fuel to reach their attack destination. Fed on a

Bushido ideology of death being preferable to defeat, they accepted that to return from a kamikaze mission invited disgrace.

The kamikaze pilots inflicted a horrifying experience on the sailors and soldiers of the US Pacific Fleet. Although hundreds of suicide aircraft were shot down before reaching their targets (the pilots did not have experience of air combat, and could not fly low beneath US radar), thousands still got through. The first mass attack of 55 kamikaze aircraft came on October 23–26, 1944, around Leyte, sinking five ships (in-cluding the carrier USS *St Lo*) and damaging 40 others, 23 severely. In April 1945, the kamikaze attacks reached a frenzied pitch off Okinawa. Around 1900 suicide aircraft attacked in "kikusui" (floating chrysanthe-mum) waves of up to 320 planes at a time. Thirty-six US ships were sunk, and three hundred and sixty-eight damaged. In total, Japan lost 5000 pilots in suicide actions dur-ing the war.

◀ *A group of kamikaze pilots are given a ceremonial cup of sake prior to their one-way mission.*

NOVEMBER 1

AIR WAR, *US*
As an indicator of Japanese despera-tion, 9000 balloons carrying explo-sive charges are released from the Japanese mainland by army forces. The balloons are meant to cross the Pacific Ocean on prevailing winds and detonate in the US. Few balloons make the journey successfully.

AIR WAR, *LEYTE GULF*
Kamikaze attacks intensify around Leyte Gulf. Today, the destroyer USS *Abner Road* is sunk and the destroyers USS *Anderson*, USS *Claxton* and USS *Ammen* are badly damaged by suicide attacks. Dive-bombers dam-age two other destroyers.

NOVEMBER 2

LAND WAR, *PALAU ISLANDS*
Japanese troops are still holding out on Mount Umurbrogol, causing heavy casualties among US forces.

▶ *Fulfiling a pledge he made nearly three years earlier, General Douglas MacArthur (second from left) returns to the Philippines on October 20, 1944.*

◀ *The escort carrier USS* **St Lo** *after being hit by a kamikaze attack on October 25 at Leyte. She later sunk.*

NOVEMBER 3

POLITICS, *PACIFIC*

Admiral Nimitz announces that Rear-Admiral Walden L. Ainsworth is now Commander, Cruisers, and Commander, Destroyers, Pacific Fleet. As a veteran of every major naval action in the south Pacific area since December 1942, Ainsworth replaces Rear-Admiral James L. Kauffman.

NOVEMBER 5

AIR WAR, *SINGAPORE*

Fifty-three B-29 bombers from the Twentieth US Army Air Force make a round trip of 5950km (3700 miles) from Calcutta to bomb coastal installations around Singapore and the Pangkalan Brandon oil refinery on the island of Sumatra.

NOVEMBER 6

AIR WAR, *LUZON*

US Hellcat fighters, Avenger torpedo planes and Helldiver dive-bombers attack Japanese airfields and shipping installations throughout southern Luzon. A heavy dogfight results after 80 Japanese fighters intercept the US force over

KEY PERSONALITIES

ADMIRAL HALSEY

Admiral William Frederick Halsey (1882–1959), an expert in the use of destroyers in the early 1930s, was attracted to the new technology and theory surrounding naval airpower during the pre-war years. Indeed in 1935, at the age of 52, he qualified as a pilot. He became one of the US Navy's most talented air power commanders, and was in command of the US Pacific Fleet's airpower when war broke out. In the difficult early months of the war, his aggressive counterstrikes, including the Doolittle Raid on April 18, 1942, led the press to nickname him "Bull" Halsey. Though he missed the Battle of Midway through ill health, he was given tactical command in the south Pacific in 1943, specifically to give more belligerence to the efforts of the naval leadership. As much as his bravery and belligerence was appreciated by the common soldier, his aggressive tendencies occasionally led him to run dangerous risks – most notably at the Battle of Leyte Gulf. His penchant for attacking the Japanese whenever possible caused him to fall for the Japanese attempt to lure him away from protecting MacArthur's men landing on Leyte. Had it not have been for mistakes on the Japanese side, then total disaster could have befallen the US forces because of his actions. Nonetheless, he alternated command of the Pacific Fleet with Admiral Spruance until the end of the war.

NOVEMBER 2–3

AIR WAR, *PACIFIC*

The Japanese attempt to reduce enemy airpower by attacking US airstrips at Tacloban, Leyte, and at Saipan and Tinian in the Mariana Islands. The attacks are extremely costly for the Japanese, many of the aircraft being brought down by accurate anti-aircraft fire.

▲ *A Japanese merchant ship carrying ammunition explodes following a direct hit on its cargo from a US dive-bomber.*

Clark Field. Fifty-eight of the Japanese aircraft are shot down in the incident, and twenty-five more later that day. More than 100 Japanese aircraft are destroyed on the ground; by November 7, that figure has risen to 327. One heavy cruiser is left sinking in Manila harbour, and ten other ships are either sunk or damaged.

NOVEMBER 7

ESPIONAGE, *TOKYO*
The Soviet spy Richard Sorge is executed in Tokyo, having been held in prison for three years.

LAND WAR, *NORTHERN BURMA*
The Chinese 22nd Division crosses the Irrawaddy River near Shwegu. The 22nd Division is part of a major thrust by Allied units to encircle the Japanese Thirty-Third Army in its positions between

Lashio and Mogok. Although the advance has been hampered by politics (General Stilwell having lost his position as Chiang Kai-shek's chief of staff and Commander of the Northern Area Combat Command), it is steadily making progress.

NOVEMBER 7–8

LAND WAR, *PALAU ISLANDS*
A Japanese force of around 200 men land on Ngeregong Island, northeast of Peleliu in the Palau Group. Although the island was previously occupied by a small unit of US Marines, it is now deserted. However, the US responds vigorously, imposing a naval blockade on the Denges Passage – the sea route taken by the Japanese to the island – before pounding the island with naval and aerial attacks.

◄ *When the Japanese tried to supply their troops fighting on Letye, the convoy was intercepted at Ormoc Bay. Here, a B-25 attacks a destroyer in the bay.*

NOVEMBER 8

LAND WAR, *BURMA*

Troops of the 7th and 17th Indian Divisions take Fort White, an important point on the Imphal–Kalemyo road near Tiddim. The British IV Corps is pushing directly south of Imphal

◄ *Men of the 7th Indian Division advancing to Fort White, northern Burma, which they captured on November 8. The fort was originally a British outpost.*

down the Kabaw Valley out on to the western side of the Pondaung Range. Its objective is to reach Pakokku to the southwest of Mandalay, cutting off forces of the Japanese Fifteenth Army as Britain's XXXIII Corps drives down on Mandalay from the north.

NOVEMBER 10

AIR WAR, *PHILIPPINES*

The Japanese attempt to run a 10-ship supply convoy through to Japanese troops on Leyte, but it is intercepted by US Third Fleet carrier aircraft just outside Ormoc Bay. The convoy is massacred, with nine of the ships (four transports and five destroyers) being sunk and the remaining destroyer badly damaged. Thirteen of the twenty Japanese aircraft providing air cover for the convoy are shot down.

LAND WAR, *CHINA*

The Japanese offensive into southern China makes further progress, capturing the US air bases at Kweilin and Liuchow in Kwangsi Province.

NOVEMBER 11

SEA WAR, *JAPAN*

The Japanese launch the aircraft carrier *Shinano*, a 69,148-tonne (68,059-ton)

vessel that is supposedly bomb-proof owing to a steel and concrete construction. She is not torpedo-proof, however, and on November 29 she is sunk by the submarine USS *Archerfish*.

NOVEMBER 12

AIR WAR, *MANILA BAY*

US carrier aircraft damage one light cruiser and two destroyers in air raids over Manila Bay. The destroyers are devastated in massive magazine explosions caused by accurate bomb and torpedo hits.

▼ *The Japanese provided air cover for supply convoys to Leyte, but the aircraft were shot out of the skies. The last moments of this Zero were caught on film.*

KEY MOMENTS

RICHARD SORGE AND THE TOKYO SPY RING

Richard Sorge (1895–1944) was one of the most influential spies of the war. Although born in Baku, Azerbaijan, in 1895, Sorge was raised in Germany where he became active in his youth in the Communist Party. He fled to Moscow in 1920 following German anti-communist activities, and there was recruited into Soviet intelligence. He returned to Germany in 1921, and worked his way up through civil service positions. In the 1930s, he received postings to China, then went to Japan to work as a newspaper correspondent and later as press attaché to the German Embassy. It was from there that Sorge did the bulk of his spying work, and he recruited a network of individuals (code-named "Ramsay") to gather his intelligence from many sources. One of them, Ozaki Hotsumi, was a senior adviser to the Japanese prime minister.

During World War II, Sorge provided some valuable intelligence to the Soviets, including the date of the German invasion of Russia, although Stalin ignored this intelligence, and that Japan would not attack the USSR in Siberia in 1941. Regarding the Pacific theatre, Sorge discovered that Japan was planning to attack the US and Allied interests in Southeast Asia and the Pacific. The last message sent read: "Japanese carrier force attacking United States Navy at Pearl Harbor, probably dawn, November 6".

In September 1941, Japanese intelligence officers started to unravel the Tokyo spy ring following routine operations – on October 18, Sorge was finally arrested. He was tortured for six days before confessing. The next three years were spent in prison, during which time he had to write a 50,000-word report detailing his espionage activities. On November 7, 1944, in Sugamo prison, he was marched into the courtyard and hanged.

NOVEMBER 13

LAND WAR, *PALAU ISLANDS*
The last elements of Japanese resistance on Bloody Ridge are wiped out.

NOVEMBER 13-14

SEA WAR, *MANILA BAY*
The Japanese cruiser *Kiso* is sunk and five destroyers severely damaged during a raid on Manila Bay by US aircraft.

NOVEMBER 14

LAND WAR, *PALAU ISLANDS*
Troops of the 81st Infantry Division reoccupy Ngeregong. They meet no Japanese resistance, which has been crushed by air and naval actions.

NOVEMBER 17

SEA WAR, *PACIFIC*
The Japanese escort carrier *Shinyo* is sunk by the submarine USS *Spadefish* in the Yellow Sea. The first torpedo out of four hit the stern, instantly disabling the turbo-electric motors and stopping the carrier. The impact detonated the poorly protected fuel tanks and caused a tremendous explosion and fire. Other hits followed, and *Shinyo* becomes a blazing inferno, begins to list rapidly to starboard and settle aft. More than 700 of her crew of 900 are killed. At this stage of the Pacific campaign, the US submarine war has been boosted by increasing numbers of British submarines being

▼ A crowd of engineers and ground crew personnel watch a US B-29 Superfortress take off from the airstrip on Saipan to begin the first B-29 mission against Tokyo.

▲ USS Intrepid *under kamikaze attack off Luzon in late November. Two Japanese aircraft hit the aircraft carrier, forcing her to return to the US for repairs.*

deployed from the Atlantic and Mediterranean to the Pacific. An Admiralty statement on November 15 reveals that British submarines have sunk 69 Japanese vessels in five days.

NOVEMBER 19

LAND WAR, *BURMA*
The British Fourteenth Army under General William Slim begins a major operation to capitalize on the Japanese defeat at Imphal and Kohima, and hopefully clear the Japanese from Burma. "Operation Extended Capital" involves the British IV Corps around Sittaung and XXXIII Corps at Mawlaik making the push across the Chindwin River, recapturing Mandalay, Rangoon and Meiktila, and destroying General Shihachi Kata-

mura's Japanese Fifteenth Army in the process. Initial objectives include the Japanese airfields at Yeu and Shwebo, the capture of which will help efficient resupply by air. To the north of British operations, Chinese and US troops formerly under the command of General Stilwell are pushing down towards Indaw.

NOVEMBER 21

SEA WAR, *WESTERN PACIFIC*
The Japanese battleship *Kongo* is sunk by the submarine USS *Sealion* in the

▲ *A British IV Corps 25-pounder in action against Japanese forces in Pinwe, Burma. The town was a railway centre and was doggedly defended by the Japanese.*

Formosa Strait. *Kongo* was actually built in England as a battlecruiser, and delivered to the Japanese in 1913. The ship was modernized in 1936–37 to gain battleship status.

NOVEMBER 24

STRATEGIC BOMBING, *TOKYO*

The USAAF launches its first long-range bombing mission on Tokyo using 111 B-29 Superfortress bombers. However, only 24 manage to drop their bombs on target.

NOVEMBER 25

KAMIKAZE, *PHILIPPINES*

Around Luzon, Japanese kamikaze aircraft severely damage four US aircraft carriers: USS *Essex*, USS *Intrepid*, USS *Hancock* and USS *Cabot*. However, Japanese shipping also has a bad day, with the heavy cruiser *Kumano* and the cruiser *Yasoshima* being sunk by US carrier aircraft.

NOVEMBER 29

AIR WAR, *IWO JIMA*

US B-24 Liberator and B-25 Mitchell bombers continue the softening up of Iwo Jima, concentrating their attacks against airfields.

NOVEMBER 30

LAND WAR, *CHINA*

As the Japanese offensive in southern China gains ground, Chiang Kai-shek

▲ *Japanese shipping under attack from US carrier aircraft in Manila Bay at the end of November.*

withdraws his 22nd and 38th Divisions from Burma and re-deploys them around Kunming.

DECEMBER 4

LAND WAR, *BURMA*

The British Fourteenth Army establishes three bridgeheads on the Chindwin River as part of Operation Extended Capital. From here, XXXIII Corps will drive southeast towards Schewbo and

Mandalay in a two-pronged attack; while, in the south, IV Corps will push down the Kabbaw Valley aiming towards Tilin and Pakokku, roughly 160km (100 miles) southwest of Mandalay itself. In the far north, the 19th Indian Division begins a decoy offensive out from Sittaung towards Indaw.

DECEMBER 6

AIR WAR, *MARIANA ISLANDS*
A US B-29 Superfortress is destroyed and two others damaged during an early morning air raid by ten Japanese Betty bombers. Six of the attackers are shot down by anti-aircraft fire.

DECEMBER 8

AIR WAR, *IWO JIMA*
The US Air Force begins one of the most intensive aerial campaigns of World War II, a 72-day bombardment of Iwo Jima by B-24 and B-25 bombers. The bombardment is preparation for the US invasion of Iwo Jima sched-

▶ *The one bright spot for Tokyo in late 1944 was southern China, where its offensive made good progress. Here, a Japanese river boat searches for the enemy.*

▲ *Admiral Nimitz (left) was made Commander-in-Chief of the US Pacific Fleet and Pacific Ocean Areas at the end of 1944. On his left is Admiral Spruance.*

uled for mid-February 1945, although the island has already sustained heavy air attacks against its shipping and shore installations.

LOGISTICS, *PACIFIC*
The commander of the US Third Fleet, Admiral William F. Halsey, proudly announces the achievements of US oiling vessels in maintaining US Navy and air operations in the Pacific. During September and October 1944, oilers had supplied the carrier task force with more than one hundred million gallons of fuel, enough to run every car in every major US city for an entire year.

DECEMBER 10

LAND WAR, *PHILIPPINES*
US troops on Leyte take the main Japanese supply base at Ormoc on the west coast of the island, the US 7th and 77th Divisions having made an amphibious landing in the area three days earlier. The US action on Leyte has followed three broad lines of advance:

▲ A US destroyer opens fire during the invasion of Mindoro. Naval support for the invasion included six escort carriers, three battleships and six cruisers.

through the north of Leyte up the Leyte Valley; across the centre towards Ormoc then northwest up the Ormoc Valley; and directly southwards following the coastlines. Fighting is heavy, but the US soldiers are making steady progress. The plight of Suzuki's Thirty-Fifth Army on Leyte is desperate, especially now the fall of Ormoc has cut his troops off from naval resupply.

LAND WAR, *CHINA*
The Ichi-Go offensive brings the Japanese victories not experienced elsewhere in the Far East. Throughout November, Japanese forces have occupied southern China up to the borders of French Indochina. Today, the advancing armies meet up with Japan's Indochinese garrison forces, thus providing a new supply route for the offensive through the Indochina to China rail link, which stretches across the entire length of China up into Mongolia.

DECEMBER 13

SEA WAR, *PHILIPPINES*
US shipping around the Philippines suffers increased suicide attacks. Today, the

cruiser USS *Nashville* and the destroyer USS *Haraden* are both damaged by kamikaze aircraft.

DECEMBER 15

LAND WAR, *BURMA*
British troops in the north of Operation Extended Capital meet up with General Stilwell's Chinese and US

▲ The crew of a US Navy Patrol Craft Escort vessel scans the sky for enemy aircraft following a kamikaze attack on the ship behind. Mindoro, December 15.

forces at Banmauk, having captured Bhamo. This combined group now focuses directly southwards towards Shwebo and Mandalay, and begins an

DECEMBER 16

▶ A line of B-29s waits to take off. The first high-altitude daylight raids on Tokyo were not a success. B-29s bombing at night at low level were more effective.

advance down the Myitkyina–Mandalay railway and the Irrawaddy River.

LAND WAR, *PHILIPPINES*

The US invasion of the Philippines spreads as the US 24th Division is landed on the island of Mindoro, just off the southwest coast of Luzon. Japanese resistance amounts to little, the Mindoro garrison numbering just 100 men. Mindoro features four abandoned airfields that will enable the Allies to extend fighter air cover to the Lingayen Gulf and Manila Bay.

AIR WAR, *PHILIPPINES*

US carrier aircraft destroy 225 Japanese aircraft on and over Luzon in three separate attacks. Japanese aircraft production has increased dramatically during 1944. In 1943, Japan produced 7147 fighters and 4189 bombers. By the end of 1944, that figure has risen to 13,811 fighters and 5100 bombers. The signifi-

cant increase in fighter, rather than bomber, production indicates that air defence rather than offensive air action is the Japanese priority. However, the US is now destroying Japanese aircraft faster than they can be built.

DECEMBER 16

POLITICS, *PACIFIC*

Douglas MacArthur is promoted to the rank of five-star general in recognition of his handling of the US campaign in the south Pacific.

AIR WAR, *SUMATRA*

British carrier aircraft bombard Japanese oil installations at Belawan-Deli.

DECEMBER 18

SEA WAR, *PHILIPPINES*

The US Navy suffers heavy losses in shipping and manpower after a typhoon hits the seas off the Philippines. The destroyers USS *Hull*, USS *Monghan* and USS *Spence* are sunk and 22 other ships damaged in the storm, while 150 aircraft are blown off

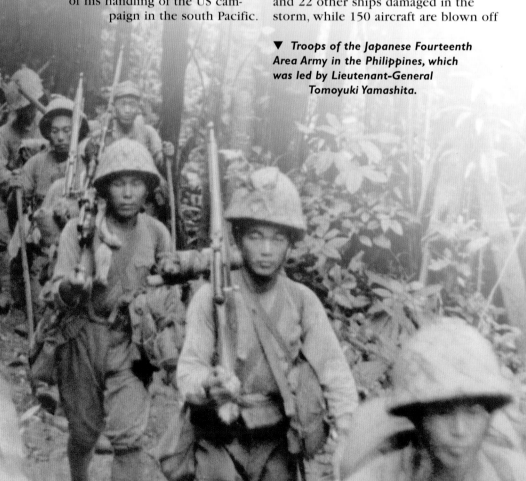

▼ Troops of the Japanese Fourteenth Area Army in the Philippines, which was led by Lieutenant-General Tomoyuki Yamashita.

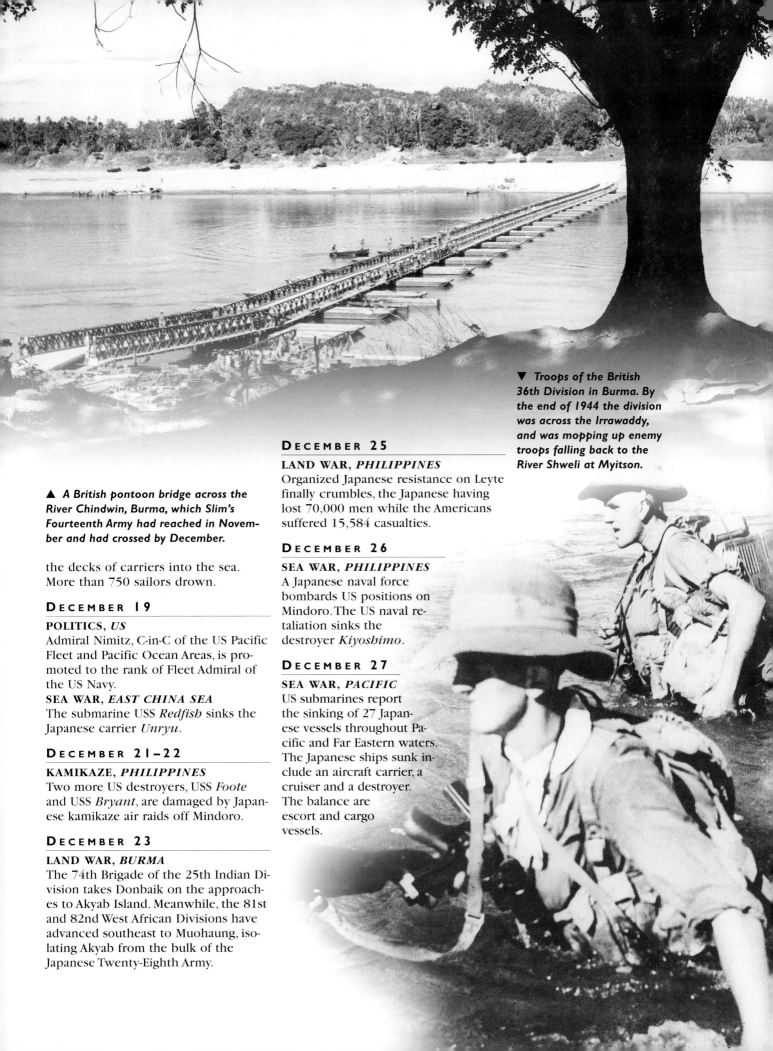

▲ *A British pontoon bridge across the River Chindwin, Burma, which Slim's Fourteenth Army had reached in November and had crossed by December.*

the decks of carriers into the sea. More than 750 sailors drown.

DECEMBER 19

POLITICS, *US*
Admiral Nimitz, C-in-C of the US Pacific Fleet and Pacific Ocean Areas, is promoted to the rank of Fleet Admiral of the US Navy.

SEA WAR, *EAST CHINA SEA*
The submarine USS *Redfish* sinks the Japanese carrier *Unryu*.

DECEMBER 21–22

KAMIKAZE, *PHILIPPINES*
Two more US destroyers, USS *Foote* and USS *Bryant*, are damaged by Japanese kamikaze air raids off Mindoro.

DECEMBER 23

LAND WAR, *BURMA*
The 74th Brigade of the 25th Indian Division takes Donbaik on the approaches to Akyab Island. Meanwhile, the 81st and 82nd West African Divisions have advanced southeast to Muohaung, isolating Akyab from the bulk of the Japanese Twenty-Eighth Army.

DECEMBER 25

LAND WAR, *PHILIPPINES*
Organized Japanese resistance on Leyte finally crumbles, the Japanese having lost 70,000 men while the Americans suffered 15,584 casualties.

DECEMBER 26

SEA WAR, *PHILIPPINES*
A Japanese naval force bombards US positions on Mindoro. The US naval retaliation sinks the destroyer *Kiyoshimo*.

DECEMBER 27

SEA WAR, *PACIFIC*
US submarines report the sinking of 27 Japanese vessels throughout Pacific and Far Eastern waters. The Japanese ships sunk include an aircraft carrier, a cruiser and a destroyer. The balance are escort and cargo vessels.

▼ *Troops of the British 36th Division in Burma. By the end of 1944 the division was across the Irrawaddy, and was mopping up enemy troops falling back to the River Shweli at Myitson.*

1945

The last year of the Pacific war saw heavy fighting on all fronts. Though US war production far outstripped that of Japan, overwhelming superiority in ships, aircraft and tanks did not translate into easy victories. On Iwo Jima and Okinawa US forces suffered heavy losses, which boded ill for the invasion of Japan itself. The Americans thus dropped atomic bombs on Japan to hasten the end of the war.

▲ Ships of the US fleet assembled off Luzon. Landing craft heading for shore can be seen in the bottom of the photograph.

JANUARY 1

LAND WAR, *CAROLINE ISLANDS*
US Army forces are landed on Fais Island in the Carolines with the objective of capturing and destroying a Japanese radio station.

JANUARY 2–8

LAND WAR, *PHILIPPINES*
The US high command in the Philippines re-deploys the Sixth Army under General Krueger from Leyte to positions off Lingayen Gulf on Luzon.

▼ A kamikaze aircraft dives towards the light cruiser USS Columbia during the Lingayen Gulf invasion on January 6, 1945. The ship was hit by two kamikaze aircraft and severely damaged.

JANUARY 3

KAMIKAZE, *LUZON*
The US escort carrier USS *Ommaney Bay* is severely damaged by a Japanese suicide aircraft. It is later scuttled.

JANUARY 4

LAND WAR, *BURMA*
Akyab Island off the west coast of Burma, previously the objective of many failed Allied offensives, is taken by British troops in an unopposed amphibious landing. While the Allies in central Burma have been making progress towards Mandalay, XV Corps is pursuing "Operation Talon", driving farther down into the Arakan and aiming for the port of Rangoon.

AIR WAR, *DUTCH EAST INDIES*
British carrier aircraft strike Japanese-controlled oil refineries at Pankalan.

JANUARY 4-9

KAMIKAZE, *LUZON*
The Japanese open a relentless aerial kamikaze campaign against US shipping around Luzon. From January 5-9 alone, the US Navy suffers at least 30 hits on shipping by suicide aircraft. In total, more than 1000 Allied personnel are killed. The confusion and turmoil in the waters around Luzon is evident by the high number of collisions between US vessels reported.

JANUARY 2-3

AIR WAR, *RYUKYU ISLANDS*
A total of 111 Japanese aircraft are destroyed on and above Formosa and the Ryukyu Islands following an attack by carrier aircraft of the US Third Fleet. Another 220 aircraft are damaged.

▼ *British M4 Sherman medium tanks and infantry on the island of Akyab following their unopposed landing on January 4.*

▲ *Indian troops of XV Corps wade across to Akyab Island in early January. The British occupied the island two days after the Japanese had evacuated it.*

JANUARY 5

LAND WAR, *BURMA*
The British 2nd Division takes the vital airfields at Yeu and Shwebo to the northwest of Mandalay.

JANUARY 5

AIR/SEA WAR, *BONIN ISLANDS*
A combined US Force of cruisers, destroyers and carrier aircraft bombard shipping and installations on Chichi Jima and Haha Jima in the Bonin Islands.

JANUARY 9

LAND WAR, *PHILIPPINES*
At 09:30 hours, the US Sixth Army opens the campaign to take Luzon. It lands the 6th and 43rd Divisions of I Corps and the 337th and 40th Divisions of XIV Corps in Lingayen Gulf at positions between Lingayen and Damortis. Japanese resistance at the beachheads is light – General Yamashita of the Fourteenth Army has pulled his troops back from the beachhead to conserve them for later combat.

JANUARY 10

LAND WAR, *BURMA*
Troops of the 28th East African Brigade, part of the British IV Corps, advance towards Pakkoku, taking Gangaw in the Kabaw Valley.

▼ *The light cruiser USS Louisville under kamikaze attack off Luzon in early January. Despite being hit twice, she remained on station to support the invasion.*

JANUARY 11

LAND WAR, *BURMA*
The British 19th Division comes under heavy counterattack from the Japanese Thirty-Third Army as it attempts to cross the Irrawaddy River at Thabeikkyin and establish a bridgehead. Thabeikkyin is only 100km (60 miles) north of Mandalay, and fighting is extremely fierce – Japanese troops make mass assaults with fixed bayonets. But

▲ *Indian Punjabi troops of the British Fourteenth Army in action near Monywa, 96km (60 miles) from Mandalay.*

Honda's Thirty-Third Army has fallen into a trap. General Slim, predicting the Japanese countermeasures, has swung troops of the British IV Corps southwards towards Pakokku to prevent Japanese troops retreating south.

JANUARY 16

LAND WAR, *NORTHERN BURMA*

The Chinese New First Army captures Namkhkam, an important position that secures the Burma Road for Allied use.

JANUARY 18

LAND WAR, *PALAU ISLANDS*

Two Japanese commando raiding groups land on Peleliu in an attempt to destroy US aircraft on the ground. The groups are wiped out and thus are unable to complete their mission.

JANUARY 20

KAMIKAZE, *LUZON*

Japanese suicide aircraft attack US naval vessels in the Formosa-Ryukyu Islands area. The carriers USS *Ticon-*

▲ *US troops cross the River Shweli in Burma over a hastily constructed bamboo bridge in pursuit of Japanese forces.*

deroga and USS *Langley* are damaged, as is the destroyer USS *Maddox*. An accidental explosion damages another carrier, USS *Hancock*.

JANUARY 20

LAND WAR, *PHILIPPINES*

US XIV Corps troops push up to the outskirts of San Miguel. After an almost uncontested landing, US forces on the island of Luzon are now locked in heavy fighting against General Yamashita's 260,000 men, as they are now less than 160km (100 miles) from Manila itself.

JANUARY 12

AIR WAR, *INDOCHINA*

US carrier aircraft operating from the South China Sea bomb Japanese airfields, shore installations and shipping in French Indochina.

JANUARY 15

AIR WAR, *FORMOSA*

US carrier aircraft sink two Japanese destroyers in renewed attacks off Formosa.

LAND WAR, *PHILIPPINES*

US forces advance out of Lingayen Bay, today crossing the Agno River at points about 24km (15 miles) inland.

DECISIVE WEAPONS

THE BATTLESHIP *YAMATO*

The battleship *Yamato* and her sister ship *Musashi* were built for the Imperial Japanese Navy in the late 1930s and early 1940s under conditions of total secrecy, as the specifications of both vessels breached international treaty limits. Work on the *Yamato* began in November 1937, and she was completed in December 1941. Her combat specifications were impressive. Her main turrets carried nine 18in guns which had a maximum range of 48km (30 miles), and she was armed with forty anti-aircraft guns of various calibres. The *Yamato* also carried six float planes for reconnaissance duties. This 69,088-tonne (68,000-ton) vessel required 2500 officers and men to crew it; yet, with the rising supremacy of naval aviation and submarine warfare, she became an anachronism from the moment she was launched.

Yamato's combat experience bore this out. In early 1944, she was damaged by a submarine torpedo from the USS *Skate*, but she was later able to participate in the Battle of the Philippine Sea. During this action she fired her main armaments, but poor visibility and fast-moving US warships made her contribution negligible. She returned home for refitting, and the lessons of the Philippine Sea led to a substantial upgrad-

ing of anti-aircraft armaments. She would have a total of 145 25mm anti-aircraft guns for her final operation, a suicide mission against US invasion forces around Okinawa in April 1945. With enough fuel for only a one-way trip, *Yamato* was spotted by US aircraft well before she reached her destination. An attack by more than 400 US carrier aircraft led to more than 20 bomb and torpedo hits. At 14:20 hours on April 7, her magazine exploded, ripping the ship apart and sending her to the bottom of the Pacific. A total of 2475 crew went down with her.

DECISIVE WEAPONS

B-29 SUPERFORTRESS

The Boeing B-29 Superfortress is best known for its role in ending World War II. On August 6, 1945, the B-29 Enola Gay dropped the first operational atomic bomb on Hiroshima; three days later, another B-29, Bockscar, dropped the second on Nagasaki. The B-29 was designed as an extreme long-range "Hemisphere Defence Weapon". When it entered service in July 1943, this huge 10-crew bomber had a range of 6598km (4100 miles) and a bomb load of 9072kg (20,000lb). It was an advanced aircraft – the gun turrets dotted around the fuselage were controlled remotely by gunners sitting inside the fuselage who aimed the weapons via periscopes. The B-29 was ideal for the vast distances of the Pacific theatre. From March 1945, B-29s began operations from five bases in the Marianas Islands, causing devastation on the Japanese mainland. Attacking mostly at night (previously, the B-29s had mainly conducted high-level daylight raids), the B-29s scattered millions of incendiaries over Japanese cities – the wood and plaster construction of Japanese housing made the buildings intensely vulnerable to fire attacks. The first such fire attack on Tokyo caused 80,000 deaths, a similar death toll to that caused by the Hiroshima bomb. Some 3970 B-29s were produced during the war, and some went on to serve in the Korean conflict of 1950–53.

◀ *A Boeing B-29 returns to Iwo Jima after a raid on Japan. Note that one of its port engines has been disabled.*

SPECIFICATIONS

CREW: 10

POWERPLANT: four 1641kW (2200hp) Wright R-3350-57 radial piston engines

PERFORMANCE: maximum speed 576kmh (358mph); service ceiling 9696m (31,800ft); range 6598km (4100 miles)

DIMENSIONS: wingspan 43.36m (142.25ft); length 30.18m (99ft); height 9.01m (29.6ft)

ARMAMENTS: 10 x 12.5mm machine guns (four-gun nose turret, two-gun turrets under nose and under and over rear fuselage); tail gun turret featuring one 20mm cannon and two 12.5mm machine guns; internal bomb load of up to 9072kg (19,958lb)

JANUARY 21

LAND WAR, *BURMA*
The 71st Brigade, 26th Indian Division, makes an amphibious jump down the Arakan to Kyaukpyu on Ramree Island, putting further pressure on the Japanese forces retreating between the west coast

▼ *A US 81mm mortar shells Japanese positions north of Lashio in northern Burma in late January.*

of Burma and the Irrawaddy. Most of the Arakan coastline is now in Allied hands.

JANUARY 23

LAND WAR, *PHILIPPINES*
US XIV Corps troops push down into southern Luzon to take Clark Field, having advanced around 113km (70 miles). Clark Field will be essential during forthcoming US operations against Iwo Jima, and General MacArthur has been leaning heavily on US commanders to take the air base. I Corps troops

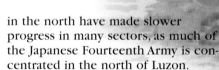

▶ *A flight of Chance Vought Corsair fighters. The Corsair was one of the best combat aircraft of World War II.*

in the north have made slower progress in many sectors, as much of the Japanese Fourteenth Army is concentrated in the north of Luzon.

JANUARY 26

LAND WAR, *BURMA*
The 7th and 17th Indian Divisions occupy Pauk, 48km (30 miles) from Pakokku. The 28th East African Brigade breaks away from Pauk and swings farther south towards Seikpyu on the Irrawaddy.

JANUARY 27

LAND WAR, *NORTHERN BURMA*
The Chinese New First Army and the Chinese Y Force meet around Mongyu, bringing together two separate lines of advance down through northern Burma. The forces now combine and drive down towards Lashio against the Japanese 56th Division. Farther west, the Chinese New Sixth Army has pushed out from Bhamo and is heading for Hsipaw, 65km (40 miles) to the southwest of Lashio.

JANUARY 28

LOGISTICS, *BURMA*
With Chinese troops having reopened the Ledo Road to Burma,

▶ **As US troops neared Manila, the city came under artillery and aerial bombardment. This bridge was demolished by the garrison to hinder enemy movements.**

the first truckloads of supplies reach China. The open flow of logistics will now help the Chinese to stem the Japanese Ichi-Go offensive into Chinese southern territories.

JANUARY 29–31

LAND WAR, *PHILIPPINES*
The US opens more fronts in the Luzon campaign by landing troops in positions around Manila Bay. XI Corps forces go ashore at San Antonio, just north of the Bataan Peninsula, on the 29th, and on the 31st the 11th Airborne Division is landed at Masugbu, south of Manila Bay, making up the southern thrust of a three-pronged assault against the Philippine capital, Manila.

FEBRUARY 1

TECHNOLOGY, AIR WAR
Chance Vought Corsair fighters make their first regular operational flight

from US Navy aircraft carriers. The Corsair will become the best carrier-launched aircraft of World War II, with its manoeuvrability, high maximum speed (671kmh/417mph) and six machine guns. The Corsair will achieve a kill ratio of eleven to one.

FEBRUARY 2

SEA WAR, *PACIFIC*
A US Navy communiqué announces that, since June 19, 1944, total Japanese shipping losses have amounted to more than 50 vessels a week. Japan's maritime assets are being decimated.

AIR WAR, *SINGAPORE*

A large force of US B-29s demolishes Singapore harbour and Japanese naval shipping moored there.

FEBRUARY 3

LAND WAR, *PHILIPPINES*

The battle for Manila begins. Japanese forces in the city are trapped between the 11th Airborne Division moving up from the south (the remainder of the 11th Airborne are parachuted into action today), XI Corps troops from the west, and units of XIV Corps from the north. The Japanese put up a ferocious defence, and the battle for the Philippines capital will go on for another month.

▶ *The "Big Three" at Yalta (left to right): Winston Churchill, a sick Franklin D. Roosevelt and Joseph Stalin. The latter agreed to declare war on Japan.*

FEBRUARY 4–11

POLITICS, *ALLIES*

British Prime Minister Churchill, US President Roosevelt and Russia's Joseph Stalin meet at Yalta in the Crimea for a six-day conference to discuss the politics of an Allied Europe as Germany faces certain defeat. Stalin also commits himself to declaring war on Japan

▲ *US troops fighting on Luzon in January. The Japanese under General Tomoyuki Yamashita fought a skilful rearguard campaign in the face of superior forces.*

within two months of Germany's final military defeat.

FEBRUARY 6

LAND WAR, *PHILIPPINES*

Some 510 Allied POWs, many taken captive by the Japanese in Bataan in 1942, are freed following a dramatic raid on a POW camp by US Rangers and Filipino insurgents. More than 200 Japanese guards are killed.

FEBRUARY 8

AIR WAR, *KURILE ISLANDS*

Ventura aircraft of the Fleet Air Arm make a rocket attack against radio and lighthouse in-

stallations at Kokutan Zaki, at the northern tip of Shimushu in the Kurile Islands.

FEBRUARY 9–12

SEA WAR, *PACIFIC*

The American submarine USS *Batfish* sinks three Japanese submarines in only four days.

▼ *The Japanese launched a large number of kamikaze attacks against the US invasion fleet off Iwo Jima. Here, the carrier Saratoga burns after one such attack.*

▲ *Soldiers of the US 5th Marine Division on the black volcanic sands of Iwo Jima. In the background is Mount Suribachi, which the Marines captured within three days.*

FEBRUARY 10

ALLIES, WAR CRIMES

The US Navy announces increased co-operation with the US Army in the gathering of evidence for the prosecution of war criminals. The US War Crimes office was established in the autumn of 1944 under the supervision of

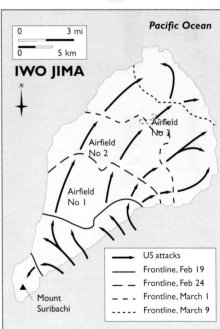

▲ *The US objective on Iwo Jima was to capture the island's three airfields to establish a forward air base for the planned Allied attack on the Japanese home islands.*

Major-General Myron C. Cramer, the Judge Advocate General of the Army.

FEBRUARY 11

AIR WAR, *PACIFIC*

Vice-Admiral George D. Murray, US Navy, Commander Air Forces, Pacific Fleet, releases figures that demonstrate US air superiority over the Pacific theatre.

▲ A US Sherman tank crashes through the entrance to Fort Santiago in Manila. The battle for the city cost the lives of 16,000 Japanese troops and 100,000 Philippine civilians.

From June 11–October 30, 1944, Pacific Fleet carrier aircraft destroyed 2472 Japanese aircraft in aerial combat and lost 123 aircraft. The ratio of US kills to losses is about 20 to 1.

FEBRUARY 13

LAND WAR, BURMA
Units of the 7th and 17th India Divisions cross the Irrawaddy River south of Pakokku at Nyaungu.

LAND WAR, PHILIPPINES
American forces capture the Nicholls Field air base and the Cavite naval base in Manila, further closing their grip around the capital.

FEBRUARY 16–27

LAND WAR, PHILIPPINES
The fortress island of Corregidor is re-occupied by US troops following a paratroop landing by men of the 11th Airborne Division on the 16th, supported by amphibious forces crossing from the Bataan Peninsula.

FEBRUARY 16–17

AIR WAR, TOKYO
US Pacific Fleet carrier aircraft make a highly successful two-day attack on Tokyo. Taking advantage of bad weather to make an undetected approach, the aircraft subsequently shoot down 322 Japanese fighters and destroy a further 177 on the ground. US aviation losses are 49 aircraft. Shipping around Tokyo also suffers heavily, with one escort carrier, three destroyers and nine coastal vessels sunk and more than twenty other ships damaged. In terms of ground installations, the Ota aircraft factory and the Musashine Tama and Tachigawa engine plants are heavily bombed.

FEBRUARY 19

LAND WAR, IWO JIMA
The US invasion of Iwo Jima begins after the island, only 13 sq km (5 sq miles) of territory, has suffered 72 days of solid bombardment. The US Marine 4th and 5th Divisions go ashore in the southeast corner of the island, landed by US V Amphibious Corps. Offshore is the US 3rd Marine Division held in reserve. The first few minutes of the landings are relatively uncontested but, once the Japanese recover, the beaches turn into places of slaughter. Despite heavy casualties, US forces manage to land 30,000 Marines throughout the day and establish a solid beachhead about 450m (1476ft) in depth. By the end of the day, units of the 5th Marine Division have moved across the southern section of the island, cutting off Japanese forces on the 150m- (500ft-) high Mount Suribachi, while the bulk of the Marine forces work their way northwards up the island.

▶ In one of the most famous scenes of World War II, soldiers of the US 5th Marine Division raise the Stars and Stripes on Mount Suribachi, February 23, 1945.

▲ *Gurkhas of the 19th Indian Division, nicknamed the Dagger Division, cross the Irrawaddy River. During its 1944–45 campaign in Burma the division fought 18 separate battles in 7 weeks.*

FEBRUARY 20

LAND WAR, *IWO JIMA*

US Marines move forward on Iwo Jima against fanatical resistance. The 277th Regiment of the US Marines defeats a night attack by a battalion-strength Japanese unit around the Motoyama Airstrip No 1 in the south of the island (Iwo Jima has three airstrips). By the morning, the airstrip is in American hands.

TECHNOLOGY, *ATOMIC BOMB*

US scientists and engineers working at the K-25 uranium plant at Oak Ridge, Tennessee, now have enough Uranium-235 to produce an atomic bomb.

POLITICS, *ALLIES*

In the aftermath of the Yalta Conference, US President Roosevelt and British Prime Minister Churchill discuss the Pacific war, pledging a shift in priorities to the East now that the defeat of Germany looks imminent.

▶ *A 17th Indian Division mortar position in Meiktila, Burma. Judging by the relaxed poses, the Japanese are some way off.*

FEBRUARY 21

LAND WAR, *BURMA*

British forces advancing from Shwebo and moving down the Chindwin meet on the Irrawaddy River near Ngazun, only 48km (30 miles) from Mandalay,

▲ *US amphibious assault vehicles knocked out by Japanese mortar and artillery fire lie abandoned on Iwo Jima.*

and establish a bridgehead. They immediately launch a major offensive towards Meiktila, directly south of Mandalay, using the 7th and 17th Indian Divisions and the 255th Indian Brigade, cutting into the rear of the Japanese Fifteenth Army.

LAND WAR, *IWO JIMA*
US Marines advance beyond the southern airstrip. Units of the 5th Marine Division make a penetration up the west coast of the island, while 4th Division troops head directly for the Motoyama Airstrip No 2 in the centre of the island. The going is extremely heavy, and the total advance for the day is around 900m (2952ft). On Mount Suribachi, US Marines fighting up the slopes gain only 100m (328ft). US casualties already exceed 3500. The US 3rd Marine division, held in reserve offshore, is now landed to boost the combat effort.

STRATEGY AND TACTICS

IWO JIMA

Why was the fight for Iwo Jima so costly? By this stage of the war, the Japanese understood that directly contesting a US amphibious landing at the beaches was too risky because of the intensity of US Navy preliminary bombardments. During the US invasion of Peleliu in the Palau Islands in September 1944, the Japanese opted for a defence-in-depth strategy, and avoided wasteful mass counterattacks. Troops were pulled back into the interior where they waited out the coastal bombardments and allowed US forces to land before engaging them heavily from pre-prepared defensive positions. The Japanese utilized this strategy on Iwo Jima. Scattered around the island were more than 800 pillboxes, bunkers, dug-in armoured vehicles and 4.8km (3 miles) of tunnels. The bunkers were well constructed from palm trunks and packed sand, and had an extremely low-profile sloping face resistant to artillery fire. All pillboxes were situated to have over-lapping fields of fire; all beaches, and the slopes leading off them, were zeroed in advance by Japanese machine guns, artillery and mortars.

The Japanese were assisted in the defence of Iwo Jima by the terrain itself. Iwo Jima is a volcanic island, its convoluted rocky landscape full of caves, ravines, ridges and other natural defensive positions. In one 400m x 600m (1312ft x 1968ft) area, US Marines had to neutralize 100 individual defensive caves. The slope of the beaches was extremely steep with crumbly volcanic ash (the Japanese embedded anti-tank mines in the slopes), and US Marines struggled simply to walk across such terrain carrying their 45kg (100lb) packs. Furthermore, US soldiers found in many places that the volcanic landscape was too hot to convert into foxholes. Ultimately, it was only the sheer tenacity of the Marines and the use of overwhelming firepower that took Iwo Jima.

AIR WAR, *IWO JIMA*
Japanese kamikaze air attacks intensify against US shipping around Iwo Jima. Today, the escort carrier USS *Bismarck Sea* is sunk and the carriers USS *Saratoga* and USS *Lunga Point* are badly damaged by kamikaze aircraft.

FEBRUARY 22

LAND WAR, *PHILIPPINES*
Troops of the Japanese Fourteenth Army defending Manila are now pushed back into the old walled city, where they continue to fight tenaciously. Meanwhile, 2000 Japanese defenders on Corregidor kill themselves by detonating a large ammunition dump.

LAND WAR, *BURMA*
British forces make another amphibious landing down the Arakan coastline, this time landing at Kangow in the Bay of Bengal.

FEBRUARY 23

LAND WAR, *IWO JIMA*
Mount Suribachi falls to US forces after a bloody battle on its slopes. Joe Rosenthal, a US combat photographer, immortalizes the moment that Marine soldiers raise the Stars and Stripes on the summit. However, the island will not be secure for another month. Fighting around the central airstrip is extremely heavy, with little progress being made. Today, only 250m (820ft) of ground is won, with Japanese fire contesting every inch of movement.

▼ *US Marine riflemen fire on Japanese positions from cover on Iwo Jima. A burning Sherman tank is on the left.*

▲ *A column of British troops passes a dead Japanese soldier during the advance on Mandalay in Burma.*

FEBRUARY 25

AIR WAR, *TOKYO*

US carrier aircraft attack the Tokyo area, concentrating efforts on shipping and industrial facilities. About three-quarters of the Ota aircraft factory is destroyed, and the Koizuma aircraft plant is badly damaged. In addition, two trains are destroyed in strafing attacks and 158 Japanese aircraft are wiped out, 47 of them in aerial combat. That night, 172 Boeing B-29 bombers devastate the city, dropping nearly 508 tonnes (500 tons) of incendiary bombs.

FEBRUARY 26

LAND WAR, *BURMA*

As British forces close in on Mandalay from the west and south, the 19th Indian Division begins an attack down the Irrawaddy from its bridgeheads around Thabeikkyin and Singu.

LAND WAR, *IWO JIMA*

The central airfield on Iwo Jima is now in US hands. The fighting for the airstrip has been heavy, and US troops have already counted 3568 lost to the Japanese for only 4000m (13,123ft) of ground taken on the island.

FEBRUARY 27–28

LAND WAR, *PHILIPPINES*

Units of XI Corps effectively clear the Bataan Peninsula. Troops from a regiment of XI Corps are landed on the southern coastline of the peninsula on the 28th, meeting up with their comrades advancing down the eastern coastline.

FEBRUARY 28

LAND WAR, *IWO JIMA*

Approximately two-thirds of Iwo Jima is now in American hands, and the centre of the US advance pushes against the southern defences of the Motoyama Airstrip No 3.

▶ *Dead Japanese soldiers on Iwo Jima. Of the island's 27,000 garrison, 20,000 were killed.*

LAND WAR, *PHILIPPINES*

Troops of the US Army 41st Division land at Puerto Princesa on Palawan Island in the southern Philippines against negligible opposition. Palawan offers excellent port facilities for US Navy operations against Japanese shipping passing to and from the Dutch East Indies.

LAND WAR, *BURMA*

Meiktila is surrounded by troops of the 17th Indian Brigade, who begin the assault on the town, which is occupied by 3500 Japanese defenders.

▲ *Bomb damage at Tokyo following a B-29 air raid. Most Japanese dwellings were made of wood, which made them very vulnerable to incendiary bombs.*

MARCH 1–31

LAND WAR, *PHILIPPINES*
Throughout March, US forces invade the many islands of the southern Philippines. By the end of the month, the Philippines are effectively in US hands, and US war leaders start to look towards the Japanese home islands themselves.

MARCH 1

AIR WAR, *RYUKYU ISLANDS*
US aircraft from Vice-Admiral Mitscher's fast carrier task force begin bombarding Okinawa in the Ryukyu chain. It is the beginning of a solid month of aerial and naval bombardment against Okinawa in preparation for the US invasion of the island scheduled for April 1.

LAND WAR, *PHILIPPINES*
US Army troops are landed on Lubang Island, just off the northern coast of Mindoro.

LAND WAR, *IWO JIMA*
US Marines manage to occupy the western end of Iwo Jima's northern-most airstrip, pushing forward after a huge bombardment by US Navy guns and US Marine artillery. Unusually, 17 Japanese prisoners are taken captive.

▼ *A lull in the fighting during the battle for Mandalay. The soldier on the right is pointing a Bren Gun, one of the finest light machine guns of the war.*

LAND WAR, *BURMA*
The British Fourteenth Army begins the assault on Meiktila, attacking through the northern suburbs of the town against a tenacious defence from Major-General Kasuya's garrison. The Japanese have converted the town into a heavy defensive outpost.

MARCH 2

LAND WAR, *IWO JIMA*
US Marines in northern Iwo Jima advance several hundred yards and capture the high ground of Hill 362. In the west, meanwhile, the US 5th Marine Division defeats a large-scale Japanese counterattack.

MARCH 3

LAND WAR, *PHILIPPINES*
Part of the US 40th Division lands on Masbate Island, just north of Leyte.

LAND WAR, *PHILIPPINES*
Having sacrificed 20,000 men in defence of the

▶ *US Marines on Iwo Jima, where over a third of the Leathernecks were either killed, wounded or suffered from battle fatigue.*

▲ A Royal Air Force B-24 Liberator photographed after droppings its bombs on the railway sidings at Na Nien, Burma.

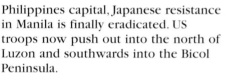

▲ US troops fighting Japanese forces on the island of Panay, which lies between Mindanao and Luzon.

Philippines capital, Japanese resistance in Manila is finally eradicated. US troops now push out into the north of Luzon and southwards into the Bicol Peninsula.

LAND WAR, *IWO JIMA*
The US advance up Iwo Jima slows to a crawl. Both the 4th

and 5th Marines have moved into rocky terrain, and the Japanese defensive fire is blistering. The 5th Marines engage in hand-to-hand fighting in an attempt to loosen the Japanese grip. A count of enemy casualties reveals that so far in the campaign 12,864 Japanese have been killed. Meanwhile, US evacuation aircraft are starting to use the southern airstrip, though they come under artillery fire when landing and taking off.

LAND WAR, *CENTRAL BURMA*
Chinese troops capture Lashio to the northeast of Mandalay. Lashio includes the northernmost of a series of vital airfields stretching throughout central and southern Burma, and each one captured provides extra logistical capability for the Allied advance.

MARCH 4

LAND WAR, *BURMA*
The 17th Indian Division takes Meiktila. The four-day battle has been ferocious, and more than 2000 Japanese have been killed. Mandalay is the next objective, where the bulk of the Japanese Fifteenth and Thirty-Third Armies are trapped.

MARCH 8

POLITICS, *US*
Vice-Admiral William Ward Smith takes command of the Service Force, US Pacific Fleet. The Service Force has a massive job in providing logistics support to US operations in the Pacific. Smith was formerly chief of staff to Admiral Kimmel, and commanded a

cruiser task group that saw action in the battles of Coral Sea and Midway.

MARCH 8-9

LAND WAR, *IWO JIMA*
Japanese forces resort to more night-infiltration actions on Iwo Jima. On this night, an infiltration is made in the 4th Marines' sector, resulting in a firefight that leaves 564 Japanese soldiers dead.

MARCH 8-10

LAND WAR, *PHILIPPINES*
US forces gain their first footholds on Mindanao in the southern Philippines.

▲ *The USS* Aaron Ward *after being hit by kamikaze aircraft off Okinawa. Note the three-bladed aircraft propeller lodged in her superstructure behind the rear guns.*

Two companies of the 24th Division are parachuted around Dipolog.

MARCH 10

LAND WAR, *PHILIPPINES*
With support provided by US Navy gunfire and USAAF ground-attack aircraft, part of the US 41st Division is landed near Zamboanga on the westernmost tip of Mindanao.

MARCH 9-10

AIR WAR, *TOKYO*
The Japanese capital is almost entirely destroyed by a massive night bombing raid by 279 B-29 Superfortress aircraft.

Nearly 2032 tonnes (2000 tons) of incendiary bombs are dropped over the city, resulting in a firestorm that kills between 80,000 and 130,000 of Tokyo's citizens. Around 300,000 buildings, most constructed from wood and plaster, are destroyed. Two nights later, 285 B-29s give Nagoya similar treatment. US aviators now have access to forward air bases captured during the US Pacific campaign. The capture of the Mariana Islands in particular has halved previous operational flying distances.

MARCH 10

POLITICS, *FRENCH INDOCHINA*
The Japanese seize the administration of French Indochina. Although Indochina had essentially been under Japanese occupation, the Japanese allowed the nominal rule of the French colonial government.

▼ *A kamikaze aircraft burns after being hit by anti-aircraft fire from the Essex class carrier USS* Wasp, *off the Ryukyu Islands in March.*

◄ *A light tank and troops of the 19th Indian Division move into their jump-off positions during the advance on Mandalay in Burma.*

MARCH 14

LAND WAR, *IWO JIMA*

The US flag is formally raised over Iwo Jima, despite continuing resistance in pockets in the far north of the island. Iwo Jima – less than 1126km (700 miles) from the Japanese homeland – is now a fully functioning air base for the US Navy, Army and Marine Corps.

MARCH 15

LAND WAR, *BURMA*

The battle for Meiktila rages for two weeks. Around the 15th, General Hoyotaro Kimura, commander of the Japanese Burma Area Army, re-deploys the best part of three divisions from the defence of Mandalay to Meiktila, with its vital rail and communication links. Troops of the 17th Indian Division are now isolated around the town by the Japanese.

MARCH 16

LAND WAR, *IWO JIMA*

Japanese resistance on Iwo Jima breaks down as US Marine forces push their

MARCH 11

KAMIKAZE, *CAROLINE ISLANDS*

The carrier USS *Randolph* is badly damaged by suicide aircraft around Ulithi Atoll in the Carolines.

LAND WAR, *IWO JIMA*

The US 3rd and 4th Marine Divisions make a good advance and capture most of Iwo Jima's east coast. The Japanese are now concentrated in a small section of territory in the north of the island.

MARCH 11–12

LAND WAR, *PHILIPPINES*

Part of the US 24th Division makes an amphibious assault from Mindoro against the island of Romblon.

▼ *The USS* Franklin *ablaze after being hit by two Japanese bombs. The subsequent fire killed 724 crew members. The ship survived after extensive repairs.*

MARCH 12–13

AIR WAR, *JAPAN*

The US strategic bombing campaign against Japan continues. On this night, the city of Osaka is wiped out by a raid of 274 US bombers.

MARCH 13

LAND WAR, *IWO JIMA*

Using explosives and bulldozers, US troops seal up 115 caves with the Japanese defenders still inside.

DECISIVE WEAPONS

YOKOSUKA MXY7 OHKA

The Ohka ("Cherry Blossom") was a rocket-powered piloted bomb designed by naval ensign Mitsuo Ohka in late 1944. Effectively, the aircraft was nothing more than a 1200kg (2646lb) warhead with wings and powered by three solid-fuel Type 4 Mark 1 Model 20 rockets. To deploy the weapon, it was first attached to the modified bomb bay of a Mitsubishi G4M bomber and flown within 40km (25 miles) of the target. Once

released, the Ohka's rockets would ignite and the pilot would then fly the bomb into his intended target. To ensure the commitment of the pilot, he was sealed into the cockpit for his one-way trip. Ohkas were a mark of Japanese desperation, and were not a total success. The first attack occurred on March 21, 1945, but all Ohkas missed their targets. Hits were achieved on the battleship USS *West Virginia* on April 1, causing severe damage. The destroyer USS *Mannert L. Abele* was sunk two weeks later, but most Ohkas did not reach launch position before their Mitsubishi transports were shot down by US fighters.

SPECIFICATIONS

CREW: 1
POWERPLANT: three solid-fuel Type 4 Mark 1 Model 20 rockets generating 800kg (1764lb) of thrust
PERFORMANCE: max speed 650kmh (403mph); range 37km (23 miles)
DIMENSIONS: wingspan 5.12m (16.79ft); length 6.07m (19.9ft); height 1.16m (3.75ft)
WARHEAD: 1200kg (2646lb)

▲ *Operation Iceberg, the US invasion of Okinawa, commences. The US fleet assembled off the island prior to the assault numbered 1400 vessels.*

way to Kitano Point, the northernmost tip of the island. A small pocket of disorganized Japanese defenders remains in the northeast, but is easily contained. Today, the central airfield comes into operation.

MARCH 16–17

AIR WAR, *JAPAN*

Kobe is devastated by 307 B-29 bombers in a night raid that kills at least 15,000 people.

MARCH 18

LAND WAR, *PHILIPPINES*

Elements of the US 40th Division land around Loilo on the southern coastline of Panay in the southern Philippines.

MARCH 18–19

AIR WAR, *JAPAN*

On March 18, US carrier aircraft attack naval installations and airfields around Kyushu Island, the southernmost territory of the Japanese homelands. The Japanese stage a major airborne retaliation, and the carriers USS *Enterprise*, USS *Yorktown* and USS *Intrepid* are damaged by bombers and suicide aircraft. Nevertheless, the US attacks continue the next day, the target locations widening to Kobe and Kure. Once again, the Japanese respond with force, and the carriers USS *Franklin*,

USS *Wasp* and USS *Essex* are damaged (the latter, ironically, by misdirected US Navy gunfire).

MARCH 19

AIR WAR, *JAPAN*

US carrier aircraft attacking the Japanese homelands switch their efforts to the Japanese Fleet in the Inland Sea. Two battleships, six aircraft carriers (heavy, light and escort), three cruisers and four destroyers are among the

▼ *Firefighters deal with the aftermath of a kamikaze attack on an aircraft carrier.*

ships badly damaged. In two days of air combat over Japan, 200 Japanese aircraft have been shot down, and 275 destroyed on the ground.

MARCH 20–21

LAND WAR, *BURMA*

Britain's XXXIII Corps takes Mandalay after house-to-house fighting. XXXIII Corps units are now re-deployed to fight around Meiktila. On the 21st, the British 36th Division advancing down from northern Burma with the Chinese New Sixth Army reaches Mandalay, and falls back under the British Fourteenth Army's jurisdiction.

MARCH 21

KAMIKAZE, *PACIFIC*

Japanese Ohka piloted bombs make their first attack against US carriers. They are unsuccessful. However, Japanese air attacks around Iwo Jima today result in the sinking of the carrier USS *Bismarck Sea*. Bombing and kamikaze raids start fires on the ship that rage out of control and force the crew to abandon the carrier.

LAND WAR, *CHINA*

Japan persists in its attempts to capture US air bases in southern China, today launching a fresh offensive towards Laohokow and Ankong.

MARCH 23–24

AIR/SEA WAR, *RYUKYU ISLANDS*

Daily air bombardments against the island of Okinawa begin today. The next day, US battleships, cruisers and destroyers add naval gunfire support to the onslaught.

MARCH 25

KAMIKAZE, *OKINAWA*

Japanese suicide aircraft damage one US destroyer, a destroyer escort, a mine-laying vessel and two high-speed transport ships.

MARCH 26

LAND WAR, *IWO JIMA*

The final pockets of Japanese resistance on Iwo Jima collapse after a suicide attack by the remaining Japanese troops. Casualties on both sides have been colossal. The US has lost 6821 Marine and navy personnel. Calculating Japanese casualties

▲ *Troops of the US 96th Division climb the sea wall on the western shore of Okinawa on April 1.*

is difficult, for many were killed inside cave complexes that were subsequently sealed. However, the US Navy estimates up to 22,000 Japanese dead.

▼ *US forces pour ashore on Okinawa. In the foreground can be seen LVT amphibious vehicles. A total of 1225 LVT-1s were built in the war.*

MARCH 27

LAND WAR, *PHILIPPINES*

The Americal Division lands on the eastern coast of Cebu. By this point, almost every island in the southern Philippines is now either under US occupation or in the process of being conquered.

KAMIKAZE, *OKINAWA*

Waves of Japanese suicide aircraft are thrown against US shipping around Okinawa. One battleship (the USS *Nevada*), one cruiser and five destroyers are among the damaged US vessels.

LAND WAR, *RYUKYU ISLANDS*

US Army 77th Division troops land on the islands of the Kerama group west of the southern tip of Okinawa, and occupy them over the next three days. The islands will provide a base for US artillery fire against Okinawa Island itself.

MARCH 27

LAND WAR, *PHILIPPINES*

US Army troops make an amphibious landing on Caballo Island, near the island of Corregidor.

MARCH 28

LAND WAR, *BURMA*

Soldiers of the Burmese National Army (BNA), an independence movement fighting on the side of the Japanese, kill some of their officers. The BNA has, over recent months, been infiltrated by the Allied Special Operations Executive (SOE), which capitalized on the low status afforded to the BNA by the Japanese Army.

MARCH 29

LAND WAR, *BURMA*

With Mandalay taken, and Britain's XXXII Corps now able to support the Indian 17th Division around Meiktila, the Japanese Burma Area Army is ordered to withdraw southwards. General Kimura uses the Mandalay-Thazi rail route to escape with a large number of troops. British forces follow closely, the ultimate objective now being the vital port of Rangoon.

KEY PERSONALITIES

FRANKLIN ROOSEVELT

President Franklin Delano Roosevelt (1882–1945) was coming towards the end of his second term in office when the Japanese attacked the US Pacific Fleet at Pearl Harbor in December 1941. Roosevelt had been tough on the Japanese prior to this incident, imposing oil and metals embargoes in 1940–41 after Japanese attacks against French Indochina. Roosevelt was told that a Japanese attack against US interests would come on December 7, but outdated military intelligence, which underestimated the range of Japanese carrier aircraft, ruled out Pearl Harbor as the target.

Following US entry into the war, Roosevelt sided with the European allies in favour of a Germany First strategy. However, the Pacific theatre still received substantial resources – at least half of US troops and around 30 percent of US aircraft were committed there in 1942. On a strategic level, Roosevelt's early war aims in the Pacific were to maintain the Chinese war effort against Japan through air supply, and ultimately halt the Japanese advance through the South Pacific. Once the war against the Japanese tipped in the US's favour and American forces neared the enemy home islands, Roosevelt decided that the use atomic bombs on Japan would save tens of thousands of US service lives and shorten the war. He never lived to see the defeat of Japan. Roosevelt died of a cerebral haemorrhage on April 12, 1945, during an unprecedented fourth term in office, having struggled with polio most of his life. Although Roosevelt could be pragmatic, especially about the political intentions of the Allies, he brought clarity and momentum to the US war effort.

AIR WAR, *JAPAN*

US aircraft from two carrier task groups attack Japanese shipping and aircraft in the Kagoshima Bay area, Kyushu, Japan.

MARCH 30

KAMIKAZE, *OKINAWA*

A Japanese suicide aircraft damages the US heavy cruiser USS *Indianapolis*.

APRIL 1

LAND WAR, *RYUKYU ISLANDS*

"Operation Iceberg", the invasion of Okinawa, begins with landings by the US Tenth Army along the southeastern

▼ *A Japanese destroyer keels over in the East China Sea following an air attack.*

huge waves of kamikaze aircraft against the 1400-strong Allied fleet. Six vessels are damaged by suicide attack, including the battleship USS *West Virginia*.

HOME FRONT, *JAPAN*

All education for Japanese schoolchildren above the age of six is cancelled, and the young are redirected into war industries to provide a boost to the Japanese labour force.

LAND WAR, *PHILIPPINES*

US Army troops are landed at Legaspi in the south of the Bicol Peninsula, trapping Japanese forces retreating down through the peninsula in the face of a strong southerly advance by US troops.

KAMIKAZE, *EAST CHINA SEA*

The British carrier HMS *Indefatigable* is hit by a kamikaze attack, suffering damage and 14 fatalities.

APRIL 2

LAND WAR, *PHILIPPINES*

US 41st Division troops land on Tawitawi, in the south of the Sulu archipelago near British North Borneo.

LAND WAR, *RYUKYU ISLANDS*

The US XXIV Corps makes good progress across southern Okinawa, reaching the east coast near the village of Tobara. However, US Marines advancing in the centre of the island are beginning to meet increasingly stiff resistance in difficult terrain. Eleven US ships are damaged today, five by suicide aircraft; one by Japanese bombers; and the remainder through collision, grounding and being struck accidentally by US naval gunfire.

▲ *The funeral of President Franklin D. Roosevelt in Washington. Roosevelt died on the verge of victory in Europe, and his loss was keenly felt by the American people.*

coast of the island around Hagushi Bay. The landings are divided into two elements: US III Marine Amphibious Corps (6th Marine Division and 1st Marine Division) takes the left flank, with the objective of advancing to the west and up into the north of the island; while, beneath it, US Army XXIV Corps (7th Infantry Division and 96th Infantry Division) begins operations to clear southern Okinawa. On this first day, re-

sistance is relatively light and the US troops establish a beachhead 5km (3 miles) deep. However, more than 130,000 Japanese soldiers of the Japanese Thirty-Second Army are waiting for them in the interior of the island.

The US invasion is not only protected by US shipping – a large British carrier force under Vice-Admiral Sir Bernard Rawlings operates against enemy positions in the Sakishima group. The Japanese Air Force immediately launches

▶ *A US soldier feeds a young child during the campaign on Okinawa. Fears about the behaviour of US troops prompted many Japanese civilians on the island to commit suicide.*

▲ *With combat raging on Okinawa, Japanese aircraft tried to sink US ships offshore. Here, a burning Zero goes down.*

APRIL 3

LAND WAR, *RYUKYU ISLANDS*
US Marines cross Okinawa and reach the east coast, cutting off Japanese troops in the Katchin Peninsula. In the south, US Army forces have reached Kuba, with Japanese resistance being light.

APRIL 5

COMMAND STRUCTURE, *PACIFIC*
The US joint chiefs of staff announce changes in the command structure of Pacific operations. General MacArthur is given command of all army forces and related resources for the Pacific theatre. Similarly, Admiral Nimitz takes charge of all US Navy units and resources throughout the Pacific.

LAND WAR, *RYUKYU ISLANDS*
US Marine units reach the Ishikawa isthmus, having advanced around 16km (10 miles) up Okinawa's west coast. Resistance is still light, with only 175 US soldiers killed in the campaign so far. Civilians prove one of the biggest problems. Okinawa has a civilian population of around 450,000, hampering offensive manoeuvres. Today alone, around 9000 civilians surrender to the Americans.

KAMIKAZE, *OKINAWA*
Japanese kamikaze aircraft attack in mass waves around Okinawa. US shipping suffers heavily, with two destroyers sunk and twenty-four other ships damaged.

POLITICS, *TOKYO*
The Japanese prime minister, Koiso Kuniaki, and his cabinet resign as

◄ *Following their capture of Pyawbwe, Burma, from the Japanese, Indian troops help to rearm a tank with ammunition.*

the war closes in on the Japanese homelands. The 78-year-old Admiral Suzuki Kantaro becomes prime minister, who begins to make ambiguous peace overtures to the Allies.

POLITICS, *MOSCOW*
In an important announcement, the Soviet foreign minister, Vyacheslav Molotov, tells the Japanese ambassador that the USSR will not renew its five-year neutrality pact with Japan. The announcement opens the possibility of Japan fighting against the Russians in Manchuria. Molotov says the change in policy is a consequence of the Japanese alliance with Germany.

APRIL 7

SEA WAR, *EAST CHINA SEA*
The Japanese Navy dispatches a large battle group to attack US shipping around Okinawa. It includes the mighty battleship *Yamato*, an Agano-class cruiser, a light cruiser and a collection of destroyers. The force is spotted by US carrier aircraft south of Kyushu, and is engaged in the East China Sea well before it reaches Okinawa. Japanese aviation losses mean that US aircraft face no aerial opposition, and in the subsequent action the *Yamato*, the Agano-class cruiser, one other cruiser and three destroyers are sunk. This signals the effective end of the Japanese Navy in the Pacific.

▼ *On Okinawa, US troops clear a cave with grenades and small-arms fire. Knocking out enemy positions was bloody and time-consuming work.*

▲ *US flamethrower tanks of the 7th Infantry Division burn out the enemy defending Hill 178 on Okinawa.*

LAND WAR, *RYUKYU ISLANDS*
Heavy Japanese resistance begins to emerge from the rocky landscape of southern Okinawa, especially around the villages of Uchitomari and Kaniku. Inland areas are laced with networks of defensive positions, and US troops are met by powerful small-arms, artillery and mortar fire. In the north, the Marines are continuing to make good progress, reaching Nago town on the west coast and Ora Bay on the east coast.

APRIL 9

LAND WAR, *RYUKYU ISLANDS*
Around half of the Motobu Peninsula is brought under US control. Enemy resistance in the area is described

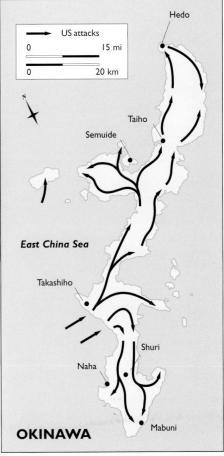

OKINAWA

▲ *The US invasion of Okinawa cost the Americans over 12,000 dead (compared to 110,000 Japanese), while at sea 36 US ships were sunk, most by kamikaze attacks. In the air, the Americans lost 763 aircraft to the Japanese 4155.*

▲ On the road to Rangoon. A column of British tanks and infantry halt after coming under Japanese sniper fire.

in a US report as "scattered and ineffective". Southern-sector operations, by contrast, are extremely slow, as the enemy begins to make repeated counterattacks from a string of heavy defensive positions known as the "Shuri Line". These positions stretch across the island for roughly 7315m (24,000ft) and include interlocking trench and pillbox systems, blockhouses, fortified caves and strongly constructed bunkers. Naval and aerial bombardments are used in an effort to smash enemy emplacements. More

than 43,000 Okinawan civilians are now under US protection.

LAND WAR, *PHILIPPINES*
US Army troops of the 41st Division make an amphibious landing on Jolo in the Sulu archipelago, to the west of Mindanao.

APRIL 10

AIR WAR, *OKINAWA*
Heavy Japanese kamikaze and bombing attacks damage the battleship USS *Missouri* and the carriers USS *Enterprise* and USS *Essex*, plus 10 other vessels.

LAND WAR, *PHILIPPINES*
US troops advancing down through Luzon reach Mauban on Lamon Bay, near the entrance to the Bicol Peninsula.

APRIL 11

LAND WAR, *BURMA*
Troops of the 7th Indian Division capture Pyawbwe, about 32km (20 miles) south of Meiktila, on the main rail route between Meiktila and Rangoon. Japanese forces are retreating south at a rapid pace.

APRIL 12

PRESIDENCY, *US*
The US president, Franklin D. Roosevelt, dies at the age of 63. Into his

▼ US Marines engaged against enemy forces on Okinawa. The soldier closest to the camera is armed with an M1 Carbine semi-automatic rifle.

place steps the US vice-president, Harry S. Truman.

LAND WAR, *RYUKYU ISLANDS*
While US troops on Okinawa are deadlocked with the Japanese defenders, more kamikaze raids hit the US Navy around the island. Suicide aircraft damage 15 ships, and a piloted bomb sinks the destroyer USS *Mannert L. Abele*.

APRIL 12–15

AIR WAR, *JAPAN*
US Pacific Fleet aircraft carry out three days of attacks over Kyushu, southern Japan. The main targets are air bases at

▲ *Allied forces in Burma land at Elephant Point, just south of Rangoon, in the final phase of the campaign to liberate the country from the Japanese.*

Kikai, Tanega, Kanoya and Kushira. A total of 246 Japanese aircraft are either destroyed or damaged in the raids.

APRIL 13

LAND WAR, *RYUKYU ISLANDS*
In the south of Okinawa, a battalion-strength Japanese force counterattacks US XXIV Corps troops. The attack is utterly destroyed by US infantry weapons supported by offshore naval gunfire.

AIR WAR, *FORMOSA*
Seafire and Hellcat fighters of the British Pacific Fleet attack Shinchiku and Kiirun airfields on Formosa. Sixteen enemy planes are shot down, one is destroyed on the

THE LIBERATION OF BURMA

Map locations: Kohima, Imphal, INDIA, Indaw, Kalewa, BURMA, Lashio, CHINA, Mandalay, Seikpyu, Meiktila, Akyab, Magwe, THAILAND, Toungoo, Irrawaddy, Sittang, Bay of Bengal, Rangoon, Madauk, Gulf of Martaban

Scale: 0 — 100 mi / 0 — 160 km

- - -▶ Allied advances
──▶ Japanese counterattacks

ground, and five others are badly damaged.

APRIL 14

LAND WAR, *RYUKYU ISLANDS*
Troops of US Marine III Amphibious Corps make good advances in northern Okinawa, reaching Hedo Point, the northernmost tip of the island, as well as securing almost all of the Motobu Penin-

◀ *British and Indian paratroopers carry out equipment checks prior to a drop near Rangoon.*

▲ *Between December 4, 1944, and May 4, 1945, the liberation of Burma was largely complete. However, it took the Allies until August 1945 to wipe out the last pockets of Japanese resistance.*

sula and moving to Momubaru town on the west coast, and Arakawa town on the east coast. Through the night of April 14/15, the Japanese in the south make three counterattacks, all of which are defeated with heavy Japanese casualties.

AIR WAR, *TOKYO*
More than 320 US B-29 bombers drop incendiary bombs on Tokyo, obliterating 16 sq km (6.3 sq miles) of the city.

APRIL 16

AIR WAR, *OKINAWA*
In one incident, a single US destroyer is attacked for more than four hours and

is hit by four bombs and two suicide aircraft. However, the destroyer manages to shoot down six enemy aircraft and remain operational. Another destroyer, the USS *Pringle*, is sunk by a suicide attack. The carrier USS *Intrepid* and the battleship USS *Missouri* are also damaged.

LAND WAR, *PHILIPPINES*
US forces land on Carabao to find that the Japanese defenders have gone. Carabao was subjected to two days of bombardment before the landings.

APRIL 16–17

LAND WAR, *RYUKYU ISLANDS*
Troops from XXIV Corps are landed on Ie Shima, a small island off Okinawa's Motobu Peninsula. Ie Shima offers an additional airfield and anchorage for US ships. Japanese resistance intensifies once the US troops advance inland, but by the end of the day the airfield is captured. By the end of the 17th, at least two-thirds of the island is in US hands.

APRIL 17

AIR WAR, *RYUKYU ISLANDS*
A US Navy communiqué reports that, in the period March 18–April 17, 1945, more than 2200 Japanese aircraft have been destroyed in the Ryukyu Islands area, with US carrier aircraft accounting for 1600 of the total. The communiqué also states that British Pacific Fleet aircraft operating off the Sakishimas and Formosa have destroyed more than 80 enemy planes.

LAND WAR, *PHILIPPINES*
The US X Corps puts the 17th Division ashore at Cotabato on Mindanao fol-

lowing heavy bombardments, one of more than 50 amphibious operations conducted around the southern Philippines between February and July 1945. The bulk of the Japanese Thirty-Fifth Army is concentrated on Mindanao, and inland fighting is heavy.

APRIL 18

LAND WAR, *RYUKYU ISLANDS*
While XXIV Corps' positions change little in southern Okinawa, US Marine Corps troops reach the northern tip of the island. On Ie Shima, US troops are struggling to dislodge Japanese defenders from dug-in positions around Iegusugu Peak.

CORRESPONDENTS, *IE SHIMA*
The famous US war correspondent Ernie Pyle is killed by a Japanese sniper

▲ *A US soldier on Okinawa loading a 57mm recoilless rifle with a perforated cartridge, which vented out propellant gases via the breech mechanism.*

at the age of 44. He had followed US soldiers in almost every theatre of their operations, and was deeply loved by the common US soldier.

APRIL 19

LAND WAR, *RYUKYU ISLANDS*
XXIV Corps begins a major offensive to dislodge the Japanese defenders from the Shuri Line in southern Okinawa. The day opens with a huge artillery

▼ *The carrier USS Bunker Hill burns after being hit by two kamikaze aircraft off Okinawa. She suffered 346 killed, 43 missing, and 264 wounded, but managed to limp back to port for repairs.*

▲ *A Vought Corsair attacks Japanese positions on Okinawa. The aircraft has just fired its whole complement of eight 5in rockets.*

barrage from US Marine and US Army guns, supported by one of the largest naval support bombardments of the Pacific war. At 06:00 hours, troops of the 7th, 27th and 96th Divisions begin the assault, and against terrible Japanese fire manage to advance about 914m (3000ft) and capture the village of Machinato.

AIR WAR, *TOKYO*
US P-51 Mustang fighters attack Atsugi airfield around Tokyo, shooting down 23 Japanese aircraft and destroying or damaging 51 others.

LAND WAR, *BURMA*
Britain's XXXIII Corps and IV Corps continue to make strong advances towards Rangoon. On the 19th, Pyinmana falls to IV Corps, a position only 64km (40 miles) from the important air base at Toungoo. On the right flank of the advance, troops of XXXIII Corps are closing up against Japanese positions on a 160km (100-mile) stretch of the Irrawaddy River.

▼ *The damage in the hangar deck of USS Sangamon following a kamikaze attack. Losses were 11 dead and 21 wounded.*

APRIL 21

APRIL 21

LAND WAR, *RYUKYU ISLANDS*

The US flag is raised over Iegusugu Peak on Ie Shima, after several days of hard fighting to dislodge Japanese defenders. The island is now under US control, although mopping-up operations continue. Japanese dead number around 100,000.

APRIL 21–25

LAND WAR, *RYUKYU ISLANDS*

XXIV Corps troops make gains on southern Okinawa. US soldiers capture Kakuza town and take key points on Hill 178, a major Japanese stronghold on the left flank of the American advance. By the 25th, the US Navy has recorded a total of 21,269 Japanese troops dead on Okinawa and the surrounding islands.

APRIL 22

LAND WAR, *PHILIPPINES*

The US 31st Division is landed on Mindanao in support of 24th Division operations in the southwest of the island. North of Mindanao, US forces consolidate their hold over Cebu Island.

▼ *A US M1 8in howitzer, nicknamed Comanche, opens fire on the island of Luzon. The M1 fired a 91kg (200lb) shell up to a range of 16,970m (55,676ft).*

▶ *The aftermath of a banzai charge on Mindanao: dead Japanese soldiers litter the ground following their assault against soldiers of the US 124th Regiment.*

APRIL 22–24

LAND WAR, *BURMA*

The Allies capture the air base and town at Toungou, having advanced 80km (50 miles) in three days. The 3000 men of the 1st Division, Indian National Army (INA), surrender to the Allies near Pyu. The INA has been fighting on the Japanese side in Burma since June 1943, and many of those who surrender are subsequently put on trial.

APRIL 25–30

KAMIKAZE, *OKINAWA*

Japanese kamikaze air attacks continue until the end of the month. More than 30 US ships are damaged.

APRIL 29

KAMIKAZE, *RYUKYU ISLANDS*

The US Navy hospital ship USS *Comfort* is hit by a Japanese kamikaze aircraft off Okinawa. Twenty-nine patients and crew are killed, another hundred are missing, and thirty-three are wounded.

LAND WAR, *RYUKYU ISLANDS*

US troops capture Machinato airfield in southern Okinawa.

LAND WAR, *BURMA*

Troops of the 20th Indian Division capture Allanmyo on the Irrawaddy, less than 64km (40 miles) from Prome.

MAY 1

AIR WAR, *RYUKYU ISLANDS*

US carrier aircraft begin strikes throughout the Ryukyu Islands, today hitting Kuro and Kuchino Islands in the north of the chain.

LAND WAR, *BORNEO*

A naval attack force, commanded by Vice-Admiral

▲ *The charred and mangled body of a Japanese soldier following a raid on a US airfield on Okinawa.*

MAY 2

LAND WAR, *PHILIPPINES*
US troops of the 158th Regiment advancing northwards through Luzon from Legaspi meet with US soldiers moving south through the Bicol Peninsula. The meeting traps Japanese forces in positions east of Naga.

MAY 3

LAND WAR, *SOUTHERN PHILIPPINES*
US Army troops go ashore at Santa Cruz in the Davao Gulf, establishing a southern flank as part of an offensive against the Japanese Thirty-Fifth

V.E. Barbey, lands a contingent of troops of the Australian 26th Brigade Group and the Royal Australian Air Force on Tarakan Island, Borneo. The 17,000 Australians have the objective of seizing the 24km (15-mile) island, which contains major oil resources and an air base which the Allies wish to use for operations over Borneo. Resistance is fierce from the start, and the campaign to take the island will be one of Australia's bloodiest battles of the war.

MAY 1–2

LAND WAR, *RYUKYU ISLANDS*
On May 1, US troops of the 7th Infantry Division make advances on the eastern flank of operations in the south of the island, reaching the village of Kuhazu. The next day, a heavy offshore bombardment from US Navy vessels destroys a number of enemy emplacements and bunkers, and allows the infantry to make further advances of around 1km (0.6 miles), relying heavily on armour and flame-throwers to make headway.

MAY 1–3

LAND WAR, *BURMA*
The British Fourteenth Army occupies Rangoon after a light-

ning advance down through Burma. On May 1, "Operation Dracula" is launched when soldiers of the Gurkha Parachute Battalion are dropped south of the city, joining the next day with a landing of the 26th Indian Division in the Gulf of Marta-ban. Rangoon is caught in a pincer movement between the southern advance and the 17th Indian Division advancing down from the north, which reaches Pegu – 64km (40 miles) from Rangoon – on May 2. The Japanese in Rangoon realize their position is untenable, and abandon the city. To the northwest, XXXIII Corps forces take Prome on May 3; Thayetmyo falls two days later.

▶ *A US Marine makes a dash for cover on Okinawa, at a site nicknamed "Death Valley". At this particular place the Marines suffered 125 casualties in 8 hours.*

▶ *A Corsair of Marine Air Group 33 at Okinawa, one of 700 US Marine aircraft that took part in the campaign.*

Army, which occupies strong positions in central Mindanao.

MAY 3-4

LAND WAR, *RYUKYU ISLANDS*
Japanese forces attempt two ambitious amphibious counterattacks in southern Okinawa. Approximately 600 Japanese soldiers try to land on the east and west coasts of Okinawa behind US lines. Predictably, the attacks are defeated, the east coast assault being repulsed at sea, while the west coast group lands but is contained and destroyed. One of the attacks is coordinated with an air strike on Yontan airfield, but Japanese aviators suffer heavy losses.

MAY 3-4

SEA/AIR WAR, *OKINAWA*
Japanese kamikaze and conventional aircraft make a major attack on US shipping around Okinawa. On May 3, three US destroyers – USS *Luce*, USS *Morrison* and USS *Little* – are sunk by suicide aircraft, and eight other vessels are severely damaged. The next day, a further 10 vessels are damaged, including the escort carrier USS Sangamon, but 168 Japanese aircraft are shot down.

MAY 4

AIR WAR, *PACIFIC*
The US Navy establishes a major air operating base on Guam known as Fleet Air Wing 18. The aircraft stationed there will be capable of major air operations over the central and western Pacific.

LAND WAR, *RYUKYU ISLANDS*
The Japanese carry out a general counterattack in southern Okinawa, firing a heavy preliminary artillery bombardment and supporting the attack with tanks and other armoured vehicles. The attack is beaten off by massive US artillery supremacy and destructive strafing by US carrier aircraft. US forces respond to the Japanese defeat by resuming the advance, beginning an assault against the key high ground of Hill 187. US estimates place the Japanese death toll in the Okinawa campaign to date at around 33,000.

MAY 4-5

SEA WAR, *SAKISHIMA GROUP*
Warships of the British Pacific Fleet bombard Miyako Island in the Sakishima Group, southeast of Okinawa. The firepower is directed against the Hirara and Nobara airfields, and is coordinated with a strike by British carrier aircraft that destroys at least 22 Japanese aircraft.

MAY 5

AIR WAR, *KOREA STRAITS*
US aircraft of Fleet Air Wing One flying from Okinawa attack Japanese vessels sailing along the coastline of western Korea. Two large oilers and five cargo ships are sunk, and fourteen other ships are left badly damaged.

▼ *American M4 Sherman tanks on Okinawa. The spare tracks attached to the front of the hulls gave additional protection to the crew.*

KAMIKAZE, *OKINAWA*
Seventeen US ships are sunk by a mass kamikaze attack off Okinawa. Yesterday, the British carriers HMS *Indomitable* and HMS *Formidable* were hit by kamikaze strikes off Japan, but suffered little damage owing to heavily armoured flight decks.

AIR WAR, *USA*
The US suffers its first civilian fatalities of the Pacific war. A Japanese bomb balloon, one of the hundreds released in the Pacific weeks earlier, kills six US civilians – a teacher and five children – in Oregon.

MAY 9

LAND WAR, *RYUKYU ISLANDS*
In celebration of the final unconditional surrender of Germany, which was signed two days ago, every US naval gun and artillery piece on and around Okinawa fires a single shell at Japanese positions. Bad weather over the last couple of days has led to reduced

▲ *Major-General Lemuel C. Shepherd, who commanded the US 6th Marine Division during the campaign on Okinawa.*

Japanese air activity over the island, although today two US destroyers are damaged by kamikaze aircraft.

MAY 10

LAND WAR, *PHILIPPINES*

Part of the US 40th Division is landed on the northern coast of Mindanao around Cagayan. The landing now means that the Japanese on Mindanao are effectively trapped between the northern, western and southern points of the US advance.

AIR WAR, *OKINAWA*

In a courageous attack, a US fighter of the 2nd Marine Aircraft Wing whose guns have jammed destroys a Japanese bomber by cutting off its tail assembly using the fighter's propeller. He attacks the Japanese bomber three times in this way before downing the aircraft.

LAND WAR, *RYUKYU ISLANDS*

The 6th Marine Division bridges the Asa River in southern Okinawa. The bridging effort is delayed for some hours by two Japanese human bomb attacks, but eventually the crossing is secured. Elsewhere in the south, particularly around the Shuri Line, US progress is slow, with hand-to-hand fighting in some sectors. The Japanese are attempting constant night attacks and night infiltration into the Tenth Army's lines.

MAY 11-12

KAMIKAZE, *OKINAWA*

Japanese suicide aircraft damage the carriers USS *Bunker Hill* and USS *Enterprise* and the destroyer USS *Evans*. The destroyer USS *Hugh W. Hadley* is also hit and damaged by an Ohka piloted bomb. The Americans, however, shoot down 93 enemy aircraft in reply – one destroyer alone shoots down 19

Japanese aircraft with sustained and intense anti-aircraft fire.

LAND WAR, *RYUKYU ISLANDS*

US forces launch a major offensive against the Okinawan capital, Naha, with elements of the 6th Marine Division penetrating the outer suburbs.

LAND WAR, *NEW GUINEA*

The 6th Australian Division attacks and occupies Wewak on the New Guinea coast. Wewak was the headquarters of the Japanese Eighteenth Army, and the remaining Japanese troops in the country are now widely dispersed and unable to mount organized resistance.

▼ *Japanese soldiers taken prisoner on Okinawa await interrogation. Only 7400 Japanese troops gave themselves up during the fighting.*

MAY 12

MAY 12

LAND WAR, *RYUKYU ISLANDS*
US Army forces are landed on Tori Shima, another island in the Ryukyu chain. The island, approximately 88km (55 miles) west of Okinawa, is captured without resistance.

MAY 13

AIR WAR, *JAPAN*
US carrier aircraft begin two days of air attacks over Kyushu, crippling its rail network, damaging its aviation production plans and destroying or damaging 272 Japanese aircraft. The aircraft carrier USS *Enterprise* is damaged by a suicide attack off the Japanese coast. All of Kyushu's airfields are now knocked out.

MAY 14

LAND WAR, *RYUKYU ISLANDS*
After a bloody five-day battle, US troops capture "Chocolate Drop Hill" east of Ishimmi and the Yonabaru airfield.

AIR WAR, *JAPAN*
The Japanese mainland is further devastated after 472 B-29 Superfortress bombers drop 2540 tonnes (2500 tons) of incendiary bombs on Nagoya. Nearly 15 sq km (6 sq miles) of the city are incinerated, and the Aichi and Mitsubishi aircraft works practically destroyed. In the air, 20 Japanese fighters are shot down by the bombers' fighter escorts.

MAY 15

POLITICS, *BURMA*
With the defeat of the Japanese Army in Burma essentially complete, the Burmese nationalist leader, Aung Sun, gives full cooperation to the Allied war effort.

▶ A column of US M4 Sherman tanks ford a river on Luzon while infantry use a makeshift bridge.

MAY 15–16

SEA WAR, *INDIAN OCEAN*
The Japanese heavy cruiser *Haguro* is sunk by a force of five British destroyers in the Malacca Strait as it attempts to evacuate Japanese Army troops from Andaman Island in the eastern Bay of Benghal.

MAY 16–18

LAND WAR, *RYUKYU ISLANDS*
US troops of the 96th Infantry Division engage in a ferocious evening battle to take "Conical Hill", southern Okinawa, against Japanese counterattacks. One company fights a one-hour grenade battle before ousting the Japanese from the summit. Another hill, known as "Sugar Loaf Hill", is taken by the 6th Marine Division on the 18th, the fifth time the summit has changed hands (it will change hands a total of 11 times during the course of the Okinawa battle). US troops have, over the last few days, advanced from the Asa to the Asato River, crushing two battalions of Japanese soldiers in the process.

◀ The wreckage of a Japanese fighter lies abandoned on a disused airstrip in Burma. By May 1945, the Japanese Fifteenth Army in Burma had largely disintegrated.

MAY 17

AIR WAR, *JAPAN*
USAAF P-51 Mustang fighters make a low-level attack on Atsugi airfield, Tokyo, and destroy or damage 42 Japanese aircraft with the loss of 1 of their number to anti-aircraft fire.

MAY 19

SEA WAR, *CHINA*
Japanese forces abandon the port of Foochow on the Chinese coast. Japanese-occupied Chinese ports have become untenable since the US capture of the Philippines, putting US air bases within striking range of Chinese coastal towns such as Amoy and Swatow, which have also been deserted by the enemy.
AIR WAR, *JAPAN*
The city of Hamamatsu is bombed by 279 Boeing B-29s.

MAY 20

LAND WAR, *RYUKYU ISLANDS*
The US Tenth Army surrounds the Japan-

◀ *After a hard-fought campaign in the Philippines, Douglas MacArthur reads the country's proclamation of liberation.*

▲ *Soldiers of the 6th Australian Division take cover from enemy fire during the capture of Wewak, off New Guinea.*

ese-held citadel of Shuri. Japanese troops make counterattacks across the southern sector, but all are repulsed. In a new variation on Japanese tactics, numbers of Japanese soldiers are found to be wearing US Marine uniforms and carrying US weapons. The US advance leads to the withdrawal of Japanese troops from the Shuri Line, although US troops still face hundreds of enemy emplacements in the far south of the island.

MAY 23

LAND WAR, *PHILIPPINES*
US X Corps and elements of the US 40th Division meet in central Mindanao in positions around Impalutao. Japanese forces are increasingly compressed into a small pocket of resistance in the east of the island, around 160km (100 miles) long by 80km (50 miles) wide.

MAY 26

LAND WAR, *BURMA*
Britain's XXXIII Corps occupies Bassein, an important railway town 128km (80 miles) to the west of Rangoon.
AIR WAR, *JAPAN*
A large B-29 raid (464 aircraft) on Tokyo nearly claims the lives of Emperor Hirohito and his family after the Imperial Palace is surrounded by fires.

MAY 27

AIR WAR, *OKINAWA*
Combined bombing and suicide attacks on US Navy vessels around Okinawa

MAY 29

sink the destroyer USS *Drexler* and damage eight other ships.

LAND WAR, *RYUKYU ISLANDS*
US infantry and Marines secure most of Naha, the Okinawan capital. Appalling rains slow the US advance even more, however. On average, US troops in the south of Okinawa have advanced only around 274m (900ft) a day.

LAND WAR, *CHINA*
Chinese Nationalist troops win an important victory in southern China by capturing the city of Nanning, the capital of Kwangsi Province. Nanning is only 128km (80 miles) from the border of Indochina, and its loss means that the Japanese Army in China is cut off from its forces in Burma, Thailand, Indochina and Malaya.

MAY 29

AIR WAR, *JAPAN*
Tokyo is devastated once again by B-29 raids, which this time burn up nearly 44 sq km (17 sq miles) of the battered city.

JUNE 1

AIR WAR, *PACIFIC*
A US naval air facility is established on Peleliu in the Palau Group.

AIR WAR, *JAPAN*
The Japanese city of Osaka is devastated by a huge B-29 raid in which 3048 tonnes (3000 tons) of incendiary munitions are dropped. Osaka becomes a non-functioning city, as most of its workforce has been dispersed.

▲ *Japanese civil defence measures: an officer instructs women civilians on the proper use of gas masks.*

JUNE 3

LAND WAR, *RYUKYU ISLANDS*
US Marines are landed on Iheya Shima in the Ryukyu Islands.

JUNE 4

LAND WAR, *RYUKYU ISLANDS*
The US 6th Marine Division makes an amphibious landing on the coastline of the Oruku Peninsula as part of a gener-

▶ *General Carl Spaatz (right) head of US Pacific air operations, with General Ira Eaker.*

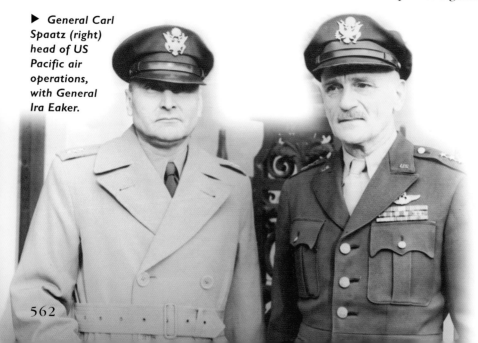

al US offensive to take Naha and its air-field in southern Okinawa. Fighting is extremely heavy.

JUNE 5

TYPHOON, *RYUKYU ISLANDS*

A huge typhoon hits the US fleet off Okinawa, causing massive destruction. Thirty-five ships are damaged, including four battleships and eight carriers.

AIR WAR, *JAPAN*

More than 3048 tonnes (3000 tons) of incendiaries are dropped over Kobe in a raid by 473 B-29 bombers.

JUNE 6

LAND WAR, *CHINA*

Japanese forces in southern China re-treat back to Kweilin, the whole Ichi-Go offensive having collapsed with the Japanese being pushed back nearly 320km (200 miles) in two weeks.

JUNE 8

AIR WAR, *JAPAN*

US carrier aircraft attack Kanoya airfield on Kyushu, inflicting further damage on Japanese homeland air resources.

SEA WAR, *JAVA SEA*

The Japanese cruiser Ashigara is torpe-doed and sunk by the British subma-rine HMS *Trenchant*.

JUNE 8-9

SEA WAR, *BORNEO*

Allied cruisers and destroyers lay down a heavy two-day bombardment on Japanese facilities around Brunei Bay, on North Borneo's northwest coast.

JUNE 9

LAND WAR, *RYUKYU ISLANDS*

US Marines go ashore on Aguni Shima in the Ryukyu chain.

LAND WAR, *PHILIPPINES*

The Japanese forces on Mindanao lose their defensive positions at Mandong, critically weakening any attempt to mount organized resistance.

JUNE 10-13

LAND WAR, *RYUKYU ISLANDS*

US forces in the Oruku Peninsula make slow progress against the Japan-ese, compressing them into an area of little more than 1000 sq m (10,800 sq ft). Many Japanese troops begin com-mitting suicide as they realize their de-feat is near. By the 13th, all resistance in the peninsula has been crushed, and a US victory on Okinawa is at last in sight.

▼ *A Japanese mother and son eat a meal in a shack amidst the rubble of a Japanese city devastated by US airpower.*

KEY PERSONALITIES

EMPEROR HIROHITO

Michinomiya Hirohito (1901–89) was the longest-reigning monarch in Japanese his-tory, taking the throne in 1926 and keep-ing it until his death in 1989. Although the figurehead of Japanese power, with a quasi-divine status among his people, Hirohito's control over the events that led to war was limited, de facto power residing in the control of the Japanese state by the mili-tary establishment. Recent research has shown that Hirohito was actually opposed both to an alliance with Germany and Italy in the Tripartite Pact, and to the Japanese war with the US. Hideki Tojo was the true instigator of the Pacific War, and it was he who rejected a note from President Roo-sevelt on December 6, 1941, that attempt-ed to avert a conflict.

Hirohito did not believe that Japan could sustain a war against the US, and even in 1942 was urging Tojo to end the conflict. By 1945, Tojo was gone from of-fice and a large number of senior politi-cians had joined the peace movement. Fol-lowing the devastation of Hiroshima and Nagasaki by atomic bombs, Hirohito broke with imperial precedent (tradition-ally, the Emperor is publicly silent) and an-nounced on radio on August 15, 1945 that Japan would accept the US demand for un-conditional surrender. In a further step, on January 1, 1946, he announced to the Japanese people that there was no divine status in his office or person. By so doing, and for his role in closing the Japanese re-sistance, Hirohito managed to escape Allied war crime trials.

JUNE 10

JUNE 10

LAND WAR, *BORNEO*

Following a two-day bombardment, Australian troops are landed at Brunei Bay (a proposed advanced base for the British Pacific Fleet) and on Labuan and Muara Islands. More than 30,000 Japanese troops are located in Borneo's interior, and at this late stage in the war the Australians do not want to waste lives with unnecessary campaigning. Consequently, the Australian troops consolidate only the coastal strip around the landing area, while Allied Special Operations Australia (SOA) units control Japanese forces inland.

JUNE 14–16

AIR WAR, *CAROLINE ISLANDS*

British carrier aircraft mount a two-day attack against remaining Japanese bases in the Caroline Islands. Such is the weakened state of the Japanese Air Force by this stage that they meet no aerial resistance.

JUNE 15

AIR WAR, *JAPAN*

The blighted city of Osaka is revisited by US B-29s, and is bombarded with a further 3048 tonnes (3000 tons) of bombs and incendiaries.

JUNE 17–18

LAND WAR, *RYUKYU ISLANDS*

Both sides on Okinawa suffer the loss of senior commanders. On the 17th, the commander of the Japanese naval base on Okinawa, Admiral Minoru Ota, commits suicide. The next day, the C-in-C of the US Tenth Army, Lieutenant-General Simon B. Buckner, is killed by shrapnel from an exploding shell, only three days before the final US victory.

▶ *Imperial twilight: the Japanese battleship* **Nagato** *stranded in home waters in mid-1945 due to severe fuel shortages.*

JUNE 20–25

LAND WAR, *BORNEO*

Australian soldiers capture major oil fields at Seria on the 20th; two days later, the island of Tarakan is finally secured. On the 25th, the Miri oil fields on Sarawak also fall into Allied hands.

JUNE 21

LAND WAR, *RYUKYU ISLANDS*

The hard-fought battle to capture Okinawa comes to an end as US forces finally overwhelm Japanese defenders in the south of the island. The Japanese commander, Lieutenant-General Ushijima Mitsuru, commits suicide. Although Japanese casualties are not confirmed, the figure is around 100,000 dead – unusually, nearly 7500 Japanese soldiers surrender. The US also

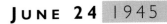

◄ *The Japanese city of Hamamatsu after the B-29 raid on June 18, which destroyed 15,160 houses and killed 1157 civilians. Air force bases and munitions factories were positioned in and around the city.*

suffers badly in the campaign, with 7613 US Marines and US Army infantry being killed, and 31,807 wounded. In addition, the US Navy loses 4900 seamen with 36 vessels sunk and 368 damaged. The air war over Okinawa has been equally bitter. Japanese aviation losses number around 8000; 4000 of these shot down during combat missions. US aviation has lost 763 aircraft. The capture of Okinawa gives the Americans an invaluable operating base only 550km (340 miles) from Japan.

POLITICS, *JAPAN*
Emperor Hirohito pleads with the Japanese cabinet to find a diplomatic way to negotiate peace with the US. US forces are now less than 643km (400 miles) away, and Japanese cities are being devastated by B-29 strikes almost every night.

JUNE 23

LAND WAR, *PHILIPPINES*
Part of the 511th Parachute Infantry Regiment is dropped on the far north coast of Luzon around Aparri. It joins with other US Army forces and advances southwards to meet US Sixth Army units moving northwards towards Tuguegarao.

JUNE 24

THAILAND, RIVER KWAI
The bridge over the River Kwai, symbol of the horrifying use of slave and POW labour by the Japanese, is destroyed in a British bombing raid. The Japanese rail link to Thailand is being cut to pieces by Allied bombing, with US forces even using new radar-guided bombs to make accurate hits on bridges and depots.

◄ *The heavy American raids on Japanese cities in 1945 made tens of thousand of people homeless, such as these two factory workers.*

JUNE 25

LAND WAR, *PHILIPPINES*

Tuguegarao and its air base fall into US hands. The next day, US troops advancing from Aparri meet up with US troops coming up from the south, thus completing the encirclement of Japanese forces in northern Luzon.

▼ *At the Potsdam Conference, Stalin (right) met the new leaders of the US and Britain: Truman (centre) and Attlee (left).*

JUNE 26

LAND WAR, *RYUKYU ISLANDS*

US Marine units are landed on Kume Shima in the Ryukyu Islands.

LAND WAR, *CHINA*

The Chinese begin to claw back southern air bases lost to the Japanese. Today, the airfield at Liuchow is recaptured.

JUNE 28

LAND WAR, *PHILIPPINES*

General MacArthur announces the

▲ *A Japanese Kaiten "human torpedo" is launched from a cruiser near Kure, Japan. Over 300 were built in 1944–45.*

effective recapture of Luzon from the Japanese. Although organized Japanese resistance has collapsed, there is much mopping-up work to do. US forces have lost 7933 men killed and 32,732 wounded retaking Luzon, as opposed to 192,000 Japanese dead.

JUNE 29

STRATEGY, *PACIFIC*

Capitalizing on the release of troops from the European theatre, US President Truman approves a joint chiefs of

▶ *USS Indianapolis, seen here shelling Saipan, delivered bomb components for "Little Boy" to Tinian. She was sunk on July 30.*

staff plan for an invasion of mainland Japan. Two operations are outlined, involving a total of 36 US divisions. The first, "Operation Olympic", proposes landing 13 divisions on Kyushu on November 1, 1945. The second, "Operation Coronet", looks to land the remaining 23 divisions on Honshu on March 1, 1946.

JULY 1

SEA WAR, *PACIFIC*

The American submarine USS *Barb* attacks enemy coastal installations at Kaihyo Island off the east coast of Karafuto. It is the first time a submarine has used rockets to attack an enemy shore position.

LAND WAR, *CHINA*

Chinese troops advancing through southern China capture Liuchow, a key town astride the main north–south rail line and featuring a large air base formerly used by US air units. USAAF forces are now working to reopen captured air bases for the strategic bombing campaign against mainland Japan.

JULY 2

HOME WAR, *JAPAN*

The Japanese Government states that the US air raids have caused five million casualties among the Japanese civilian population.

JULY 3–5

LAND WAR, *BORNEO*

Australian forces capture the airfield at Sepinggang. Two days later, further troops are landed at Balikpapen Bay, and the Australian 7th Division is now making good advances into Borneo's interior and along its coastline.

JULY 5

LAND WAR, *PHILIPPINES*

General MacArthur announces that the Philippines are now liberated from Japanese control. The Philippines campaign has been the largest operation for US forces in the Pacific, and the Japanese have lost well over 200,000 men. However, many other Japanese troops remain on the island – around 50,000 will surrender at the end of the war.

POLITICS, *AUSTRALIA*

The Australian prime minister, John Curtin, dies at the age of 60. Curtin had held the post since October 1941, and although his political power was tenuous at times he had fully mobilized Australia for war, often against internal government opposition. More than 30,000 people attend his funeral in Perth on July 9.

POLITICS, *US*

General Carl A. "Tooey" Spaatz is appointed head of US Strategic Air Forces in the Pacific. Spaatz had formerly commanded the US bombing effort against Germany, and now he will oversee the air campaign against Japan and the deployment of the atomic bombs.

▲ *A victim of US airpower. The battleship* Ise *lies wrecked in Kure harbour after being hit 23 times by bombs dropped from aircraft belonging to Task Force 38.*

▲ Under mortar and small-arms fire, British Lee tanks near a Japanese position during mopping-up operations in Burma.

JULY 7–10

AIR WAR, *JAPAN*
US carrier aircraft attack Japanese airfields on the Tokyo plain. A total of 173 Japanese machines are destroyed, utterly overwhelmed by more than 1000 US fighter-bombers. Japan still has huge numbers of aircraft on the mainland, although many are committed to suicide missions. Japan also has an appalling deficit of trained pilots, and veteran US aviators easily pick off young crews with only a few hours' flying experience.

JULY 13

POLITICS, *ITALY*
In a largely symbolic gesture, Italy declares war on Japan.

POLITICS, *JAPAN*
The Japanese ambassador in Moscow, Naotake Sato, meets with the Soviet foreign minister, Molotov, and discusses possible peace initiatives with the Allies that do not involve Japan's unconditional surrender.

JULY 14–15

AIR WAR, *JAPAN*
US carrier-based aircraft bomb rail facilities, industrial targets and shipping around northern Honshu and Hokkaido, causing substantial infrastructure damage and sinking the destroyer *Tachibana*. Supporting the attacks is a naval group of battleships, cruisers and destroyers under Rear-Admiral J.F. Shafroth, which attacks coastal targets around Kamaishi, Honshu, on the 14th; and steel and iron works around Muroran, Hokkaido, on the 15th. This is the first time US warships have fired directly at Japan, and such attacks now become daily events.

JULY 16

TECHNOLOGY, *ATOMIC BOMB*
The first atomic bomb is successfully exploded in the

◄ A member of the Japanese Fifteenth Army in Burma (right) who chose to give himself up to the British.

desert at Alamogordo, New Mexico. The bomb is a 20-kiloton device (explosive force equivalent to 20,320 tonnes/20,000 tons of TNT) and raises a mushroom cloud that towers to 12,200m (40,000ft).

POLITICS, *POTSDAM*
Churchill, Stalin and Roosevelt meet in Potsdam to discuss the strategy of completing World War II, and the politics of dividing up conquered Europe. They are told of the successful detonation of the first atomic bomb.

JULY 18

AIR WAR, *JAPAN*
US carrier aircraft from the Third Fleet attack Yokosuka naval base and airfields around Tokyo. Japan's last big warship, the battleship *Nagato*, is sunk.

SEA WAR, *JAPAN*
The coastal city of Hitachi is pounded by a fierce one-hour bombardment

◄ *A B-29 Superfortress accompanied by a swarm of North American P-51 Mustang fighters. With drop tanks the P-51 had an operational range of 2080km (1300 miles).*

(an island located between Japan and mainland Asia). Once ashore, they blow up a Japanese train before escaping.

JULY 24

SEA WAR, *PHILIPPINES*
The US destroyer USS *Underhill* is critically damaged by a Japanese piloted torpedo, and is later scuttled. The Japanese piloted torpedoes (Kaiten) were essentially Long Lance torpedoes fitted with an operating compartment and a conning tower for use by a single crewman.

JULY 24-25

AIR WAR, *JAPAN*
The remaining strength of the Japanese Navy is further devastated by a two-day

STRATEGY AND TACTICS

THE INVASION OF JAPAN

Although the atomic bombs removed the need for a conventional invasion of Japan, the campaign was planned in detail and forces gathered for its execution. The invasion had two proposed stages. First, Operation Olympic would land the US Sixth Army, 13 divisions strong, on Kyushu in the far south of Japan on November 1, 1945, securing key naval and aviation bases and pulling enemy forces down into the south of Japan. Then, on March 1, 1946, Operation Coronet would be launched against Tokyo. Here, the US Eighth Army and US First Army, totalling 14 divi-

sions, would land in a pincer movement around Tokyo itself, driving with heavy armoured forces to Kumagaya and Koga and isolating the capital for capture.

Despite undeniable US superiority in the Pacific at this stage of the war, there were deep fears about levels of US casualties. The experience of island clearance in places such as Iwo Jima and Okinawa led US Army and Marine Corps chiefs to predict some 500,000 US casualties to take Japan. This level of human loss was unacceptable to the US president and his staff, and the preference was for the deployment of atomic bombs.

from US Navy warships, which fire 2032 tonnes (2000 tons) of shells.

JULY 19

KAMIKAZE, *OKINAWA*
The US destroyer USS *Thatcher* is hit and badly damaged in a suicide attack.

JULY 21-25

POLITICS, ATOMIC BOMB
At the Potsdam Conference, Roosevelt and Churchill agree to the use of the atomic bomb; and, after Tokyo issues a rebuttal of Allied surrender demands, President Truman gives the order that the A-bomb can be used operationally after August 3.

JULY 23

RAID, *KARAFUTO*
The submarine USS *Barb* lands US raiding forces on the east coast of Karafuto

DECISIVE WEAPONS

THE MANHATTAN PROJECT

The "Manhattan Project" was the codename for the US atomic weapons programme. The origins of the project go back to 1939, when top US scientists, including the influential Albert Einstein, persuaded President Roosevelt of the military possibilities for fission chain re-actions of atomic elements. Official work began in February 1940 with a grant of $6000, but on December 6, 1941 – with war raging in Europe and threatening in the Far East – the programme was substantially upgraded and placed under the jurisdiction of the Office of Scientific Research and Development. The War Department took joint management following the Japanese attack on Pearl Harbor.

The programme assumed the name Manhattan Project in 1942 after the US Army engineers of the Manhattan district, who were given the task of constructing the initial plants for the work.

Scientists such as Ernest Orlando Lawrence and Philip Hauge Alberson spent the next three years working on methods of producing usable amounts of uranium-235 and plutonium-239 suitable for the fission process. Most of this work was conducted at the Oak Ridge reactor plant near Knoxville, Tennessee; the metallurgical department of the University of Chicago; and the Hanford Engineer Works near Pasco, Washington.

The job of turning fissionable material into a nuclear weapon fell to Robert Oppenheimer and the staff of his laboratory established in 1943 in the desert at Los Alamos, New Mexico. Oppenheimer had to devise a weapon that could create a supercritical mass of fissionable material to produce an explosion, and in the summer of 1945 the Hanford Works gave him enough plutonium-239 to conduct his first test. On July 16, 1945, the first atomic bomb was exploded at Alamogordo, New Mexico, producing a blast the equivalent of 20,320 tonnes (20,000 tons) of TNT, sending a mushroom cloud 12,200m (40,000ft) into the air and fusing the desert sand into glass. The US, having ultimately invested two billion dollars in the Manhattan Project, now had its atomic bomb.

▲ *Enola Gay, the B-29 Superfortress commanded by Colonel Paul W. Tibbets that dropped the first atomic bomb on August 6, 1945.*

attack by carrier aircraft over the Inland Sea, hitting Kure Naval Base and airfields at Nagoya, Osaka and Miho. Three battleships, one escort carrier and two heavy cruisers are sunk. Kure is hit again three days later, and one aircraft carrier and five other vessels are sunk.

JULY 26

POLITICS, *PACIFIC*
The Potsdam Declaration is delivered to the Japanese Government. It calls for

JULY 28

KAMIKAZE, *OKINAWA*
The US destroyer USS *Callaghan* is hit and sunk by Japanese kamikaze aircraft around Okinawa. USS *Callaghan* will be the last Allied warship in the Pacific campaign to be sunk by a kamikaze attack, although the next day a suicide plane damages the destroyer USS *Cassin Young*.

POLITICS, JAPAN
The Japanese Government rejects the Potsdam Declaration: the peacemakers in the cabinet are overridden by belligerent military leaders such as Korechika Anami, the war minister; and army chief of staff Yoshijiro Umezu.

JULY 30

SEA WAR, *PHILIPPINE SEA*
The US heavy cruiser USS *Indianapolis* is sunk by a Japanese submarine in the Philippine Sea, having first delivered to Tinian the uranium for the atomic bomb. Only 316 of the 1196 crew survive, many dying slowly over three days in the remote Philippine Sea, suffering dehydration, shark attacks and drowning.

AUGUST 1

AIR/SEA WAR, *WAKE ISLAND*
US carrier aircraft and battleships bombard Japanese forces on Wake Island. The Japanese reply with coastal guns, damaging the battleship USS *Pennsylvania*.

AUGUST 2

POLITICS, *POTSDAM*
The Potsdam Conference comes to an end with a clear Allied commitment to deploy the atomic bomb to bring about the defeat of Japan.

AIR WAR, *JAPAN*
B-29 raids devastate Nagasaki and Toyama. The next day, B-29s drop huge volumes of sea mines around the Japanese coast, blockading harbours. In recent months, air-dropped sea mines have been sinking more Japanese ships than US submarines.

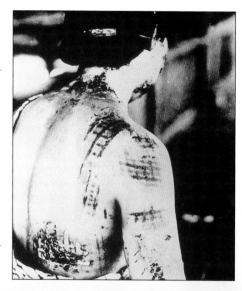

▲ The atomic blast produced heat rays that caused terrible injuries. Here, a kimono pattern was branded onto skin.

the unconditional surrender of Japan, the alternative being Japan's "prompt and utter destruction".

ATOMIC BOMB, *MARIANA ISLANDS*
The cruiser USS *Indianapolis* delivers a lethal consignment – enough uranium-235 to make the first atomic bomb – to Tinian air base in the Mariana Islands. A USAAF bomber unit, the 509th Composite Group, has been specially created and trained for the deployment of the atomic bomb against Japan.

▼ Hiroshima after the atomic blast. By the end of December 1945, 140,000 of its 350,000 inhabitants had died either during the blast or from radiation poisoning.

AUGUST 4

LAND WAR, *BURMA*

The final organized elements of the Japanese Twenty-Eighth Army are destroyed in heavy battle around the Pegu Yoma range, nearly 8500 of the 10,000 Japanese troops being killed. Although Burma is in Allied hands, isolated concentrations of Japanese troops remain throughout southern Burma, pushed up against the Irrawaddy and Sittang rivers.

AUGUST 4–6

AIR WAR, *JAPAN*

US B-29 bombers drop leaflets over Japan warning that, without a surrender, strategic bombing will destroy 12 more cities. On the night of August 5/6, six cities are totally devastated during incendiary attacks.

▼ *The ruins of Nagasaki following the dropping of the second atomic bomb on Japan by the Americans. After the bomb was dropped "black rain" fell in some areas, carrying radioactive materials from within the rising cloud of fission products.*

AUGUST 6

ATOMIC BOMB, *HIROSHIMA*

A 20-kiloton atomic bomb is dropped over the city of Hiroshima from the B-29 Enola Gay, piloted by Colonel Paul Tibbets. The initial blast kills around 100,000 people, leaving most of the survivors wounded and irradiated.

AUGUST 7

TECHNOLOGY, *JAPAN*

Japan flies its first and only turbojet aircraft, the Nakajima Kikka ("Orange Blossom"). The Kikka is essentially a smaller version of Germany's Me 262, and only 19 prototypes are built before the war comes to an end.

AUGUST 8

POLITICS, *SOVIET UNION*

The USSR declares war on Japan.

AUGUST 9

ATOMIC BOMB, *NAGASAKI*

Nagasaki is devastated by a second atomic bomb, this time dropped from the B-29 Bockscar. Around 35,000 people are killed and 60,000 wounded.

▲ *The B-29 nicknamed Bockscar dropped the atomic bomb on Nagasaki. Today, about a million visitors each year view Bockscar in the US Air Force Museum.*

SEA WAR, *JAPAN*

US battleships and cruisers attack Japanese industrial targets along the coast of Honshu, Japan.

LAND WAR, *MANCHURIA*

A huge Soviet offensive deploying more than 1.5 million troops is launched against the Japanese Army in Manchuria. The Japanese defence by the Kwantung Army crumbles, and the Soviet forces drive at speed towards the southern Manchurian coast.

▲ *President Truman announces Japan's surrender to members of the press at the White House in Washington.*

AUGUST 10

POLITICS, *JAPAN*
Emperor Hirohito tells the Japanese Government that he wishes to accept the terms of the Potsdam Declaration, and to announce Japan's unconditional surrender to the Allies.

AUGUST 11

POLITICS, *PACIFIC*
General MacArthur is declared the Allied Supreme Commander, giving him the authority to accept

THE SOVIET INVASION OF MANCHURIA

the Japanese surrender on behalf of all the Allied nations.

AUGUST 13–14

AIR WAR, *TOKYO*
As a further incentive to get the Japanese to surrender, around 1600 US aircraft bomb Tokyo.

◀ *In accordance with their emperor's wishes, the military leaders of Japan's forces surrendered to the Allies. Here, General Takazo Numata (left) and Admiral Kaigye Chudo (centre) arrive at Rangoon to surrender their units.*

▲ *For the invasion of Manchuria the Soviets massed 1.6 million troops and 5550 tanks. The Japanese had 1 million troops and 1200 obsolete tanks.*

AUGUST 15

POLITICS, *JAPAN*
Emperor Hirohito breaks imperial silence and makes a radio broadcast to the Japanese people. He tells of his move to surrender Japan's forces, and asks the Japanese people not to resist the Allies. The next day, Hirohito orders Japanese troops at home and throughout the Pacific to lay down their arms.

AUGUST 17

AIR WAR, *JAPAN*
Carrier aircraft from the Third Fleet attack Japanese air bases around Tokyo, encountering surprisingly heavy opposition from Japanese aircraft.

POLITICS, *CHINA*
The Chinese Communist leadership tells the US Government that it wants territorial gains from any postwar settlement with Japan. The Soviet Union pledges to return Manchuria to China within three months of the end of hostilities with Japan.

AUGUST 17

POLITICS, *JAPAN*
General Prince Higashikuni becomes Japan's new prime minister, and forms a new cabinet to oversee the Japanese surrender to the Allies.

POLITICS, *DUTCH EAST INDIES*
Nationalist leaders in the Dutch East Indies declare independence from the Netherlands, renaming the country the Independent Republic of Indonesia.

AUGUST 18

INDIAN NATIONAL ARMY, *FORMOSA*
The Indian National Army's leader, Subhas Chandra Bose is killed in an air crash.

AUGUST 18–20

LAND WAR, *MANCHURIA*

In a massive offensive from the west, north and east, Soviet forces overwhelm the Kwantung Army in central Manchuria, capturing the cities of Harbin, Tsitsihar and Changchun in three successive days of campaigning.

AUGUST 21

SURRENDER, *MARSHALL ISLANDS*

The Japanese garrison at Mili Atoll in the Marshall Islands becomes the first to surrender in the Pacific theatre.

AUGUST 23

LAND WAR, *MANCHURIA*

Soviet forces reach the coastline of southern Manchuria, concluding a 12-day defeat of the Kwantung Army. It is the quickest campaign in Soviet history, killing 80,000 Japanese soldiers for Soviet losses of 8000 dead and 22,000 wounded.

AUGUST 25

ALLIES, *JAPAN*

US carrier aircraft begin uncontested flights over Japan, monitoring the surrender of Japanese military facilities and also locating and supplying Allied prisoners of war formerly held in Japanese camps.

AUGUST 27

SEA WAR, *TOKYO*

Vessels of the US Third Fleet anchor

◄ *Foreign Minister Mamoru Shigemitsu (in top hat and tails) and representatives of the Japanese armed forces on the USS Missouri during the surrender ceremony.*

▲ *US aircraft fly in formation during the surrender ceremonies in Tokyo Bay, a photograph that amply illustrates US military might.*

themselves in Sagami Bay in the approaches to Tokyo harbour.

AUGUST 28

OCCUPATION, *JAPAN*

The first US troops land in Japan. They are US Air Force technicians who go to inspect Atsugi airfield near Tokyo.

SURRENDER, *BURMA*

Japanese officers sign surrender documents in Rangoon, finalizing the defeat of Japan in Burma.

AUGUST 29–31

SURRENDER, *PACIFIC*

Japanese forces throughout the Pacific theatre begin to surrender en masse, with troops on Singapore, Marcus Island and the Philippines capitulating to the US and British.

AUGUST 30

OCCUPATION, *JAPAN*

US occupation forces begin major landings in Tokyo Bay with the US Third Fleet and its aircraft providing security. Yokosuka Naval Base is officially handed over to the Allies. General MacArthur makes it his Supreme Allied Command headquarters.

SEPTEMBER 2

SURRENDER, *USS MISSOURI*

The Japanese foreign minister, Mamoru Shigemitsu, and General Yoshijiro

Umezo sign the final Instrument of Surrender aboard the US battleship USS *Missouri* anchored in Tokyo Bay. General MacArthur's signature concludes Japanese hostilities with all Allied nations, and it is MacArthur who will oversee the occupation of Japan. The Japanese surrender brings the Pacific war, and World War II, to an end.

▼ *Having just landed, US Marines smash Japanese field artillery pieces and small arms at Yokosuka Naval Base in Japan on August 29, 1945.*